OXFORD WORLD'S CLASSICS

THE ITALIAN

ANN RADCLIFFE (née Ward) was b
was in trade, but she passed much
of more prosperous and socially ele
moved to Bath, where she may hav
and Harriet Lee, early innovators ir
drama. She married in 1787 William   .... became proprietor and editor of the *English Chronicle*. It was apparently with his
encouragement that she took up writing as a pastime. Her first attempts in the genre of romance, *The Castles of Athlin and Dunbayne*
(1789) and *A Sicilian Romance* (1790), were published anonymously.
They received some favourable attention from the reviewers, but it
was *The Romance of the Forest* (1791) which established her as the
supreme practitioner of the Gothic mode, then variously dubbed 'the
Terrorist System of Novel Writing', 'the hobgoblin-romance', or eventually, as a tribute to her influence, 'the Radcliffe romance'. Two further novels published in her lifetime, *The Mysteries of Udolpho* (1794)
and *The Italian* (1797), served to consolidate her reputation as 'the
Great Enchantress'. Her works were translated into many languages.
Radcliffe was also an enthusiastic traveller. She authored a work based
on her sole excursion to the Continent, *A Journey Made in the Summer
of 1794, through Holland and the Western Frontier of Germany ... To
Which Are Added Observations of a Tour to the Lakes* (1795). But the
tours of southern Europe undertaken in the novels were more exotic,
based on travel books, fashionable landscape paintings, and a vivid
imagination; the scene-painting sometimes heightened by verse. Walter
Scott was to describe Radcliffe as 'the first poetess of romantic fiction'.
In spite of her celebrity, Radcliffe clung to privacy, and retired from
publishing in 1797. In later life she suffered from asthma, and died of
an attack in 1823. A final novel, *Gaston de Blondeville*, was published
in 1826, together with a narrative poem, *St Alban's Abbey*, extracts
from her travel diaries, and a memoir of the author by Thomas Noon
Talfourd.

E. J. CLERY is Research Fellow in English at Sheffield Hallam Uni-
versity and author of *The Rise of Supernatural Fiction, 1762–1800* (1995).
Other works include the revised edition of Horace Walpole's *The
Castle of Otranto* (1996) for Oxford World's Classics.

FREDERICK GARBER is Professor of English at the State University
of New York at Binghampton and author of *Thoreau's Redemptive
Imagination*.

OXFORD WORLD'S CLASSICS

*For over 100 years Oxford World's Classics have brought
readers closer to the world's great literature. Now with over 700
titles—from the 4,000-year-old myths of Mesopotamia to the
twentieth century's greatest novels—the series makes available
lesser-known as well as celebrated writing.*

*The pocket-sized hardbacks of the early years contained
introductions by Virginia Woolf, T. S. Eliot, Graham Greene,
and other literary figures which enriched the experience of reading.
Today the series is recognized for its fine scholarship and
reliability in texts that span world literature, drama and poetry,
religion, philosophy and politics. Each edition includes perceptive
commentary and essential background information to meet the
changing needs of readers.*

OXFORD WORLD'S CLASSICS

ANN RADCLIFFE

The Italian

or the

Confessional of the Black Penitents

A ROMANCE

Edited by
FREDERICK GARBER

With an Introduction and Notes by
E. J. CLERY

OXFORD
UNIVERSITY PRESS

OXFORD

UNIVERSITY PRESS

Great Clarendon Street, Oxford OX2 6DP

Oxford University Press is a department of the University of Oxford.
It furthers the University's objective of excellence in research, scholarship,
and education by publishing worldwide in

Oxford New York

Athens Auckland Bangkok Bogotá Buenos Aires Calcutta
Cape Town Chennai Dar es Salaam Delhi Florence Hong Kong Istanbul
Karachi Kuala Lumpur Madrid Melbourne Mexico City Mumbai
Nairobi Paris São Paulo Singapore Taipei Tokyo Toronto Warsaw

with associated companies in Berlin Ibadan

Oxford is a registered trade mark of Oxford University Press
in the UK and in certain other countries

Published in the United States
by Oxford University Press Inc., New York

British Library Cataloguing in Publication Data

Data available

Library of Congress Cataloging in Publication Data

Data available

ISBN 978–0–19–953740–2

2

Printed in Great Britain by
Clays Ltd, St Ives plc

CONTENTS

INTRODUCTION

IN 1797, when *The Italian* first appeared, Ann Radcliffe was the acknowledged queen of romance. Her previous two works, *The Romance of the Forest* and *The Mysteries of Udolpho*, had been not only popular successes, but also artistic triumphs, winning high praise in the periodical reviews. Earlier Gothic novels by Horace Walpole and Clara Reeve[1] had been noted for their controversial use of the supernatural. They were considered novelties by a reading public accustomed to the realist fictions of Richardson and Fielding. Radcliffe's achievement was to bring Gothic into the mainstream of literary production. In deference to the realist credo she retained merely the *suspicion* of the supernatural, making up for its absence by inventive use of effects of suspense and dread. In addition, she introduced to Gothic fiction a poetic sensibility which became her trade mark, exhibited in lengthy landscape descriptions and in the characterization of her tender but indomitable heroines. Success inspired a host of imitators, but no one could rival her on her own ground. The only serious challenge came from the German *schauerromane* or 'terror fiction', which dealt in unrestrained sensationalism,[2] and above all from a home-grown example of that genre, M. G. Lewis's *The Monk*, a *succès de scandale* in 1796.

The Italian has often been discussed as a riposte to *The Monk*, but in truth Radcliffe had little need to assert her pre-eminence. This could be gauged financially: she received £500 from her publishers for the copyright of *The Mysteries of Udolpho*, a sum so large that another publisher wagered £10 that the report of it was untrue. For *The Italian*, the payment was raised to £800—approximately £60,000 at today's rates. In the same period another reputable writer, Charlotte Smith, was paid £50 per volume

---

[1] Respectively, *The Castle of Otranto* (1764) and *The Old English Baron* (first published as *The Champion of Virtue* in 1777).

[2] Notably Schiller's *Die Geisterseher* and Karl Grosse's *Der Genius*, translated in 1795 and 1796, respectively as *The Ghost-Seer* and *Horrid Mysteries*.

for her novels; in 1803 Jane Austen, notoriously, would receive
£10 for the first version of *Northanger Abbey*. Moreover, although the critical reception of *The Italian* left something to be
desired, it was of a kind which confirmed Radcliffe's 'genius':
there were many favourable references to her other writings,
some adverse comment on the inevitably declining power of her
device of the 'explained supernatural', but also continued enthusiasm for her landscape-painting, and she was found to have
excelled herself in her portraits of villainy. No mention any-
where of 'Monk' Lewis. However, it was at this point that Radcliffe
chose to retire from the field, aged only 32. In the coming years
her novels went through many editions; they were adapted as
stage productions, condensed into chapbooks, and lesser novelists continued to ring the changes on her titles (*The Mysteries of
the Forest*, *The Monk of Udolpho*, *Italian Mysteries*, etc.), and
even on her name ('Mary Anne Radcliffe', pseudonymous author of *Manfroné; or, The One-Handed Monk*).[3] Nothing more
was heard of Radcliffe herself before her death in 1823, apart
from the unfounded rumour that an overactive imagination had
driven her insane.

The contrast between Radcliffe's literary celebrity and her
secluded life had always been striking, even before her retirement. For while women at that time were expected to shun publicity—and the abuse levelled at the outspoken feminist Mary
Wollstonecraft was a salutary reminder of this—other female authors such as Frances Burney and Hannah More were able to
mingle discreetly in London literary circles. Radcliffe appears not
to have entered public life at all, and it was only in the obituaries
of the 1820s that a few bare facts emerged. She was born Miss
Ward, the daughter of a London tradesman, though the family
had genteel connections. As a girl, she benefited from visits to
the home of an uncle, Thomas Bentley, a partner in the fashionable Wedgwood potteries, and a man of culture and progressive
ideas, who entertained some of the leading literary and artistic
figures of the day. In 1787 she married William Radcliffe, a graduate

---

[3] The authorship of *Manfroné* was claimed by Louisa Theresa Bellenden Ker;
see *The Feminist Companion to English Literature* (London, 1990).

of Oxford with legal training, who soon became proprietor and editor of the *English Chronicle*. The couple were childless, and memoirs based on William Radcliffe's report emphasize that he encouraged her to take up writing as a pastime.

If her biography appears to be a record of uneventful domesticity, her work is testament to the extraordinary energy of a vagabond imagination. In *Literary Women*, Ellen Moers declared Radcliffe the inventor of 'travelling heroinism': 'the Gothic novel was a device to send maidens on distant and exciting journeys without offending the proprieties . . . a feminine substitute for the picaresque.'[4] Radcliffe's own delight in travelling is clear from published accounts of trips she made with her husband in England, Holland, and Germany. There is no question but that she would have gone further afield if she could, but war with France put large areas of Europe off-limits during the greater part of her adult life. She was forced to rely on travel literature, topographical art, and her own invention for the locales in her novels, which covered an ever-increasing geographical range. *The Castles of Athlin and Dunbayne* was subtitled *A Highland Tale*; *A Sicilian Romance* also speaks for itself. In *The Romance of the Forest*, the heroine journeys through central and southern France and the Alps. *The Mysteries of Udolpho* follows a hectic itinerary from Gascony and the Pyrenees through the Midi to the Italian Appenines and back. *The Italian* explores new regions: Naples and its environs, the mountains of the Garganus, the shore of the Adriatic, and Rome. The last two works, especially, contain a wealth of information (not all of it accurate) regarding the topography, geology, and botany of the places they describe. These details were culled from the travel books that were so popular in the period, and indeed, Radcliffe on a few occasions did not resist the temptation to borrow whole passages.[5] But most important and influential was her ability to conjure distant scenes in the language of the sublime or the picturesque; a rocky defile, pastoral uplands gilded by the setting sun, a seashore under a stormy sky. Byron, in *Childe Harold's Pilgrimage*,

[4] Ellen Moers, *Literary Women* (The Women's Press, 1978), 126.

[5] See J. M. S. Tompkins, 'Ramond de Carbonnières, Grosley and Mrs Radcliffe', *Review of English Studies* (July 1929), 294–301.

paid tribute to the influence of Radcliffe on his youthful fantasy-image of Venice.[6]

Attitudes to Italy

Exoticism was evidently a vital part of the appeal of Radcliffe's fiction. Walpole had set his 'Gothic Story' in Italy, but there is little apart from the place-name Otranto to suggest foreignness in that work. Radcliffe, on the other hand, is wholeheartedly engaged in the exploration of national difference. The 'otherness' of Italy is the constant theme of her fifth novel, and it is a source both of terror and delight. Clara McIntyre has justly observed that the title, *The Italian*, is an anomaly since, although the villain Schedoni is implied, every other character is also Italian.[7] Perhaps it should instead be taken to designate a complete 'myth' of national character as described by Roland Barthes in *Mythologies*—a generic 'Italianity'.[8] Radcliffe was writing at the beginning of the age of nationalism, and the activities of travel and cultural comparison were important aids to conceptualizing distinct nation-states. British tourists, whether they were actual travellers or merely of the armchair variety, were engaged in a continual process of defining and sifting differences, ready to assimilate certain aspects of a foreign culture, rejecting others in order to reinforce the boundaries of British selfhood.

Throughout the eighteenth century, Italy formed the highlight of any European tour. Travellers were drawn there, above all, to view the remains of the Roman Empire. At the time, knowledge of Latin, classical history and literature, and appreciation of classical art, were the essential attributes of the ruling class. The British, enjoying a period of civil peace and commerce-driven imperial expansion, liked to describe theirs as a new 'Augustan' age. The visit to Rome, which was almost obligatory for young men of means and rank, was therefore less a humble pilgrimage

[6] Canto IV, verse xviii.

[7] Clara McIntyre, *Ann Radcliffe in Relation to her Time* (New Haven and London, 1920), 70.

[8] Roland Barthes, *Mythologies*, trans. Annette Lavers (London, 1972), 121.

than a triumphant gesture of identification. While there, they had their portraits painted, standing amid imposing relics, and returned home bearing as trophies classical medals or urns.

In *The Italian*, Radcliffe communicates some of this enthusiasm for classical culture. Her sex was not altogether a barrier, for although the female mind was not considered capable of the exertions required for studying Latin, women could and did share the taste in classicism through plays, operas, and the visual arts, not forgetting Josiah Wedgwood's Etruscan urns; by the 1790s, even women's fashions were taking a classical turn. Naples was a significant choice of location, since from 1764 to 1799 Sir William Hamilton, the Envoy to the Neopolitan Court, made it a centre of British virtu; his wife, Lady Emma Hamilton, was well known (among other things) for her 'postures' based on figures from the vases and statuary discovered at nearby Herculaneum and Pompeii. *The Italian* is set in the mid-eighteenth century (the frame narrative is dated 1764) rather than in gothic times.[9] The heroine, Ellena, is therefore able to earn a living for a while by copying designs from the excavations at Herculaneum, only uncovered twenty years before. Her work hangs in the cabinet of the illustrious Marchese di Vivaldi. His wife, the Marchesa, her wickedness notwithstanding, is similarly a connoisseur of the antique. She collects drawings of ancient ruins which suggest the work of the contemporary engraver Giovanni Battista Piranesi; specifically the series entitled the *Vedute*, which show the monuments of past glory looming out of strong shadow, their size exaggerated by the insect-like modern-day figures who stray into their haunted precincts. The influence of Piranesi's visual style can be found in some of the most powerful word-pictures in the novel. Vivaldi's adventures in the delapidated fortress of Paluzzi, and the later scene in the ruined villa of the Barone di Cambrusca, owe a great deal to the *Vedute*;[10] while the description of the prison of the

---

[9] Here, as in my Introduction to *The Castle of Otranto* (Oxford, 1996), I use 'gothic' with an initial lower case to refer to the historical period, which for Radcliffe and her contemporaries extended from the fall of the Roman Empire to the reign of James I, and 'Gothic' with an initial capital to refer to the 18th-c. aesthetic movement.

[10] See also p. 195 for what seems like a precise reference.

Inquisition points to Piranesi's most famous series, the *Carceri d'Invenzione*, 'Prisons of the Imagination'.

As the popularity of Piranesi's work at the time suggests (Walter Scott, for instance, owned a complete set of the *Vedute*), the attraction of Italy did not lie solely in the past. It was also valued for its artistic achievements in modern times, from the Renaissance onwards, particularly in painting and music. Again, there was a strong element of cultural consumerism and snob appeal. British aristocrats filled their stately homes, built on the principles of the Italian architect Palladio, with Old Masters shipped from Italy, and went to London to attend performances of the celebrated Italian opera. It is no accident that Radcliffe's hero and heroine, Vincentio di Vivaldi and Ellena Rosalba, share the names of two of Italy's more prominent cultural exporters in the period, the composer Vivaldi and the artist Rosalba Carriera; nor that they both prove to be fine singers. It is well known that Radcliffe shared the widespread enthusiasm for another artist, Salvator Rosa, who was responsible for a picturesque image of Italy distinctly at odds with the tranquil classical canvases of Claude Lorrain. Dubbed 'savage Rosa' by the poet James Thomson, his landscape paintings were famous for their rough and strangely threatening loveliness: wind-blown heaths, twisted trees, *banditti* lurking in caves or on clifftops. They were dramatic tableaux in search of a narrative, and this is what Radcliffe so successfully supplied.

British interest in the disturbing art of Piranesi and Rosa is a good indicator of the ambivalence of British attitudes to Italy generally, composed on the one hand of acquisitive admiration, and on the other of fear and revulsion. Jacobean tragedy had established the negative stereotype of the Italian, characterized by unbridled passion and exorbitant cruelty. Although Radcliffe was ready to utilize happier clichés, for instance in her portrayal of Vivaldi's affectionate and impetuous servant Paolo, it is the dark side of the national type that motivates her story.

Roman Catholicism

The subtitle of the novel, *The Confessional of the Black Penitents*, makes plain the basis of the nightmare vision of Italy: the Roman Catholic Church. Whereas the classical heritage united Western Europe in the eighteenth century, religious difference led to alienation and antagonism, and Italy was in this respect regarded by Protestant nations as the epicentre of spiritual corruption. The confessional privileged in Radcliffe's title was intrinsically sinister for the novel's first audience. Before her readers had begun the first line, they would have been prepared to encounter the dark influence of the Catholic priesthood. The confessional, Protestants argued, gave priests a licence to meddle in matters of individual conscience, extracting secrets, imposing penances or levying indulgences, usurping the divine prerogative to pardon sins and pretending to guarantee a place in heaven. It was taken for granted that members of monastic orders were social parasites, who distorted the word of God in pursuit of their own interests and governed their flock by keeping them in a state of ignorance and superstition. The order of 'the Black Penitents' is an emblematic invention, its blackness a moral and intellectual quality, its austerities mere play-acting.

But although Radcliffe invites such assumptions, she was by no means a straightforward bigot. The prelude that initiates the main narrative is a small masterpiece of ideological self-consciousness and formal dexterity. A party of English travellers enters the portico of the church of Santa Maria del Pianto in Naples, just as the reader approaches the main body of the text through this introductory frame. We share the travellers' visual perspective, first as they admire the architecture, then as they examine closely a loitering figure of singular and menacing appearance. Seamlessly, we are made complicit with their ideological viewpoint, when they are told by a friar that the mysterious man is an assassin who has found sanctuary within the church. '"Do your altars, then, protect the murderer?" said the Englishman. . . . "of what avail are your laws, if the most atrocious criminal may thus find shelter from them?"' (p. 2) The Englishman's horror is ours:

here is a confusion of the spiritual and the temporal, a scandalous survival of an earlier age. The strict separation of religious and civil functions had been one of the guiding tenets of Britain's Glorious Revolution of 1688; it was regarded as a prerequisite of the secular nation-state. The friar responds by observing that the protection of criminals by the Church is not uncommon—and nor, indeed, was the scenario of the outraged British tourist. Two recent and popular travel books had drawn attention to this very phenomenon. In *A View of Society and Manners in Italy*, John Moore blamed the frequency of assassinations in Italy on the custom of sanctuary; while in *Observations and Reflections Made in the Course of a Journey through France, Italy and Germany*, Hester Thrale Piozzi related the story of a friar who had murdered a woman in a church in Naples under scandalous circumstances, and gone unpunished.[11]

The encounter between the self-righteous Englishman and the transgressive Italian should not, therefore, be taken at face value. Radcliffe employs it as a trope, a familiar handle for her readers. Outbursts against the iniquities of foreign lands were an indispensable component of the 'splenetic' mode of travel writing, whose most illustrious practitioner was Tobias Smollett. Radcliffe had herself made humorous obeisance to the tradition in her own contribution to the travel genre, *A Journey Made in the Summer of 1794*.[12] The words of the Englishman at the start of *The Italian* are, in effect, in double quotation marks; on closer inspection we note that his clichéd responses are met by the friar or the travellers' Italian companion with a suavity that quite undermines his own ironic gesture of submission, when he 'gravely bows' at the friar's logic. We then see him falling under the influence of his surroundings, the gloom created by stained-glass, dark wood, and black veiling. The observer has become the object of observation. Finally, we remark his last, shuddering, backward glance at the

[11] Moore, *View of Society* (London, 1781), 460; Piozzi, *Observations and Reflections*, ed. Herbert Barrows (1789; Ann Arbor, 1967), 237.

[12] Radcliffe, *A Journey Made in the Summer of 1794, Through Holland and the Western Frontier of Germany, with a Return Down the Rhine: To Which are Added Observations During a Tour of the Lakes of Lancashire, Westmoreland, and Cumberland* (London, 1795), 102–5.

confessional box as the criminal steals away from it, and his eagerness to read the narrative promised him by his Italian friend, which will explain the mystery of the place. It is a volume we will read alongside him, our *alter ego*; but he vanishes into it, never to re-emerge.

Radcliffe's work has often been described as anti-Catholic, together with the greater part of early Gothic fiction. Unquestionably, she voices some prejudices, and exploits popular preconceptions about Catholicism from time to time to produce an instant atmosphere of enigma and foreboding. But her twentieth-century critics have tended, on their part, to rely on a fixed and simplified notion of British Protestant attitudes which does not do justice to Radcliffe's most engaged and complex treatment of religion, *The Italian*. A review of changes in the politics of religion through the eighteenth century will suggest ways in which Radcliffe and other Gothic writers in fact participated in a gradual liberalizing of religious ideas.

The Revolution of 1688—the forced abdication of the reigning Catholic monarch James II—was carried out in the name of a Protestant succession, but it also served the interests of an emerging political and economic order. The new regime was pledged to uphold the autonomy of Parliament, individual liberties, and security of property, while the Church of England was allotted the role of quiescent handmaiden to the secular state. The Toleration Act of 1689 was chiefly designed to conciliate Protestant Dissenters, but it did enshrine the broad principle that national peace and prosperity were best served by minimal state interference in religious opinion. If it failed to extend the same degree of liberty to Catholics and atheists, this was for reasons expressed by Locke in his *Letter Concerning Toleration*, and widely shared: the 'bonds of human society' were threatened by Catholics, whose teachings advised them not to keep faith with heretics and questioned the sovereignty of non-Catholic rulers, and by atheists, whose denial of the existence of God 'dissolves all'. These sects represented a 'secret evil' in the commonwealth.[13]

[13] See John Locke, *Epistola de Tolerantia: A Letter on Toleration*, ed. R. Klibansky, trans. J. W. Gough (Oxford, 1968), 131–5.

The deposed Catholic Stuarts continued to challenge the legitimacy of the Protestant order in Britain throughout the first half of the eighteenth century. In response, a steady stream of anti-Catholic, and implicitly anti-Stuart, propaganda flowed from the presses, reaching flood proportions in the immediate aftermath of the Jacobite rebellions of 1715 and 1745, and at moments of crisis in the frequent wars with the Catholic states of France and Spain. The same points were repeatedly made. In political terms, the Roman Catholic Church, always inclined to repression and violence, would favour an absolutist regime: it was inimical to national interests, since Catholics must give their primary allegiance to a foreign prince, the Pope. Economically, Catholicism was disastrous: monasteries full of idle monks and nuns drained the economy, while the common people were kept in a state of poverty and inertia, not helped by the vast number of non-working holy days. Popery was incompatible with individual freedom of conscience; in Catholic lands superstition and idolatry were used to sustain ignorant compliance; and if brainwashing failed, there was persecution, the inquisitorial system established to root out heresy by means of anonymous denunciation, torture, and execution.

These were the charges which were persistently levelled, especially in order to rally support for government action at moments of pressure.[14] Yet there was a sense of strain and contradiction here. The propaganda denounced the violence of Popery and the threat it represented to civil order. But the propaganda itself brought religion centrally into the realm of politics: it was an incitement to violence and ran the risk of arousing popular passions which could not necessarily be controlled. After 1746 and the final defeat of the Stuart cause, attempts began to remove this contradiction. Attitudes to Catholicism started to stratify. The hegemonic classes, secure in their inheritance, gradually move towards increased tolerance of Catholics, most concretely through legislative reform, but accompanied at the same time by a growing sense of certain aesthetic possibilities contained in Catholicism.

[14] See Colin Haydon, *Anti-Catholicism in Eighteenth-Century England, c.1714–80. A Political and Social Study* (Manchester and New York, 1993).

It is in this context of increasing tolerance among the educated elite, that Gothic writing first makes its appearance in the second half of the century. By 'Gothic writing' I mean something broader than Gothic fiction beginning with Walpole. For instance, Radcliffe's treatment of Catholicism in her early work owes a great deal to a neglected sub-genre of loco-descriptive poetry.[15] In this poetic mode, the sight of a ruined monastic building provides the poet with an excuse to denounce the reign of superstition and despotism and congratulate her or himself on living in more enlightened times. William Shenstone's 'The Ruined Abbey; or, The Effects of Superstition' can serve as an example.[16] The wandering bard is led into a grove where 'An Abbey's rude remains attract thy view'.[17] But the vista is obstructed with branches, and the bard is next urged to 'Produce thine axe', with an elaborate apology to a 'favourite pine . . . that screens the vast remains'. The motive for this unmitigated act of seeing, apparently so desirable, is twofold. First, and most obviously, the aim is instruction; the abbey in its ruined state is food for the 'philosophic mind'. The rest of the poem duly ranges over the violent history of Catholicism in England and the 'thousand horrid forms' of Popery with becoming moral outrage conveyed in ferocious rhetoric. What raises these ruminations beyond the standard rhetoric is indicated by the word 'sweetly' in the injunction, 'thither oft thine eye | Shall wander sweetly'. This is the other reason for looking at the Abbey: pleasure. It makes all the difference. The viewer-philosopher is separated from the scene of violence in the manner of sublime experience. In this case, however, the distance is temporal rather than physical, and the feelings inspired are less of awe, than of rather nauseating smugness. In this manner, denunciation becomes as stylized and ritualistic as a genuflection. It is devoid of heat, generalized, retrospective, without immediate

[15] The fullest account of the relation of the taste for monastic ruins to Gothic writing is Maurice Lévy's *The Roman 'Gothique' Anglais, 1764–1824* (Toulouse, 1968), 9–47, 143–53, 216–17; I am also indebted here to Robert Miles, who makes the case against equating Gothic with fiction alone in *Gothic Writing 1750–1820* (London and New York, 1993).

[16] First published in Shenstone's posthumous *Collected Works* (1764–9).

[17] Ibid. 61.

political referent. What seems at first sight a continuity is in fact a dislocation. Anti-Catholicism is here reified as literary form and subordinated to the secular, cultural realm. It becomes a facet of individual 'taste'. There is an investment of pleasure, derived from a sense of stability and security.

By the late 1770s, any right-thinking, cultivated person faced with a gothic building in a state of disrepair would know how to respond: with a mixture of aesthetic enthusiasm and strenuous but unfocused disapproval. In the sphere of political reform, however, the course of liberalization did not run so smoothly. In 1780 the Gordon Riots erupted over an attempt to repeal restrictions on Catholics, leaving 285 dead, and revealing a gulf between popular prejudice and an increasingly liberal elite. It was as if the rioters were protesting the loss of their traditional hate-figures.[18] And it was a reminder that the link between religion and violence could not so easily be reduced to a poetic convention. No further attempt to change the law was made until 1791, when the ideological landscape had radically altered.

In the meantime, Radcliffe began her career as an exponent of Gothic taste and aestheticized Catholicism. In her first novel, *The Castles of Athlin and Dunbayne*, reflection on 'ancient superstition' follows the introduction of an abbey with clockwork predictability.[19] In fact it is a telling indication of the conventionality of this motif, that although the story is set in the Middle Ages, the abbey is *already a ruin*. *A Sicilian Romance*, contains the first of many lyrical evocations of monastic architecture that she would write. She describes the abbey of St Augustin in terms which deftly combine censure and reverie: 'The dim glass of the high-arched windows, stained with the colourings of monkish fictions, and shaded by the thick trees that environed the edifice, spread around a sacred gloom, which inspired the beholder with congenial feelings.' The spectacle also inspires, in the approved manner, a militant ode to Superstition, calling on the monk-

---

[18] This was Burke's interpretation; see Robert Hole, *Pulpits, Politics and Public Order in England, 1760–1832* (Cambridge, 1989), 57.

[19] Radcliffe, *The Castles of Athlin and Dunbayne*, ed. Alison Milbank (Oxford and New York, 1995), 102.

created monster to 'Cease your ruin! . . . Cease your wild terrific sway!'.[20]

In the same novel, however, she begins to integrate the monastery as a plot element, specifically with a view to dramatizing the subjection of women in society. Here again, the hint has been given by 'liberal' treatments of Catholicism. Anna Laetitia Aikin's essay 'On Monastic Institutions' begins with a witty play on topographical convention, as the rambling author stumbles upon the inevitable abbey and gives vent to her distaste 'like a good protestant', before being moved to reflect, unexpectedly, on a few of the past benefits of monasticism.[21] For instance, while convents were often complicit with oppressive patriarchy, providing a dumping-ground for 'surplus' women, or serving as a threat to encourage submission to a mercenary marriage, they could also provide a refuge from male violence and a certain independence. Both possibilities are sketched in *A Sicilian Romance*. The negative view is forcefully put by Adeline in *The Romance of the Forest*: to be a nun is to be

[e]xcluded from the cheerful intercourse of society—from the pleasant view of nature—almost from the light of day—condemned to forego the delights of a world, which imagination painted in the gayest and most alluring colours, and whose hues were, perhaps, not the less captivating because they were only ideal:—such was the state, to which I was destined.[22]

These feelings are echoed by Blanche De Villefort in *The Mysteries of Udolpho*, as she tries to dissuade her friend Emily from seeking sanctuary in the convent of St Claire.[23] Yet here, as in *The Italian*, there emerges an alternative sentiment, idealizing the

---

[20] Radcliffe, *A Sicilian Romance*, ed. Alison Milbank (Oxford and New York, 1993), 117, 118.

[21] J. and A. L. Aikin, *Miscellaneous Pieces in Prose* (London, 1773). Lucy Aikin attributes all the pieces in this volume, apart from a poem and the prose fragment 'Sir Bertram', to Anna Laetitia Aikin rather than her brother; *Memoirs of John Aikin, M.D.* (2 vols., London, 1823), i. 21.

[22] Radcliffe, *The Romance of the Forest*, ed. Chloe Chard (Oxford and New York, 1986), 37.

[23] Radcliffe, *The Mysteries of Udolpho*, ed. Bonamy Dobrée (Oxford and New York, 1970), 489.

convent community as a refuge for women, a place where they could escape crisis in the patriarchal family and secure some autonomy. This aspiration had been articulated by the early feminist Mary Astell a century before, in her proposal for a 'Protestant nunnery'.[24] In *The Italian*, Olivia is saved from her violent husband by recourse to religious vows, and eventually finds happiness under the mild regime of the convent of Santa Maria della Pieta.

But by the time Radcliffe came to write *The Italian*, arguments for or against convents must have seemed beside the point. Britain was at war with an atheist state. In France, the monastic orders had been abolished, church property confiscated, and the Cathedral of Notre Dame renamed the Temple of Reason under a programme of radical dechristianization. Priests were required to take an oath of loyalty to the Republic and 'refractories' were either banished or executed; by the end of the Reign of Terror in 1794 more than 900 clergy had been killed, and upwards of 24,000 had emigrated, many of them to Britain. The revolutionary army under Napoleon was invading northern Italy; in 1798 the Papal States were captured and renamed the Roman republic, and Pope Pius VI was imprisoned.

The French Revolution

The French Revolution demanded a complete reordering of attitudes towards religion, as of so much else. At first, it had seemed to follow the 'natural' evolution towards the separation of religious and secular spheres already experienced in Britain, and many across the Channel applauded each new piece of restrictive legislation passed by the revolutionary government in Paris. But soon the dominant sentiment in Britain shifted and, in the words of E. P. Thompson, 'there is a drastic redirection of hatred; the Pope was displaced from the seat of commination and in his place was elevated Tom Paine'.[25] Significantly, when a Catholic

---

[24] See Ruth Perry, *The Celebrated Mary Astell* (Chicago and London, 1986), ch. 5.

[25] *The Making of the English Working Class*, 2nd edn. (Harmondsworth, 1980), 430.

Relief Bill was next broached in Parliament, in 1791, it passed into law without opposition.

The Italian is set in the pre-revolutionary 1750s, but its concerns are dictated by the mid-1790s. At this moment, all the old certainties were thrown into question. When Tom Paine in *The Age of Reason* (1794) condemned the 'adulterous connection of church and state' his words echoed Locke's demands of a century before; but in the new circumstances these words were found highly provocative. Those who had initially welcomed the declining power of the Catholic Church in France were appalled by its complete annihilation. Moderates struggled to reorientate themselves in this altered world, among them Ann Radcliffe.

Although contemporaries and some later admirers were eager to characterize the author as an otherworldly enchantress, it is worth remembering that her husband William was editor of a national newspaper. The *English Chronicle* was a staunchly Whig, oppositional publication. It had greeted the storming of the Bastille with rapture. In 1794, while the Terror raged in Paris, the Radcliffes made a tour on the Continent, skirting the battle lines of the revolutionary war, in Holland and the Rhineland. The next year they published a co-written account of their trip.[26] This included, in addition to minutely detailed reports on recent battles and sieges in the region, descriptions of the wretched plight of prisoners-of-war and of the Radcliffes' own flight down the Rhine before the advancing French army.

Radcliffe's response to the French Revolution in *The Italian*, though subtle, is unmistakable. The novel's prelude, discussed above, is typical of her method. It prepares for a perfectly conventional picture of Catholic malignity, and apparently confirms in the reader a complacent, British and Protestant set of assumptions. But insensibly the contours of the perspective begin to alter, and the reader is brought into a curious empathy with the Catholic Other.

[26] Radcliffe, *Journey Made in the Summer of 1794*. Ann Radcliffe's name alone appears on the title-page, but a preface by her explains that it has been produced collaboratively. It is important to note that Radcliffe does not cede sole responsibility for the political commentary to her husband, as has sometimes been suggested.

The characterization of the villain Schedoni is perhaps the clearest example of post-revolutionary revisionism. At first we see merely a scheming, evil-natured monk; a stock figure, albeit a particularly impressive one, for whom a lineage can be traced from Thomas Leland's *Longsword* (1762), through Walpole's *The Mysterious Mother* (1768), William Hutchison's *The Hermitage* (1772), and Radcliffe's own Abbot in *A Sicilian Romance*, to M. G. Lewis's *The Monk*. In the accustomed manner of Gothic monks, he is ambitious and unscrupulous. He sees an opportunity to ingratiate himself with the Marchesa di Vivaldi, by destroying the budding romance between the young Vivaldi and Ellena of which she disapproves. As so often, the role of confessor is the perfect means of doing mischief. But once Ellena's identity is revealed, the reader is forced to view Schedoni quite differently. Suddenly he is a man with a past, tormented by an unspeakable secret. By the end, in spite of acknowledged crimes, his bearing under sentence of death is capable of commanding respect: 'his firmness or his hardihood never forsook him' (p. 364).

Note, however, that a choice is offered between 'firmness' or 'hardihood'. The degree to which we are called on to sympathize with Schedoni's sufferings has sometimes been exaggerated by the critics, eager to find in him a descendant of Milton's fallen angel, Satan, or a precursor to the Byronic hero. Nevertheless, it is certain that the development of some psychological complexity in Schedoni does away with his formulaic role as embodiment of religious corruption. Even one of Radcliffe's most partial contemporary commentators could not contain his disappointment at this turn of events, describing the monk's change 'from demon to man' as unnatural.[27] Furthermore—and this is the vital point of difference between Radcliffe's villain and Lewis's Ambrosio in *The Monk*—it is revealed that Schedoni committed all his crimes as a layman, and only subsequently joined a religious order as a method of concealment: a rebuttal, then, of the cliché of the monk whose twisted nature is a result of his unnatural monastic existence.

[27] [Thomas Talfourd], 'Memoir of the Author' prefixed to Ann Radcliffe, *Gaston de Blondeville* (4 vols., London, 1826), i. 130.

With Schedoni, a revision of conventions which lets Catholicism off the hook is internalized in the form of a divided psyche. Elsewhere, reparations are almost ludicrously mechanical. The powerful impression of the cruel Abbess at San Stefano, where Ellena is incarcerated, is eventually countered by that of the kind Abbess of Our Lady of Pity.[28] Then there is an effort to redress the balance in the very chambers of the Inquisition, by introducing a *nice* inquisitor. This bizarre invention serves no direct purpose in the plot. It can most readily be interpreted as a symptom of the collective loss of nerve among the Protestant elite in Britain: confidence in the progress of a secular society must falter in the face of French atheism. The Revolution had not gone according to plan, and any religious institution now deserved a second look. Perhaps even the Inquisition couldn't be all bad.[29] Later, the sacrament of confession is also redeemed, this time on the grounds of narrative utility, when Radcliffe opts to ignore the imperative seal of silence and has Father Ansaldo divulge Schedoni's past history.[30]

The Fantasy of the Inquisition

Such devices are a relatively superficial symptom of post-revolutionary feeling. Another widespread phenomenon of those bewildering times was a fascination with conspiracy theories, which in a subtle, even subliminal manner led to acceptance of a culture of persecution and rule by terror, paralysing the naturally humanitarian instincts even of liberal writers. The political anxieties of the day permeate *The Italian*, and manifest themselves most dramatically in what might be called its 'inquisitorial form'. Just as

[28] Her faith, which is described at some length on pp. 299–300, seems close to Unitarianism or even Deism; she remains, however, nominally a Catholic.

[29] Montague Summers amusingly recorded his dismay at finding a description of the countenance of the Grand Inquisitor with 'openness and judgement . . . its chief characteristics', in another novel of 1797, *The Inquisitor* (*The Gothic Quest* (London, 1968), 193).

[30] See Sister Mary Muriel Tarr, *Catholicism in Gothic Fiction: A Study of the Nature and Function of Catholic Materials in Gothic Fiction in England (1762–1820)* (Washington, DC, 1946), 39–42, on Radcliffe's mishandling of Catholic institutions.

heresy had undermined the hegemony of the Papacy in the Middle Ages, in the mid-1790s it was rumoured that secret confederacies were spreading throughout Europe, intent on the overthrow of civilization. The year *The Italian* was published, 1797, was also the year when such rumours were triumphantly yet terrifyingly vindicated by John Robison's *Proofs of a Conspiracy Against All the Religions and Governments of Europe, Carried on in the Secret Meetings of Free Masons, Illuminati, and Reading Societies* and the Abbé Barruel's *Memoirs Illustrating the History of Jacobinism*. Prior to this, the British public had been familiarized with a poetics of conspiracy elaborated by German horror fiction in translation, *Herman of Unna*, *Horrid Mysteries*, and above all, Schiller's *The Ghost-Seer*, with its figure of the inscrutable Armenian, often identified as a prototype for Schedoni. At the same time fears of foreign contamination had been supplemented by suspicions of the enemy within: the growing network of Corresponding Societies in England and Scotland; republican plots in Ireland. But conspiracy theories were not confined to the side of reaction. Demonization of the enemy was the common denominator of extreme revolutionary and of conservative rhetoric, as suspicion on both sides of the Channel led to escalating persecution. In France, there was the Committee of Public Safety and its reign of terror; in Britain, the Committee of Secrecy, the suspension of Habeas Corpus, and the infamous Treason Trials of 1794.

The charge of treason was the chief instrument of rule by terror; in this period of crisis, the characteristic procedures of government control were inquisitorial, proactive, and self-enclosed: a system of spies, arrest on suspicion, indefinite imprisonment, physical and mental torture, trial under the presumption of guilt, the pressing threat of execution. Historians of the medieval Inquisition note that the charge of heresy was modelled on the charge of treason in ancient Roman law. In the aftermath of the French Revolution, it was as if the fanaticism associated with the Inquisition now animated the secular persecution of treason, at the very moment when established religion itself was facing obsolescence on the Continent; a curious return of the repressed.

The image of a secret tribunal along the lines of the Holy Inquisition was as terrifying as the conspiracies it was supposed to combat. It forms part of a collective nightmare ubiquitous in the mid-1790s. Wordsworth in Book x of *The Prelude* speaks of the hold of this fantasy upon him, as he struggled to assimilate the experience of the Terror:

> Such ghastly visions had I of despair
> And tyranny, and implements of death,
> And long orations which in dreams I pleaded
> Before unjust Tribunals, with a voice
> Labouring, a brain confounded . . .

But he then goes on to say, and this reversal is key to an understanding of *The Italian*, 'amid the awe | Of unintelligible chastisement, | I felt a kind of sympathy with power'.[31] In her novel Radcliffe ostensibly condemns the Inquisition, yet at the same time she mimics its procedures in the narration. This 'kind of sympathy with power' was a capitulation to the atmosphere of paranoia dominant at that moment, a replication of the devices of repression, practised upon the mind and nerves of the reader. Everyone who has read any Radcliffe will be familiar with her concealments, her false leads, her techniques of suspense. Victor Sage has discussed *The Mysteries of Udolpho* as a 'tissue of verbal misunderstandings', and shown how 'the whole text forms a kind of via negativa, in which uncertainty about the truth-status of anything we are reading, or the characters are experiencing, is essential to its narrative effect'.[32] With *The Italian* these experiments are taken much further. Whereas in *Udolpho* interpretative error is principally derived from the limited knowledge and overactive imagination of the heroine, in *The Italian* the workings of deception are far more various, pervasive, and difficult to dispel. The narrator turns Grand Inquisitor, and

---

[31] William Wordsworth, *The Prelude: The 1805 Text*, ed. Stephen Gill, 2nd edn. (Oxford and New York, 1970), Book x, lines 374–8, 414–16.

[32] 'The Epistemology of Error: Reading and Isolation in *The Mysteries of Udolpho*', *Qwerty*, 6 (1996), 107.

the reader is implicated simultaneously as victim and accomplice.

The novel is characterized by a number of manoeuvres analogous to inquisitorial procedure: suspicion, mystification, torture, confession. These are fluid features rather than linear stages, and they constantly shift in their effect from characters to reader. Nevertheless, confession is the desired end of the process; confession, rather than truth. Insofar as inquisition constitutes a judicial method in *The Italian*, a means of resolving the mystery from the past that threatens to overwhelm the present with disaster, there will be no attempt to derive knowledge from a dispassionate survey of evidence. Truth, defined as the adherence of evidence to reality, will not appear. Instead, suspicion has a determining priority. This priority is thematized at an early stage through the character of Schedoni, who, we are told 'cared not for truth. . . . At length, from a habit of intricacy and suspicion, his vitiated mind could receive nothing for truth, which was simple and easily comprehended' (p. 34). When at a later stage Schedoni, on the defensive, temporarily forgets these habits, he is reminded by a suspicious peasant, 'Now, it is not one time in ten that any thing can be proved, Signor, as you well know, yet we none of us believe it the less for that!' (p. 278). This indifference to truth is not unique to the villain. Vivaldi, by the time he faces the tribunal of the Inquisition, has already shown a tendency to place suspicion before verifiable fact, especially by his indulgence in superstition. Under the threat of torture he finally gives way and passes on the unauthorized rumours which will inculpate and eventually condemn his enemy, Schedoni. Irresistibly he is drawn into collusion with an authority that judges by supposition and condemns on the basis of confession alone; a confession which may be obtained by any means—lies and deception, enticement, threat, or act of violence. At the start of his confinement Vivaldi had boldly declared, 'It is not the truth, which you seek; it is not the guilty, whom you punish; the innocent, having no crimes to confess, are the victims of your cruelty, or, to escape from it, become criminal, and proclaim a lie' (p. 203). By the end, his interests have become identified with those of the Inquisition; his future happiness will be ensured by its agency, all objections forgotten.[33]

Suspicion is similarly fundamental to the experience of reading *The Italian*. The reader must accompany Vivaldi down the path of inquisitorial consciousness. In contrast to the accusatory procedure, which depends upon one private individual bringing a charge against another, a tribunal of the inquisition acts on the presupposition of crime, and then sets about discovering the criminal. The tribunal is 'at once the Prosecutor, Witness, and Judge!' (p. 206), as Vivaldi recognizes, appalled. It relies upon informers and secret denunciation. From the start of *The Italian* this role is taken primarily by the narrator, though Vivaldi with his active imagination aids and abets. Father Schedoni, from his first introduction, is freely incriminated through the 'anonymous' medium of narration (see pp. 34–5), supplemented by the irrational prejudice of Vivaldi. Regardless of the fact that this first impression turns out to be accurate, what is significant is that no sufficient evidence is produced to support it until about halfway through the novel, when we witness Schedoni's proposal to murder Ellena. Presentiment is the operative principle of the narrative's progression.

Deliberate mystification serves to confuse judgement still further. The insistent imagery of veils and veiling in the novel has been the subject of some interesting critical discussion; taken alternatively as symbolic of division or of oblique revelation.[34]

---

[33] Vivaldi's willingness to swear an oath 'to reveal the truth' before an authority he regards as unjust (201–2, cf. 326) relates interestingly to J. C. D. Clark's theory of eighteenth-century Britain as a 'confessional state' (*English Society, 1688–1832* (Cambridge, 1985)). Here confession represents a formal submission to established faith which is the basis of citizenship; oaths were required for most forms of professional advancement, and confession in this sense was therefore an invitation to hypocrisy and self-division. It should not be confused with the function of confession as it appears in Michel Foucault's *The History of Sexuality: An Introduction* (Harmondsworth, 1979): an articulation of inner depth, the essential 'truth' of the individual.

[34] See Elizabeth Broadwell, 'The Veil Image in Ann Radcliffe's *The Italian*', *South Atlantic Bulletin*, 40 (1975); Eve Kosofsky Sedgwick, *The Coherence of Gothic Conventions* (New York and London, 1986), 98–140; and Susan C. Greenfield, 'Veiled Desire: Mother–Daughter Love and Sexual Imagery in Ann Radcliffe's *The Italian*', *The Eighteenth Century: Theory and Interpretation*, 33 (1992), 73–89.

The story begins with the veil which tantalizes the enquiring eye of Vivaldi, at once concealing and exposing Ellena's charms. Here, as at the start of *The Monk*, this moment of decorous striptease signals looming disaster. The obstruction of vision, a metaphor for understanding, is always dangerous. In *The Italian* the veil and its equivalents are for the most part a tool of arbitrary power: the monk's habit masks identity and grants unwarranted prestige; Ellena is pressured to 'take the veil'; the nun's veil she wears becomes the pretext for Vivaldi's arrest; imprisoned by the Inquisition, Vivaldi is blindfolded by a black veil, his guards are strangely masked and the chamber of the tribunal is rendered more ominous by arrangements of black canopies and screens; the cultivation of irrational fear through superstition is itself a blind. The confessional box, with its grille emphasizing the absolute authority of the priest and the subordination of the confessant by an artful combination of access and concealment, can serve as a paradigm of veiling as a relation of power. Solitary confinement is an extension of this relation; mental isolation imposed as physical constraint. Radcliffe shows the principal horror of imprisonment to be the threat to reason: it involves vulnerability to deception, the tendency to speculate, and indulge in imaginary fears and conclusions. Ellena is saved by information passed to her by an ally within her prison-convent. Vivaldi, in contrast, is bewildered and disarmed by a maze of misinformation.

The reader is similarly isolated and repeatedly misled. One example of this appears in the very first epigraph at the start of Chapter I, a quotation from *The Mysterious Mother*, a play by Horace Walpole, that asks 'What is this secret sin . . .?'. The epigraphs are themselves a form of veiling, suggesting hidden knowledge, a key to the text which lies elsewhere. The reference to *The Mysterious Mother* implies the 'secret sin' of incest; a hint compounded much later in the novel by a rambling inset narrative told by a guide to Schedoni and Ellena, concerning the wicked Barone di Cambrusca and his daughter who 'had lived too long' (p. 270). The reader is incarcerated in a fabric of misleading expectations—as will become plain by the end of the novel. It is enough to say here that no promise is more delusory than that made in the prelude: 'the facts are what you require, and from these [the narrator] has not deviated' (p. 4). The destabilizing force of the introductory encounter between the English tourist and the Italian assassin is neither redeemed nor exorcized.

Torture, referred to euphemistically by the Inquisition as 'being put to the question', is represented as a state of anticipation in *The Italian*. We are persuaded that Vivaldi suffers more through dread and uncertainty than he could do on the rack. The formal correlative of this suffering is, of course, suspense. In addition to the hovering suggestions already referred to, Radcliffe creates suspense, more effectively here than in any of her previous works, through a series of interrupted inset narratives, and most forcibly, by switching between the two equally tense plotlines concerning Ellena and Vivaldi in the second half.[35]

The desired result of the Inquisition is confession, and the readerly equivalent of confession is affect: immersion in feeling. The final truth of the narration does not lie in moral instruction, as it did, at least nominally, in the rest of Radcliffe's oeuvre and indeed nearly all eighteenth-century fiction. The point of this text lies in the sensations that it arouses.[36] It represents a convergence of the inquisitorial method with the self-interrogations of Rousseau in the *Confessions*, a sacred text of the cult of sensibility. The politics of such a reader-position are that of compliant, depoliticized surrender to the emotion of the moment, whether of terror or of pleasure, without seeking very far into causes or consequences.[37] Walter Scott's complaint about the 'loose stitches'

[35] See Mark M. Hennelly, Jr, ' "The Slow Torture of Delay": Reading *The Italian*', *Studies in the Humanities*, 14: 1 (1987), 1–17.

[36] The dialogue between the story-telling peasant and Schedoni, which David Punter in *The Literature of Terror* has described as 'a masterly parody of the twists and turns of Gothic fiction itself' (rev. edn. (2 vols.; London and New York, 1996), i. 64), significantly ends with a failure of evidence and an appeal to affect: ' "I have listened too long to this idle history," said the Confessor, "there seems to be no rational foundation for it . . ." "Well Signor, 'tis plain you know the rest already, or you never would go without it . . . I am sure it made my hair stand on end to hear of it, what an unaccountable—" ' (285).

[37] Other critics have tended to see this process as a form of positive consciousness-raising. For Syndy M. Conger, 'nightmare provokes self-examination and growth in readers' ('Sensibility Restored: Radcliffe's Answer to Lewis's *The Monk*', in Kenneth W. Graham (ed.), *Gothic Fictions: Prohibition/ Transgression* (New York,

in the novel is relevant here.[38] We will never know why Schedoni reacts so strongly to the unfinished tale of the Barone di Cambrusca, nor how the thrilling effect of the disembodied voice was created in the court of the Inquisition, nor indeed Father Nicola Zampari's real motives for denouncing Schedoni. Ignorance is integral to affect, and there will be no ultimate enlightenment, no overview, no security in the valedictory words of an omniscient narrator. In place of the conventional maxims on the wisdom of divine providence which concluded earlier works by Radcliffe, there is a burst of joy, a will to happiness in the face of ineradicable darkness.[39]

The Italian is generally regarded as Radcliffe's most accomplished and exciting novel; it is the work in which she makes the most direct commitment to the pleasures of the imagination for their own sake, moving didacticism into the background. In this sense, it participates in a shift towards an escapist model of popular fiction which continues to hold good today. It is ironic, then, that Radcliffe should have been pushed in this direction, to a great extent, by her attempt to come to terms with the politics of Revolution. When the moderate Girondins went to the guillotine in 1793, the expectations and assumptions of their counterparts in England, reform-minded Whigs like Radcliffe and her husband, also expired. Consciously, Radcliffe moderated her criticism of Catholicism in response to atheist republicanism. Perhaps more unconsciously, she allowed her narrative technique to be drawn into the vortex of doubt and suspicion at the centre of the Revolution debate, and tacitly endorsed the practices of terrorist

1989, 114); for Punter the reader is a 'creative participant' (*Literature of Terror*, 85); while Hennelly proposes that 'the reader begins to appreciate . . . that a Gothic tormentor can finally become a Gothic mentor' ('Slow Torture of Delay', 4).

[38] *Sir Walter Scott on Novelists and Fiction*, ed. Ioan Williams (London, 1968), 108–9.

[39] Charlotte Brontë was observant of this combination of Utopianism and despair in the novel. In *Shirley*, II. xii, she juxtaposes the response of the child, Rose Yorke, midway through reading *The Italian*—'you feel as if you were far away from England,—really in Italy—under another sort of sky. . . . It makes me long to travel'—and that of the pragmatic Caroline Helstone, who while she agrees that it 'seemed to open with such promise', describes the tale as ending 'in disappointment, vanity, and vexation of spirit'.

government which emerged from the post-revolutionary back-lash.

The Italian can usefully be read alongside the contemporary work of the Jacobin novelists, who made fiction the vehicle of their radical convictions. Novels such as *Caleb Williams* and *St Leon* by William Godwin, *Maria; or the Wrongs of Woman* by Mary Wollstonecraft, and *Secresy* by Eliza Fenwick, share a concern with the dangerous allure of superstition (irrational beliefs being equated with subservience to a mystified social hierarchy), conflict with arbitrary power, and the experience of wrongful imprisonment. These writers, like Radcliffe, were responding to the most powerful reactionary statement on recent events, *Reflections on the Revolution in France* (1790), in which Edmund Burke, the former champion of the American Revolution, made a plea for mystery and irrational faith as the vital basis of social stability. Jacobin fiction rejected this argument while drawing on devices popularized by Gothic writers such as Radcliffe. The effect on Radcliffe herself was more ambiguous. Avoiding meta-language, she absorbed the ideological problems of her time, and out of them forged a compelling mode of narration which would inspire a new generation of writers, including Walter Scott, Charles Maturin, James Hogg, Thomas De Quincy, and Mary and Percy Shelley.

E. J. C.

NOTE ON THE TEXT

THE text used in this volume is taken from the first edition of 1797. In the same year a second edition appeared, also from Cadell and Davies of London, and there were other editions in Dublin, New York, and Philadelphia, as well as a number of translations. The date of the last edition published in Radcliffe's lifetime is 1811; it is erroneously styled the second edition, and although it shows hundreds of changes, the author is unlikely to have participated.

Obvious printing errors have been silently altered in the present version. The original punctuation, grammar and spelling (apart from the long 's') have been retained, although they are occasionally erratic. For instance, 'Shakespeare' alternates with 'Shakspeare' in the attribution of epigraphs; '*Maestro*', the servant Paulo's favourite term of address, is not always italicized, and once appears with an added acute accent over the 'e'. Such inconsistencies were not uncommon in eighteenth-century publishing.

SELECT BIBLIOGRAPHY

1. *Bibliography*

Frank, Frederick S., *The First Gothics: A Critical Guide to the English Gothic Novel* (New York and London, 1987).

——*Gothic Fiction: A Master List of Twentieth-Century Criticism and Selected Texts* (London, 1988).

McNutt, D. J., *The Eighteenth-Century Gothic Novel: An Annotated Bibliography of Criticism and Selected texts* (Folkestone, 1975).

Rogers, Deborah D., *Ann Radcliffe: A Bio-Bibliography* (Westport, Conn., and London, 1996).

Spector, Robert Donald, *The English Gothic: A Bibliographic Guide to Writers from Horace Walpole to Mary Shelley* (London and Westport, Conn., 1984).

Summers, Montague, *A Gothic Bibliography* (New York, 1941).

2. *On Gothic Writing*

Baker, E. A., *The Novel of Sentiment and the Gothic Romance* (The History of the English Novel, v; New York, 1929).

Birkhead, Edith, *The Tale of Terror: A Study of the Gothic Romance* (London, 1921).

Botting, Fred, *Gothic* (London and New York, 1996).

Castle, Terry, *The Female Thermometer: Eighteenth-Century Culture and the Invention of the Uncanny* (Oxford and New York, 1995).

Clery, E. J., *The Rise of Supernatural Fiction, 1762–1800* (Cambridge, 1995).

Day, William Patrick, *In the Circles of Fear and Desire: A Study of Gothic Fantasy* (Chicago and London, 1985).

Delamotte, Eugenia, *Perils of the Night: A Feminist Study of Nine-teenth-Century Gothic* (New York and Oxford, 1990).

Ellis, Kate F., *The Contested Castle: Gothic Novels and the Subversion of Domestic Ideology* (Urbana, Ill., and Chicago, 1989).

Fleenor, Juliann E. (ed.), *The Female Gothic* (Montreal and London, 1983).

Haggerty, George E., *Gothic Fiction/ Gothic Form* (University Park, Pa., and London, 1989).

Howard, Jacqueline, *Reading Gothic Fiction: A Bakhtinian Approach* (Oxford, 1994).

Howells, Coral Ann, *Love, Mystery and Misery: Feeling in Gothic Fiction* (1978; 2nd edn., London, 1996).

Kelly, Gary, *English Fiction of the Romantic Period, 1789–1830* (London and New York, 1989).

Kiely, Robert, *The Romantic Novel in England* (Cambridge, Mass., 1972).

Kilgour, Maggie, *The Rise of the Gothic Novel* (London and New York, 1995).

Lévy, Maurice, *Le Roman 'gothique' anglais, 1764–1824* (1968; 2nd edn., Paris, 1996).

Miles, Robert, *Gothic Writing 1750–1820: A Genealogy* (London and New York, 1993).

——(ed.), *Female Gothic Writing*, special number of *Women's Writing*, 1: 2 (1994).

Napier, Elizabeth, *The Failure of Gothic: Problems of Disjunction in an Eighteenth-Century Literary Form* (Oxford, 1987).

Punter, David, *The Literature of Terror*, 2 vols. (1980; 2nd edn., London and New York, 1996).

Railo, Eino, *The Haunted Castle: A Study of the Elements of English Romanticism* (London and New York, 1927).

Sage, Victor, *Horror Fiction in the Protestant Tradition* (Basingstoke and London, 1988).

Sedgwick, Eve K., *The Coherence of Gothic Conventions* (New York, 1980).

Summers, Montague, *The Gothic Quest: A History of the Gothic Novel* (London, 1938).

Todorov, Tzvetan, *The Fantastic: A Structural Approach to a Literary Genre* (Ithaca, NY, 1975).

Tompkins, J. M. S., *The Popular Novel in England, 1770–1800* (London, 1932).

Varma, Devendra P., *The Gothic Flame* (London, 1957).

3. *On Radcliffe and* The Italian

Canuel, Mark, '"Holy Hypocrisy" and the Government of Belief: Religion and Nationalism in the Gothic', *Studies in Romanticism*, 34 (Winter 1995), 507–30.

Conger, Syndy M., 'Sensibility Restored: Radcliffe's Answer to Lewis's

The Monk', in Kenneth W. Graham (ed.), *Gothic Fictions: Prohibition/Transgression* (New York, 1989), 113–49.

Cottom, Daniel, *The Civilized Imagination: A Study of Ann Radcliffe, Jane Austen, and Sir Walter Scott* (Cambridge, 1985).

Durant, David, 'Ann Radcliffe and the Conservative Gothic', *Studies in English Literature*, 22 (1982), 519–29.

Grant, Aline, *Ann Radcliffe: A Biography* (Denver, 1951).

Greenfield, Susan C., 'Veiled Desire: Mother–Daughter Love and Sexual Imagery in Ann Radcliffe's *The Italian*', *The Eighteenth Century: Theory and Interpretation*, 33 (1992), 73–89.

Hennelly, Mark M., Jr., ' "The Slow Torture of Delay": Reading *The Italian*', *Studies in the Humanities*, 14: 1 (1987), 1–17.

Howells, Coral Ann, 'The Pleasures of the Woman's Text: Ann Radcliffe's Subtle Transgressions in *The Mysteries of Udolpho* and *The Italian*', in Kenneth W. Graham (ed.), *Gothic Fictions*, 158–61.

McIntyre, C. F., *Ann Radcliffe in Relation to Her Time* (New Haven, 1920).

Miles, Robert, *Gothic Writing 1750–1820: A Genealogy* (London and New York, 1993).

——*Ann Radcliffe: The Great Enchantress* (Manchester and New York, 1995).

Murray, E. B., *Ann Radcliffe* (New York, 1972).

Punter, David, *The Literature of Terror*, 2 vols., vol. i, 2nd edn. (London and New York, 1996).

Rogers, Deborah D. (ed.), *The Critical Response to Ann Radcliffe* (London and Westport, Conn., 1994).

Sage, Victor, *Horror Fiction in the Protestant Tradition* (Basingstoke and London, 1988).

Saglia, Diego, 'Looking at the Other: Cultural Difference and the Traveller's Gaze in *The Italian*', *Studies in the Novel*, 28: 1 (1996), 12–37.

Schmitt, Cannon, 'Techniques of Terror, Technologies of Nationality: Ann Radcliffe's *The Italian*', *English Literary History*, 61 (1994), 853–76.

Shuttleworth, Sally, 'Psychiatric Discourse and the Novel of the Romantic Era: Ann Radcliffe's *The Italian* and William Godwin's *Caleb Williams*', in B. Castel, J. A. Leith, and A. W. Riley (eds.), *Muse and Reason: The Relation of Arts and Sciences 1650–1850. A Royal Society Symposium, Queen's Quarterly* (1994), 179–202.

Spacks, Patricia Meyer, 'Female Orders of Narrative: *Clarissa* and *The*

Italian', in J. Douglas Canfield and J. Paul Hunter (eds.), *Rhetorics of Order / Ordering Rhetorics in English Neoclassical Literature* (Newark, London, and Toronto, 1989), 158–72.

Stoler, John F., *Ann Radcliffe: The Novel of Terror and Suspense* (New York, 1980).

Todd, Janet, 'Posture and Imposture: The Gothic Manservant in Ann Radcliffe's *The Italian*', *Women and Literature*, 2 (1982), 25–38.

Tompkins, J. M. S., *The Work of Mrs Radcliffe and its Influence on Later Writers* (1921; repr. New York, 1980).

Ware, Malcolm, *Sublimity in the Novels of Ann Radcliffe* (Uppsala and Copenhagen, 1963).

CHRONOLOGY OF ANN RADCLIFFE

1764 9 July, born in London, daughter of William Ward, a haberdasher, and Ann Ward (née Oates). Related on her father's side to the surgeon Colonel Cheseldon and on her mother's side to the Bishop of Gloucester.

1772 Moves to Bath, where she may have attended Sophia Lee's school for young ladies. Family visits paid to the London home of Thomas Bentley, partner of Josiah Wedgwood and Radcliffe's uncle by marriage.

1787 Marries William Radcliffe, Oxford graduate, parliamentary reporter and proprietor of the *English Chronicle*. Encouraged by husband in first writing ventures.

1789 *The Castles of Athlin and Dunbayne*, a short novel, published anonymously.

1790 *A Sicilian Romance*, 2 vols., published anonymously.

1791 *The Romance of the Forest, Interspersed with some Pieces of Poetry*, 3 vols. First edition published anonymously; authorship acknowledged in advertisement to second edition the following year.

1794 *The Mysteries of Udolpho, A Romance, Interspersed with some Pieces of Poetry*, 4 vols. Literary reputation established with popular success of novel at home and abroad. Makes tour of war-torn Netherlands and Germany with husband, travelling down the Rhine as far as the Swiss border. Tour of the Lake District in autumn.

1795 *A Journey Made in the Summer of 1794, through Holland and the Western Frontier of Germany, with a Return Down the Rhine: To Which Are Added Observations During a Tour of the Lakes of Lancashire and Westmoreland, and Cumberland*. Death of father.

1796 Death of mother.

1797 *The Italian, or the Confessional of the Black Penitents*,[1] 3 vols.

---

[1] Although the title-page of the 1st edn. of *The Italian* bears the date '1797', the novel was advertised as having been published in the *Oracle and Public Advertiser* of 12 Dec. 1796 and the *St James's Chronicle* of 13–15 Dec. 1796; see James Raven and Antonia Forster, *English Novels 1770–1799: A Bibliographical Survey* (Oxford, 1998).

Ceases publishing, owing to new-found financial independence. Tour of Kent and south-east coast.

1798 Subject of laudatory essay (attributed to S. T. Coleridge) in the *Critical Review*.

1801 Tour of Southampton, Portsmouth, and Isle of Wight.

1802 *Gaston de Blondeville* completed after visiting Kenilworth Castle, but 'laid aside, so disinclined had she become to publication' (Talfourd). Increasingly shuns literary society.

1810 Anonymous 'Ode to Terror' printed in which it is asserted that Radcliffe has gone mad and died of 'the horrors'.

1816 Publication of *The Poems of Ann Radcliffe*, an unauthorized reprint of poems from the novels.

1823 7 February, dies of asthmatic fever after bout of delirium. Claim made in the *Monthly Review* that 'she died in a state of mental desolation not to be described'.

1826 'On the Supernatural in Poetry', *New Monthly Magazine*, 7. *Gaston de Blondeville, or the Court of Henry III Keeping Festival in Ardenne, A Romance* and *St Alban's Abbey, A Metrical Tale* published posthumously in 4-vol. set prefaced by Thomas Talfourd's 'Memoir of the Life and Writings of Mrs Radcliffe'.

THE

ITALIAN,

OR THE

CONFESSIONAL of the BLACK PENITENTS.

A ROMANCE.

BY

ANN RADCLIFFE,

AUTHOR OF THE MYSTERIES OF UDOLPHO, &c. &c.

He, wrapt in clouds of myſtery and ſilence,
Broods o'er his paſſions, bodies them in deeds,
And ſends them forth on wings of Fate to others :
Like the inviſible Will, that guides us,
Unheard, unknown, unſearchable !

IN THREE VOLUMES.

VOL. I.

LONDON:

Printed for T. CADELL Jun. and W. DAVIES
(Succeſſors to Mr. CADELL) in the STRAND.

1797.

Title-page of the first edition, 1797

THE ITALIAN

OR THE

CONFESSIONAL OF THE
BLACK PENITENTS[1]

———

ABOUT the year 1764, some English travellers in Italy, during one
of their excursions in the environs of Naples, happened to stop
before the portico of the *Santa Maria del Pianto*,* a church belonging to a very ancient convent of the order of the *Black Penitents*.
The magnificence of this portico, though impaired by time, excited
so much admiration, that the travellers were curious to survey the
structure to which it belonged, and with this intention they
ascended the marble steps that led to it.

Within the shade of the portico, a person with folded arms, and
eyes directed towards the ground, was pacing behind the pillars
the whole extent of the pavement, and was apparently so engaged
by his own thoughts, as not to observe that strangers were approaching. He turned, however, suddenly, as if startled by the sound of
steps, and then, without further pausing, glided to a door that
opened into the church, and disappeared.

There was something too extraordinary in the figure of this man,
and too singular in his conduct, to pass unnoticed by the visitors.
He was of a tall thin figure, bending forward from the shoulders;
of a sallow complexion, and harsh features, and had an eye, which,
as it looked up from the cloke that muffled the lower part of his
countenance, seemed expressive of uncommon ferocity.

The travellers, on entering the church, looked round for the
stranger, who had passed thither before them, but he was no
where to be seen, and, through all the shade of the long aisles,
only one other person appeared. This was a friar of the adjoining
convent, who sometimes pointed out to strangers the objects in
the church, which were most worthy of attention, and who now,
with this design, approached the party that had just entered.

The interior of this edifice had nothing of the shewy ornament and general splendor, which distinguish the churches of Italy, and particularly those of Naples; but it exhibited a simplicity and grandeur of design, considerably more interesting to persons of taste, and a solemnity of light and shade much more suitable to promote the sublime elevation of devotion.

When the party had viewed the different shrines and whatever had been judged worthy of observation, and were returning through an obscure aisle towards the portico, they perceived the person who had appeared upon the steps, passing towards a confessional on the left, and, as he entered it, one of the party pointed him out to the friar, and enquired who he was; the friar turning to look after him, did not immediately reply, but, on the question being repeated, he inclined his head, as in a kind of obeisance, and calmly replied, 'He is an assassin.'

'An assassin!' exclaimed one of the Englishmen; 'an assassin and at liberty!'

An Italian gentleman, who was of the party, smiled at the astonishment of his friend.

'He has sought sanctuary here,' replied the friar; 'within these walls he may not be hurt.'

'Do your altars, then, protect the murderer?' said the Englishman.

'He could find shelter no where else,' answered the friar meekly.

'This is astonishing!' said the Englishman; 'of what avail are your laws, if the most atrocious criminal may thus find shelter from them? But how does he contrive to exist here! He is, at least, in danger of being starved?'

'Pardon me,' replied the friar; 'there are always people willing to assist those, who cannot assist themselves; and as the criminal may not leave the church in search of food, they bring it to him here.'

'Is this possible!' said the Englishman, turning to his Italian friend.

'Why, the poor wretch must not starve,' replied the friend; 'which he inevitably would do, if food were not brought to him! But have you never, since your arrival in Italy, happened to see a person in the situation of this man? It is by no means an uncommon one.'*

'Never!' answered the Englishman, 'and I can scarcely credit what I see now!'

'Why, my friend,' observed the Italian, 'if we were to shew no mercy to such unfortunate persons, assassinations are so frequent, that our cities would be half depopulated.'

In notice of this profound remark, the Englishman could only gravely bow.

'But observe yonder confessional,' added the Italian, 'that beyond the pillars on the left of the aisle, below a painted window. Have you discovered it? The colours of the glass throw, instead of light, a shade over that part of the church, which, perhaps, prevents your distinguishing what I mean!'

The Englishman looked whither his friend pointed, and observed a confessional of oak, or some very dark wood, adjoining the wall, and remarked also, that it was the same, which the assassin had just entered. It consisted of three compartments, covered with a black canopy. In the central division was the chair of the confessor, elevated by several steps above the pavement of the church; and on either hand was a small closet, or box, with steps leading up to a grated partition, at which the penitent might kneel, and, concealed from observation, pour into the ear of the confessor, the consciousness of crimes that lay heavy on his heart.

'You observe it?' said the Italian.

'I do,' replied the Englishman; 'it is the same, which the assassin has passed into; and I think it one of the most gloomy spots I ever beheld; the view of it is enough to strike a criminal with despair!'

'We, in Italy, are not so apt to despair,' replied the Italian smilingly.

'Well, but what of this confessional?' enquired the Englishman. 'The assassin entered it!'

'He has no relation, with what I am about to mention,' said the Italian; 'but I wish you to mark the place, because some very extraordinary circumstances belong to it.'

'What are they?' said the Englishman.

'It is now several years since the confession, which is connected with them, was made at that very confessional,' added the Italian; 'the view of it, and the sight of this assassin, with your surprize at the liberty which is allowed him, led me to a recollection of the story. When you return to the hotel, I will communicate it to you, if you have no pleasanter way of engaging your time.'

'I have a curiosity to hear it,' replied the Englishman, 'cannot you relate it now?'

'It is much too long to be related now; that would occupy a week; I have it in writing, and will send you the volume. A young student of Padua, who happened to be at Naples soon after this horrible confession became public'——

'Pardon me,' interrupted the Englishman, 'that is surely very extraordinary? I thought confessions were always held sacred by the priest, to whom they were made.'

'Your observation is reasonable,' rejoined the Italian; 'the faith of the priest is never broken, except by an especial command from an higher power; and the circumstances must even then be very extraordinary to justify such a departure from the law. But, when you read the narrative, your surprise on this head will cease. I was going to tell you, that it was written by a student of Padua, who, happening to be here soon after the affair became public, was so much struck with the facts, that, partly as an exercise, and partly in return for some trifling services I had rendered him, he committed them to paper for me. You will perceive from the work, that this student was very young, as to the arts of composition, but the facts are what you require, and from these he has not deviated. But come, let us leave the church.'

'After I have taken another view of this solemn edifice,' replied the Englishman, 'and particularly of the confessional you have pointed to my notice!'

While the Englishman glanced his eye over the high roofs, and along the solemn perspectives of the Santa del Pianto, he perceived the figure of the assassin stealing from the confessional across the choir, and, shocked on again beholding him, he turned his eyes, and hastily quitted the church.

The friends then separated, and the Englishman, soon after returning to his hotel, received the volume. He read as follows:

VOLUME I

CHAPTER I

What is this secret sin; this untold tale,
That art cannot extract, nor penance cleanse?
MYSTERIOUS MOTHER*

IT was in the church of San Lorenzo at Naples, in the year 1758, that Vincentio di Vivaldi first saw Ellena Rosalba. The sweetness and fine expression of her voice attracted his attention to her figure, which had a distinguished air of delicacy and grace; but her face was concealed in her veil. So much indeed was he fascinated by the voice, that a most painful curiosity was excited as to her countenance, which he fancied must express all the sensibility of character that the modulation of her tones indicated. He listened to their exquisite expression with a rapt attention, and hardly withdrew his eyes from her person till the matin service had concluded; when he observed her leave the church with an aged lady, who leaned upon her arm, and who appeared to be her mother.

Vivaldi immediately followed their steps, determined to obtain, if possible, a view of Ellena's face, and to discover the home to which she should retire. They walked quickly, looking neither to the right or left, and as they turned into the Strada di Toledo he had nearly lost them; but quickening his pace, and relinquishing the cautious distance he had hitherto kept, he overtook them as they entered on the Terrazzo Nuovo, which runs along the bay of Naples, and leads towards the Gran Corso. He overtook them; but the fair unknown still held her veil close, and he knew not how to introduce himself to her notice, or to obtain a view of the features, which excited his curiosity. He was embarrassed by a respectful timidity, that mingled with his admiration, and which kept him silent, notwithstanding his wish to speak.

In descending the last steps of the *Terrazzo*, however, the foot of the elder lady faltered, and, while Vivaldi hastened to assist her, the breeze from the water caught the veil, which Ellena had no longer a hand sufficiently disengaged to confine, and, wafting it partially aside, disclosed to him a countenance more touchingly beautiful than he had dared to image. Her features were of the Grecian outline, and, though they expressed the tranquillity of an elegant mind, her dark blue eyes sparkled with intelligence. She was assisting her companion so anxiously, that she did not immediately observe the admiration she had inspired; but the moment her eyes met those of Vivaldi, she became conscious of their effect, and she hastily drew her veil.

The old lady was not materially hurt by her fall, but, as she walked difficultly, Vivaldi seized the opportunity thus offered, and insisted that she should accept his arm. She refused this with many acknowledgments; but he pressed the offer so repeatedly and respectfully, that, at length, she accepted it, and they walked towards her residence together.

On the way thither, he attempted to converse with Ellena, but her replies were concise, and he arrived at the end of the walk while he was yet considering what he could say, that might interest and withdraw her from this severe reserve. From the style of their residence, he imagined that they were persons of honourable, but moderate independence. The house was small, but exhibited an air of comfort, and even of taste. It stood on an eminence, surrounded by a garden and vineyards, which commanded the city and bay of Naples, an ever-moving picture, and was canopied by a thick grove of pines and majestic date-trees; and, though the little portico and colonnade in front were of common marble, the style of architecture was elegant. While they afforded a shelter from the sun, they admitted the cooling breezes that rose from the bay below, and a prospect of the whole scope of its enchanting shores.

Vivaldi stopped at the little gate, which led into the garden, where the elder lady repeated her acknowledgments for his care, but did not invite him to enter; and he, trembling with anxiety and sinking with disappointment, remained for a moment gazing upon Ellena, unable to take leave, yet irresolute what to say that might prolong the interview, till the old lady again bade him good-day. He then summoned courage enough to request he might be allowed to enquire after her health, and, having obtained her permission, his eyes bade adieu to Ellena, who, as they were parting, ventured to thank him for the care he had taken of her aunt. The sound of her voice, and this acknowledgment of obligation, made him less willing to go than before, but at length he tore himself away. The beauty of her countenance haunting his imagination, and the touching accents of her voice still vibrating on his heart, he descended to the shore below her residence, pleasing himself with the consciousness of being near her, though he could no longer behold her; and sometimes hoping that he might again see her, however distantly, in a balcony of the house, where the silk awning seemed to invite the breeze from the sea. He lingered hour after hour, stretched beneath the umbrageous pines that waved over the shore, or traversing, regardless of the heat, the base of the cliffs that crowned it; recalling to his fancy the enchantment of her smile, and seeming still to listen to the sweetness of her accents.

In the evening he returned to his father's palace at Naples, thoughtful yet pleased, anxious yet happy; dwelling with delightful hope on the remembrance of the thanks he had received from Ellena, yet not daring to form any plan as to his future conduct. He returned time enough to attend his mother in her evening ride on the Corso, where, in every gay carriage that passed, he hoped to see the object of his constant thought; but she did not appear. His mother, the Marchesa di Vivaldi, observed his anxiety and unusual silence, and asked him some questions, which she meant should lead to an explanation of the change in his manners; but his replies only excited a stronger curiosity, and, though she forbore to press her enquiries, it was probable that she might employ a more artful means of renewing them.

Vincentio di Vivaldi was the only son of the Marchese di Vivaldi, a nobleman of one of the most ancient families of the kingdom of Naples, a favourite possessing an uncommon share of influence at Court, and a man still higher in power than in rank. His pride of birth was equal to either, but it was mingled with the justifiable pride of a principled mind; it governed his conduct in morals as well as in the jealousy of ceremonial distinctions, and elevated his practice as well as his claims. His pride was at once his vice and his virtue, his safeguard and his weakness.

The mother of Vivaldi, descended from a family as ancient as that of his father, was equally jealous of her importance; but her pride was that of birth and distinction, without extending to morals. She was of violent passions, haughty, vindictive, yet crafty and deceitful; patient in stratagem, and indefatigable in pursuit of vengeance, on the unhappy objects who provoked her resentment. She loved her son, rather as being the last of two illustrious houses, who was to re-unite and support the honour of both, than with the fondness of a mother.

Vincentio inherited much of the character of his father, and very little of that of his mother. His pride was as noble and generous as that of the Marchese; but he had somewhat of the fiery passions of the Marchesa, without any of her craft, her duplicity, or vindictive thirst of revenge. Frank in his temper, ingenuous in his sentiments, quickly offended, but easily appeased; irritated by any appearance of disrespect, but melted by a concession, a high sense of honor rendered him no more jealous of offence, than a delicate humanity made him ready for reconciliation, and anxious to spare the feelings of others.

On the day following that, on which he had seen Ellena, he returned to the villa Altieri, to use the permission granted him of enquiring after the health of Signora Bianchi. The expectation of seeing Ellena agitated him with impatient joy and trembling hope, which still encreased as he approached her residence, till, having reached the garden-gate, he was obliged to rest for a few moments to recover breath and composure.

Having announced himself to an old female servant, who came to the gate, he was soon after admitted to a small vestibule, where he found Signora Bianchi winding balls of silk, and alone; though from the position of a chair which stood near a frame for embroidery, he judged that Ellena had but just quitted the apartment. Signora Bianchi received him with a reserved politeness, and seemed very cautious in her replies to his enquiries after her niece, who, he hoped, every moment, would appear. He lengthened his visit till there was no longer an excuse for doing so; till he had exhausted every topic of conversation, and till the silence of Signora Bianchi seemed to hint, that his departure was expected. With a heart saddened by disappointment, and having obtained only a reluctant permission to enquire after the health of that lady on some future day, he then took leave.

On his way through the garden he often paused to look back upon the house, hoping to obtain a glimpse of Ellena at a lattice; and threw a glance around him, almost expecting to see her seated beneath the shade of the luxuriant plantains;* but his search was every where vain, and he quitted the place with the slow and heavy step of despondency.

The day was employed in endeavours to obtain intelligence concerning the family of Ellena, but of this he procured little that was satisfactory. He was told, that she was an orphan, living under the care of her aunt, Signora Bianchi; that her family, which had never been illustrious, was decayed in fortune, and that her only dependence was upon this aunt. But he was ignorant of what was very true, though very secret, that she assisted to support this aged relative, whose sole property was the small estate on which they lived, and that she passed whole days in embroidering silks, which were disposed of to the nuns of a neighbouring convent, who sold them to the Neapolitan ladies, that visited their grate, at a very high advantage. He little thought, that a beautiful robe, which he had often seen his mother wear, was worked by Ellena; nor that some copies from the antique, which ornamented a cabinet of the Vivaldi palace, were drawn by her hand. If he had known these circumstances, they would only have served to encrease the passion, which, since they were proofs of a disparity of fortune, that would certainly render his family repugnant to a connection with hers, it would have been prudent to discourage.

Ellena could have endured poverty, but not contempt; and it was to protect herself from this effect of the narrow prejudices of the world around her, that she had so cautiously concealed from it a knowledge of the industry, which did honor to her character. She was not ashamed of poverty, or of the industry which overcame it, but her spirit shrunk from the senseless smile and humiliating condescension, which prosperity sometimes gives to indigence. Her mind was not yet strong enough, or her views sufficiently enlarged, to teach her a contempt of the sneer of vicious folly, and to glory in the dignity of virtuous independence. Ellena was the sole support of her aunt's declining years; was patient to her infirmities, and consoling to her sufferings; and repaid the fondness of a mother with the affection of a daughter. Her mother she had never known, having lost her while she was an infant, and from that period Signora Bianchi had performed the duties of one for her.

Thus innocent and happy in the silent performance of her duties and in the veil of retirement, lived Ellena Rosalba, when she first saw Vincentio di Vivaldi. He was not of a figure to pass unobserved when seen, and Ellena had been struck by the spirit and dignity of his air, and by his countenance, so frank, noble, and full of that kind of expression, which announces the energies of the soul. But she was cautious of admitting a sentiment more tender than admiration, and endeavoured to dismiss his image from her mind, and by engaging in her usual occupations, to recover the state of tranquillity, which his appearance had somewhat interrupted.

Vivaldi, mean while, restless from disappointment, and impatient from anxiety, having passed the greater part of the day in enquiries, which repaid him only with doubt and apprehension, determined to return to the villa Altieri, when evening should conceal his steps, consoled by the certainty of being near the object of his thoughts, and hoping, that chance might favour him once more with a view, however transient, of Ellena.

The Marchesa Vivaldi held an assembly this evening, and a suspicion concerning the impatience he betrayed, induced her to detain him about her person to a late hour, engaging him to select the music for her orchestra, and to superintend the performance of a new piece, the work of a composer whom she had brought into fashion. Her assemblies were among the most brilliant and crowded in Naples, and the nobility, who were to be at the palace this evening, were divided into two parties as to the merits of the musical genius, whom she patronized, and those of another candidate for fame. The performance of the evening, it was expected, would finally decide the victory. This, therefore, was a night of great importance and anxiety to the Marchesa, for she was as jealous of the reputation of her favourite composer as of her own, and the welfare of her son did but slightly divide her cares.

The moment he could depart unobserved, he quitted the assembly, and, muffling himself in his cloak, hastened to the villa Altieri, which lay at a short distance to the west of the city. He reached it unobserved, and, breathless with impatience, traversed the boundary of the garden; where, free from ceremonial restraint, and near the object of his affection, he experienced for the few first moments a joy as exquisite as her presence could have inspired. But this delight faded with its novelty, and in a short time he felt as forlorn as if he was separated for ever from Ellena, in whose presence he but lately almost believed himself.

The night was far advanced, and, no light appearing from the house, he concluded the inhabitants had retired to rest, and all hope of seeing her vanished from his mind. Still, however, it was sweet to be near her, and he anxiously sought to gain admittance to the gardens, that he might approach the window where it was possible she reposed. The boundary, formed of trees and thick shrubs, was not difficult to be passed, and he found himself once more in the portico of the villa.

It was nearly midnight, and the stillness that reigned was rather soothed than interrupted by the gentle dashing of the waters of the bay below, and by the hollow murmurs of Vesuvius,* which threw up, at intervals its sudden flame on the horizon, and then left it to darkness. The solemnity of the scene accorded with the temper of his mind, and he listened in deep attention for the returning sounds, which broke upon the ear like distant thunder muttering imperfectly from the clouds. The pauses of silence, that succeeded each groan of the mountain, when expectation listened for the rising sound, affected the imagination of Vivaldi at this time with particular awe, and, rapt in thought, he continued to gaze upon the sublime and shadowy outline of the shores, and on the sea, just discerned beneath the twilight of a cloudless sky. Along its grey surface many vessels were pursuing their silent course, guided over the deep waters only by the polar star, which burned with steady lustre. The air was calm, and rose from the bay with most balmy and refreshing coolness; it scarcely stirred the heads of the broad pines that overspread the villa; and bore no sounds but of the waves and the groans of the far-off mountain, —till a chaunting of deep voices swelled from a distance. The solemn character of the strain engaged his attention; he perceived that it was a requiem, and he endeavoured to discover from what quarter it came. It advanced, though distantly, and then passed away on the air. The circumstance struck him; he knew it was usual in some parts of Italy to chaunt this strain over the bed of the dying; but here the mourners seemed to walk the earth, or the air. He was not doubtful as to the strain itself;—once before he had heard it, and attended with circumstances which made it impossible that he should ever forget it. As he now listened to the choral voices softening in distance, a few pathetic notes brought full upon his remembrance the divine melody he had heard Ellena utter in the church of San Lorenzo. Overcome by the recollection, he started away, and, wandering over the garden, reached another side of the villa, where he soon heard the voice of Ellena herself, performing the midnight hymn to the Virgin, and accompanied by a lute, which she touched with most affecting and delicate expression. He stood for a moment entranced, and scarcely daring to breathe, lest he should lose any note of that meek and holy strain, which seemed to flow from a devotion almost saintly. Then, looking round to discover the object of his admiration, a light issuing from among the bowery foliage of a clematis led him to a lattice, and shewed him Ellena. The lattice had been thrown open to admit the cool air, and he had a full view of her and the apartment. She was rising from a small altar where she had concluded the service; the glow of devotion was still upon her countenance as she raised her eyes, and with a rapt earnestness fixed them on the heavens. She still held the lute, but no longer awakened it, and seemed lost to every surrounding object. Her fine hair was negligently bound up in a silk net, and some tresses that had escaped it, played on her neck, and round her beautiful countenance, which now was not even partially concealed by a veil. The light drapery of her dress, her whole figure, air, and attitude, were such as might have been copied for a Grecian nymph.

Vivaldi was perplexed and agitated between the wish of seizing an opportunity, which might never again occur, of pleading his love, and the fear of offending, by intruding upon her retirement at so sacred an hour; but, while he thus hesitated, he heard her sigh, and then with a sweetness peculiar to her accent, pronounce his name. During the trembling anxiety, with which he listened to what might follow this mention of his name, he disturbed the clematis that surrounded the lattice, and she turned her eyes towards the window; but Vivaldi was entirely concealed by the foliage. She, however, rose to close the lattice; as she approached which, Vivaldi, unable any longer to command himself, appeared before her. She stood fixed for an instant, while her countenance changed to an ashy paleness; and then, with trembling haste closing the lattice, quitted the apartment. Vivaldi felt as if all his hopes had vanished with her.

After lingering in the garden for some time without perceiving a light in any other part of the building, or hearing a sound proceed from it, he took his melancholy way to Naples. He now began to ask himself some questions, which he ought to have urged before, and to enquire wherefore he sought the dangerous pleasure of seeing Ellena, since her family was of such a condition as rendered the consent of his parents to a marriage with her unattainable.

He was lost in revery on this subject, sometimes half resolved to seek her no more, and then shrinking from a conduct, which seemed to strike him with the force of despair, when, as he emerged from the dark arch of a ruin, that extended over the road, his steps were crossed by a person in the habit of a monk, whose face was shrouded by his cowl still more than by the twilight. The stranger, addressing him by his name, said, 'Signor! your steps are watched; beware how you revisit Altieri!' Having uttered this, he disappeared, before Vivaldi could return the sword he had half drawn into the scabbard, or demand an explanation of the words he had heard. He called loudly and repeatedly, conjuring the unknown person to appear, and lingered near the spot for a considerable time; but the vision came no more.

Vivaldi arrived at home with a mind occupied by this incident, and tormented by the jealousy to which it gave rise; for, after indulging various conjectures, he concluded with believing the notice, of which he had been warned, to be that of a rival, and that the danger which menaced him, was from the poniard of jealousy. This belief discovered to him at once the extent of his passion, and of the imprudence, which had thus readily admitted it; yet so far was this new prudence from overcoming his error, that, stung with a torture more exquisite than he had ever known, he resolved, at every event, to declare his love, and sue for the hand of Ellena. Unhappy young man, he knew not the fatal error, into which passion was precipitating him!

On his arrival at the Vivaldi palace, he learned, that the Marchesa had observed his absence, had repeatedly enquired for him, and had given orders that the time of his return should be mentioned to her. She had, however, retired to rest; but the Marchese, who had attended the King on an excursion to one of the royal villas on the bay, returned home soon after Vincentio; and, before he had withdrawn to his apartment, he met his son with looks of unusual displeasure, but avoided saying any thing, which either explained or alluded to the subject of it; and, after a short conversation, they separated.

Vivaldi shut himself in his apartment to deliberate, if that may deserve the name of deliberation, in which a conflict of passions, rather than an exertion of judgment, prevailed. For several hours he traversed his suite of rooms, alternately tortured by the remembrance of Ellena, fired with jealousy, and alarmed for the consequence of the imprudent step, which he was about to take. He knew the temper of his father, and some traits of the character of his mother, sufficiently to fear that their displeasure would be irreconcilable concerning the marriage he meditated; yet, when he considered that he was their only son, he was inclined to admit a hope of forgiveness, notwithstanding the weight which the circumstance must add to their disappointment. These reflexions were frequently interrupted by fears lest Ellena had already disposed of her affections to this imaginary rival. He was, however, somewhat consoled by remembering the sigh she had uttered, and the tenderness, with which she had immediately pronounced his name. Yet, even if she were not averse to his suit, how could he solicit her hand, and hope it would be given him, when he should declare that this must.be in secret? He scarcely dared to believe that she would condescend to enter a family who disdained to receive her; and again despondency overcame him.

The morning found him as distracted as the night had left him; his determination, however, was fixed; and this was, to sacrifice what he now considered as a delusive pride of birth, to a choice which he believed would ensure the happiness of his life. But, before he ventured to declare himself to Ellena, it appeared necessary to ascertain whether he held an interest in her heart, or whether she had devoted it to the rival of his love, and who this rival really was. It was so much easier to wish for such information than to obtain it, that, after forming a thousand projects, either the delicacy of his respect for Ellena, or his fear of offending her, or an apprehension of discovery from his family before he had secured an interest in her affections, constantly opposed his views of an enquiry.

In this difficulty he opened his heart to a friend, who had long possessed his confidence, and whose advice he solicited with somewhat more anxiety and sincerity than is usual on such occasions. It was not a sanction of his own opinion that he required, but the impartial judgment of another mind. Bonarmo, however little he might be qualified for the office of an adviser, did not scruple to give his advice. As a means of judging whether Ellena was disposed to favour Vivaldi's addresses, he proposed that, according to the custom of the country, a serenade should be given; he maintained, that, if she was not disinclined towards him, some sign of approbation would appear; and if otherwise, that she would remain silent and invisible. Vivaldi objected to this coarse and inadequate mode of expressing a love so sacred as his, and he had too lofty an opinion of Ellena's mind and delicacy, to believe, that the trifling homage of a serenade would either flatter her self-love, or interest her in his favour; nor, if it did, could he venture to believe, that she would display any sign of approbation.

His friend laughed at his scruples and at his opinion of what he called such romantic delicacy, that his ignorance of the world was his only excuse for having cherished them. But Vivaldi interrupted this raillery, and would neither suffer him for a moment to speak thus of Ellena, or to call such delicacy romantic. Bonarmo, however, still urged the serenade as at least a possible means of discovering her disposition towards him before he made a formal avowal of his suit; and Vivaldi, perplexed and distracted with apprehension and impatience to terminate his present state of suspense, was at length so far overcome by his own difficulties, rather than by his friend's persuasion, that he consented to make the adventure of a serenade on the approaching night. This was adopted rather as a refuge from despondency, than with any hope of success; for he still believed that Ellena would not give any hint, that might terminate his uncertainty.

Beneath their cloaks they carried musical instruments, and, muffling up their faces, so that they could not be known, they proceeded in thoughtful silence on the way to the villa Altieri. Already they had passed the arch, in which Vivaldi was stopped by the stranger on the preceding night, when he heard a sudden sound near him, and, raising his head from the cloak, he perceived the same figure! Before he had time for exclamation, the stranger crossed him again. 'Go not to the villa Altieri,' said he in a solemn voice, 'lest you meet the fate you ought to dread.'

'What fate?' demanded Vivaldi, stepping back; 'Speak, I conjure you!'

But the monk was gone, and the darkness of the hour baffled observation as to the way of his departure.

'*Dio mi guardi!*' exclaimed Bonarmo, 'this is almost beyond belief! but let us return to Naples; this second warning ought to be obeyed.'

'It is almost beyond endurance,' exclaimed Vivaldi; 'which way did he pass?'

'He glided by me,' replied Bonarmo, 'and he was gone before I could cross him!'

'I will tempt the worst at once,' said Vivaldi; 'if I have a rival, it is best to meet him. Let us go on.'

Bonarmo remonstrated, and represented the serious danger that threatened from so rash a proceeding. 'It is evident that you have a rival,' said he, 'and your courage cannot avail you against hired bravos.' Vivaldi's heart swelled at the mention of a rival. 'If you think it dangerous to proceed, I will go alone,' said he.

Hurt by this reproof, Bonarmo accompanied his friend in silence, and they reached without interruption the boundary of the villa. Vivaldi led to the place by which he had entered on the preceding night, and they passed unmolested into the garden.

'Where are these terrible bravos of whom you warned me?' said Vivaldi, with taunting exultation.

'Speak cautiously,' replied his friend; 'we may, even now, be within their reach.'

'They also may be within ours,' observed Vivaldi.

At length, these adventurous friends came to the orangery, which was near the house, when, tired by the ascent, they rested to recover breath, and to prepare their instruments for the serenade. The night was still, and they now heard, for the first time, murmurs as of a distant multitude; and then the sudden splendor of fire-works broke upon the sky. These arose from a villa on the western margin of the bay, and were given in honour of the birth of one of the royal princes. They soared to an immense height, and, as their lustre broke silently upon the night, it lightened on the thousand up-turned faces of the gazing crowd, illumined the waters of the bay, with every little boat that skimmed its surface, and shewed distinctly the whole sweep of its rising shores, the stately city of Naples on the strand below, and, spreading far among the hills, its terraced roofs crowded with spectators, and the Corso tumul-tuous with carriages and blazing with torches.

While Bonarmo surveyed this magnificent scene, Vivaldi turned his eyes to the residence of Ellena, part of which looked out from among the trees, with a hope that the spectacle would draw her to a balcony; but she did not appear, nor was there any light, that might indicate her approach.

While they still rested on the turf of the orangery, they heard a sudden rustling of the leaves, as if the branches were disturbed by some person who endeavoured to make his way between them, when Vivaldi demanded who passed. No answer was returned, and a long silence followed.

'We are observed,' said Bonarmo, at length, 'and are even now, perhaps, almost beneath the poinard of the assassin: let us be gone.'

'O that my heart were as secure from the darts of love, the assassin of my peace,' exclaimed Vivaldi, 'as yours is from those of bravos! My friend, you have little to interest you, since your thoughts have so much leisure for apprehension.'

'My fear is that of prudence, not of weakness,' retorted Bonarmo, with acrimony; 'you will find, perhaps, that I have none, when you most wish me to possess it.'

'I understand you,' replied Vivaldi; 'let us finish this business, and you shall receive reparation, since you believe yourself injured: I am as anxious to repair an offence, as jealous of receiving one.'

'Yes,' replied Bonarmo, 'you would repair the injury you have done your friend with his blood.'

'Oh! never, never!' said Vivaldi, falling on his neck. 'Forgive my hasty violence; allow for the distraction of my mind.'

Bonarmo returned the embrace. 'It is enough,' said he; 'no more, no more! I hold again my friend to my heart.'

While this conversation passed, they had quitted the orangery, and reached the walls of the villa, where they took their station under a balcony that overhung the lattice, through which Vivaldi had seen Ellena on the preceding night. They tuned their instruments, and opened the serenade with a duet.

Vivaldi's voice was a fine tenor, and the same susceptibility, which made him passionately fond of music, taught him to modulate its cadence with exquisite delicacy, and to give his emphasis with the most simple and pathetic expression. His soul seemed to breathe in the sounds,—so tender, so imploring, yet so energetic. On this night, enthusiasm inspired him with the highest eloquence, perhaps, which music is capable of attaining; what might be its effect on Ellena he had no means of judging, for she did not appear either at the balcony or the lattice, nor gave any hint of applause. No sounds stole on the stillness of the night, except those of the serenade, nor did any light from within the villa break upon the obscurity without; once, indeed, in a pause of the instruments, Bonarmo fancied he distinguished voices near him, as of persons who feared to be heard, and he listened attentively, but without ascertaining the truth. Sometimes they seemed to sound heavily in his ear, and then a death-like silence prevailed. Vivaldi affirmed the sound to be nothing more than the confused murmur of the distant multitude on the shore, but Bonarmo was not thus easily convinced.

The musicians, unsuccessful in their first endeavour to attract attention, removed to the opposite side of the building, and placed themselves in front of the portico, but with as little success; and, after having exercised their powers of harmony and of patience for above an hour, they resigned all further effort to win upon the obdurate Ellena. Vivaldi, notwithstanding the feebleness of his first hope of seeing her, now suffered an agony of disappointment; and Bonarmo, alarmed for the consequence of his despair, was as anxious to persuade him that he had no rival, as he had lately been pertinacious in affirming that he had one.

At length, they left the gardens, Vivaldi protesting that he would not rest till he had discovered the stranger, who so wantonly destroyed his peace, and had compelled him to explain his ambiguous warnings; and Bonarmo remonstrating on the imprudence and difficulty of the search, and representing that such conduct would probably be the means of spreading a report of his attachment, where most he dreaded it should be known.

Vivaldi refused to yield to remonstrance or considerations of any kind. 'We shall see,' said he, 'whether this demon in the garb of a monk, will haunt me again at the accustomed place; if he does, he shall not escape my grasp; and if he does not, I will watch as vigilantly for his return, as he seems to have done for mine. I will lurk in the shade of the ruin, and wait for him, though it be till death!'

Bonarmo was particularly struck by the vehemence with which he pronounced the last words, but he no longer opposed his purpose, and only bade him consider whether he was well armed, 'For,' he added, 'you may have need of arms there, though you had no use for them at the villa Altieri. Remember that the stranger told you that your steps were watched.'

'I have my sword,' replied Vivaldi, 'and the dagger which I usually wear; but I ought to enquire what are your weapons of defence.'

'Hush!' said Bonarmo, as they turned the foot of a rock that overhung the road, 'we are approaching the spot; yonder is the arch!' It appeared duskily in the perspective, suspended between two cliffs, where the road wound from sight, on one of which were the ruins of the Roman fort it belonged to, and on the other, shadowing pines, and thickets of oak that tufted the rock to its base.

They proceeded in silence, treading lightly, and often throwing a suspicious glance around, expecting every instant that the monk would steal out upon them from some recess of the cliffs. But they passed on unmolested to the arch-way. 'We are here before him, however,' said Vivaldi as they entered the darkness. 'Speak low, my friend,' said Bonarmo, 'others besides ourselves may be shrouded in this obscurity. I like not the place.'

'Who but ourselves would chuse so dismal a retreat?' whispered Vivaldi, 'unless indeed, it were banditti; the savageness of the spot would, in truth, suit their humour, and it suits well also with my own.'

'It would suit their purpose too, as well as their humour,' observed Bonarmo. 'Let us remove from this deep shade, into the more open road, where we can as closely observe who passes.'

Vivaldi objected that in the road they might themselves be observed, 'and if we are seen by my unknown tormentor, our design is defeated, for he comes upon us suddenly, or not at all, lest we should be prepared to detain him.'

Vivaldi, as he said this, took his station within the thickest gloom of the arch, which was of considerable depth, and near a flight of steps that was cut in the rock, and ascended to the fortress. His friend stepped close to his side. After a pause of silence, during which Bonarmo was meditating, and Vivaldi was impatiently watching, 'Do you really believe,' said the former, 'that any effort to detain him would be effectual? He glided past me with a strange facility, it was surely more than human!'

'What is it you mean?' enquired Vivaldi.

'Why, I mean that I could be superstitious. This place, perhaps, infests my mind with congenial gloom, for I find that, at this moment, there is scarcely a superstition too dark for my credulity.'

Vivaldi smiled. 'And you must allow,' added Bonarmo, 'that he has appeared under circumstances somewhat extraordinary. How should he know your name, by which, you say, he addressed you at the first meeting? How should he know from whence you came, or whether you designed to return? By what magic could he become acquainted with your plans?'

'Nor am I certain that he is acquainted with them,' observed Vivaldi; 'but if he is, there was no necessity for superhuman means to obtain such knowledge.'

'The result of this evening surely ought to convince you that he is acquainted with your designs,' said Bonarmo. 'Do you believe it possible that Ellena could have been insensible to your attentions, if her heart had not been pre-engaged, and that she would not have shewn herself at a lattice?'

'You do not know Ellena,' replied Vivaldi, 'and therefore I once more pardon you the question. Yet had she been disposed to accept my addresses, surely some sign of approbation,'—he checked himself.

'The stranger warned you not to go to the villa Altieri,' resumed Bonarmo, 'he seemed to anticipate the reception, which awaited you, and to know a danger, which hitherto you have happily escaped.'

'Yes, he anticipated too well that reception,' said Vivaldi, losing his prudence in passionate exclamation; 'and he is himself, perhaps, the rival, whom he has taught me to suspect. He has assumed a disguise only the more effectually to impose upon my credulity, and to deter me from addressing Ellena. And shall I tamely lie in wait for his approach? Shall I lurk like a guilty assassin for this rival?'

'For heaven's sake!' said Bonarmo, 'moderate these transports; consider where you are. This surmise of yours is in the highest degree improbable.' He gave his reasons for thinking so, and these convinced Vivaldi, who was prevailed upon to be once more patient.

They had remained watchful and still for a considerable time, when Bonarmo saw a person approach the end of the arch-way nearest to Altieri. He heard no step, but he perceived a shadowy figure station itself at the entrance of the arch, where the twilight of this brilliant climate was, for a few paces, admitted. Vivaldi's eyes were fixed on the road leading towards Naples, and he, therefore, did not perceive the object of Bonarmo's attention, who, fearful of his friend's precipitancy, forbore to point out immediately what he observed, judging it more prudent to watch the motions of this unknown person, that he might ascertain whether it really were the monk. The size of the figure, and the dark drapery in which it seemed wrapt, induced him, at length, to believe that this was the expected stranger; and he seized Vivaldi's arm to direct his attention to him, when the form gliding forward disappeared in the gloom, but not before Vivaldi had understood the occasion of his friend's gesture and significant silence. They heard no foot-step pass them, and, being convinced that this person, whatever he was, had not left the arch-way, they kept their station in watchful stillness. Presently they heard a rustling, as of garments, near them, and Vivaldi, unable longer to command his patience, started from his concealment, and with arms extended to prevent any one from escaping, demanded who was there.

The sound ceased, and no reply was made. Bonarmo drew his sword, protesting he would stab the air till he found the person who lurked there; but that if the latter would discover himself, he should receive no injury. This assurance Vivaldi confirmed by his promise. Still no answer was returned; but as they listened for a voice, they thought something passed them, and the avenue was not narrow enough to have prevented such a circumstance. Vivaldi rushed forward, but did not perceive any person issue from the arch into the highway, where the stronger twilight must have discovered him.

'Somebody certainly passed,' whispered Bonarmo, 'and I think I hear a sound from yonder steps, that lead to the fortress.'

'Let us follow,' cried Vivaldi, and he began to ascend.

'Stop, for heaven's sake stop!' said Bonarmo; 'consider what you are about! Do not brave the utter darkness of these ruins; do not pursue the assassin to his den!'

'It is the monk himself!' exclaimed Vivaldi, still ascending; 'he shall not escape me!'

Bonarmo paused a moment at the foot of the steps, and his friend disappeared; he hesitated what to do, till ashamed of suffering him to encounter danger alone, he sprang to the flight, and not without difficulty surmounted the rugged steps.

Having reached the summit of the rock, he found himself on a terrace, that ran along the top of the arch-way and had once been fortified; this, crossing the road, commanded the defile each way. Some remains of massy walls, that still exhibited loops for archers, were all that now hinted of its former use. It led to a watch-tower almost concealed in thick pines, that crowned the opposite cliff, and had thus served not only for a strong battery over the road, but, connecting the opposite sides of the defile, had formed a line of communication between the fort and this out-post.

Bonarmo looked round in vain for his friend, and the echoes of his own voice only, among the rocks, replied to his repeated calls. After some hesitation whether to enter the walls of the main building, or to cross to the watch-tower, he determined on the former, and entered a rugged area, the walls of which, following the declivities of the precipice, could scarcely now be traced. The citadel, a round tower, of majestic strength, with some Roman arches scattered near, was all that remained of this once important fortress; except, indeed, a mass of ruins near the edge of the cliff, the construction of which made it difficult to guess for what purpose it had been designed.

Bonarmo entered the immense walls of the citadel, but the utter darkness within checked his progress, and, contenting himself with calling loudly on Vivaldi, he returned to the open air.

As he approached the mass of ruins, whose singular form had interested his curiosity, he thought he distinguished the low accents of a human voice, and while he listened in anxiety, a person rushed forth from a doorway of the ruin, carrying a drawn sword. It was Vivaldi himself. Bonarmo sprang to meet him; he was pale and breathless, and some moments elapsed before he could speak, or appeared to hear the repeated enquiries of his friend.

'Let us go,' said Vivaldi, 'let us leave this place!'

'Most willingly,' replied Bonarmo, 'but where have you been, and who have you seen, that you are thus affected.'

'Ask me no more questions, let us go,' repeated Vivaldi.

They descended the rock together, and when, having reached the arch-way, Bonarmo enquired, half sportively, whether they should remain any longer on the watch, his friend answered, 'No!' with an emphasis that startled him. They passed hastily on the way to Naples, Bonarmo repeating enquiries which Vivaldi seemed reluctant to satisfy, and wondering no less at the cause of this sudden reserve, than anxious to know whom he had seen.

'It was the monk, then,' said Bonarmo; 'you secured him at last?'

'I know not what to think,' replied Vivaldi, 'I am more perplexed than ever.'

'He escaped you then?'

'We will speak of this in future,' said Vivaldi; 'but be it as it may, the business rests not here. I will return in the night of to-morrow with a torch; dare you venture yourself with me?'

'I know not,' replied Bonarmo, 'whether I ought to do so, since I am not informed for what purpose.'

'I will not press you to go,' said Vivaldi; 'my purpose is already known to you.'

'Have you really failed to discover the stranger—have you still doubts concerning the person you pursued?'

'I have doubts, which to-morrow night, I hope, will dissipate.'

'This is very strange!' said Bonarmo, 'It was but now that I witnessed the horror, with which you left the fortress of Paluzzi, and already you speak of returning to it! And why at night—why not in the day, when less danger would beset you?'

'I know not as to that,' replied Vivaldi, 'you are to observe that day-light never pierces within the recess, to which I penetrated; we must search the place with torches at whatsoever hour we would examine it.'

'Since this is necessary,' said Bonarmo, 'how happens it that you found your way in total darkness?'

'I was too much engaged to know how; I was led on, as by an invisible hand.'

'We must, notwithstanding,' observed Bonarmo, 'go in day-time, if not by day-light, provided I accompany you. It would be little less than insanity to go twice to a place, which is probably infested with robbers, and at their own hour of midnight.'

'I shall watch again in the accustomed place,' replied Vivaldi, 'before I use my last resource, and this cannot be done during the day. Besides, it is necessary that I should go at a particular hour, the hour when the monk has usually appeared.'

'He did escape you, then?' said Bonarmo, 'and you are still ignorant concerning who he is?'

Vivaldi rejoined only with an enquiry whether his friend would accompany him. 'If not,' he added, 'I must hope to find another companion.'

Bonarmo said, that he must consider of the proposal, and would acquaint him with his determination before the following evening.

While this conversation concluded, they were in Naples, and at the gates of the Vivaldi palace, where they separated for the remainder of the night.

CHAPTER II

OLIVIA. Why what would you?
VIOLA.   Make me a willow cabin at your gate,
         And call upon my soul within the house;
         Write loyal cantos of contemned love,
         And sing them loud even in the dead of night:
         Halloo your name to the reverberate hills,
         And make the babbling gossip of the air
         Cry out, Olivia! O! you should not rest
         Between the elements of air and earth,
         But you should pity me.
                              TWELFTH NIGHT*

SINCE Vivaldi had failed to procure an explanation of the words of the monk, he determined to relieve himself from the tortures of suspence, respecting a rival, by going to the villa Altieri, and declaring his pretensions. On the morning immediately following his late adventure, he went thither, and on enquiring for Signora Bianchi, was told that she could not be seen. With much difficulty he prevailed upon the old house-keeper to deliver a request that he might be permitted to wait upon her for a few moments. Permission was granted him, when he was conducted into the very apartment where he had formerly seen Ellena. It was unoccupied and he was told that Signora Bianchi would be there presently.

During this interval, he was agitated at one moment with quick impatience, and at another with enthusiastic pleasure, while he gazed on the altar whence he had seen Ellena rise, and where, to his fancy, she still appeared; and on every object, on which he knew her eyes had lately dwelt. These objects, so familiar to her, had in the imagination of Vivaldi acquired somewhat of the sacred character she had impressed upon his heart, and affected him in some degree as her presence would have done. He trembled as he took up the lute she had been accustomed to touch, and, when he awakened the chords, her own voice seemed to speak. A drawing, half-finished, of a dancing nymph remained on a stand, and he immediately understood that her hand had traced the lines. It was a copy from Herculaneum,* and, though a copy, was touched with the spirit of original genius. The light steps appeared almost to move, and the whole figure displayed the airy lightness of exquisite grace. Vivaldi perceived this to be one of a set that ornamented the apartment, and observed with surprise, that they were the particular subjects, which adorned his father's cabinet,* and which he had understood to be the only copies permitted from the originals in the royal museum.

Every object, on which his eyes rested, seemed to announce the presence of Ellena; and the very flowers that so gaily embellished the apartment, breathed forth a perfume, which fascinated his senses and affected his imagination. Before Signora Bianchi appeared, his anxiety and apprehension had encreased so much, that, believing he should be unable to support himself in her presence, he was more than once upon the point of leaving the house. At length, he heard her approaching step from the hall, and his breath almost forsook him. The figure of Signora Bianchi was not of an order to inspire admiration, and a spectator might have smiled to see the perturbation of Vivaldi, his faultering step and anxious eye, as he advanced to meet the venerable Bianchi, as he bowed upon her faded hand, and listened to her querulous voice. She received him with an air of reserve, and some moments passed before he could recollect himself sufficiently to explain the purpose of his visit; yet this, when he discovered it, did not apparently surprise her. She listened with composure, though with somewhat of a severe countenance, to his protestations of regard for her niece, and when he implored her to intercede for him in obtaining the hand of Ellena, she said, 'I cannot be ignorant that a family of your rank must be averse to an union with one of mine; nor am I unacquainted that a full sense of the value of birth is a marking feature in the characters of the Marchese and Marchesa di Vivaldi. This proposal must be disagreeable or, at least, unknown to them; and I am to inform you, Signor, that, though Signora di Rosalba is their inferior in rank, she is their equal in pride.'

Vivaldi disdained to prevaricate, yet was shocked to own the truth thus abruptly. The ingenuous manner, however, with which he at length did this, and the energy of a passion too eloquent to be misunderstood, somewhat soothed the anxiety of Signora Bianchi, with whom other considerations began to arise. She considered that from her own age and infirmities she must very soon, in the course of nature, leave Ellena a young and friendless orphan; still somewhat dependent upon her own industry, and entirely so on her discretion. With much beauty and little knowledge of the world, the dangers of her future situation appeared in vivid colours to the affectionate mind of Signora Bianchi; and she sometimes thought that it might be right to sacrifice considerations, which in other circumstances would be laudable, to the obtaining for her niece the protection of a husband and a man of honour. If in this instance she descended from the lofty integrity, which ought to have opposed her consent that Ellena should clandestinely enter any family, her parental anxiety may soften the censure she deserved.

But, before she determined upon this subject, it was necessary to ascertain that Vivaldi was worthy of the confidence she might repose in him. To try, also, the constancy of his affection, she gave little present encouragement to his hopes. His request to see Ellena she absolutely refused, till she should have considered further of his proposals; and his enquiry whether he had a rival, and, if he had, whether Ellena was disposed to favour him, she evaded, since she knew that a reply would give more encouragement to his hopes, than it might hereafter be proper to confirm.

Vivaldi, at length, took his leave, released, indeed, from absolute despair, but scarcely encouraged to hope; ignorant that he had a rival, yet doubtful whether Ellena honoured himself with any share of her esteem.

He had received permission to wait upon Signora Bianchi on a future day, but till that day should arrive time appeared motionless; and, since it seemed utterly impossible to endure this interval of suspence, his thoughts on the way to Naples were wholy engaged in contriving the means of concluding it, till he reached the well-known arch, and looked round, though hopelessly, for his mysterious tormentor. The stranger did not appear; and Vivaldi pursued the road, determined to re-visit the spot at night, and also to return privately to villa Altieri, where he hoped a second visit might procure for him some relief from his present anxiety.

When he reached home he found that the Marchese, his father, had left an order for him to await his arrival; which he obeyed; but the day passed without his return. The Marchesa, when she saw him, enquired, with a look that expressed much, how he had engaged himself of late, and completely frustrated his plans for the evening, by requiring him to attend her to Portici. Thus he was prevented from receiving Bonarmo's determination, from watching at Paluzzi, and from revisiting Ellena's residence.

He remained at Portici the following evening, and, on his return to Naples, the Marchese being again absent, he continued ignorant of the intended subject of the interview. A note from Bonarmo brought a refusal to accompany him to the fortress, and urged him to forbear so dangerous a visit. Being for this night unprovided with a companion for the adventure, and unwilling to go alone, Vivaldi deferred it to another evening; but no consideration could deter him from visiting the villa Altieri. Not chusing to solicit his friend to accompany him thither, since he had refused his first request, he took his solitary lute, and reached the garden at an earlier hour than usual.

The sun had been set above an hour, but the horizon still retained somewhat of a saffron brilliancy, and the whole dome of the sky had an appearance of transparency, peculiar to this enchanting climate, which seemed to diffuse a more soothing twilight over the reposing world. In the south-east the outline of Vesuvius appeared distinctly, but the mountain itself was dark and silent.

Vivaldi heard only the quick and eager voices of some Lazaroni* at a distance on the shore, as they contended at the simple game of maro.* From the bowery lattices of a small pavilion within the orangery, he perceived a light, and the sudden hope, which it occasioned, of seeing Ellena, almost overcame him. It was impossible to resist the opportunity of beholding her, yet he checked the impatient step he was taking, to ask himself, whether it was honorable thus to steal upon her retirement, and become an unsuspected observer of her secret thoughts. But the temptation was too powerful for this honorable hesitation; the pause was momentary; and, stepping lightly towards the pavilion, he placed himself near an open lattice, so as to be shrouded from observation by the branches of an orange-tree, while he obtained a full view of the apartment. Ellena was alone, sitting in a thoughtful attitude and holding her lute, which she did not play. She appeared lost to a consciousness of surrounding objects, and a tenderness was on her countenance, which seemed to tell him that her thoughts were engaged by some interesting subject. Recollecting that, when last he had seen her thus, she pronounced his name, his hope revived, and he was going to discover himself and appear at her feet, when she spoke, and he paused.

'Why this unreasonable pride of birth!' said she; 'A visionary prejudice destroys our peace. Never would I submit to enter a family averse to receive me; they shall learn, at least, that I inherit nobility of soul. O! Vivaldi! but for this unhappy prejudice!'—

Vivaldi, while he listened to this, was immovable; he seemed as if entranced; the sound of her lute and voice recalled him, and he heard her sing the first stanza of the very air, with which he had opened the serenade on a former night, and with such sweet pathos as the composer must have felt when he was inspired with the idea.

She paused at the conclusion of the first stanza, when Vivaldi, overcome by the temptation of such an opportunity for expressing his passion, suddenly struck the chords of the lute, and replied to her in the second. The tremor of his voice, though it restrained his tones, heightened its eloquence. Ellena instantly recollected it; her colour alternately faded and returned; and, before the verse concluded, she seemed to have lost all consciousness. Vivaldi was now advancing into the pavilion, when his approach recalled her; she waved him to retire, and before he could spring to her support, she rose and would have left the place, had he not interrupted her and implored a few moments attention.

'It is impossible,' said Ellena.

'Let me only hear you say that I am not hateful to you,' rejoined Vivaldi; 'that this intrusion has not deprived me of the regard, with which but now you acknowledged you honoured me.'—

'Oh, never, never!' interrupted Ellena, impatiently; 'forget that I ever made such acknowledgment; forget that you ever heard it; I know not what I said.'

'Ah, beautiful Ellena! do you think it possible I ever can forget it? It will be the solace of my solitary hours, the hope that shall sustain me.'—

'I cannot be detained Signor,' interrupted Ellena, still more embarrassed, 'or forgive myself for having permitted such a conversation;' but as she spoke the last words, an involuntary smile seemed to contradict their meaning. Vivaldi believed the smile in spite of the words; but, before he could express the lightning joy of conviction, she had left the pavilion; he followed through the garden—but she was gone.

From this moment Vivaldi seemed to have arisen into a new existence; the whole world to him was Paradise; that smile seemed impressed upon his heart for ever. In the fulness of present joy, he believed it impossible that he could ever be unhappy again, and defied the utmost malice of future fortune. With footsteps light as air, he returned to Naples, nor once remembered to look for his old monitor on the way.

The Marchese and his mother being from home, he was left at his leisure to indulge the rapturous recollection, that pressed upon his mind, and of which he was impatient of a moment's interruption. All night he either traversed his apartment with an agitation equal to that, which anxiety had so lately inflicted, or composed and destroyed letters to Ellena; sometimes fearing that he had written too much, and at others feeling that he had written too little; recollecting circumstances which he ought to have mentioned, and lamenting the cold expression of a passion, to which it appeared that no language could do justice.

By the hour when the domestics had risen, he had, however, completed a letter somewhat more to his satisfaction, and he dispatched it to the villa Altieri by a confidential person; but the servant had scarcely quitted the gates, when he recollected new arguments, which he wished to urge, and expressions to change of the utmost importance to enforce his meaning, and he would have given half the world to have recalled the messenger.

In this state of agitation he was summoned to attend the Marchese, who had been too much engaged of late to keep his own appointment. Vivaldi was not long in doubt as to the subject of this interview.

'I have wished to speak with you,' said the Marchese, assuming an air of haughty severity, 'upon a subject of the utmost importance to your honour and happiness; and I wished, also, to give you an opportunity of contradicting a report, which would have occasioned me considerable uneasiness, if I could have believed it. Happily I had too much confidence in my son to credit this; and I affirmed that he understood too well what was due both to his family and himself, to take any step derogatory from the dignity of either. My motive for this conversation, therefore, is merely to afford you a moment for refuting the calumny I shall mention, and to obtain for myself authority for contradicting it to the persons who have communicated it to me.'

Vivaldi waited impatiently for the conclusion of this exordium, and then begged to be informed of the subject of the report.

'It is said,' resumed the Marchese, 'that there is a young woman, who is called Ellena Rosalba,—I think that is the name;—do you know any person of the name?'

'Do I know!' exclaimed Vivaldi, 'but pardon me, pray proceed, my Lord.'

The Marchese paused, and regarded his son with sternness, but without surprise. 'It is said, that a young person of this name has contrived to fascinate your affections, and'——

'It is most true, my Lord, that Signora Rosalba has won my

affections,' interrupted Vivaldi with honest impatience, 'but without contrivance.'

'I will not be interrupted,' said the Marchese, interrupting in his turn. 'It is said that she has so artfully adapted her temper to yours, that, with the assistance of a relation who lives with her, she has reduced you to the degrading situation of her devoted suitor.'

'Signora Rosalba has, my Lord, exalted me to the honour of being her suitor,' said Vivaldi, unable longer to command his feelings. He was proceeding, when the Marchese abruptly checked him, 'You avow your folly then!'

'My Lord, I glory in my choice.'

'Young man,' rejoined his father, 'as this is the arrogance and romantic enthusiasm of a boy, I am willing to forgive it for once, and observe me, only for once. If you will acknowledge your error, instantly dismiss this new favourite.'—

'My Lord!'

'You must instantly dismiss her,' repeated the Marchese with sterner emphasis; 'and, to prove that I am more merciful than just, I am willing, on this condition, to allow her a small annuity as some reparation for the depravity, into which you have assisted to sink her.'

'My Lord!' exclaimed Vivaldi aghast, and scarcely daring to trust his voice, 'my Lord!—depravity?' struggling for breath. 'Who has dared to pollute her spotless fame by insulting your ears with such infamous falsehood? Tell me, I conjure you, instantly tell me, that I may hasten to give him his reward. Depravity!—an annuity—an annuity! O Ellena! Ellena!' As he pronounced her name tears of tenderness mingled with those of indignation.

'Young man,' said the Marchese, who had observed the violence of his emotion with strong displeasure and alarm, 'I do not lightly give faith to report, and I cannot suffer myself to doubt the truth of what I have advanced. You are deceived, and your vanity will continue the delusion, unless I condescend to exert my authority, and tear the veil from your eyes. Dismiss her instantly, and I will adduce proof of her former character which will stagger even your faith, enthusiastic as it is.'

'Dismiss her!' repeated Vivaldi, with calm yet stern energy, such as his father had never seen him assume; 'My Lord, you have never yet doubted my word, and I now pledge you that honourable word, that Ellena is innocent. Innocent! O heavens, that it should ever be necessary to affirm so, and, above all, that it should ever be necessary for me to vindicate her!'

'I must indeed lament that it ever should,' replied the Marchese coldly. 'You have pledged your word, which I cannot question. I believe, therefore, that you are deceived; that you think her virtuous, notwithstanding your midnight visits to her house. And grant she is, unhappy boy! what reparation can you make her for the infatuated folly, which has thus stained her character? What'——

'By proclaiming to the world, my Lord, that she is worthy of becoming my wife,' replied Vivaldi, with a glow of countenance, which announced the courage and the exultation of a virtuous mind.

'Your wife!' said the Marchese, with a look of ineffable disdain, which was instantly succeeded by one of angry alarm.—'If I believed you could so far forget what is due to the honour of your house, I would for ever disclaim you as my son.'

'O! why,' exclaimed Vivaldi, in an agony of conflicting passions, 'why should I be in danger of forgetting what is due to a father, when I am only asserting what is due to innocence; when I am only defending her, who has no other to defend her! Why may not I be permitted to reconcile duties so congenial! But, be the event what it may, I will defend the oppressed, and glory in the virtue, which teaches me, that it is the first duty of humanity to do so. Yes, my Lord, if it must be so, I am ready to sacrifice inferior duties to the grandeur of a principle, which ought to expand all hearts and impel all actions. I shall best support the honour of my house by adhering to its dictates.'

'Where is the principle,' said the Marchese, impatiently, 'which shall teach you to disobey a father; where is the virtue which shall instruct you to degrade your family?'

'There can be no degradation, my Lord, where there is no vice,' replied Vivaldi; 'and there are instances, pardon me, my Lord, there are some few instances in which it is virtuous to disobey.'

'This paradoxical morality,' said the Marchese, with passionate displeasure, 'and this romantic language, sufficiently explain to me the character of your associates, and the innocence of her, whom you defend with so chivalric an air. Are you to learn, Signor, that you belong to your family, not your family to you; that you are only a guardian of its honour, and not at liberty to dispose of yourself? My patience will endure no more!'

Nor could the patience of Vivaldi endure this repeated attack on the honor of Ellena. But, while he yet asserted her innocence, he endeavoured to do so with the temper, which was due to the presence of a father; and, though he maintained the independence of a man, he was equally anxious to preserve inviolate the duties of a son. But unfortunately the Marchese and Vivaldi differed in opinion concerning the limits of these duties; the first extending them to passive obedience, and the latter conceiving them to conclude at a point, wherein the happiness of an individual is so deeply concerned as in marriage. They parted mutually inflamed; Vivaldi unable to prevail with his father to mention the name of his infamous informant, or to acknowledge himself convinced of Ellena's innocence; and the Marchese equally unsuccessful in his endeavours to obtain from his son a promise that he would see her no more.

Here then was Vivaldi, who only a few short hours before had experienced a happiness so supreme as to efface all impressions of the past, and to annihilate every consideration of the future; a joy so full that it permitted him not to believe it possible that he could ever again taste of misery; he, who had felt as if that moment was as an eternity, rendering him independent of all others,—even he was thus soon fallen into the region of time and of suffering.

The present conflict of passion appeared endless; he loved his father, and would have been more shocked to consider the vexation he was preparing for him, had he not been resentful of the contempt he expressed for Ellena. He adored Ellena; and, while he felt the impractability of resigning his hopes, was equally indignant of the slander, which affected her name, and impatient to avenge the insult upon the original defamer.

Though the displeasure of his father concerning a marriage with Ellena had been already foreseen, the experience of it was severer and more painful than he had imagined; while the indignity offered to Ellena was as unexpected as intolerable. But this circumstance furnished him with an additional argument for addressing her; for, if it had been possible that his love could have paused, his honour seemed now engaged in her behalf; and, since he had been a means of sullying her fame, it became his duty to restore it. Willingly listening to the dictates of a duty so plausible, he determined to persevere in his original design. But his first efforts were directed to discover her slanderer, and recollecting, with surprize, those words of the Marchese, which had confessed a knowledge of his evening visits to the villa Altieri, the doubtful warnings of the monk seemed explained. He believed that this man was at once the spy of his steps, and the defamer of his love, till the inconsistency of such conduct with the seeming friendliness of his admonitions, struck Vivaldi and compelled him to believe the contrary.

Meanwhile, the heart of Ellena had been little less tranquil. It was divided by love and pride; but had she been acquainted with the circumstances of the late interview between the Marchese and Vivaldi, it would have been divided no longer, and a just regard for her own dignity would instantly have taught her to subdue, without difficulty, this infant affection.

Signora Bianchi had informed her niece of the subject of Vivaldi's visit; but she had softened the objectionable circumstances that attended his proposal, and had, at first, merely hinted that it was not to be supposed his family would approve a connection with any person so much their inferior in rank as herself. Ellena, alarmed by this suggestion, replied, that, since she believed so, she had done right to reject Vivaldi's suit; but her sigh, as she said this, did not escape the observation of Signora Bianchi, who ventured to add, that she had not *absolutely* rejected his offers.

While in this and future conversations, Ellena was pleased to perceive her secret admiration thus justified by an approbation so indisputable as that of her aunt, and was willing to believe that the circumstance, which had alarmed her just pride, was not so humiliating as she at first imagined, Bianchi was careful to conceal the real considerations, which had induced her to listen to Vivaldi, being well assured that they would have no weight with Ellena, whose generous heart and inexperienced mind would have revolted from mingling any motives of interest with an engagement so sacred as that of marriage. When, however, from further deliberation upon the advantages, which such an alliance must secure for her niece, Signora Bianchi determined to encourage his views, and to direct the mind of Ellena, whose affections were already engaged on her side, the opinions of the latter were found less ductile than had been expected. She was shocked at the idea of entering clandestinely the family of Vivaldi. But Bianchi, whose infirmities urged her wishes, was now so strongly convinced of the prudence of such an engagement for her niece, that she determined to prevail over her reluctance, though she perceived that this must be by means more gradual and persuasive than she had believed necessary. On the evening, when Vivaldi had surprised from Ellena an acknowledgment of her sentiments, her embarrassment and vexation, on her returning to the house, and relating what had occurred, sufficiently expressed to Signora Bianchi the exact situation of her heart. And when, on the following morning, his letter arrived, written with the simplicity and energy of truth, the aunt neglected not to adapt her remarks upon it, to the character of Ellena, with her usual address.

Vivaldi, after the late interview with the Marchese, passed the remainder of the day in considering various plans, which might discover to him the person, who had abused the credulity of his father; and in the evening he returned once more to the villa Altieri, not in secret, to serenade the dark balcony of his mistress, but openly, and to converse with Signora Bianchi, who now received him more courteously than on his former visit. Attributing the anxiety in his countenance to the uncertainty, concerning the disposition of her niece, she was neither surprised or offended, but ventured to relieve him from a part of it, by encouraging his hopes. Vivaldi dreaded lest she should enquire further respecting the sentiments of his family, but she spared both his delicacy and her own on this point; and, after a conversation of considerable length, he left the villa Altieri with a heart somewhat soothed by approbation, and lightened by hope, although he had not obtained a sight of Ellena. The disclosure she had made of her sentiments on the preceding evening, and the hints she had received as to those of his family, still wrought upon her mind with too much effect to permit an interview.

Soon after his return to Naples, the Marchesa, whom he was surprised to find disengaged, sent for him to her closet,* where a scene passed similar to that which had occurred with his father, except that the Marchesa was more dexterous in her questions, and more subtle in her whole conduct; and that Vivaldi, never for a moment, forgot the decorum which was due to a mother. Managing his passions, rather than exasperating them, and deceiving him with respect to the degree of resentment she felt from his choice, she was less passionate than the Marchese in her observations and menaces, perhaps, only because she entertained more hope than he did of preventing the evil she contemplated.

Vivaldi quitted her, unconvinced by her arguments, unsubdued by her prophecies, and unmoved in his designs. He was not alarmed, because he did not sufficiently understand her character to apprehend her purposes. Despairing to effect these by open violence, she called in an auxiliary of no mean talents, and whose character and views well adapted him to be an instrument in her hands. It was, perhaps, the baseness of her own heart, not either depth of reflexion or keenness of penetration, which enabled her to understand the nature of his; and she determined to modulate that nature to her own views.

There lived in the Dominican convent of the Spirito Santo, at
Naples, a man called father Schedoni;* an Italian, as his name
imported, but whose family was unknown, and from some circumstances, it appeared, that he wished to throw an impenetrable veil
over his origin. For whatever reason, he was never heard to
mention a relative, or the place of his nativity, and he had artfully
eluded every enquiry that approached the subject, which the
curiosity of his associates had occasionally prompted. There were
circumstances, however, which appeared to indicate him to be a
man of birth, and of fallen fortune; his spirit, as it had sometimes
looked forth from under the disguise of his manners, seemed lofty;
it shewed not, however, the aspirings of a generous mind, but rather
the gloomy pride of a disappointed one. Some few persons in the
convent, who had been interested by his appearance, believed that
the peculiarities of his manners, his severe reserve and unconquerable silence, his solitary habits and frequent penances, were the
effect of misfortunes preying upon a haughty and disordered spirit;
while others conjectured them the consequence of some hideous
crime gnawing upon an awakened conscience.

He would sometimes abstract himself from the society for whole
days together, or when with such a disposition he was compelled
to mingle with it, he seemed unconscious where he was, and continued shrouded in meditation and silence till he was again alone.
There were times when it was unknown whither he had retired,
notwithstanding that his steps had been watched, and his customary haunts examined. No one ever heard him complain. The
elder brothers of the convent said that he had talents, but denied
him learning; they applauded him for the profound subtlety
which he occasionally discovered in argument, but observed that he
seldom perceived truth when it lay on the surface; he could follow
it through all the labyrinths of disquisition, but overlooked it,
when it was undisguised before him. In fact he cared not for truth,
nor sought it by bold and broad argument, but loved to exert the
wily cunning of his nature in hunting it through artificial per-
plexities. At length, from a habit of intricacy and suspicion, his
vitiated mind could receive nothing for truth, which was simple
and easily comprehended.

Among his associates no one loved him, many disliked him, and
more feared him. His figure was striking, but not so from grace;
it was tall, and, though extremely thin, his limbs were large and
uncouth, and as he stalked along, wrapt in the black garments of
his order, there was something terrible in its air; something almost

super-human. His cowl, too, as it threw a shade over the livid paleness of his face, encreased its severe character, and gave an effect
to his large melancholy eye, which approached to horror. His was
not the melancholy of a sensible and wounded heart, but apparently that of a gloomy and ferocious disposition. There was
something in his physiognomy extremely singular, and that can
not easily be defined. It bore the traces of many passions, which
seemed to have fixed the features they no longer animated. An
habitual gloom and severity prevailed over the deep lines of his
countenance; and his eyes were so piercing that they seemed to
penetrate, at a single glance, into the hearts of men, and to read
their most secret thoughts; few persons could support their
scrutiny, or even endure to meet them twice. Yet, notwithstanding
all this gloom and austerity, some rare occasions of interest had
called forth a character upon his countenance entirely different;
and he could adapt himself to the tempers and passions of persons,
whom he wished to conciliate, with astonishing facility, and
generally with complete triumph. This monk, this Schedoni, was
the confessor and secret adviser of the Marchesa di Vivaldi. In the
first effervescence of pride and indignation, which the discovery
of her son's intended marriage occasioned, she consulted him on
the means of preventing it, and she soon perceived that his talents
promised to equal her wishes. Each possessed, in a considerable
degree, the power of assisting the other; Schedoni had subtlety
with ambition to urge it; and the Marchesa had inexorable pride,
and courtly influence; the one hoped to obtain a high benefice for
his services, and the other to secure the imaginary dignity of her
house, by her gifts. Prompted by such passions, and allured by
such views, they concerted in private, and unknown even to the
Marchese, the means of accomplishing their general end.

Vivaldi, as he quitted his mother's closet, had met Schedoni in
the corridor leading thither. He knew him to be her confessor, and
was not much surprised to see him, though the hour was an unusual
one. Schedoni bowed his head, as he passed, and assumed a meek
and holy countenance; but Vivaldi, as he eyed him with a penetrating glance, now recoiled with involuntary emotion; and it seemed
as if a shuddering presentiment of what this monk was preparing
for him, had crossed his mind.

CHAPTER III

—— Art thou any thing?
Art thou some God, some Angel, or some Devil
That mak'st my blood cold, and my hair to stand?
Speak to me, what thou art.

JULIUS CÆSAR *

VIVALDI, from the period of his last visit to Altieri, was admitted a frequent visitor to Signora Bianchi, and Ellena was, at length, prevailed upon to join the party, when the conversation was always on indifferent topics. Bianchi, understanding the disposition of her niece's affections, and the accomplished mind and manners of Vivaldi, judged that he was more likely to succeed by silent attentions than by a formal declaration of his sentiments. By such declaration, Ellena, till her heart was more engaged in his cause, would, perhaps, have been alarmed into an absolute rejection of his addresses, and this was every day less likely to happen, so long as he had an opportunity of conversing with her.

Signora Bianchi had acknowledged to Vivaldi that he had no rival to apprehend; that Ellena had uniformly rejected every admirer who had hitherto discovered her within the shade of her retirement, and that her present reserve proceeded more from considerations of the sentiments of his family than from disapprobation of himself. He forbore, therefore, to press his suit, till he should have secured a stronger interest in her heart, and in this hope he was encouraged by Signora Bianchi, whose gentle remonstrances in his favour became every day more pleasing and more convincing.

Several weeks passed away in this kind of intercourse, till Ellena, yielding to the representations of Signora Bianchi, and to the pleadings of her own heart, received Vivaldi as an acknowledged admirer, and the sentiments of his family were no longer remembered, or, if remembered, it was with a hope that they might be overcome by considerations more powerful.

The lovers, with Signora Bianchi and a Signor Giotto, a distant relation of the latter, frequently made excursions in the delightful environs of Naples; for Vivaldi was no longer anxious to conceal his attachment, but wished to contradict any report injurious to his love, by the publicity of his conduct; while the consideration, that Ellena's name had suffered by his late imprudence, contributed, with the unsuspecting innocence and sweetness of her manners towards him, who had been the occasion of her injuries, to mingle a sacred pity with his love, which obliterated all family politics from his mind, and bound her irrecoverably to his heart.

These excursions sometimes led them to Puzzuoli, Baia, or the woody cliffs of Pausilippo, and as, on their return, they glided along the moon-light bay, the melodies of Italian strains seemed to give enchantment to the scenery of its shore. At this cool hour the voices of the vine-dressers were frequently heard in trio, as they reposed, after the labour of the day, on some pleasant promontory, under the shade of poplars; or the brisk music of the dance from fishermen, on the margin of the waves below. The boatmen rested on their oars, while their company listened to voices modulated by sensibility to finer eloquence, than is in the power of art alone to display; and at others, while they observed the airy natural grace, which distinguishes the dance of the fishermen and peasants of Naples. Frequently as they glided round a promontory, whose shaggy masses impended far over the sea, such magic scenes of beauty unfolded, adorned by these dancing groups on the bay beyond, as no pencil could do justice to. The deep clear waters reflected every image of the landscape, the cliffs, branching into wild forms, crowned with groves, whose rough foliage often spread down their steeps in picturesque luxuriance; the ruined villa on some bold point, peeping through the trees; peasants' cabins hanging on the precipices, and the dancing figures on the strand—all touched with the silvery tint and soft shadows of moon-light. On the other hand, the sea trembling with a long line of radiance, and shewing in the clear distance the sails of vessels stealing in every direction along its surface, presented a prospect as grand as the landscape was beautiful.

One evening that Vivaldi sat with Ellena and Signora Bianchi, in the very pavilion where he had overheard that short but interesting soliloquy, which assured him of her regard, he pleaded with more than his usual earnestness for a speedy marriage. Bianchi did not oppose his arguments; she had been unwell for some time, and, believing herself to be declining fast, was anxious to have their nuptials concluded. She surveyed with languid eyes, the scene that spread before the pavilion. The strong effulgence which a setting-sun threw over the sea, shewing innumerable gaily painted ships, and fishing-boats returning from Santa Lucia into the port of Naples, had no longer power to cheer her. Even the Roman tower that terminated the mole* below, touched as it was with the slanting rays; and the various figures of fishermen, who lay smoking beneath its walls, in the long shadow, or stood in the sunshine on the beach, watching the approaching boats of their comrades, combined a picture which was no longer interesting. 'Alas!' said she, breaking from meditative silence, 'this sun so glorious, which lights up all the various colouring of these shores, and the glow of those majestic mountains; alas! I feel that it will not long shine for me—my eyes must soon close upon the prospect for ever!'

To Ellena's tender reproach for this melancholy suggestion Bianchi replied only by expressing an earnest wish to witness the certainty of her being protected; adding, that this must be soon, or she should not live to see it. Ellena, extremely shocked both by this presage of her aunt's fate, and by the direct reference made to her own condition in the presence of Vivaldi, burst into tears, while he, supported by the wishes of Signora Bianchi, urged his suit with encreased interest.

'This is not a time for fastidious scruples,' said Bianchi, 'now that a solemn truth calls out to us. My dear girl, I will not disguise my feelings; they assure me I have not long to live. Grant me then the only request I have to make, and my last hours will be comforted.'

After a pause she added, as she took the hand of her niece, 'This will, no doubt, be an awful separation to us both; and it must also be a mournful one, Signor,' turning to Vivaldi, 'for she has been as a daughter to me, and I have, I trust, fulfilled to her the duties of a mother. Judge then, what will be her feelings when I am no more. But it will be your care to soothe them.'

Vivaldi looked at Ellena, and would have spoken; her aunt, however, proceeded. 'My own feelings would now be little less poignant, if I did not believe that I was confiding her to a tenderness, which cannot diminish; that I should prevail with her to accept the protection of a husband. To you, Signor, I commit the legacy of my child. Watch over her future moments, guard her from inquietude as vigilantly as I have done, and, if possible, from misfortune! I have yet much to say, but my spirits are exhausted.'

While he listened to this sacred charge, and recollected the injury Ellena had already sustained for his sake, by the cruel obliquy which the Marchese had thrown upon her character, he suffered a degree of generous indignation, of which he scarcely could conceal the cause, and a succeeding tenderness that almost melted him to tears; and he secretly vowed to defend her fame and protect her peace, at the sacrifice of every other consideration.

Bianchi, as she concluded her exhortation, gave Ellena's hand to Vivaldi, who received it with emotion such as his countenance, only, could express, and with solemn fervour raising his eyes to heaven, vowed that he never would betray the confidence thus reposed in him, but would watch over the happiness of Ellena with a care as tender, as anxious, and as unceasing as her own; that from this moment he considered himself bound by ties not less sacred than those which the church confers, to defend her as his wife, and would do so to the latest moment of his existence. As he said this, the truth of his feelings appeared in the energy of his manner.

Ellena, still weeping, and agitated by various considerations, spoke not, but withdrawing the handkerchief from her face, she looked at him through her tears, with a smile so meek, so affectionate, so timid, yet so confiding, as expressed all the mingled emotions of her heart, and appealed more eloquently to his, than the most energetic language could have done.

Before Vivaldi left the villa, he had some further conversation with Signora Bianchi, when it was agreed that the nuptials should be solemnized on the following week, if Ellena could be prevailed on to confirm her consent so soon; and that when he returned the next day, her determination would probably be made known to him.

He departed for Naples once more with the lightly-bounding steps of joy, which, however, when he arrived there, was somewhat alloyed by a message from the Marchese, demanding to see him in his cabinet. Vivaldi anticipated the subject of the interview, and obeyed the summons with reluctance.

He found his father so absorbed in thought, that he did not immediately perceive him. On raising his eyes from the floor, where discontent and perplexity seemed to have held them, he fixed a stern regard on Vivaldi. 'I understand,' said he, 'that you persist in the unworthy pursuit against which I warned you. I have left you thus long to your own discretion, because I was willing to afford you an opportunity of retracting with grace the declaration, which you have dared to make me of your principles and intentions; but your conduct has not therefore been the less observed. I am informed that your visits have been as frequent at the residence of the unhappy young woman, who was the subject of our former conversation, as formerly, and that you are as much infatuated.'

'If it is Signora Rosalba, whom your lordship means,' said Vivaldi, 'she is not unhappy; and I do not scruple to own, that I am as sincerely attached to her as ever. Why, my dear father,' continued he, subduing the feelings which this degrading mention of Ellena had aroused, 'why will you persist in opposing the happiness of your son; and above all, why will you continue to think unjustly of her, who deserves your admiration, as much as my love?'

'As I am not a lover,' replied the Marchese, 'and that the age of boyish credulity is past with me, I do not wilfully close my mind against examination, but am directed by proof and yield to conviction.'

'What proof is it, my Lord, that has thus easily convinced you?' said Vivaldi; 'Who is it that persists in abusing your confidence, and in destroying my peace?'

The Marchese haughtily reproved his son for such doubts and questions, and a long conversation ensued, which seemed neither to reconcile the interests or the opinions of either party. The Marchese persisted in accusation and menace; and Vivaldi in defending Ellena, and in affirming, that his affections and intentions were irrecoverable.

Not any art of persuasion could prevail with the Marchese to adduce his proofs, or deliver up the name of his informer; nor any menace awe Vivaldi into a renunciation of Ellena; and they parted mutually dissatisfied. The Marchese had failed on this occasion to act with his usual policy, for his menaces and accusations had aroused spirit and indignation, when kindness and gentle remonstrance would certainly have awakened filial affection, and might have occasioned a contest in the breast of Vivaldi. Now, no struggle of opposing duties divided his resolution. He had no hesitation on the subject of their dispute; but, regarding his father as a haughty oppressor who would rob him of his most sacred right; and as one who did not scruple to stain the name of the innocent and the defenceless, when his interest required it, upon the doubtful authority of a base informer, he suffered neither pity or remorse to mingle with the resolution of asserting the freedom of his nature; and was even more anxious than before, to conclude a marriage which he believed would secure his own happiness, and the reputation of Ellena.

He returned, therefore, on the following day to the villa Altieri, with encreased impatience to learn the result of Signora Bianchi's further conversation with her niece, and the day on which the nuptials might be solemnized. On the way thither, his thoughts were wholly occupied by Ellena, and he proceeded mechanically, and without observing where he was, till the shade which the well-known arch threw over the road recalled him to local circumstances, and a voice instantly arrested his attention. It was the voice of the monk, whose figure again passed before him. 'Go not to the villa Altieri,' it said solemnly, 'for death is in the house!'

Before Vivaldi could recover from the dismay into which this abrupt assertion and sudden appearance had thrown him, the stranger was gone. He had escaped in the gloom of the place, and seemed to have retired into the obscurity, from which he had so suddenly emerged, for he was not seen to depart from under the archway. Vivaldi pursued him with his voice, conjuring him to appear, and demanding who was dead; but no voice replied.

Believing that the stranger could not have escaped unseen from the arch by any way, but that leading to the fortress above, Vivaldi began to ascend the steps, when, considering that the more certain means of understanding this awful assertion would be, to go immediately to the villa Altieri, he left this portentous ruin, and hastened thither.

An indifferent person would probably have understood the words of the monk to allude to Signora Bianchi, whose infirm state of health rendered her death, though sudden, not improbable; but to the affrighted fancy of Vivaldi, the dying Ellena only appeared. His fears, however probabilities might sanction, or the event justify them, were natural to ardent affection; but they were accompanied by a presentiment as extraordinary as it was horrible; —it occurred to him more than once, that Ellena was murdered. He saw her wounded, and bleeding to death; saw her ashy countenance, and her wasting eyes, from which the spirit of life was fast departing, turned piteously on himself, as if imploring him to save her from the fate that was dragging her to the grave. And, when he reached the boundary of the garden, his whole frame trembled so, with horrible apprehension, that he rested a while, unable to venture further towards the truth. At length, he summoned courage to dare it, and, unlocking a private gate, of which he had lately received the key, because it spared him a considerable distance of the road to Naples, he approached the house. Every place around it was silent and forsaken; many of the lattices were closed, and, as he endeavoured to collect from every trivial circumstance some conjecture, his spirits still sunk as he advanced, till, having arrived within a few paces of the portico, all his fears were confirmed. He heard from within a feeble sound of lamentation, and then some notes of that solemn and peculiar kind of recitative, which is in some parts of Italy the requiem of the dying. The sounds were so low and distant that they only murmured on his ear; but, without pausing for information, he rushed into the portico, and knocked loudly at the folding doors, now closed against him.

After repeated summonses, Beatrice, the old house-keeper, appeared. She did not wait for Vivaldi's enquiries. 'Alas! Signor,' said she, 'alas-a-day! who would have thought it; who would have expected such a change as this! It was only yester-evening that you was here,—she was then as well as I am; who would have thought that she would be dead to-day?'

'She *is* dead, then!' exclaimed Vivaldi, struck to the heart; 'she *is* dead!' staggering towards a pillar of the hall, and endeavouring to support himself against it. Beatrice, shocked at his condition, would have gone for assistance, but he waved her to stay. 'When did she die,' said he, drawing breath with difficulty, 'how and where?'

'Alas! here in the villa, Signor,' replied Beatrice, weeping; 'who would have thought that I should live to see this day! I hoped to have laid down my old bones in peace.'

'What has caused her death?' interrupted Vivaldi impatiently, 'and when did she die?'

'About two of the clock this morning, Signor; about two o'clock. O miserable day, that I should live to see it!'

'I am better,' said Vivaldi, raising himself; 'lead me to her apartment,—I must see her. Do not hesitate, lead me on.'

'Alas! Signor, it is a dismal sight; why should you wish to see her? Be persuaded; do not go, Signor; it is a woeful sight!'

'Lead me on,' repeated Vivaldi sternly; 'or if you refuse, I will find the way myself.'

Beatrice, terrified by his look and gesture, no longer opposed him, begging only that he would wait till she had informed her lady of his arrival; but he followed her closely up the staircase and along a corridor that led round the west side of the house, which brought him to a suite of chambers darkened by the closed lattices, through which he passed towards the one where the body lay. The requiem had ceased, and no sound disturbed the awful still-ness that prevailed in these deserted rooms. At the door of the last apartment, where he was compelled to stop, his agitation was such, that Beatrice, expecting every instant to see him sink to the floor, made an effort to support him with her feeble aid, but he gave a signal for her to retire. He soon recovered himself and passed into the chamber of death, the solemnity of which might have affected him in any other state of his spirits; but these were now too severely pressed upon by real suffering to feel the influence of local circumstances. Approaching the bed on which the corpse was laid, he raised his eyes to the mourner who hung weeping over it, and beheld—Ellena! who, surprized by this sudden intrusion, and still more by the agitation of Vivaldi, repeatedly demanded the occasion of it. But he had neither power or inclination to explain a circumstance, which must deeply wound the heart of Ellena, since it would have told that the same event, which excited her grief, accidentally inspired his joy.

He did not long intrude upon the sacredness of sorrow, and the short time he remained was employed in endeavours to command his own emotion and to soothe her's.

When he left Ellena, he had some conversation with Beatrice, as to the death of Signora Bianchi, and understood that she had retired to rest on the preceding night apparently in her usual state of health. 'It was about one in the morning, Signor,' continued Beatrice, 'I was waked out of my first sleep by a noise in my lady's chamber. It is a grievous thing to me, Signor, to be waked from my first sleep, and I, Santa Maria forgive me! was angry at being disturbed! So I would not get up, but laid my head upon the pillow again, and tried to sleep; but presently I heard the noise again; nay now, says I, somebody must be up in the house, that's certain. I had scarcely said so, Signor, when I heard my young lady's voice calling "Beatrice! Beatrice!" Ah! poor young lady! she was indeed in a sad fright, as well she might. She was at my door in an instant, and looked as pale as death, and trembled so! "Beatrice," said she, "rise this moment; my aunt is dying." She did not stay for my answer, but was gone directly. Santa Maria protect me! I thought I should have swooned outright.'

'Well, but your lady?' said Vivaldi, whose patience the tedious circumlocution of old Beatrice had exhausted.

'Ah! my poor lady! Signor, I thought I never should have been able to reach her room; and when I got there, I was scarcely more alive than herself.—There she lay on her bed! O it was a grievous sight to see! there she lay, looking so piteously; I saw she was dying. She could not speak, though she tried often, but she was sensible, for she would look so at Signora Ellena, and then try again to speak; it almost broke one's heart to see her. Something seemed to lie upon her mind, and she tried almost to the last to tell it; and as she grasped Signora Ellena's hand, she would still look up in her face with such doleful expression as no one who had not a heart of stone could bear. My poor young mistress was quite overcome by it, and cried as if her heart would break. Poor young lady! she has lost a friend indeed, such a one as she must never hope to see again.'

'But she shall find one as firm and affectionate as the last!' exclaimed Vivaldi fervently.

'The good Saint grant it may prove so!' replied Beatrice, doubtingly. 'All that could be done for our dear lady,' she continued, 'was tried, but with no avail. She could not swallow what the Doctor offered her. She grew fainter and fainter, yet would often utter such deep sighs, and then would grasp my hand so hard! At last she turned her eyes from Signora Ellena, and they grew duller and fixed, and she seemed not to see what was before her. Alas! I knew then she was going; her hand did not press mine as it had done a minute or two before, and a deadly coldness was upon it. Her face changed so too in a few minutes! This was about two o'clock, and she died before her confessor could administer.'

Beatrice ceased to speak, and wept; Vivaldi almost wept with her, and it was some time before he could command his voice sufficiently to enquire, what were the symptoms of Signora Bianchi's disorder, and whether she had ever been thus suddenly attacked before.

'Never, Signor!' replied the old house-keeper; 'and though, to be sure, she has long been very infirm, and going down, as one may say, yet,'—

'What is it you mean?' said Vivaldi.

'Why, Signor, I do not know what to think about my lady's death. To be sure, there is nothing certain; and I may only get scoffed at, if I speak my mind abroad, for nobody would believe me, it is so strange, yet I must have my own thoughts, for all that.'

'Do speak intelligibly,' said Vivaldi, 'you need not apprehend censure from me.'

'Not from you, Signor, but if the report should get abroad, and it was known that I had set it a-going.'

'That never shall be known from me,' said Vivaldi, with encreased impatience, 'tell me, without fear, all that you conjecture.'

'Well then, Signor, I will own, that I do not like the suddenness of my lady's death, no, nor the manner of it, nor her appearance after death!'

'Speak explicitly, and to the point,' said Vivaldi.

'Nay, Signor, there are some folks that will not understand if you speak ever so plain, I am sure I speak plain enough. If I might tell my mind,—I do not believe she came fairly by her death at last!'

'How!' said Vivaldi, 'your reasons?'

'Nay, Signor, I have given them already; I said I did not like the suddenness of her death, nor her appearance after, nor'—

'Good heaven!' interrupted Vivaldi, 'you mean poison!'

'Hush, Signor, hush! I do not say that; but she did not seem to die naturally.'

'Who has been at the villa lately?' said Vivaldi, in a tremulous voice.

'Alas! Signor, nobody has been here; she lived so privately that she saw nobody.'

'Not one person?' said Vivaldi, 'consider well, Beatrice, had she no visitor?'

'Not of a long while, Signor, no visitors but yourself and her cousin Signor Giotto. The only other person that has been within these walls for many weeks, to the best of my remembrance, is a sister of the Convent, who comes for the silks my young lady embroiders.'

'Embroiders! What convent?'

'The Santa Maria della Pieta,* yonder, Signor; if you will step this way to the window, I will shew it you. Yonder, among the woods on the hill-side, just above those gardens that stretch down to the bay. There is an olive ground close beside it, and observe, Signor, there is a red and yellowish ridge of rocks rises over the woods higher still, and looks as if it would fall down upon those old spires. Have you found it, Signor?'

'How long is it since this sister came here?' said Vivaldi.

'Three weeks at least, Signor.'

'And you are certain that no other person has called within that time?'

'No other, Signor, except the fisherman and the gardener, and a man who brings maccaroni, and such sort of things; for it is such a long way to Naples, Signor, and I have so little time.

'Three weeks, say you! You said three weeks, I think? Are you certain as to this?'

'Three weeks, Signor! Santa della Pieta! Do you believe, Signor, that we could fast for three weeks! Why, they call almost every day.'

'I speak of the nun,' said Vivaldi.

'O yes, Signor,' replied Beatrice; 'it is that, at least, since she was here.'

'This is strange!' said Vivaldi, musing, 'but I will talk with you some other time. Meanwhile, I wish you could contrive that I should see the face of your deceased lady, without the knowledge of Signora Ellena. And, observe me, Beatrice, be strictly silent as to your surmises concerning her death: do not suffer any negligence to betray your suspicions to your young mistress. Has she any suspicions herself of the same nature?'

Beatrice replied, that she believed Signora Ellena had none; and promised faithfully to observe his injunctions.

He then left the villa, meditating on the circumstances he had just learned, and on the prophetic assertion of the monk, between whom, and the cause of Bianchi's sudden death, he could not forbear surmising there was some connection; and it now occurred to him, and for the first time, that this monk, this mysterious stranger, was no other than Schedoni, whom he had observed of late going more frequently than usual, to his mother's apartment. He almost started, in horror of the suspicion, to which this conjecture led, and precipitately rejected it, as a poison that would destroy his own peace for ever. But though he instantly dismissed the suspicion, the conjecture returned to his mind, and he endeavoured to recollect the voice and figure of the stranger, that he might compare them with those of the confessor. The voices were, he thought, of a different tone, and the persons of a different height and proportion. This comparison, however, did not forbid him to surmise that the stranger was an agent of the confessor's; that he was, at least, a secret spy upon his actions, and the defamer of Ellena; while both, if indeed there were two persons concerned, appeared to be at the command of his parents. Fired with indignation of the unworthy arts that he believed to have been employed against him, and impatient to meet the slanderer of Ellena, he determined to attempt some decisive step towards a discovery of the truth, and either to compel the confessor to reveal it to him, or to search out his agent, who, he fancied, was occasionally a resident within the ruins of Paluzzi.

The inhabitants of the convent, which Beatrice had pointed out, did not escape his consideration, but no reason appeared for supposing them the enemies of his Ellena, who, on the contrary, he understood had been for some years amicably connected with them. The embroidered silks, of which the old servant had spoken, sufficiently explained the nature of the connection, and discovering more fully the circumstances of Ellena's fortune, her conduct heightened the tender admiration, with which he had hitherto regarded her.

The hints for suspicion which Beatrice had given respecting the cause of her mistress's decease, incessantly recurred to him; and it appeared extraordinary, and sometimes in the highest degree improbable, that any person could be sufficiently interested in the death of a woman apparently so blameless, as to administer poison to her. What motive could have prompted so horrible a deed, was still more inexplicable. It was true that she had long been in a declining state; yet the suddenness of her departure and the singularity of some circumstances preceding as well as some appearances that had followed it, compelled Vivaldi to doubt as to the cause. He believed, however, that, after having seen the corpse, his doubts must vanish; and Beatrice had promised, that, if he could return in the evening, when Ellena had retired to rest, he should be permitted to visit the chamber of the deceased. There was something repugnant to his feelings, in going thus secretly, or, indeed, at all, to the residence of Ellena at this delicate period, yet it was necessary he should introduce there some medical professor, on whose judgment he could rest, respecting the occasion of Bianchi's death; and as he believed he should so soon acquire the right of vindicating the honour of Ellena, that consideration did not so seriously affect him as otherwise it would have done. The enquiry which called him thither was, besides, of a nature too solemn and important to be lightly resigned; he had, therefore, told Beatrice he would be punctual to the hour she appointed. His intention to search for the monk was thus again interrupted.

CHAPTER IV

Unfold th' impenetrable mystery,
That sets your soul and you at endless discord.

MYSTERIOUS MOTHER*

WHEN Vivaldi returned to Naples, he enquired for the Marchesa, of whom he wished to ask some questions concerning Schedoni, which, though he scarcely expected they would be explicitly answered, might yet lead to part of the truth he sought for.

The Marchesa was in her closet, and Vivaldi found the confessor with her. 'This man crosses me, like my evil genius,' said he to himself as he entered, 'but I will know whether he deserves my suspicions before I leave the room.'

Schedoni was so deeply engaged in conversation, that he did not immediately perceive Vivaldi, who stood for a moment examining his countenance, and tracing subjects for curiosity in its deep lines. His eyes, while he spoke, were cast downward, and his features were fixed in an expression at once severe and crafty. The Marchesa was listening with deep attention, her head inclined towards him, as if to catch the lowest murmur of his voice, and her face picturing the anxiety and vexation of her mind. This was evidently a conference, not a confession.

Vivaldi advancing, the monk raised his eyes; his countenance suffered no change, as they met those of Vivaldi. He rose, but did not take leave, and returned the slight and somewhat haughty salutation of Vivaldi, with an inclination of the head, that indicated a pride without pettishness, and a firmness bordering on contempt.

The Marchesa, on perceiving her son, was somewhat embarrassed, and her brow, before slightly contracted by vexation, now frowned with severity. Yet it was an involuntary emotion, for she endeavoured to chace the expression of it with a smile. Vivaldi liked the smile still less than the frown.

Schedoni seated himself quietly, and began, with almost the ease of a man of the world, to converse on general topics. Vivaldi, however, was reserved and silent; he knew not how to begin a conversation, which might lead to the knowledge he desired, and the Marchesa did not relieve him from the difficulty. His eye and his ear assisted him to conjecture at least, if not to obtain the information he wished; and, as he listened to the deep tones of Schedoni's voice, he became almost certain, that they were not the accents of his unknown adviser, though he considered, at the same moment, that it was not difficult to disguise, or to feign a voice. His stature seemed to decide the question more reasonably; for the figure of Schedoni appeared taller than that of the stranger; and though there was something of resemblance in their air, which Vivaldi had never observed before, he again considered, that the habit of the same order, which each wore, might easily occasion an artificial resemblance. Of the likeness, as to countenance, he could not judge, since the stranger's had been so much shrouded by his cowl, that Vivaldi had never distinctly seen a single feature. Schedoni's hood was now thrown back, so that he could not compare even the air of their heads under similar circumstances; but as he remembered to have seen the confessor on a former day approaching his mother's closet with the cowl shading his face, the same gloomy severity seemed to characterize both, and nearly the same terrible portrait was drawn on his fancy. Yet this again might be only an artificial effect, a character which the cowl alone gave to the head; and any face seen imperfectly beneath its dark shade, might have appeared equally severe. Vivaldi was still extremely perplexed in his opinion. One circumstance, however, seemed to throw some light on his judgment. The stranger had appeared in the habit of a monk, and, if Vivaldi's transient observation might be trusted, he was of the very same order with that of Schedoni. Yet if he were Schedoni, or even his agent, it was not probable that he would have shewn himself in a dress that might lead to a discovery of his person. That he was anxious for concealment, his manner had strongly proved; it seemed then, that this habit of a monk was only a disguise, assumed for the purpose of misleading conjecture. Vivaldi, however, determined to put some questions to Schedoni, and at the same time to observe their effect on his countenance. He took occasion to notice some drawings of ruins, which ornamented the cabinet of the Marchesa, and to say that the fortress of Paluzzi was worthy of being added to her collection.* 'You have seen it lately, perhaps, reverend father,' added Vivaldi, with a penetrating glance.

'It is a striking relique of antiquity,' replied the confessor.

'That arch,' resumed Vivaldi, his eye still fixed on Schedoni, 'that arch suspended between two rocks, the one overtopped by the towers of the fortress, the other shadowed with pine and broad oak, has a fine effect. But a picture of it would want human figures.

Now either the grotesque shapes of banditti lurking within the ruin, as if ready to start out upon the traveller, or a friar rolled up in his black garments, just stealing forth from under the shade of the arch, and looking like some supernatural messenger of evil, would finish the piece.'

The features of Schedoni suffered no change during this speech. 'Your picture is complete,' said he, 'and I cannot but admire the facility with which you have classed the monks together with banditti.'

'Your pardon, holy father,' said Vivaldi, 'I did not draw a parallel between them.'

'O! no offence, Signor,' replied Schedoni, with a smile some-what ghastly.

During the latter part of this conversation, if conversation it may be called, the Marchesa had followed a servant, who had brought her a letter, out of the apartment, and as the confessor appeared to await her return, Vivaldi determined to press his enquiry. 'It appears, however,' said he, 'that Palluzzi, if not haunted by robbers, is at least frequented by ecclesiastics; for I have seldom passed it without seeing one of the order, and that one has appeared so suddenly, and vanished so suddenly, that I have been almost compelled to believe he was literally a spiritual being!'

'The convent of the Black Penitents is not far distant,' observed the confessor.

'Does the dress of this convent resemble that of your order, reverend father? for I observed that the monk I speak of was habited like yourself; aye, and he was about your stature, and very much resembled you.'

'That well may be, Signor,' replied the confessor calmly; 'there are many brethren who, no doubt, resemble each other; but the brothers of the Black Penitents are clothed in sackcloth; and the death's head on the garment, the peculiar symbol of this order, would not have escaped your observation; it could not, therefore, be a member of their society whom you have seen.'

'I am not inclined to think that it was,' said Vivaldi; 'but be it who it may, I hope soon to be better acquainted with him, and to tell him truths so strong, that he shall not be permitted even to affect the misunderstanding of them.'

'You will do right, if you have cause of complaint against him,' observed Schedoni.

'And *only* if I have cause of complaint, holy father? Are strong truths to be told only when there is direct cause of complaint? Is it only when we are injured that we are to be sincere?' He believed that he had now detected Schedoni, who seemed to have betrayed a consciousness that Vivaldi had reason for complaint against the stranger.

'You will observe, reverend father, that I have not said I am injured,' he added. 'If you know that I am, this must be by other means than by my words; I have not even expressed resentment.'

'Except by your voice and eye, Signor,' replied Schedoni drily. 'When a man is vehement and disordered, we usually are inclined to suppose he feels resentment, and that he has cause of complaint, either real or imaginary. As I have not the honour of being acquainted with the subject you allude to, I cannot decide to which of the two your cause belongs.'

'I have never been in doubt as to that,' said Vivaldi haughtily; 'and if I had, you will pardon me, holy father, but I should not have requested your decision. My injuries are, alas! too real; and I now think it is also too certain to whom I may attribute them. The secret adviser, who steals into the bosom of a family only to poison its repose, the informer—the base asperser of innocence, stand revealed in one person before me.'

Vivaldi delivered these words with a tempered energy, at once dignified and pointed, which seemed to strike directly to the heart of Schedoni; but, whether it was his conscience or his pride that took the alarm, did not certainly appear. Vivaldi believed the former. A dark malignity overspread the features of the monk, and at that moment Vivaldi thought he beheld a man, whose passions might impel him to the perpetration of almost any crime, how hideous soever. He recoiled from him, as if he had suddenly seen a serpent in his path, and stood gazing on his face, with an attention so wholly occupied as to be unconscious that he did so.

Schedoni almost instantly recovered himself; his features relaxed from their first expression, and that portentous darkness passed away from his countenance; but with a look that was still stern and haughty, he said, 'Signor, however ignorant I may be of the subject of your discontent, I can not misunderstand that your resentment is, to some extent or other, directed against myself as the cause of it. Yet I will not suppose, Signor; I say I will not suppose,' raising his voice significantly, 'that you have dared to brand me with the ignominious titles you have just uttered; but'—

'I have applied them to the author of my injuries,' interrupted Vivaldi; 'you, father, can best inform me whether they applied to yourself.'

'I have then nothing to complain of,' said Schedoni, adroitly, and with a sudden calmness, that surprised Vivaldi. 'If you directed them against the author of your injuries, whatever they may be, I am satisfied.'

The chearful complacency, with which he spoke this, renewed the doubts of Vivaldi, who thought it nearly impossible that a man conscious of guilt could assume, under the very charge of it, the tranquil and dignified air, which the confessor now displayed. He began to accuse himself of having condemned him with passionate rashness, and gradually became shocked at the indecorum of his conduct towards a man of Schedoni's age and sacred profession. Those expressions of countenance, which had so much alarmed him, he was now inclined to think the effect of a jealous and haughty honour, and he almost forgot the malignity, which had mingled with Schedoni's pride, in sorrow for the offence that had provoked it. Thus, not less precipitate in his pity than his anger, and credulous alike to the passion of the moment, he was now as eager to apologize for his error, as he had been hasty in committing it. The frankness, with which he apologized and lamented the impropriety of his conduct, would have won an easy forgiveness from a generous heart. Schedoni listened with apparent complacency and secret contempt. He regarded Vivaldi as a rash boy, who was swayed only by his passions; but while he suffered deep resentment for the evil in his character, he felt neither respect nor kindness for the good, for the sincerity, the love of justice, the generosity, which threw a brilliancy even on his foibles. Schedoni, indeed, saw only evil in human nature.

Had the heart of Vivaldi been less generous, he would now have distrusted the satisfaction, which the confessor assumed, and have discovered the contempt and malignity, that lurked behind the smile thus imperfectly masking his countenance. The confessor perceived his power, and the character of Vivaldi lay before him as a map. He saw, or fancied he saw every line and feature of its plan, and the relative proportions of every energy and weakness of its nature. He believed, also, he could turn the very virtues of this young man against himself, and he exulted, even while the smile of good-will was yet upon his countenance, in anticipating the moment that should avenge him for the past outrage, and which, while Vivaldi was ingenuously lamenting it, he had apparently forgotten.

Schedoni was thus ruminating evil against Vivaldi, and Vivaldi was considering how he might possibly make Schedoni atonement for the affront he had offered him, when the Marchesa returned to the apartment; and perceived in the honest countenance of Vivaldi some symptoms of the agitation which had passed over it; his complexion was flushed, and his brow slightly contracted. The face of Schedoni told nothing but complacency, except that now and then when he looked at Vivaldi, it was with half-shut eyes, that indicated treachery, or, at least, cunning, trying to conceal exasperated pride.

The Marchesa, with displeasure directed against her son, enquired the reason of his emotion; but he, stung with consciousness of his conduct towards the monk, could neither endure to explain it, or to remain in her presence, and saying that he would confide his honour to the discretion of the holy father, who would speak only too favourably of his fault, he abruptly left the room.

When he had departed, Schedoni gave, with seeming reluctance, the explanation which the Marchesa required, but was cautious not to speak too favourably of Vivaldi's conduct, which, on the contrary, he represented as much more insulting than it really was; and, while he aggravated the offensive part of it, he suppressed all mention of the candour and self-reproach, which had followed the charge. Yet this he managed so artfully that he appeared to extenuate Vivaldi's errors, to lament the hastiness of his temper, and to plead for a forgiveness from his irritated mother. 'He is very young,' added the monk, when he perceived that he had sufficiently exasperated the Marchesa against her son; 'he is very young, and youth is warm in its passions and precipitate in its judgments. He was, besides, jealous, no doubt, of the friendship, with which you are pleased to honour me; and it is natural that a son should be jealous of the attention of such a mother.'

'You are too good, father,' said the Marchesa; her resentment encreasing towards Vivaldi in proportion as Schedoni displayed his artificial candour and meekness.

'It is true,' continued the confessor, 'that I perceive all the inconveniences to which my attachment, I should say my duty to your family exposes me; but I willingly submit to these, while it is yet possible that my advice may be a means of preserving the honour of your house unsullied, and of saving this inconsiderate young man from future misery and unavailing repentance.'

During the warmth of this sympathy in resentment, the Marchesa and Schedoni mutually, and sincerely, lost their remembrance of the unworthy motives, by which each knew the other to be influenced, as well as that disgust which those who act together to the same bad end, can seldom escape from feeling towards their associates. The Marchesa, while she commended the fidelity of Schedoni, forgot his views and her promises as to a rich benefice; while the confessor imputed her anxiety for the splendor of her son's condition to a real interest in his welfare, not a care of her own dignity. After mutual compliments had been exchanged, they proceeded to a long consultation concerning Vivaldi, and it was agreed, that their efforts for what they termed his preservation should no longer be confined to remonstrances.

CHAPTER V

What if it be a poison, which the friar
Subtly hath ministered? ——
SHAKESPEARE*

VIVALDI, when his first feelings of pity and compunction for having insulted an aged man, the member of a sacred profession, were past, and when he looked with a more deliberate eye upon some circumstances of the confessor's conduct, perceived that suspicion was again gathering on his mind. But, regarding this as a symptom of his own weakness, rather than as a hint of truth, he endeavoured, with a magnanimous disdain, to reject every surmise that boded unfavourably of Schedoni.

When evening arrived, he hastened towards the villa Altieri, and, having met without the city, according to appointment, a physician, upon whose honor and judgment he thought he might rely, they proceeded on their way together. Vivaldi had forgotten, during the confusion of his last interview with Ellena, to deliver up the key of the garden-gate, and he now entered it as usual, though he could not entirely overcome the reluctance, which he felt on thus visiting, in secret and at night, the dwelling of Ellena. Under no other circumstances, however, could the physician, whose opinion was so necessary to his peace, be introduced without betraying a suspicion, which must render her unhappy, probably for ever.

Beatrice, who had watched for them in the portico, led the way to the chamber where the corpse was laid out; and Vivaldi, though considerably affected when he entered, soon recovered composure enough to take his station on one side of the bed, while the physician placed himself on the other. Unwilling to expose his emotion to

the observation of a servant, and desirous also of some private conversation with the physician, he took the lamp from Beatrice and
dismissed her. As the light glared upon the livid face of the corpse,
Vivaldi gazed with melancholy surprize, and an effort of reason
was necessary to convince him, that this was the same countenance
which only one evening preceding was animated like his own;
which had looked upon him in tears, while, with anxiety the most
tender, she had committed the happiness of her niece to his care,
and had, alas! too justly predicted her approaching dissolution. The
circumstances of that scene now appeared to him like a vision, and
touched every fibre of his heart. He was fully sensible of the importance of the trust committed to him, and, as he now hung over
the pale and deserted form of Bianchi, he silently renewed his
solemn vows to Ellena, to deserve the confidence of her departed
guardian.

Before Vivaldi had courage enough to ask the opinion of the
physician, who was still viewing the face of the deceased with very
earnest attention and disapproving countenance, his own suspicions strengthened from some circumstances of her appearance;
and particularly from the black tint that prevailed over her complexion, it seemed to him, that her death had been by poison. He
feared to break a silence, which prolonged his hope of the contrary,
feeble though it was; and the physician, who probably was apprehensive for the consequence of delivering his real thought, did not
speak.

'I read your opinion,' said Vivaldi, at length, 'it coincides with
my own.'

'I know not as to that, Signor,' replied the physician, 'though I
think I perceive what is yours. Appearances are unfavourable, yet
I will not take upon me to decide from them, that it is as you suspect. There are other circumstances, under which similar appearances might occur.' He gave his reasons for this assertion,
which were plausible even to Vivaldi, and concluded with requesting to speak with Beatrice, 'for I wish to understand,' said he,
'what was the exact situation of this lady for some hours previous
to her decease.'

After a conversation of some length with Beatrice, whatever
might be the opinion resulting from his enquiries, he adhered
nearly to his former assertions; pronouncing that so many contradictory circumstances appeared, as rendered it impossible for him
to decide, whether Bianchi had died by poison, or otherwise. He
stated more fully than he had done before, the reasons, which must

render the opinion of any medical person, on this subject, doubtful. But, whether it was that he feared to be responsible for a decision, which would accuse some person of murder, or that he really was inclined to believe that Bianchi died naturally, it is certain he seemed disposed to adopt the latter opinion; and that he was very anxious to quiet the suspicions of Vivaldi. He so far succeeded, indeed, as to convince him that it would be unavailing to pursue the enquiry, and almost compelled him to believe, that she had departed according to the common course of nature.

Vivaldi, having lingered awhile over the death-bed of Bianchi, and taken a last farewel of her silent form, quitted the chamber and the house as softly as he had approached, and unobserved, as he believed, by Ellena or any other person. The morning dawned over the sea, when he returned into the garden, and a few fishermen, loitering on the beach, or putting off their little boats from the shore, were the only persons visible at this early hour. The time, however, was passed for renewing the enquiry he had purposed at Paluzzi, and the brightening dawn warned him to retire. To Naples, therefore, he returned, with spirits somewhat soothed by a hope, that Bianchi had not fallen prematurely, and by the certainty that Ellena was well. On the way thither, he passed the fort without interruption, and, having parted with the physician, was admitted into his father's mansion by a confidential servant.

CHAPTER VI

—— For here have been
Some six or seven, who did hide their faces
Even from darkness.
                                        SHAKESPEARE*

ELLENA, on thus suddenly losing her aunt, her only relative, the friend of her whole life, felt as if left alone in the world. But it was not in the first moments of affliction that this feeling occurred. Her own forlorn situation was not even observed, while affection, pity, and irresistible grief for Bianchi, occupied her heart.

Bianchi was to be interred in the church belonging to the convent of Santa Maria della Pieta. The body, attired according to the custom of the country, and decorated with flowers, was carried on an open bier to the place of interment, attended only by priests and torch-bearers. But Ellena could not endure thus lightly to part with the reliques of a beloved friend, and being restrained by custom from following the corpse to the grave, she repaired first to the convent, to attend the funeral service. Her sorrow did not allow her to join in the choral symphonies of the nuns, but their sacred solemnity was soothing to her spirits, and the tears she shed while she listened to the lengthening notes, assuaged the force of grief.

When the service concluded, she withdrew to the parlour of the lady Abbess, who mingled with her consolations many entreaties that Ellena would make the convent her present asylum; and her affliction required little persuasion on this subject. It was her wish to retire hither, as to a sanctuary, which was not only suitable to her particular circumstances, but especially adapted to the present state of her spirits. Here she believed that she should sooner acquire resignation, and regain tranquillity, than in a place less consecrated to religion; and, before she took leave of the Abbess, it was agreed, that she should be received as a boarder. To acquaint Vivaldi with her intention was, indeed, her chief motive for returning to the villa Altieri, after this her resolution had been taken. Her affection and esteem had been gradual in their progress, and had now attained a degree of strength, which promised to decide the happiness or misery of her whole life. The sanction given by her aunt to this choice, and particularly the very solemn manner in which, on the evening preceding her death, she bequeathed Ellena to his care, had still further endeared him to her heart, and imparted a sacredness to the engagement, which made her consider Vivaldi as her guardian and only surviving protector. The more tenderly she lamented her deceased relative, the more tenderly she thought of Vivaldi; and her love for the one was so intimately connected with her affection for the other, that each seemed strengthened and exalted by the union.

When the funeral was over, they met at Altieri.

He was neither surprized or averse to her withdrawing awhile to a convent; for there was a propriety in retiring, during the period of her grief, from a home where she had no longer a guardian, which delicacy seemed to demand. He only stipulated, that he might be permitted to visit her in the parlour of the convent, and to claim, when decorum should no longer object to it, the hand, which Bianchi had resigned to him.

Notwithstanding that he yielded to this arrangement without complaining, it was not entirely without repining; but being assured by Ellena of the worthiness of the Abbess of the Santa Maria della Pieta, he endeavoured to silence the secret murmurs of his heart with the conviction of his judgment.

Meanwhile, the deep impression made by his unknown tormentor, the monk, and especially by his prediction of the death of Bianchi, remained upon his mind, and he once more determined to ascertain, if possible, the true nature of this portentous visitant, and what were the motives which induced him thus to haunt his footsteps and interrupt his peace. He was awed by the circumstances which had attended the visitations of the monk, if monk it was; by the suddenness of his appearance, and departure; by the truth of his prophecies; and, above all, by the solemn event which had verified his last warning; and his imagination, thus elevated by wonder and painful curiosity, was prepared for something above the reach of common conjecture, and beyond the accomplishment of human agency. His understanding was sufficiently clear and strong to teach him to detect many errors of opinion, that prevailed around him, as well as to despise the common superstitions of his country, and, in the usual state of his mind, he probably would not have paused for a moment on the subject before him; but his passions were now interested and his fancy awakened, and, though he was unconscious of this propensity, he would, perhaps, have been somewhat disappointed, to have descended suddenly from the region of fearful sublimity, to which he had soared—the world of terrible shadows—to the earth, on which he daily walked, and to an explanation simply natural.

He designed to visit again, at midnight, the fortress of Paluzzi, and not to watch for the appearance of the stranger, but to carry torches into every recess of the ruin, and discover, at least, whether it was haunted by other human beings than himself. The chief difficulty, which had hitherto delayed him, was that of finding a person, in whom he could confide, to accompany him in the search, since his former adventure had warned him never to renew it alone. Signor Bonarmo persisted absolutely, and, perhaps, wisely, to refuse his request on this subject; and, as Vivaldi had no other acquaintance, to whom he chose to give so much explanation of the affair as might induce compliance, he at length determined to take with him Paulo, his own servant.

On the evening, previous to the day of Ellena's departure to the Santa della Pieta, Vivaldi went to Altieri, to bid her adieu. During this interview his spirits were more than usually depressed; and, though he knew that her retirement was only for a short period, and had as much confidence in the continuance of her affection, as is, perhaps, possible to a lover, Vivaldi felt as if he was parting with her for ever. A thousand vague and fearful conjectures, such as he had never till this moment admitted, assailed him, and amongst them, it appeared probable, that the arts of the nuns might win her from the world, and sacrifice her to the cloister. In her present state of sorrow this seemed to be even more than probable, and not all the assurances which Ellena gave him, and in these parting moments she spoke with less reserve than she had hitherto done, could entirely re-assure his mind. 'It should seem, Ellena, by these boding fears,' said he, imprudently, 'that I am parting with you for ever; I feel a weight upon my heart, which I cannot throw off. Yet I consent that you shall withdraw awhile to this convent, convinced of the propriety of the step; and I ought, also, to know that you will soon return; that I shall soon take you from its walls as my wife, never more to leave me, never more to pass from my immediate care and tenderness. I ought to feel assured of all this; yet so apt are my fears that I cannot confide in what is probable, but rather apprehend what is possible. And is it then possible that I yet may lose you; and is it only probable that you may be mine for ever? How, under such circumstances, could I weakly consent to your retirement? Why did I not urge you to bestow immediately those indissoluble bands, which no human force can burst asunder? How could I leave the destiny of all my peace within the reach of a possibility, which it was once in my power to have removed! Which it *was* in my power!—It is, perhaps, still in my power. O Ellena! let the severities of custom yield to the security of my happiness. If you do go to the Santa Maria, let it be only to visit its altar!'

Vivaldi delivered this expostulation with a rapidity, that left no pause for Ellena to interrupt him. When, at length, he concluded, she gently reproached him for doubting the continuance of her regard, and endeavoured to sooth his apprehensions of misfortune, but would not listen to his request. She represented, that not only the state of her spirits required retirement, but that respect to the memory of her aunt demanded it; and added gravely, that if he had so little confidence in the steadiness of her opinions, as to doubt the constancy of her affection, and for so short a period, unless her vows were secured to him, he had done imprudently to elect her for the companion of his whole life.

Vivaldi, then ashamed of the weakness he had betrayed, besought her forgiveness, and endeavoured to appease apprehensions which passion only made plausible, and which reason reproved;

notwithstanding which, he could recover neither tranquillity nor confidence; nor could Ellena, though her conduct was supported and encouraged by justness of sentiment, entirely remove the oppression of spirits she had felt from almost the first moment of this interview. They parted with many tears; and Vivaldi, before he finally took his leave, frequently returned to claim some promise, or to ascertain some explanation, till Ellena remarked with a forced smile, that these resembled eternal adieus, rather than those of only a few days; an observation which renewed all his alarm, and furnished an excuse for again delaying his departure. At length he tore himself away, and left the villa Altieri; but as the time was yet too early to suit his purposed enquiry at Paluzzi, he returned to Naples.

Ellena, meanwhile, endeavouring to dissipate melancholy recollections by employment, continued busied in preparation for her departure on the following day, till a late hour of the night. In the prospect of quitting, though only for so short a period, the home where she had passed almost every day since the dawn of her earliest remembrance, there was something melancholy, if not solemn. In leaving these well-known scenes, where, it might be said, the shade of her deceased relative seemed yet to linger, she was quitting all vestige of her late happiness, all note of former years and of present consolation; and she felt as if going forth into a new and homeless world. Her affection for the place encreased as the passing time diminished, and it seemed as if the last moment of her stay would be precisely that, in which the villa Altieri would be most valued.

In her favourite apartments she lingered for a considerable time; and in the room where she had supped on the night immediately preceding the death of Signora Bianchi, she indulged many tender and mournful recollections, and probably would have continued to indulge them much longer, had not her attention been withdrawn by a sudden rustling of the foliage that surrounded the window, when, on raising her eyes, she thought she perceived some person pass quickly from before it. The lattices had, as usual, been left open to admit the fresh breeze from the bay below, but she now rose with some alarm to close them, and had scarcely done so when she heard a distant knocking from the portico, and in the next instant the screams of Beatrice in the hall.

Alarmed for herself, Ellena had, however, the courage to advance to the assistance of her old servant, when, on entering the passage leading to the hall, three men, masked and muffled up in cloaks, appeared, advancing from the opposite extremity. While she fled, they pursued her to the apartment she had quitted. Her breath and her courage were gone, yet she struggled to sustain herself, and endeavoured to ask with calmness what was their errand. They gave no reply, but threw a veil over her face, and, seizing her arms, led her almost unresisting, but supplicating, towards the portico.

In the hall, Ellena perceived Beatrice bound to a pillar; and another ruffian, who was also masked, watching over and menacing her, not by words, but gestures. Ellena's shrieks seemed to recall the almost lifeless Beatrice, for whom she supplicated as much as for herself; but entreaty was alike unavailing for each, and Ellena was borne from the house and through the garden. All consciousness had now forsaken her. On recovering, she perceived herself in a carriage, which was driven with great rapidity, and that her arms were within the grasp of some persons, whom, when her recollection returned more fully, she believed to be the men, who had carried her from the villa. The darkness prevented her from observing their figures, and to all her questions and entreaties a death-like silence was observed.

During the whole night the carriage proceeded rapidly, stopping only while the horses were changed, when Ellena endeavoured to interest by her cries the compassion of the people at the post-houses, and by her cries only, for the blinds were closely drawn. The postilions, no doubt, imposed on the credulity of these people, for they were insensible to her distress, and her immediate companions soon overcame the only means that had remained by which she could make it known.

For the first hours, a tumult of terror and amazement occupied her mind, but, as this began to subside, and her understanding to recover its clearness, grief and despondency mingled with her fears. She saw herself separated from Vivaldi, probably for ever, for she apprehended that the strong and invisible hand which governed her course, would never relinquish its grasp till it had placed her irrecoverably beyond the reach of her lover. A conviction that she should see him no more came, at intervals, with such overwhelming force, that every other consideration and emotion disappeared before it; and at these moments she lost all anxiety as to the place of her destination, and all fear as to her personal safety.

As the morning advanced and the heat encreased, the blinds were let down a little to admit air, and Ellena then perceived, that only two of the men, who had appeared at the villa Altieri, were in the carriage, and that they were still disguised in cloaks and visors. She had no means of judging through what part of the country she was travelling, for above the small openings which the blinds left she could see only the towering tops of mountains, or sometimes the veiny precipices and tangled thickets, that closely impended over the road.

About noon, as she judged from the excessive heat, the carriage stopped at a post-house, and ice-water was handed through the window, when, as the blind was lowered to admit it, she perceived herself on a wild and solitary plain, surrounded by mountains and woods. The people at the door of the post-house seemed 'unused to pity or be pitied.'* The lean and sallow countenance of poverty stared over their gaunt bones, and habitual discontent had fixed the furrows of their cheeks. They regarded Ellena with only a feeble curiosity, though the affliction in her looks might have interested almost any heart that was not corroded by its own sufferings; nor did the masked faces of her companions excite a much stronger attention.

Ellena accepted the cool refreshment offered her, the first she had taken on the road. Her companions having emptied their glasses drew up the blind, and, notwithstanding the almost intolerable heat of noon, the carriage proceeded. Fainting under its oppression, Ellena entreated that the windows might be open, when the men, in compliance with their own necessity rather than with her request, lowered the blinds, and she had a glimpse of the lofty region of the mountains, but of no object that could direct her conjecture concerning where she was. She saw only pinnacles and vast precipices of various-tinted marbles, intermingled with scanty vegetation, such as stunted pinasters, dwarf oak and holly, which gave dark touches to the many-coloured cliffs, and sometimes stretched in shadowy masses to the deep vallies, that, winding into obscurity, seemed to invite curiosity to explore the scenes beyond. Below these bold precipices extended the gloomy region of olive-trees, and lower still other rocky steeps sunk towards the plains, bearing terraces crowned with vines, and where often the artificial soil was propped by thickets of juniper, pomegranate and oleander.

Ellena, after having been so long shut in darkness, and brooding over her own alarming circumstances, found temporary, though feeble, relief in once more looking upon the face of nature; till, her spirits being gradually revived and elevated by the grandeur of the images around her, she said to herself, 'If I am condemned to misery, surely I could endure it with more fortitude in scenes like these, than amidst the tamer landscapes of nature! Here, the objects seem to impart somewhat of their own force, their own sublimity, to the soul.* It is scarcely possible to yield to the pressure of misfortune while we walk, as with the Deity, amidst his most stupendous works!'

But soon after the idea of Vivaldi glancing athwart her memory, she melted into tears; the weakness however was momentary, and during the rest of the journey she preserved a strenuous equality of mind.

It was when the heat and the light were declining that the carriage entered a rocky defile, which shewed, as through a telescope reversed, distant plains, and mountains opening beyond, lighted up with all the purple splendor of the setting sun. Along this deep and shadowy perspective a river, which was seen descending among the cliffs of a mountain, rolled with impetuous force, fretting and foaming amidst the dark rocks in its descent, and then flowing in a limpid lapse to the brink of other precipices, whence again it fell with thundering strength to the abyss, throwing its misty clouds of spray high in the air, and seeming to claim the sole empire of this solitary wild. Its bed took up the whole breadth of the chasm, which some strong convulsion of the earth seemed to have formed, not leaving space even for a road along its margin. The road, therefore, was carried high among the cliffs, that impended over the river, and seemed as if suspended in air; while the gloom and vastness of the precipices, which towered above and sunk below it, together with the amazing force and uproar of the falling waters, combined to render the pass more terrific than the pencil could describe, or language can express. Ellena ascended it, not with indifference but with calmness; she experienced somewhat of a dreadful pleasure in looking down upon the irresistible flood; but this emotion was heightened into awe, when she perceived that the road led to a slight bridge, which, thrown across the chasm at an immense height, united two opposite cliffs, between which the whole cataract of the river descended. The bridge, which was defended only by a slender railing, appeared as if hung amidst the clouds. Ellena, while she was crossing it, almost forgot her misfortunes. Having reached the opposite side of the glen, the road gradually descended the precipices for about half a mile, when it opened to extensive prospects over plains and towards distant mountains—the sunshine landscape, which had long appeared to bound this shadowy pass. The transition was as the passage through the vale of death to the bliss of eternity; but the idea of its resemblance did not long remain with Ellena. Perched high among the cliffs of a mountain, which might be said to terminate one of the jaws of this terrific gorge, and which was one of the loftiest of a chain that surrounded the plains, appeared the spires and long terraces of a monastery; and she soon understood that her journey was to conclude there.

At the foot of this mountain her companions alighted, and obliged her to do the same, for the ascent was too steep and irregular to admit of a carriage. Ellena followed unresistingly, like a lamb to the sacrifice, up a path that wound among the rocks, and was cooly overshadowed by thickets of almond trees, figs, broad-leaved myrtle, and ever-green rose bushes, intermingled with the strawberry tree, beautiful in fruit and blossoms, the yellow jasmine, the delightful *acacia mimosa*, and a variety of other fragrant plants. These bowers frequently admitted glimpses of the glowing country below, and sometimes opened to expansive views bounded by the snowy mountains of Abruzzo. At every step were objects which would have afforded pleasure to a tranquil mind; the beautifully variegated marbles, that formed the cliffs immediately above, their fractured masses embossed with mosses and flowers of every vivid hue that paints the rainbow; the elegance of the shrubs that tufted, and the majestic grace of the palms which waved over them, would have charmed almost any other eye than Ellena's, whose spirit was wrapt in care, or than those of her companions, whose hearts were dead to feeling. Partial features of the vast edifice she was approaching, appeared now and then between the trees; the tall west window of the cathedral with the spires that overtopped it; the narrow pointed roofs of the cloisters; angles of the insurmountable walls, which fenced the garden from the precipices below, and the dark portal leading into the chief court; each of these, seen at intervals beneath the gloom of cypress and spreading cedar, seemed as if menacing the unhappy Ellena with hints of future suffering. She passed several shrines and images half hid among the shrubs and the cliffs; and, when she drew near the monastery, her companions stopped at a little chapel which stood beside the path, where, after examining some papers, an act which she observed with surprise, they drew aside, as if to consult respecting herself. Their conversation was delivered in voices so low, that she could not catch a single tone distinctly, and it is probable that if she could, this would not have assisted her in conjecturing who they were; yet the profound silence they had hitherto observed had much encreased her curiosity, now that they spoke.

One of them soon after quitted the chapel and proceeded alone to the monastery, leaving Ellena in the custody of his comrade, whose pity she now made a last, though almost hopeless, effort to interest. He replied to all her entreaties only by a waving of the hand, and an averted face; and she endeavoured to meet with fortitude and to endure with patience, the evil which she could neither avoid nor subdue. The spot where she awaited the return of the ruffian, was not of a character to promote melancholy, except, indeed, that luxurious and solemn kind of melancholy, which a view of stupendous objects inspires. It overlooked the whole extent of plains, of which she had before caught partial scenes, with the vast chain of mountains, which seemed to form an insurmountable rampart to the rich landscape at their feet. Their towering and fantastic summits, crowding together into dusky air, like flames tapering to a point, exhibited images of peculiar grandeur, while each minuter line and feature withdrawing, at this evening hour, from observation, seemed to resolve itself into the more gigantic masses, to which the dubious tint, the solemn obscurity, that began to prevail over them, gave force and loftier character. The silence and deep repose of the landscape, served to impress this character more awfully on the heart, and while Ellena sat wrapt in the thoughtfulness it promoted, the vesper-service of the monks breathing softly from the cathedral above, came to her ear; it was a music which might be said to win on silence, and was in perfect unison with her feelings; solemn, deep, and full, it swelled in holy peels, and rolled away in murmurs, which attention pursued to the last faint note that melted into air. Ellena's heart owned the power of this high minstrelsy; and while she caught for a moment the sweeter voices of the nuns mingling in the chorus, she indulged a hope that they would not be wholly insensible to her sufferings, and that she should receive some consolation from sympathy as soft as these tender-breathing strains appeared to indicate.

She had rested nearly half an hour on the turfy slope before the chapel, when she perceived through the twilight, two monks descending from the monastery towards the spot where she sat. As they drew near, she distinguished their dress of grey stuff,* the hood, the shaven head, where only a coronet of white hair was left, and other ensigns of their particular order. On reaching the chapel they accosted her companion, with whom they retired a few paces, and conversed. Ellena heard, for the first time, the sound of her conductor's voice, and though this was but faintly, she marked it well. The other ruffian did not yet appear, but it seemed evident that these friars had left the convent in consequence of his information; and sometimes, when she looked upon the taller of the two, she fancied she saw the person of the very man whose absence she had remarked, a conjecture which strengthened while she more accurately noticed him. The portrait had certainly much resemblance in height and bulk; and the same gaunt awkwardness, which even the cloak of the ruffian had not entirely shrouded, obtruded itself from under the folded garments of the recluse. If countenance, too, might be trusted, this same friar had a ruffian's heart, and his keen and cunning eye seemed habitually upon the watch for prey. His brother of the order shewed nothing strongly characteristic either in his face or manner.

After a private conversation of some length, the friars approached Ellena, and told her, that she must accompany them to the convent; when her disguised conductor, having resigned her to them, immediately departed and descended the mountain.

Not a word was uttered by either of the party as they pursued the steep tract leading to the gates of this secluded edifice, which were opened to them by a lay-brother, and Ellena entered a spacious court. Three sides of this were enclosed by lofty buildings, lined with ranges of cloisters; the fourth opened to a garden, shaded with avenues of melancholy cypress, that extended to the cathedral, whose fretted windows and ornamented spires appeared to close the perspective. Other large and detached buildings skirted the gardens on the left, while, on the right, spacious olive-grounds and vineyards spread to the cliffs that formed a barrier to all this side of the domain of the convent.

The friar, her conductor, crossed the court to the north wing, and there ringing a bell, a door was opened by a nun, into whose hands Ellena was given. A significant look was exchanged between the devotees, but no words; the friar departed, and the nun, still silent, conducted her through many solitary passages, where not even a distant foot-fall echoed, and whose walls were roughly painted with subjects indicatory of the severe superstitions of the place, tending to inspire melancholy awe. Ellena's hope of pity vanished as her eyes glanced over these symbols of the disposition of the inhabitants, and on the countenance of the nun characterised by a gloomy malignity, which seemed ready to inflict upon others some portion of the unhappiness she herself suffered. As she glided forward with soundless step, her white drapery, floating along these solemn avenues, and her hollow features touched with the mingled light and shadow which the partial rays of a taper she held occasioned, she seemed like a spectre newly risen from the grave, rather than a living being. These passages terminated in the parlour of the Abbess, where the nun paused, and, turning to Ellena, said, 'It is the hour of vespers; you will wait here till our lady of the convent leaves the church; she would speak with you.'

'To what saint is the convent dedicated,' said Ellena, 'and who, sister, presides over it?'

The nun gave no reply, and after having eyed the forlorn stranger for a moment, with inquisitive ill-nature, quitted the room. The unhappy Ellena had not been left long to her own reflections, when the Abbess appeared; a stately lady, apparently occupied with opinions of her own importance, and prepared to receive her guest with rigour and supercilious haughtiness. This Abbess, who was herself a woman of some distinction, believed that of all possible crimes, next to that of sacrilege, offences against persons of rank were least pardonable. It is not surprising, therefore, that, supposing Ellena, a young woman of no family, to have sought clandestinely to unite herself with the noble house of Vivaldi, she should feel for her, not only disdain, but indignation, and that she should readily consent, not only to punish the offender, but at the same time, to afford means of preserving the ancient dignity of the offended.

'I understand,' said the Abbess, on whose appearance the alarmed Ellena had arisen, 'I understand,' said she, without making any signal for her to be seated, 'that you are the young person who is arrived from Naples.'

'My name is Ellena di Rosalba,' said her auditor, recovering some degree of courage from the manner which was designed to depress her.

'I know nothing of your name,' replied the Superior; 'I am informed only that you are sent here to acquire a knowledge of yourself and of your duties. Till the period shall be passed, for which you are given into my charge, I shall scrupulously observe the obligations of the troublesome office, which my regard for the honour of a noble family, has induced me to undertake.'

By these words, the author and the motives of this extraordinary transaction were at once revealed to Ellena, who was for some moments almost overwhelmed by the sudden horrors that gathered on her mind, and stood silent and motionless. Fear, shame, and indignation, alternately assailed her; and the sting of offended honour, on being suspected, and thus accused of having voluntarily disturbed the tranquillity, and sought the alliance of any family, and especially of one who disdained her, struck forcibly to her heart, till the pride of conscious worth revived her courage and fortified her patience, and she demanded by whose will she had been torn from her home, and by whose authority she was now detained, as it appeared, a prisoner.

The Abbess, unaccustomed to have her power opposed, or her words questioned, was for a moment too indignant to reply; and Ellena observed, but no longer with dismay, the brooding tempest ready to burst over her head. 'It is I only, who am injured,' said she to herself, 'and shall the guilty oppressor triumph, and the innocent sufferer sink under the shame that belongs only to guilt! Never will I yield to a weakness so contemptible. The consciousness of deserving well will recall my presence of mind, which, permitting me to estimate the characters of my oppressors by their actions, will enable me also to despise their power.'

'I must remind you,' said the Abbess, at length, 'that the questions you make are unbecoming in your situation; and that contrition and humility are the best extenuations of error. You may withdraw.'

'Most true,' replied Ellena, bowing with dignity to the Superior; 'and I most willingly resign them to my oppressors.'

Ellena forbore to make further enquiry or remonstrance, and perceiving that reproach would not only be useless, but degrading to herself, she immediately obeyed the mandate of the Abbess, and determined, since she must suffer, to suffer, if possible, with firmness and dignity.

She was conducted from the parlour by the nun who had admitted her, and as she passed through the refectory where the nuns, just returned from vespers, were assembled, their inquisitive glances, their smiles and busy whispers, told her, that she was not only an object of curiosity, but of suspicion, and that little sympathy could be expected from hearts, which even the offices of hourly devotion had not purified from the malignant envy, that taught them to exalt themselves upon the humiliation of others.

The little room, to which Ellena was led, and where, to her great satisfaction, she was left alone, rather deserved the denomination of a cell than of a chamber; since, like those of the nuns, it had only one small lattice; and a mattress, one chair, and a table, with a crucifix and a prayer-book were all its furniture. Ellena, as she surveyed her melancholy habitation, suppressed a rising sigh, but she could not remain unaffected by recollections, which, on this view of her altered state, crowded to her mind; nor think of Vivaldi far away, perhaps for ever, and probably, even ignorant of her destination, without bitter tears. But she dried them, as the idea of the Marchesa obtruded on her thoughts, for other emotions than those of grief possessed her. It was to the Marchesa that she especially attributed her present situation; and it now appeared, that the family of Vivaldi had not only been reluctant, but absolutely averse to a connection with hers, contrary to the suggestions of Signora Bianchi, who had represented, that it might be supposed only, from their known character, that they would disapprove of the alliance, but would of course be reconciled to an event, which their haughtiest displeasure never could revoke. This discovery of their absolute rejection awakened all the proper pride, which the mistaken prudence of her aunt, and her affection for Vivaldi had lulled to rest; and she now suffered the most acute vexation and remorse, for having yielded her consent to enter clandestinely into any family. The imaginary honours of so noble an alliance vanished, when the terms of obtaining them were considered; and now, that the sound mind of Ellena was left to its own judgment, she looked with infinitely more pride and preference upon the industrious means, which had hitherto rendered her independent, than on all distinction which might be reluctantly conferred. The consciousness of innocence, which had supported her in the presence of the Superior, began to falter. 'Her accusation was partly just!' said Ellena, 'and I deserve punishment, since I could, even for a moment, submit to the humiliation of desiring an alliance, which I knew would be unwillingly conferred. But it is not yet too late to retrieve my own esteem by asserting my independence, and resigning Vivaldi for ever. By resigning him! by abandoning him who loves me,—abandoning him to misery! Him, whom I cannot even think of without tears,—to whom my vows have been given,—who may claim me by the sacred remembrance of my dying friend,—him, to whom my whole heart is devoted! O! miserable alternative!—that I can no longer act justly, but at the expence of all my future happiness! Justly! And would it then be just to abandon him who is willing to resign every thing for me,—abandon him to ceaseless sorrow, that the prejudices of his family may be gratified?'

Poor Ellena perceived that she could not obey the dictates of a just pride, without such opposition from her heart as she had never experienced before. Her affections were now too deeply engaged to permit her to act with firmness, at the price of long-suffering. The consideration of resigning Vivaldi was so very grievous, that she could scarcely endure to pause upon it for a moment; yet, on the other hand, when she thought of his family, it appeared that she never could consent to make a part of it. She would have blamed the erroneous judgment of Signora Bianchi, whose persuasions had so much assisted in reducing her to the present alternative, had not the tenderness with which she cherished her memory, rendered this impossible. All, that now remained for her, was to endeavour patiently to endure present evils, which she could not conquer; for, to forsake Vivaldi as the price of liberty, should liberty be offered her on such terms, or to accept him in defiance of honourable pride, should he ever effect her release, appeared to her distracted thoughts almost equally impracticable. But, as the probability of his never being able to discover her abode, returned to her consideration, the anguish she suffered told how much more she dreaded to lose than to accept Vivaldi, and that love was, after all, the most powerful affection of her heart.

CHAPTER VII

The bell then beating one!
SHAKESPEARE*

VIVALDI, meanwhile, ignorant of what had occurred at villa Altieri, repaired as he had proposed, to Paluzzi, attended by his servant Paulo. It was deep night before he left Naples, and so anxious was he to conceal himself from observation, that though Paulo carried a torch, he did not permit it to be lighted, till after he should have remained some time within the arch-way, thinking it most prudent to watch a while in secret for his unknown adviser, before he proceeded to examine the fort.

His attendant, Paulo, was a true Neapolitan, shrewd, inquisitive, insinuating, adroit; possessing much of the spirit of intrigue, together with a considerable portion of humour, which displayed itself not so much in words, as in his manner and countenance, in the archness of his dark, penetrating eye, and in the exquisite adaptation of his gesture to his idea. He was a distinguished favourite with his master, who, if he had not humour himself, had a keen relish of it in others, and who certainly did possess wit, with all its lively accompaniments, in an eminent degree. Vivaldi had been won by the *naïveté* and humour of this man, to allow him an unusual degree of familiarity in conversation; and, as they now walked together towards Paluzzi, he unfolded to Paulo as much of his former adventure there as he judged necessary to interest his curiosity and excite his vigilance. The relation did both. Paulo, however, naturally courageous, was incredulous to superstition of any kind; and, having quickly perceived that his master was not altogether indisposed to attribute to a supernatural cause the extraordinary occurrences at Paluzzi, he began, in his manner, to rally him; but Vivaldi was not in temper to endure jesting; his mood was grave, even to solemnity, and he yielded, though reluctantly, to the awe which, at intervals, returned upon him with the force of a magical spell, binding up all his faculties to sternness, and fixing them in expectation. While he was nearly regardless of defence against human agency, his servant was, however, preparing for that alone; and very properly represented the imprudence of going to Paluzzi in darkness. Vivaldi observed that they could not watch for the monk otherwise than in darkness, since the torch which lighted them would also warn him, and he had very particular reasons for watching before he proceeded to examine. He added, that after a certain time had elapsed, the torch might be lighted at a neighbouring cottage. Paulo objected, that in the meanwhile, the person for whom they watched might escape; and Vivaldi compromised the affair. The torch was lighted, but concealed within a hollow of the cliffs, that bordered the road, and the centinels took their station in darkness, within the deep arch, near the spot where Vivaldi had watched with Bonarmo. As they did this, the distant chime of a convent informed Vivaldi that midnight was turned. The sound recalled to his mind the words of Schedoni, concerning the vicinity of the convent of the *Black Penitents*, to Paluzzi, and he asked Paulo whether this was the chime of that convent. Paulo replied that it was, and that a remarkable circumstance had taught him to remember *the Santa del Pianto*, or *Our Lady of Tears*. 'The place, Signor, would interest you,' said Paulo; 'for there are some odd stories told of it; and I am inclined to think, this unknown monk must be one of that society, his conduct is so strange.'

'You believe then, that I am willing to give faith to wonderful stories,' said Vivaldi, smiling. 'But what have you heard, that is so extraordinary, respecting this convent? Speak low, or we may be discovered.'

'Why, Signor, the story is not generally known,' said Paulo in a whisper; 'I half promised never to reveal it.'

'If you are under any promise of secresy,' interrupted Vivaldi, 'I forbid you to tell this wonderful tale, which, however, seems somewhat too big to rest within your brain.'

'The story would fain expand itself to your's, Signor,' said Paulo; 'and, as I did not absolutely promise to conceal it, I am very willing to reveal it.'

'Proceed, then,' said Vivaldi; 'but let me once more caution you to speak low.'

'You are obeyed, Signor. You must know, then, *Maestro*,* that it was on the eve of the festival of *Santo Marco*, and about six years since'——

'Peace!' said Vivaldi. They were silent; but every thing remaining still, Paulo, after some time, ventured to proceed, though in a yet lower whisper. 'It was on the eve of the *Santo Marco*, and when the last bell had rung, that a person'——He stopped again, for a rustling sound passed near him.

'You are too late,' said a sudden voice beside Vivaldi, who instantly recognized the thrilling accents of the monk.—'It is past midnight; she departed an hour ago. Look to your steps!'

Though thrilled by this well-known voice, Vivaldi scarcely yielded to his feelings for a moment, but, checking the question which would have asked 'who departed?' he, by a sudden spring, endeavoured to seize the intruder, while Paulo, in the first hurry of his alarm, fired a pistol, and then hastened for the torch. So certainly did Vivaldi believe himself to have leaped upon the spot whence the voice proceeded, that, on reaching it, he instantly extended his arms, and searching around, expected every moment to find his enemy in his grasp. Darkness again baffled his attempt.

'You are known,' cried Vivaldi; 'you shall see me at the *Santa del Pianto!* What, oh! Paulo, the torch!—the torch!'

Paulo, swift as the wind, appeared with it. 'He passed up those steps in the rock, Signor; I saw the skirts of his garments ascending!'

'Follow me, then,' said Vivaldi, mounting the steps. 'Away, away, *Maestro!*' said Paulo, impatiently; 'but, for Heaven's sake, name no more the convent of the *Santa del Pianto*; our lives may answer it!'

He followed to the terrace above, where Vivaldi, holding high the torch, looked round for the monk. The place, however, as far as his eye could penetrate, was forsaken and silent. The glare of the torch enlightened only the rude walls of the citadel, some points of the cliff below, and some tall pines that waved over them, leaving in doubtful gloom many a recess of the ruin, and many a tangled thicket, that spread among the rocks beyond.

'Do you perceive any person, Paulo?' said Vivaldi, waving the torch in the air to rouse the flame.

'Among those arches on the left, Signor, those arches that stand duskily beyond the citadel, I thought I saw a shadowy sort of a figure pass. He might be a ghost, by his silence, for aught I know, *Maestro*; but he seems to have a good mortal instinct in taking care of himself, and to have as swift a pair of heels to assist in carrying him off, as any Lazaro* in Naples need desire.'

'Fewer words, and more caution!' said Vivaldi, lowering the torch, and pointing it towards the quarter which Paulo had mentioned. 'Be vigilant, and tread lightly.'

'You are obeyed, Signor; but their eyes will inform them, though their ears refuse, while we hold a light to our own steps.'

'Peace, with this buffoonery!' said Vivaldi, somewhat sternly; 'follow in silence, and be on your guard.'

Paulo submitted, and they proceeded towards the range of arches, which communicated with the building, whose singular structure had formerly arrested the attention of Bonarmo, and whence Vivaldi himself had returned with such unexpected precipitancy and consternation.

On perceiving the place he was approaching, he suddenly stopped, and Paulo observing his agitation, and probably not relishing the adventure, endeavoured to dissuade him from further research: 'For we know not who may inhabit this gloomy place, Signor, or their numbers, and we are only two of us after all! Besides, Signor, it was through that door, yonder;' and he pointed to the very spot whence Vivaldi had so fearfully issued; 'through that door, that I fancied, just now, I saw something pass.'

'Are you certain as to this?' said Vivaldi, with increased emotion. 'What was its form?'

'It was so dusky thereabout, *Maestro*, that I could not distinguish.'

Vivaldi's eyes were fixed upon the building, and a violent conflict of feelings seemed to shake his soul. A few seconds decided it. 'I will go on,' said he, 'and terminate, at any hazard, this state of intolerable anxiety. Paulo, pause a moment, and consider well whether you can depend on your courage, for it may be severely tried. If you can, descend with me in silence, and I warn you to be wary; if you cannot, I will go alone.'

'It is too late now, Signor, to ask myself that question,' replied Paulo, with a submissive air; 'and if I had not settled it long ago, I should not have followed you thus far. My courage, Signor, you never doubted before.'

'Come on then,' said Vivaldi. He drew his sword, and entering the narrow door-way, the torch, which he had now resigned to Paulo, shewed a stone passage, that was, however, interminable to the eye.

As they proceeded, Paulo observed, that the walls were stained in several places with what appeared to be blood, but prudently forbore to point this out to his master, observing the strict injunction of silence he had received.

Vivaldi stepped cautiously, and often paused to listen, after which he went on with a quicker pace, making signs only to Paulo to follow, and be vigilant. The passage terminated in a stair-case, that seemed to lead to vaults below. Vivaldi remembered the light which had formerly appeared there, and, as recollection of the past gathered on his mind, he faultered in his purpose.

Again he paused, looked back upon Paulo, but was going forward, when Paulo himself seized his arm. 'Stop! Signor,' said he in a low voice. 'Do you not distinguish a figure standing yonder, in the gloom?'

Vivaldi looked onward, and perceived, indistinctly, something as of human form, but motionless and silent. It stood at the dusky extremity of the avenue, near the stair-case. Its garments, if garments they were, were dark; but its whole figure was so faintly traced to the eye, that it was impossible to ascertain whether this was the monk. Vivaldi took the light, and held it forward, endeavouring to distinguish the object before he ventured further; but the enquiry was useless, and, resigning the torch to Paulo, he rushed on. When he reached the head of the stair-case, however, the form, whatever it might be, was gone. Vivaldi had heard no footstep. Paulo pointed out the exact spot where it had stood, but no vestige of it appeared. Vivaldi called loudly upon the monk, but he heard only the lengthening echoes of his own voice revolving among the chambers below, and, after hesitating a while on the head of the stairs, he descended.

Paulo had not followed down many steps, when he called out, 'It is there! Signor; I see it again! and now it flits away through the door that opens to the vaults!'

Vivaldi pursued so swiftly, that Paulo could scarcely follow fast enough with the light; and, as at length he rested to take breath, he perceived himself in the same spacious chamber to which he had formerly descended. At this moment Paulo perceived his countenance change. 'You are ill, Signor,' said he. 'In the name of our holy Saint, let us quit this hideous place. Its inhabitants can be nothing good, and no good can come of our remaining here.'

Vivaldi made no reply; he drew breath with difficulty, and his eyes remained fixed on the ground, till a noise, like the creaking of a heavy hinge, rose in a distant part of the vault. Paulo turned his eyes, at the same instant, towards the place whence it came, and they both perceived a door in the wall slowly opened, and immediately closed again, as if the person within had feared to be discovered. Each believed, from the transient view he had of it, that this was the same figure which had appeared on the stair-case, and that it was the monk himself. Reanimated by this belief, Vivaldi's nerves were instantly rebraced, and he sprang to the door, which was unfastened, and yielded immediately to his impetuous hand. 'You shall not deceive me now,' cried he, as he entered; 'Paulo! keep guard at the door!'

He looked round the second vault, in which he now found himself, but no person appeared; he examined the place, and particularly the walls, without discovering any aperture, either of door or window, by which the figure could have quitted the chamber; a strongly-grated casement, placed near the roof, was all that admitted air, and probably light. Vivaldi was astonished! 'Have you seen any thing pass?' said he to Paulo.

'Nothing, *Maestro*,' replied the servant.

'This is almost incredible,' exclaimed Vivaldi; ''tis certain, this form can be nothing human!'

'If so, Signor,' observed Paulo, 'why should it fear us? as surely it does; or why should it have fled?'

'That is not so certain,' rejoined Vivaldi; 'it may have fled only to lead us into evil. But bring hither the torch; here is something in the wall which I would examine.'

Paulo obeyed. It was merely a ruggedness in the stones, not the partition of a door, that had excited his curiosity. 'This is inexplicable!' exclaimed Vivaldi, after a long pause. 'What motive could any human being have for thus tormenting me.'

'Or any being superhuman, either, my Signor?' said Paulo.

'I am warned of evils that await me,' continued Vivaldi, musing; 'of events that are regularly fulfilled; the being who warns me, crosses my path perpetually, yet, with the cunning of a demon, as constantly eludes my grasp, and baffles my pursuit! It is incomprehensible, by what means he glides thus away from my eye, and fades, as if into air, at my approach! He is repeatedly in my presence, yet is never to be found!'

'It is most true, Signor,' said Paulo, 'that he is never to be found, and therefore let me entreat you to give up the pursuit. This place is enough to make one believe in the horrors of purgatory! Let us go, Signor.'

'What but spirit could have quitted this vault so mysteriously,' continued Vivaldi, not attending to Paulo; 'what but spirit!'——

'I would fain prove,' said the servant, 'that substance can quit it as easily; I would fain evaporate through that door myself.'

He had scarcely spoken the words, when the door closed, with a thundering clap that echoed through all the vaults; and Vivaldi and Paulo stood for a moment aghast! and then both hastened to open it, and to leave the place. Their consternation may be easily conceived, when they found that all their efforts at the door were ineffectual. The thick wood was inlaid with solid bars of iron; and was of such unconquerable strength, that it evidently guarded what had been designed for a prison, and appeared to be the keep or dungeon of the ancient fort.

'Ah, Signor mio!' said Paulo, 'if this was a spirit, 'tis plain he knew we were not so, by his luring us hither. Would we could exchange natures with him for a moment; for I know not how, as mere mortal men, we can ever squeeze ourselves out of this scrape. You must allow, *Maestro*, that this was not one of the evils he warned you of; or, if he did, it was through my organs, for I entreated you.'——

'Peace, good Signor *Buffo!*' said Vivaldi; 'a truce with this nonsense, and assist in searching for some means of escape.'

Vivaldi again examined the walls, and as unsuccessfully as before; but in one corner of the vault lay an object, which seemed to tell the fate of one who had been confined here, and to hint his own: it was a garment covered with blood. Vivaldi and his servant discovered it at the same instant; and a dreadful foreboding of their own destiny fixed them, for some moments, to the spot. Vivaldi first recovered himself, when instead of yielding to despondency, all his faculties were aroused to devise some means for escaping; but Paulo's hopes seemed buried beneath the dreadful vestments upon which he still gazed. 'Ah, my Signor!' said he, at length, in a faultering accent, 'who shall dare to raise that garment?

What if it should conceal the mangled body whose blood has stained it!'

Vivaldi, shudderingly, turned to look on it again.

'It moves!' exclaimed Paulo; 'I see it move!' as he said which, he started to the opposite side of the chamber. Vivaldi stepped a few paces back, and as quickly returned; when, determined to know the event at once, he raised the garment upon the point of his sword, and perceived, beneath, other remains of dress, heaped high together, while even the floor below was stained with gore.

Believing that fear had deceived the eyes of Paulo, Vivaldi watched this horrible spectacle for some time, but without perceiving the least motion; when he became convinced, that not any remains of life were shrouded beneath it, and that it contained only articles of dress, which had belonged to some unfortunate person, who had probably been decoyed hither for plunder, and afterwards murdered. This belief, and the repugnance he felt to dwell upon the spectacle, prevented him from examining further, and he turned away to a remote part of the vault. A conviction of his own fate, and of his servant's, filled his mind for a while with despair. It appeared that he had been ensnared by robbers, till, as he recollected the circumstances which had attended his entrance, and the several peculiar occurrences connected with the arch-way, this conjecture seemed highly improbable. It was unreasonable, that robbers should have taken the trouble to decoy, when they might at first have seized him; still more so, that they would have persevered so long in the attempt; and most of all, that when he had formerly been in their power, they should have neglected their opportunity, and suffered him to leave the ruin unmolested. Yet, granting that all this, improbable as it was, were, however, possible, the solemn warnings and predictions of the monk, so frequently delivered, and so faithfully fulfilled, could have no connection with the schemes of banditti. It appeared, therefore, that Vivaldi was not in the hands of robbers; or, if he were, that the monk, at least, had no connection with them; yet it was certain that he had just heard the voice of this monk beneath the arch; that his servant had said, he saw the vestments of one ascending the steps of the fort; and that they had both reason, afterward, to believe it was his shadowy figure, which they had pursued to the very chamber where they were now confined.

As Vivaldi considered all these circumstances, his perplexity encreased, and he was more than ever inclined to believe, that the form, which had assumed the appearance of a monk, was something superhuman.

'If this being had *appeared only*,' said he to himself, 'I should, perhaps, have thought it the perturbed spirit of him, who doubtless has been murdered here, and that it led me hither to discover the deed, that his bones might be removed to holy ground; but this monk, or whatever it is, was neither silent, nor apparently anxious concerning himself; he spoke only of events connected with my peace, and predicted of the future, as well as reverted to the past! If he had either hinted of himself, or had been wholly silent, his appearance, and manner of eluding pursuit, is so extraordinary, that I should have yielded, for once, perhaps, to the tales of our grandfathers, and thought he was the spectre of a murdered person.'

As Vivaldi expressed his incredulity, however, he returned to examine the garment once more, when, as he raised it, he observed, what had before escaped his notice, black drapery mingled with the heap beneath; and, on lifting this also on the point of his sword, he perceived part of the habiliment of a monk! He started at the discovery, as if he had seen the apparition, which had so long been tempting his credulity. Here were the vest and scapulary, rent and stained with blood! Having gazed for a moment, he let them drop upon the heap; when Paulo, who had been silently observing him, exclaimed,

'Signor! that should be the garment of the demon who led us hither. Is it a winding-sheet for us, *Maestro?* Or was it one for the body he inhabited while on earth!'

'Neither, I trust,' replied Vivaldi, endeavouring to command the perturbation he suffered, and turning from the spectacle; 'therefore we will try once more to regain our liberty.'

This was a design, however, beyond his accomplishment; and, having again attacked the door, raised Paulo to the grated window, and vociferated for release with his utmost strength, in which he was very ably seconded by Paulo, he abandoned, for the present, all further attempts, and, weary and desponding, threw himself on the ground of the dungeon.

Paulo bitterly lamented his master's rashness in penetrating to this remote spot, and bewailed the probability of their being famished.

'For, supposing, Signor, that we were not decoyed hither for plunder and butchery, and supposing that we are not surrounded by malicious spirits, which San Januarius forbid I should take upon me to affirm is impossible! supposing all this, Signor, yet still there remains almost a certainty of our being starved to death;

for how is it possible that any body can hear our cries, in a place so remote from all resort, and buried, as one may say, under ground, as this is?'

'Thou art an excellent comforter,' said Vivaldi, groaning.

'You must allow, Signor, that you are even with me,' replied Paulo; 'and that you are as excellent a conductor.'

Vivaldi gave no answer, but lay on the ground, abandoned to agonizing thought. He had now leisure to consider the late words of the monk, and to conjecture, for he was in a mood for conjecturing the worst, that they not only alluded to Ellena, but that his saying 'she had departed an hour ago,' was a figurative manner of telling that she had died then. This was a conjecture which dispelled almost all apprehension for himself. He started from the ground, and paced his prison with quick and unequal steps; it was now no longer a heavy despondency that oppressed him, but an acute anxiety that stung him, and, with the tortures of suspense, brought also those of passionate impatience and horror concerning the fate of Ellena. The longer he dwelt upon the possibility of her death, the more probable it appeared. This monk had already forewarned him of the death of Bianchi; and when he recollected the suspicious circumstances which had attended it, his terrors for Ellena increased. The more he yielded to his feelings, the more violent they became, till, at length, his ungovernable impatience and apprehensions arose almost to frenzy.

Paulo forgot, for a while, his own situation in the superior sufferings of his master, and now, at least, endeavoured to perform the offices of a comforter, for he tried to calm Vivaldi's mind, by selecting the fairest circumstances for hope which the subject admitted, and he passed without noticing, or, if noticing, only lightly touched upon, the most prominent possibilities of evil. His master, however, was insensible to all he said, till he mentioned again the convent del Pianto; and this subject, as it seemed connected with the monk, who had hinted the fate of Ellena, interested the unhappy Vivaldi, who withdrew awhile from his own reflections, to listen to a recital which might assist his conjectures.

Paulo complied with his command, but not without reluctance. He looked round the empty vault, as if he feared that some person might be lurking in the obscurity, who would overhear, and even answer him.

'We are tolerably retired here too, Signor,' said he, recollecting himself; 'one may venture to talk secrets with little danger of being discovered. However, *Maestro*, it is best to make matters quite sure; and therefore, if you will please to take a seat on the ground, I will stand beside you and relate all I know of the convent of *Our Lady of Tears*, which is not much after all.'

Vivaldi, having seated himself, and bidden Paulo do the same, the servant began in a low voice——'It was on the vigil of the *Santo Marco*, just after the last vesper-bell had tolled—You never was at the *Santa Maria del Pianto*, Signor, or you would know what a gloomy old church it has.—It was in a confessional in one of the side aisles of this church, and just after the last bell had ceased, that a person, so muffled up, that neither face nor shape could be distinguished, came and placed himself on the steps of one of the boxes adjoining the confessional chair; but if he had been as airily dressed as yourself, Signor, he might have been just as well concealed; for that dusky aisle is lighted only by one lamp, which hangs at the end next the painted window, except when the tapers at the shrine of San Antonio happen to be burning at the other extremity, and even then the place is almost as gloomy as this vault. But that is, no doubt, contrived for the purpose, that people may not blush for the sins they confess; and, in good faith, this is an accommodation which may bring more money to the poor's box, for the monks have a shrewd eye that way, and'——

'You have dropt the thread of your story,' said Vivaldi.

'True, Signor, let me recollect where I lost it.—Oh! at the steps of the confessional;—the stranger knelt down upon them, and for some time poured such groans into the ear of the confessor, as were heard all along the aisle. You are to know, Signor, that the brothers of *Santa del Pianto* are of the order of *Black Penitents*; and people who have more sins than ordinary to confess, sometimes go there, to consult with the grand penitentiary* what is to be done. Now it *happened*, that Father Ansaldo, the grand penitentiary himself, was in the chair, as is customary on the vigil of the *Santo Marco*; and he gently reproved the penitent for bewailing so loud, and bade him take comfort; when the other replied only by a groan deeper than before, but it was not so loud, and then proceeded to confess. But what he did confess, Signor, I know not; for the confessor, you know, never must divulge, except, indeed, on very extra-ordinary occasions. It was, however, something so very strange and horrible, that the grand penitentiary suddenly quitted the chair, and before he reached the cloisters he fell into strong con-vulsions. On recovering himself, he asked the people about him, whether the penitent, who had visited such a confessional, naming it, was gone; adding, that if he was still in the church, it was proper he should be detained. He described, at the same time, as well as he could, the sort of figure he had dimly seen approaching the confessional just before he had received the confession, at recollecting which, he seemed ready to go off again into his convulsions. One of the fathers, who had crossed the aisle, on his way to the cloisters, upon the first alarm of Ansaldo's disorder, remembered that a person, such as was described, had passed him hastily. He had seen a tall figure, muffled up in the habit of a white friar,* gliding swiftly along the aisle, towards the door which opened into the outer court of the convent; but he was himself too much engaged to notice the stranger particularly. Father Ansaldo thought this must be the person; and the porter was summoned, and asked whether he had observed such an one pass. He affirmed that he had not seen any person go forth from the gate within the last quarter of an hour; which might be true enough, you know, Signor, if the rogue had been off his post. But he further said, that no one had entered, during the whole evening, habited in white, as the stranger was described to be: so the porter proved himself to be a vigilant watchman; for he must have been fast asleep too, or how could this personage have entered the convent, and left it again, without being seen by him!'

'In white, was he?' said Vivaldi; 'if he had been in black, I should have thought this must have been the monk, my tormentor.'

'Why, you know, Signor, that occurred to me before,' observed Paulo, 'and a man might easily change his dress, if that were all.'

'Proceed,' said Vivaldi.

'Hearing this account from the porter,' continued Paulo, 'the fathers believed, one and all, that the stranger must be secreted within the walls; and the convent, with every part of the precincts, was searched; but no person was found!'

'This must certainly be the monk,' said Vivaldi, 'notwithstanding the difference of his habit; there surely cannot be two beings in the world, who would conduct themselves in this same mysterious manner!'

He was interrupted by a low sound, which seemed, to his distracted fancy, to proceed from a dying person. Paulo also heard it; he started, and they both listened with intense and almost intolerable expectation.

'Ah!' said Paulo, at length, 'it was only the wind.'

'It was no more,' said Vivaldi; 'proceed therefore.'

'From the period of this strange confession,' resumed Paulo, 'Father Ansaldo was never properly himself; he'——

'Doubtless the crime confessed related to himself,' observed Vivaldi.

'Why, no, Signor, I never heard that that was the case; and some remarkable circumstances, which followed, seemed to prove it otherwise. About a month after the time I have mentioned, on the evening of a sultry day, when the monks were retiring from the last service'——

'Hark!' cried Vivaldi.

'I hear whispers,' said Paulo, whispering himself.

'Be still!' said Vivaldi.

They listened attentively, and heard a murmuring, as of voices; but could not ascertain whether they came from the adjoining vault, or arose from beneath the one in which they were. The sound returned at intervals; and the persons who conversed, whatever they were, seemingly restrained their voices, as if they feared to be heard. Vivaldi considered whether it were better to discover himself, and call for assistance, or to remain still.

'Remember, Signor,' said Paulo, 'what a chance we have of being starved, unless we venture to discover ourselves to these people, or whatever they are.'

'Venture!' exclaimed Vivaldi. 'What has such a wretch as I to do with fear? O, Ellena, Ellena!'

He instantly called loudly to the person whom he believed he had heard, and was seconded by Paulo; but their continued vociferations availed them nothing; no answer was returned; and even the indistinct sounds, which had awakened their attention, were heard no more.

Exhausted by their efforts, they laid down on the floor of the dungeon, abandoning all further attempts at escape till the morning light might assist them.

Vivaldi had no further spirits to enquire for the remainder of Paulo's narrative. Almost despairing for himself, he could not feel an interest concerning strangers; for he had already perceived, that it could not afford him information connected with Ellena; and Paulo, who had roared himself hoarse, was very willing to be silent.

CHAPTER VIII

Who may she be that steals through yonder cloister,
And, as the beam of evening tints her veil,
Unconsciously discloses saintly features,
Inform'd with the high soul of saintly virtue?

DURING several days after Ellena's arrival at the monastery of San Stefano, she was not permitted to leave the room. The door was locked upon her, and not any person appeared except the nun, who brought her a scanty portion of food, and who was the same, that had first admitted her into that part of the convent appropriated to the abbess.

On the fourth day, when, probably, it was believed that her spirits were subdued by confinement, and by her experience of the suffering she had to expect from resistance, she was summoned to the parlour. The abbess was alone, and the air of austerity, with which she regarded Ellena, prepared the latter to endure.

After an exordium on the heinousness of her offence, and the necessity there was for taking measures to protect the peace and dignity of a noble family, which her late conduct had nearly destroyed; the abbess informed her, that she must determine either to accept the veil, or the person whom the Marchesa di Vivaldi had, of her great goodness, selected for her husband.

'You never can be sufficiently grateful,' added the abbess, 'for the generosity the Marchesa displays, in allowing you a choice on the subject. After the injury you have endeavoured to inflict upon her and her family, you could not expect that any indulgence would be shewn you. It was natural to suppose, that the Marchesa would have punished you with severity; instead of which, she allows you to enter into our society; or, if you have not strength of mind sufficient to enable you to renounce a sinful world, she permits you to return into it, and gives you a suitable partner to support you through its cares and toils,—a partner much more suitable to your circumstances than him, to whom you had the temerity to lift your eye.'

Ellena blushed at this coarse appeal to her pride, and persevered in a disdainful silence. Thus to give to injustice the colouring of mercy, and to acts most absolutely tyrannical the softening tints

of generosity, excited her honest indignation. She was not, however, shocked by a discovery of the designs formed against her,
since, from the moment of her arrival at San Stefano, she had
expected something terribly severe, and had prepared her mind to
meet it with fortitude; for she believed, that, so supported, she
should weary the malice of her enemies, and finally triumph over
misfortune. It was only when she thought of Vivaldi that her
courage failed, and that the injuries she endured seemed too heavy
to be long sustained.

'You are silent!' said the abbess, after a pause of expectation. 'Is
it possible, then, that you can be ungrateful for the generosity of
the Marchesa? But, though you may at present be insensible to
her goodness, I will forbear to take advantage of your indiscretion,
and will still allow you liberty of choice. You may retire to your
chamber, to consider and to decide. But remember, that you must
abide by the determination you shall avow; and, that you will be
allowed no appeal from the alternatives, which are now placed
before you.—If you reject the veil, you must accept the husband
who is offered you.'

'It is unnecessary,' said Ellena, with an air of dignified tranquillity, 'that I should withdraw for the purposes of considering
and deciding. My resolution is already taken, and I reject each of
the offered alternatives. I will neither condemn myself to a cloister,
or to the degradation, with which I am threatened on the other
hand. Having said this, I am prepared to meet whatever suffering
you shall inflict upon me; but be assured, that my own voice never
shall sanction the evils to which I may be subjected, and that the
immortal love of justice, which fills all my heart, will sustain my
courage no less powerfully than the sense of what is due to my own
character. You are now acquainted with my sentiments and my
resolutions; I shall repeat them no more.'

The abbess, whose surprise had thus long suffered Ellena to
speak, still fixed upon her a stern regard, as she said, 'Where is it
that you have learned these heroics, and acquired the rashness
which thus prompts you to avow them!—the boldness which
enables you to insult your Superior, a priestess of your holy religion, even in her sanctuary!'

'The sanctuary is prophaned,' said Ellena, mildly, but with
dignity: 'it is become a prison. It is only when the Superior ceases
to respect the precepts of that holy religion, the precepts which
teach her justice and benevolence, that she herself is no longer
respected. The very sentiment which bids us revere its mild and

beneficent laws, bids us also reject the violators of them: when you command me to reverence my religion, you urge me to condemn yourself.'

'Withdraw!' said the abbess, rising impatiently from her chair; 'your admonition, so becomingly delivered, shall not be forgotten.'

Ellena willingly obeyed, and was led back to her cell, where she sat down pensively, and reviewed her conduct. Her judgment approved of the frankness, with which she had asserted her rights, and of the firmness, with which she had reproved a woman, who had dared to demand respect from the very victim of her cruelty and oppression. She was the more satisfied with herself, because she had never, for an instant, forgotten her own dignity so far, as to degenerate into the vehemence of passion, or to faulter with the weakness of fear. Her conviction of the abbess's unworthy character was too clear to allow Ellena to feel abashed in her presence; for she regarded only the censure of the good, to which she had ever been as tremblingly alive, as she was obdurately insensible to that of the vicious.

Ellena, having now asserted her resolutions, determined to avoid, if possible, all repetition of scenes like the last, and to repel by silence only, whatever indignity might be offered her. She knew that she must suffer, and she resolved to endure. Of the three evils, which were placed before her, that of confinement, with all its melancholy accompaniments, appeared considerably less severe, than either the threatened marriage, or a formal renunciation of the world; either of which would devote her, during life, to misery, and that by her own act. Her choice, therefore, had been easy, and the way was plain before her. If she could endure with calmness the hardships which she could not avoid, half their weight would be unfelt; and she now most strenuously endeavoured to attain the strength of mind, which was necessary to support such equanimity.

For several days after the late interview with the abbess, she was kept a close prisoner; but on the fifth evening she was permitted to attend vespers. As she walked through the garden to the chapel, the ordinary freshness of the open air, and the verdure of the trees and shrubs were luxuries to her, who had so long been restricted from the common blessings of nature. She followed the nuns to a chapel where they usually performed their devotions, and was there seated among the novices. The solemnity of the service, and particularly of those parts, which were accompanied by music, touched all her heart, and soothed and elevated her spirit.

Among the voices of the choir, was one whose expression immediately fixed her attention; it seemed to speak a loftier sentiment of devotion than the others, and to be modulated by the melancholy of an heart, that had long since taken leave of this world. Whether it swelled with the high peal of the organ, or mingled in low and trembling accents with the sinking chorus, Ellena felt that she understood all the feelings of the breast from which it flowed; and she looked to the gallery where the nuns were assembled, to discover a countenance, that might seem to accord with the sensibility expressed in the voice. As no strangers were admitted to the chapel, some of the sisters had thrown back their veils, and she saw little that interested her in their various faces; but the figure and attitude of a nun, kneeling in a remote part of the gallery, beneath a lamp, which threw its rays aslant her head, perfectly agreed with the idea she had formed of the singer, and the sound seemed to approach immediately from that direction. Her face was concealed by a black veil, whose transparency, however, permitted the fairness of her complexion to appear; but the air of her head, and the singularity of her attitude, for she was the only person who remained kneeling, sufficiently indicated the superior degree of fervency and penitence, which the voice had expressed.

When the hymn had ceased, she rose from her knees, and Ellena, soon after, observing her throw back her veil, discovered, by the lamp, which shed its full light upon her features, a countenance, that instantly confirmed her conjecture. It was touched with a melancholy kind of resignation; yet grief seemed still to occasion the paleness, and the air of languor, that prevailed over it, and which disappeared only when the momentary energy of devotion seemed to lift her spirit above this world, and to impart to it somewhat of a seraphic grandeur. At those moments her blue eyes were raised towards Heaven, with such meek, yet fervent love, such sublime enthusiasm as the heads of Guido* sometimes display, and which renewed, with Ellena, all the enchanting effects of the voice she had just heard.

While she regarded the nun with a degree of interest which rendered her insensible to every other object in the chapel, she fancied she could perceive the calmness in her countenance to be that of despair, rather than of resignation; for, when her thoughts were not elevated in prayer, there was frequently a fixedness in her look, too energetic for common suffering, or for the temper of mind, which may lead to perfect resignation. It had, however, much that attached the sympathy of Ellena, and much that seemed to speak a similarity of feeling. Ellena was not only soothed, but in some degree comforted, while she gazed upon her; a selfishness which may, perhaps, be pardoned, when it is considered, that she thus knew there was one human being, at least, in the convent, who must be capable of feeling pity, and willing to administer consolation. Ellena endeavoured to meet her eye, that she might inform her of the regard she had inspired, and express her own unhappiness; but the nun was so entirely engaged by devotion, that she did not succeed.

As they left the chapel, however, the nun passed close by Ellena, who threw back her veil, and fixed upon her a look so supplicating and expressive, that the nun paused, and in her turn regarded the novice, not with surprize only, but with a mixture of curiosity and compassion. A faint blush crossed her cheek, her spirits seemed to faulter, and she was unwilling to withdraw her eyes from Ellena: but it was necessary that she should continue in the procession, and, bidding her farewel by a smile of ineffable pity, she passed on to the court, while Ellena followed with attention still fixed upon the sister, who soon disappeared beyond the doorway of the Abbess's apartment, and Ellena had nearly reached her own, before her thoughts were sufficiently disengaged to permit her to enquire the name of the stranger.

'It is sister Olivia whom you mean, perhaps,' said her conductress.

'She is very handsome,' said Ellena.

'Many of the sisters are so,' replied Margaritone, with an air of pique.

'Undoubtedly,' said Ellena; 'but she, whom I mean, has a most touching countenance; frank, noble, full of sensibility; and there is a gentle melancholy in her eye, which cannot but interest all who observe her.'

Ellena was so fascinated by this interesting nun, that she forgot she was describing her to a person, whose callous heart rendered her insensible to the influence of any countenance, except, perhaps, the commanding one of the lady abbess; and to whom, therefore, a description of the fine traits, which Ellena felt, was as unintelligible as would have been an Arabic inscription.

'She is passed the bloom of youth,' continued Ellena, still anxious to be understood; 'but she retains all its interesting graces, and adds to them the dignity of'——

'If you mean that she is of middle age,' interrupted Margaritone, peevishly, 'it is sister Olivia you mention, for we are all younger than she is.'

Ellena, raising her eyes almost unconsciously, as the nun spoke this, fixed them upon a face sallow, meagre, seemingly near fifty years an inhabitant of this world; and she could scarcely suppress the surprize she felt, on perceiving such wretched vanity lingering among the chilled passions of so repulsive a frame, and within the sequestered shade of a cloister. Margaritone, still jealous of the praise bestowed on Olivia, repelled all further enquiry, and, having attended Ellena to her cell, locked her up for the night.

On the following evening Ellena was again permitted to attend vespers, and, on the way to the chapel, the hope of seeing her interesting favourite reanimated her spirits. In the same part of the gallery, as on the preceding night, she again appeared, and kneeling, as before, beneath the lamp, in private orison, for the service was not begun.

Ellena endeavoured to subdue the impatience she felt to express her regard, and to be noticed by the holy sister, till she should have finished. When the nun rose, and observed Ellena, she lifted her veil, and, fixing on her the same enquiring eye, her countenance brightened into a smile so full of compassion and intelligence, that Ellena, forgetting the decorums of the place, left her seat to approach her; it seemed as if the soul, which beamed forth in that smile, had long been acquainted with hers. As she advanced, the nun dropped her veil, a reproof which she immediately understood, and she withdrew to her seat; but her attention remained fixed on the nun during the whole service.

At the conclusion, when they left the chapel, and she saw Olivia pass without noticing her, Ellena could scarcely restrain her tears; she returned in deep dejection to her room. The regard of this nun was not only delightful, but seemed necessary to her heart, and she dwelt, with fond perseverance, on the smile that had expressed so much, and which threw one gleam of comfort, even through the bars of her prison.

Her reverie was soon interrupted by a light step, that approached her cell, and in the next moment the door was unlocked, and Olivia herself appeared. Ellena rose with emotion to meet her; the nun held forth her hand to receive hers.

'You are unused to confinement,' said she, curtsying mournfully, and placing on the table a little basket containing refreshment, 'and our hard fare'——

'I understand you,' said Ellena, with a look expressive of her gratitude; 'you have a heart that can pity, though you inhabit these walls;—you have suffered too, and know the delicate generosity of softening the sorrows of others, by any attention that may tell them your sympathy. O! if I could express how much the sense of this affects me!'

Tears interrupted her. Olivia pressed her hand, looked steadily upon her face, and was somewhat agitated, but she soon recovered apparent tranquillity, and said, with a serious smile, 'You judge rightly, my sister, respecting my sentiments, however you may do concerning my sufferings. My heart is not insensible to pity, nor to you, my child. You were designed for happier days than you can hope to find within these cloisters!'

She checked herself as if she had allowed too much, and then added, 'But you may, perhaps, be peaceful; and since it consoles you to know that you have a friend near you, believe me that friend —but believe it in silence. I will visit you when I am permitted— but do not enquire for me; and if my visits are short, do not press me to lengthen them.'

'How good this is!' said Ellena, in a faultering voice. 'How sweet too it is! you will visit me, and I am pitied by you!'

'Hush!' said the nun, expressively; 'no more; I may be observed. Good night, my sister; may your slumbers be light!'

Ellena's heart sunk. She had not spirits to say, 'Good night!' but her eyes, covered with tears, said more. The nun turned her own away suddenly, and, pressing her hand in silence, left the cell. Ellena, firm and tranquil under the insults of the abbess, was now melted into tears by the kindness of a friend. These gentle tears were refreshing to her long-oppressed spirits, and she indulged them. Of Vivaldi she thought with more composure than she had done since she left the villa Altieri; and something like hope began to revive in her heart, though reflection offered nothing to support it.

On the following morning, she perceived that the door of her cell had not been closed. She rose impatiently, and, not without a hope of liberty, immediately passed it. The cell, opening upon a short passage, which communicated with the main building, and which was shut up by a door, was secluded, and almost insulated from every other chamber; and this door being now secured, Ellena was as truly a prisoner as before. It appeared then, that the nun had omitted to fasten the cell only for the purpose of allowing her more space to walk in the passage, and she was grateful for the attention. Still more she was so, when, having traversed it, she perceived one extremity terminate in a narrow stair-case, that appeared to lead to other chambers.

She ascended the winding steps hastily, and found they led only to a door, opening into a small room, where nothing remarkable appeared, till she approached the windows, and beheld thence an horizon, and a landscape spread below, whose grandeur awakened all her heart. The consciousness of her prison was lost, while her eyes ranged over the wide and freely-sublime scene without. She perceived that this chamber was within a small turret, projecting from an angle of the convent over the walls, and suspended, as in air, above the vast precipices of granite, that formed part of the mountain. These precipices were broken into cliffs, which, in some places, impended far above their base, and, in others, rose, in nearly perpendicular lines, to the walls of the monastery, which they supported. Ellena, with a dreadful pleasure, looked down them, shagged as they were with larch, and frequently darkened by lines of gigantic pine bending along the rocky ledges, till her eye rested on the thick chesnut woods that extended over their winding base, and which, softening to the plains, seemed to form a gradation between the variegated cultivation there, and the awful wildness of the rocks above. Round these extensive plains were tumbled the mountains, of various shape and attitude, which Ellena had admired on her approach to San Stefano; some shaded with forests of olive and almond trees, but the greater part abandoned to the flocks, which, in summer, feed on their aromatic herbage, and on the approach of winter, descend to the sheltered plains of the *Tavogliere di Puglia*.*

On the left opened the dreadful pass which she had traversed, and the thunder of whose waters now murmured at a distance. The accumulation of overtopping points, which the mountains of this dark perspective exhibited, presented an image of grandeur superior to any thing she had seen while within the pass itself.

To Ellena, whose mind was capable of being highly elevated, or sweetly soothed, by scenes of nature, the discovery of this little turret was an important circumstance. Hither she could come, and her soul, refreshed by the views it afforded, would acquire strength to bear her, with equanimity, thro' the persecutions that might await her. Here, gazing upon the stupendous imagery around her, looking, as it were, beyond the awful veil which obscures the features of the Deity, and conceals Him from the eyes of his creatures, dwelling as with a present God in the midst of his sublime works; with a mind thus elevated, how insignificant would appear to her the transactions, and the sufferings of this world! How poor the boasted power of man, when the fall of a single cliff from these mountains would with ease destroy thousands of his race assembled on the plains below! How would it avail them, that they were accoutred for battle, armed with all the instruments of destruction that human invention ever fashioned? Thus man, the giant who now held her in captivity, would shrink to the diminutiveness of a fairy; and she would experience, that his utmost force was unable to enchain her soul, or compel her to fear him, while he was destitute of virtue.

Ellena's attention was recalled from the scene without by a sound from within the gallery, and she then heard a key turning in the door of the passage. Fearing that it was sister Margaritone who approached, and who, informed by her absence of the consolatory turret she had discovered, would perhaps debar her from ever returning to it, Ellena descended with a palpitating heart, and found that nun in the cell. Surprize and severity were in her countenance, when she enquired by what means Ellena had unclosed the door, and whither she had been.

Ellena answered without any prevarication, that she had found the door unfastened, and that she had visited the turret above; but she forbore to express a wish to return thither, judging that such an expression would certainly exclude her in future. Margaritone, after sharply rebuking her for prying beyond the passage, and setting down the breakfast she had brought, left the room, the door of which she did not forget to secure. Thus Ellena was at once deprived of so innocent a means of consolation as her pleasant turret had afforded.

During several days, she saw only the austere nun, except when she attended vespers; where, however, she was so vigilantly observed, that she feared to speak with Olivia, even by her eyes. Olivia's were often fixed upon her face, and with a kind of expression which Ellena, when she did venture to look at her, could not perfectly interpret. It was not only of pity, but of anxious curiosity, and of something also like fear. A blush would sometimes wander over her cheek, which was succeeded by an extreme paleness, and by an air of such universal languor as precedes a fainting fit: but the exercises of devotion seemed frequently to recal her fleeting spirits, and to elevate them with hope and courage.

When she left the chapel, Ellena saw Olivia no more that night; but on the following morning she came with breakfast to the cell. A character of peculiar sadness was on her brow.

'O! how glad I am to see you!' said Ellena; 'and how much I have regretted your long absence! I was obliged to remember constantly what you had enjoined, to forbear enquiring after you.'

The nun replied with a melancholy smile, 'I come in obedience to our lady abbess,' said she, as she seated herself on Ellena's mattress.

'And did you not wish to come?' said Ellena, mournfully.

'I did wish it,' replied Olivia; 'but'—and she hesitated.

'Whence then this reluctance?' enquired Ellena.

Olivia was silent a moment.

'You are a messenger of evil news!' said Ellena; 'you are only reluctant to afflict me.'

'It is as you say,' replied Olivia; 'I am only reluctant to afflict you; and I fear you have too many attachments to the world, to allow you to receive, without sorrow, what I have to communicate. I am ordered to prepare you for the vows, and to say, that, since you have rejected the husband which was proposed to you, you are to accept the veil; that many of the customary forms are to be dispensed with; and that the ceremony of taking the black veil, will follow without delay that of receiving the white one.'

The nun paused; and Ellena said, 'You are an unwilling bearer of this cruel message; and I reply only to the lady abbess, when I declare, that I never will accept either; that force may send me to the altar, but that it never shall compel me to utter vows which my heart abhors; and if I am constrained to appear there, it shall be only to protest against her tyranny, and against the form intended to sanction it.'

To Olivia this answer was so far from being displeasing, that it appeared to give her satisfaction.

'I dare not applaud your resolution,' said she; 'but I will not condemn it. You have, no doubt, connections in the world which would render a seclusion from it afflicting. You have relations, friends, from whom it would be dreadful to part?'

'I have neither,' said Ellena, sighing.

'No! Can that be possible? and yet you are so unwilling to retire!'

'I have only one friend,' replied Ellena, 'and it is of him they would deprive me!'

'Pardon, my love, the abruptness of these enquiries,' said Olivia; 'yet, while I entreat your forgiveness, I am inclined to offend again, and to ask your name.'

'That is a question I will readily answer. My name is Ellena di Rosalba.'

'How?' said Olivia, with an air of deliberation; 'Ellena di'——

'Di Rosalba,' repeated her companion; 'and permit me to ask your motive for the enquiry: do you know any person of my name?'

'No,' replied the nun, mournfully; 'but your features have some resemblance to those of a friend I once had.'

As she said this, her agitation was apparent, and she rose to go. 'I must not lengthen my visit, lest I should be forbidden to repeat it,' said she. 'What answer shall I give to the abbess? If you are determined to reject the veil, allow me to advise you to soften your refusal as much as possible; I am, perhaps, better acquainted with her character than you are; and O, my sister! I would not see you pining away your existence in this solitary cell.'

'How much I am obliged by the interest you express for my welfare,' said Ellena, 'and by the advice you offer! I will yield my judgment in this instance to yours; you shall modulate my refusal as you think proper: but remember that it must be absolute; and beware, lest the abbess should mistake gentleness for irresolution.'

'Trust me, I will be cautious in all that relates to you,' said Olivia. 'Farewell! I will visit you, if possible, in the evening. In the mean time the door shall be left open, that you may have more air and prospect than this cell affords. That staircase leads to a pleasant chamber.'

'I have visited it already,' replied Ellena, 'and have to thank you for the goodness, which permitted me to do so. To go thither will greatly soothe my spirits; if I had some book, and my drawing-instruments, I could almost forget my sorrows there.'

'Could you so?' said the nun, with an affectionate smile. 'Adieu! I will endeavour to see you in the evening. If sister Margaritone returns, be careful not to enquire for me; nor once ask her for the little indulgence I give you.'

Olivia withdrew, and Ellena retired to the chamber above, where she lost for a while all sense of sorrow amidst the great scenery, which its windows exhibited.

At noon, the step of Margaritone summoned Ellena from her retreat, and she was surprised that no reproof followed this second discovery of her absence. Margaritone only said, that the abbess had the goodness to permit Ellena to dine with the novices, and that she came to conduct her to their table.

Ellena did not rejoice in this permission, preferring to remain in her solitary turret, to the being exposed to the examining eyes of strangers; and she followed dejectedly, through the silent passages to the apartment where they were assembled. She was not less surprised than embarrassed to observe, in the manners of young people residing in a convent, an absence of that decorum, which includes beneath its modest shade every grace that ought to adorn the female character, like the veil which gives dignity to their air and softness to their features. When Ellena entered the room, the eyes of the whole company were immediately fixed upon her; the young ladies began to whisper and smile, and shewed, by various means, that she was the subject of conversation, not otherwise than censorious. No one advanced to meet and to encourage her, to welcome her to the table, or still less display one of those nameless graces, with which a generous and delicate mind delights to reanimate the modest and the unfortunate.

Ellena took a chair in silence; and, though she had at first felt forlorn and embarrassed by the impertinent manners of·her companions, a consciousness of innocence gradually revived her spirits, and enabled her to resume an air of dignity, which repressed this rude presumption.

Ellena returned to her cell, for the first time, with eagerness. Margaritone did not fasten the door of it, but she was careful to secure that of the passage; and even this small indulgence she seemed to allow with a surly reluctance, as if compelled to obey the command of a superior. The moment she was gone, Ellena withdrew to her pleasant turret, where, after having suffered from the coarse manners of the novices, her gratitude was the more lively, when she perceived the delicate attention of her beloved nun. It appeared that she had visited the chamber in Ellena's absence, and had caused to be brought thither a chair and a table, on which were placed some books, and a knot of fragrant flowers. Ellena did not repress the grateful tears, which the generous feelings of Olivia excited; and she forbore, for some moments, to examine the books, that the pleasing emotions she experienced might not be interrupted.

On looking into these books, however, she perceived, that some of them treated of mystical subjects, which she laid aside with disappointment; but in others she observed a few of the best Italian poets, and a volume or two of Guicciardini's history.* She was somewhat surprised, that the poets should have found their way to the library of a nun, but was too much pleased with the discovery to dwell on the enquiry.

Having arranged her books, and set her little room in order, she seated herself at a window, and, with a volume of Tasso,*

endeavoured to banish every painful remembrance from her mind.
She continued wandering in the imaginary scenes of the poet, till
the fading light recalled her to those of reality. The sun was set,
but the mountain-tops were still lighted up by his beams, and a
tint of glorious purple coloured all the west, and began to change
the snowy points on the horizon. The silence and repose of the vast
scene, promoted the tender melancholy that prevailed in her heart;
she thought of Vivaldi, and wept—of Vivaldi, whom she might,
perhaps, never see again, though she doubted not that he would be
indefatigable in searching for her. Every particular of their last
conversation, when he had so earnestly lamented the approaching
separation, even while he allowed of its propriety, came to her
mind; and, while she witnessed, in imagination, the grief and distraction, which her mysterious departure and absence must have
occasioned him, the fortitude, with which she had resisted her own
sufferings, yielded to the picture of his.

The vesper-bell, at length, summoned her to prepare for mass,
and she descended to her cell to await the arrival of her conductress.
It was Margaritone, who soon appeared; but in the chapel she, as
usual, saw Olivia, who, when the service had concluded, invited
her into the garden of the convent. There, as she walked beneath
the melancholy cypresses, that, ranged on either side the long
walks, formed a majestic canopy, almost excluding the evening
twilight, Olivia conversed with her on serious, but general, topics,
carefully avoiding any mention of the abbess, and of the affairs of
Ellena. The latter, anxious to learn the effect of her repeated
rejection of the veil, ventured to make some enquiries, which the
nun immediately discouraged, and as cautiously checked the grateful effusions of her young friend for the attentions she had
received.

Olivia accompanied Ellena to her cell, and there no longer
scrupled to relieve her from uncertainty. With a mixture of frankness and discretion, she related as much of the conversation, that
had passed between herself and the abbess, as it appeared necessary for Ellena to know, from which it seemed that the former was
as obstinate, as the latter was firm.

'Whatever may be your resolution,' added the nun, 'I earnestly
advise you, my sister, to allow the Superior some hope of compliance, lest she proceed to extremities.'

'And what extremity can be more terrible,' replied Ellena, 'than
either of those, to which she would now urge me? Why should I
descend to practice dissimulation?'

'To save yourself from undeserved sufferings,' said Olivia mournfully.

'Yes, but I should then incur deserved ones,' observed Ellena; 'and forfeit such peace of mind as my oppressors never could restore to me.' As she said this, she looked at the nun with an expression of gentle reproach and disappointment.

'I applaud the justness of your sentiment,' replied Olivia, regarding her with tenderest compassion. 'Alas! that a mind so noble should be subjected to the power of injustice and depravity!'

'Not subjected,' said Ellena, 'do not say subjected. I have accustomed myself to contemplate those sufferings; I have chosen the least of such as were given to my choice, and I will endure them with fortitude; and can you then say that I am subjected?'

'Alas, my sister! you know not what you promise,' replied Olivia; 'you do not comprehend the sufferings which may be preparing for you.'

As she spoke, her eyes filled with tears, and she withdrew them from Ellena, who, surprised at the extreme concern on her countenance, entreated she would explain herself.

'I am not certain, myself, as to this point,' said Olivia; 'and if I were, I should not dare to explain it.'

'Not dare!' repeated Ellena, mournfully. 'Can benevolence like yours know fear, when courage is necessary to prevent evil?'

'Enquire no further!' said Olivia; but no blush of conscious duplicity stained her cheek. 'It is sufficient that you understand the consequence of open resistance to be terrible, and that you consent to avoid it.'

'But how avoid it, my beloved friend, without incurring a consequence which, in my apprehension, would be yet more dreadful? How avoid it, without either subjecting myself to a hateful marriage, or accepting the vows? Either of these events would be more terrible to me, than any thing with which I may be menaced.'

'Perhaps not,' said the nun. 'Imagination cannot draw the horrors of —— But, my sister, let me repeat, that I would save you! O, how willingly save you from the evils preparing! and that the only chance of doing so is, by prevailing with you to abandon at least the appearance of resistance.'

'Your kindness deeply affects me,' said Ellena; 'and I am fearful of appearing insensible of it, when I reject your advice; yet I cannot adopt it. The very dissimulation, which I should employ in self-defence, might be a means of involving me in destruction.'

As Ellena concluded, and her eyes glanced upon the nun,

unaccountable suspicion occurred to her, that Olivia might be insincere, and that, at this very moment, when she was advising dissimulation, she was endeavouring to draw Ellena into some snare, which the abbess had laid. She sickened at this dreadful supposition, and dismissed it without suffering herself to examine its probability. That Olivia, from whom she had received so many attentions, whose countenance and manners announced so fair a mind, and for whom she had conceived so much esteem and affection, should be cruel and treacherous, was a suspicion that gave her more pain, than the actual imprisonment in which she suffered; and when she looked again upon her face, Ellena was consoled by a clear conviction, that she was utterly incapable of perfidy.

'If it were possible that I could consent to practise deceit,' resumed Ellena, after a long pause, 'what could it avail me? I am entirely in the power of the abbess, who would soon put my sincerity to the proof; when a discovery of my duplicity would only provoke her vengeance, and I should be punished even for having sought to avoid injustice.'

'If deceit is at any time excusable,' replied Olivia, reluctantly, 'it is when we practise it in self-defence. There are some rare situations, when it may be resorted to without our incurring ignominy, and yours is one of those. But I will acknowledge, that all the good I expect is from the delay which temporizing may procure you. The Superior, when she understands there is a probability of obtaining your consent to her wishes, may be willing to allow you the usual time of preparation for the veil, and meanwhile something may occur to rescue you from your present situation.'

'Ah! could I but believe so!' said Ellena; 'but, alas! what power can rescue me? And I have not one relative remaining even to attempt my deliverance. To what possibility do you allude?'

'The Marchesa may relent.'

'Does, then, your possibility of good rest with her, my dear friend? If so, I am in despair again; for such a chance of benefit, there would certainly be little policy in forfeiting one's integrity.'

'There are also other possibilities, my sister,' said Olivia; 'but hark! what bell is that? It is the chime which assembles the nuns in the apartment of the abbess, where she dispenses her evening benediction. My absence will be observed. Good night, my sister. Reflect on what I have advised; and remember, I conjure you, to consider, that the consequence of your decision must be solemn, and may be fatal.'

The nun spoke this with a look and emphasis so extraordinary, that Ellena at once wished and dreaded to know more; but before she had recovered from her surprize, Olivia had left the room.

CHAPTER IX

——— He, like the tenant
Of some night-haunted ruin, bore an aspect
Of horror, worn to habitude.
MYSTERIOUS MOTHER*

THE adventurous Vivaldi, and his servant Paulo, after passing the night of Ellena's departure from villa Altieri in one of the subterraneous chambers of the fort of Paluzzi, and yielding, at length, to exhausted nature, awoke in terror and utter darkness, for the flambeau had expired. When a recollection of the occurrences of the preceding evening returned, they renewed their efforts for liberty with ardour. The grated window was again examined, and being found to overlook only a confined court of the fortress, no hope appeared of escaping.

The words of the monk returned with Vivaldi's first recollections, to torture him with apprehension, that Ellena was no more; and Paulo, unable either to console or to appease his master, sat down dejectedly beside him. Paulo had no longer a hope to suggest, or a joke to throw away; and he could not forbear seriously remarking, that to die of hunger was one of the most horrible means of death, or lamenting the rashness which had made them liable to so sad a probability.

He was in the midst of a very pathetic oration, of which, however, his master did not hear a single word, so wholly was his attention engaged by his own melancholy thoughts, when on a sudden he became silent, and then, starting to his feet, exclaimed, 'Signor, what is yonder? Do you see nothing?'

Vivaldi looked round.

'It is certainly a ray of light,' continued Paulo; 'and I will soon know where it comes from.'

As he said this he sprung forward, and his surprize almost equalled his joy when he discovered that the light issued through the door of the vault, which stood a little open. He could scarcely believe his senses, since the door had been strongly fastened on the preceding night, and he had not heard its ponderous bolts undrawn. He threw it widely open, but recollecting himself, stopped to look into the adjoining vault before he ventured forth; when Vivaldi darted past him, and bidding him follow instantly, ascended to the day. The courts of the fortress were silent and vacant, and Vivaldi reached the arch-way without having observed a single person, breathless with speed, and scarcely daring to believe that he had regained his liberty.

Beneath the arch he stopped to recover breath, and to consider whether he should take the road to Naples, or to the villa Altieri, for it was yet early morning, and at an hour when it appeared improbable that Ellena's family would be risen. The apprehension of her death had vanished as Vivaldi's spirits revived, which the pause of hesitation sufficiently announced: but even this was the pause only of an instant; a strong anxiety concerning her determined him to proceed to the villa Altieri, notwithstanding the unsuitableness of the hour, since he could, at least, reconnoitre her residence, and await till some sign of the family having risen should appear.

'Pray, Signor,' said Paulo, while his master was deliberating, 'do not let us stop here lest the enemy should appear again; and do, Signor, take the road which is nearest to some house where we may get breakfast, for the fear of starving has taken such hold upon me, that it has nearly anticipated the reality of it already.'

Vivaldi immediately departed for the villa. Paulo, as he danced joyfully along, expressed all the astonishment that filled his mind, as to the cause of their late imprisonment and escape; but Vivaldi, who had now leizure to consider the subject, could not assist him in explaining it. The only certainty that appeared, was, that he had not been confined by robbers; and what interest any person could have in imprisoning him for the night, and suffering him to escape in the morning, did not appear.

On entering the garden at Altieri, he was surprized to observe that several of the lower lattices were open at this early hour, but surprize changed to terror, when, on reaching the portico, he heard a moaning of distress from the hall, and when, after loudly calling, he was answered by the piteous cries of Beatrice. The hall door was fastened, and, Beatrice being unable to open it, Vivaldi, followed by Paulo, sprang through one of the unclosed lattices; when on reaching the hall, he found the housekeeper bound to a pillar, and learned that Ellena had been carried off during the night by armed men.

For a moment he was almost stupified by the shock of this intelligence, and then asked Beatrice a thousand questions concerning the affair, without allowing her time to answer one of them. When, however, he had patience to listen, he learned that the ruffians were four in number; that they were masked; that two of them had carried Ellena through the garden, while the others, after binding Beatrice to a pillar, threatening her with death if she made any noise, and watching over her till their comrades had secured their prize, left her a prisoner. This was all the information she could give respecting Ellena.

Vivaldi, when he could think coolly, believed he had discovered the instigators and the design of the whole affair, and the cause, also, of his late confinement. It appeared that Ellena had been carried off by order of his family, to prevent the intended marriage, and that he had been decoyed into the fort of Paluzzi, and kept a prisoner there, to prevent him from intercepting the scheme, which his presence at the villa Altieri would effectually have done. He had himself spoken of his former adventure at Paluzzi; and it now appeared, that his family had taken advantage of the curiosity he had expressed, to lead him into the vaults. The event of this design was the more certain, since, as the fort lay in the direct road to the villa Altieri, Vivaldi could not go thither without being observed by the creatures of the Marchesa, who, by an artful manœuvre, might make him their prisoner, without employing violence.

As he considered these circumstances, it appeared certain, also, that father Schedoni was in truth the monk who had so long haunted his steps; that he was the secret adviser of his mother, and one of the authors of the predicted misfortunes, which, it seemed, he possessed a too certain means of fulfilling. Yet Vivaldi, while he admitted the probability of all this, reflected with new astonishment on the conduct of Schedoni, during his interview with him in the Marchesa's cabinet;—the air of dignified innocence, with which he had repressed accusation, the apparent simplicity, with which he had pointed out circumstances respecting the stranger, that seemed to make against himself; and Vivaldi's opinion of the confessor's duplicity began to waver. 'Yet what other person,' said he, 'could be so intimately acquainted with my concerns, or have an interest sufficiently strong for thus indefatigably thwarting me, except this confessor, who is, no doubt, well rewarded for his perseverance? The monk can be no other than Schedoni, yet it is strange that he should have forborn to disguise his person, and should appear in his mysterious office in the very habit he usually wears!'

Whatever might be the truth as to Schedoni, it was evident that Ellena had been carried away by order of Vivaldi's family, and he immediately returned towards Naples with an intention of demanding her at their hands, not with any hope of their compliance, but believing that they might accidentally afford him some lights on the subject. If, however, he should fail to obtain any hint that might assist him in traceing the route she had been carried, he determined to visit Schedoni, accuse him of perfidy, urge him to a full explanation of his conduct, and, if possible, obtain from him a knowledge of Ellena's place of confinement.

When, at length, he obtained an interview with the Marchese, and, throwing himself at his feet, supplicated that Ellena might be restored to her home, the unaffected surprize of his father overwhelmed him with astonishment and despair. The look and manner of the Marchese could not be doubted; Vivaldi was convinced that he was absolutely ignorant of any step which had been taken against Ellena.

'However ungraciously you have conducted yourself,' said the Marchese, 'my honour has never yet been sullied by duplicity; however I may have wished to break the unworthy connection you have formed, I should disdain to employ artifice as the means. If you really design to marry this person, I shall make no other effort to prevent such a measure, than by telling you the consequence you are to expect;—from thenceforth I will disown you for my son.'

The Marchese quitted the apartment when he had said this, and Vivaldi made no attempt to detain him. His words expressed little more than they had formerly done, yet Vivaldi was shocked by the absolute menace now delivered. The stronger passion of his heart, however, soon overcame their effect; and this moment, when he began to fear that he had irrecoverably lost the object of his dearest affections, was not the time, in which he could long feel remoter evils, or calculate the force of misfortunes which never might arrive. The nearer interest pressed solely upon his mind, and he was conscious only to the loss of Ellena.

The interview, which followed with his mother, was of a different character from that, which had occurred with the Marchese. The keen dart of suspicion, however, sharpened as it was by love and by despair, pierced beyond the veil of her duplicity; and Vivaldi as quickly detected her hypocrisy as he had yielded his conviction to the sincerity of the Marchese. But his power rested here; he possessed no means of awakening her pity or actuating her justice, and could not obtain even a hint, that might guide him in his search of Ellena.

Schedoni, however, yet remained to be tried; Vivaldi had no longer a doubt as to his having caballed with the Marchesa, and that he had been an agent in removing Ellena. Whether he was the person who haunted the ruins of Paluzzi, still remained to be proved, for, though several circumstances seemed to declare that he was, others, not less plausible, asserted the contrary.

On leaving the Marchesa's apartment, Vivaldi repaired to the convent of the Spirito Santo, and enquired for father Schedoni. The lay-brother who opened the gate, informed him that the father was in his cell, and Vivaldi stepped impatiently into the court requesting to be shewn thither.

'I dare not leave the gate, Signor,' said the brother, 'but if you cross the court, and ascend that stair-case which you see yonder beyond the door-way on your right, it will lead you to a gallery, and the third door you will come to is father Schedoni's.'

Vivaldi passed on without seeing another human being, and not a sound disturbed the silence of this sanctuary, till, as he ascended the stairs, a feeble note of lamentation proceeded from the gallery, and he concluded it was uttered by some penitent at confession.

He stopped, as he had been directed, at the third door, when, as he gently knocked, the sound ceased, and the same profound silence returned. Vivaldi repeated his summons, but, receiving no answer, he ventured to open the door. In the dusky cell within no person appeared, but he still looked round, expecting to discover some one in the dubious gloom. The chamber contained little more than a mattress, a chair, a table, and a crucifix; some books of devotion were upon the table, one or two of which were written in unknown characters; several instruments of torture lay beside them. Vivaldi shuddered as he hastily examined these, though he did not comprehend the manner of their application, and he left the chamber, without noticing any other object, and returned to the court. The porter said, that since father Schedoni was not in his cell, he was probably either in the church or in the gardens, for that he had not passed the gates during the morning.

'Did he pass yester-evening?' said Vivaldi, eagerly.

'Yes, he returned to vespers,' replied the brother with surprize.

'Are you certain as to that, my friend?' rejoined Vivaldi, 'are you certain that he slept in the convent last night?'

'Who is it that asks the question?' said the lay-brother, with displeasure, 'and what right has he to make it? You are ignorant of the rules of our house, Signor, or you would perceive such questions to be unnecessary; any member of our community is liable to be severely punished if he sleep a night without these walls, and father Schedoni would be the last among us so to trespass. He is one of the most pious of the brotherhood; few indeed have courage to imitate his severe example. His voluntary sufferings are sufficient for a saint. He pass the night abroad? Go, Signor, yonder is the church, you will find him there, perhaps.'

Vivaldi did not linger to reply. 'The hypocrite!' said he to himself as he crossed to the church, which formed one side of the quadrangle; 'but I will unmask him.'

The church, which he entered, was vacant and silent like the court. 'Whither can the inhabitants of this place have withdrawn themselves?' said he; 'wherever I go, I hear only the echoes of my own footsteps; it seems as if death reigned here over all! But, perhaps, it is one of the hours of general meditation, and the monks have only retired to their cells.'

As he paced the long aisles, he suddenly stopped to catch the startling sound that murmured through the lofty roof; but it seemed to be only the closing of a distant door. Yet he often looked forward into the sacred gloom, which the painted windows threw over the remote perspective, in the expectation of perceiving a monk. He was not long disappointed; a person appeared, standing silently in an obscure part of the cloister, cloathed in the habit of this society, and he advanced towards him.

The monk did not avoid Vivaldi, or even turn to observe who was approaching, but remained in the same attitude, fixed like a statue. This tall and gaunt figure had, at a distance, reminded him of Schedoni, and Vivaldi, as he now looked under the cowl, discovered the ghastly countenance of the confessor.

'Have I found you at last?' said Vivaldi. 'I would speak with you, father, in private. This is not a proper place for such discourse as we must hold.'

Schedoni made no reply, and Vivaldi, once again looking at him, observed that his features were fixed, and his eyes bent towards the ground. The words of Vivaldi seemed not to have reached his understanding, nor even to have made any impression on his senses.

He repeated them in a louder tone, but still not a single line of Schedoni's countenance acknowledged their influence. 'What means this mummery?' said he, his patience exhausted, and his indignation aroused; 'This wretched subterfuge shall not protect you, you are detected, your stratagems are known! Restore Ellena di Rosalba to her home, or confess where you have concealed her.'

Schedoni was still silent and unmoved. A respect for his age and profession withheld Vivaldi from seizing and compelling him to answer; but the agony of impatience and indignation which he suffered, formed a striking contrast to the death-like apathy of the monk. 'I now also know you,' continued Vivaldi, 'for my tor- mentor at Paluzzi, the prophet of evils, which you too well practised the means of fulfilling, the predictor of the death of Signora Bianchi.' Schedoni frowned. 'The forewarner of Ellena's depar- ture; the phantom who decoyed me into the dungeons of Paluzzi; the prophet and the artificer of all my misfortunes.'

The monk raised his eyes from the ground, and fixed them with terrible expression upon Vivaldi, but was still silent.

'Yes, father,' added Vivaldi, 'I know and will proclaim you to the world. I will strip you of the holy hypocrisy in which you shroud yourself; announce to all your society the despicable artifices you have employed, and the misery you have occasioned. Your character shall be announced aloud.'

While Vivaldi spoke, the monk had withdrawn his eyes, and fixed them again on the ground. His countenance had resumed its usual expression.

'Wretch! restore to me Ellena di Rosalba!' cried Vivaldi, with the sudden anguish of renewed despair. 'Tell me at least, where she may be found, or you shall be compelled to do so. Whither, whither have you conveyed her?'

As he pronounced this in loud and passionate accents, several ecclesiastics entered the cloisters, and were passing on to the body of the church, when his voice arrested their attention. They paused, and perceiving the singular attitude of Schedoni, and the frantic gesticulations of Vivaldi, hastily advanced towards them. 'For- bear!' said one of the strangers, as he seized the cloak of Vivaldi, 'do you not observe!'

'I observe a hypocrite,' replied Vivaldi, stepping back and dis- engaging himself, 'I observe a destroyer of the peace, it was his duty to protect. I'——

'Forbear this desperate conduct,' said the priest, 'lest it provoke the just vengeance of Heaven! Do you not observe the holy office in which he is engaged?' pointing to the monk, 'Leave the church while you are permitted to do so in safety; you suspect not the punishment you may provoke.'

'I will not quit the spot till you answer my enquiries,' said

Vivaldi to Schedoni, without deigning even to look upon the priest; 'Where, I repeat, is Ellena di Rosalba?'

The confessor was still silent and unmoved. 'This is beyond all patience, and all belief,' continued Vivaldi. 'Speak! Answer me, or dread what I may unfold. Yet silent! Do you know the convent *del Pianto?* Do you know the confessional of the *Black Penitents?*'

Vivaldi thought he perceived the countenance of the monk suffer some change. 'Do you remember that terrible night,' he added, 'when, on the steps of that confessional, a tale was told?'——

Schedoni raised his eyes, and fixing them once more on Vivaldi, with a look that seemed intended to strike him to the dust, 'Avaunt!' cried he in a tremendous voice; 'avaunt! sacrilegious boy! Tremble for the consequence of thy desperate impiety!'

As he concluded, he started from his position, and gliding with the silent swiftness of a shadow along the cloister, vanished in an instant. Vivaldi, when attempting to pursue him, was seized by the surrounding monks. Insensible to his sufferings, and exasperated by his assertions, they threatened, that if he did not immediately leave the convent, he should be confined, and undergo the severe punishment to which he had become liable, for having disturbed and even insulted one of their holy order while performing an act of penance.

'He has need of such acts,' said Vivaldi; 'but when can they restore the happiness his treachery has destroyed? Your order is disgraced by such a member, reverend fathers; your'——

'Peace!' cried a monk, 'he is the pride of our house; he is severe in his devotion, and in self-punishment terrible beyond the reach of——But I am throwing away my commendations, I am talking to one who is not permitted to value or to understand the sacred mysteries of our exercises.'

'Away with him to the *Padre Abbate!*' cried an enraged priest; 'away with him to the dungeon!'

'Away! away!' repeated his companions, and they endeavoured to force Vivaldi through the cloisters. But with the sudden strength which pride and indignation lent him, he burst from their united hold, and, quitting the church by another door, escaped into the street.

Vivaldi returned home in a state of mind that would have engaged the pity of any heart, which prejudice or self-interest had not hardened. He avoided his father, but sought the Marchesa, who, triumphant in the success of her plan, was still insensible to the sufferings of her son.

When the Marchesa had been informed of his approaching marriage, she had, as usual, consulted with her confessor on the means of preventing it, who had advised the scheme she adopted, a scheme which was the more easily carried into effect, since the Marchesa had early in life been acquainted with the abbess of San Stefano, and knew, therefore, enough of her character and disposition to confide, without hesitation, the management of this important affair to her discretion. The answer of the abbess to her proposal, was not merely acquiescent, but zealous, and it appeared that she too faithfully justified the confidence reposed in her. After this plan had been so successfully prosecuted, it was not to be hoped that the Marchesa would be prevailed upon to relinquish it by the tears, the anguish, or all the varied sufferings of her son. Vivaldi now reproved the easiness of his own confidence in having hoped it, and quitted her cabinet with a despondency that almost reached despair.

The faithful Paulo obeyed the hasty summons of his master, but he had not succeeded in obtaining intelligence of Ellena; and Vivaldi, having dismissed him again on the same enquiry, retired to his apartment, where the excess of grief, and a feeble hope of devising some successful mode of remedy, alternately agitated and detained him.

In the evening, restless and anxious for change, though scarcely knowing whither to bend his course, he left the palace, and strolled down to the sea-beach. A few fishermen and lazzaroni only were loitering along the strand, waiting for boats from St. Lucia. Vivaldi, with folded arms, and his hat drawn over his face to shade his sorrow from observation, paced the edge of the waves, listening to their murmur, as they broke gently at his feet, and gazing upon their undulating beauty, while all consciousness was lost in melancholy reverie concerning Ellena. Her late residence appeared at a distance, rising over the shore. He remembered how often from thence they had together viewed this lovely scene! Its features had now lost their charm; they were colourless and uninteresting, or impressed only mournful ideas. The sea fluctuating beneath the setting sun, the long mole and its light-house tipped with the last rays, fishermen reposing in the shade, little boats skimming over the smooth waters, which their oars scarcely dimpled; these were images that brought to his recollection the affecting evening when he had last seen this picture from the villa Altieri, when, seated in the orangery with Ellena and Bianchi, on the night preceding the death of the latter, Ellena herself had so solemnly been given to his

care, and had so affectingly consented to the dying request of her
relative. The recollection of that scene came to Vivaldi with all
the force of contrast, and renewed all the anguish of despair; he
paced the beach with quicker steps, and long groans burst from his
heart. He accused himself of indifference and inactivity, for having
been thus long unable to discover a single circumstance which
might direct his search; and though he knew not whither to go, he
determined to leave Naples immediately, and return no more to his
father's mansion till he should have rescued Ellena.

Of some fishermen who were conversing together upon the
beach, he enquired whether they could accommodate him with a
boat, in which he meant to coast the bay; for it appeared probable
that Ellena had been conveyed from Altieri by water, to some town
or convent on the shore, the privacy and facility of such a mode of
conveyance being suitable to the designs of her enemies.

'I have but one boat, Signor,' said a fisherman, 'and that is busy
enough in going to and fro between here and Santa Lucia, but my
comrade, here, perhaps can serve you. What, Carlo, can you help
the Signor to your little skiff? the other, I know, has enough to do
in the trade.'

His comrade, however, was too much engaged with a party of
three or four men, who were listening in deep attention round him,
to reply; Vivaldi advancing to urge the question, was struck by the
eagerness with which he delivered his narrative, as well as the un-
couthness of his gesticulation; and he paused a moment in attention. One of the auditors seemed to doubt of something that had
been asserted. 'I tell you,' replied the narrator, 'I used to carry fish
there, two and three times a week, and very good sort of people they
were; they have laid out many a ducat with me in their time. But
as I was saying, when I got there, and knocked upon the door, I
heard, all of a sudden, a huge groaning, and presently I heard the
voice of the old housekeeper herself, roaring out for help; but I
could give her none, for the door was fastened; and, while I ran
away for assistance to old Bartoli, you know old Bartoli, he lives
by the road side as you go to Naples; well, while I ran to him, comes
a Signor, and jumps through the window and sets her at liberty at
once. So then, I heard the whole story.'——

'What story?' said Vivaldi, 'and of whom do you speak?'

'All in good time, *Maestro*, you shall hear,' said the fisherman,
who looking at him for a moment, added, 'Why, Signor, it should
be you I saw there, you should be the very Signor that let Beatrice
loose.'

Vivaldi, who had scarcely doubted before, that it was Altieri of which the man had spoken, now asked a thousand questions respecting the route the ruffians had taken Ellena, but obtained no relief to his anxiety.

—'I should not wonder,' said a Lazzaro who had been listening to the relation; 'I should not wonder if the carriage that passed Bracelli early on the same morning, with the blinds drawn up, though it was so hot that people could scarcely breathe in the open air, should prove to be it which carried off the lady!'

This hint was sufficient to reanimate Vivaldi, who collected all the information the Lazzaro could give, which was, however, little more than that a carriage, such as he described, had been seen by him, driving furiously through Bracelli, early on the morning mentioned as that of Signora di Rosalba's departure. Vivaldi had now no doubt as to its being the one which conveyed her away, and he determined to set out immediately for that place, where he hoped to obtain from the post-master further intelligence concerning the road she had pursued.

With this intention he returned once more to his father's mansion, not to acquaint him with his purpose, or to bid him farewell, but to await the return of his servant Paulo, who he meant should accompany him in the search. Vivaldi's spirits were now animated with hope, slender as were the circumstances that supported it; and, believing his design to be wholly unsuspected by those who would be disposed to interrupt it, he did not guard either against the measures, which might impede his departure from Naples, or those which might overtake him on his journey.

CHAPTER X

What, would'st thou have a serpent sting thee twice?

SHAKESPEARE*

THE Marchesa, alarmed at some hints dropped by Vivaldi in the late interview between them, and by some circumstances of his latter conduct, summoned her constant adviser, Schedoni. Still suffering with the insult he had received in the church of the *Spirito Santo*, he obeyed with sullen reluctance, yet not without a malicious hope of discovering some opportunity for retaliation. That insult, which had pointed forth his hypocrisy, and ridiculed the solemn abstraction he assumed, had sunk deep in his heart, and, fermenting the direst passions of his nature, he meditated a terrible revenge. It had subjected him to mortifications of various kinds. Ambition, it has already appeared, was one of his strongest motives of action, and he had long since assumed a character of severe sanctity, chiefly for the purposes of lifting him to promotion. He was not beloved in the society of which he was a member; and many of the brotherhood, who had laboured to disappoint his views, and to detect his errors, who hated him for his pride, and envied him for his reputed sanctity, now gloried in the mortification he had received, and endeavoured to turn the circumstance to their own advantage. They had not scrupled already to display by insinuation and pointed sneers, their triumph, and to menace his reputation; and Schedoni, though he deserved contempt, was not of a temper to endure it.

But above all, some hints respecting his past life, which had fallen from Vivaldi, and which occasioned him so abruptly to leave the church, alarmed him. So much terror, indeed, had they excited, that it is not improbable that he would have sealed his secret in death, devoting Vivaldi to the grave, had he not been restrained by the dreaded vengeance of the Vivaldi family. Since that hour he had known no peace, and had never slept; he had taken scarcely any food, and was almost continually on his knees upon the steps of the high altar. The devotees who beheld him, paused and admired; such of the brothers as disliked him, sneered and passed on. Schedoni appeared alike insensible to each; lost to this world, and preparing for a higher.

The torments of his mind and the severe penance he had observed, had produced a surprising change in his appearance, so that he resembled a spectre rather than a human being. His visage was wan and wasted, his eyes were sunk and become nearly motionless, and his whole air and attitudes exhibited the wild energy of something—not of this earth.

When he was summoned by the Marchesa, his conscience whispered this to be the consequence of circumstances, which Vivaldi had revealed; and, at first, he had determined not to attend her; but, considering that if it was so, his refusal would confirm suspicion, he resolved to trust once more to the subtilty of his address for deliverance.

With these apprehensions, tempered by this hope, he entered the Marchesa's closet. She almost started on observing him, and could not immediately withdraw her eyes from his altered visage, while Schedoni was unable wholly to conceal the perturbation which such earnest observation occasioned. 'Peace rest with you, daughter!' said he, and he seated himself, without lifting his eyes from the floor.

'I wished to speak with you, father, upon affairs of moment,' said the Marchesa gravely, 'which are probably not unknown to you.' She paused, and Schedoni bowed his head, awaiting in anxious expectation what was to follow.

'You are silent, father,' resumed the Marchesa. 'What am I to understand by this?'

'That you have been misinformed,' replied Schedoni, whose apt conscience betrayed his discretion.

'Pardon me,' said the Marchesa, 'I am too well informed, and should not have requested your visit if any doubt had remained upon my mind.'

'Signora! be cautious of what you credit,' said the confessor imprudently; 'you know not the consequence of a hasty credulity.'

'Would that mine were a rash credulity!' replied the Marchesa; 'but—we are betrayed.'

'We?' repeated the monk, beginning to revive: 'What has happened?'

The Marchesa informed him of Vivaldi's absence, and inferred from its length, for it was now several days since his departure, that he had certainly discovered the place of Ellena's confinement, as well as the authors of it.

Schedoni differed from her, but hinted, that the obedience of youth was hopeless, unless severer measures were adopted.

'Severer!' exclaimed the Marchesa; 'good father, is it not severe enough to confine her for life?'

'I mean severer with respect to your son, lady,' replied Schedoni. 'When a young man has so far overcome all reverence for an holy ordinance as publicly to insult its professors, and yet more, when that professor is in the very performance of his duties, it is time he should be controlled with a strong hand. I am not in the practice of advising such measures, but the conduct of Signor Vivaldi is such as calls aloud for them. Public decency demands it. For myself, indeed, I should have endured patiently the indignity which has been offered me, receiving it as a salutary mortification, as one of those inflictions that purify the soul from the pride which even the holiest men may unconsciously cherish. But I am no longer permitted to consider myself; the public good requires that an example should be made of the horrible impiety of which your son, it grieves me, daughter, to disclose it!—your son, unworthy of such a mother! has been guilty.'

It is evident that in the style, at least, of this accusation, Schedoni suffered the force of his resentment to prevail over the usual subtilty of his address, the deep and smooth insinuation of his policy.

'To what do you allude, righteous father?' enquired the astonished Marchesa; 'what indignity, what impiety has my son to answer for? I entreat you will speak explicitly, that I may prove I can lose the mother in the strict severity of the judge.'

'That is spoken with the grandeur of sentiment, which has always distinguished you, my daughter! Strong minds perceive that justice is the highest of the moral attributes, mercy is only the favourite of weak ones.'

Schedoni had a view in this commendation beyond that of confirming the Marchesa's present resolution against Vivaldi. He wished to prepare her for measures, which might hereafter be necessary to accomplish the revenge he meditated, and he knew that by flattering her vanity, he was most likely to succeed. He praised her, therefore, for qualities he wished her to possess, encouraged her to reject general opinions by admiring as the symptoms of a superior understanding, the convenient morality upon which she had occasionally acted; and, calling sternness justice, extolled that for strength of mind, which was only callous insensibility.

He then described to her Vivaldi's late conduct in the church of the *Spirito Santo*, exaggerated some offensive circumstances of it, invented others, and formed of the whole an instance of monstrous impiety and unprovoked insult.

The Marchesa listened to the relation with no less indignation than surprize, and her readiness to adopt the confessor's advice allowed him to depart with renovated spirits and most triumphant hopes.

Meanwhile, the Marchese remained ignorant of the subject of the conference with Schedoni. His opinions had formerly been sounded, and having been found decidedly against the dark policy it was thought expedient to practise, he was never afterwards consulted respecting Vivaldi. Parental anxiety and affection began to revive as the lengthened absence of his son was observed. Though jealous of his rank, he loved Vivaldi; and, though he had never positively believed that he designed to enter into a sacred engagement with a person, whom the Marchese considered to be so much his inferior as Ellena, he had suffered doubts, which gave him considerable uneasiness. The present extraordinary absence of Vivaldi renewed his alarm. He apprehended that if she was discovered at this moment, when the fear of losing her for ever, and the exasperation, which such complicated opposition occasioned, had awakened all the passions of his son, this rash young man might be prevailed upon to secure her for his own by the indissoluble vow. On the other hand, he dreaded the effect of Vivaldi's despair, should he fail in the pursuit; and thus, fearing at one moment that for which he wished in the next, the Marchese suffered a tumult of mind inferior only to his son's.

The instructions, which he delivered to the servants whom he sent in pursuit of Vivaldi, were given under such distraction of thought, that scarcely any person perfectly understood his commission; and, as the Marchesa had been careful to conceal from him her knowledge of Ellena's abode, he gave no direction concerning the route to *San Stefano*.

While the Marchese at Naples was thus employed, and while Schedoni was forming further plans against Ellena, Vivaldi was wandering from village to village, and from town to town, in pursuit of her, whom all his efforts had hitherto been unsuccessful to recover. From the people at the post-house at Bracelli, he had obtained little information that could direct him; they only knew that a carriage, such as had been already described to Vivaldi, with the blinds drawn up, changed horses there on the morning, which he remembered to be that of Ellena's departure, and had proceeded on the road to Morgagni.

When Vivaldi arrived thither, all trace of Ellena was lost; the master of the post could not recollect a single circumstance connected with the travellers, and, even if he had noticed them, it would have been insufficient for Vivaldi's purpose, unless he had also observed the road they followed; for at this place several roads branched off into opposite quarters of the country; Vivaldi, therefore, was reduced to chuse one of these, as chance or fancy directed; and, as it appeared probable that the Marchesa had conveyed Ellena to a convent, he determined to make enquiries at every one on his way.

He had now passed over some of the wildest tracts of the Apennine, among scenes, which seemed abandoned by civilized society to the banditti who haunted their recesses. Yet even here amidst wilds that were nearly inaccessible, convents, with each its small dependent hamlet, were scattered, and, shrouded from the world by woods and mountains, enjoyed unsuspectedly many of its luxuries, and displayed, unnoticed, some of its elegance. Vivaldi, who had visited several of these in search of Ellena, had been surprized at the refined courtesy and hospitality, with which he was received.

It was on the seventh day of his journey, and near sun-set, that he was bewildered in the woods of Rugieri. He had received a direction for the road he was to take at a village some leagues distant, and had obeyed it confidently till now, when the path was lost in several tracts that branched out among the trees. The day was closing, and Vivaldi's spirits began to fail, but Paulo, light of heart and ever gay, commended the shade and pleasant freshness of the woods, and observed, that if his master did lose his way, and was obliged to remain here for the night, it could not be so very unlucky, for they could climb up among the branches of a chestnut, and find a more neat and airy lodging than any inn had yet afforded them.

While Paulo was thus endeavouring to make the best of what might happen, and his master was sunk in reverie, they suddenly heard the sound of instruments and voices from a distance. The gloom, which the trees threw around, prevented their distinguishing objects afar off, and not a single human being was visible, nor any trace of his art, beneath the shadowy scene. They listened to ascertain from what direction the sounds approached, and heard a chorus of voices, accompanied by a few instruments, performing the evening service.

'We are near a convent, Signor,' said Paulo, 'listen! they are at their devotions.'

'It is as you say,' replied Vivaldi; 'and we will make the best of our way towards it.'

'Well, Signor! I must say, if we find as good doings here as we had at the Capuchin's, we shall have no reason to regret our beds *al-fresco* among the chestnut branches.'

'Do you perceive any walls or spires beyond the trees?' said Vivaldi, as he led the way.

'None, Signor,' replied Paulo; 'yet we draw nearer the sounds. Ah, Signor! do you hear that note? How it dies away! And those instruments just touched in symphony! This is not the music of peasants; a convent must be near, though we do not see it.'

Still as they advanced, no walls appeared, and soon after the music ceased; but other sounds led Vivaldi forward to a pleasant part of the woods, where, the trees opening, he perceived a party of pilgrims seated on the grass.* They were laughing and convers- ing with much gaiety, as each spread before him the supper, which he drew from his scrip;* while he, who appeared to be the *Father- director** of the pilgrimage, sat with a jovial countenance in the midst of the company, dispensing jokes and merry stories, and receiving in return a tribute from every scrip. Wines of various sorts were ranged before him, of which he drank abundantly, and seemed not to refuse any dainty that was offered.

Vivaldi, whose apprehensions were now quieted, stopped to observe the groupe, as the evening rays, glancing along the skirts of the wood, threw a gleam upon their various countenances, shew- ing, however, in each a spirit of gaiety that might have charac- terized the individuals of a party of pleasure, rather than those of a pilgrimage. The *Father-director* and his flock seemed perfectly to understand each other; the Superior willingly resigned the solemn austerity of his office, and permitted the company to make them- selves as happy as possible, in consideration of receiving plenty of the most delicate of their viands; yet somewhat of dignity was mingled with his condescensions, that compelled them to receive even his jokes with a degree of deference, and perhaps they laughed at them less for their spirit than because they were favors.

Addressing the Superior, Vivaldi requested to be directed how he might regain his way. The father examined him for a moment before he replied, but observing the elegance of his dress, and a certain air of distinction; and perceiving, also, that Paulo was his servant, he promised his services, and invited him to take a seat at his right hand, and partake of the supper.

Vivaldi, understanding that the party was going his road, accepted the invitation; when Paulo, having fastened the horses to a tree, soon became busy with the supper. While Vivaldi conversed with the father, Paulo engrossed all the attention of the pilgrims near him; they declared he was the cleverest and the merriest fellow they had ever seen, and often expressed a wish that he was going as far with them as to the shrine in a convent of Carmelites, which terminated their pilgrimage. When Vivaldi understood that this shrine was in the church of a convent, partly inhabited by nuns,* and that it was little more than a league and a half distant, he determined to accompany them, for it was as possible that Ellena was confined there as in any other cloister; and of her being imprisoned in some convent, he had less doubt, the more he considered the character and views of his mother. He set forward, therefore, with the pilgrims, and on foot, having resigned his horse to the weary *Father-director*.

Darkness closed over them long before they reached the village where they designed to pass the night; but they beguiled the way with songs and stories, now and then, only, stopping at command of the Father, to repeat some prayer or sing a hymn. But, as they drew near a village, at the base of the mountain on which the shrine stood, they halted to arrange themselves in procession; and the Superior having stopped short in the midst of one of his best jokes, dismounted Vivaldi's horse, placed himself at their head, and beginning a loud strain, they proceeded in full chorus of melancholy music.

The peasants, hearing their sonorous voices, came forth to meet and conduct them to their cabins. The village was already crowded with devotees, but these poor peasants, looking up to them with love and reverence, made every possible contrivance to accommodate all who came; notwithstanding which, when Paulo soon after turned into his bed of straw, he had more reasons than one to regret his chestnut mattress.

Vivaldi passed an anxious night, waiting impatiently for the dawning of that day, which might possibly restore to him Ellena. Considering that a pilgrim's habit would not only conceal him from suspicion, but allow him opportunities for observation, which his own dress would not permit, he employed Paulo to provide him one. The address of the servant, assisted by a single ducat, easily procured it, and at an early hour he set forward on his enquiry.

CHAPTER XI

Bring roses, violets, and the cold snow-drop,
Beautiful in tears, to strew the path-way
Of our saintly sister.

A FEW devotees only had begun to ascend the mountain, and Vivaldi kept aloof even from these, pursuing a lonely track, for his thoughtful mind desired solitude. The early breeze sighing among the foliage, that waved high over the path, and the hollow dashing of distant waters, he listened to with complacency, for these were sounds which soothed yet promoted his melancholy mood; and he sometimes rested to gaze upon the scenery around him, for this too was in harmony with the temper of his mind. Disappointment had subdued the wilder energy of the passions, and produced a solemn and lofty state of feeling; he viewed with pleasing sadness the dark rocks and precipices, the gloomy mountains and vast solitudes, that spread around him; nor was the convent he was approaching a less sacred feature of the scene, as its gray walks and pinnacles appeared beyond the dusky groves. 'Ah! if it should enclose her!' said Vivaldi, as he caught a first glimpse of its hall. 'Vain hope! I will not invite your illusions again, I will not expose myself to the agonies of new disappointment; I will search, but not expect. Yet, if she should be there!'

Having reached the gates of the convent, he passed with hasty steps into the court; where his emotion encreased as he paused a moment and looked round its silent cloisters. The porter only appeared, when Vivaldi, fearful lest he should perceive him not to be a pilgrim, drew his hood over his face, and, gathering up his garments still closer in his folded arms, passed on without speaking, though he knew not which of the avenues before him led to the shrine. He advanced, however, towards the church, a stately edifice, detached, and at some little distance, from the other parts of the convent. Its highly vaulted aisles, extending in twilight perspective, where a monk, or a pilgrim only, now and then crossed, whose dark figures, passing without sound, vanished like shadows; the universal stillness of the place, the gleam of tapers from the high altar, and of lamps, which gave a gloomy pomp to every shrine in the church:—all these circumstances conspired to impress a sacred awe upon his heart.

He followed some devotees through a side aisle to a court, that was overhung by a tremendous rock, in which was a cave, containing the shrine of *our Lady of Mount Carmel*. This court was enclosed by the rock, and by the choir of the church, except that to the south a small opening led the eye to a glimpse of the landscape below, which, seen beyond the dark jaws of the cliff, appeared free, and light, and gaily coloured, melting away into the blue and distant mountains.

Vivaldi entered the cave, where, enclosed within a filigree screen of gold, lay the image of the saint, decorated with flowers and lighted up by innumerable lamps and tapers. The steps of the shrine were thronged with kneeling pilgrims, and Vivaldi, to avoid singularity, kneeled also; till a high peal of the organ, at a distance, and the deep voices of choiristers announced that the first mass was begun. He left the cave, and, returning into the church, loitered at an extremity of the aisles, where he listened awhile to the solemn harmony pealing along the roofs, and softening away in distance. It was such full and entrancing music as frequently swells in the high festivals of the Sicilian church, and is adapted to inspire that sublime enthusiasm, which sometimes elevates its disciples. Vivaldi, unable to endure long the excess of feeling, which this harmony awakened, was leaving the church, when suddenly it ceased, and the tolling of a bell sounded in its stead. This seemed to be the knell of death, and it occurred to him, that a dying person was approaching to receive the last sacrament; when he heard remotely a warbling of female voices, mingling with the deeper tones of the monks, and with the hollow note of the bell, as it struck at intervals. So sweetly, so plaintively, did the strain grow on the air, that those, who listened, as well as those, who sung, were touched with sorrow, and seemed equally to mourn for a departing friend.

Vivaldi hastened to the choir, the pavement of which was strewn with palm-branches and fresh flowers. A pall of black velvet lay upon the steps of the altar, where several priests were silently attending. Every where appeared the ensigns of solemn pomp and ceremony, and in every countenance the stillness and observance of expectation. Meanwhile the sounds drew nearer, and Vivaldi perceived a procession of nuns approaching from a distant aisle.

As they advanced, he distinguished the lady abbess leading the train, dressed in her pontifical robes, with the mitre on her head; and well he marked her stately step, moving in time to the slow minstrelsy, and the air of proud yet graceful dignity, with which she characterized herself. Then followed the nuns, according to their several orders, and last came the novices, carrying lighted tapers, and surrounded by other nuns, who were distinguished by a particular habit.

Having reached a part of the church appropriated for their reception, they arranged themselves in order. Vivaldi with a palpitating heart enquired the occasion of this ceremony, and was told that a nun was going to be professed.

'You are informed, no doubt, brother,' added the prior who gave him this intelligence, 'that on the morning of our high festival, our *lady*'s day, it is usual for such as devote themselves to heaven, to receive the veil. Stand bye a while, and you will see the ceremony.'

'What is the name of the novice who is now to receive it?' said Vivaldi, in a voice whose tremulous accents betrayed his emotion.

The friar glanced an eye of scrutiny upon him, as he replied, 'I know not her name, but if you will step a little this way, I will point her out to you.'

Vivaldi, drawing his hood over his face, obeyed in silence.

'It is she on the right of the abbess,' said the stranger, 'who leans on the arm of a nun, she is covered with a white veil, and is taller than her companions.'

Vivaldi observed her with a fearful eye, and, though he did not recognize the person of Ellena, yet, whether it was that his fancy was possessed with her image, or that there was truth in his surmise, he thought he perceived a resemblance of her. He enquired how long the novice had resided in the convent, and many other particulars, to which the stranger either could not or dared not reply.

With what anxious solicitude did Vivaldi endeavour to look through the veils of the several nuns in search of Ellena, whom he believed the barbarous policy of his mother might already have devoted to the cloister! With a solicitude still stronger, he tried to catch a glimpse of the features of the novices, but their faces were shaded by hoods, and their white veils, though thrown half back, were disposed in such artful folds that they concealed them from observation, as effectually as did the pendant lawn the features of the nuns.

The ceremony began with the exhortation of the *Father-Abbot*, delivered with solemn energy; then the novice kneeling before him, made her profession, for which Vivaldi listened with intense attention, but it was delivered in such low and trembling accents, that he could not ascertain even the tone. But during the anthem that mingled with the ensuing part of the service, he thought he distinguished the voice of Ellena, that touching and well-known voice, which in the church of San Lorenzo had first attracted his attention. He listened, scarcely daring to draw breath, lest he should lose a note; and again he fancied her voice spoke in a part of the plaintive response delivered by the nuns.

Vivaldi endeavoured to command his emotion, and to await with patience some further unfolding of the truth; but when the priest prepared to withdraw the white veil from the face of the novice, and throw the black one over her, a dreadful expectation that she was Ellena seized him, and he with difficulty forbore stepping forward and discovering himself on the instant.

The veil was at length withdrawn, and a very lovely face appeared, but not Ellena's. Vivaldi breathed again, and waited with tolerable composure for the conclusion of the ceremony; till, in the solemn strain that followed the putting on of the black veil, he heard again the voice, which he was now convinced was her's. Its accents were low, and mournful, and tremulous, yet his heart acknowledged instantaneously their magic influence.

When this ceremony had concluded, another began; and he was told it was that of a noviciation. A young woman, supported by two nuns, advanced to the altar, and Vivaldi thought he beheld Ellena. The priest was beginning the customary exhortation, when she lifted her half-veil, and, shewing a countenance where meek sorrow was mingled with heavenly sweetness, raised her blue eyes, all bathed in tears, and waved her hand as if she would have spoken. —It was Ellena herself.

The priest attempted to proceed.

'I protest in the presence of this congregation,' said she solemnly, 'that I am brought hither to pronounce vows which my heart disclaims. I protest'——

A confusion of voices interrupted her, and at the same instant she perceived Vivaldi rushing towards the altar. Ellena gazed for a moment, and then, stretching forth her supplicating hands towards him, closed her eyes, and sunk into the arms of some persons round her, who vainly endeavoured to prevent him from approaching and assisting her. The anguish, with which he bent over her lifeless form, and called upon her name, excited the commiseration even of the nuns, and especially of Olivia, who was most assiduous in efforts to revive her young friend.

When Ellena unclosed her eyes, and looking up, once more

beheld Vivaldi, the expression, with which she regarded him, told that her heart was unchanged, and that she was unconscious of the miseries of imprisonment while he was with her. She desired to withdraw, and, assisted by Vivaldi and Olivia, was leaving the church, when the abbess ordered that she should be attended by the nuns only; and, retiring from the altar, she gave directions that the young stranger should be conducted to the parlour of the convent.

Vivaldi, though he refused to obey an imperious command, yielded to the entreaties of Ellena, and to the gentle remonstrances of Olivia; and, bidding Ellena farewell for a while, he repaired to the parlour of the abbess. He was not without some hope of awakening her to a sense of justice, or of pity; but he found that her notions of right were inexorably against him, and that pride and resentment usurped the influence of every other feeling. She began her lecture with expressing the warm friendship she had so long cherished for the Marchesa, proceeded to lament that the son of a friend, whom she so highly esteemed, should have forgotten his duty to his parents, and the observance due to the dignity of his house, so far as to seek connection with a person of Ellena di Rosalba's inferior station; and concluded with a severe reprimand for having disturbed the tranquillity of her convent and the decorum of the church by his intrusion.

Vivaldi listened with submitting patience to this mention of morals and decorum from a person, who, with the most perfect self-applause, was violating some of the plainest obligations of humanity and justice; who had conspired to tear an orphan from her home, and who designed to deprive her for life of liberty, with all the blessings it inherits. But, when she proceeded to speak of Ellena with the caustic of severe reprobation, and to hint at the punishment, which her public rejection of the vows had incurred, the patience of Vivaldi submitted no longer; indignation and contempt rose high against the Superior, and he exhibited a portrait of herself in the strong colours of truth. But the mind, which compassion could not persuade, reason could not appal; selfishness had hardened it alike to the influence of each; her pride only was affected, and she retaliated the mortification she suffered by menace and denunciation.

Vivaldi, on quitting her apartment, had no other resource than an application to the *Abate*,* whose influence, at least, if not his authority, might assuage the severity of her power. In this Abate, a mildness of temper, and a gentleness of manner were qualities of less value than is usually and deservedly imputed to them; for, being connected with feebleness of mind, they were but the pleasing merits of easy times, which in an hour of difficulty never assumed the character of virtues, by inducing him to serve those, for whom he might feel. And thus, with a temper and disposition directly opposite to those of the severe and violent abbess, he was equally selfish, and almost equally culpable, since by permitting evil, he was nearly as injurious in his conduct as those who planned it. Indolence and timidity, a timidity the consequence of want of clear perception, deprived him of all energy of character; he was prudent rather than wise, and so fearful of being thought to do wrong that he seldom did right.

To Vivaldi's temperate representations and earnest entreaties that he would exert some authority towards liberating Ellena, he listened with patience; acknowledged the hardships of her situation; lamented the unhappy divisions between Vivaldi and his family; and then declined advancing a single step in so delicate an affair. Signora di Rosalba, he said, was in the care of the abbess, over whom he had no right of control in matters relative to her domestic concerns. Vivaldi then supplicated, that, though he possessed no authority, he would, at least, intercede or remonstrate against so unjust a procedure as that of detaining Ellena a prisoner, and assist in restoring her to the home, from which she had been forcibly carried.

'And this, again,' replied the Abate, 'does not come within my jurisdiction; and I make it a rule never to encroach upon that of another person.'

'And can you endure, holy father,' said Vivaldi, 'to witness a flagrant act of injustice and not endeavour to counteract it? not even step forward to rescue the victim when you perceive the preparation for the sacrifice?'

'I repeat, that I never interfere with the authority of others,' replied the Superior; 'having asserted my own, I yield to them in their sphere, the obedience which I require in mine.'

'Is power then,' said Vivaldi, 'the infallible test of justice? Is it morality to obey where the command is criminal? The whole world have a claim upon the fortitude, the active fortitude of those who are placed as you are, between the alternative of confirming a wrong by your consent, or preventing it by your resistance. Would that your heart expanded towards that world, reverend father!'

'Would that the whole world were wrong that you might have the glory of setting it right!' said the Abate, smiling. 'Young man!

you are an enthusiast, and I pardon you. You are a knight of chivalry, who would go about the earth fighting with every body by way of proving your right to do good; it is unfortunate that you are born somewhat too late.'

'Enthusiasm in the cause of humanity'—said Vivaldi, but he checked himself; and despairing of touching a heart so hardened by selfish prudence, and indignant at beholding an apathy so vicious in its consequence, he left the Abate without other effort. He perceived that he must now have recourse to further stratagem, a recourse which his frank and noble mind detested, but he had already tried, without success, every other possibility of rescuing the innocent victim of the Marchesa's prejudice and pride.

Ellena meanwhile had retired to her cell, agitated by a variety of considerations, and contrary emotions, of which, however, those of joy and tenderness were long predominant. Then came anxiety, apprehension, pride, and doubt, to divide and torture her heart. It was true that Vivaldi had discovered her prison, but, if it were possible, that he could release her, she must consent to quit it with him; a step from which a mind so tremblingly jealous of propriety as hers, recoiled with alarm, though it would deliver her from captivity. And how, when she considered the haughty character of the Marchese di Vivaldi, the imperious and vindictive nature of the Marchesa, and, still more, their united repugnance to a connection with her, how could she endure to think, even for a moment, of intruding herself into such a family! Pride, delicacy, good sense seemed to warn her against a conduct so humiliating and vexatious in its consequences, and to exhort her to preserve her own dignity by independence; but the esteem, the friendship, the tender affection, which she had cherished for Vivaldi, made her pause, and shrink with emotions, of little less than horror, from the eternal renunciation, which so dignified a choice required. Though the encouragement, which her deceased relative had given to this attachment, seemed to impart to it a sacred character, that considerably soothed the alarmed delicacy of Ellena, the approbation thus implied, had no power to silence her own objections, and she would have regretted the mistaken zeal, which had contributed to lead her into the present distressing situation, had she revered the memory of her aunt, or loved Vivaldi, less. Still, however, the joy, which his presence had occasioned, and which the consciousness that he was still near her had prolonged, was not subdued, though it was frequently obscured, by such anxious considerations. With jealous and indiscreet solicitude, she now recollected every look, and the accent of every word, which had told that his affection was undiminished, thus seeking, with inconsistent zeal, for a conviction of the very tenderness, which but a moment before she had thought it would be prudent to lament, and almost necessary to renounce.

She awaited with extreme anxiety the appearance of Olivia, who might probably know the result of Vivaldi's conference with the abbess, and whether he was yet in the convent.

In the evening Olivia came, a messenger of evil; and Ellena, informed of the conduct of the abbess, and the consequent departure of Vivaldi, perceived all her courage, and all the half-formed resolutions, which a consideration of his family had suggested, faulter and expire. Sensible only of grief and despondency, she ascertained, for the first time, the extent of her affection and the severity of her situation. She perceived, also, that the injustice, which his family had exercised towards her, absolved her from all consideration of their displeasure, otherwise than as it might affect herself; but this was a conviction, which it were now probably useless to admit.

Olivia not only expressed the tenderest interest in her welfare, but seemed deeply affected with her situation; and, whether it was, that the nun's misfortunes bore some resemblance to Ellena's, or from whatever cause, it is remarkable that her eyes were often filled with tears, while she regarded her young friend, and she betrayed so much emotion that Ellena noticed it with surprise. She was, however, too delicate to hint any curiosity on the subject; and too much engaged by a nearer interest, to dwell long upon the circumstance.

When Olivia withdrew, Ellena retired to her turret, to soothe her spirits with a view of serene and majestic nature, a recourse which seldom failed to elevate her mind and soften the asperities of affliction. It was to her like sweet and solemn music, breathing peace over the soul—like the oaten stop of Milton's Spirit,

> Who with his soft pipe, and smooth-dittied song,
> Well knew to still the wild winds when they roar
> And hush the waving woods.*

While she sat before a window, observing the evening light beaming up the valley, and touching all the distant mountains with misty purple, a reed as sweet, though not as fanciful, sounded from among the rocks below. The instrument and the character of the strain were such as she had been unaccustomed to hear within the walls of San Stefano, and the tone diffused over her spirits a pleasing melancholy, that rapt all her attention. The liquid cadence, as it trembled and sunk away, seemed to tell the dejection of no vulgar feelings, and the exquisite taste, with which the complaining notes were again swelled, almost convinced her, that the musician was Vivaldi.

On looking from the lattice, she perceived a person perched on a point of the cliff below, whither it appeared almost impracticable for any human step to have climbed, and preserved from the precipice only by some dwarf shrubs that fringed the brow. The twilight did not permit her immediately to ascertain whether it was Vivaldi, and the situation was so dangerous that she hoped it was not he. Her doubts were removed, when, looking up, he perceived Ellena, and she heard his voice.

Vivaldi had learned from a lay-brother of the convent, whom Paulo had bribed, and who, when he worked in the garden, had sometimes seen Ellena at the window, that she frequented this remote turret; and, at the hazard of his life, he had now ventured thither, with a hope of conversing with her.

Ellena, alarmed at his tremendous situation, refused to listen to him, but he would not leave the spot till he had communicated a plan concerted for her escape, and, entreating that she would confide herself to his care, assured her she would be conducted wherever she judged proper. It appeared that the brother had consented to assist his views, in consideration of an ample reward, and to admit him within the walls on this evening, when, in his pilgrim's habit, he might have an opportunity of again seeing Ellena. He conjured her to attend, if possible, in the convent parlour during supper, explaining, in a few words, the motive for this request, and the substance of the following particulars:

The Lady-abbess, in observance of the custom upon high festivals, gave a collation to the *Padre-abate*, and such of the priests as had assisted at the vesper-service. A few strangers of distinction and pilgrims were also to partake of the entertainments of this night, among which was included a concert to be performed by the nuns. At the collation was to be displayed a profusion of delicacies, arranged by the sisters, who had been busy in preparing the pastry and confectionary during several days, and who excelled in these articles no less than in embroidery and other ingenious arts. This supper was to be given in the abbess's outer parlour, while she herself, attended by some nuns of high rank, and a few favourites, was to have a table in the inner apartment, where, separated only by the grate, she could partake of the conversation of the holy fathers. The tables were to be ornamented with artificial flowers, and a variety of other fanciful devices upon which the ingenuity of the sisters had been long employed, who prepared for these festivals with as much vanity, and expected them to dissipate the gloomy monotony of their usual life, with as much eagerness of delight, as a young beauty anticipates a first ball.

On this evening, therefore, every member of the convent would be engaged either by amusement or business, and to Vivaldi, who had been careful to inform himself of these circumstances, it would be easy, with the assistance of the brother, to obtain admittance, and mingle himself among the spectators, disguised in his pilgrim's habit. He entreated, therefore, that Ellena would contrive to be in the abbess's apartment this evening, when he would endeavour to convey to her some further particulars of the plan of escape, and would have mules in waiting at the foot of the mountain, to conduct her to the villa Altieri, or to the neighbouring convent of the Santa della Pieta. Vivaldi secretly hoped that she might be prevailed with to give him her hand on quitting San Stefano, but he forbore to mention this hope, lest it should be mistaken for a condition, and that Ellena might be either reluctant to accept his assistance, or, accepting it, might consider herself bound to grant a hasty consent.

To his mention of escape she listened with varying emotion; at one moment attending to it with hope and joy, as promising her only chance of liberation from an imprisonment, which was probably intended to last for her life, and of restoring her to Vivaldi; and at another, recoiling from the thought of departing with him, while his family was so decidedly averse to their marriage. Thus, unable to form any instant resolution on the subject, and entreating that he would leave his dangerous station before the thickening twilight should encrease the hazard of his descent, Ellena added, that she would endeavour to obtain admittance to the apartment of the abbess, and to acquaint him with her final determination. Vivaldi understood all the delicacy of her scruples, and though they afflicted him, he honoured the good sense and just pride that suggested them.

He lingered on the rock till the last moments of departing light, and then, with a heart fluttering with hopes and fears, bade Ellena farewel, and descended; while she watched his progress through the silent gloom, faintly distinguishing him gliding along ledges of the precipice, and making his adventurous way from cliff to cliff, till the winding thickets concealed him from her view. Still anxious, she remained at the lattice, but he appeared no more; no voice announced disaster; and, at length, she returned to her cell, to deliberate on the subject of her departure.

Her considerations were interrupted by Olivia, whose manner indicated something extraordinary; the usual tranquillity of her countenance was gone, and an air of grief mingled with apprehension appeared there. Before she spoke, she examined the passage and looked round the cell. 'It is as I feared,' said she abruptly; 'my suspicions are justified, and you, my child, are sacrificed, unless it were possible for you to quit the convent this night.'

'What is it that you mean?' said the alarmed Ellena.

'I have just learned,' resumed the nun, 'that your conduct this morning, which is understood to have thrown a premeditated insult upon the abbess, is to be punished with what they *call* imprisonment; alas! why should I soften the truth,—with what I believe is death itself, for who ever returned alive from that hideous chamber!'

'With death!' said Ellena, aghast; 'Oh, heavens! how have I deserved death?'

'That is not the question, my daughter, but how you may avoid it. Within the deepest recesses of our convent, is a stone chamber, secured by doors of iron, to which such of the sisterhood as have been guilty of any heinous offence have, from time to time, been consigned. This condemnation admits of no reprieve; the unfortunate captive is left to languish in chains and darkness, receiving only an allowance of bread and water just sufficient to prolong her sufferings, till nature, at length, sinking under their intolerable pressure, obtains refuge in death. Our records relate several instances of such horrible punishment, which has generally been inflicted upon nuns, who, weary of the life which they have chosen under the first delusions of the imagination, or which they have been compelled to accept by the rigour or avarice of parents, have been detected in escaping from the convent.'

The nun paused, but Ellena remaining wrapt in silent thought, she resumed: 'One miserable instance of this severity has occurred within my memory. I saw the wretched victim enter that apartment—never more to quit it alive! I saw, also, her poor remains laid at rest in the convent garden! During nearly two years she languished upon a bed of straw, denied even the poor consolation of conversing through the grate with such of the sisters as pitied her; and who of us was there that did not pity her! A severe punishment was threatened to those, who should approach with any compassionate intention; thank God! I incurred it, and I endured it, also, with secret triumph.'

A gleam of satisfaction passed over Olivia's countenance as she spoke this; it was the sweetest that Ellena had ever observed there. With a sympathetic emotion, she threw herself on the bosom of the nun, and wept; for some moments they were both silent. Olivia, at length said, 'Do you not believe, my child, that the officious and offended abbess will readily seize upon the circumstance of your disobedience, as a pretence for confining you in that fatal chamber? The wishes of the Marchesa will thus surely be accomplished, without the difficulty of exacting your obedience to the vows. Alas! I have received proof too absolute of her intention, and that to-morrow is assigned as the day of your sacrifice; you may, perhaps, be thankful that the business of the festival has obliged her to defer executing the sentence even till to-morrow.'

Ellena replied only with a groan, as her head still drooped upon the shoulder of the nun; she was not now hesitating whether to accept the assistance of Vivaldi, but desponding lest his utmost efforts for her deliverance should be vain.

Olivia, who mistook the cause of her silence, added, 'Other hints I could give, which are strong as they are dreadful, but I will forbear. Tell me how it is possible I may assist you; I am willing to incur a second punishment, in endeavouring to relieve a second sufferer.'

Ellena's tears flowed fast at this new instance of the nun's generosity. 'But if they should discover you in assisting me to leave the convent,' she said, in a voice convulsed by her gratitude,—'O! if they should discover you!'——

'I can ascertain the punishment,' Olivia replied with firmness, 'and do not fear to meet it.'

'How nobly generous this is!' said the weeping Ellena; 'I ought not to suffer you to be thus careless of yourself!'

'My conduct is not wholly disinterested,' the nun modestly replied; 'for I think I could endure any punishment with more fortitude than the sickening anguish of beholding such suffering as I have witnessed. What are bodily pains in comparison with the subtle, the exquisite tortures of the mind! Heaven knows I can support my own afflictions, but not the view of those of others when they are excessive. The instruments of torture I believe I could endure, if my spirit was invigorated with the consciousness of a generous purpose; but pity touches upon a nerve that vibrates instantly to the heart, and subdues resistance. Yes, my child, the agony of pity is keener than any other, except that of remorse, and even in remorse, it is, perhaps, the mingling unavailing pity, that points the sting. But, while I am indulging this egotism, I am, perhaps, increasing your danger of the suffering I deprecate.'

Ellena, thus encouraged by the generous sympathy of Olivia, mentioned Vivaldi's purposed visit of this evening; and consulted with her on the probability of procuring admittance for herself to the abbess's parlour. Reanimated by this intelligence, Olivia advised her to repair not only to the supper-room, but to attend the previous concert, to which several strangers would be admitted, among whom might probably be Vivaldi. When to this, Ellena objected her dread of the abbess's observation, and of the immediate seclusion that would follow, Olivia soothed her fears of discovery, by offering her the disguise of a nun's veil, and promising not only to conduct her to the apartment, but to afford her every possible assistance towards her escape.

'Among the crowd of nuns, who will attend in that spacious apartment,' Olivia added, 'it is improbable you would be distinguished, even if the sisters were less occupied by amusement, and the abbess were at leisure to scrutinize. As it is, you will hazard little danger of discovery; the Superior, if she thinks of you at all, will believe that you are still a prisoner in your cell, but this is an evening of too much importance to her vanity, for any consideration, distinct from that emotion, to divide her attention. Let hope, therefore, support you, my child, and do you prepare a few lines to acquaint Vivaldi with your consent to his proposal, and with the urgency of your circumstances; you may, perhaps, find an opportunity of conveying them through the grate.'

They were still conversing on this subject, when a particular chime sounded, which Olivia said summoned the nuns to the concert-room; and she immediately hastened for a black veil, while Ellena wrote the few lines that were necessary for Vivaldi.

END OF THE FIRST VOLUME

VOLUME II

CHAPTER I

That lawn conceals her beauty
As the thin cloud, just silver'd by the rays,
The trembling moon: think ye 'tis shrouded from
The curious eye?

WRAPT in Olivia's veil, Ellena descended to the music-room, and
mingled with the nuns, who were assembled within the grate.
Among the monks and pilgrims without it, were some strangers in
the usual dress of the country, but she did not perceive any person
who resembled Vivaldi; and she considered, that, if he were present, he would not venture to discover himself, while her nun's
veil concealed her as effectually from him as from the lady Abbess.
It would be necessary, therefore, to seek an opportunity of withdrawing it for a moment at the grate, an expedient, which must
certainly expose her to the notice of strangers.

On the entrance of the lady Abbess, Ellena's fear of observation rendered her insensible to every other consideration; she
fancied, that the eyes of the Superior were particularly directed
upon herself. The veil seemed an insufficient protection from their
penetrating glances, and she almost sunk with the terror of instant
discovery.

The Abbess, however, passed on, and, having conversed for a
few moments with the *padre Abate* and some visitors of distinction, took her chair; and the performance immediately opened
with one of those solemn and impressive airs, which the Italian
nuns know how to give with so much taste and sweetness. It
rescued even Ellena for a moment from a sense of danger, and she
resigned herself to the surrounding scene, of which the *coup-
d'œil** was striking and grand. In a vaulted apartment of considerable extent, lighted by innumerable tapers, and where even the
ornaments, though pompous, partook of the solemn character of
the institution, were assembled about fifty nuns, who, in the

interesting habit of their order, appeared with graceful plainness. The delicacy of their air, and their beauty, softened by the lawn that thinly veiled it, were contrasted by the severe majesty of the lady Abbess, who, seated on an elevated chair, apart from the audience, seemed the Empress of the scene, and by the venerable figures of the father *Abate* and his attendant monks, who were arranged without that screen of wire-work, extending the whole breadth of the apartment, which is called the grate. Near the holy father were placed the strangers of distinction, dressed in the splendid Neapolitan habit, whose gay colouring and airy elegance opposed well with the dark drapery of the ecclesiastics; their plumed hats loftily overtopping the half-cowled heads and grey locks of the monks. Nor was the contrast of countenances less striking; the grave, the austere, the solemn, and the gloomy, intermingling with the light, the blooming, and the debonaire, expressed all the various tempers, that render life a blessing or a burden, and, as with the spell of magic, transform this world into a transient paradise or purgatory. In the back ground of the picture stood some pilgrims, with looks less joyous and more demure than they had worn on the road the preceding day; and among them were some inferior brothers and attendants of the convent. To this part of the chamber Ellena frequently directed her attention, but did not distinguish Vivaldi; and, though she had taken a station near the grate, she had not courage indecorously to withdraw her veil before so many strangers. And thus, if he even were in the apartment, it was not probable he would venture to come forward.

The concert concluded without his having been discovered by Ellena; and she withdrew to the apartment, where the collation was spread, and where the Abbess and her guests soon after appeared. Presently, she observed a stranger, in a pilgrim's habit, station himself near the grate; his face was partly muffled in his cloak, and he seemed to be a spectator rather than a partaker of the feast.

Ellena, who understood this to be Vivaldi, was watchful for an opportunity of approaching, unseen by the Abbess, the place where he had fixed himself. Engaged in conversation with the ladies around her, the Superior soon favoured Ellena's wish, who, having reached the grate, ventured to lift her veil for one instant. The stranger, letting his cloak fall, thanked her with his eyes for her condescension, and she perceived, that he was not Vivaldi! Shocked at the interpretation, which might be given to a conduct apparently so improper, as much as by the disappointment, which

Vivaldi's absence occasioned, she was hastily retiring, when another stranger approached with quick steps, whom she instantly knew, by the grace and spirit of his air, to be Vivaldi; but, determined not to expose herself a second time to the possibility of a mistake, she awaited for some further signal of his identity, before she discovered herself. His eyes were fixed upon her in earnest attention for some moments, before he drew aside the cloak from his face. But he soon did so;—and it was Vivaldi himself.

Ellena, perceiving that she was known, did not raise her veil, but advanced a few steps towards the grate. Vivaldi there deposited a small folded paper, and before she could venture to deliver her own billet, he had retired among the crowd. As she stepped forward to secure his letter, she observed a nun hastily approach the spot where he had laid it, and she paused. The garment of the Recluse wafted it from the place where it had been partly concealed; and when Ellena perceived the nun's foot rest upon the paper, she with difficulty disguised her apprehensions.

A friar, who from without the grate addressed the sister, seemed with much earnestness, yet with a certain air of secrecy, communicating some important intelligence. The fears of Ellena suggested that he had observed the action of Vivaldi, and was making known his suspicions; and she expected, every instant, to see the nun lift up the paper, and deliver it to the Abbess.

From this immediate apprehension, however, she was released when the sister pushed it gently aside, without examination, a circumstance that not less surprized than relieved her. But, when the conference broke up, and the friar, hastily retreating among the crowd, disappeared from the apartment, and the nun approached and whispered the Superior, all her terrors were renewed. She scarcely doubted, that Vivaldi was detected, and that his letter was designedly left where it had been deposited, for the purpose of alluring her to betray herself. Trembling, dismayed, and almost sinking with apprehension, she watched the countenance of the Abbess, while the nun addressed her, and thought she read her own fate in the frown that appeared there.

Whatever might be the intentions or the directions of the Superior, no active measure was at present employed; the Recluse, having received an answer, retired quietly among the sisters, and the Abbess resumed her usual manner. Ellena, however, supposing she was now observed, did not dare to seize the paper, though she believed it contained momentous information, and feared that the time was now escaping, which might facilitate her deliverance. Whenever she ventured to look round, the eyes of the Abbess seemed pointed upon her, and she judged from the position of the nun, for the veil concealed her face, that she also was vigilantly regarding her.

Above an hour had elapsed in this state of anxious suspense, when the collation concluded, and the assembly broke up; during the general bustle of which, Ellena ventured to the grate, and secured the paper. As she concealed it in her robe, she scarcely dared to enquire by a hasty glance whether she had been observed, and would have withdrawn immediately to examine the contents, had she not perceived, at the same instant, the Abbess quitting the apartment. On looking round for the nun, Ellena discovered that she was gone.

Ellena followed distantly in the Abbess's train; and, as she drew nearer to Olivia, gave a signal, and passed on to her cell. There, once more alone, and having secured the door, she sat down to read Vivaldi's billet, trying to command her impatience, and to understand the lines, over which her sight rapidly moved, when in the eagerness of turning over the paper, the lamp dropt from her trembling hand and expired. Her distress now nearly reached despair. To go forth into the convent for a light was utterly impracticable, since it would betray that she was no longer a prisoner, and not only would Olivia suffer from a discovery of the indulgence she had granted, but she herself would be immediately confined. Her only hope rested upon Olivia's arrival before it might be too late to practice the instructions of Vivaldi, if, indeed, they were still practicable; and she listened with intense solicitude for an approaching footstep, while she yet held, ignorant of its contents, the billet, that probably would decide her fate. A thousand times she turned about the eventful paper, endeavoured to trace the lines with her fingers, and to guess their import, thus enveloped in mystery; while she experienced all the various torture that the consciousness of having in her very hand the information, on a timely knowledge of which her life, perhaps, depended, without being able to understand it, could inflict.

Presently she heard advancing steps, and a light gleamed from the passage before she considered they might be some other than Olivia's; and that it was prudent to conceal the billet she held. The consideration, however, came too late to be acted upon; for, before the rustling paper was disposed of, a person entered the cell, and Ellena beheld her friend. Pale, trembling, and silent, she took the lamp from the nun, and, eagerly running over Vivaldi's note, learned, that at the time it was written, brother Jeronimo was in waiting without the gate of the nun's garden, where Vivaldi designed to join him immediately, and conduct her by a private way beyond the walls. He added, that horses were stationed at the foot of the mountain, to convey her wherever she should judge proper; and conjured her to be expeditious, since other circumstances, besides the universal engagement of the Recluses, were at that moment particularly favourable to an escape.

Ellena, desponding and appalled, gave the paper to Olivia, requesting she would read it hastily, and advise her how to act. It was now an hour and a half since Vivaldi had said, that success depended upon expedition, and that he had probably watched at the appointed place; in such an interval, how many circumstances might have occurred to destroy every possibility of a retreat, which it was certain the engagement of the Abbess and the sisters no longer favoured!

The generous Olivia, having read the billet, partook of all her young friend's distress, and was as willing, as Ellena was anxious, to dare every danger for the chance of obtaining deliverance.

Ellena could feel gratitude for such goodness even at this moment of agonizing apprehension. After a pause of deep consideration, Olivia said, 'In every avenue of the convent we are now liable to meet some of the nuns; but my veil, though thin, has hitherto protected you, and we must hope it may still assist your purpose. It will be necessary, however, to pass through the refectory, where such of the sisters as did not partake of the collation, are assembled at supper, and will remain so, till the first mattin* calls them to the chapel. If we wait till then, I fear it will be to no purpose to go at all.'

Ellena's fears perfectly agreed with those of Olivia; and entreating that another moment might not be lost in hesitation, and that she would lead the way to the nun's garden, they quitted the cell together.

Several of the sisters passed them, as they descended to the refectory, but without particularly noticing Ellena; who, as she drew near that alarming apartment, wrapt her veil closer, and leaned with heavier pressure upon the arm of her faithful friend. At the door they were met by the Abbess, who had been overlooking the nuns assembled at supper, and missing Olivia had enquired for her. Ellena shrunk back to elude observation, and to let the Superior pass; but Olivia was obliged to answer to the summons. Having, however, unveiled herself, she was permitted to proceed; and Ellena, who had mingled with the crowd that surrounded the Abbess, and thus escaped detection, followed Olivia with faltering steps, through the refectory. The nuns were luckily too much engaged by the entertainment, at this moment, to look round them, and the fugitive reached, unsuspected, an opposite door.

In the hall, to which they descended, the adventurers were frequently crossed by servants bearing dishes from the refectory to the kitchen; and, at the very moment when they were opening the door, that led into the garden, a sister, who had observed them, demanded whether they had yet heard the mattin-bell, since they were going towards the chapel.

Terrified at this critical interruption, Ellena pressed Olivia's arm, in signal of silence, and was hastening forward, when the latter, more prudent, paused, and calmly answering the question, was then suffered to proceed.

As they crossed the garden towards the gate, Ellena's anxiety lest Vivaldi should have been compelled to leave it, encreased so much, that she had scarcely power to proceed. 'O if my strength should fail before I reach it!' she said softly to Olivia, 'or if I should reach it too late!'

Olivia tried to cheer her, and pointed out the gate, on which the moonlight fell; 'At the end of this walk only,' said Olivia, 'see!— where the shadows of the trees open, is our goal.'

Encouraged by the view of it, Ellena fled with lighter steps along the alley; but the gate seemed to mock her approach, and to retreat before her. Fatigue overtook her in this long alley, before she could overtake the spot so anxiously sought, and, breathless and exhausted, she was once more compelled to stop, and once more in the agony of terror exclaimed—'O, if my strength should fail before I reach it!—O, if I should drop even while it is within my view.'

The pause of a moment enabled her to proceed, and she stopped not again till she arrived at the gate; when Olivia suggested the prudence of ascertaining who was without, and of receiving an answer to the signal, which Vivaldi had proposed, before they ventured to make themselves known. She then struck upon the wood, and, in the anxious pause that followed, whispering voices were distinctly heard from without, but no signal spoke in reply to the nun's.

'We are betrayed!' said Ellena softly, 'but I will know the worst at once;' and she repeated the signal, when, to her unspeakable joy, it was answered by three smart raps upon the gate. Olivia, more distrustful, would have checked the sudden hope of her friend, till some further proof had appeared, that it was Vivaldi who waited without, but her precaution came too late; a key already grated in the lock; the door opened, and two persons muffled in their garments appeared at it. Ellena was hastily retreating, when a well-known voice recalled her, and she perceived, by the rays of a half-hooded lamp, which Jeronimo held, Vivaldi.

'O heavens!' he exclaimed, in a voice tremulous with joy, as he took her hand, 'is it possible that you are again my own! If you could but know what I have suffered during this last hour!'— Then observing Olivia, he drew back, till Ellena expressed her deep sense of obligation to the nun.

'We have no time to lose,' said Jeronimo sullenly; 'we have stayed too long already, as you will find, perhaps.'

'Farewel, dear Ellena!' said Olivia, 'may the protection of heaven never leave you!'

The fears of Ellena now gave way to affectionate sorrow, as, weeping on the bosom of the nun, she said 'farewel! O farewel, my dear, my tender friend! I must never, never see you more, but I shall always love you; and you have promised, that I shall hear from you; remember the convent della Pieta!'

'You should have settled this matter within,' said Jeronimo, 'we have been here these two hours already.'

'Ah Ellena!' said Vivaldi, as he gently disengaged her from the nun, 'do I then hold only the second place in your heart?'

Ellena, as she dismissed her tears, replied with a smile more eloquent than words; and when she had again and again bade adieu to Olivia, she gave him her hand, and quitted the gate.

'It is moonlight,' observed Vivaldi to Jeronimo, 'your lamp is useless, and may betray us.'

'It will be necessary in the church,' replied Jeronimo, 'and in some circuitous avenues we must pass, for I dare not lead you out through the great gates, Signor, as you well know.'

'Lead on, then,' replied Vivaldi, and they reached one of the cypress walks, that extended to the church; but, before they entered it, Ellena paused and looked back to the garden gate, that she might see Olivia once again. The nun was still there, and Ellena perceived her faintly in the moonlight, waving her hand in signal of a last adieu. Ellena's heart was full; she wept, and lingered, and returned the signal, till the gentle violence of Vivaldi withdrew her from the spot.

'I envy your friend those tears,' said he, 'and feel jealous of the tenderness that excites them. Weep no more, my Ellena.'

'If you knew her worth,' replied Ellena, 'and the obligations I owe her!'—Her voice was lost in sighs, and Vivaldi only pressed her hand in silence.

As they traversed the gloomy walk, that led to the church, Vivaldi said, 'Are you certain, father, that not any of the brothers are doing penance at the shrines in our way?'

'Doing penance on a festival, Signor! they are more likely, by this time, to be taking down the ornaments.'

'That would be equally unfortunate for us,' said Vivaldi; 'cannot we avoid the church, father?'

Jeronimo assured him, that this was impossible; and they immediately entered one of its lonely aisles, where he unhooded the lamp, for the tapers, which had given splendour, at an earlier hour, to the numerous shrines, had expired, except those at the high altar, which were so remote, that their rays faded into twilight long before they reached the part of the church where the fugitives passed. Here and there, indeed, a dying lamp shot a tremulous gleam upon the shrine below, and vanished again, serving to mark the distances in the long perspective of arches, rather than to enlighten the gloomy solitude; but no sound, not even of a whisper, stole along the pavement.

They crossed to a side door communicating with the court, and with the rock, which enshrined the image of *our Lady of mount Carmel*. There, the sudden glare of tapers issuing from the cave, alarmed the fugitives, who had begun to retreat, when Jeronimo, stepping forward to examine the place, assured them, there was no symptom of any person being within, and that lights burned day and night around the shrine.

Revived by this explanation, they followed into the cave, where their conductor opened a part of the wire-work enclosing the saint, and led them to the extremity of the vault, sunk deep within which appeared a small door. While Ellena trembled with apprehension, Jeronimo applied a key, and they perceived, beyond the door, a narrow passage winding away into the rock. The monk was leading on, but Vivaldi, who had the suspicions of Ellena, paused at the entrance, and demanded whither he was conducting them.

'To the place of your *destination*,' replied the brother, in a hollow voice; an answer which alarmed Ellena, and did not satisfy Vivaldi. 'I have given myself to your guidance,' he said, 'and have confided

to you what is dearer to me than existence. Your life,' pointing to
the short sword concealed beneath his pilgrim's vest, 'your life,
you may rely upon my word, shall answer for your treachery. If
your purpose is evil, pause a moment, and repent, or you shall not
quit this passage alive.'

'Do you menace me!' replied the brother, his countenance
darkening. 'Of what service would be my death to you? Do you
not know that every brother in the convent would rise to avenge it?'

'I know only that I will make sure of one traitor, if there be one,'
said Vivaldi, 'and defend this lady against your host of monks;
and, since you also know this, proceed accordingly.'

At this instant it occurring to Ellena, that the passage in question
probably led to the prison-chamber, which Olivia had described
as situated within some deep recess of the convent, and that
Jeronimo had certainly betrayed them, she refused to go further.
'If your purpose is honest,' said she, 'why do you not conduct us
through some direct gate of the convent; why are we brought into
these subterraneous labyrinths?'

'There is no direct gate but that of the portal,' Jeronimo replied,
'and this is the only other avenue leading beyond the walls.' 'And
why can we not go out through the portal?' Vivaldi asked.

'Because it is beset with pilgrims, and lay brothers,' replied
Jeronimo, 'and though you might pass them safely enough, what
is to become of the lady? But all this you knew before, Signor; and
was willing enough to trust me, then. The passage we are entering
opens upon the cliffs, at some distance. I have run hazard enough
already, and will waste no more time; so if you do not chuse to go
forward, I will leave you, and you may act as you please.'

He concluded with a laugh of derision, and was re-locking the
door, when Vivaldi, alarmed for the probable consequence of his
resentment, and somewhat re-assured by the indifference he discovered as to their pursuing the avenue or not, endeavoured to
appease him, as well as to encourage Ellena; and he succeeded
in both.

As he followed in silence through the gloomy passage, his
doubts were, however, not so wholly vanquished, but that he was
prepared for attack, and while he supported Ellena with one hand,
he held his sword in the other.

The avenue was of considerable length, and before they reached
its extremity, they heard music from a distance, winding along the
rocks. 'Hark!' cried Ellena, 'Whence come those sounds?
Listen!'

'From the cave we have left,' replied Jeronimo, 'and it is midnight by that; it is the last chaunt of the pilgrims at the shrine of our Lady. Make haste, Signor, I shall be called for.'

The fugitives now perceived, that all retreat was cut off, and that, if they had lingered only a few moments longer in the cave, they should have been surprized by those devotees, some one of whom, however, it appeared possible might wander into this avenue, and still interrupt their escape. When Vivaldi told his apprehensions, Jeronimo, with an arch sneer, affirmed there was no danger of that, 'for the passage,' he added, 'is known only to the brothers of the convent.'

Vivaldi's doubts vanished when he further understood, that the avenue led only from the cliffs without to the cave, and was used for the purpose of conveying secretly to the shrine, such articles as were judged necessary to excite the superstitious wonder of the devotees.

While he proceeded in thoughtful silence, a distant chime sounded hollowly through the chambers of the rock. 'The mattin-bell strikes!' said Jeronimo, in seeming alarm, 'I am summoned. Signora quicken your steps;' an unnecessary request for Ellena already passed with her utmost speed; and she now rejoiced on perceiving a door in the remote winding of the passage, which she believed would emancipate her from the convent. But, as she advanced, the avenue appeared extending beyond it; and the door, which stood a little open allowed her a glimpse of a chamber in the cliff, duskily lighted.

Vivaldi, alarmed by the light, enquired, when he had passed, whether any person was in the chamber, and received an equivocal answer from Jeronimo, who, however, soon after pointed to an arched gate that terminated the avenue. They proceeded with lighter steps, for hope now cheared their hearts, and, on reaching the gate, all apprehension vanished. Jeronimo gave the lamp to Vivaldi, while he began to unbar and unlock the door, and Vivaldi had prepared to reward the brother for his fidelity, before they perceived that the door refused to yield. A dreadful imagination seized on Vivaldi. Jeronimo turning round, coolly said, 'I fear we are betrayed; the second lock is shot! I have only the key of the first.'

'We *are* betrayed,' said Vivaldi, in a resolute tone, 'but do not suppose, that your dissimulation conceals you. I understand by whom we are betrayed. Recollect my late assertion, and consider once more, whether it is your interest to intercept us.'

'My Signor,' replied Jeronimo, 'I do not deceive you when I

protest by our holy Saint, that I have not caused this gate to be fastened, and that I would open it if I could. The lock, which holds it, was not shot an hour ago. I am the more surprized at what has happened, because this place is seldom passed, even by the holiest footstep; and I fear, whoever has passed now, has been led hither by suspicion, and comes to intercept your flight.'

'Your wily explanation, brother, may serve you for an inferior occasion, but not on this,' replied Vivaldi, 'either, therefore, unclose the gate, or prepare for the worst. You are not now to learn,* that, however slightly I may estimate my own life, I will never abandon this lady 'to the horrors, which your community have already prepared for her.'

Ellena, summoning her fleeting spirits, endeavoured to calm the indignation of Vivaldi, and to prevent the consequence of his suspicions, as well as to prevail with Jeronimo, to unfasten the gate. Her efforts were, however, followed by a long altercation; but, at length, the art or the innocence of the brother, appeased Vivaldi, who now endeavoured to force the gate, while Jeronimo in vain represented its strength, and the certain ruin, that must fall upon himself, if it should be discovered he had concurred in destroying it.

The gate was immoveable; but, as no other chance of escaping appeared, Vivaldi was not easily prevailed with to desist; all possibility of retreating too was gone, since the church and the cave were now crowded with devotees, attending the mattin service.

Jeronimo, however, seemingly did not despair of effecting their release, but he acknowledged that they would probably be compelled to remain concealed in this gloomy avenue all night, and perhaps the next day. At length, it was agreed, that he should return to the church, to examine whether a possibility remained of the fugitives passing unobserved to the great portal; and, having conducted them back to the chamber, of which they had taken a passing glimpse, he proceeded to the shrine.

For a considerable time after his departure, they were not without hope; but, their confidence diminishing as his delay encreased, their uncertainty at length became terrible; and it was only for the sake of Vivaldi, from whom she scrupulously concealed all knowledge of the particular fate, which she was aware must await her in the convent, that Ellena appeared to endure it with calmness. Notwithstanding the plausibility of Jeronimo, suspicion of his treachery returned upon her mind. The cold and earthy air of this chamber was like that of a sepulchre; and when she looked round, it appeared exactly to correspond with the description given by Olivia of the prison where the nun had languished and expired. It was walled and vaulted with the rock, had only one small grated aperture in the roof to admit air, and contained no furniture, except one table, a bench, and the lamp, which dimly shewed the apartment. That a lamp should be found burning in a place so remote and solitary, amazed her still more when she recollected the assertion of Jeronimo,—that even holy steps seldom passed this way; and when she considered also, that he had expressed no surprize at a circumstance, according to his own assertion, so unusual. Again it appeared, that she had been betrayed into the very prison, designed for her by the Abbess; and the horror, occasioned by this supposition, was so great, that she was on the point of disclosing it to Vivaldi, but an apprehension of the distraction, into which his desperate courage might precipitate him, restrained her.

While these considerations occupied Ellena, and it appeared that any certainty would be less painful than this suspense, she frequently looked round the chamber in search of some object, which might contradict or confirm her suspicion, that this was the death-room of the unfortunate nun. No such circumstance appeared, but as her eyes glanced, with almost phrenzied eagerness, she perceived something shadowy in a remote corner of the floor; and on approaching, discovered what seemed a dreadful hieroglyphic, a mattrass of straw, in which she thought she beheld the death-bed of the miserable recluse; nay more, that the impression it still retained, was that which her form had left there.

While Vivaldi was yet entreating her to explain the occasion of the horror she betrayed, the attention of each was withdrawn by a hollow sigh, that rose near them. Ellena caught unconsciously the arm of Vivaldi, and listened, aghast, for a return of the sound, but all remained still.

'It surely was not fancied!' said Vivaldi, after a long pause, 'you heard it also?'

'I did!' replied Ellena.

'It was a sigh, was it not?' he added.

'O yes, and such a sigh!'

'Some person is concealed near us,' observed Vivaldi, looking round; 'but be not alarmed, Ellena, I have a sword.'

'A sword! alas! you know not——But hark! there, again!'

'That was very near us!' said Vivaldi. 'This lamp burns so sickly!'——and he held it high, endeavouring to penetrate the furthest gloom of the chamber. 'Hah! who goes there?' he cried, and stepped suddenly forward; but no person appeared, and a silence as of the tomb, returned.

'If you are in sorrow, speak!' Vivaldi, at length, said; 'from fellow-sufferers you will meet with sympathy. If your designs are evil—tremble, for you shall find I am desperate.'

Still no answer was returned, and he carried forward the lamp to the opposite end of the chamber, where he perceived a small door in the rock. At the same instant he heard from within, a low tremulous sound, as of a person in prayer, or in agony. He pressed against the door, which, to his surprise, yielded immediately, and discovered a figure kneeling before a crucifix, with an attention so wholly engaged, as not to observe the presence of a stranger, till Vivaldi spoke. The person then rose from his knees, and turning, shewed the silvered temples and pale features of an aged monk. The mild and sorrowful character of the countenance, and the lambent lustre of eyes, which seemed still to retain somewhat of the fire of genius, interested Vivaldi, and encouraged Ellena, who had followed him.

An unaffected surprize appeared in the air of the monk; but Vivaldi, notwithstanding the interesting benignity of his countenance, feared to answer his enquiries, till the father hinted to him, that an explanation was necessary, even to his own safety. Encouraged by his manner, rather than intimidated by this hint, and perceiving, that his situation was desperate, Vivaldi confided to the friar some partial knowledge of his embarrassment.

While he spoke, the father listened with deep attention, looked with compassion alternately upon him and Ellena; and some harassing objection seemed to contend with the pity, which urged him to assist the strangers. He enquired how long Jeronimo had been absent, and shook his head significantly when he learned that the gate of the avenue was fastened by a double lock. 'You are betrayed, my children,' said he, 'you have trusted with the simplicity of youth, and the cunning of age has deceived you.'

The terrible conviction affected Ellena to tears; and Vivaldi, scarcely able to command the indignation which a view of such treachery excited, was unable to offer her any consolation.

'You, my daughter, I remember to have seen in the church this morning,' observed the friar; 'I remember too, that you protested against the vows you were brought thither to seal. Alas! my child, was you aware of the consequence of such a proceeding?'

'I had only a choice of evils,' Ellena replied.

'Holy father,' said Vivaldi, 'I will not believe, that you are one of those who either assisted in or approved the persecution of innocence. If you were acquainted with the misfortunes of this lady, you would pity, and save her; but there is now no time for detail; and I can only conjure you, by every sacred consideration, to assist her to leave the convent! If there were leisure to inform you of the unjustifiable means, which have been employed to bring her within these walls—if you knew that she was taken, an orphan, from her home at midnight—that armed ruffians brought her hither—and at the command of strangers—that she has not a single relation surviving to assert her right of independence, or reclaim her of her persecutors.——O! holy father, if you knew all this!'——Vivaldi was unable to proceed.

The friar again regarded Ellena with compassion, but still in thoughtful silence. 'All this may be very true,' at length he said, 'but'——and he hesitated.

'I understand you, father,' said Vivaldi—'you require proof; but how can proof be adduced here? You must rely upon the honour of my word. And, if you are inclined to assist us, it must be immediately!—while you hesitate, we are lost. Even now I think I hear the footsteps of Jeronimo.'

He stepped softly to the door of the chamber, but all was yet still. The friar, too, listened, but he also deliberated; while Ellena, with clasped hands and a look of eager supplication and terror, awaited his decision.

'No one is approaching,' said Vivaldi, 'it is not yet too late!— Good father! if you would serve us, dispatch.'

'Poor innocent!' said the friar, half to himself, 'in this chamber— in this fatal place!'—

'In this chamber!' exclaimed Ellena, anticipating his meaning. 'It was in this chamber, then, that a nun was suffered to perish! and I, no doubt, am conducted hither to undergo a similar fate!'

'In this chamber!' re-echoed Vivaldi, in a voice of desperation. 'Holy father, if you are indeed disposed to assist us, let us act this instant; the next, perhaps, may render your best intentions unavailing!'

The friar, who had regarded Ellena while she mentioned the nun, with the utmost surprize, now withdrew his attention; a few tears fell on his cheek, but he hastily dried them, and seemed struggling to overcome some grief, that was deep in his heart.

Vivaldi, finding that entreaty had no power to hasten his decision, and expecting every moment to hear the approach of

Jeronimo, paced the chamber in agonizing perturbation, now pausing at the door to listen, and then calling, though almost hopelessly, upon the humanity of the friar. While Ellena, looking round the room in shuddering horror, repeatedly exclaimed, 'On this very spot! in this very chamber! O what sufferings have these walls witnessed! what are they yet to witness!'

Vivaldi now endeavoured to soothe the spirits of Ellena, and again urged the friar to employ this critical moment in saving her; 'O heaven!' said he, 'if she is now discovered, her fate is certain!'

'I dare not say what that fate would be,' interrupted the father, 'or what my own, should I consent to assist you; but, though I am old, I have not quite forgotten to feel for others! They may oppress the few remaining years of my age, but the blooming days of youth should flourish; and they shall flourish, my children, if my power can aid you. Follow me to the gate; we will see whether my key cannot unfasten all the locks that hold it.'

Vivaldi and Ellena immediately followed the feeble steps of the old man, who frequently stopped to listen whether Jeronimo, or any of the brothers, to whom the latter might have betrayed Ellena's situation, were approaching; but not an echo wandered along the lonely avenue, till they reached the gate, when distant footsteps beat upon the ground.

'They are approaching, father!' whispered Ellena. 'O, if the key should not open these locks instantly, we are lost! Hark! now I hear their voices—they call upon my name! Already they have discovered we have left the chamber.'

While the friar, with trembling hands, applied the key, Vivaldi endeavoured at once to assist him, and to encourage Ellena.

The locks gave way, and the gate opened at once upon the moonlight mountains. Ellena heard once more, with the joy of liberty, the midnight breeze passing among the pensile* branches of the palms, that loftily overshadowed a rude platform before the gate, and rustling with fainter sound among the pendent shrubs of the surrounding cliffs.

'There is no leisure for thanks, my children,' said the friar, observing they were about to speak. 'I will fasten the gate, and endeavour to delay your pursuers, that you may have time to escape. My blessing go with you!'

Ellena and Vivaldi had scarcely a moment to bid him 'farewel!' before he closed the door, and Vivaldi, taking her arm, was hastening towards the place where he had ordered Paulo to wait with the horses, when, on turning an angle of the convent wall, they perceived a long train of pilgrims issuing forth from the portal, at a little distance.

Vivaldi drew back; yet dreading every moment, that he lingered near the monastery, to hear the voice of Jeronimo, or other persons, from the avenue, he was sometimes inclined to proceed at any hazard. The only practicable path leading to the base of the mountain, however, was now occupied by these devotees, and to mingle with them was little less than certain destruction. A bright moonlight shewed distinctly every figure, that moved in the scene, and the fugitives kept within the shadow of the walls, till, warned by an approaching footstep, they crossed to the feet of the cliffs that rose beyond some palmy hillocks on the right, whose dusky recesses promised a temporary shelter. As they passed with silent steps along the winding rocks, the tranquillity of the landscape below afforded an affecting contrast with the tumult and alarm of their minds.

Being now at some distance from the monastery, they rested under the shade of the cliffs, till the procession of devotees, which were traced descending among the thickets and hollows of the mountain, should be sufficiently remote. Often they looked back to the convent, expecting to see lights issue from the avenue, or the portal; and attended in mute anxiety for the sullen murmurs of pursuit; but none came on the breeze; nor did any gleaming lamp betray the steps of a spy.

Released, at length, from immediate apprehension, Ellena listened to the mattin-hymn of the pilgrims, as it came upon the still air and ascended towards the cloudless heavens. Not a sound mingled with the holy strain, and even in the measured pause of voices only the trembling of the foliage above was distinguished. The responses, as they softened away in distance, and swelled again on the wafting breeze, appeared like the music of spirits, watching by night upon the summits of the mountains, and answering each other in celestial airs, as they walk their high boundary, and overlook the sleeping world.

'How often, Ellena, at this hour,' said Vivaldi, 'have I lingered round your dwelling, consoled by the consciousness of being near you! Within those walls, I have said, she reposes; they enclose my world, all without is to me a desart. Now, I am in your presence! O Ellena! now that you are once more restored to me, suffer not the caprice of possibility again to separate us! Let me lead you to the first altar that will confirm our vows.'

Vivaldi forgot, in the anxiety of a stronger interest, the delicate silence he had resolved to impose upon himself, till Ellena should be in a place of safety.

'This is not a moment,' she replied, with hesitation, 'for conversation; our situation is yet perilous, we tremble on the very brink of danger.'

Vivaldi immediately rose; 'Into what imminent danger,' said he, 'had my selfish folly nearly precipitated you! We are lingering in this alarming neighbourhood, when that feeble strain indicates the pilgrims to be sufficiently remote to permit us to proceed!'

As he spoke, they descended cautiously among the cliffs, often looking back to the convent, where, however, no light appeared, except what the moon shed over the spires and tall windows of its cathedral. For a moment, Ellena fancied she saw a taper in her favourite turret, and a belief, that the nuns, perhaps the Abbess herself, were searching for her there, renewed her terror and her speed. But the rays were only those of the moon, striking through opposite casements of the chamber; and the fugitives reached the base of the mountain without further alarm, where Paulo appeared with horses. 'Ah! Signormio,' said the servant, 'I am glad to see you alive and merry; I began to fear, by the length of your stay, that the monks had clapped you up to do penance for life. How glad I am to see you Maéstro!'

'Not more so than I am to see you, good Paulo. But where is the pilgrim's cloak I bade you provide?'

Paulo displayed it, and Vivaldi, having wrapt it round Ellena, and placed her on horseback, they took the road towards Naples, Ellena designing to take refuge in the convent della Pieta. Vivaldi, however, apprehending that their enemies would seek them on this road, proposed leaving it as soon as practicable, and reaching the neighbourhood of Villa Altieri by a circuitous way.

They soon after arrived at the tremendous pass, through which Ellena had approached the monastery, and whose horrors were considerably heightened at this dusky hour, for the moonlight fell only partially upon the deep barriers of the gorge, and frequently the precipice, with the road on its brow, was entirely shadowed by other cliffs and woody points that rose above it. But Paulo, whose spirits seldom owned the influence of local scenery, jogged merrily along, frequently congratulating himself and his master on their escape, and carolling briskly to the echoes of the rocks, till Vivaldi, apprehensive for the consequence of this loud gaiety, desired him to desist.

'Ah Signormio! I must obey you,' said he, 'but my heart was

never so full in my life; and I would fain sing, to unburden it of some of this joy. That scrape we got into in the dungeon there, at what's the name of the place? was bad enough, but it was nothing to this, because here I was left out of it; and you, *Maestro*, might have been murdered again and again, while I, thinking of nothing at all, was quietly airing myself on the mountain by moonlight.

But what is that yonder in the sky, Signor? It looks for all the world like a bridge; only it is perched so high, that nobody would think of building one in such an out-of-the-way place, unless to cross from cloud to cloud, much less would take the trouble of clambering up after it, for the pleasure of going over.'

Vivaldi looked forward, and Ellena perceived the Alpine bridge, she had formerly crossed with so much alarm, in the moonlight perspective, airily suspended between tremendous cliffs, with the river far below, tumbling down the rocky chasm. One of the supporting cliffs, with part of the bridge, was in deep shade, but the other, feathered with foliage, and the rising surges at its foot, were strongly illumined; and many a thicket wet with the spray, sparkled in contrast to the dark rock it overhung. Beyond the arch, the long-drawn prospect faded into misty light.

'Well, to be sure!' exclaimed Paulo, 'to see what curiosity will do! If there are not some people have found their way up to the bridge already.'

Vivaldi now perceived figures upon the slender arch, and, as their indistinct forms glided in the moonshine, other emotions than those of wonder disturbed him, lest these might be pilgrims going to the shrine of our Lady, and who would give information of his route. No possibility, however, appeared of avoiding them, for the precipices that rose immediately above, and fell below, forbade all excursion, and the road itself was so narrow, as scarcely to admit of two horses passing each other.

'They are all off the bridge now, and without having broken their necks, perhaps!' said Paulo, 'where, I wonder, will they go next! Why surely, Signor, this road does not lead to the bridge yonder; we are not going to pick our way in the air too? The roar of those waters has made my head dizzy already; and the rocks here are as dark as midnight, and seem ready to tumble upon one; they are enough to make one despair to look at them; you need not have checked my mirth, Signor.'

'I would fain check your loquacity,' replied Vivaldi. 'Do, good Paulo, be silent and circumspect, those people may be near us, though we do not yet see them.'

'The road does lead to the bridge, then, Signor!' said Paulo dolourously. 'And see! there they are again; winding round that rock, and coming towards us.'

'Hush! they are pilgrims,' whispered Vivaldi, 'we will linger under the shade of these rocks, while they pass. Remember, Paulo, that a single indiscreet word may be fatal; and that if they hail us, I alone am to answer.'

'You are obeyed, Signor.'

The fugitives drew up close under the cliffs, and proceeded slowly, while the words of the devotees, as they advanced, became audible.

'It gives one some comfort,' said Paulo, 'to hear cheerful voices, in such a place as this. Bless their merry hearts! theirs seems a pilgrimage of pleasure; but they will be demure enough, I warrant, by and bye. I wish I'——

'Paulo! have you so soon forgot?' said Vivaldi sharply.

The devotees, on perceiving the travellers, became suddenly silent; till he who appeared to be the *Father-director*, as they passed, said 'Hail! in the name of *Our Lady of Mount Carmel!*' and they repeated the salutation in chorus.

'Hail!' replied Vivaldi, 'the first mass is over,' and he passed on.

'But if you make haste, you may come in for the second,' said Paulo, jogging after.

'You have just left the shrine, then?' said one of the party, 'and can tell us'—

'Poor pilgrims, like yourselves,' replied Paulo, 'and can tell as little. Good morrow, fathers, yonder peeps the dawn!'

He came up with his master, who had hurried forward with Ellena, and who now severely reproved his indiscretion; while the voices of the Carmelites, singing the mattin-hymn, sunk away among the rocks, and the quietness of solitude returned.

'Thank heaven! we are quit of this adventure,' said Vivaldi.

'And now we have only the bridge to get over,' rejoined Paulo, 'and, I hope, we shall all be safe.'

They were now at the entrance of it; as they passed the trembling planks, and looked up the glen, a party of people appeared advancing on the road the fugitives had left, and a chorus of other voices than those of the Carmelites, were heard mingling with the hollow sound of the waters.

Ellena, again alarmed, hastened forward, and Vivaldi, though he endeavoured to appease her apprehension of pursuit, encouraged her speed.

'These are nothing but more pilgrims Signora,' said Paulo, 'or they would not send such loud shouts before them; they must needs think we can hear.'

The travellers proceeded as fast as the broken road would permit; and were soon beyond the reach of the voices; but as Paulo turned to look whether the party was within sight, he perceived two persons, wrapt in cloaks, advancing under the brow of the cliffs, and within a few paces of his horse's heels. Before he could give notice to his master, they were at his side.

'Are you returning from the shrine of *our Lady*?' said one of them.

Vivaldi, startled by the voice, looked round, and demanded who asked the question?

'A brother pilgrim,' replied the man, 'one who has toiled up these steep rocks, till his limbs will scarcely bear him further. Would that you would take compassion on him, and give him a ride.'

However compassionate Vivaldi might be to the sufferings of others, this was not a moment when he could indulge his disposition, without endangering the safety of Ellena; and he even fancied the stranger spoke in a voice of dissimulation. His suspicions strengthened when the traveller, not repulsed by a refusal, enquired the way he was going, and proposed to join his party; 'For these mountains, they say, are infested with banditti,' he added, 'and a large company is less likely to be attacked than a small one.'

'If you are so very weary, my friend,' said Vivaldi, 'how is it possible you can keep pace with our horses? though I acknowledge you have done wonders in overtaking them.'

'The fear of these banditti,' replied the stranger, 'urged us on.'

'You have nothing to apprehend from robbers,' said Vivaldi, 'if you will only moderate your pace; for a large company of pilgrims are on the road, who will soon overtake you.'

He then put an end to the conversation, by clapping spurs to his horse, and the strangers were soon left far behind. The inconsistency of their complaints with their ability, and the whole of their manner, were serious subjects of alarm to the fugitives; but when they had lost sight of them, they lost also their apprehensions; and having, at length, emerged from the pass, they quitted the high road to Naples, and struck into a solitary one that led westward towards Aquila.

CHAPTER II

Thus sang th' unletter'd Swain to th' oaks and rills,
While the still morn went forth with sandals gray,
And now the sun had stretch'd out all the hills,
And now was dropt into the western bay.——

MILTON*

FROM the summit of a mountain, the morning light shewed the travellers the distant lake of Celano, gleaming at the feet of other lofty mountains of the Appennine, far in the south. Thither Vivaldi judged it prudent to direct his course, for the lake lay so remote from the immediate way to Naples, and from the neighbourhood of San Stefano, that it's banks promised a secure retreat. He considered, also, that among the convents scattered along those delightful banks, might easily be found a priest, who would solemnize their nuptials, should Ellena consent to an immediate marriage.

The travellers descended among olive woods, and soon after were directed by some peasants at work, into a road that leads from Aquila to the town of Celano, one of the very few roads which intrudes among the wild mountains, that on every side sequester the lake. As they approached the low grounds, the scent of orange blossoms breathed upon the morning air, and the spicy myrtle sent forth all its fragrance from among the cliffs, which it thickly tufted. Bowers of lemon and orange spread along the valley; and among the cabins of the peasants, who cultivated them, Vivaldi hoped to obtain repose and refreshment for Ellena.

The cottages, however, at which Paulo enquired were unoccupied, the owners being all gone forth to their labour: and the travellers, again ascending, found themselves soon after among mountains inhabited by the flocks, where the scent of the orange was exchanged for the aromatic perfume of the pasturage.

'My Signor!' said Paulo, 'is not that a shepherd's horn sounding at a distance? If so, the Signora may yet obtain some refreshment.'

While Vivaldi listened, a hautboy and a pastoral drum were heard considerably nearer.

They followed the sound over the turf, and came within view

of a cabin, sheltered from the sun by a tuft of almond trees. It was a dairy-cabin belonging to some shepherds, who at a short distance were watching their flocks, and, stretched beneath the shade of chestnuts, were amusing themselves by playing upon these rural instruments; a scene of Arcadian manners* frequent at this day, upon the mountains of Abruzzo. The simplicity of their appearance, approaching to wildness, was tempered by a hospitable spirit. A venerable man, the chief shepherd, advanced to meet the strangers; and, learning their wants, conducted them into his cool cabin, where cream, cheese made of goat's milk, honey extracted from the delicious herbage of the mountains, and dried figs were quickly placed before them.

Ellena, overcome with the fatigue of anxiety, rather than that of travelling, retired, when she had taken breakfast, for an hour's repose; while Vivaldi rested on the bench before the cottage, and Paulo, keeping watch, discussed his breakfast, together with the circumstances of the late alarm, under the shade of the almond trees.

When Ellena again appeared, Vivaldi proposed, that they should rest here during the intense heat of the day; and, since he now considered her to be in a place of temporary safety, he ventured to renew the subject nearest his heart; to represent the evils, that might overtake them, and to urge an immediate solemnization of their marriage.

Thoughtful and dejected, Ellena attended for some time in silence to the arguments and pleadings of Vivaldi. She secretly acknowledged the justness of his representations, but she shrunk, more than ever, from the indelicacy, the degradation of intruding herself into his family; a family, too, from whom she had not only received proofs of strong dislike, but had suffered terrible injustice, and been menaced with still severer cruelty. These latter circumstances, however, released her from all obligations of delicacy or generosity, so far as concerned only the authors of her suffering; and she had now but to consider the happiness of Vivaldi and herself. Yet she could not decide thus precipitately on a subject, which so solemnly involved the fortune of her whole life; nor forbear reminding Vivaldi, affectionately, gratefully, as she loved him, of the circumstances which with-held her decision.

'Tell me yourself,' said she, 'whether I ought to give my hand, while your family—your mother'——She paused, and blushed, and burst into tears.

'Spare me the view of those tears,' said Vivaldi, 'and a recollection of the circumstances that excite them. O, let me not think of my mother, while I see you weep! Let me not remember, that her injustice and cruelty destined you to perpetual sorrow!'

Vivaldi's features became slightly convulsed, while he spoke; he rose, paced the room with quick steps, and then quitted it, and walked under the shade of the trees in front of the cabin.

In a few moments, however, he commanded his emotion and returned. Again he placed himself on the bench beside Ellena, and taking her hand, said solemnly, and in a voice of extreme sensibility, 'Ellena, you have long witnessed how dear you are to me; you cannot doubt my love; you have long since promised— solemnly promised, in the presence of her who is now no more, but whose spirit may even at this moment look down upon us,— of her, who bequeathed you to my tenderest care, to be mine for ever. By these sacred truths, by these affecting recollections! I conjure you, abandon me not to despair, nor in the energy of a just resentment, sacrifice the son to the cruel and mistaken policy of the mother! You, nor I, can conjecture the machinations, which may be spread for us, when it shall be known that you have left San Stefano. If we delay to exchange our vows, I know, and I feel— that you are lost to me for ever!'

Ellena was affected, and for some moments unable to reply. At length, drying her tears, she said tenderly, 'Resentment can have no influence on my conduct towards you; I think I feel none towards the Marchesa—for she is your mother. But pride, insulted pride, has a right to dictate, and ought to be obeyed; and the time is now, perhaps, arrived when, if I would respect myself, I must renounce you.'——

'Renounce me!' interrupted Vivaldi, 'renounce me! And is it, then, possible you could renounce me?' he repeated, his eyes still fixed upon her face with eagerness and consternation. 'Tell me at once, Ellena, is it possible?'

'I fear it is not,' she replied.

'You fear! alas! if you *fear*, it is too possible, and I have lost you already! Say, O! say but, that you *hope* it is not, and I, too, will hope again.'

The anguish, with which he uttered this, awakened all her tenderness, and, forgetting the reserve she had imposed upon herself, and every half-formed resolution, she said, with a smile of ineffable sweetness, 'I will neither fear nor hope in this instance; I will obey the dictates of gratitude, of affection, and will *believe* that I never can renounce you, while you are unchanged.'

'Believe!' repeated Vivaldi, 'only believe! And why that mention of gratitude; and why that unnecessary reservation? Yet even this assurance, feebly as it sustains my hopes, is extorted; you see my misery, and from pity, from *gratitude*, not affection, would assuage it. Besides, you will neither fear, nor hope! Ah, Ellena! did love ever yet exist without fear—and without hope? O! never, never! I fear and hope with such rapid transition; every assurance, every look of yours gives such force either to the one, or to the other, that I suffer unceasing anxiety. Why, too, that cold, that heart-breaking mention of gratitude? No, Ellena! it is too certain that you do not love me!—My mother's cruelty has estranged your heart from me!'

'How much you mistake!' said Ellena. 'You have already received sacred testimonies of my regard; if you doubt their sincerity, pardon me, if I so far respect myself as to forbear entreating you will believe them.'

'How calm, how indifferent, how circumspect, how prudent!' exclaimed Vivaldi in tones of mournful reproach. 'But I will not distress you; forgive me for renewing this subject at this time. It was my intention to be silent till you should have reached a place of more permanent security than this; but how was it possible, with such anxiety pressing upon my heart, to persevere in that design. And what have I gained by departing from it?—increase of anxiety—of doubt—of fear!'

'Why will you persist in such self-inflictions?' said Ellena. 'I cannot endure that you should doubt my affection, even for a moment. And how can you suppose it possible, that I ever can become insensible of your's; that I can ever forget the imminent danger you have voluntarily incurred for my release, or, remembering it, can cease to feel the warmest gratitude?'

'That is the very word which tortures me beyond all others!' said Vivaldi; 'is it then, only a sense of obligation you own for me? O! rather say you hate me, than suffer me to deceive my hopes with assurances of a sentiment so cold, so circumscribed, so dutiful as that of gratitude!'

'With me the word has a very different acceptation,' replied Ellena smiling. 'I understand it to imply all that is tender and generous in affection; and the sense of duty which you say it includes, is one of the sweetest and most sacred feelings of the human heart.'

'Ah Ellena! I am too willing to be deceived, to examine your definition rigorously; yet I believe it is your smile, rather than the accuracy of your explanation, that persuades me to a confidence in your affection; and I will trust, that the gratitude *you* feel is thus tender and comprehensive. But, I beseech you, name the word no more! Its sound is like the touch of the Torpedo,* I perceive my confidence chilled even while I listen to my own pronunciation of it.'

The entrance of Paulo interrupted the conversation, who advancing with an air of mystery and alarm, said in a low voice,

'Signor! as I kept watch under the almond trees, who should I see mounting up the road from the valley yonder, but the two barefooted Carmelites, that overtook us in the pass of Chiari! I lost them again behind the woods, but I dare say they are coming this way, for the moment they spy out this dairy-hut, they will guess something good is to be had here; and the shepherds would believe their flocks would all die, if'——

'I see them at this moment emerging from the woods,' said Vivaldi, 'and now, they are leaving the road and crossing this way. Where is our host, Paulo!'

'He is without, at a little distance, Signor. Shall I call him?'

'Yes,' replied Vivaldi, 'or, stay; I will call him myself. Yet, if they see me'——

'Aye, Signor; or, for that matter, if they see me. But we cannot help ourselves now; for if we call the host, we shall betray ourselves, and, if we do not call him, he will betray us; so they must find us out, be it as it may.'

'Peace! peace! let me think a moment,' said Vivaldi. While Vivaldi undertook to think, Paulo was peeping about for a hiding place, if occasion should require one.

'Call our host immediately,' said Vivaldi, 'I must speak with him.'

'He passes the lattice at this instant,' said Ellena.

Paulo obeyed, and the shepherd entered the cabin.

'My good friend,' said Vivaldi, 'I must entreat that you will not admit those friars, whom you see coming this way, nor suffer them to know what guests you have. They have been very troublesome to us already, on the road; I will reward you for any loss their sudden departure may occasion you.'

'Nay for that matter, friend,' said Paulo, 'it is their visit only that can occasion you loss, begging the Signor's pardon; their departure never occasioned loss to any body. And to tell you the truth, for my master will not speak out, we were obliged to look pretty sharply about us, while they bore us company, or we have reason to think our pockets would have been the lighter. They are designing people, friend, take my word for it; banditti, perhaps, in disguise. The dress of a Carmelite would suit their purpose, at this time of the pilgrimage. So be pretty blunt with them, if they want to come in here; and you will do well, when they go, to send somebody to watch which way they take, and see them clear off, or you may lose a stray lamb, perhaps.'

The old shepherd lifted up his eyes and hands, 'To see how the world goes!' said he. 'But thank you, Maestro, for your warning; they shall not come within my threshold, for all their holy seeming, and it's the first time in my life I ever said nay to one of their garb, and mine has been a pretty long one, as you may guess, perhaps, by my face. How old, Signor, should you take me to be? I warrant you will guess short of the matter tho'; for on these high mountains'——

'I will guess when you have dismissed the travellers,' said Vivaldi, 'after having given them some hasty refreshment without; they must be almost at the door, by this time. Dispatch, friend.'

'If they should fall foul upon me, for refusing them entrance,' said the shepherd, 'you will come out to help me, Signor? for my lads are at some distance.'

Vivaldi assured him that they would, and he left the cabin.

Paulo ventured to peep at the lattice, on what might be going forward without. 'They are gone round to the door, Signor, I fancy,' said he, 'for I see nothing of them this way; if there was but another window! What foolish people to build a cottage with no window near the door! But I must listen.'

He stepped on tip-toe to the door, and bent his head in attention.

'They are certainly spies from the monastery,' said Ellena to Vivaldi, 'they follow us so closely! If they were pilgrims, it is improbable, too, that their way should lie through this unfrequented region, and still more so, that they should not travel in a larger party. When my absence was discovered, these people were sent, no doubt, in pursuit of me, and having met the devotees whom we passed, they were enabled to follow our route.'

'We shall do well to act upon this supposition,' replied Vivaldi, 'but, though I am inclined to believe them emissaries from San Stefano, it is not improbable that they are only Carmelites returning to some convent on the lake of Celano.'

'I cannot hear a syllable, Signor,' said Paulo. 'Pray do listen yourself! and there is not a single chink in this door to afford one consolation. Well! if ever I build a cottage, there shall be a window near——'

'Listen!' said Vivaldi.

'Not a single word, Signor!' cried Paulo, after a pause, 'I do not even hear a voice!—But now I hear steps, and they are coming to the door, too; they shall find it no easy matter to open it, though;' he added, placing himself against it. 'Ay, ay, you may knock, friend, till your arm aches, and kick and lay about you—no matter for that.'

'Silence! let us know who it is,' said Vivaldi; and the old shepherd's voice was heard without. 'They are gone, Signors,' said he, 'you may open the door.'

'Which way did they go?' asked Vivaldi, when the man entered. 'I cannot say, as to that, Signor, because I did not happen to see them at all; and I have been looking all about, too.'

'Why, I saw them myself, crossing this way from the wood yonder,' said Paulo.

'And there is nothing to shelter them from our view between the wood, and this cottage, friend,' added Vivaldi; 'What can they have done with themselves?'

'For that matter, gone into the wood again, perhaps,' said the shepherd.

Paulo gave his master a significant look, and added, 'It is likely enough, friend; and you may depend upon it they are lurking there for no good purpose. You will do well to send somebody to look after them; your flocks will suffer for it, else. Depend upon it, they design no good.'

'We are not used to such sort of folks in these parts,' replied the shepherd, 'but if they mean any harm, they shall find we can help ourselves.' As he concluded, he took down a horn from the roof, and blew a shrill blast that made the mountains echo; when immediately the younger shepherds were seen running from various quarters towards the cottage.

'Do not be alarmed, friend;' said Vivaldi, 'these travellers mean you no harm, I dare say, whatever they may design against us. But, as I think them suspicious persons, and should not like to overtake them on the road, I will reward one of your lads if you will let him go a little ways towards Celano, and examine whether they are lurking on that route.'

The old man consented, and, when the shepherds came up, one of them received directions from Vivaldi.

'And be sure you do not return, till you have found them,' added Paulo.

'No master,' replied the lad, 'and I will bring them safe here, you may trust me.'

'If you do, friend, you will get your head broke for your trouble. You are only to discover where they are, and to watch where they go,' said Paulo.

Vivaldi, at length, made the lad comprehend what was required of him, and he departed; while the old shepherd went out to keep guard.

The time of his absence was passed in various conjectures by the party in the cabin, concerning the Carmelites. Vivaldi still inclined to believe they were honest people returning from a pilgrimage, but Paulo was decidedly against this opinion. 'They are waiting for us on the road, you may depend upon it, Signor,' said the latter. 'You may be certain they have some *great design* in hand, or they would never have turned their steps from this dairy-house when once they had spied it, and that they did spy it, we are sure.'

'But if they have in hand the great design you speak of, Paulo,' said Vivaldi, 'it is probable that they have spied us also, by their taking this obscure road. Now it must have occurred to them when they saw a dairy-hut, in so solitary a region, that we might probably be found within—yet they have not examined. It appears, therefore, they have no design against us. What can you answer to this Paulo? I trust the apprehensions of Signora di Rosalba are unfounded.'

'Why! do you suppose, Signor, they would attack us when we were safe housed, and had these good shepherds to lend us a helping hand? No, Signor, they would not even have shewn themselves, if they could have helped it; and being once sure we were here, they would skulk back to the woods, and lurk for us in the road they knew we must go, since, as it happens, there is only one.'

'How is it possible,' said Ellena, 'that they can have discovered us here, since they did not approach the cabin to enquire.'

'They came near enough for their purpose, Signora, I dare say; and, if the truth were known, they spied my face looking at them through the lattice.'

'Come, come,' said Vivaldi, 'you are an ingenious tormentor, indeed, Paulo. Do you suppose they saw enough of thy face last night by moonlight, in that dusky glen, to enable them to recollect it again at a distance of forty yards? Revive, my Ellena, I think every appearance is in our favour.'

'Would I could think so too!' said she, with a sigh.

'O! for that matter, Signora,' rejoined Paulo, 'there is nothing to be afraid of; they should find tough work of it, if they thought proper to attack us, lady.'

'It is not an open attack that we have to fear,' replied Ellena, 'but they may surround us with their snares, and defy resistance.'

However Vivaldi might accede to the truth of this remark, he would not appear to do so, but tried to laugh away her apprehensions; and Paulo was silenced for a while, by a significant look from his master.

The shepherd's boy returned much sooner than they had expected, and he probably saved his time, that he might spare his labour, for he brought no intelligence of the Carmelites. 'I looked for them among the woods along the road side in the hollow, yonder, too,' said the lad, 'and then I mounted the hill further on, but I could see nothing of them far or near, nor of a single soul, except our goats, and some of them do stray wide enough, sometimes; they lead me a fine dance often. They sometimes, Signor, have wandered as far as Monte Nuvola, yonder, and got to the top of it, up among the clouds, and the crags, where I should break my neck if I climbed; and the rogues seemed to know it, too, for when they have seen me coming, scrambling up, puffing and blowing, they have ceased their capering, and stood peeping over a crag so sly, and so quiet, it seemed as if they were laughing at me; as much as to say, "Catch us if you can." '

Vivaldi, who during the latter part of this speech had been consulting with Ellena, whether they should proceed on their way immediately, asked the boy some further questions concerning the Carmelites; and becoming convinced that they had either not taken the road to Celano, or, having taken it, were at a considerable distance, he proposed setting out, and proceeding leisurely, 'For I have now little apprehension of these people,' he added, 'and a great deal lest night should overtake us before we reach the place of our destination, since the road is mountainous and wild, and, further, we are not perfectly acquainted with it.'

Ellena approving the plan, they took leave of the good shepherd, who could with difficulty be prevailed with to accept any recompence for his trouble, and who gave them some further directions as to the road; and their way was long cheered by the sound of the tabor* and the sweetness of the hautboy,* wafted over the wild.

When they descended into the woody hollow mentioned by the boy, Ellena sent forth many an anxious look beneath the deep shade; while Paulo, sometimes silent, and at others whistling and singing loudly, as if to overcome his fears, peeped under every bough that crossed the road, expecting to discover his friends the Carmelites lurking within its gloom.

Having emerged from this valley, the road lay over mountains covered with flocks, for it was now the season when they had quitted the plains of Apulia, to feed upon the herbage for which this region is celebrated; and it was near sun-set, when, from a summit to which the travellers had long been ascending, the whole lake of Celano, with its vast circle of mountains, burst at once upon their view.

'Ah Signor!' exclaimed Paulo, 'what a prospect is here! It reminds me of home; it is almost as pleasant as the bay of Naples! I should never love it like that though, if it were an hundred times finer.'

The travellers stopped to admire the scene, and to give their horses rest, after the labour of the ascent. The evening sun, shooting athwart a clear expanse of water, between eighteen and twenty leagues in circumference, lighted up all the towns and villages, and towered castles, and spiry convents, that enriched the rising shores; brought out all the various tints of cultivation, and coloured with beamy purple the mountains which on every side formed the majestic background of the landscape. Vivaldi pointed out to Ellena the gigantic Velino in the north, a barrier mountain, between the territories of Rome and Naples. Its peaked head towered far above every neighbouring summit, and its white precipices were opposed to the verdant points of the Majella, snow-crowned, and next in altitude, loved by the flocks. Westward, near woody hills, and rising immediately from the lake, appeared Monte Salviano, covered with wild sage, as its name imports, and once pompous with forests of chestnut; a branch from the Appennine extended to meet it. 'See,' said Vivaldi, 'where Monte-Corno stands like a ruffian, huge, scared, threatening, and horrid!—and in the south, where the sullen mountain of San Nicolo shoots up, barren and rocky! From thence, mark how other overtopping ridges of the mighty Appennine darken the horizon far along the east, and circle to approach the Velino in the north!'

'Mark too,' said Ellena, 'how sweetly the banks and undulating plains repose at the feet of the mountains; what an image of beauty and elegance they oppose to the awful grandeur that overlooks and guards them! Observe, too, how many a delightful valley, opening from the lake, spreads its rice and corn fields, shaded with groves of the almond, far among the winding hills; how gaily vineyards

and olives alternately chequer the acclivities; and how gracefully
the lofty palms bend over the higher cliffs.'

'Ay, Signora!' exclaimed Paulo, 'and have the goodness to
observe how like are the fishing boats, that sail towards the
hamlet below, to those one sees upon the bay of Naples. They are
worth all the rest of the prospect, except indeed this fine sheet of
water, which is almost as good as the bay, and that mountain, with
its sharp head, which is almost as good as Vesuvius—if it would
but throw out fire!'*

'We must despair of finding a mountain in this neighbourhood,
so *good* as to do that, Paulo,' said Vivaldi, smiling at this stroke of
nationality; 'though, perhaps, many that we now see, have once
been volcanic.'

'I honour them for that, Signor; and look at them with double
satisfaction; but *our* mountain is the only mountain in the world.
O! to see it of a dark night! what a blazing it makes! and what a
height it will shoot to! and what a light it throws over the sea! No
other mountain can do so. It seems as if the waves were all on fire.
I have seen the reflection as far off as Capri, trembling all across
the gulf, and shewing every vessel as plain as at noon day; ay, and
every sailor on the deck. You never saw such a sight, Signor.'

'Why you do, indeed, seem to have forgotten that I ever did,
Paulo, and also that a volcano can do any mischief. But let us
return, Ellena, to the scene before us. Yonder, a mile or two within
the shore, is the town of Celano, whither we are going.'

The clearness of an Italian atmosphere permitted him to discriminate the minute though very distant features of the landscape;
and on an eminence rising from the plains of a valley, opening to
the west, he pointed out the modern Alba, crowned with the ruins
of its ancient castle, still visible upon the splendor of the horizon,
the prison and tomb of many a Prince, who, 'fallen from his
high estate,'* was sent from Imperial Rome to finish here the sad
reverse of his days; to gaze from the bars of his tower upon solitudes where beauty or grandeur administered no assuaging feelings
to him, whose life had passed amidst the intrigues of the world,
and the feverish contentions of disappointed ambition; to him,
with whom reflection brought only remorse, and anticipation
despair; whom 'no horizontal beam enlivened in the crimson
evening of life's dusty day.'*

'And to such a scene as this,' said Vivaldi, 'a Roman Emperor
came, only for the purpose of witnessing the most barbarous
exhibition; to indulge the most savage delights! Here, Claudius

celebrated the accomplishment of his arduous work, an aqueduct to carry the overflowing waters of the Celano to Rome, by a naval fight, in which hundreds of wretched slaves perished for his amusement! Its pure and polished surface was stained with human blood, and roughened by the plunging bodies of the slain, while the gilded gallies of the Emperor floated gaily around, and these beautiful shores were made to echo with applauding yells, worthy of the furies!'*

'We scarcely dare to trust the truth of history, in some of its traits of human nature,' said Ellena.

'Signor,' cried Paulo, 'I have been thinking that while we are taking the air, so much at our ease, here, those Carmelites may be spying at us from some hole or corner that we know nothing of, and may swoop upon us, all of a sudden, before we can help ourselves. Had we not better go on, Signor?'

'Our horses are, perhaps, sufficiently rested,' replied Vivaldi, 'but, if I had not long since dismissed all suspicion of the evil intention of those strangers, I should not willingly have stopped for a moment.'

'But pray let us proceed,' said Ellena.

'Ay, Signora, it is best to be of the safe side,' observed Paulo. 'Yonder, below, is Celano, and I hope we shall get safe housed there, before it is quite dark, for here we have no mountain, that will light us on our way! Ah! if we were but within twenty miles of Naples, now,—and it was an *illumination* night!'—

As they descended the mountain, Ellena, silent and dejected, abandoned herself to reflection. She was too sensible of the difficulties of her present situation, and too apprehensive of the influence, which her determination must have on all her future life, to be happy, though escaped from the prison of San Stefano, and in the presence of Vivaldi, her beloved deliverer and protector. He observed her dejection with grief, and, not understanding all the finer scruples that distressed her, interpreted her reserve into indifference towards himself. But he forbore to disturb her again with a mention of his doubts, or fears; and he determined not to urge the subject of his late entreaties, till he should have placed her in some secure asylum, where she might feel herself at perfect liberty to accept or to reject his proposal. By acting with an honour so delicate, he unconsciously adopted a certain means of increasing her esteem and gratitude, and deserved them the more, since he had to endure the apprehension of losing her by the delay thus occasioned to their nuptials.

They reached the town of Celano before the evening closed; when Vivaldi was requested by Ellena to enquire for a convent, where she might be lodged for the night. He left her at the inn, with Paulo for her guard, and proceeded on his search. The first gate he knocked upon belonged to a convent of Carmelites. It appeared probable, that the pilgrims of that order, who had occasioned him so much disquietude, were honest brothers of this house; but as it was probable also, that if they were emissaries of the Abbess of San Stefano, and came to Celano, they would take up their lodging with a society of their own class, in preference to that of any other, Vivaldi thought it prudent to retire from their gates without making himself known. He passed on, therefore, and soon after arrived at a convent of Dominicans, where he learned, that there were only two houses of nuns in Celano, and that these admitted no other boarders than permanent ones.

Vivaldi returned with this intelligence to Ellena, who endeavoured to reconcile herself to the necessity of remaining where she was; but Paulo, ever active and zealous, brought intelligence, that at a little fishing town, at some distance, on the bank of the lake, was a convent of Ursalines, remarkable for their hospitality to strangers. The obscurity of so remote a place, was another reason for preferring it to Celano, and Vivaldi proposing to remove thither, if Ellena was not too weary to proceed, she readily assented, and they immediately set off.

'It happens to be a fine night,' said Paulo, as they left Celano, 'and so, Signor, we cannot well lose our way; besides, they say, there is but one. The town we are going to lies yonder on the edge of the lake, about a mile and a half off. I think I can see a gray steeple or two, a little to the right of that wood where the water gleams so.'

'No, Paulo,' replied Vivaldi, after looking attentively. 'I perceive what you mean; but those are not the points of steeples, they are only the tops of some tall cypresses.'

'Pardon me, Signor, they are too tapering for trees; that must surely be the town. This road, however, will lead us right, for there is no other to puzzle us, as they say.'

'This cool and balmy air revives me,' said Ellena; 'and what a soothing shade prevails over the scene! How softened, yet how distinct, is every near object; how sweetly dubious the more removed ones; while the mountains beyond character themselves sublimely upon the still glowing horizon.'

'Observe, too,' said Vivaldi, 'how their broken summits, tipt with the beams that have set to our lower region, exhibit the portraiture of towers and castles, and embattled ramparts, which seemed designed to guard them against the enemies, that may come by the clouds.'

'Yes,' replied Ellena, 'the mountains themselves display a sublimity, that seems to belong to a higher world; their besiegers ought not to be of this earth; they can be only spirits of the air.'

'They can be nothing else, Signora,' said Paulo, 'for nothing of this earth can reach them. See! lady, they have some of the qualities of your spirits, too; see! how they change their shapes and colours, as the sun-beams sink. And now, how gray and dim they grow! See but how fast they vanish!'

'Every thing reposes,' said Vivaldi. 'Who would willingly travel in the day, when Italy has such nights as this!'

'Signor, that *is* the town before us,' said Paulo, 'for now I can discern, plain enough, the spires of convents; and there goes a light! Hah, hah! and there is a bell, too, chiming from one of the spires! The monks are going to mass; would we were going to supper, Signor!'

'That chime is nearer than the place you point to, Paulo, and I doubt whether it comes from the same quarter.'

'Hark! Signor, the air wafts the sound! and now it is gone again.'

'Yes, I believe you are right, Paulo, and that we have not far to go.'

The travellers descended the gradual slopes, towards the shore; and Paulo, some time after, exclaimed, 'See, Signor, where another light glides along! See! it is reflected on the lake.'

'I hear the faint dashing of waves, now,' said Ellena, 'and the sound of oars, too. But observe, Paulo, the light is not in the town, it is in the boat that moves yonder.'

'Now it retreats, and trembles in a lengthening line upon the waters,' said Vivaldi. 'We have been too ready to believe what we wish and have yet far to go.'

The shore they were approaching formed a spacious bay for the lake, immediately below. Dark woods seemed to spread along the banks, and ascend among the cultivated slopes towards the mountains; except where, here and there, cliffs, bending over the water, were distinguished through the twilight by the whiteness of their limestone precipices. Within the bay, the town became gradually visible; lights twinkled between the trees, appearing and vanishing, like the stars of a cloudy night; and, at length was heard the melancholy song of boatmen, who were fishing near the shore.

Other sounds soon after struck the ear. 'O, what merry notes!' exclaimed Paulo, 'they make my heart dance. See! Signora, there is a group, footing it away so gaily on the bank of the lake, yonder, by those trees. O, what a merry set! Would I were among them! that is, I mean, if you, *Maestro*, and the Signora were not here.'

'Well corrected, Paulo.'

'It is a festival, I fancy,' observed Vivaldi. 'These peasants of the lake can make the moments fly as gaily as the voluptuaries of the city, it seems.'

'O! what merry music!' repeated Paulo. 'Ah! how often I have footed it as joyously on the beach at Naples, after sun-set, of a fine night, like this; with such a pleasant fresh breeze to cool one! Ah! there are none like the fishermen of Naples for a dance by moon-light; how lightly they do trip it! O! if I was but there now! That is, I mean, if you, *Maestro*, and the Signora were there too. O! what merry notes!'

'We thank you, good Signor Paulo,' said Vivaldi, 'and I trust we shall all be there soon; when you shall trip it away, with as joyous an heart as the best of them.'

The travellers now entered the town, which consisted of one street, straggling along the margin of the lake; and having enquired for the Ursaline convent, were directed to it's gates. The portress appeared immediately upon the ringing of the bell, and carried a message to the Abbess, who as quickly returned an invitation to Ellena. She alighted, and followed the portress to the parlour, while Vivaldi remained at the gate, till he should know whether she approved of her new lodging. A second invitation induced him, also, to alight; he was admitted to the grate, and offered refreshment, which, however, he declined staying to accept, as he had yet a lodging to seek for the night. The Abbess, on learning this circumstance, courteously recommended him to a neighbouring society of Benedictines, and desired him to mention her name to the Abbot.

Vivaldi then took leave of Ellena, and, though it was only for a few hours, he left her with dejection, and with some degree of apprehension for her safety, which, though circumstances could not justify him in admitting, he could not entirely subdue. She shared his dejection, but not his fears, when the door closed after him, and she found herself once more among strangers. The forlornness of her feelings could not be entirely overcome by the attentions of the Abbess; and there was a degree of curiosity, and even of scrutiny, expressed in the looks of some of the sisters, which seemed more than was due to a stranger. From such examination she eagerly escaped to the apartment allotted for her, and to the repose from which she had so long been withheld.

Vivaldi, meanwhile, had found an hospitable reception with the Benedictines, whose sequestered situation made the visit of a stranger a pleasurable novelty to them. In the eagerness of conversation, and, yielding to the satisfaction which the mind receives from exercising ideas that have long slept in dusky indolence, and to the pleasure of admitting new ones, the Abbot and a few of the brothers sat with Vivaldi to a late hour. When, at length, the traveller was suffered to retire, other subjects than those, which had interested his host, engaged his thoughts; and he revolved the means of preventing the misery that threatened him, in a serious separation from Ellena. Now, that she was received into a respectable asylum, every motive for silence upon this topic was done away. He determined, therefore, that on the following morning, he would urge all his reasons and entreaties for an immediate marriage; and among the brothers of the Benedictine, he had little doubt of prevailing with one to solemnize the nuptials, which he believed would place his happiness and Ellena's peace, beyond the influence of malignant possibilities.

CHAPTER III

I under fair pretence of friendly ends,
And well-placed words of glozing courtesy,
Baited with reasons not unplausible,
Wind me into the easy-hearted man,
And hug him into snares.

MILTON*

WHILE Vivaldi and Ellena were on the way from San Stefano, the Marchese Vivaldi was suffering the utmost vexation, respecting his son; and the Marchesa felt not less apprehension, that the abode of Ellena might be discovered; yet this fear did not withhold her from mingling in all the gaieties of Naples. Her assemblies were, as usual, among the most brilliant of that voluptuous city, and she patronized, as zealously as before, the strains of her favourite composer. But, notwithstanding this perpetual dissipation, her thoughts frequently withdrew themselves from the scene, and dwelt on gloomy forebodings of disappointed pride.

A circumstance, which rendered her particularly susceptible to such disappointment at this time, was, that overtures of alliance had been lately made to the Marchese, by the father of a lady, who was held suitable, in every consideration, to become his daughter; and whose wealth rendered the union particularly desirable at a time, when the expences of such an establishment as was necessary to the vanity of the Marchesa, considerably exceeded his income, large as it was.

The Marchesa's temper had been thus irritated by the contemplation of her son's conduct in an affair, which so materially affected the fortune, and, as she believed, the honour of his family; when a courier from the Abbess of San Stefano brought intelligence of the flight of Ellena with Vivaldi. She was in a disposition, which heightened disappointment into fury; and she forfeited, by the transports to which she yielded, the degree of pity that otherwise was due to a mother, who believed her only son to have sacrificed his family and himself to an unworthy passion. She believed, that he was now married, and irrecoverably lost. Scarcely able to endure the agony of this conviction, she sent for her ancient adviser Schedoni, that she might, at least, have the relief of expressing her emotions; and of examining whether there remained a possibility of dissolving these long-dreaded nuptials. The phrenzy of passion, however, did not so far overcome her circumspection as to compel her to acquaint the Marchese with the contents of the Abbess's letter, before she had consulted with her Confessor. She knew that the principles of her husband were too just, upon the grand points of morality, to suffer him to adopt the measures she might judge necessary; and she avoided informing him of the marriage of his son, until the means of counteracting it should have been suggested and accomplished, however desperate such means might be.

Schedoni was not to be found. Trifling circumstances encrease the irritation of a mind in such a state as was her's. The delay of an opportunity for unburthening her heart to Schedoni, was hardly to be endured; another and another messenger were dispatched to her Confessor.

'My mistress has committed some great sin, truely!' said the servant, who had been twice to the convent within the last half hour. 'It must lie heavy on her conscience, in good truth, since she cannot support it for one half hour. Well! the rich have this comfort, however, that, let them be ever so guilty, they can buy themselves innocent again, in the twinkling of a ducat. Now a poor man might be a month before he recovered his innocence, and that, too, not till after many a bout of hard flogging.'

In the evening Schedoni came, but it was only to confirm her worst fear. He, too, had heard of the escape of Ellena, as well as that she was on the lake of Celano, and was married to Vivaldi. How he had obtained this information he did not chuse to disclose, but he mentioned so many minute circumstances in confirmation of it's truth, and appeared to be so perfectly convinced of the facts he related, that the Marchesa believed them, as implicitly as himself; and her passion and despair transgressed all bounds of decorum.

Schedoni observed, with dark and silent pleasure, the turbulent excess of her feelings; and perceived that the moment was now arrived, when he might command them to his purpose, so as to render his assistance indispensable to her repose; and probably so as to accomplish the revenge he had long meditated against Vivaldi, without hazarding the favour of the Marchesa. So far was he from attempting to sooth her sufferings, that he continued to irritate her resentment, and exasperate her pride; effecting this, at the same time, with such imperceptible art, that he appeared only to be palliating the conduct of Vivaldi, and endeavouring to console his distracted mother.

'This is a rash step, certainly,' said the Confessor; 'but he is young, very young, and, therefore, does not foresee the consequence to which it leads. He does not perceive how seriously it will affect the dignity of his house;—how much it will depreciate his consequence with the court, with the nobles of his own rank, and even with the plebeians, with whom he has condescended to connect himself. Intoxicated with the passions of youth, he does not weigh the value of those blessings, which wisdom and the experience of maturer age know how to estimate. He neglects them *only* because he does not perceive their influence in society, and that lightly to resign them, is to degrade himself in the view of almost every mind. Unhappy young man! he is to be pitied fully as much as blamed.'

'Your excuses, reverend father,' said the tortured Marchesa, 'prove the goodness of your heart; but they illustrate, also, the degeneracy of his mind, and detail the full extent of the effects which he has brought upon his family. It affords me no consolation to know, that this degradation proceeds from his head, rather than his heart; it is sufficient that he has incurred it, and that no possibility remains of throwing off the misfortune.'

'Perhaps that is affirming too much,' observed Schedoni.

'How, father!' said the Marchesa.

'Perhaps a possibility does remain,' said he.

'Point it out to me, good father! I do not perceive it.'

'Nay, my lady,' replied the subtle Schedoni, correcting himself, 'I am by no means assured, that such possibility does exist. My solicitude for your tranquillity, and for the honour of your house, makes me so unwilling to relinquish hope, that, perhaps, I only imagine a possibility in your favour. Let me consider.——Alas! the misfortune, severe as it is, must be endured;—there remain no means of escaping from it.'

'It was cruel of you, father, to suggest a hope which you could not justify,' observed the Marchesa.

'You must excuse my extreme solicitude, then,' replied the Confessor. 'But how is it possible for me to see a family of your ancient estimation brought into such circumstances; its honours blighted by the folly of a thoughtless boy, without feeling sorrow and indignation, and looking round for even some desperate means of delivering it from disgrace.' He paused.

'Disgrace!' exclaimed the Marchesa, 'father, you—you—

Disgrace!—The word is a strong one, but——it is, alas! just. And shall we submit to this?—Is it possible we *can* submit to it?'

'There is no remedy,' said Schedoni, coolly.

'Good God!' exclaimed the Marchesa, 'that there should be no law to prevent, or, at least, to punish such criminal marriages!'

'It is much to be lamented,' replied Schedoni.

'The woman who obtrudes herself upon a family, to dishonour it,' continued the Marchesa, 'deserves a punishment nearly equal to that of a state criminal, since she injures those who best support the state. She ought to suffer'——

'Not nearly, but quite equal,' interrupted the Confessor, 'she deserves——death!'

He paused, and there was a moment of profound silence, till he added—'for death only can obliviate the degradation she has occasioned; her death alone can restore the original splendor of the line she would have sullied.'

He paused again, but the Marchesa still remaining silent, he added, 'I have often marvelled that our lawgivers should have failed to perceive the justness, nay the necessity, of such punishment!'

'It is astonishing,' said the Marchesa, thoughtfully, 'that a regard for their own honour did not suggest it.'

'Justice does not the less exist, because her laws are neglected,' observed Schedoni. 'A sense of what she commands lives in our breasts; and when we fail to obey that sense, it is to weakness, not to virtue, that we yield.'

'Certainly,' replied the Marchesa, 'that truth never yet was doubted.'

'Pardon me, I am not so certain as to that,' said the Confessor, 'when justice happens to oppose prejudice, we are apt to believe it virtuous to disobey her. For instance, though the law of justice demands the death of this girl, yet because the law of the land forbears to enforce it, you, my daughter, even you! though possessed of a man's spirit, and his clear perceptions, would think that virtue bade her live, when it was only fear!'

'Hah!' exclaimed the Marchesa, in a low voice, 'What is that you mean? You shall find I have a man's courage also.'

'I speak without disguise,' replied Schedoni, 'my meaning requires none.'

The Marchesa mused, and remained silent.

'I have done my duty,' resumed Schedoni, at length. 'I have pointed out the only way that remains for you to escape dishonour. If my zeal is displeasing——but I have done.'

'No, good father, no,' said the Marchesa; 'you mistake the cause of my emotion. New ideas, new prospects, open!—they confuse, they distract me! My mind has not yet attained sufficient strength to encounter them; some woman's weakness still lingers at my heart.'

'Pardon my inconsiderate zeal,' said Schedoni, with affected humility, 'I have been to blame. If your's is a weakness, it is, at least, an amiable one, and, perhaps, deserves to be encouraged, rather than conquered.'

'How, father! If it deserves encouragement, it is not a weakness, but a virtue.'

'Be it so,' said Schedoni, coolly, 'the interest I have felt on this subject, has, perhaps, misled my judgment, and has made me unjust. Think no more of it, or, if you do, let it be only to pardon the zeal I have testified.'

'It does not deserve pardon, but thanks,' replied the Marchesa, 'not thanks only, but reward. Good father, I hope it will some time be in my power to prove the sincerity of my words.'

The Confessor bowed his head.

'I trust that the services you have rendered me, shall be gratefully repaid—rewarded, I dare not hope, for what benefit could possibly reward a service so vast, as it may, perhaps, be in your power to confer upon my family! What recompence could be balanced against the benefit of having rescued the honour of an ancient house!'

'Your goodness is beyond my thanks, or my desert,' said Schedoni, and he was again silent.

The Marchesa wished him to lead her back to the point, from which she herself had deviated, and he seemed determined, that she should lead him thither. She mused, and hesitated. Her mind was not yet familiar with atrocious guilt; and the crime which Schedoni had suggested, somewhat alarmed her. She feared to think, and still more to name it; yet, so acutely susceptible was her pride, so stern her indignation, and so profound her desire of vengeance, that her mind was tossed as on a tempestuous ocean, and these terrible feelings threatened to overwhelm all the residue of humanity in her heart. Schedoni observed all its progressive movements, and, like a gaunt tyger, lurked in silence, ready to spring forward at the moment of opportunity.

'It is your advice, then, father,' resumed the Marchesa, after a long pause,—'it is your opinion—that Ellena.'——She hesitated, desirous that Schedoni should anticipate her meaning; but he chose to spare his own delicacy rather than that of the Marchesa.

'You think, then, that this insidious girl deserves'——She paused again, but the Confessor, still silent, seemed to wait with submission for what the Marchesa should deliver.

'I repeat, father, that it is your opinion this girl deserves severe punishment.'——

'Undoubtedly,' replied Schedoni, 'Is it not also your own?'

'That not any punishment can be too severe?' continued the Marchesa. 'That justice, equally with necessity, demands——her life? Is not this your opinion too?'

'O! pardon me,' said Schedoni, 'I may have erred; that only *was* my opinion; and when I formed it, I was probably too much under the influence of zeal to be just. When the heart is warm, how is it possible that the judgment can be cool.'

'It is *not* then, your opinion, holy father,' said the Marchesa with displeasure.

'I do not absolutely say that,' replied the Confessor.—But I leave it to your better judgment to decide upon its justness.'

As he said this, he rose to depart. The Marchesa was agitated and perplexed, and requested he would stay; but he excused himself by alledging, that it was the hour when he must attend a particular mass.

'Well then, holy father, I will occupy no more of your valuable moments at present; but you know how highly I estimate your advice, and will not refuse, when I shall at some future time request it.'

'I cannot refuse to accept an honour,' replied the Confessor, with an air of meekness, 'but the subject you allude to is delicate'——

'And therefore I must value, and require your opinion upon it,' rejoined the Marchesa.

'I would wish you to value your own,' replied Schedoni; 'you cannot have a better director.'

'You flatter, father.'

'I only reply, my daughter.'

'On the evening of to-morrow,' said the Marchesa, gravely, 'I shall be at vespers in the church of San Nicolo; if you should happen to be there, you will probably see me, when the service is over, and the congregation is departed, in the north cloister. We can there converse on the subject nearest my heart, and without observation.——Farewell!'

'Peace be with you, daughter! and wisdom council your thoughts!' said Schedoni, 'I will not fail to visit San Nicolo.'

He folded his hands upon his breast, bowed his head, and left the apartment with the silent footstep, that indicates weariness and conscious duplicity.

The Marchesa remained in her closet, shaken by ever-varying passions, and ever-fluctuating opinions; meditating misery for others, and inflicting it only upon herself.

CHAPTER IV

Along the roofs sounds the low peal of Death,
And Conscience trembles to the boding note;
She views his dim form floating o'er the aisles,
She hears mysterious murmurs in the air,
And voices, strange and potent, hint the crime
That dwells in thought, within her secret soul.

THE Marchesa repaired, according to her appointment, to the church of San Nicolo, and, ordering her servants to remain with the carriage at a side-door, entered the choir, attended only by her woman.

When vespers had concluded, she lingered till nearly every person had quitted the choir, and then walked through the solitary aisles to the north cloister. Her heart was as heavy as her step; for when is it that peace and evil passions dwell together? As she slowly paced the cloisters, she perceived a monk passing between the pillars, who, as he approached, lifted his cowl, and she knew him to be Schedoni.

He instantly observed the agitation of her spirits, and that her purpose was not yet determined, according to his hope. But, though his mind became clouded, his countenance remained unaltered; it was grave and thoughtful. The sternness of his vulture-eye was, however, somewhat softened, and its lids were contracted by subtlety.

The Marchesa bade her woman walk apart, while she conferred with her Confessor.

'This unhappy boy,' said she, when the attendant was at some distance, 'How much suffering does his folly inflict upon his family! My good father, I have need of all your advice and consolation. My mind is perpetually haunted by a sense of my misfortune; it has no respite; awake or in my dream, this ungrateful son alike pursues me! The only relief my heart receives is when conversing with you—my only counsellor, my only disinterested friend.'

The Confessor bowed. 'The Marchese is, no doubt, equally afflicted with yourself,' said he; 'but he is, notwithstanding, much more competent to advise you on this delicate subject than I am.'

'The Marchese has prejudices, father, as you well know; he is a sensible man, but he is sometimes mistaken, and he is incorrigible in error. He has the faults of a mind that is merely well disposed; he is destitute of the discernment and the energy which would make it great. If it is necessary to adopt a conduct, that departs in the smallest degree from those common rules of morality which he has cherished, without examining them, from his infancy, he is shocked, and shrinks from action. He cannot discriminate the circumstances, that render the same action virtuous or vicious. How then, father, are we to suppose he would approve of the bold inflictions we meditate?'

'Most true!' said the artful Schedoni, with an air of admiration.

'We, therefore, must not consult him,' continued the Marchesa, 'lest he should now, as formerly, advance and maintain objections, to which we cannot yield. What passes in conversation with you, father, is sacred, it goes no farther.'

'Sacred as a confession!' said Schedoni, crossing himself.

'I know not,'—resumed the Marchesa, and hesitated; 'I know not'—she repeated in a yet lower voice, 'how this girl may be disposed of; and this it is which distracts my mind.'

'I marvel much at that,' said Schedoni. 'With opinions so singularly just, with a mind so accurate, yet so bold as you have displayed, is it possible that you can hesitate as to what is to be done! You, my daughter, will not prove yourself one of those ineffectual declaimers, who can think vigorously, but cannot act so! One way, only, remains for you to pursue, in the present instance; it is the same which your superior sagacity pointed out, and taught me to approve. Is it necessary for me to persuade *her*, by whom I am convinced! There is only one way.'

'And on that I have been long meditating,' replied the Marchesa, 'and, shall I own my weakness? I cannot yet decide.'

'My daughter! can it be possible that you should want courage to soar above vulgar prejudice, in action, though not in opinion?' said Schedoni, who, perceiving that his assistance was necessary to fix her fluctuating mind, gradually began to steal forth from the prudent reserve, in which he had taken shelter.

'If this person was condemned by the law,' he continued, 'you would pronounce her sentence to be just; yet you dare not, I am humbled while I repeat it, you dare not dispense justice yourself!'

The Marchesa, after some hesitation, said, 'I have not the shield of the law to protect me, father: and the boldest virtue may pause, when it reaches the utmost verge of safety.'

'Never!' replied the Confessor, warmly; 'virtue never trembles; it is her glory, and sublimest attribute to be superior to danger; to despise it. The best principle is not virtue till it reaches this elevation.'

A philosopher might, perhaps, have been surprized to hear two persons seriously defining the limits of virtue, at the very moment in which they meditated the most atrocious crime; a man of the world would have considered it to be mere hypocrisy; a supposition which might have disclosed his general knowledge of manners, but would certainly have betrayed his ignorance of the human heart.

The Marchesa was for some time silent and thoughtful, and then repeated deliberately, 'I have not the shield of the law to protect me.'

'But you have the shield of the church,' replied Schedoni; 'you should not only have protection, but absolution.'

'Absolution!—Does virtue—justice, require absolution, father?'

'When I mentioned absolution for the action which you perceive to be so just and necessary,' replied Schedoni, 'I accommodated my speech to vulgar prejudice, and to vulgar weakness. And, forgive me, that since you, my daughter, descended from the loftiness of your spirit to regret the shield of the law, I endeavoured to console you, by offering a shield to conscience. But enough of this; let us return to argument. This girl is put out of the way of committing more mischief, of injuring the peace and dignity of a distinguished family; she is sent to an eternal sleep, before her time.—Where is the crime, where is the evil of this? On the contrary, you perceive, and you have convinced me, that it is only strict justice, only self-defence.'

The Marchesa was attentive, and the Confessor added, 'She is not immortal; and the few years more, that might have been allotted her, she deserves to forfeit, since she would have employed them in cankering the honour of an illustrious house.'

'Speak low, father,' said the Marchesa, though he spoke almost in a whisper; 'the cloister appears solitary, yet some person may lurk behind those pillars. Advise me how this business may be managed; I am ignorant of the particular means.'

'There is some hazard in the accomplishment of it, I grant,' replied Schedoni; 'I know not whom you may confide in.—The men who make a trade of blood'——

'Hush!' said the Marchesa, looking round through the twilight— 'a step!'

'It is the Friar's, yonder, who crosses to the choir,' replied Schedoni.

They were watchful for a few moments, and then he resumed the subject. 'Mercenaries ought not to be trusted,'—

'Yet who but mercenaries'—interrupted the Marchesa, and instantly checked herself. But the question thus implied, did not escape the Confessor.

'Pardon my astonishment,' said he, 'at the inconsistency, or, what shall I venture to call it? of your opinions! After the acuteness you have displayed on some points, is it possible you can doubt, that principle may both prompt and perform the deed? Why should we hesitate to do what we judge to be right?'

'Ah! reverend father,' said the Marchesa, with emotion, 'but where shall we find another like yourself—another, who not only can perceive with justness, but will act with energy.'

Schedoni was silent.

'Such a friend is above all estimation; but where shall we seek him?'

'Daughter!' said the Monk, emphatically, 'my zeal for your family is also above all calculation.'

'Good father,' replied the Marchesa, comprehending his full meaning, 'I know not how to thank you.'

'Silence is sometimes eloquence,' said Schedoni, significantly.

The Marchesa mused; for her conscience also was eloquent. She tried to overcome its voice, but it would be heard; and sometimes such starts of horrible conviction came over her mind, that she felt as one who, awaking from a dream, opens his eyes only to measure the depth of the precipice on which he totters. In such moments she was astonished, that she had paused for an instant upon a subject so terrible as that of murder. The sophistry of the Confessor, together with the inconsistencies which he had betrayed, and which had not escaped the notice of the Marchesa, even at the time they were uttered, though she had been unconscious of her own, then became more strongly apparent, and she almost determined to suffer the poor Ellena to live. But returning passion, like a wave that has recoiled from the shore, afterwards came with recollected energy, and swept from her feeble mind the barriers, which reason and conscience had begun to rear.

'This confidence with which you have thought proper to honour me,' said Schedoni, at length, and paused; 'This affair, so momentous'——

'Ay, this affair,' interrupted the Marchesa, in a hurried manner, —'but when, and where, good father? Being once convinced, I am anxious to have it settled.'

'That must be as occasion offers,' replied the Monk, thoughtfully.—'On the shore of the Adriatic, in the province of Apulia, not far from Manfredonia, is a house that might suit the purpose. It is a lone dwelling on the beach, and concealed from travellers, among the forests, which spread for many miles along the coast.'

'And the people?' said the Marchesa.

'Ay, daughter, or why travel so far as Apulia? It is inhabited by one poor man, who sustains a miserable existence by fishing. I know him, and could unfold the reasons of his solitary life;—but no matter, it is sufficient that *I know him.*'

'And would trust him, father?'

'Ay, lady, with the life of this girl——though scarcely with my own.'

'How! If he is such a villain he may not be trusted! think further. But now, you objected to a mercenary, yet this man is one!'

'Daughter, he may be trusted, when it is in such a case; he is safe and sure. I have reason to know him.'

'Name your reasons, father.'

The Confessor was silent, and his countenance assumed a very peculiar character; it was more terrible than usual, and overspread with a dark, cadaverous hue of mingled anger and guilt. The Marchesa started involuntarily as, passing by a window, the evening gleam that fell there, discovered it; and for the first time she wished, that she had not committed herself so wholly to his power. But the die was now cast; it was too late to be prudent; and she again demanded his reasons.

'No matter,' said Schedoni, in a stifled voice——'she dies!'

'By his hands?' asked the Marchesa, with strong emotion. 'Think, once more, father.'

They were both again silent and thoughtful. The Marchesa, at length, said, 'Father, I rely upon your integrity and prudence;' and she laid a very flattering emphasis upon the word integrity.

'But I conjure you to let this business be finished quickly, suspense is to me the purgatory of this world, and not to trust the accomplishment of it to a second person.' She paused, and then added, 'I would not willingly owe so vast a debt of obligation to any other than yourself.'

'Your request, daughter, that I would not confide this business to a second person,' said Schedoni, with displeasure, 'cannot be accorded to. Can you suppose, that I, myself'——

'Can I doubt that principle may both prompt and perform the deed,' interrupted the Marchesa with quickness, and anticipating his meaning, while she retorted upon him his former words. 'Why should we hesitate to do what we judge to be right?'

The silence of Schedoni alone indicated his displeasure, which the Marchesa immediately understood.

'Consider, good father,' she added significantly, 'how painful it must be to me, to owe so infinite an obligation to a stranger, or to any other than so highly valued a friend as yourself.'

Schedoni, while he detected her meaning, and persuaded himself that he despised the flattery, with which she so thinly veiled it, unconsciously suffered his self-love to be soothed by the compliment. He bowed his head, in signal of consent to her wish.

'Avoid violence, if that be possible,' she added, immediately comprehending him, 'but let her die quickly! The punishment is due to the crime.'

The Marchesa happened, as she said this, to cast her eyes upon the inscription over a Confessional, where appeared, in black letters, these awful words, '*God hears thee!*' It appeared an awful warning. Her countenance changed; it had struck upon her heart. Schedoni was too much engaged by his own thoughts to observe, or understand her silence. She soon recovered herself; and considering that this was a common inscription for Confessionals, disregarded what she had at first considered as a peculiar admonition; yet some moments elapsed, before she could renew the subject.

'You was speaking of a place, father,' resumed the Marchesa—— 'you mentioned a'——

'Ay,' muttered the Confessor, still musing,—'in a chamber of that house there is'——

'What noise is that?' said the Marchesa, interrupting him. They listened. A few low and querulous notes of the organ sounded at a distance, and stopped again.

'What mournful music is that?' said the Marchesa in a faultering voice, 'It was touched by a fearful hand! Vespers were over long ago!'

'Daughter,' said Schedoni, somewhat sternly, 'you said you had a man's courage. Alas! you have a woman's heart.'

'Excuse me, father; I know not why I feel this agitation, but I will command it. That chamber?'——

'In that chamber,' resumed the Confessor, 'is a secret door, constructed long ago.'——

'And for what purpose constructed?' said the fearful Marchesa.

'Pardon me, daughter; 'tis sufficient that it is there; we will make a good use of it. Through that door—in the night—when she sleeps'——

'I comprehend you,' said the Marchesa, 'I comprehend you. But why, you have your reasons, no doubt, but why the necessity of a secret door in a house which you say is so lonely—inhabited by only one person?'

'A passage leads to the sea,' continued Schedoni, without replying to the question. 'There, on the shore, when darkness covers it; there, plunged amidst the waves, no stain shall hint of'——

'Hark!' interrupted the Marchesa, starting, 'that note again!'

The organ sounded faintly from the choir, and paused, as before. In the next moment, a slow chaunting of voices was heard, mingling with the rising peal, in a strain particularly melancholy and solemn.

'Who is dead?' said the Marchesa, changing countenance; 'it is a requiem!'

'Peace be with the departed!' exclaimed Schedoni, and crossed himself; 'Peace rest with his soul!'

'Hark! to that chaunt!' said the Marchesa, in a trembling voice; 'it is a first requiem; the soul has but just quitted the body!'

They listened in silence. The Marchesa was much affected; her complexion varied at every instant; her breathings were short and interrupted, and she even shed a few tears, but they were those of despair, rather than of sorrow. 'That body is now cold,' said she to herself, 'which but an hour ago was warm and animated! Those fine senses are closed in death! And to this condition would I reduce a being like myself! Oh, wretched, wretched mother! to what has the folly of a son reduced thee!'

She turned from the Confessor, and walked alone in the cloister. Her agitation encreased; she wept without restraint, for her veil and the evening gloom concealed her, and her sighs were lost amidst the music of the choir.

Schedoni was scarcely less disturbed, but his were emotions of apprehension and contempt. 'Behold, what is woman!' said he——

'The slave of her passions, the dupe of her senses! When pride and revenge speak in her breast, she defies obstacles, and laughs at crimes! Assail but her senses, let music, for instance, touch some feeble chord of her heart, and echo to her fancy, and lo! all her perceptions change:—she shrinks from the act she had but an instant before believed meritorious, yields to some new emotion, and sinks —the victim of a sound! O, weak and contemptible being!'

The Marchesa, at least, seemed to justify his observations. The desperate passions, which had resisted every remonstrance of reason and humanity, were vanquished only by other passions; and, her senses touched by the mournful melody of music, and her superstitious fears awakened by the occurrence of a requiem for the dead, at the very moment when she was planning murder, she yielded, for a while, to the united influence of pity and terror. Her agitation did not subside; but she returned to the Confessor.

'We will converse on this business at some future time,' said she; 'at present, my spirits are disordered. Good night, father! Remember me in your orisons.'

'Peace be with you, lady!' said the Confessor, bowing gravely, 'You shall not be forgotten. Be resolute, and yourself.'

The Marchesa beckoned her woman to approach, when, drawing her veil closer, and leaning upon the attendant's arm, she left the cloister. Schedoni remained for a moment on the spot, looking after her, till her figure was lost in the gloom of the long perspective; he then, with thoughtful steps, quitted the cloister by another door. He was disappointed, but he did not despair.

CHAPTER V

The lonely mountains o'er,
And the resounding shore,
A voice of weeping heard, and loud lament!
From haunted spring, and dale,
Edg'd with poplar pale,
The parting genius is with sighing sent;
With flower-inwoven tresses torn
The nymphs in twilight shade of tangled thicket mourn.

MILTON*

WHILE the Marchesa and the Monk were thus meditating conspiracies against Ellena, she was still in the Ursaline convent on the lake of Celano. In this obscure sanctuary, indisposition, the consequence of the long and severe anxiety she had suffered, compelled her to remain. A fever was on her spirits, and an universal lassitude prevailed over her frame; which became the more effectual, from her very solicitude to conquer it. Every approaching day she hoped she should be able to pursue her journey homeward, yet every day found her as incapable of travelling as the last, and the second week was already gone, before the fine air of Celano, and the tranquillity of her asylum, began to revive her. Vivaldi, who was her daily visitor at the grate of the convent; and who, watching over her with intense solicitude, had hitherto forbore to renew a subject, which, by agitating her spirits, might affect her health, now, that her health strengthened, ventured gradually to mention his fears lest the place of her retreat should be discovered, and lest he yet might irrecoverably lose her, unless she would approve of their speedy marriage. At every visit he now urged the subject, represented the dangers that surrounded them, and repeated his arguments and entreaties; for now, when he believed that time was pressing forward fatal evils, he could no longer attend to the delicate scruples, that bade him be sparing in entreaty. Ellena, had she obeyed the dictates of her heart, would have rewarded his attachment and his services, by a frank approbation of his proposal; but the objections which reason exhibited against such a concession, she could neither overcome or disregard.

Vivaldi, after he had again represented their present dangers, and claimed the promise of her hand, received in the presence of her deceased relative, Signora Bianchi, gently ventured to remind her, that an event as sudden as lamentable, had first deferred their nuptials, and that if Bianchi had lived, Ellena would have bestowed, long since, the vows he now solicited. Again he intreated her, by every sacred and tender recollection, to conclude the fearful uncertainty of their fate, and to bestow upon him the right to protect her, before they ventured forth from this temporary asylum.

Ellena immediately admitted the sacredness of the promise, which she had formerly given, and assured Vivaldi that she considered herself as indissolubly bound to wed him as if it had been given at the altar; but she objected to a confirmation of it, till his family should seem willing to receive her for their daughter; when, forgetting the injuries she had received from them, she would no longer refuse their alliance. She added, that Vivaldi ought to be more jealous of the dignity of the woman, whom he honoured with his esteem, than to permit her making a greater concession.

Vivaldi felt the full force of this appeal; he recollected, with anguish, circumstances of which she was happily ignorant, but which served to strengthen with him the justness of her reproof. And, as the aspersions which the Marchese had thrown upon her name, crowded to his memory, pride and indignation swelled his heart, and so far overcame apprehension of hazard, that he formed a momentary resolution to abandon every other consideration, to that of asserting the respect which was due to Ellena, and to forbear claiming her for his wife, till his family should make acknowledgment of their error, and willingly admit her in the rank of their child. But this resolution was as transient as plausible; other considerations, and former fears pressed upon him. He perceived the strong improbability, that they would ever make a voluntary sacrifice of their pride to his love; or yield mistakes, nurtured by prejudice and by willing indulgence, to truth and a sense of justice. In the mean time, the plans, which would be formed for separating him from Ellena, might succeed, and he should lose her for ever. Above all, it appeared, that the best, the only method, which remained for confuting the daring aspersions that had affected her name, was, by proving the high respect he himself felt for her, and presenting her to the world in the sacred character of his wife. These considerations quickly determined him to persevere in his suit; but it was impossible to urge them to Ellena, since the circumstances they must unfold, would not only shock her delicacy and afflict her heart, but would furnish the proper pride she cherished with new arguments against approaching a family, who had thus grossly insulted her.

While these considerations occupied him, the emotion they occasioned did not escape Ellena's observation; it encreased, as he reflected on the impossibility of urging them to her, and on the hopelessness of prevailing with her, unless he could produce new arguments in his favour. His unaffected distress awakened all her tenderness and gratitude; she asked herself whether she ought any longer to assert her own rights, when by doing so, she sacrificed the peace of him, who had incurred so much danger for her sake, who had rescued her from severe oppression, and had so long and so well proved the strength of his affection.

As she applied these questions, she appeared to herself an unjust and selfish being, unwilling to make any sacrifice for the tranquillity of him, who had given her liberty, even at the risk of his life. Her very virtues, now that they were carried to excess, seemed to her to border upon vices; her sense of dignity, appeared to be narrow pride; her delicacy weakness; her moderated affection cold ingratitude; and her circumspection, little less than prudence degenerated into meanness.

Vivaldi, as apt in admitting hope as fear, immediately perceived her resolution beginning to yield, and he urged again every argument which was likely to prevail over it. But the subject was too important for Ellena, to be immediately decided upon; he departed with only a faint assurance of encouragement; and she forbade him to return till the following day, when she would acquaint him with her final determination.

This interval was, perhaps, the most painful he had ever experienced. Alone, and on the banks of the lake, he passed many hours in alternate hope and fear; in endeavouring to anticipate the decision, on which seemed suspended all his future peace, and abruptly recoiling from it, as often as imagination represented it to be adverse.

Of the walls, that enclosed her, he scarcely ever lost sight; the view of them seemed to cherish his hopes, and, while he gazed upon their rugged surface, Ellena alone was pictured on his fancy; till his anxiety to learn her disposition towards him arose to agony, and he would abruptly leave the spot. But an invisible spell still seemed to attract him back again, and evening found him pacing slowly beneath the shade of those melancholy boundaries that concealed his Ellena.

Her day was not more tranquil. Whenever prudence and decorous pride forbade her to become a member of the Vivaldi family, as constantly did gratitude, affection, irresistible tenderness plead the cause of Vivaldi. The memory of past times returned; and the very accents of the deceased seemed to murmur from the grave, and command her to fulfil the engagement, which had soothed the dying moments of Bianchi.

On the following morning, Vivaldi was at the gates of the convent, long before the appointed hour, and he lingered in dreadful impatience, till the clock struck the signal for his entrance.

Ellena was already in the parlour; she was alone, and rose in disorder on his approach. His steps faultered, his voice was lost, and his eyes only, which he fixed with a wild earnestness on her's, had power to enquire her resolution. She observed the paleness of his countenance, and his emotion, with a mixture of concern and approbation. At that moment, he perceived her smile, and hold out her hand to him; and fear, care, and doubt vanished at once from his mind. He was incapable of thanking her, but sighed deeply as he pressed her hand, and, overcome with joy, supported himself against the grate that separated them.

'You are, then, indeed my own!' said Vivaldi, at length recovering his voice—'We shall be no more parted—you are mine for ever! But your countenance changes! O heaven! surely I have not mistaken! Speak! I conjure you, Ellena; relieve me from these terrible doubts!'

'I am yours, Vivaldi,' replied Ellena faintly, 'oppression can part us no more.'

She wept, and drew her veil over her eyes.

'What mean those tears?' said Vivaldi, with alarm. 'Ah! Ellena,' he added in a softened voice, 'should tears mingle with such moments as these! Should your tears fall upon my heart now! They tell me, that your consent is given with reluctance—with grief; that your love is feeble, your heart—yes Ellena! that your whole heart is no longer mine!'

'They ought rather to tell you,' replied Ellena, 'that it is all your own; that my affection never was more powerful than now, when it can overcome every consideration with respect to your family, and urge me to a step which must degrade me in their eyes,—and, I fear, in my own.'

'O retract that cruel assertion!' interrupted Vivaldi, 'Degrade you in your own!—degrade you in their eyes!' He was much agitated; his countenance was flushed, and an air of more than usual dignity dilated his figure.

'The time shall come, my Ellena,' he added with energy, 'when they shall understand your worth, and acknowledge your excellence. O! that I were an Emperor, that I might shew to all the world how much I love and honour you!'

Ellena gave him her hand, and, withdrawing her veil, smiled on him through her tears, with gratitude and reviving courage.

Before Vivaldi retired to the convent, he obtained her consent to consult with an aged Benedictine, whom he had engaged in his interest, as to the hour at which the marriage might be solemnized with least observation. The priest informed him, that at the conclusion of the vesper-service, he should be disengaged for several hours; and that, as the first hour after sun-set was more solitary than almost any other, the brotherhood being then assembled in the refectory, he would meet Vivaldi and Ellena at that time, in a chapel on the edge of the lake, a short distance from the Benedictine convent, to which it belonged, and celebrate their nuptials.

With this proposal, Vivaldi immediately returned to Ellena; when it was agreed that the party should assemble at the hour mentioned by the priest. Ellena, who had thought it proper to mention her intention to the Abbess of the Ursalines, was, by her permission, to be attended by a lay-sister; and Vivaldi was to meet her without the walls, and conduct her to the altar. When the ceremony was over, the fugitives were to embark in a vessel, hired for the purpose, and, crossing the lake, proceed towards Naples. Vivaldi again withdrew to engage a boat, and Ellena to prepare for the continuance of her journey.

As the appointed hour drew near, her spirits sunk, and she watched with melancholy foreboding, the sun retiring amidst stormy clouds, and his rays fading from the highest points of the mountains, till the gloom of twilight prevailed over the scene. She then left her apartment, took a grateful leave of the hospitable Abbess, and, attended by the lay-sister, quitted the convent.

Immediately without the gate she was met by Vivaldi, whose look, as he put her arm within his, gently reproached her for the dejection of her air.

They walked in silence towards the chapel of San Sebastian. The scene appeared to sympathize with the spirits of Ellena. It was a gloomy evening, and the lake, which broke in dark waves upon the shore, mingled its hollow sounds with those of the wind, that bowed the lofty pines, and swept in gusts among the rocks. She observed with alarm the heavy thunder clouds, that rolled along the sides of the mountains, and the birds circling swiftly over the waters, and scudding away to their nests among the cliffs; and she noticed to Vivaldi, that, as a storm seemed approaching, she wished to avoid crossing the lake. He immediately ordered Paulo to dismiss the boat, and to be in waiting with a carriage, that, if the weather should become clear, they might not be detained longer than was otherwise necessary.

As they approached the chapel, Ellena fixed her eyes on the mournful cypresses which waved over it, and sighed. 'Those,' she said, 'are funereal mementos—not such as should grace the altar of marriage! Vivaldi, I could be superstitious.—Think you not they are portentous of future misfortune? But forgive me; my spirits are weak.'

Vivaldi endeavoured to soothe her mind, and tenderly reproached her for the sadness she indulged. Thus they entered the chapel. Silence, and a kind of gloomy sepulchral light, prevailed within. The venerable Benedictine, with a brother, who was to serve as guardian to the bride, were already there, but they were kneeling, and engaged in prayer.

Vivaldi led the trembling Ellena to the altar, where they waited till the Benedictines should have finished, and these were moments of great emotion. She often looked round the dusky chapel, in fearful expectation of discovering some lurking observer; and, though she knew it to be very improbable, that any person in this neighbourhood could be interested in interrupting the ceremony, her mind involuntarily admitted the possibility of it. Once, indeed, as her eyes glanced over a casement, Ellena fancied she distinguished a human face laid close to the glass, as if to watch what was passing within; but when she looked again, the apparition was gone. Notwithstanding this, she listened with anxiety to the uncertain sounds without, and sometimes started as the surges of the lake dashed over the rock below, almost believing she heard the steps and whispering voices of men in the avenues of the chapel. She tried, however, to subdue apprehension, by considering, that if this were true, an harmless curiosity might have attracted some inhabitants of the convent hither, and her spirits became more composed, till she observed a door open a little way, and a dark countenance looking from behind it. In the next instant it retreated, and the door was closed.

Vivaldi, who perceived Ellena's complexion change, as she laid her hand on his arm, followed her eyes to the door, but, no person appearing, he enquired the cause of her alarm.

'We are observed,' said Ellena, 'some person appeared at that door!'

'And if we are observed, my love,' replied Vivaldi, 'who is there in this neighbourhood whose observation we can have reason to fear? Good father, dispatch,' he added, turning to the priest, 'you forget that we are waiting.'

The officiating priest made a signal that he had nearly concluded his orison; but the other brother rose immediately, and spoke with Vivaldi, who desired that the doors of the chapel might be fastened to prevent intrusion.

'We dare not bar the gates of this holy temple,' replied the Benedictine, 'it is a sanctuary, and never may be closed.'

'But you will allow me to repress idle curiosity,' said Vivaldi, 'and to enquire who watches beyond that door? The tranquillity of this lady demands thus much.'

The brother assented, and Vivaldi stepped to the door; but perceiving no person in the obscure passage beyond it, he returned with lighter steps to the altar, from which the officiating priest now rose.

'My children,' said he, 'I have made you wait,—but an old man's prayers are not less important than a young man's vows, though this is not a moment when you will admit that truth.'

'I will allow whatever you please, good father,' replied Vivaldi, 'if you will administer those vows, without further delay;—— time presses.'

The venerable priest took his station at the altar, and opened the book. Vivaldi placed himself on his right hand, and with looks of anxious love, endeavoured to encourage Ellena, who, with a dejected countenance, which her veil but ill concealed, and eyes fixed on the ground, leaned on her attendant sister. The figure and homely features of this sister; the tall stature and harsh visage of the brother, clothed in the gray habit of his order; the silvered head and placid physiognomy of the officiating priest, enlightened by a gleam from the lamp above, opposed to the youthful grace and spirit of Vivaldi, and the milder beauty and sweetness of Ellena, formed altogether a group worthy of the pencil.

The priest had begun the ceremony, when a noise from without again alarmed Ellena, who observed the door once more cautiously opened, and a man bend forward his gigantic figure from behind it. He carried a torch, and its glare, as the door gradually unclosed, discovered other persons in the passage beyond, looking forward over his shoulder into the chapel. The fierceness of their air, and the strange peculiarity of their dress, instantly convinced Ellena that they were not inhabitants of the Benedictine convent, but some terrible messengers of evil. Her half-stifled shriek alarmed Vivaldi, who caught her before she fell to the ground; but, as he had not faced the door, he did not understand the occasion of her terror, till the sudden rush of footsteps made him turn, when he observed several men armed, and very singularly habited, advancing towards the altar.

'Who is he that intrudes upon this sanctuary?' he demanded sternly, while he half rose from the ground where Ellena had sunk.

'What sacrilegious footsteps,' cried the priest, 'thus rudely violate this holy place?'

Ellena was now insensible; and the men continuing to advance, Vivaldi drew his sword to protect her.

The priest and Vivaldi now spoke together, but the words of neither could be distinguished, when a voice, tremendous from its loudness, like bursting thunder, dissipated the cloud of mystery.

'You Vincentio di Vivaldi, and of Naples,' it said, 'and you Ellena di Rosalba, of Villa Altieri, we summon you to surrender, in the name of the most holy Inquisition!'*

'The Inquisition!' exclaimed Vivaldi, scarcely believing what he heard. 'Here is some mistake!'

The official repeated the summons, without deigning to reply.

Vivaldi, yet more astonished, added, 'Do not imagine you can so far impose upon my credulity, as that I can believe myself to have fallen within the cognizance of the Inquisition.'

'You may believe what you please, Signor,' replied the chief officer, 'but you and that lady are our prisoners.'

'Begone, impostor!' said Vivaldi, springing from the ground, where he had supported Ellena, 'or my sword shall teach you to repent your audacity!'

'Do you insult an officer of the Inquisition!' exclaimed the ruffian. 'That holy Community will inform you what you incur by resisting it's mandate.'

The priest interrupted Vivaldi's retort, 'If you are really officers of that tremendous tribunal,' he said, 'produce some proof of your office. Remember this place is sanctified, and tremble for the consequence of imposition. You do wrong to believe, that I will deliver up to you persons who have taken refuge here, without an unequivocal demand from that dread power.'

'Produce your form of summons,' demanded Vivaldi, with haughty impatience.

'It is here,' replied the official, drawing forth a black scroll, which he delivered to the priest, 'Read, and be satisfied!'

The Benedictine started the instant he beheld the scroll, but he received and deliberately examined it. The kind of parchment, the impression of the seal, the particular form of words, the private signals, understood only by the initiated—all announced this to be a true instrument of arrestation from the *Holy Office*.* The scroll dropped from his hand, and he fixed his eyes, with surprize and unutterable compassion, upon Vivaldi, who stooped to reach the parchment, when it was snatched by the official.

'Unhappy young man!' said the priest, 'it is too true; you are summoned by that awful power, to answer to your crime, and I am spared from the commission of a terrible offence!'

Vivaldi appeared thunderstruck. 'For what crime, holy father, am I called upon to answer? This is some bold and artful imposture, since it can delude even you! What crime—what offence?'

'I did not think you had been thus hardened in guilt!' replied the priest, 'Forbear! add not the audacity of falsehood, to the head-long passions of youth. You understand too well your crime.'

'Falsehood!' retorted Vivaldi, 'But your years, old man, and those sacred vestments, protect you. For these ruffians, who have dared to implicate that innocent victim,' pointing to Ellena, 'in the charge, they shall have justice from my vengeance.'

'Forbear! forbear!' said the priest, seizing his arm, 'have pity on yourself and on her. Know you not the punishment you incur from resistance?'

'I know nor care not,' replied Vivaldi, 'but I will defend Ellena di Rosalba to the last moment. Let them approach if they dare.'

'It is on her, on her who lies senseless at your feet,' said the priest, 'that they will wreck their vengeance for these insults; on her—the partner of your guilt.'

'The partner of my guilt!' exclaimed Vivaldi, with mingled astonishment and indignation——'of my guilt!'

'Rash young man! does not the very veil she wears betray it? I marvel how it could pass my observation!'

'You have stolen a nun from her convent,' said the chief officer, 'and must answer for the crime. When you have wearied yourself with these heroics, Signor, you must go with us; our patience is wearied already.'

Vivaldi observed, for the first time, that Ellena was shrouded in a nun's veil; it was the one which Olivia had lent, to conceal her from the notice of the Abbess, on the night of her departure from

San Stefano, and which, in the hurry of that departure, she had forgotten to leave with the nun. During this interval, her mind had been too entirely occupied by cares and apprehension to allow her once to notice, that the veil she wore was other than her usual one; but it had been too well observed by some of the Ursaline sisters.

Though he knew not how to account for the circumstance of the veil, Vivaldi began to perceive others which gave colour to the charge brought against him, and to ascertain the wide circumference of the snare that was spread around him. He fancied, too, that he perceived the hand of Schedoni employed upon it, and that his dark spirit was now avenging itself for the exposure he had suffered in the church of the Spirito Santo, and for all the consequent mortifications. As Vivaldi was ignorant of the ambitious hopes which the Marchesa had encouraged in father Schedoni, he did not see the improbability, that the Confessor would have dared to hazard her favour by this arrest of her son; much less could he suspect, that Schedoni, having done so, had secrets in his possession, which enabled him safely to defy her resentment, and bind her in silence to his decree.

With the conviction, that Schedoni's was the master-hand that directed the present manœuvre, Vivaldi stood aghast, and gazing in silent unutterable anguish on Ellena, who, as she began to revive, stretched forth her helpless hands, and called upon him to save her. 'Do not leave me,' said she in accents the most supplicating, 'I am safe while you are with me.'

At the sound of her voice, he started from his trance, and turning fiercely upon the ruffians, who stood in sullen watchfulness around, bade them depart, or prepare for his fury. At the same instant they all drew their swords, and the shrieks of Ellena, and the supplications of the officiating priest, were lost amidst the tumult of the combatants.

Vivaldi, most unwilling to shed blood, stood merely on the defensive, till the violence of his antagonists compelled him to exert all his skill and strength. He then disabled one of the ruffians; but his skill was insufficient to repel the other two, and he was nearly overcome, when steps were heard approaching, and Paulo rushed into the chapel. Perceiving his master beset, he drew his sword, and came furiously to his aid. He fought with unconquerable audacity and fierceness, till nearly at the moment when his adversary fell, other ruffians entered the chapel, and Vivaldi with his faithful servant was wounded, and, at length, disarmed.

Ellena, who had been withheld from throwing herself between

the combatants, now, on observing that Vivaldi was wounded, renewed her efforts for liberty, accompanied by such agony of supplication and complaint, as almost moved to pity the hearts of the surrounding ruffians.

Disabled by his wounds, and also held by his enemies, Vivaldi was compelled to witness her distress and danger, without a hope of rescuing her. In frantic accents he called upon the old priest to protect her.

'I dare not oppose the orders of the Inquisition,' replied the Benedictine, 'even if I had sufficient strength to defy it's officials. Know you not, unhappy young man, that it is death to resist them?'

'Death!' exclaimed Ellena, 'death!'

'Ay lady, too surely so!'

'Signor, it would have been well for you,' said one of the officers, 'if you had taken my advice; you will pay dearly for what you have done,' pointing to the ruffian, who lay severely wounded on the ground.

'My master will not have that to pay for, friend,' said Paulo, 'for if you must know, that is a piece of my work; and, if my arms were now at liberty, I would try if I could not match it among one of you, though I am so slashed.'

'Peace, good Paulo! the deed was mine,' said Vivaldi; then addressing the official, 'For myself I care not, I have done my duty —but for her!—Can you look upon her, innocent and helpless as she is, and not relent! Can you, will you, barbarians! drag her, also, to destruction, upon a charge too so daringly false?'

'Our relenting would be of no service to her,' replied the official, 'we must do our duty. Whether the charge is true or false, she must answer to it before her judges.'

'What charge?' demanded Ellena.

'The charge of having broken your nun's vows,' replied the priest.

Ellena raised her eyes to heaven; 'Is it even so!' she exclaimed.

'You hear she acknowledges the crime,' said one of the ruffians.

'She acknowledges no crime,' replied Vivaldi; 'she only perceives the extent of the malice that persecutes her. O! Ellena, must I then abandon you to their power! leave you for ever!'

The agony of this thought re-animated him with momentary strength; he burst from the grasp of the officials, and once more clasped Ellena to his bosom, who, unable to speak, wept, with the anguish of a breaking heart, as her head sunk upon his shoulder.

The ruffians around them so far respected their grief, that, for a moment, they did not interrupt it.

Vivaldi's exertion was transient; faint from sorrow, and from loss of blood, he became unable to support himself, and was compelled again to relinquish Ellena.

'Is there no help?' said she, with agony; 'will you suffer him to expire on the ground?'

The priest directed, that he should be conveyed to the Benedictine convent, where his wounds might be examined, and medical aid administered. The disabled ruffians were already carried thither; but Vivaldi refused to go, unless Ellena might accompany him. It was contrary to the rules of the place, that a woman should enter it, and before the priest could reply, his Benedictine brother eagerly said, that they dared not transgress the law of the convent.

Ellena's fears for Vivaldi entirely overcame those for herself, and she entreated, that he would suffer himself to be conveyed to the Benedictines; but he could not be prevailed with to leave her. The officials, however, prepared to separate them; Vivaldi in vain urged the useless cruelty of dividing him from Ellena, if, as they had hinted, she also was to be carried to the Inquisition; and as ineffectually demanded, whither they really designed to take her.

'We shall take good care of her, Signor,' said an officer, 'that is sufficient for you. It signifies nothing whether you are going the same way, you must not go together.'

'Why, did you ever hear, Signor, of arrested persons being suffered to remain in company?' said another ruffian, 'Fine plots they would lay; I warrant they would not contradict each other's evidence a tittle.'

'You shall not separate me from my master, though,' vociferated Paulo; 'I demand to be sent to the Inquisition with him, or to the devil, but all is one for that.'

'Fair and softly,' replied the officer; 'you shall be sent to the Inquisition first, and to the devil afterwards; you must be tried before you are condemned.'

'But waste no more time,' he added to his followers, and pointing to Ellena, 'away with her.'

As he said this, they lifted Ellena in their arms. 'Let me loose!' cried Paulo, when he saw they were carrying her from the place, 'let me loose, I say!' and the violence of his struggles burst asunder the cords which held him; a vain release, for he was instantly seized again.

Vivaldi, already exhausted by the loss of blood and the anguish of his mind, made, however, a last effort to save her; he tried to raise himself from the ground, but a sudden film came over his sight, and his senses forsook him, while yet the name of Ellena faultered on his lips.

As they bore her from the chapel, she continued to call upon Vivaldi, and alternately to supplicate that she might once more behold him, and take one last adieu. The ruffians were inexorable, and she heard his voice no more, for he no longer heard—no longer was able to reply to her's.

'O! once again!' she cried in agony, 'One word, Vivaldi! Let me hear the sound of your voice yet once again!' But it was silent.

As she quitted the chapel, with eyes still bent towards the spot where he lay, she exclaimed, in the piercing accents of despair, 'Farewel, Vivaldi!—O! for ever——ever, farewel!'

The tone, in which she pronounced the last 'farewel!' was so touching, that even the cold heart of the priest could not resist it; but he impatiently wiped away the few tears, that rushed into his eyes, before they were observed. Vivaldi heard it—it seemed to arouse him from death!—he heard her mournful voice for the last time, and, turning his eyes, saw her veil floating away through the portal of the chapel. All suffering, all effort, all resistance were vain; the ruffians bound him, bleeding as he was, and conveyed him to the Benedictine convent, together with the wounded Paulo, who unceasingly vociferated on the way thither, 'I demand to be sent to the Inquisition! I demand to be sent to the Inquisition!'

CHAPTER VI

In earliest Greece to thee, with partial choice,
The grief-full Muse address'd her infant tongue;
The maids and matrons on her awful voice,
Silent and pale, in wild amazement hung.

COLLINS'S ODE TO FEAR*

THE wounds of Vivaldi, and of his servant, were pronounced, by the Benedictine who had examined and dressed them, to be not dangerous, but those of one of the ruffians were declared doubtful. Some few of the brothers displayed much compassion and kindness towards the prisoners; but the greater part seemed fearful of expressing any degree of sympathy for persons who had fallen within the cognizance of the Holy Office, and even kept aloof from the chamber, in which they were confined. To this self-restriction, however, they were not long subjected; for Vivaldi and Paulo were compelled to begin their journey as soon as some short rest had sufficiently revived them. They were placed in the same carriage, but the presence of two officers prevented all interchange of conjecture as to the destination of Ellena, and with respect to the immediate occasion of their misfortune. Paulo, indeed, now and then hazarded a surmise, and did not scruple to affirm, that the Abbess of San Stefano was their chief enemy; that the Carmelite friars, who had overtaken them on the road, were her agents; and that, having traced their route, they had given intelligence where Vivaldi and Ellena might be found.

'I guessed we never should escape the Abbess,' said Paulo, 'though I would not disturb you, Signor mio, nor the poor lady Ellena, by saying so. But your Abbesses are as cunning as Inquisitors, and are so fond of governing, that they had rather, like them, send a man to the devil, than send him no where.'

Vivaldi gave Paulo a significant look, which was meant to repress his imprudent loquacity, and then sunk again into silence and the abstractions of deep grief. The officers, mean while, never spoke, but were observant of all that Paulo said, who perceived their watchfulness, but because he despised them as spies, he thoughtlessly despised them also as enemies, and was so far from concealing opinions, which they might repeat to his prejudice, that he had a pride in exaggerating them, and in daring the worst, which the exasperated tempers of these men, shut up in the same carriage with him, and compelled to hear whatever he chose to say against the institution to which they belonged, could effect. Whenever Vivaldi, recalled from his abstractions by some bold assertion, endeavoured to check his imprudence, Paulo was contented to solace his conscience, instead of protecting himself, by saying, 'It is their own fault; they would thrust themselves into my company ; let them have enough of it; and, if ever they take me before their reverences, the Inquisitors, *they* shall have enough for it too. I will play up such a tune in the Inquisition as is not heard there every day. I will jingle all the bells on their fool's caps, and tell them a little honest truth, if they make me smart for it ever so.'

Vivaldi, aroused once more, and seriously alarmed for the consequences which honest Paulo might be drawing upon himself, now insisted on his silence, and was obeyed.

They travelled during the whole night, stopping only to change horses. At every post house, Vivaldi looked for a carriage that might inclose Ellena, but none appeared, nor any sound of wheels told him that she followed.

With the morning light he perceived the dome of St. Peter, appearing faintly over the plains that surrounded Rome, and he understood, for the first time, that he was going to the prisons of the Inquisition in that city. The travellers descended upon the Campania, and then rested for a few hours at a small town on its borders.

When they again set forward, Vivaldi perceived that the guard was changed, the officer who had remained with him in the apartment of the inn only appearing among the new faces which surrounded him. The dress and manners of these men differed considerably from those of the other. Their conduct was more temperate, but their countenances expressed a darker cruelty, mingled with a sly demureness, and a solemn self-importance, that announced them at once as belonging to the Inquisition. They were almost invariably silent; and when they did speak, it was only in a few sententious words. To the abounding questions of Paulo, and the few earnest entreaties of his master, to be informed of the place of Ellena's destination, they made not the least reply; and listened to all the flourishing speeches of the servant against Inquisitors and the Holy Office with the most profound gravity.

Vivaldi was struck with the circumstance of the guard being changed, and still more with the appearance of the party, who now composed it. When he compared the manners of the late, with those of the present guard, he thought he discovered in the first the mere ferocity of ruffians; but in the latter, the principles of cunning and cruelty, which seemed particularly to characterize Inquisitors; he was inclined to believe, that a stratagem had enthralled him, and that now, for the first time, he was in the custody of the *Holy Office.*

It was near midnight when the prisoners entered the *Porto del Popolo*, and found themselves in the midst of the Carnival at Rome. The *Corso*, through which they were obliged to pass, was crowded with gay carriages and masks, with processions of musicians, monks, and mountebanks, was lighted up with innumerable flambeaux, and resounded with the heterogeneous rattling of wheels, the music of serenaders, and the jokes and laughter of the revellers, as they sportively threw about their sugar-plumbs. The heat of the weather made it necessary to have the windows of the coach open; and the prisoners, therefore, saw all that passed without. It was a scene, which contrasted cruelly with the feelings and circumstances of Vivaldi; torn as he was from her he most loved, in dreadful uncertainty as to her fate, and himself about to be brought before a tribunal, whose mysterious and terrible proceedings appalled even the bravest spirits. Altogether, this was one of the most striking examples, which the chequer-work of human life could shew, or human feelings endure. Vivaldi sickened as he looked upon the splendid crowd, while the carriage made its way slowly with it; but Paulo, as he gazed, was reminded of the Corso of Naples, such as it appeared at the time of Carnival, and, comparing the present scene with his native one, he found fault with every thing he beheld. The dresses were tasteless, the equipages without splendor, the people without spirit; yet, such was the propensity of his heart to sympathize with whatever was gay, that, for some moments, he forgot that he was a prisoner on his way to the Inquisition; almost forgot that he was a Neapolitan; and, while he exclaimed against the dullness of a Roman carnival, would have sprung through the carriage window to partake of its spirit, if his fetters and his wounds had not withheld him. A deep sigh from Vivaldi recalled his wandering imagination; and, when he noticed again the sorrow in his master's look, all his lightly joyous spirits fled.

'My *maestro*, my dear *maestro!'*—he said, and knew not how to finish what he wished to express.

At that moment they passed the theatre of San Carlo, the doors of which were thronged with equipages, where Roman ladies, in their gala habits, courtiers in their fantastic dresses, and masks of all descriptions, were hastening to the opera. In the midst of this gay bustle, where the carriage was unable to proceed, the officials of the Inquisition looked on in solemn silence, not a muscle of their features relaxing in sympathy, or yielding a single wrinkle of the self-importance that lifted their brows; and, while they regarded with secret contempt those, who could be thus lightly pleased, the people, in return, more wisely, perhaps, regarded with contempt the proud moroseness, that refused to partake of innocent pleasures, because they were trifling, and shrunk from countenances furrowed with the sternness of cruelty. But, when their office was distinguished, part of the crowd pressed back from the carriage in affright, while another part advanced with curiosity; though, as the majority retreated, space was left for the carriage to move on. After quitting the Corso, it proceeded for some miles through dark and deserted streets, where only here and there a lamp, hung on high before the image of a saint, shed it's glimmering light, and where a melancholy and universal silence prevailed. At intervals, indeed, the moon, as the clouds passed away, shewed, for a moment, some of those mighty monuments of Rome's eternal name, those sacred ruins, those gigantic skeletons, which once enclosed a soul, whose energies governed a world! Even Vivaldi could not behold with indifference the grandeur of these reliques, as the rays fell upon the hoary walls and columns, or pass among these scenes of ancient story, without feeling a melancholy awe, a sacred enthusiasm, that withdrew him from himself. But the illusion was transient; his own misfortunes pressed too heavily upon him to be long unfelt, and his enthusiasm vanished like the moonlight.

A returning gleam lighted up, soon after, the rude and extensive area, which the carriage was crossing. It appeared, from it's desolation, and the ruins scattered distantly along its skirts, to be a part of the city entirely abandoned by the modern inhabitants to the reliques of its former grandeur. Not even the shadow of a human being crossed the waste, nor any building appeared, which might be supposed to shelter one. The deep tone of a bell, however, rolling on the silence of the night, announced the haunts of man to be not far off; and Vivaldi perceived in the distance, to which he was approaching, an extent of lofty walls and towers, that, as far as the gloom would permit his eye to penetrate, bounded the horizon. He judged these to be the prisons of the Inquisition. Paulo pointed them out at the same moment. 'Ah, Signor!' said he despondingly, 'that is the place! what strength! If, my Lord, the Marchese were but to see where we are going! Ah!'——

He concluded with a deep sigh, and sunk again into the state of apprehension and mute expectation, which he had suffered from the moment that he quitted the Corso.

The carriage having reached the walls, followed their bendings to a considerable extent. These walls, of immense height, and strengthened by innumerable massy bulwarks, exhibited neither window or grate, but a vast and dreary blank; a small round tower only, perched here and there upon the summit, breaking their monotony.

The prisoners passed what seemed to be the principal entrance, from the grandeur of its portal, and the gigantic loftiness of the towers that rose over it; and soon after the carriage stopped at an arch-way in the walls, strongly barricadoed. One of the escort alighted, and, having struck upon the bars, a folding door within was immediately opened, and a man bearing a torch appeared behind the barricado, whose countenance, as he looked through it, might have been copied for the

'Grim-visaged comfortless Despair'

of the Poet.*

No words were exchanged between him and the guard; but on perceiving who were without, he opened the iron gate, and the prisoners, having alighted, passed with the two officials beneath the arch, the guard following with a torch. They descended a flight of broad steps, at the foot of which another iron gate admitted them to a kind of hall; such, however, it at first appeared to Vivaldi, as his eyes glanced through its gloomy extent, imperfectly ascertaining it by the lamp, which hung from the centre of the roof. No person appeared, and a death-like silence prevailed; for neither the officials nor the guard yet spoke; nor did any distant sound contradict the notion, that they were traversing the chambers of the dead. To Vivaldi it occurred, that this was one of the burial vaults of the victims, who suffered in the Inquisition, and his whole frame thrilled with horror. Several avenues, opening from the apartment, seemed to lead to distant quarters of this immense fabric, but still no footstep whispering along the pavement, or voice murmuring through the arched roofs, indicated it to be the residence of the living.

Having entered one of the passages, Vivaldi perceived a person clothed in black, and who bore a lighted taper, crossing silently in the remote perspective; and he understood too well from his habit, that he was a member of this dreadful tribunal.

The sound of footsteps seemed to reach the stranger, for he turned, and then paused, while the officers advanced. They then made signs to each other, and exchanged a few words, which neither Vivaldi or his servant could understand, when the stranger, pointing with his taper along another avenue, passed away. Vivaldi followed him with his eyes, till a door at the extremity of the passage opened, and he saw the Inquisitor enter an apartment, whence a great light proceeded, and where several other figures, habited like himself, appeared waiting to receive him. The door immediately closed; and, whether the imagination of Vivaldi was affected, or that the sounds were real, he thought, as it closed, he distinguished half-stifled groans, as of a person in agony.

The avenue, through which the prisoners passed, opened, at length, into an apartment gloomy like the first they had entered, but more extensive. The roof was supported by arches, and long arcades branched off from every side of the chamber, as from a central point, and were lost in the gloom, which the rays of the small lamps, suspended in each, but feebly penetrated.

They rested here, and a person soon after advanced, who appeared to be the jailor, into whose hands Vivaldi and Paulo were delivered. A few mysterious words having been exchanged, one of the officials crossed the hall, and ascended a wide stair-case, while the other, with the jailor and the guard, remained below, as if awaiting his return.

A long interval elapsed, during which the stillness of the place was sometimes interrupted by a closing door, and, at others, by indistinct sounds, which yet appeared to Vivaldi like lamentations and extorted groans. Inquisitors, in their long black robes, issued, from time to time, from the passages, and crossed the hall to other avenues. They eyed the prisoners with curiosity, but without pity. Their visages, with few exceptions, seemed stamped with the characters of demons. Vivaldi could not look upon the grave cruelty, or the ferocious impatience, their countenances severally expressed, without reading in them the fate of some fellow creature, the fate, which these men seemed going, even at this moment, to confirm; and, as they passed with soundless steps, he shrunk from observation, as if their very looks possessed some supernatural power, and could have struck death. But he followed their fleeting figures, as they proceeded on their work of horror, to where the last glimmering ray faded into darkness, expecting to see other doors of other chambers open to receive them. While meditating upon these horrors, Vivaldi lost every selfish consideration in astonishment and indignation of the sufferings, which the frenzied wickedness of man prepares for man, who, even at the moment of infliction, insults his victim with assertions of the justice and necessity of such procedure. 'Is this possible!' said Vivaldi internally, 'Can this be in human nature!—Can such horrible perversion of right be permitted! Can man, who calls himself endowed with reason, and immeasurably superior to every other created being, argue himself into the commission of such horrible folly, such inveterate cruelty, as exceeds all the acts of the most irrational and ferocious brute. Brutes do not deliberately slaughter their species; it remains for man only, man, proud of his prerogative of reason, and boasting of his sense of justice, to unite the most terrible extremes of folly and wickedness!'

Vivaldi had been no stranger to the existence of this tribunal; he had long understood the nature of the establishment, and had often received particular accounts of its customs and laws; but, though he had believed before, it was now only that conviction appeared to impress his understanding. A new view of human nature seemed to burst, at once, upon his mind, and he could not have experienced greater astonishment, if this had been the first moment, in which he had heard of the institution. But, when he thought of Ellena, considered that she was in the power of this tribunal, and that it was probable she was at this moment within the same dreadful walls, grief, indignation, and despair irritated him almost to frenzy. He seemed suddenly animated with supernatural strength, and ready to attempt impossibilities for her deliverance. It was by a strong effort for self command, that he forbore bursting the bonds, which held him, and making a desperate attempt to seek her through the vast extent of these prisons. Reflection, however, had not so entirely forsaken him, but that he saw the impossibility of succeeding in such an effort, the moment he had conceived it, and he forbore to rush upon the certain destruction, to which it must have led. His passions, thus restrained, seemed to become virtues, and to display themselves in the energy of his courage and his fortitude. His soul became stern and vigorous in despair, and his manner and countenance assumed a calm dignity, which seemed to awe, in some degree, even his guards. The pain of his wounds was no longer felt; it appeared as if the strength of his intellectual self had subdued the infirmities of the body, and, perhaps, in these moments of elevation, he could have endured the torture without shrinking.

Paulo, meanwhile, mute and grave, was watchful of all that passed; he observed the revolutions in his master's mind, with grief first, and then with surprize, but he could not imitate the noble fortitude, which now gave weight and steadiness to Vivaldi's thoughts. And when he looked on the power and gloom around him, and on the visages of the passing Inquisitors, he began to repent, that he had so freely delivered his opinion of this tribunal, in the presence of its agents, and to perceive, that if he played up the kind of tune he had threatened, it would probably be the last he should ever be permitted to perform in this world.

At length, the chief officer descended the stair-case, and immediately bade Vivaldi follow him. Paulo was accompanying his master, but was withheld by the guard, and told he was to be disposed of in a different way. This was the moment of his severest trial; he declared he would not be separated from his master.

'What did I demand to be brought here for,' he cried, 'if it was not that I might go shares with the Signor in all his troubles? This is not a place to come to for pleasure, I warrant; and I can promise ye, gentlemen, I would not have come within an hundred miles of you, if it had not been for my master's sake.'

The guards roughly interrupted him, and were carrying him away, when Vivaldi's commanding voice arrested them. He returned to speak a few words of consolation to his faithful servant, and, since they were to be separated, to take leave of him.

Paulo embraced his knees, and, while he wept, and his words were almost stifled by sobs, declared no force should drag him from his master, while he had life; and repeatedly appealed to the guards, with—'What did I demand to be brought here for? Did ever any body come here to seek pleasure? What right have you to prevent my going shares with my master in his troubles?'

'We do not intend to deny you that pleasure, friend,' replied one of the guards.

'Don't you? Then heaven bless you!' cried Paulo, springing from his knees, and shaking the man by the hand with a violence, that would nearly have dislocated the shoulder of a person less robust.

'So come with us,' added the guard, drawing him away from Vivaldi. Paulo now became outrageous, and, struggling with the guards, burst from them, and again fell at the feet of his master, who raised and embraced him, endeavouring to prevail with him to submit quietly to what was inevitable, and to encourage him with hope.

'I trust that our separation will be short,' said Vivaldi, 'and that we shall meet in happier circumstances. My innocence must soon appear.'

'We shall never, never meet again, Signor mio, in this world,' said Paulo, sobbing violently, 'so don't make me hope so. That old Abbess knows what she is about too well to let us escape; or she would not have catched us up so cunningly as she did; so what signifies innocence! O! if my old lord, the Marchese, did but know where we are!'

Vivaldi interrupted him, and turning to the guards said, 'I recommend my faithful servant to your compassion, he is innocent. It will some time, perhaps, be in my power to recompence you for any indulgence you may allow him, and I shall value it a thousand times more highly, than any you could shew to myself! Farewel, Paulo,——farewel! Officer, I am ready.'

'O stay! Signor, for one moment—stay!' said Paulo.

'We can wait no longer,' said the guard, and again drew Paulo away, who looking piteously after Vivaldi, alternately repeated, 'Farewel, dear maestro! farewel dear, dear maestro!' and 'What did I demand to be brought here for? What did I demand to be brought here for?—what was it for, if not to go shares with my maestro?' till Vivaldi was beyond the reach of sight and of hearing.

Vivaldi, having followed the officer up the stair-case, passed through a gallery to an anti-chamber, where, being delivered into the custody of some persons in waiting, his conductor disappeared beyond a folding door, that led to an inner apartment. Over this door was an inscription in Hebrew characters, traced in blood-colour. Dante's inscription on the entrance of the infernal regions, would have been suitable to a place, where every circumstance and feature seemed to say, '*Hope, that comes to all, comes not here!*'

Vivaldi conjectured, that in this chamber they were preparing for him the instruments, which were to extort a confession; and though he knew little of the regular proceedings of this tribunal, he had always understood, that the torture was inflicted upon the accused person, till he made confession of the crime, of which he was suspected. By such a mode of proceeding, the innocent were certain of suffering longer than the guilty; for, as they had nothing to confess, the Inquisitor, mistaking innocence for obstinacy, persevered in his inflictions, and it frequently happened that he compelled the innocent to become criminal, and assert a falsehood, that they might be released from anguish, which they could no longer sustain. Vivaldi considered this circumstance undauntedly;

every faculty of his soul was bent up to firmness and endurance. He believed that he understood the extent of the charge, which would be brought against him, a charge as false, as a specious confirmation of it, would be terrible in it's consequence both to Ellena and himself. Yet every art would be practised to bring him to an acknowledgment of having carried off a nun, and he knew also, that, since the prosecutor and the witnesses are never confronted with the prisoner in cases of severe accusation, and since their very names are concealed from him, it would be scarcely possible for him to prove his innocence. But he did not hesitate an instant whether to sacrifice himself for Ellena, determining rather to expire beneath the merciless inflictions of the Inquisitors, than to assert a falsehood, which must involve her in destruction.

The officer, at length, appeared, and, having beckoned Vivaldi to advance, uncovered his head, and bared his arms. He then led him forward through the folding door into the chamber; having done which, he immediately withdrew, and the door, which shut out Hope, closed after him.

Vivaldi found himself in a spacious apartment, where only two persons were visible, who were seated at a large table, that occupied the centre of the room. They were both habited in black; the one, who seemed by his piercing eye, and extraordinary physiognomy, to be an Inquisitor, wore on his head a kind of black turban, which heightened the natural ferocity of his visage; the other was uncovered, and his arms bared to the elbows. A book, with some instruments of singular appearance, lay before him. Round the table were several unoccupied chairs, on the backs of which appeared figurative signs, at the upper end of the apartment, a gigantic crucifix stretched nearly to the vaulted roof; and, at the lower end, suspended from an arch in the wall, was a dark curtain, but whether it veiled a window, or shrouded some object or person, necessary to the designs of the Inquisitor, there were little means of judging. It was, however, suspended from an arch such as sometimes contains a casement, or leads to a deep recess.*

The Inquisitor called on Vivaldi to advance, and, when he had reached the table, put a book into his hands, and bade him swear to reveal the truth, and keep for ever secret whatever he might see or hear in the apartment.

Vivaldi hesitated to obey so unqualified a command. The Inquisitor reminded him, by a look, not to be mistaken, that he was absolute here; but Vivaldi still hesitated. 'Shall I consent to my own condemnation?' said he to himself, 'The malice of demons like these may convert the most innocent circumstances into matter of accusation, for my destruction, and I must answer whatever questions they choose to ask. And shall I swear, also, to conceal whatever I may witness in this chamber, when I know that the most diabolical cruelties are hourly practised here?'

The Inquisitor, in a voice which would have made a heart less fortified than was Vivaldi's tremble, again commanded him to swear; at the same time, he made a signal to the person, who sat at the opposite end of the table, and who appeared to be an inferior officer.

Vivaldi was still silent, but he began to consider that, unconscious as he was of crime, it was scarcely possible for his words to be tortured into a self-accusation; and that, whatever he might witness, no retribution would be prevented, no evil withheld by the oath, which bound him to secresy, since his most severe denunciation could avail nothing against the supreme power of this tribunal. As he did not perceive any good, which could arise from refusing the oath; and saw much immediate evil from resistance, he consented to receive it. Notwithstanding this, when he put the book to his lips, and uttered the tremendous vow prescribed to him, hesitation and reluctance returned upon his mind, and an icy coldness struck to his heart. He was so much affected, that circumstances, apparently the most trivial, had at this moment influence upon his imagination. As he accidentally threw his eyes upon the curtain, which he had observed before without emotion, and now thought it moved, he almost started in expectation of seeing some person, an Inquisitor perhaps, as terrific as the one before him, or an Accuser as malicious as Schedoni, steal from behind it.

The Inquisitor having administered the oath, and the attendant having noted it in his book, the examination began. After demanding, as is usual, the names and titles of Vivaldi and his family, and his place of residence, to which he fully replied, the Inquisitor asked, whether he understood the nature of the accusation on which he had been arrested.

'The order for my arrestation informed me,' replied Vivaldi.

'Look to your words!' said the Inquisitor, 'and remember your oath. What was the ground of accusation?'

'I understood,' said Vivaldi, 'that I was accused of having stolen a nun from her sanctuary.'

A faint degree of surprise appeared on the brow of the Inquisitor. 'You confess it, then?' he said, after the pause of a moment, and making a signal to the Secretary, who immediately noted Vivaldi's words.

'I solemnly deny it,' replied Vivaldi, 'the accusation is false and malicious.'

'Remember the oath you have taken!' repeated the Inquisitor, 'learn also, that mercy is shewn to such as make full confession; but that the torture is applied to those, who have the folly and the obstinacy to withhold the truth.'

'If you torture me till I acknowledge the justness of this accusation,' said Vivaldi, 'I must expire under your inflictions, for suffering never shall compel me to assert a falsehood. It is not the truth, which you seek; it is not the guilty, whom you punish; the innocent, having no crimes to confess, are the victims of your cruelty, or, to escape from it, become criminal, and proclaim a lie.'

'Recollect yourself,' said the Inquisitor, sternly. 'You are not brought hither to accuse, but to answer accusation. You say you are innocent; yet acknowledge yourself to be acquainted with the subject of the charge which is to be urged against you! How could you know this, but from the voice of conscience?'

'From the words of your own summons,' replied Vivaldi, 'and from those of your officials who arrested me.'

'How!' exclaimed the Inquisitor, 'note that,' pointing to the Secretary; 'he says by the words of our summons; now we know, that you never read that summons. He says also by the words of our officials;—it appears, then, he is ignorant, that death would follow such a breach of confidence.'

'It is true, I never did read the summons,' replied Vivaldi, 'and as true, that I never asserted I did; the friar, who read it, told of what it accused me, and your officials confirmed the testimony.'

'No more of this equivocation!' said the Inquisitor, 'Speak only to the question.'

'I will not suffer my assertions to be misrepresented,' replied Vivaldi, 'or my words to be perverted against myself. I have sworn to speak the truth only; since you believe I violate my oath, and doubt my direct and simple words, I will speak no more.'

The Inquisitor half rose from his chair, and his countenance grew paler. 'Audacious heretic!' he said, 'will you dispute, insult, and disobey, the commands of our most holy tribunal! You will be taught the consequence of your desperate impiety.—To the torture with him!'

A stern smile was on the features of Vivaldi; his eyes were calmly fixed on the Inquisitor, and his attitude was undaunted and firm. His courage, and the cool contempt, which his looks expressed, seemed to touch his examiner, who perceived that he had not a common mind to operate upon. He abandoned, therefore, for the present, terrific measures, and, resuming his usual manner, proceeded in the examination.

'Where were you arrested?'

'At the chapel of San Sebastian, on the lake of Celano.'

'You are certain as to this?' asked the Inquisitor, 'you are sure it was not at the village of Legano, on the high road between Celano and Rome?'

Vivaldi, while he confirmed his assertion, recollected with some surprize that Legano was the place where the guard had been changed, and he mentioned the circumstance. The Inquisitor, however, proceeded in his questions, without appearing to notice it. 'Was any person arrested with you?'

'You cannot be ignorant,' replied Vivaldi, 'that Signora di Rosalba, was seized at the same time, upon the false charge of being a nun, who had broken her vows, and eloped from her convent; nor that Paulo Mendrico, my faithful servant! was also made a prisoner, though upon what pretence he was arrested I am utterly ignorant.'

The Inquisitor remained for some moments in thoughtful silence, and then enquired slightly concerning the family of Ellena, and her usual place of residence. Vivaldi, fearful of making some assertion that might be prejudicial to her, referred him to herself; but the inquiry was repeated.

'She is now within these walls,' replied Vivaldi, hoping to learn from the manner of his examiner, whether his fears were just, 'and can answer these questions better than myself.'

The Inquisitor merely bade the Notary write down her name, and then remained for a few moments meditating. At length, he said, 'Do you know where you now are?'

Vivaldi, smiling at the question, replied, 'I understand that I am in the prisons of the Inquisition, at Rome.'

'Do you know what are the crimes that subject persons to the cognizance of the Holy Office?'

Vivaldi was silent.

'Your conscience informs *you*, and your silence confirms *me*. Let me admonish you, once more, to make a full confession of your guilt; remember that this is a merciful tribunal, and shews favour to such as acknowledge their crimes.'

Vivaldi smiled; but the Inquisitor proceeded.

'It does not resemble some severe, yet just courts, where immediate execution follows the confession of a criminal. No! it is merciful, and though it punishes guilt, it never applies the torture but in cases of necessity, when the obstinate silence of the prisoner requires such a measure. You see, therefore, what you may avoid, and what expect.'

'But if the prisoner has nothing to confess?' said Vivaldi,— 'Can your tortures make him guilty? They may force a weak mind to be guilty of falsehood; to escape present anguish, a man may unwarily condemn himself to the death! You will find that I am not such an one.'

'Young man,' replied the Inquisitor, 'you will understand too soon, that we never act, but upon sure authority; and will wish, too late, that you had made an honest confession. Your silence cannot keep from us a knowledge of your offences; we are in possession of facts; and your obstinacy can neither wrest from us the truth, or pervert it. Your most secret offences are already written on the tablets of the Holy Office; your conscience cannot reflect them more justly.—Tremble, therefore, and revere. But understand, that, though we have sufficient proof of your guilt, we require you to confess; and that the punishment of obstinacy is as certain, as that of any other offence.'

Vivaldi made no reply, and the Inquisitor, after a momentary silence, added, 'Was you ever in the church of the Spirito Santo, at Naples?'

'Before I answer the question,' said Vivaldi, 'I require the name of my accuser.'

'You are to recollect that you have no right to demand any thing in this place,' observed the Inquisitor, 'nor can you be ignorant that the name of the Informer is always kept sacred from the knowledge of the Accused. Who would venture to do his duty, if his name was arbitrarily to be exposed to the vengeance of the criminal against whom he informs? It is only in a particular process that the Accuser is brought forward.'

'The names of the Witnesses?' demanded Vivaldi. 'The same justice conceals them also from the knowledge of the Accused,' replied the Inquisitor.

'And is no justice left for the Accused?' said Vivaldi. 'Is he to be tried and condemned without being confronted with either his Prosecutor, or the Witnesses!'

'Your questions are too many,' said the Inquisitor, 'and your answers too few. The Informer is not also the Prosecutor; the

Holy Office, before which the information is laid, is the Prosecutor, and the dispenser of justice; its Public Accuser lays the circumstances, and the testimonies of the Witnesses, before the Court. But too much of this.'

'How!' exclaimed Vivaldi, 'is the tribunal at once the Prosecutor, Witness, and Judge! What can private malice wish for more, than such a court of *justice*, at which to arraign it's enemy? The stiletto of the Assassin is not so sure, or so fatal to innocence. I now perceive, that it avails me nothing to be guiltless; a single enemy is sufficient to accomplish my destruction.'

'You have an enemy then?' observed the Inquisitor.

Vivaldi was too well convinced that he had one, but there was not sufficient proof, as to the person of this enemy, to justify him in asserting that it was Schedoni. The circumstance of Ellena having been arrested, would have compelled him to suspect another person as being at least accessary to the designs of the Confessor, had not credulity started in horror from the supposition, that a mother's resentment could possibly betray her son into the prisons of the Inquisition, though this mother had exhibited a temper of remorseless cruelty towards a stranger, who had interrupted her views for that son.

'You have an enemy then?' repeated the Inquisitor.

'That I am here sufficiently proves it,' replied Vivaldi. 'But I am so little any man's enemy, that I know not who to call mine.'

'It is evident, then, that you have no enemy,' observed the subtle Inquisitor, 'and that this accusation is brought against you by a respecter of truth, and a faithful servant of the Roman interest.'

Vivaldi was shocked to perceive the insidious art, by which he had been betrayed into a declaration apparently so harmless, and the cruel dexterity with which it had been turned against him. A lofty and contemptuous silence was all that he opposed to the treachery of his examiner, on whose countenance appeared a smile of triumph and self-congratulation, the life of a fellow creature being, in his estimation, of no comparative importance with the self-applauses of successful art; the art, too, upon which he most valued himself—that of his profession.

The Inquisitor proceeded, 'You persist, then, in withholding the truth?' He paused, but Vivaldi making no reply, he resumed.

'Since it is evident, from your own declaration, that you have no enemy, whom private resentment might have instigated to accuse you; and, from other circumstances which have occurred in your conduct, that you are conscious of more than you have confessed,—

it appears, that the accusation which has been urged against you, is not a malicious slander. I exhort you, therefore, and once more conjure you, by our holy faith, to make an ingenuous confession of your offences, and to save yourself from the means, which must of necessity be enforced to obtain a confession before your trial commences. I adjure you, also, to consider, that by such open conduct only, can mercy be won to soften the justice of this most righteous tribunal!'

Vivaldi, perceiving that it was now necessary for him to reply, once more solemnly asserted his innocence of the crime alledged against him in the summons, and of the consciousness of any act, which might lawfully subject him to the notice of the Holy Office.

The Inquisitor again demanded what was the crime alledged, and, Vivaldi having repeated the accusation, he again bade the Secretary note it, as he did which, Vivaldi thought he perceived upon his features something of a malignant satisfaction, for which he knew not how to account. When the Secretary had finished, Vivaldi was ordered to subscribe his name and quality to the depositions, and he obeyed.

The Inquisitor then bade him consider of the admonition he had received, and prepare either to confess on the morrow, or to undergo the question. As he concluded, he gave a signal, and the officer, who had conducted Vivaldi into the chamber, immediately appeared.

'You know your orders,' said the Inquisitor, 'receive your prisoner, and see that they are obeyed.'

The official bowed, and Vivaldi followed him from the apartment in melancholy silence.

CHAPTER VII

Call up the Spirit of the ocean, bid
Him raise the storm! The waves begin to heave,
To curl, to foam; the white surges run far
Upon the dark'ning waters, and mighty
Sounds of strife are heard. Wrapt in the midnight
Of the clouds, sits Terror, meditating
Woe. Her doubtful form appears and fades,
Like the shadow of Death, when he mingles
With the gloom of the sepulchre, and broods
In lonely silence. Her spirits are abroad!
They do her bidding! Hark, to that shriek!
The echoes of the shore have heard!

ELLENA, meanwhile, when she had been carried from the chapel of San Sebastian, was placed upon a horse in waiting, and, guarded by the two men who had seized her, commenced a journey, which continued with little interruption during two nights and days. She had no means of judging whither she was going, and listened in vain expectation, for the feet of horses, and the voice of Vivaldi, who, she had been told, was following on the same road.

The steps of travellers seldom broke upon the silence of these regions, and, during the journey, she was met only by some market-people passing to a neighbouring town, or now and then by the vine-dressers or labourers in the olive grounds; and she descended upon the vast plains of Apulia, still ignorant of her situation. An encampment, not of warriors, but of shepherds, who were leading their flocks to the mountains of Abruzzo, enlivened a small tract of these levels, which were shadowed on the north and east by the mountainous ridge of the Garganus, stretching from the Apennine far into the Adriatic.

The appearance of the shepherds was nearly as wild and savage as that of the men, who conducted Ellena; but their pastoral instruments of flageolets* and tabors spoke of more civilized feelings, as they sounded sweetly over the desert. Her guards rested, and refreshed themselves with goat's milk, barley cakes, and almonds, and the manners of these shepherds, like those she had formerly met with on the mountains, proved to be more hospitable than their air had indicated.

After Ellena had quitted this pastoral camp, no vestige of a human residence appeared for several leagues, except here and there the towers of a decayed fortress, perched upon the lofty acclivities she was approaching, and half concealed in the woods. The evening of the second day was drawing on, when her guards drew near the forest, which she had long observed in the distance, spreading over the many-rising steeps of the Garganus. They entered by a track, a road it could not be called, which led among oaks and gigantic chestnuts, apparently the growth of centuries, and so thickly interwoven, that their branches formed a canopy which seldom admitted the sky. The gloom which they threw around, and the thickets of cystus, juniper, and lenticus, which flourished beneath the shade, gave a character of fearful wildness to the scene.

Having reached an eminence, where the trees were more thinly scattered, Ellena perceived the forests spreading on all sides among hills and vallies, and descending towards the Adriatic, which bounded the distance in front. The coast, bending into a bay, was rocky and bold. Lofty pinnacles, wooded to their summits, rose over the shores, and cliffs of naked marble of such gigantic proportions, that they were awful even at a distance, obtruded themselves far into the waves, breasting their eternal fury. Beyond the margin of the coast, as far as the eye could reach, appeared pointed mountains, darkened with forests, rising ridge over ridge in many successions. Ellena, as she surveyed this wild scenery, felt as if she was going into eternal banishment from society. She was tranquil, but it was with the quietness of exhausted grief, not of resignation; and she looked back upon the past, and awaited the future, with a kind of out-breathed despair.

She had travelled for some miles through the forest, her guards only now and then uttering to each other a question, or an observation concerning the changes which had taken place in the bordering scenery, since they last passed it, when night began to close in upon them.

Ellena perceived her approach to the sea, only by the murmurs of its surge upon the rocky coast, till, having reached an eminence, which was, however, no more than the base of two woody mountains that towered closely over it, she saw dimly it's gray surface spreading in the bay below. She now ventured to ask how much further she was to go, and whether she was to be taken on board one of the little vessels, apparently fishing smacks, that she could just discern at anchor.

'You have not far to go now,' replied one of the guards, surlily; 'you will soon be at the end of your journey, and at rest.'

They descended to the shore, and presently came to a lonely dwelling, which stood so near the margin of the sea, as almost to be washed by the waves. No light appeared at any of the lattices; and, from the silence that reigned within, it seemed to be uninhabited. The guard had probably reason to know otherwise, for they halted at the door, and shouted with all their strength. No voice, however, answered to their call, and, while they persevered in efforts to rouse the inhabitants, Ellena anxiously examined the building, as exactly as the twilight would permit. It was of an ancient and peculiar structure, and, though scarcely important enough for a mansion, had evidently never been designed for the residence of peasants.

The walls, of unhewn marble, were high, and strengthened by bastions; and the edifice had turretted corners, which, with the porch in front, and the sloping roof, were falling fast into numerous symptoms of decay. The whole building, with it's dark windows and soundless avenues, had an air strikingly forlorn and solitary. A high wall surrounded the small court in which it stood, and probably had once served as a defence to the dwelling; but the gates, which should have closed against intruders, could no longer perform their office; one of the folds had dropped from it's fastenings, and lay on the ground almost concealed in a deep bed of weeds, and the other creaked on its hinges to every blast, at each swing seeming ready to follow the fate of it's companion.

The repeated calls of the guard, were, at length, answered by a rough voice from within; when the door of the porch was lazily unbarred, and opened by a man, whose visage was so misery-struck, that Ellena could not look upon it with indifference, though wrapt in misery of her own. The lamp he held threw a gleam athwart it, and shewed the gaunt ferocity of famine, to which the shadow of his hollow eyes added a terrific wildness. Ellena shrunk while she gazed. She had never before seen villainy and suffering so strongly pictured on the same face, and she observed him with a degree of thrilling curiosity, which for a moment excluded from her mind all consciousness of the evils to be apprehended from him.

It was evident that this house had not been built for his reception; and she conjectured, that he was the servant of some cruel agent of the Marchesa di Vivaldi.

From the porch, she followed into an old hall, ruinous, and destitute of any kind of furniture. It was not extensive but lofty, for it seemed to ascend to the roof of the edifice, and the chambers above opened around it into a corridor.

Some half-sullen salutations were exchanged between the guard and the stranger, whom they called Spalatro, as they passed into a chamber, where, it appeared that he had been sleeping on a mattress laid in a corner. All the other furniture of the place, were two or three broken chairs and a table. He eyed Ellena with a shrewd contracted brow, and then looked significantly at the guard, but was silent, till he desired them all to sit down, adding, that he would dress some fish for supper. Ellena discovered that this man was the master of the place; it appeared also that he was the only inhabitant; and, when the guard soon after informed her their journey concluded here, her worst apprehensions were confirmed. The efforts she made to sustain her spirits, were no longer success-ful. It seemed that she was brought hither by ruffians to a lonely house on the sea-shore, inhabited by a man, who had 'villain' engraved in every line of his face, to be the victim of inexorable pride and an insatiable desire of revenge. After considering these circumstances, and the words, which had just told her, she was to go no further, conviction struck like lightning upon her heart; and, believing she was brought hither to be assassinated, horror chilled all her frame, and her senses forsook her.

On recovering, she found herself surrounded by the guard and the stranger, and she would have supplicated for their pity, but that she feared to exasperate them by betraying her suspicions. She complained of fatigue, and requested to be shewn to her room. The men looked upon one another, hesitated, and then asked her to partake of the fish that was preparing. But Ellena having declined the invitation with as good a grace as she could assume, they con-sented that she should withdraw. Spalatro, taking the lamp, lighted her across the hall, to the corridor above, where he opened the door of a chamber, in which he said she was to sleep.

'Where is my bed?' said the afflicted Ellena fearfully as she looked round.

'It is there—on the floor,' replied Spalatro, pointing to a miser-able mattress, over which hung the tattered curtains of what had once been a canopy. 'If you want the lamp,' he added, 'I will leave it, and come for it in a minute or two.'

'Will you not let me have a lamp for the night,' she said in a supplicating and timid voice.

'For the night!' said the man gruffly; 'What! to set fire to the house.'

Ellena still entreated that he would allow her the comfort of a light.

'Ay, ay,' replied Spalatro, with a look she could not comprehend, 'it would be a great comfort to you, truly! You do not know what you ask.'

'What is it that you mean?' said Ellena, eagerly; 'I conjure you, in the name of our holy church, to tell me!'

Spalatro stepped suddenly back, and looked upon her with surprise, but without speaking.

'Have mercy on me!' said Ellena, greatly alarmed by his manner; 'I am friendless, and without help!'

'What do you fear,' said the man, recovering himself; and then, without waiting her reply, added—'Is it such an unmerciful deed to take away a lamp?'

Ellena, who again feared to betray the extent of her suspicions, only replied, that it would be merciful to leave it, for that her spirits were low, and she required light to cheer them in a new abode.

'We do not stand upon such conceits here,' replied Spalatro, 'we have other matters to mind. Besides, it's the only lamp in the house, and the company below are in darkness while I am losing time here. I will leave it for two minutes, and no more.' Ellena made a sign for him to put down the lamp; and, when he left the room, she heard the door barred upon her.

She employed these two minutes in examining the chamber, and the possibility it might afford of an escape. It was a large apartment, unfurnished and unswept of the cobwebs of many years. The only door she discovered was the one, by which she had entered, and the only window a lattice, which was grated. Such preparation for preventing escape seemed to hint how much there might be to escape from.

Having examined the chamber, without finding a single circumstance to encourage hope, tried the strength of the bars, which she could not shake, and sought in vain for an inside fastening to her door, she placed the lamp beside it, and awaited the return of Spalatro. In a few moments he came, and offered her a cup of sour wine with a slice of bread; which, being somewhat soothed by this attention, she did not think proper to reject.

Spalatro then quitted the room, and the door was again barred. Left once more alone, she tried to overcome apprehension by prayer; and after offering up her vespers with a fervent heart, she became more confiding and composed.

But it was impossible that she could so far forget the dangers of her situation, as to seek sleep, however wearied she might be, while the door of her room remained unsecured against the intrusion of the ruffians below; and, as she had no means of fastening it, she determined to watch during the whole night. Thus left to solitude and darkness, she seated herself upon the mattress to await the return of morning, and was soon lost in sad reflection; every minute occurrence of the past day, and of the conduct of her guards, moved in review before her judgment; and, combining these with the circumstances of her present situation, scarcely a doubt as to the fate designed for her remained. It seemed highly improbable, that the Marchesa di Vivaldi had sent her hither merely for imprisonment, since she might have confined her in a convent, with much less trouble; and still more so, when Ellena considered the character of the Marchesa, such as she had already experienced it. The appearance of this house, and of the man who inhabited it, with the circumstance of no woman being found residing here, each and all of these signified, that she was brought hither, not for long imprisonment, but for death. Her utmost efforts for fortitude or resignation could not overcome the cold tremblings, the sickness of heart, the faintness and universal horror, that assailed her. How often, with tears of mingled terror and grief, did she call upon Vivaldi—Vivaldi, alas! far distant—to save her; how often exclaim in agony, that she should never, never see him more!

She was spared, however, the horror of believing that he was an inhabitant of the Inquisition. Having detected the imposition, which had been practised towards herself, and that she was neither on the way to the Holy Office, nor conducted by persons belonging to it, she concluded, that the whole affair of Vivaldi's arrest, had been planned by the Marchesa, merely as a pretence for confining him, till she should be placed beyond the reach of his assistance. She hoped, therefore, that he had only been sent to some private residence belonging to his family, and that, when her fate was decided, he would be released, and she be the only victim. This was the sole consideration, that afforded any degree of assuagement to her sufferings.

The people below sat till a late hour. She listened often to their distant voices, as they were distinguishable in the pauses of the surge, that broke loud and hollow on the shore; and every time the creaking hinges of their room door moved, apprehended they were coming to her. At length, it appeared they had left the apartment, or had fallen asleep there, for a profound stillness reigned whenever the murmur of the waves sunk. Doubt did not long deceive her, for, while she yet listened, she distinguished footsteps ascending to the corridor. She heard them approach her chamber, and stop at the door; she heard, also, the low whisperings of their voices, as they seemed consulting on what was to be done, and she scarcely ventured to draw breath, while she intensely attended to them. Not a word, however, distinctly reached her, till, as one of them was departing, another called out in a half-whisper, 'It is below on the table, in my girdle; make haste.' The man came back, and said something in a lower voice, to which the other replied, 'she sleeps,' or Ellena was deceived by the hissing consonants of some other words. He then descended the stairs; and in a few minutes she perceived his comrade also pass away from the door; she listened to his retreating steps, till the roaring of the sea was alone heard in their stead.

Ellena's terrors were relieved only for a moment. Considering the import of the words, it appeared that the man who had descended, was gone for the stiletto of the other, such an instrument being usually worn in the girdle, and from the assurance, 'she sleeps,' he seemed to fear that his words had been overheard; and she listened again for their steps; but they came no more.

Happily for Ellena's peace, she knew not that her chamber had a door, so contrived as to open without sound, by which assassins might enter unsuspectedly at any hour of the night. Believing that the inhabitants of this house had now retired to rest, her hopes and her spirits began to revive; but she was yet sleepless and watchful. She measured the chamber with unequal steps, often starting as the old boards shook and groaned where she passed; and often pausing to listen whether all was yet still in the corridor. The gleam, which a rising moon threw between the bars of her window, now began to shew many shadowy objects in the chamber, which she did not recollect to have observed while the lamp was there. More than once, she fancied she saw something glide along towards the place where the mattress was laid, and, almost congealed with terror, she stood still to watch it; but the illusion, if such it was, disappeared where the moon-light faded, and even her fears could not give shape to it beyond. Had she not known that her chamber-door remained strongly barred, she would have believed this was an assassin stealing to the bed where it might be supposed she slept. Even now the thought occurred to her, and vague as it was, had power to strike an anguish, almost deadly, through her heart, while she considered that her immediate situation was nearly as perilous as the one she had imagined. Again she listened, and scarcely dared to breathe; but not the lightest sound occurred in the pauses of the waves, and she believed herself convinced that no person except herself was in the room. That she was deceived in this belief, appeared from her unwillingness to approach the mattress, while it was yet involved in shade. Unable to overcome her reluctance, she took her station at the window, till the strengthening rays should allow a clearer view of the chamber, and in some degree restore her confidence; and she watched the scene without as it gradually became visible. The moon, rising over the ocean, shewed it's restless surface spreading to the wide horizon; and the waves, which broke in foam upon the rocky beach below, retiring in long white lines far upon the waters. She listened to their measured and solemn sound, and, somewhat soothed by the solitary grandeur of the view, remained at the lattice till the moon had risen high into the heavens; and even till morning began to dawn upon the sea, and purple the eastern clouds.

Re-assured, by the light that now pervaded her room, she returned to the mattress; where anxiety at length yielded to her weariness, and she obtained a short repose.

CHAPTER VIII

And yet I fear you; for you are fatal then,
When your eyes roll so.   -   -   -   -
-   -   -   -   -   -   -   -   -   -
Alas! why gnaw you so your nether lip?
Some bloody passion shakes your very frame:
These are portents; but yet I hope, I hope,
They do not point on me.   SHAKSPEARE*

ELLENA was awakened from profound sleep, by a loud noise at the door of her chamber; when, starting from her mattress, she looked around her with surprise and dismay, as imperfect recollections of the past began to gather on her mind. She distinguished the undrawing of iron bars, and then the countenance of Spalatro at her door, before she had a clear remembrance of her situation— that she was a prisoner in a house on a lonely shore, and that this man was her jailor. Such sickness of the heart returned with these convictions, such faintness and terror, that unable to support her trembling frame, she sunk again upon the mattress, without demanding the reason of this abrupt intrusion.

'I have brought you some breakfast,' said Spalatro, 'if you are awake to take it; but you seem to be asleep yet. Surely you have had sleep sufficient for one night; you went to rest soon enough.'

Ellena made no reply, but, deeply affected with a sense of her situation, looked with beseeching eyes at the man, who advanced, holding forth an oaten cake and a bason of milk. 'Where shall I set them?' said he, 'you must needs be glad of them, since you had no supper.'

Ellena thanked him, and desired he would place them on the floor, for there was neither table nor chair in the room. As he did this, she was struck with the expression of his countenance, which exhibited a strange mixture of archness and malignity. He seemed congratulating himself upon his ingenuity, and anticipating some occasion of triumph; and she was so much interested, that her observation never quitted him while he remained in the room. As his eyes accidentally met her's, he turned them away, with the abruptness of a person who is conscious of evil intentions, and fears lest they should be detected; nor once looked up till he hastily left the chamber, when she heard the door secured as formerly.

The impression, which his look had left on her mind, so wholly engaged her in conjecture, that a considerable time elapsed before she remembered that he had brought the refreshment she so much required; but, as she now lifted it to her lips, a horrible suspicion arrested her hand; it was not, however, before she had swallowed a small quantity of the milk. The look of Spalatro, which occasioned her surprise, had accompanied the setting down of the breakfast, and it occurred to her, that poison was infused in this liquid. She was thus compelled to refuse the sustenance, which was become necessary to her, for she feared to taste even of the oaten cake, since Spalatro had offered it, but the little milk she had unwarily taken, was so very small that she had no apprehension concerning it.

The day, however, was passed in terror, and almost in despondency; she could neither doubt the purpose, for which she had been brought hither, nor discover any possibility of escaping from her persecutors; yet that propensity to hope, which buoys up the human heart, even in the severest hours of trial, sustained, in some degree, her fainting spirits.

During these miserable hours of solitude and suspense, the only alleviation to her suffering arose from a belief, that Vivaldi was safe, at least from danger, though not from grief; but she now understood too much of the dexterous contrivances of the

Marchesa, his mother, to think it was practicable for him to escape from her designs, and again restore her to liberty.

All day Ellena either leaned against the bars of her window, lost in reverie, while her unconscious eyes were fixed upon the ocean, whose murmurs she no longer heard; or she listened for some sound from within the house, that might assist her conjectures, as to the number of persons below, or what might be passing there. The house, however, was profoundly still, except when now and then a footstep sauntered along a distant passage, or a door was heard to close; but not the hum of a single voice arose from the lower rooms, nor any symptom of there being more than one person, beside herself, in the dwelling. Though she had not heard her former guards depart, it appeared certain that they were gone, and that she was left alone in this place with Spalatro. What could be the purport of such a proceeding, Ellena could not imagine; if her death was designed, it seemed strange that one person only should be left to the hazard of the deed, when three must have rendered the completion of it certain. But this surprise vanished, when her suspicion of poison returned; for it was probable, that these men had believed their scheme to be already nearly accomplished, and had abandoned her to die alone, in a chamber from whence escape was impracticable, leaving Spalatro to dispose to her remains. All the incongruities she had separately observed in their conduct, seemed now to harmonize and unite in one plan; and her death, designed by poison, and that poison to be conveyed in the disguise of nourishment, appeared to have been the object of it. Whether it was that the strength of this conviction affected her fancy, or that the cause was real, Ellena, remembering at this moment that she had tasted the milk, was seized with an universal shuddering, and thought she felt that the poison had been sufficiently potent to affect her, even in the inconsiderable quantity she might have taken.

While she was thus agitated, she distinguished footsteps loitering near her door, and attentively listening, became convinced, that some person was in the corridor. The steps moved softly, sometimes stopping for an instant, as if to allow time for listening, and soon after passed away.

'It is Spalatro!' said Ellena; 'he believes that I have taken the poison, and he comes to listen for my dying groans! Alas! he is only come somewhat too soon, perhaps!'

As this horrible supposition occurred, the shuddering returned with encreased violence, and she sunk, almost fainting, on the mattress; but the fit was not of long continuance. When it gradually left her, and recollection revived, she perceived, however, the prudence of suffering Spalatro to suppose she had taken the beverage he brought her, since such belief would at least procure some delay of further schemes, and every delay afforded some possibility for hope to rest upon. Ellena, therefore, poured through the bars of her window, the milk, which she believed Spalatro had designed should be fatal in its consequence.

It was evening, when she again fancied footsteps were lingering near her door, and the suspicion was confirmed, when, on turning her eyes, she perceived a shade on the floor, underneath it, as of some person stationed without. Presently the shadow glided away, and at the same time she distinguished departing steps treading cautiously.

'It is he!' said Ellena; 'he still listens for my moans!'

This further confirmation of his designs affected her nearly as much as the first; when anxiously turning her looks towards the corridor, the shadow again appeared beneath the door, but she heard no step. Ellena now watched it with intense solicitude and expectation; fearing every instant that Spalatro would conclude her doubts by entering the room. 'And O! when he discovers that I live,' thought she, 'what may I not expect during the first moments of his disappointment! What less than immediate death!'

The shadow, after remaining a few minutes stationary, moved a little, and then glided away as before. But it quickly returned, and a low sound followed, as of some person endeavouring to unfasten bolts without noise. Ellena heard one bar gently undrawn, and then another; she observed the door begin to move, and then to give way, till it gradually unclosed, and the face of Spalatro presented itself from behind it. Without immediately entering, he threw a glance round the chamber, as if he wished to ascertain some circumstance before he ventured further. His look was more than usually haggard as it rested upon Ellena, who apparently reposed on her mattress.

Having gazed at her for an instant, he ventured towards the bed with quick and unequal steps; his countenance expressed at once impatience, alarm, and the consciousness of guilt. When he was within a few paces, Ellena raised herself, and he started back as if a sudden spectre had crossed him. The more than usual wildness and wanness of his looks, with the whole of his conduct, seemed to confirm all her former terrors; and, when he roughly asked her how she did, Ellena had not sufficient presence of mind to answer that she was ill. For some moments, he regarded her with an earnest and sullen attention, and then a sly glance of scrutiny, which he threw round the chamber, told her that he was enquiring whether she had taken the poison. On perceiving that the bason was empty, he lifted it from the floor, and Ellena fancied a gleam of satisfaction passed over his visage.

'You have had no dinner,' said he, 'I forgot you; but supper will soon be ready; and you may walk up the beach till then, if you will.'

Ellena, extremely surprised and perplexed by this offer of a seeming indulgence, knew not whether to accept or reject it. She suspected that some treachery lurked within it. The invitation appeared to be only a stratagem to lure her to destruction, and she determined to decline accepting it; when again she considered, that to accomplish this, it was not necessary to withdraw her from the chamber, where she was already sufficiently in the power of her persecutors. Her situation could not be more desperate than it was at present, and almost any change might make it less so.

As she descended from the corridor, and passed through the lower part of the house, no person appeared but her conductor; and she ventured to enquire, whether the men who had brought her hither were departed. Spalatro did not return an answer, but led the way in silence to the court, and, having passed the gates, he pointed toward the west, and said she might walk that way.

Ellena bent her course towards the 'many-sounding waves,'* followed at a short distance by Spalatro, and, wrapt in thought, pursued the windings of the shore, scarcely noticing the objects around her; till, on passing the foot of a rock, she lifted her eyes to the scene that unfolded beyond, and observed some huts scattered at a considerable distance, apparently the residence of fishermen. She could just distinguish the dark sails of some skiffs turning the cliffs, and entering the little bay, where the hamlet margined the beach; but, though she saw the sails lowered, as the boats approached the shore, they were too far off to allow the figures of the men to appear. To Ellena, who had believed that no human habitation, except her prison, interrupted the vast solitudes of these forests and shores, the view of the huts, remote as they were, imparted a feeble hope, and even somewhat of joy. She looked back, to observe whether Spalatro was near; he was already within a few paces; and, casting a wistful glance forward to the remote cottages, her heart sunk again.

It was a lowering evening, and the sea was dark and swelling; the screams of the sea-birds too, as they wheeled among the clouds, and sought their high nests in the rocks, seemed to indicate an approaching storm. Ellena was not so wholly engaged by selfish sufferings, but that she could sympathise with those of others, and she rejoiced that the fishermen, whose boats she had observed, had escaped the threatening tempest, and were safely sheltered in their little homes, where, as they heard the loud waves break along the coast, they could look with keener pleasure upon the social circle, and the warm comforts around them. From such considerations however, she returned again to a sense of her own forlorn and friendless situation.

'Alas!' said she, 'I have no longer a home, a circle to smile welcomes upon me! I have no longer even one friend to support, to rescue me! I—a miserable wanderer on a distant shore! tracked, perhaps, by the footsteps of the assassin, who at this instant eyes his victim with silent watchfulness, and awaits the moment of opportunity to sacrifice her!'

Ellena shuddered as she said this, and turned again to observe whether Spalatro was near. He was not within view; and, while she wondered, and congratulated herself on a possibility of escaping, she perceived a Monk walking silently beneath the dark rocks that overbrowed the beach. His black garments were folded round him; his face was inclined towards the ground, and he had the air of a man in deep meditation.

'His, no doubt, are worthy musings!' said Ellena, as she observed him, with mingled hope and surprise. 'I may address myself, without fear, to one of his order. It is probably as much his wish, as it is his duty, to succour the unfortunate. Who could have hoped to find on this sequestered shore so sacred a protector! his convent cannot be far off.'

He approached, his face still bent towards the ground, and Ellena advanced slowly, and with trembling steps, to meet him. As he drew near, he viewed her askance, without lifting his head; but she perceived his large eyes looking from under the shade of his cowl, and the upper part of his peculiar countenance. Her confidence in his protection began to fail, and she faultered, unable to speak, and scarcely daring to meet his eyes. The Monk stalked past her in silence, the lower part of his visage still muffled in his drapery, and as he passed her looked neither with curiosity, nor surprise.

Ellena paused, and determined, when he should be at some distance, to endeavour to make her way to the hamlet, and throw herself upon the humanity of it's inhabitants, rather than solicit the pity of this forbidding stranger. But in the next moment she heard a step behind her, and, on turning, saw the Monk again approaching. He stalked by as before, surveying her, however, with a sly and scrutinizing glance from the corners of his eyes. His air and countenance were equally repulsive, and still Ellena could not summon courage enough to attempt engaging his compassion; but shrunk as from an enemy. There was something also terrific in the silent stalk of so gigantic a form; it announced both power and treachery. He passed slowly on to some distance, and disappeared among the rocks.

Ellena turned once more with an intention of hastening towards the distant hamlet, before Spalatro should observe her, whose strange absence she had scarcely time to wonder at; but she had not proceeded far, when suddenly she perceived the Monk again at her shoulder. She started, and almost shrieked; while he regarded her with more attention than before. He paused a moment, and seemed to hesitate; after which he again passed on in silence. The distress of Ellena encreased; he was gone the way she had designed to run, and she feared almost equally to follow him, and to return to her prison. Presently he turned, and passed her again, and Ellena hastened forward. But, when fearful of being pursued, she again looked back, she observed him conversing with Spalatro. They appeared to be in consultation, while they slowly advanced, till, probably observing her rapid progress, Spalatro called on her to stop, in a voice that echoed among all the rocks. It was a voice, which would not be disobeyed. She looked hopelessly at the still distant cottages, and slackened her steps. Presently the Monk again passed before her, and Spalatro had again disappeared. The frown, with which the former now regarded Ellena, was so terrific, that she shrunk trembling back, though she knew him not for her persecutor, since she had never consciously seen Schedoni. He was agitated, and his look became darker.

'Whither go you?' said he in a voice that was stifled by emotion.

'Who is it, father, that asks the question?' said Ellena, endeavouring to appear composed.

'Whither go you, and who are you?' repeated the Monk more sternly.

'I am an unhappy orphan,' replied Ellena, sighing deeply, 'If you are, as your habit denotes, a friend to the charities, you will regard me with compassion.'

Schedoni was silent, and then said—'Who, and what is it that you fear?'

'I fear—even for my life,' replied Ellena, with hesitation. She observed a darker shade pass over his countenance. 'For your life!' said he, with apparent surprise, 'who is there that would think it worth the taking.'

Ellena was struck with these words.

'Poor insect!' added Schedoni, 'who would crush thee?'

Ellena made no reply; she remained with her eyes fixed in amazement upon his face. There was something in his manner of pronouncing this, yet more extraordinary than in the words themselves. Alarmed by his manner, and awed by the encreasing gloom, and swelling surge, that broke in thunder on the beach, she at length turned away, and again walked towards the hamlet which was yet very remote.

He soon overtook her; when rudely seizing her arm, and gazing earnestly on her face, 'Who is it, that you fear?' said he, 'say who!'

'That is more than I dare say,' replied Ellena, scarcely able to sustain herself.

'Hah! is it even so!' said the Monk, with encreasing emotion. His visage now became so terrible, that Ellena struggled to liberate her arm, and supplicated that he would not detain her. He was silent, and still gazed upon her, but his eyes, when she had ceased to struggle, assumed the fixt and vacant glare of a man, whose thoughts have retired within themselves, and who is no longer conscious to surrounding objects.

'I beseech you to release me!' repeated Ellena, 'it is late, and I am far from home.'

'That is true,' muttered Schedoni, still grasping her arm, and seeming to reply to his own thoughts rather than to her words,— 'that is very true.'

'The evening is closing fast,' continued Ellena, 'and I shall be overtaken by the storm.'

Schedoni still mused, and then muttered—'The storm, say you? Why ay, let it come.'

As he spoke, he suffered her arm to drop, but still held it, and walked slowly towards the house. Ellena, thus compelled to accompany him, and yet more alarmed both by his looks, his incoherent answers, and his approach to her prison, renewed her supplications and her efforts for liberty, in a voice of piercing distress, adding, 'I am far from home, father; night is coming on. See how the rocks darken! I am far from home, and shall be waited for.'

'That is false!' said Schedoni, with emphasis; 'and you know it to be so.'

'Alas! I do,' replied Ellena, with mingled shame and grief, 'I have no friends to wait for me!'

'What do those deserve, who deliberately utter falsehoods,' continued the Monk, 'who deceive, and flatter young men to their destruction?'

'Father!' exclaimed the astonished Ellena.

'Who disturb the peace of families—who trepan,* with wanton arts, the heirs of noble houses—who—hah! what do such deserve?'

Overcome with astonishment and terror, Ellena remained silent. She now understood that Schedoni, so far from being likely to prove a protector, was an agent of her worst, and as she had believed her only enemy; and an apprehension of the immediate and terrible vengeance, which such an agent seemed willing to accomplish, subdued her senses; she tottered, and sunk upon the beach. The weight, which strained the arm Schedoni held, called his attention to her situation.

As he gazed upon her helpless and faded form, he became agitated. He quitted it, and traversed the beach in short turns, and with hasty steps; came back again, and bent over it—his heart seemed sensible to some touch of pity. At one moment, he stepped towards the sea, and taking water in the hollows of his hands, threw it upon her face; at another, seeming to regret that he had done so, he would stamp with sudden fury upon the shore, and walk abruptly to a distance. The conflict between his design and his conscience was strong, or, perhaps, it was only between his passions. He, who had hitherto been insensible to every tender feeling, who, governed by ambition and resentment had contributed, by his artful instigations, to fix the baleful resolution of the Marchesa di Vivaldi, and who was come to execute her purpose,—even he could not now look upon the innocent, the wretched Ellena, without yielding to the momentary weakness, as he termed it, of compassion.

While he was yet unable to baffle the new emotion by evil passions, he despised that which conquered him. 'And shall the weakness of a girl,' said he, 'subdue the resolution of a man! Shall the view of her transient sufferings unnerve my firm heart, and compel me to renounce the lofty plans I have so ardently, so laboriously imagined, at the very instant when they are changing into realities! Am I awake! Is one spark of the fire, which has so long smouldered within my bosom, and consumed my peace, alive! Or am I tame and abject as my fortunes? hah! as my fortunes! Shall the spirit of my family yield for ever to circumstances? The question rouses it, and I feel it's energy revive within me.'

He stalked with hasty steps towards Ellena, as if he feared to trust his resolution with a second pause. He had a dagger concealed beneath his Monk's habit; as he had also an assassin's heart shrouded by his garments. He had a dagger—but he hesitated to use it, the blood which it might spill, would be observed by the peasants of the neighbouring hamlet, and might lead to a discovery. It would be safer, he considered, and easier, to lay Ellena, senseless as she was, in the waves; their coldness would recal her to life, only at the moment before they would suffocate her.

As he stooped to lift her, his resolution faultered again, on beholding her innocent face, and in that moment she moved. He started back, as if she could have known his purpose, and, knowing it, could have avenged herself. The water, which he had thrown upon her face, had gradually revived her; she unclosed her eyes, and, on perceiving him, shrieked and attempted to rise. His resolution was subdued, so tremblingly fearful is guilt in the moment when it would execute it's atrocities. Overcome with apprehensions, yet agitated with shame and indignation against himself for being so, he gazed at her for an instant in silence, and then abruptly turned away his eyes and left her. Ellena listened to his departing steps, and, raising herself, observed him retiring among the rocks that led towards the house. Astonished at his conduct, and surprised to find that she was alone, Ellena renewed all her efforts to sustain herself, till she should reach the hamlet so long the object of her hopes; but she had proceeded only a few paces, when Spalatro again appeared swiftly approaching. Her utmost exertion availed her nothing; her feeble steps were soon overtaken, and Ellena perceived herself again his prisoner. The look with which she resigned herself, awakened no pity in Spalatro, who uttered some taunting jest upon the swiftness of her flight, as he led her back to her prison, and proceeded in sullen watchfulness. Once again, then, she entered the gloomy walls of that fatal mansion, never more, she now believed, to quit them with life, a belief, which was strengthened when she remembered that the Monk on leaving her, had taken the way hither; for, though she knew not how to account for his late forbearance, she could not suppose that he would long be merciful. He appeared no more, however, as she passed to her chamber, where Spalatro left her again to solitude and terror, and she heard that fateful door again barred upon her. When his retreating steps had ceased to sound, a stilness, as of the grave, prevailed in the house; like the dead calm, which sometimes precedes the horrors of a tempest.

CHAPTER IX

I am settled, and bend up
Each corporal agent to this terrible feat.
SHAKSPEARE*

SCHEDONI had returned from the beach to the house, in a state of perturbation, that defied the controul of even his own stern will. On the way thither he met Spalatro, whom, as he dispatched him to Ellena, he strictly commanded not to approach his chamber till he should be summoned.

Having reached his apartment, he secured the door, though not any person, except himself, was in the house, nor any one expected, but those who he knew would not dare to intrude upon him. Had it been possible to have shut out all consciousness of himself, also, how willingly would he have done so! He threw himself into a chair, and remained for a considerable time motionless, and lost in thought, yet the emotions of his mind were violent and contradictory. At the very instant when his heart reproached him with the crime he had meditated, he regretted the ambitious views he must relinquish if he failed to perpetrate it, and regarded himself with some degree of contempt for having hitherto hesitated on the subject. He considered the character of his own mind with astonishment, for circumstances had drawn forth traits, of which, till now, he had no suspicion. He knew not by what doctrine to explain the inconsistencies, the contradictions, he experienced, and, perhaps, it was not one of the least that in these moments of direful and conflicting passions, his reason could still look down upon their operations, and lead him to a cool, though brief examination of his own nature. But the subtlety of self-love still eluded his enquiries, and he did not detect that pride was even at this instant of self-examination, and of critical import, the master-spring of his mind. In the earliest dawn of his character this passion had displayed its predominancy, whenever occasion permitted, and it's influence had led to some of the chief events of his life.

The Count di Marinella, for such had formerly been the title of the Confessor, was the younger son of an ancient family, who resided in the duchy of Milan, and near the feet of the Tyrolean Alps, on such estates of their ancestors, as the Italian wars of a former century had left them. The portion, which he had received at the death of his father, was not large, and Schedoni was not of a disposition to improve his patrimony by slow diligence, or to submit to the restraint and humiliation, which his narrow finances would have imposed. He disdained to acknowledge an inferiority of fortune to those, with whom he considered himself equal in rank; and, as he was destitute of generous feeling, and of sound judgment, he had not that loftiness of soul, which is ambitious of true grandeur. On the contrary, he was satisfied with an ostentatious display of pleasures and of power, and, thoughtless of the consequence of dissipation, was contented with the pleasures of the moment, till his exhausted resources compelled him to pause, and to reflect. He perceived, too late for his advantage, that it was necessary for him to dispose of part of his estate, and to confine himself to the income of the remainder. Incapable of submitting with grace to the reduction, which his folly had rendered expedient, he endeavoured to obtain by cunning, the luxuries that his prudence had failed to keep, and which neither his genius or his integrity could command. He withdrew, however, from the eyes of his neighbours, unwilling to submit his altered circumstances to their observation.

Concerning several years of his life, from this period, nothing was generally known; and, when he was next discovered, it was in the Spirito Santo convent at Naples, in the habit of a Monk, and under the assumed name of Schedoni. His air and countenance were as much altered as his way of life; his looks had become gloomy and severe, and the pride, which had mingled with the gaiety of their former expression, occasionally discovered itself under the disguise of humility, but more frequently in the austerity of silence, and in the barbarity of penance.

The person who discovered Schedoni, would not have recollected him, had not his remarkable eyes first fixed his attention, and then revived remembrance. As he examined his features, he traced the faint resemblance of what Marinella had been, to whom he made himself known.

The Confessor affected to have forgotten his former acquaintance, and assured him, that he was mistaken respecting himself, till the stranger so closely urged some circumstances, that the former was no longer permitted to dissemble. He retired, in some emotion, with the stranger, and, whatever might be the subject of their conference, he drew from him, before he quitted the convent, a tremendous vow, to keep secret from the brotherhood his knowledge of Schedoni's family, and never to reveal without those walls, that he had seen him. These requests he had urged in a manner, that at once surprised and awed the stranger, and which at the same time that it manifested the weight of Schedoni's fears, bade the former tremble for the consequence of disobedience; and he shuddered even while he promised to obey. Of the first part of the promise he was probably strictly observant; whether he was equally so of the second, does not appear; it is certain, that after this period, he was never more seen or heard of at Naples.

Schedoni, ever ambitious of distinction, adapted his manners to the views and prejudices of the society with whom he resided, and became one of the most exact observers of their outward forms, and almost a prodigy for self-denial and severe discipline. He was pointed out by the fathers of the convent to the juniors as a great example, who was, however, rather to be looked up to with reverential admiration, than with an hope of emulating his sublime virtues. But with such panegyrics their friendship for Schedoni concluded. They found it convenient to applaud the austerities, which they declined to practise; it procured them a character for sanctity, and saved them the necessity of earning it by mortifications of their own; but they both feared and hated Schedoni for his pride and his gloomy austerities, too much, to gratify his ambition by any thing further than empty praise. He had been several years in the society, without obtaining any considerable advancement, and with the mortification of seeing persons, who had never emulated his severity, raised to high offices in the church. Somewhat too late he discovered, that he was not to expect any substantial favour from the brotherhood, and then it was that his restless and disappointed spirit first sought preferment by other avenues. He had been some years Confessor to the Marchesa di Vivaldi, when the conduct of her son awakened his hopes, by showing him, that he might render himself not only useful but necessary to her, by his councils. It was his custom to study the characters of those around him, with a view of adapting them to his purposes, and, having ascertained that of the Marchesa, these hopes were encouraged. He perceived that her passions were strong, her judgment weak; and he understood, that, if circumstances should ever enable him to be serviceable in promoting the end at which any one of those passions might aim, his fortune would be established.

At length, he so completely insinuated himself into her

confidence, and became so necessary to her views, that he could demand his own terms, and this he had not failed to do, though with all the affected delicacy and finesse that his situation seemed to require. An office of high dignity in the church, which had long vainly excited his ambition, was promised him by the Marchesa, who had sufficient influence to obtain it; her condition was that of his preserving the honour of her family, as she delicately termed it, which she was careful to make him understand could be secured only by the death of Ellena. He acknowledged, with the Marchesa, that the death of this fascinating young woman was the only means of preserving that honour, since, if she lived, they had every evil to expect from the attachment and character of Vivaldi, who would discover and extricate her from any place of confinement, however obscure or difficult of access, to which she might be conveyed. How long and how arduously the Confessor had aimed to oblige the Marchesa, has already appeared. The last scene was now arrived, and he was on the eve of committing that atrocious act, which was to secure the pride of her house, and to satisfy at once his ambition and his desire of vengeance; when an emotion new and surprising to him, had arrested his arm, and compelled his resolution to falter. But this emotion was transient, it disappeared almost with the object that had awakened it; and now, in the silence and retirement of his chamber, he had leisure to recollect his thoughts, to review his schemes, to re-animate his resolution, and to wonder again at the pity, which had almost won him from his purpose. The ruling passion of his nature once more resumed it's authority, and he determined to earn the honour, which the Marchesa had in store for him.

After some cool, and more of tumultuous, consideration, he resolved that Ellena should be assassinated that night, while she slept, and afterwards conveyed through a passage of the house communicating with the sea, into which the body might be thrown and buried, with her sad story, beneath the waves. For his own sake, he would have avoided the danger of shedding blood, had this appeared easy; but he had too much reason to know she had suspicions of poison, to trust to a second attempt by such means; and again his indignation rose against himself, since by yielding to a momentary compassion, he had lost the opportunity afforded him of throwing her unresistingly into the surge.

Spalatro, as has already been hinted, was a former confident of the Confessor, who knew too truly, from experience, that he could be trusted, and had, therefore, engaged him to assist on this occasion. To the hands of this man he consigned the fate of the unhappy Ellena, himself recoiling from the horrible act he had willed; and intending by such a step to involve Spalatro more deeply in the guilt, and thus more effectually to secure his secret.

The night was far advanced before Schedoni's final resolution was taken, when he summoned Spalatro to his chamber to instruct him in his office. He bolted the door, by which the man had entered, forgetting that themselves were the only persons in the house, except the poor Ellena, who, unsuspicious of what was conspiring, and her spirits worn out by the late scene, was sleeping peacefully on her mattress above. Schedoni moved softly from the door he had secured, and, beckoning Spalatro to approach, spoke in a low voice, as if he feared to be overheard. 'Have you perceived any sound from her chamber lately?' said he, 'Does she sleep, think you?'

'No one has moved there for this hour past, at least,' replied Spalatro, 'I have been watching in the corridor, till you called, and should have heard if she had stirred, the old floor shakes so with every step.'

'Then hear me, Spalatro,' said the Confessor. 'I have tried, and found thee faithful, or I should not trust thee in a business of confidence like this. Recollect all I said to thee in the morning, and be resolute and dexterous, as I have ever found thee.'

Spalatro listened in gloomy attention, and the Monk proceeded, 'It is late; go, therefore, to her chamber; be certain that she sleeps. Take this,' he added, 'and this,' giving him a dagger and a large cloak—'You know how you are to use them.'

He paused, and fixed his penetrating eyes on Spalatro, who held up the dagger in silence, examined the blade, and continued to gaze upon it, with a vacant stare, as if he was unconscious of what he did.

'You know your business,' repeated Schedoni, authoritatively, 'dispatch! time wears; and I must set off early.'

The man made no reply.

'The morning dawns already,' said the Confessor, still more urgently, 'Do you faulter? do you tremble? Do I not know you?'

Spalatro put up the poinard in his bosom without speaking, threw the cloak over his arm, and moved with a loitering step towards the door.

'Dispatch!' repeated the Confessor, 'why do you linger?'

'I cannot say I like this business, Signor,' said Spalatro surlily. 'I know not why I should always do the most, and be paid the least.'

'Sordid villain!' exclaimed Schedoni, 'you are not satisfied then!'

'No more a villain than yourself, Signor,' retorted the man, throwing down the cloak, 'I only do your business; and 'tis you that are sordid, for you would take all the reward, and I would only have a poor man have his dues. Do the work yourself, or give me the greater profit.'

'Peace!' said Schedoni, 'dare no more to insult me with the mention of reward. Do you imagine I have sold myself! 'Tis my will that she dies; this is sufficient; and for you—the price you have asked has been granted.'

'It is too little,' replied Spalatro, 'and besides, I do not like the work.—What harm has she done me?'

'Since when is it, that you have taken upon you to moralize?' said the Confessor, 'and how long are these cowardly scruples to last? This is not the first time you have been employed; what harm had others done you! You forget that I know you, you forget the past.'

'No, Signor, I remember it too well, I wish I could forget; I remember it too well.—I have never been at peace since. The bloody hand is always before me! and often of a night, when the sea roars, and storms shake the house, *they* have come, all gashed as I left them, and stood before my bed! I have got up, and ran out upon the shore for safety!'

'Peace!' repeated the Confessor, 'where is this frenzy of fear to end? To what are these visions, painted in blood, to lead? I thought I was talking with a man, but find I am speaking only to a baby, possessed with his nurse's dreams! Yet I understand you,— you shall be satisfied.'

Schedoni, however, had for once misunderstood this man, when he could not believe it possible that he was really averse to execute what he had undertaken. Whether the innocence and beauty of Ellena had softened his heart, or that his conscience did torture him for his past deeds, he persisted in refusing to murder her. His conscience, or his pity, was of a very peculiar kind however; for, though he refused to execute the deed himself, he consented to wait at the foot of a back stair-case, that communicated with Ellena's chamber, while Schedoni accomplished it, and afterward to assist in carrying the body to the shore. 'This is a compromise between conscience and guilt, worthy of a demon,' muttered Schedoni, who appeared to be insensible that he had made the same compromise with himself not an hour before; and whose extreme reluctance at this moment, to perpetrate with his own hand, what he had willingly designed for another, ought to have reminded him of that compromise.

Spalatro, released from the immediate office of an executioner, endured silently the abusive, yet half-stifled, indignation of the Confessor, who also bade him remember, that, though he now shrunk from the most active part of this transaction, he had not always been restrained, in offices of the same nature, by equal compunction; and that not only his means of subsistence, but his very life itself, was at his mercy. Spalatro readily acknowledged that it was so; and Schedoni knew, too well, the truth of what he had urged, to be restrained from his purpose, by any apprehension of the consequence of a discovery from this ruffian.

'Give me the dagger, then,' said the Confessor, after a long pause, 'take up the cloak, and follow to the stair-case. Let me see, whether your valour will carry you thus far.'

Spalatro resigned the stiletto, and threw the cloak again over his arm. The Confessor stepped to the door, and, trying to open it, 'It is fastened!' said he in alarm, 'some person has got into the house,—it is fastened!'

'That well may be, Signor,' replied Spalatro, calmly, 'for I saw you bolt it yourself, after I came into the room.'

'True,' said Schedoni, recovering himself; 'that is true.'

He opened it, and proceeded along the silent passages, towards the private stair-case, often pausing to listen, and then stepping more lightly;—the terrific Schedoni, in this moment of meditative guilt, feared even the feeble Ellena. At the foot of the stair-case, he again stopped to listen. 'Do you hear any thing?' said he in a whisper.

'I hear only the sea,' replied the man.

'Hush! it is something more!' said Schedoni; 'that is the murmur of voices!'

They were silent. After a pause of some length, 'It is, perhaps, the voice of the spectres I told you of, Signor,' said Spalatro, with a sneer. 'Give me the dagger,' said Schedoni.

Spalatro, instead of obeying, now grasped the arm of the Confessor, who, looking at him for an explanation of this extraordinary action, was still more surprised to observe the paleness and horror of his countenance. His starting eyes seemed to follow some object along the passage, and Schedoni, who began to partake of his feelings, looked forward to discover what occasioned this dismay, but could not perceive any thing that justified it. 'What is it you fear?' said he at length.

Spalatro's eyes were still moving in horror, 'Do you see nothing!' said he pointing. Schedoni looked again, but did not distinguish any object in the remote gloom of the passage, whither Spalatro's sight was now fixed.

'Come, come,' said he, ashamed of his own weakness, 'this is not a moment for such fancies. Awake from this idle dream.'

Spalatro withdrew his eyes, but they retained all their wildness. 'It was no dream,' said he, in the voice of a man who is exhausted by pain, and begins to breathe somewhat more freely again. 'I saw it as plainly as I now see you.'

'Dotard! what did you see!' enquired the Confessor.

'It came before my eyes in a moment, and shewed itself distinctly and outspread.'

'What shewed itself?' repeated Schedoni.

'And then it beckoned—yes, it beckoned me, with that blood-stained finger! and glided away down the passage, still beckoning——till it was lost in the darkness.'

'This is very frenzy!' said Schedoni, excessively agitated. 'Arouse yourself, and be a man!'

'Frenzy! would it were, Signor. I saw that dreadful hand—I see it now—it is there again!—there!'

Schedoni, shocked, embarrassed, and once more infected with the strange emotions of Spalatro, looked forward expecting to discover some terrific object, but still nothing was visible to him, and he soon recovered himself sufficiently to endeavour to appease the fancy of this conscience-struck ruffian. But Spalatro was insensible to all he could urge, and the Confessor, fearing that his voice, though weak and stifled, would awaken Ellena, tried to withdraw him from the spot, to the apartment they had quitted.

'The wealth of San Loretto should not make me go that way, Signor,' replied he, shuddering—'that was the way *it* beckoned, it vanished that way!'

Every emotion now yielded with Schedoni, to that of apprehension lest Ellena, being awakened, should make his task more horrid by a struggle, and his embarrassment encreased at each instant, for neither command, menace, or entreaty could prevail with Spalatro to retire, till the Monk luckily remembered a door, which opened beyond the stair-case, and would conduct them by another way to the opposite side of the house. The man consented so to depart, when, Schedoni unlocking a suit of rooms, of which he had always kept the keys, they passed in silence through an extent of desolate chambers, till they reached the one, which they had lately left.

Here, relieved from apprehension respecting Ellena, the Confessor expostulated more freely with Spalatro, but neither argument or menace could prevail, and the man persisted in refusing to return to the stair-case, though protesting, at the same time, that he would not remain alone in any part of the house; till the wine, with which the Confessor abundantly supplied him, began to overcome the terrors of his imagination. At length, his courage was so much re-animated, that he consented to resume his station, and await at the foot of the stairs the accomplishment of Schedoni's dreadful errand, with which agreement they returned thither by the way they had lately passed. The wine, with which Schedoni also had found it necessary to strengthen his own resolution, did not secure him from severe emotion, when he found himself again near Ellena; but he made a strenuous effort for self-subjection, as he demanded the dagger of Spalatro.

'You have it already, Signor,' replied the man.

'True,' said the Monk; 'ascend softly, or our steps may awaken her.'

'You said I was to wait at the foot of the stairs, Signor, while you'——

'True, true, true!' muttered the Confessor, and had begun to ascend, when his attendant desired him to stop. 'You are going in darkness, Signor, you have forgotten the lamp. I have another here.'

Schedoni took it angrily, without speaking, and was again ascending, when he hesitated, and once more paused. 'The glare will disturb her,' thought he, 'it is better to go in darkness.— Yet——'. He considered, that he could not strike with certainty without light to direct his hand, and he kept the lamp, but returned once more to charge Spalatro not to stir from the foot of the stairs till he called, and to ascend to the chamber upon the first signal.

'I will obey, Signor, if you, on your part, will promise not to give the signal till all is over.'

'I do promise,' replied Schedoni. 'No more!'

Again he ascended, nor stopped till he reached Ellena's door, where he listened for a sound; but all was as silent as if death already reigned in the chamber. This door was, from long disuse, difficult to be opened; formerly it would have yielded without sound, but now Schedoni was fearful of noise from every effort he made to move it. After some difficulty, however, it gave way, and he perceived, by the stillness within the apartment, that he had not disturbed Ellena. He shaded the lamp with the door for a moment, while he threw an enquiring glance forward, and when he did venture farther, held part of his dark drapery before the light, to prevent the rays from spreading through the room.

As he approached the bed, her gentle breathings informed him that she still slept, and the next moment he was at her side. She lay in deep and peaceful slumber, and seemed to have thrown herself upon the mattress, after having been wearied by her griefs; for, though sleep pressed heavily on her eyes, their lids were yet wet with tears.

While Schedoni gazed for a moment upon her innocent countenance, a faint smile stole over it. He stepped back. 'She smiles in her murderer's face!' said he, shuddering, 'I must be speedy.'

He searched for the dagger, and it was some time before his trembling hand could disengage it from the folds of his garment; but, having done so, he again drew near, and prepared to strike. Her dress perplexed him; it would interrupt the blow, and he stooped to examine whether he could turn her robe aside, without waking her. As the light passed over her face, he perceived that the smile had vanished—the visions of her sleep were changed, for tears stole from beneath her eye-lids, and her features suffered a slight convulsion. She spoke! Schedoni, apprehending that the light had disturbed her, suddenly drew back, and, again irresolute, shaded the lamp, and concealed himself behind the curtain, while he listened. But her words were inward and indistinct, and convinced him that she still slumbered.

His agitation and repugnance to strike encreased with every moment of delay, and, as often as he prepared to plunge the poinard in her bosom, a shuddering horror restrained him. Astonished at his own feelings, and indignant at what he termed a dastardly weakness, he found it necessary to argue with himself, and his rapid thoughts said, 'Do I not feel the necessity of this act! Does not what is dearer to me than existence—does not my consequence depend on the execution of it? Is she not also beloved by the young Vivaldi?—have I already forgotten the church of the Spirito Santo?' This consideration re-animated him; vengeance nerved his arm, and drawing aside the lawn* from her bosom, he once more raised it to strike; when, after gazing for an instant, some new cause of horror seemed to seize all his frame, and he stood for some moments aghast and motionless like a statue. His respiration was short and laborious, chilly drops stood on his forehead, and all his faculties of mind seemed suspended. When he recovered, he stooped to examine again the miniature, which had occasioned this revolution, and which had lain concealed beneath the lawn that he withdrew. The terrible certainty was almost confirmed, and forgetting, in his impatience to know the truth, the imprudence of suddenly discovering himself to Ellena at this hour of the night, and with a dagger at his feet, he called loudly 'Awake! awake! Say, what is your name? Speak! speak quickly!'

Ellena, aroused by a man's voice, started from her mattress, when, perceiving Schedoni, and by the pale glare of the lamp, his haggard countenance, she shrieked, and sunk back on the pillow. She had not fainted; and believing that he came to murder her, she now exerted herself to plead for mercy. The energy of her feelings enabled her to rise and throw herself at his feet. 'Be merciful, O father! be merciful!' said she, in a trembling voice.

'Father!' interrupted Schedoni, with earnestness; and then, seeming to restrain himself, he added, with unaffected surprise, 'Why are you thus terrified?' for he had lost, in new interests and emotions, all consciousness of evil intention, and of the singularity of his situation. 'What do you fear?' he repeated.

'Have pity, holy father!' exclaimed Ellena in agony.

'Why do you not say whose portrait that is?' demanded he, forgetting that he had not asked the question before.

'Whose portrait?' repeated the Confessor in a loud voice.

'Whose portrait!' said Ellena, with extreme surprise.

'Ay, how came you by it? Be quick—whose resemblance is it?'

'Why should you wish to know?' said Ellena.

'Answer my question,' repeated Schedoni, with encreasing sternness.

'I cannot part with it, holy father,' replied Ellena, pressing it to her bosom, 'you do not wish me to part with it!'

'Is it impossible to make you answer my question!' said he, in extreme perturbation, and turning away from her, 'has fear utterly confounded you!' Then, again stepping towards her, and seizing her wrist, he repeated the demand in a tone of desperation.

'Alas! he is dead! or I should not now want a protector,' replied Ellena, shrinking from his grasp, and weeping.

'You trifle,' said Schedoni, with a terrible look, 'I once more demand an answer—whose picture?'——

Ellena lifted it, gazed upon it for a moment, and then pressing it to her lips said, 'This was my father.'

'Your father!' he repeated in an inward voice, 'your father!' and shuddering, turned away.

Ellena looked at him with surprise. 'I never knew a father's

care,' she said, 'nor till lately did I perceive the want of it.—
But now.'——

'His name?' interrupted the Confessor.

'But now' continued Ellena—'if you are not as a father to me—
to whom can I look for protection?'

'His name?' repeated Schedoni, with sterner emphasis.

'It is sacred,' replied Ellena, 'for he was unfortunate!'

'His name?' demanded the Confessor, furiously.

'I have promised to conceal it, father.'

'On your life, I charge you tell it; remember, on your life!'

Ellena trembled, was silent, and with supplicating looks
implored him to desist from enquiry, but he urged the question
more irresistibly. 'His name then,' said she, 'was Marinella.'

Schedoni groaned and turned away; but in a few seconds,
struggling to command the agitation that shattered his whole
frame, he returned to Ellena, and raised her from her knees, on
which she had thrown herself to implore mercy.

'The place of his residence?' said the Monk.

'It was far from hence,' she replied; but he demanded an unequivocal answer, and she reluctantly gave one.

Schedoni turned away as before, groaned heavily, and paced
the chamber without speaking; while Ellena, in her turn, enquired
the motive of his questions, and the occasion of his agitation. But
he seemed not to notice any thing she said, and, wholly given up
to his feelings, was inflexibly silent, while he stalked, with measured
steps, along the room, and his face, half hid by his cowl, was bent
towards the ground.

Ellena's terror began to yield to astonishment, and this emotion
encreased, when, Schedoni approaching her, she perceived tears
swell in his eyes, which were fixt on her's, and his countenance soften
from the wild disorder that had marked it. Still he could not speak.
At length he yielded to the fulness of his heart, and Schedoni, the
stern Schedoni, wept and sighed! He seated himself on the mattress
beside Ellena, took her hand, which she affrighted attempted to
withdraw, and when he could command his voice, said, 'Unhappy
child!——behold your more unhappy father!' As he concluded,
his voice was overcome by groans, and he drew the cowl entirely
over his face.

'My father!' exclaimed the astonished and doubting Ellena—
'my father!' and fixed her eyes upon him. He gave no reply, but
when, a moment after, he lifted his head, 'Why do you reproach
me with those looks!' said the conscious Schedoni.

'Reproach you!—reproach my father!' repeated Ellena, in accents softening into tenderness, '*Why* should I reproach my father!'

'*Why!*' exclaimed Schedoni, starting from his seat, 'Great God!'

As he moved, he stumbled over the dagger at his foot; at that moment it might be said to strike into his heart. He pushed it hastily from sight. Ellena had not observed it; but she observed his labouring breast, his distracted looks, and quick steps, as he walked to and fro in the chamber; and she asked, with the most soothing accents of compassion, and looks of anxious gentleness, what made him so unhappy, and tried to assuage his sufferings. They seemed to encrease with every wish she expressed to dispel them; at one moment he would pause to gaze upon her, and in the next would quit her with a frenzied start.

'Why do you look so piteously upon me, father?' Ellena said, 'why are you so unhappy? Tell me, that I may comfort you.'

This appeal renewed all the violence of remorse and grief, and he pressed her to his bosom, and wetted her cheek with his tears. Ellena wept to see him weep, till her doubts began to take alarm. Whatever might be the proofs, that had convinced Schedoni of the relationship between them, he had not explained these to her, and, however strong was the eloquence of nature which she witnessed, it was not sufficient to justify an entire confidence in the assertion he had made, or to allow her to permit his caresses without trembling. She shrunk, and endeavoured to disengage herself; when, immediately understanding her, he said, 'Can you doubt the cause of these emotions? these signs of paternal affection?'

'Have I not reason to doubt,' replied Ellena, timidly, 'since I never witnessed them before?'

He withdrew his arms, and, fixing his eyes earnestly on hers, regarded her for some moments in expressive silence. 'Poor Innocent!' said he, at length, 'you know not how much your words convey!—It is too true, you never have known a father's tenderness till now!'

His countenance darkened while he spoke, and he rose again from his seat. Ellena, meanwhile, astonished, terrified and oppressed by a variety of emotions, had no power to demand his reasons for the belief that so much agitated him, or any explanation of his conduct; but she appealed to the portrait, and endeavoured, by tracing some resemblance between it and Schedoni, to decide her doubts. The countenance of each was as different in character as in years. The miniature displayed a young man rather handsome, of a gay and smiling countenance; yet the smile expressed triumph, rather than sweetness, and his whole air and features were distinguished by a consciousness of superiority that rose even to haughtiness.

Schedoni, on the contrary, advanced in years, exhibited a severe physiognomy, furrowed by thought, no less than by time, and darkened by the habitual indulgence of morose passions. He looked as if he had never smiled since the portrait was drawn; and it seemed as if the painter, prophetic of Schedoni's future disposition, had arrested and embodied that smile, to prove hereafter that cheerfulness had once played upon his features.

Though the expression was so different between the countenance, which Schedoni formerly owned, and that he now wore, the same character of haughty pride was visible in both; and Ellena did trace a resemblance in the bold outline of the features, but not sufficient to convince her, without farther evidence, that each belonged to the same person, and that the Confessor had ever been the young cavalier in the portrait. In the first tumult of her thoughts, she had not had leisure to dwell upon the singularity of Schedoni's visiting her at this deep hour of the night, or to urge any questions, except vague ones, concerning the truth of her relationship to him. But now, that her mind was somewhat recollected, and that his looks were less terrific, she ventured to ask a fuller explanation of these circumstances, and his reasons for the late extraordinary assertion. 'It is past midnight, father,' said Ellena, 'you may judge then how anxious I am to learn, what motive led you to my chamber at this lonely hour?'

Schedoni made no reply.

'Did you come to warn me of danger?' she continued, 'had you discovered the cruel designs of Spalatro? Ah! when I supplicated for your compassion on the shore this evening, you little thought what perils surrounded me! or you would——'

'You say true!' interrupted he, in a hurried manner, 'but name the subject no more. Why will you persist in returning to it?'

His words surprized Ellena, who had not even alluded to the subject till now; but the returning wildness of his countenance, made her fearful of dwelling upon the topic, even so far as to point out his error.

Another deep pause succeeded, during which Schedoni continued to pace the room, sometimes stopping for an instant, to fix his eyes on Ellena, and regarding her with an earnestness that seemed to partake of frenzy, and then gloomily withdrawing his regards, and sighing heavily, as he turned away to a distant part of the room. She, meanwhile, agitated with astonishment at his conduct, as well as at her own circumstances, and with the fear of offending him by further questions, endeavoured to summon courage to solicit the explanation which was so important to her tranquillity. At length she asked, how she might venture to believe a circumstance so surprising, as that of which he had just assured her, and to remind him that he had not yet disclosed his reason for admitting the belief.

The Confessor's feelings were eloquent in reply; and, when at length they were sufficiently subdued, to permit him to talk coherently, he mentioned some circumstances concerning Ellena's family, that proved him at least to have been intimately acquainted with it; and others, which she believed were known only to Bianchi and herself, that removed every doubt of his identity.

This, however, was a period of his life too big with remorse, horror, and the first pangs of parental affection, to allow him to converse long; deep solitude was necessary for his soul. He wished to plunge where no eye might restrain his emotions, or observe the overflowing anguish of his heart. Having obtained sufficient proof to convince him that Ellena was indeed his child, and assured her that she should be removed from this house on the following day, and be restored to her home, he abruptly left the chamber.

As he descended the stair-case, Spalatro stepped forward to meet him, with the cloak which had been designed to wrap the mangled form of Ellena, when it should be carried to the shore. 'Is it done?' said the ruffian, in a stifled voice, 'I am ready;' and he spread forth the cloak, and began to ascend.

'Hold! villain, hold!' said Schedoni, lifting up his head for the first time, 'Dare to enter that chamber, and your life shall answer for it.'

'What!' exclaimed the man, shrinking back astonished—'will not *her*'s satisfy you!'

He trembled for the consequence of what he had said, when he observed the changing countenance of the Confessor. But Schedoni spoke not: the tumult in his breast was too great for utterance, and he pressed hastily forward. Spalatro followed. 'Be pleased to tell me what I am to do,' said he, again holding forth the cloak.

'Avaunt!' exclaimed the other, turning fiercely upon him; 'leave me.'

'How!' said the man, whose spirit was now aroused, 'has *your* courage failed too, Signor? If so, I will prove myself no dastard, though you called me one; I'll do the business myself.'

'Villain! fiend!' cried Schedoni, seizing the ruffian by the throat, with a grasp that seemed intended to annihilate him; when, recollecting that the fellow was only willing to obey the very instructions he had himself but lately delivered to him, other emotions succeeded to that of rage; he slowly liberated him, and in accents broken, and softening from sternness, bade him retire to rest. 'Tomorrow,' he added, 'I will speak further with you. As for this night——I have changed my purpose. Begone!'

Spalatro was about to express the indignation, which astonishment and fear had hitherto overcome, but his employer repeated his command in a voice of thunder, and closed the door of his apartment with violence, as he shut out a man, whose presence was become hateful to him. He felt relieved by his absence, and began to breathe more freely, till, remembering that this accomplice had just boasted that he was no dastard, he dreaded lest, by way of proving the assertion, he should attempt to commit the crime, from which he had lately shrunk. Terrified at the possibility, and even apprehending that it might already have become a reality, he rushed from the room, and found Spalatro in the passage leading to the private stair-case; but, whatever might have been his purpose, the situation and looks of the latter were sufficiently alarming. At the approach of Schedoni, he turned his sullen and malignant countenance towards him, without answering the call, or the demand as to his business there; and with slow steps obeyed the order of his master, that he should withdraw to his room. Thither Schedoni followed, and, having locked him in it for the night, he repaired to the apartment of Ellena, which he secured from the possibility of intrusion. He then returned to his own, not to sleep, but to abandon himself to the agonies of remorse and horror; and he yet shuddered like a man, who has just recoiled from the brink of a precipice, but who still measures the gulf with his eye.

CHAPTER X

—————But their way
Lies through the perplexed paths of this drear wood,
The nodding horror of whose shady brows
Threats the forlorn and wandering passenger.

MILTON*

ELLENA, when Schedoni had left her, recollected all the particulars, which he had thought proper to reveal concerning her
family, and, comparing them with such circumstances as the late
Bianchi had related on the same subject, she perceived nothing
that was contradictory between the two accounts. But she knew
not even yet enough of her own story, to understand why Bianchi
had been silent as to some particulars, which had just been disclosed. From Bianchi she had always understood, that her mother
had married a nobleman of the duchy of Milan, and of the house of
Marinella; that the marriage had been unfortunate; and that she
herself, even before the death of the Countess, had been committed
to the care of Bianchi, the only sister of that lady. Of this event, or
of her mother, Ellena had no remembrance; for the kindness of
Bianchi had obliterated from her mind the loss and the griefs of
her early infancy; and she recollected only the accident which had
discovered to her, in Bianchi's cabinet, after the death of the latter,
the miniature and the name of her father. When she had enquired
the reason of this injunction, Bianchi replied, that the degraded
fortune of her house rendered privacy desirable; and answered her
further questions concerning her father, by relating, that he had
died while she was an infant. The picture, which Ellena had discovered, Bianchi had found among the trinkets of the departed
Countess, and designed to present it at some future period to
Ellena, when her discretion might be trusted with a knowledge
of her family. This was the whole of what Signora Bianchi had
judged it necessary to explain, though in her last hours it appeared
that she wished to reveal more; but it was then too late.

Though Ellena perceived that many circumstances of the relations given by Schedoni, and by Signora Bianchi, coincided, and
that none were contradictory, except that of his death, she could
not yet subdue her amazement at this discovery, or even the doubts

which occasionally recurred to her as to it's truth. Schedoni, on the contrary, had not even appeared surprised, when she assured him, that she always understood her father had been dead many years; though when she asked if her mother too was living, both his distress and his assurances confirmed the relation made by Bianchi.

When Ellena's mind became more tranquil, she noticed again the singularity of Schedoni's visit to her apartment at so sacred an hour; and her thoughts glanced back involuntarily to the scene of the preceding evening on the sea-shore, and the image of her father appeared in each, in the terrific character of an agent of the Marchesa di Vivaldi. The suspicions, however, which she had formerly admitted, respecting his designs, were now impatiently rejected, for she was less anxious to discover truth, than to release herself from horrible suppositions; and she willingly believed that Schedoni, having misunderstood her character, had only designed to assist in removing her beyond the reach of Vivaldi. The ingenuity of hope suggested also, that, having just heard from her conductors, or from Spalatro, some circumstances of her story, he had been led to a suspicion of the relationship between them, and that in the first impatience of parental anxiety, he had disregarded the hour, and come, though at midnight, to her apartment to ascertain the truth.

While she soothed herself with this explanation of a circumstance, which had occasioned her considerable surprise, she perceived on the floor the point of a dagger peeping from beneath the curtains! Emotions almost too horrible to be sustained, followed this discovery; she took the instrument, and gazed upon it aghast and trembling, for a suspicion of the real motive of Schedoni's visit glanced upon her mind. But it was only for a moment; such a supposition was too terrible to be willingly endured; she again believed that Spalatro alone had meditated her destruction, and she thanked the Confessor as her deliverer, instead of shrinking from him as an assassin. She now understood that Schedoni, having discovered the ruffian's design, had rushed into the chamber to save a stranger from his murderous poniard, and had unconsciously rescued his own daughter, when the portrait at her bosom informed him of the truth. With this conviction Ellena's eyes overflowed with gratitude, and her heart was hushed to peace.

Schedoni, meanwhile, shut up in his chamber, was agitated by feelings of a very opposite nature. When their first excess was exhausted, and his mind was calm enough to reflect, the images

that appeared on it struck him with solemn wonder. In pursuing
Ellena at the criminal instigation of the Marchesa di Vivaldi, it
appeared that he had been persecuting his own child; and in thus
consenting to conspire against the innocent, he had in the event
been only punishing the guilty, and preparing mortification for
himself on the exact subject to which he had sacrificed his conscience. Every step that he had taken with a view of gratifying his
ambition was retrograde, and while he had been wickedly intent
to serve the Marchesa and himself, by preventing the marriage of
Vivaldi and Ellena, he had been laboriously counteracting his own
fortune. An alliance with the illustrious house of Vivaldi, was
above his loftiest hope of advancement, and this event he had himself nearly prevented by the very means which had been adopted,
at the expence of every virtuous consideration, to obtain an
inferior promotion. Thus by a singular retribution, his own crimes
had recoiled upon himself.

Schedoni perceived the many obstacles, which lay between him
and his newly awakened hopes, and that much was to be overcome
before those nuptials could be publicly solemnized, which he was
now still more anxious to promote, than he had lately been to prevent. The approbation of the Marchesa was, at least, desirable, for
she had much at her disposal, and without it, though his daughter
might be the wife of Vivaldi, he himself would be no otherwise
benefited at present than by the honour of the connection. He had
some peculiar reasons for believing, that her consent might be
obtained, and, though there was hazard in delaying the nuptials
till such an experiment had been made, he resolved to encounter it,
rather than forbear to solicit her concurrence. But, if the Marchesa
should prove inexorable, he determined to bestow the hand of
Ellena, without her knowledge, and in doing so, he well knew that
he incurred little danger from her resentment, since he had secrets
in his possession, the consciousness of which must awe her into a
speedy neutrality. The consent of the Marchese, as he despaired
of obtaining it, he did not mean to solicit, and the influence of the
Marchesa was such, that Schedoni did not regard that as essential.

The first steps, however, to be taken, were those that might
release Vivaldi from the Inquisition, the tremendous prison into
which Schedoni himself, little foreseeing that he should so soon
wish for his liberation, had caused him to be thrown. He had
always understood, indeed, that if the Informer forbore to appear
against the Accused in this Court, the latter would of course be
liberated; and he also believed, that Vivaldi's freedom could be

obtained whenever he should think proper to apply to a person at Naples, whom he knew to be connected with the *Holy Office* of Rome. How much the Confessor had suffered his wishes to deceive him, may appear hereafter. His motives for having thus confined Vivaldi, were partly those of self-defence. He dreaded the discovery and the vengeance, which might follow the loss of Ellena, should Vivaldi be at liberty immediately to pursue his enquiries. But he believed that all trace of her must be lost, after a few weeks had elapsed, and that Vivaldi's sufferings from confinement in the Inquisition would have given interests to his mind, which must weaken the one he felt for Ellena. Yet, though in this instance self-defence had been a principal motive with Schedoni, a desire of revenging the insult he had received in the church of the Spirito Santo, and all the consequent mortifications he experienced, had been a second; and, such was the blackness of his hatred, and the avarice of his revenge, that he had not considered the suffering, which the loss of Ellena would occasion Vivaldi, as sufficient retaliation.

In adopting a mode of punishment so extraordinary as that of imprisonment in the Inquisition, it appears, therefore, that Schedoni was influenced, partly by the difficulty of otherwise confining Vivaldi, during the period for which confinement was absolutely necessary to the success of his own schemes, and partly by a desire of inflicting the tortures of terror. He had also been encouraged by his discovery of this opportunity for conferring new obligations on the Marchesa. The very conduct, that must have appeared to the first glance of an honest mind fatal to his interests, he thought might be rendered beneficial to them, and that his dexterity could so command the business, as that the Marchesa should eventually thank him as the deliverer of her son, instead of discovering and execrating him as his Accuser; a scheme favoured by the unjust and cruel rule enacted by the tribunal he approached, which permitted anonymous Informers.

To procure the arrestation of Vivaldi, it had been only necessary to send a written accusation, without a name, to the *Holy Office*, with a mention of the place where the accused person might be seized; but the suffering in consequence of this did not always proceed further than the *question*; since, if the Informer failed to discover himself to the Inquisitors, the prisoner, after many examinations, was released, unless he happened unwarily to criminate himself. Schedoni, as he did not intend to prosecute, believed, therefore, that Vivaldi would of course be discharged after a certain period, and supposing it also utterly impossible that he could ever discover his Accuser, the Confessor determined to appear anxious and active in effecting his release. This character of a deliverer, he knew he should be the better enabled to support by means of a person officially connected with the *Holy Office*, who had already unconsciously assisted his views. In the apartment of this man, Schedoni had accidentally seen a formula of arrestation against a person suspected of Heresy, the view of which had not only suggested to him the plan he had since adopted, but had in some degree assisted him to carry it into effect. He had seen the scroll only for a short time, but his observations were so minute, and his memory so clear, that he was able to copy it with at least sufficient exactness to impose upon the Benedictine priest, who had, perhaps, seldom or never seen a real instrument of this kind. Schedoni had employed this artifice for the purpose of immediately securing Vivaldi, apprehending that, while the Inquisitors were slowly deliberating upon his arrest, he might quit Celano, and elude discovery. If the deception succeeded, it would enable him also to seize Ellena, and to mislead Vivaldi respecting her destination. The charge of having carried off a nun might appear to be corroborated by many circumstances, and Schedoni would probably have made these the subject of real denunciation, had he not foreseen the danger and the trouble in which it might implicate himself; and that, as the charge could not be substantiated, Ellena would finally escape. As far as his plan now went, it had been successful; some of the bravoes whom he hired to personate officials, had conveyed Vivaldi to the town, where the real officers of the Inquisition were appointed to receive him; while the others carried Ellena to the shore of the Adriatic. Schedoni had much applauded his own ingenuity, in thus contriving, by the matter of the forged accusation, to throw an impenetrable veil over the fate of Ellena, and to secure himself from the suspicions or vengeance of Vivaldi, who, it appeared, would always believe that she had died, or was still confined in the unsearchable prisons of the Inquisition.

Thus he had betrayed himself in endeavouring to betray Vivaldi, whose release, however, he yet supposed could be easily obtained; but how much his policy had, in this instance, outrun his sagacity, now remained to be proved.

The subject of Schedoni's immediate perplexity was, the difficulty of conveying Ellena back to Naples; since, not chusing to appear at present in the character of her father, he could not decorously accompany her thither himself, nor could he prudently entrust her to the conduct of any person, whom he knew in this neighbourhood. It was, however, necessary to form a speedy determination, for he could neither endure to pass another day in a scene, which must continually impress him with the horrors of the preceding night, nor that Ellena should remain in it; and the morning light already gleamed upon his casements.

After some further deliberation, he resolved to be himself her conductor, as far at least as through the forests of the Garganus, and at the first town where conveniencies could be procured, to throw aside his Monk's habit, and, assuming the dress of a layman, accompany her in this disguise towards Naples, till he should either discover some secure means of sending her forward to that city, or a temporary asylum for her in a convent on the way.

His mind was scarcely more tranquil, after having formed this determination, than before, and he did not attempt to repose himself even for a moment. The circumstances of the late discovery were almost perpetually recurring to his affrighted conscience, accompanied by a fear that Ellena might suspect the real purpose of his midnight visit; and he alternately formed and rejected plausible falsehoods, that might assuage her curiosity, and delude her apprehension.

The hour arrived, however, when it was necessary to prepare for departure, and found him still undecided as to the explanation he should form.

Having released Spalatro from his chamber, and given him directions to procure horses and a guide immediately from the neighbouring hamlet, he repaired to Ellena's room, to prepare her for this hasty removal. On approaching it, a remembrance of the purpose, with which he had last passed through these same passages and stair-case, appealed so powerfully to his feelings, that he was unable to proceed, and he turned back to his own apartment to recover some command over himself. A few moments restored to him his usual address, though not his tranquillity, and he again approached the chamber; it was now, however, by way of the corridor. As he unbarred the door, his hand trembled; but, when he entered the room, his countenance and manner had resumed their usual solemnity, and his voice only would have betrayed, to an attentive observer, the agitation of his mind.

Ellena was considerably affected on seeing him again, and he examined with a jealous eye the emotions he witnessed. The smile with which she met him was tender, but he perceived it pass away

from her features, like the aërial colouring that illumines a mountain's brow; and the gloom of doubt and apprehension again overspread them. As he advanced, he held forth his hand for her's,
when, suddenly perceiving the dagger he had left in the chamber,
he involuntarily withdrew his proffered courtesy, and his countenance changed. Ellena, whose eyes followed his to the object
that attracted them, pointed to the instrument, took it up, and
approaching him said, 'This dagger I found last night in my
chamber! O my father!'—

'That dagger!' said Schedoni, with affected surprize.

'Examine it,' continued Ellena, while she held it up, 'Do you
know to whom it belongs? and who brought it hither?'

'What is it you mean?' asked Schedoni, betrayed by his feelings.

'Do you know, too, for what purpose it was brought?' said
Ellena mournfully.

The Confessor made no reply, but irresolutely attempted to
seize the instrument.

'O yes, I perceive you know too well,' continued Ellena, 'here,
my father, while I slept'——

'Give me the dagger,' interrupted Schedoni, in a frightful
voice.

'Yes, my father, I will give it as an offering of my gratitude,'
replied Ellena, but as she raised her eyes, filled with tears, his look
and fixed attitude terrified her, and she added with a still more persuasive tenderness, 'Will you not accept the offering of your child,
for having preserved her from the poniard of an assassin?'

Schedoni's looks became yet darker; he took the dagger in
silence, and threw it with violence to the furthest end of the chamber, while his eyes remained fixed on her's. The force of the action
alarmed her; 'Yes, it is in vain that you would conceal the truth,'
she added, weeping unrestrainedly, 'your goodness cannot avail;
I know the whole.'——

The last words aroused Schedoni again from his trance, his
features became convulsed, and his look furious. 'What do you
know?' he demanded in a subdued voice, that seemed ready to
burst in thunder.

'All that I owe you,' replied Ellena, 'that last night, while I
slept upon this mattress, unsuspicious of what was designed
against me, an assassin entered the chamber with that instrument
in his hand, and——'

A stifled groan from Schedoni checked Ellena; she observed his
rolling eyes, and trembled; till, believing that his agitation was

occasioned by indignation against the assassin, she resumed, 'Why should you think it necessary to conceal the danger which has threatened me, since it is to you that I owe my deliverance from it? O! my father, do not deny me the pleasure of shedding these tears of gratitude, do not refuse the thanks, which are due to you! While I slept upon that couch, while a ruffian stole upon my slumber— it was you, yes! can I ever forget that it was my father, who saved me from his poniard!'

Schedoni's passions were changed, but they were not less violent; he could scarcely controul them, while he said in a tremulous tone—'It is enough, say no more;' and he raised Ellena, but turned away without embracing her.

His strong emotion, as he paced in silence the furthest end of the apartment, excited her surprize, but she then attributed it to a remembrance of the perilous moment, from which he had rescued her.

Schedoni, meanwhile, to whom her thanks were daggers, was trying to subdue the feelings of remorse that tore his heart; and was so enveloped in a world of his own, as to be for some time unconscious of all around him. He continued to stalk in gloomy silence along the chamber, till the voice of Ellena, entreating him rather to rejoice that he had been permitted to save her, than so deeply to consider dangers which were past, again touched the chord that vibrated to his conscience, and recalled him to a sense of his situation. He then bade her prepare for immediate departure, and abruptly quitted the room.

Vainly hoping that in flying from the scene of his meditated crime, he should leave with it the acuteness of remembrance, and the agonizing stings of remorse, he was now more anxious than ever to leave this place. Yet he should still be accompanied by Ellena, and her innocent looks, her affectionate thanks, inflicted an anguish, which was scarcely endurable. Sometimes, thinking that her hatred, or what to him would be still severer, her contempt, must be more tolerable than this gratitude, he almost resolved to undeceive her respecting his conduct, but as constantly and impatiently repelled the thought with horror, and finally determined to suffer her to account for his late extraordinary visit in the way she had chosen.

Spalatro, at length, returned from the hamlet with horses, but without having procured a guide to conduct the travellers through a tract of the long-devolving forests of the Garganus, which it was necessary for them to pass. No person had been willing to undertake so arduous a task; and Spalatro, who was well acquainted with all the labyrinths of the way, now offered his services.

Schedoni, though he could scarcely endure the presence of this man, had no alternative but to accept him, since he had dismissed the guide who had conducted him hither. Of personal violence Schedoni had no apprehension, though he too well understood the villainy of his proposed companion; for he considered that he himself should be well armed, and he determined to ascertain that Spalatro was without weapons; he knew also, that in case of a contest, his own superior stature would easily enable him to overcome such an antagonist.

Every thing being now ready for departure, Ellena was summoned, and the Confessor led her to his own apartment, where a slight breakfast was prepared.

Her spirits being revived by the speed of this departure, she would again have expressed her thanks, but he peremptorily interrupted her, and forbade any further mention of gratitude.

On entering the court where the horses were in waiting, and perceiving Spalatro, Ellena shrunk and put her arm within Schedoni's for protection. 'What recollections does the presence of that man revive!' said she, 'I can scarcely venture to believe myself safe, even with you, when he is here.'

Schedoni made no reply, till the remark was repeated, 'You have nothing to fear from him,' muttered the Confessor, while he hastened her forward, 'and we have no time to lose in vague apprehension.'

'How!' exclaimed Ellena, 'is not he the assassin from whom you saved me! I cannot doubt, that you know him to be such, though you would spare me the pain of believing so.'

'Well, well, be it so,' replied the Confessor; 'Spalatro, lead the horses this way.'

The party were soon mounted, when, quitting this eventful mansion, and the shore of the Adriatic, as Ellena hoped for ever, they entered upon the gloomy wilderness of the Garganus. She often turned her eyes back upon the house with emotions of inexpressible awe, astonishment, and thankfulness, and gazed while a glimpse of it's turretted walls could be caught beyond the dark branches, which, closing over it, at length shut it from her view. The joy of this departure, however, was considerably abated by the presence of Spalatro, and her fearful countenance enquired of Schedoni the meaning of his being suffered to accompany them. The Confessor was reluctant to speak concerning a man, of whose very existence he would willingly have ceased to think. Ellena guided her horse still closer to Schedoni's, but, forbearing to urge the enquiry otherwise than by looks, she received no reply, and endeavoured to quiet her apprehensions, by considering that he would not have permitted this man to be their guide, unless he had believed he might be trusted. This consideration, though it relieved her fears, encreased her perplexity respecting the late designs of Spalatro, and her surprise that Schedoni, if he had really understood them to be evil, should endure his presence. Every time she stole a glance at the dark countenance of this man, rendered still darker by the shade of the trees, she thought 'assassin' was written in each line of it, and could scarcely doubt that he, and not the people who had conducted her to the mansion, had dropped the dagger in her chamber. Whenever she looked round through the deep glades, and on the forest-mountains that on every side closed the scene, and seemed to exclude all cheerful haunt of man, and then regarded her companions, her heart sunk, notwithstanding the reasons she had for believing herself in the protection of a father. Nay, the very looks of Schedoni himself, more than once reminding her of his appearance on the sea-shore, renewed the impressions of alarm and even of dismay, which she had there experienced. At such moments it was scarcely possible for her to consider him as her parent, and, in spite of every late appearance, strange and unaccountable doubts began to gather on her mind.

Schedoni, meanwhile, lost in thought, broke not, by a single word, the deep silence of the solitudes through which they passed. Spalatro was equally mute, and equally engaged by his reflections on the sudden change in Schedoni's purpose, and by wonder as to the motive, which could have induced him to lead Ellena in safety, from the very spot whither she was brought by his express command to be destroyed. He, however, was not so wholly occupied, as to be unmindful of his situation, or unwatchful of an opportunity of serving his own interests, and retaliating upon Schedoni for the treatment he had received on the preceding night.

Among the various subjects that distracted the Confessor, the difficulty of disposing of Ellena, without betraying at Naples that she was his relative, was not the least distressing. Whatever might be the reason which could justify such feelings, his fears of a premature discovery of the circumstance to the society with whom he lived, were so strong, as often to produce the most violent effect upon his countenance, and it was, perhaps, when he was occupied by this subject, that it's terrific expression revived with Ellena the late scene upon the shore. His embarrassment was not less, as to the excuse to be offered the Marchesa, for having failed to fulfil his engagement, and respecting the means by which he might interest her in favour of Ellena, and even dispose her to approve the marriage, before she should be informed of the family of this unfortunate young woman. Perceiving all the necessity for ascertaining the probabilities of such consent, before he ventured to make an avowal of her origin, he determined not to reveal himself till he should be perfectly sure that the discovery would be acceptable to the Marchesa. In the mean time, as it would be necessary to say something of Ellena's birth, he meant to declare, that he had discovered it to be noble, and her family worthy, in every respect, of a connection with that of the Vivaldi.

An interview with the Marchesa, was almost equally wished for and dreaded by the Confessor. He shuddered at the expectation of meeting a woman, who had instigated him to the murder of his own child, which, though he had been happily prevented from committing it, was an act that would still be wished for by the Marchesa. How could he endure her reproaches, when she should discover that he had failed to accomplish her will! How conceal the indignation of a father, and dissimulate all a father's various feelings, when, in reply to such reproaches, he must form excuses, and act humility, from which his whole soul would revolt! Never could his arts of dissimulation have been so severely tried, not even in the late scenes with Ellena, never have returned upon himself in punishment so severe, as in that which awaited him with the Marchesa. And from it's approach, the cool and politic Schedoni often shrunk in such horror, that he almost determined to avoid it at any hazard, and secretly to unite Vivaldi and Ellena, without even soliciting the consent of the Marchesa.

A desire, however, of the immediate preferment, so necessary to his pride, constantly checked this scheme, and finally made him willing to subject every honest feeling, and submit to any meanness, however vicious, rather than forego the favourite object of his erroneous ambition. Never, perhaps, was the paradoxical union of pride and abjectness, more strongly exhibited than on this occasion.

While thus the travellers silently proceeded, Ellena's thoughts often turned to Vivaldi, and she considered, with trembling anxiety, the effect which the late discovery was likely to have upon their future lives. It appeared to her, that Schedoni must approve of a connection thus flattering to the pride of a father, though he would probably refuse his consent to a private marriage. And, when she further considered the revolution, which a knowledge of her family might occasion towards herself in the minds of the Vivaldi, her prospects seemed to brighten, and her cares began to dissipate. Judging that Schedoni must be acquainted with the present situation of Vivaldi, she was continually on the point of mentioning him, but was as constantly restrained by timidity, though, had she suspected him to be an inhabitant of the Inquisition, her scruples would have vanished before an irresistible interest. As it was, believing that he, like herself, had been imposed upon by the Marchesa's agents, in the disguise of officials, she concluded, as has before appeared, that he now suffered a temporary imprisonment by order of his mother, at one of the family villas. When, however, Schedoni, awaking from his reverie, abruptly mentioned Vivaldi, her spirits fluttered with impatience to learn his exact situation, and she enquired respecting it.

'I am no stranger to your attachment,' said Schedoni, evading the question, 'but I wish to be informed of some circumstances relative to it's commencement.'

Ellena, confused, and not knowing what to reply, was for a moment silent, and then repeated her enquiry.

'Where did you first meet?' said the Confessor, still disregarding her question. Ellena related, that she had first seen Vivaldi, when attending her aunt from the church of San Lorenzo. For the present she was spared the embarrassment of further explanation by Spalatro, who, riding up to Schedoni, informed him they were approaching the town of Zanti. On looking forward, Ellena perceived houses peeping from among the forest-trees, at a short distance, and presently heard the cheerful bark of a dog, that sure herald and faithful servant of man!

Soon after the travellers entered Zanti, a small town surrounded by the forest, where, however, the poverty of the inhabitants seemed to forbid a longer stay than was absolutely necessary for repose, and a slight refreshment. Spalatro led the way to a cabin, in which the few persons, that journied this road were usually entertained. The appearance of the people, who owned it, was as wild as their country, and the interior of the dwelling was so dirty and comfortless, that Schedoni, preferring to take his repast in the open air, a table was spread under the luxuriant shade of the forest-trees, at a little distance. Here, when the host had withdrawn, and Spalatro had been dispatched to examine the post-horses, and to procure a lay-habit for the Confessor, the latter, once more alone with Ellena, began to experience again somewhat of the embarrassments of conscience; and Ellena, whenever her eyes glanced upon him, suffered a solemnity of fear that rose almost to terror. He, at length, terminated this emphatic silence, by renewing his mention of Vivaldi, and his command that Ellena should relate the history of their affection. Not daring to refuse, she obeyed, but with as much brevity as possible, and Schedoni did not interrupt her by a single observation. However eligible their nuptials now appeared to him, he forbore to give any hint of approbation, till he should have extricated the object of her regards from his perilous situation. But, with Ellena, this very silence implied the opinion it was meant to conceal, and, encouraged by the hope it imparted, she ventured once more to ask, by whose order Vivaldi had been arrested; whither he had been conveyed, and the circumstances of his present situation.

Too politic to intrust her with a knowledge of his actual condition, the Confessor spared her the anguish of learning that he was a prisoner in the Inquisition. He affected ignorance of the late transaction at Celano, but ventured to believe, that both Vivaldi and herself had been arrested by order of the Marchesa, who, he conjectured, had thrown him into temporary confinement, a measure which she, no doubt, had meant to enforce also towards Ellena.

'And you, my father,' observed Ellena, 'what brought you to my prison,—you who was not informed with the Marchesa's designs? What accident conducted you to that remote solitude, just at the moment when you could save your child!'

'Informed of the Marchesa's designs!' said Schedoni, with embarrassment and displeasure: 'Have you ever imagined that I could be accessary—that I could consent to assist, I mean could consent to be a confidant of such atrocious'——Schedoni, bewildered, confounded, and half betrayed, checked himself.

'Yet you have said, the Marchesa meant only to confine me!' observed Ellena; 'was that design so atrocious? Alas, my father! I know too well that her plan was more atrocious, and since you had too much reason to know this, why do you say that imprisonment only was intended for me? But your solicitude for my tranquillity leads you to'——

'What means,' interrupted the suspicious Schedoni, 'can I particularly have of understanding the Marchesa's schemes? I repeat, that I am not her confidant; how then is it to be supposed I should know that they extended further than to imprisonment?'

'Did you not save me from the arm of the assassin!' said Ellena tenderly; 'did not you wrench the very dagger from his grasp!'

'I had forgotten, I had forgotten,' said the Confessor, yet more embarrassed.

'Yes, good minds are ever thus apt to forget the benefits they confer,' replied Ellena. 'But you shall find, my father, that a grateful heart is equally tenacious to remember them; it is the indelible register of every act that is dismissed from the memory of the benefactor.'

'Mention no more of benefits,' said Schedoni, impatiently; 'let silence on this subject henceforth indicate your wish to oblige me.'

He rose, and joined the host, who was at the door of his cabin. Schedoni wished to dismiss Spalatro as soon as possible, and he enquired for a guide to conduct him through that part of the forest, which remained to be traversed. In this poor town, a person willing to undertake that office was easily to be found, but the host went in quest of a neighbour whom he had recommended.

Meanwhile Spalatro returned, without having succeeded in his commission. Not any lay-habit could be procured, upon so short a notice, that suited Schedoni. He was obliged, therefore, to continue his journey to the next town at least, in his own dress, but the necessity was not very serious to him, since it was improbable that he should be known in this obscure region.

Presently the host appeared with his neighbour, when Schedoni, having received satisfactory answers to his questions, engaged him for the remainder of the forest-road, and dismissed Spalatro. The ruffian departed with sullen reluctance and evident ill-will, circumstances which the Confessor scarcely noticed, while occupied by the satisfaction of escaping from the presence of the atrocious partner of his conscience. But Ellena, as he passed her, observed the malignant disappointment of his look, and it served only to heighten the thankfulness his departure occasioned her.

It was afternoon before the travellers proceeded. Schedoni had calculated that they could easily reach the town, at which they designed to pass the night, before the close of evening, and he had been in no haste to depart during the heat of the day. Their track now lay through a country less savage, though scarcely less wild than that they had passed in the morning. It emerged from the interior towards the border of the forest; they were no longer enclosed by impending mountains; the withdrawing shades were no longer impenetrable to the eye, but now and then opened to gleams of sunshine-landscape, and blue distances; and in the immediate scene, many a green glade spread it's bosom to the sun. The grandeur of the trees, however, did not decline; the plane, the oak, and the chestnut still threw a pomp of foliage round these smiling spots, and seemed to consecrate the mountain streams, that descended beneath their solemn shade.

To the harassed spirits of Ellena the changing scenery was refreshing, and she frequently yielded her cares to the influence of majestic nature. Over the gloom of Schedoni, no scenery had, at any moment, power; the shape and paint of external imagery gave neither impression or colour to his fancy. He contemned the sweet illusions, to which other spirits are liable, and which often confer a delight more exquisite, and not less innocent, than any, which deliberative reason can bestow.

The same thoughtful silence, that had wrapt him at the beginning of the journey, he still preserved, except when occasionally he asked a question of the guide concerning the way, and received answers too loquacious for his humour. This loquacity, however, was not easily repressed, and the peasant had already begun to relate some terrible stories of murder, committed in these forests upon people, who had been hardy enough to venture into them without a guide, before the again abstracted Schedoni even noticed that he spoke. Though Ellena did not give much credit to these narratives, they had some effect upon her fears, when soon after she entered the deep shades of a part of the forest, that lay along a narrow defile, whence every glimpse of cheerful landscape was again excluded by precipices, which towered on either side. The stillness was not less effectual than the gloom, for no sounds were heard, except such as seemed to characterize solitude, and impress it's awful power more deeply on the heart,——the hollow dashing of torrents descending distantly, and the deep sighings of the wind, as it passed among trees, which threw their broad arms over the cliffs, and crowned the highest summits. Onward, through the narrowing windings of the defile, no living object appeared; but, as Ellena looked fearfully back, she thought she distinguished a human figure advancing beneath the dusky umbrage that closed the view. She communicated her suspicion to Schedoni, though not her fears, and they stopped for a moment, to observe further. The object advanced slowly, and they perceived the stature of a man, who, having continued to approach, suddenly paused, and then glided away behind the foliage that crossed the perspective, but not before Ellena fancied she discriminated the figure of Spalatro. None but a purpose the most desperate, she believed, could have urged him to follow into this pass, instead of returning, as he had pretended, to his home. Yet it appeared improbable, that he alone should be willing to attack two armed persons, for both Schedoni and the guide had weapons of defence. This consideration afforded her only a momentary respite from apprehension, since it was possible that he might not be alone, though only one person had yet been seen among the shrouding branches of the woods. 'Did you not think he resembled Spalatro?' said Ellena to the Confessor, 'was he not of the same stature and air? You are well armed, or I should fear for you, as well as for myself.'

'I did not observe a resemblance,' replied Schedoni, throwing a glance back, 'but whoever he is, you have nothing to apprehend from him, for he has disappeared.'

'Yes, Signor, so much the worse,' observed the guide, 'so much the worse, if he means us any harm, for he can steal along the rocks behind these thickets, and strike out upon us before we are aware of him. Or, if he knows the path that runs among those old oaks yonder, on the left, where the ground rises, he has us sure at the turning of the next cliff.'

'Speak lower,' said Schedoni, 'unless you mean that he should benefit by your instructions.'

Though the Confessor said this without any suspicion of evil intention from the guide, the man immediately began to justify himself, and added, 'I'll give him a hint of what he may expect, however, if he attacks us.' As he spoke, he fired his trombone* in the air, when every rock reverberated the sound, and the faint and fainter thunder retired in murmurs through all the windings of the defile. The eagerness, with which the guide had justified himself, produced an effect upon Schedoni contrary to what he designed; and the Confessor, as he watched him suspiciously, observed, that after he had fired, he did not load his piece again. 'Since you have given the enemy sufficient intimation where to find us,' said Schedoni, 'you will do well to prepare for his reception; load again, friend. I have arms too, and they are ready.'

While the man sullenly obeyed, Ellena, again alarmed, looked back in search of the stranger, but not any person appeared beneath the gloom, and no footstep broke upon the stillness. When, however, she suddenly heard a rustling noise, she looked to the bordering thickets, almost expecting to see Spalatro break from among them, before she perceived that it was only the sounding pinions of birds, which, startled by the report of the trombone from their high nests in the cliffs, winged their way from danger.

The suspicions of the Confessor had, probably, been slight, for they were transient; and when Ellena next addressed him, he had again retired within himself. He was ruminating upon an excuse to be offered the Marchesa, which might be sufficient both to assuage her disappointment and baffle her curiosity, and he could not, at present, fabricate one that might soothe her resentment, without risk of betraying his secret.

Twilight had added its gloom to that of the rocks, before the travellers distinguished the town, at which they meant to pass the night. It terminated the defile, and its grey houses could scarcely be discerned from the precipice upon which they hung, or from the trees that embosomed them. A rapid stream rolled below, and over it a bridge conducted the wanderers to the little inn, at which they were to take up their abode. Here, quietly lodged, Ellena dismissed all present apprehension of Spalatro, but she still believed she had seen him, and her suspicions, as to the motive of his extraordinary journey, were not appeased.

As this was a town of ampler accommodation than the one they had left, Schedoni easily procured a lay-habit, that would disguise him for the remainder of the journey; and Ellena was permitted to lay aside the nun's veil, for one of a more general fashion; but, in dismissing it, she did not forget that it had been the veil of Olivia, and she preserved it as a sacred relique of her favourite recluse.

The distance between this town and Naples was still that of several days journey, according to the usual mode of travelling; but the most dangerous part of the way was now overcome, the road having emerged from the forests; and when Schedoni, on the following morning, was departing, he would have discharged the guide, had not the host assured him, he would find one still necessary in the open, but wild, country through which he must pass. Schedoni's distrust of this guide had never been very serious, and, as the result of the preceding evening proved favourable, he had restored him so entirely to his confidence, as willingly to engage him for the present day. In this confidence, however, Ellena did not perfectly coincide; she had observed the man while he loaded the trombone, on Schedoni's order, and his evident reluctance had almost persuaded her, that he was in league with some person who designed to attack them; a conjecture, perhaps, the more readily admitted while her mind was suffering from the impression of having seen Spalatro. She now ventured to hint her distrust to the Confessor, who paid little attention to it, and reminded her, that sufficient proof of the man's honesty had appeared, in their having been permitted to pass in safety, a defile so convenient for the purpose of rapine as that of yesterday. To a reply apparently so reasonable, Ellena could oppose nothing, had she even dared to press the topic; and she recommenced the journey with gayer hopes.

END OF THE SECOND VOLUME

VOLUME III

CHAPTER I

Mark where yon ruin frowns upon the steep,
The giant-spectre of departed power!
Within those shadowy walls and silent chambers
Have stalked the crimes of days long past!

ON this day, Schedoni was more communicative than on the preceding one. While they rode apart from the guide, he conversed with Ellena on various topics relative to herself, but without once alluding to Vivaldi; and even condescended to mention his design of disposing of her in a convent at some distance from Naples, till it should be convenient for him to acknowledge her for his daughter. But the difficulty of finding a suitable situation embarrassed him, and he was disconcerted by the awkwardness of introducing her himself to strangers, whose curiosity would be heightened by a sense of their interest.

These circumstances induced him the more easily to attend to the distress of Ellena, on her learning that she was again to be placed at a distance from her home, and among strangers; and the more willingly to listen to the account she gave of the convent of Santa Maria della Pieta, and to her request of returning thither. But in whatever degree he might be inclined to approve, he listened without consenting, and Ellena had only the consolation of perceiving that he was not absolutely determined to adopt his first plan.

Her thoughts were too deeply engaged upon her future prospects to permit leisure for present fears, or probably she would have suffered some return of those of yesterday, in traversing the lonely plains and rude vallies, through which the road lay. Schedoni was thankful to the landlord, who had advised him to keep the guide, the road being frequently obscured amongst the wild heaths that stretched around, and the eye often sweeping over long tracts of country, without perceiving a village, or any human dwelling.

During the whole morning, they had not met one traveller, and they continued to proceed beneath the heat of noon, because Schedoni had been unable to discover even a cottage, in which shelter and repose might be obtained.

It was late in the day when the guide pointed out the grey walls of an edifice, which crowned the acclivity they were approaching. But this was so shrouded among woods, that no feature of it could be distinctly seen, and it did but slightly awaken their hopes of approaching a convent, which might receive them with hospitality.

The high banks overshadowed with thickets, between which the road ascended, soon excluded even a glimpse of the walls; but, as the travellers turned the next projection, they perceived a person on the summit of the road, crossing as if towards some place of residence, and concluded that the edifice they had seen was behind the trees, among which he had disappeared.

A few moments brought them to the spot, where, retired at a short distance among the woods that browed the hill, they discovered the extensive remains of what seemed to have been a villa, and which, from the air of desolation it exhibited, Schedoni would have judged to be wholly deserted, had he not already seen a person enter. Wearied and exhausted, he determined to ascertain whether any refreshment could be procured from the inhabitants within, and the party alighted before the portal of a deep and broad avenue of arched stone, which seemed to have been the grand approach to the villa. The entrance was obstructed by fallen fragments of columns, and by the underwood that had taken root amongst them. The travellers, however, easily overcame these interruptions: but as the avenue was of considerable extent, and as its only light proceeded from the portal, except what a few narrow loops in the walls admitted, they soon found themselves involved in an obscurity that rendered the way difficult, and Schedoni endeavoured to make himself heard by the person he had seen. The effort was unsuccessful, but, as they proceeded, a bend in the passage shewed a distant glimmering of light, which served to guide them to the opposite entrance, where an arch opened immediately into a court of the villa. Schedoni paused here in disappointment, for every object seemed to bear evidence of abandonment and desolation; and he looked, almost hopelessly, round the light colonnade which ran along three sides of the court, and to the trees that waved over the fourth, in search of the person, who had been seen from the road. No human figure stole upon the vacancy; yet the apt fears of Ellena almost imagined the form of Spalatro gliding behind the columns, and she started as the air shook over the wild plants that wreathed them, before she discovered that it was not the sound of steps. At the extravagance of her suspicions, however, and the weakness of her terrors, she blushed, and endeavoured to resist that propensity to fear, which nerves long pressed upon had occasioned in her mind.

Schedoni, meanwhile, stood in the court, like the evil spirit of the place, examining its desolation, and endeavouring to ascertain whether any person lurked in the interior of the building. Several doorways in the colonnade appeared to lead to chambers of the villa, and, after a short hesitation, Schedoni, having determined to pursue his inquiry, entered one of them, and passed through a marble hall to a suite of rooms, whose condition told how long it was since they had been inhabited. The roofs had entirely vanished, and even portions of the walls had fallen, and lay in masses amongst the woods without.

Perceiving that it was as useless as difficult to proceed, the confessor returned to the court, where the shade of the palmetos,* at least, offered an hospitable shelter to the wearied travellers. They reposed themselves beneath the branches, on some fragments of a marble fountain, whence the court opened to the extensive landscape, now mellowed by the evening beams, and partook of the remains of a repast, which had been deposited in the wallet of the guide.

'This place appears to have suffered from an earthquake, rather than from time,' said Schedoni, 'for the walls, though shattered, do not seem to have decayed, and much that has been strong lies in ruin, while what is comparatively slight remains uninjured; these are certainly symptoms of partial shocks of the earth. Do you know any thing of the history of this place, friend?'

'Yes, Signor,' replied the guide.

'Relate it, then.'

'I shall never forget the earthquake that destroyed it, Signor; for it was felt all through the Garganus. I was then about sixteen, and I remember it was near an hour before midnight that the great shock was felt. The weather had been almost stifling for several days, scarcely a breath of air had stirred, and slight tremblings of the ground were noticed by many people. I had been out all day, cutting wood in the forest with my father, and tired enough we were, when——'

'This is the history of yourself,' said Schedoni, interrupting him, 'Who did this place belong to?'

'Did any person suffer here?' said Ellena.

'The Baróne di Cambrusca lived here,' replied the guide.

'Hah! the Baróne!' repeated Schedoni, and sunk into one of his customary fits of abstraction.

'He was a Signor little loved in the country,' continued the guide, 'and some people said it was a judgment upon him for——'

'Was it not rather a judgment upon the country,' interrupted the Confessor, lifting up his head, and then sinking again into silence.

'I know not for that, Signor, but he had committed crimes enough to make one's hair stand on end. It was here that he——'

'Fools are always wondering at the actions of those above them,' said Schedoni, testily; 'Where is the Baróne now?'

'I cannot tell, Signor, but most likely where he deserves to be, for he has never been heard of since the night of the earthquake, and it is believed he was buried under the ruins.'

'Did any other person suffer?' repeated Ellena.

'You shall hear, Signora,' replied the peasant, 'I happen to know something about the matter, because a cousin of our's lived in the family at the time, and my father has often told me all about it, as well as of the late lord's goings-on. It was near midnight when the great shock came, and the family, thinking of nothing at all, had supped, and been asleep some time. Now it happened, that the Baróne's chamber was in a tower of the old building, at which people often wondered, because, said they, why should he chuse to sleep in the old part when there are so many fine rooms in the new villa? but so it was.'

'Come, dispatch your meal,' said Schedoni, awaking from his deep musing, 'the sun is setting, and we have yet far to go.'

'I will finish the meal and the story together, Signor, with your leave,' replied the guide. Schedoni did not notice what he said, and, as the man was not forbidden, he proceeded with his relation.

'Now it happened, that the Baróne's chamber was in that old tower,—if you will look this way, Signora, you may see what is left of it.'

Ellena turned her attention to where the guide pointed, and perceived the shattered remains of a tower rising beyond the arch, through which she had entered the court.

'You see that corner of a windowcase, left in the highest part of the wall, Signora,' continued the guide, 'just by that tuft of ash, that grows out of the stone.'

'I observe,' said Ellena.

'Well, that was one of the windows of the very chamber, Signora, and you see scarcely any thing else is left of it. Yes, there is the door-case, too, but the door itself is gone; that little staircase, which you see beyond it, led up to another story, which nobody now would guess had ever been; for roof, and flooring, and all are fallen. I wonder how that little staircase in the corner happened to hold so fast!'

'Have you almost done?' inquired Schedoni, who had not apparently attended to any thing the man said, and now alluded to the refreshment he was taking.

'Yes, Signor, I have not a great deal more to tell, or to eat either, for that matter,' replied the guide; 'but you shall hear. Well, yonder was the very chamber, Signora; at that door-case, which is still in the wall, the Baróne came in; ah! he little thought, I warrant, that he should never more go out at it! How long he had been in the room I do not know, nor whether he was asleep, or awake, for there is nobody that can tell; but when the great shock came, it split the old tower at once, before any other part of the buildings. You see that heap of ruins, yonder, on the ground, Signora, there lie the remains of the chamber; the Baróne, they say, was buried under them!'

Ellena shuddered while she gazed upon this destructive mass. A groan from Schedoni startled her, and she turned towards him, but, as he appeared shrouded in meditation, she again directed her attention to this awful memorial. As her eye passed upon the neighbouring arch, she was struck with the grandeur of its proportions, and with its singular appearance, now that the evening rays glanced upon the overhanging shrubs, and darted a line of partial light athwart the avenue beyond. But what was her emotion, when she perceived a person gliding away in the perspective of the avenue, and, as he crossed where the gleam fell, distinguished the figure and countenance of Spalatro! She had scarcely power faintly to exclaim, 'Steps go there!' before he had disappeared; and, when Schedoni looked round, the vacuity and silence of solitude every where prevailed.

Ellena now did not scruple positively to affirm that she had seen Spalatro, and Schedoni, fully sensible that, if her imagination had not deluded her, the purpose of his thus tracing their route must be desperate, immediately rose, and, followed by the peasant, passed into the avenue to ascertain the truth, leaving Ellena alone in the court. He had scarcely disappeared before the danger of his adventuring into that obscure passage, where an assassin might strike unseen, forcibly occurred to Ellena, and she loudly conjured him to return. She listened for his voice, but heard only his retreating steps; when, too anxious to remain where she was, she hastened to the entrance of the avenue. But all was now hushed; neither voice, nor steps were distinguished. Awed by the gloom of the place, she feared to venture further, yet almost equally dreaded to remain alone in any part of the ruin, while a man so desperate as Spalatro was hovering about it.

As she yet listened at the entrance of the avenue, a faint cry, which seemed to issue from the interior of the villa, reached her. The first dreadful surmise that struck Ellena was, that they were murdering her father, who had probably been decoyed, by another passage, back into some chamber of the ruin; when, instantly forgetting every fear for herself, she hastened towards the spot whence she judged the sound to have issued. She entered the hall, which Schedoni had noticed, and passed on through a suite of apartments beyond. Every thing here, however, was silent, and the place apparently deserted. The suite terminated in a passage, that seemed to lead to a distant part of the villa, and Ellena, after a momentary hesitation, determined to follow it.

She made her way with difficulty between the half-demolished walls, and was obliged to attend so much to her steps, that she scarcely noticed whither she was going, till, the deepening shade of the place recalling her attention, she perceived herself among the ruins of the tower, whose history had been related by the guide; and, on looking up, observed she was at the foot of the staircase, which still wound up the wall, that had led to the chamber of the Baróne.

At a moment less anxious, the circumstance would have affected her; but now, she could only repeat her calls upon the name of Schedoni, and listen for some signal that he was near. Still receiving no answer, nor hearing any further sound of distress, she began to hope that her fears had deceived her, and having ascertained that the passage terminated here, she quitted the spot.

On regaining the first chamber, Ellena rested for a moment to recover breath; and, while she leaned upon what had once been a window, opening to the court, she heard a distant report of fire-arms. The sound swelled, and seemed to revolve along the avenue through which Schedoni had disappeared.—Supposing that the combatants were engaged at the farthest entrance, Ellena was preparing to go thither, when a sudden step moved near her, and, on turning, she discovered, with a degree of horror that almost deprived her of recollection, Spalatro himself stealing along the very chamber in which she was.

That part of the room which she stood in, fell into a kind of recess; and whether it was this circumstance that prevented him from immediately perceiving her, or that, his chief purpose being directed against another object, he did not chuse to pause here, he passed on with skulking steps; and, before Ellena had determined whither to go, she observed him cross the court before her, and enter the avenue. As he had passed, he looked up at the window: and it was certain he then saw her, for he instantly faultered, but in the next moment proceeded swiftly, and disappeared in the gloom.

It seemed that he had not yet encountered Schedoni, but it also occurred to Ellena, that he was gone into the avenue for the purpose of waiting to assassinate him in the darkness. While she was meditating some means of giving the Confessor a timely alarm of his danger, she once more distinguished his voice. It approached from the avenue, and Ellena immediately calling aloud that Spalatro was there, entreated him to be on his guard. In the next instant a pistol was fired there.

Among the voices that succeeded the report, Ellena thought she distinguished groans. Schedoni's voice was in the next moment heard again, but it seemed faint and low. The courage which she had before exerted was now exhausted; she remained fixed to the spot, unable to encounter the dreadful spectacle that probably awaited her in the avenue, and almost sinking beneath the expectation of it.

All was now hushed; she listened for Schedoni's voice, and even for a footstep—in vain. To endure this state of uncertainty much longer was scarcely possible, and Ellena was endeavouring to collect fortitude to meet a knowledge of the worst, when suddenly a feeble groaning was again heard. It seemed near, and to be approaching still nearer. At that moment, Ellena, on looking towards the avenue, perceived a figure covered with blood, pass into the court. A film, which drew over her eyes, prevented her noticing farther. She tottered a few paces back, and caught at the fragment of a pillar, by which she supported herself. The weakness was transient; immediate assistance appeared necessary to the wounded person, and pity soon predominating over horror, she recalled her spirits, and hastened to the court.

When, on reaching it, she looked round in search of Schedoni, he was no where to be seen; the court was again solitary and silent, till she awakened all its echoes with the name of *father*. While she repeated her calls, she hastily examined the colonnade, the separated chamber which opened immediately from it, and the shadowy ground beneath the palmetos, but without discovering any person.

As she turned towards the avenue, however, a track of blood on the ground told her too certainly where the wounded person had passed. It guided her to the entrance of a narrow passage, that seemingly led to the foot of the tower; but here she hesitated, fearing to trust the obscurity beyond. For the first time, Ellena conjectured, that not Schedoni, but Spalatro might be the person she had seen, and that, though he was wounded, vengeance might give him strength to strike his stiletto at the heart of whomsoever approached him, while the duskiness of the place would favour the deed.

She was yet at the entrance of the passage, fearful to enter, and reluctant to leave it, listening for a sound, and still hearing at intervals, swelling though feeble groans; when quick steps were suddenly heard advancing up the grand avenue, and presently her own name was repeated loudly in the voice of Schedoni. His manner was hurried as he advanced to meet her, and he threw an eager glance round the court. 'We must be gone,' said he, in a low tone, and taking her arm within his. 'Have you seen any one pass?'

'I have seen a wounded man enter the court,' replied Ellena, 'and feared he was yourself.'

'Where?—Which way did he go!' inquired Schedoni, eagerly, while his eyes glowed, and his countenance became fell.

Ellena, instantly comprehending his motive for the question, would not acknowledge that she knew whither Spalatro had withdrawn; and, reminding him of the danger of their situation, she entreated that they might quit the villa immediately.

'The sun is already set,' she added. 'I tremble at what may be the perils of this place at such an obscure hour, and even at what may be those of our road at a later!'

'You are sure he was wounded?' said the Confessor.

'Too sure,' replied Ellena, faintly.

'Too sure!' sternly exclaimed Schedoni.

'Let us depart, my father; O let us go this instant!' repeated Ellena.

'What is the meaning of all this!' asked Schedoni, with anger. 'You cannot, surely, have the weakness to pity this fellow!'

'It is terrible to see any one suffer,' said Ellena. 'Do not, by remaining here, leave me a possibility of grieving for you. What anguish it would occasion you, to see me bleed; judge, then, what must be mine, if you are wounded by the dagger of an assassin!'

Schedoni stifled the groan which swelled from his heart, and abruptly turned away.

'You trifle with me,' he said, in the next moment: 'you do not know that the villain is wounded. I fired at him, it is true, at the instant I saw him enter the avenue, but he has escaped me. What reason have you for your supposition?'

Ellena was going to point to the track of blood on the ground, at a little distance, but checked herself; considering that this might guide him on to Spalatro, and again she entreated they might depart, adding, 'O! spare yourself, and him!'

'What! spare an assassin!' said Schedoni, impatiently.

'An assassin! He *has*, then, attempted your life?' exclaimed Ellena.

'Why no, not absolutely that,' said Schedoni, recollecting himself, 'but—what does the fellow do here? Let me pass, I will find him.'

Ellena still hung upon his garment, while, with persuasive tenderness, she endeavoured to awaken his humanity. 'O! if you had ever known what it was to expect instant death,' she continued, 'you would pity this man now, as he, perhaps, has sometimes pitied others! I have known such suffering, my father, and can, therefore, feel even for him!'

'Do you know for *whom* you are pleading?' said the distracted Schedoni, while every word she had uttered seemed to have penetrated his heart. The surprize which this question awakened in Ellena's countenance, recalled him to a consciousness of his imprudence; he recollected that Ellena did not certainly know the office, with which Spalatro had been commissioned against her: and when he considered that this very Spalatro, whom Ellena had with such simplicity supposed to have, at some time, spared a life through pity, had in truth spared her own, and, yet more, had been eventually a means of preventing him from destroying his own child, the Confessor turned in horror from his design; all his passions changed, and he abruptly quitted the court, nor paused till he reached the farthest extremity of the avenue, where the guide was it waiting with the horses.

A recollection of the conduct of Spalatro respecting Ellena had thus induced Schedoni to spare him; but this was all; it did not prevail with him to inquire into the condition of this man, or to mitigate his punishment; and, without remorse, he now left him to his fate.

With Ellena it was otherwise; though she was ignorant of the obligation she owed him, she could not know that any human being was left under such circumstances of suffering and solitude, without experiencing very painful emotion; but, considering how expeditiously Spalatro had been able to remove himself, she endeavoured to hope that his wound was not mortal.

The travellers, mounting their horses in silence, left the ruin, and were for some time too much engaged by the impression of the late occurrences, to converse together. When, at length, Ellena inquired the particulars of what had passed in the avenue, she understood that Schedoni, on pursuing Spalatro, had seen him there only for a moment. Spalatro had escaped by some way unknown to the Confessor, and had regained the interior of the ruin, while his pursuers were yet following the avenue. The cry, which Ellena had imagined to proceed from the interior, was uttered, as it now appeared, by the guide, who, in his haste, had fallen over some fragments of the wall that lay scattered in the avenue: the first report of arms had been from the trombone, which Schedoni had discharged on reaching the portal; and the last, when he fired a pistol,* on perceiving Spalatro passing from the court.

'We have had trouble enough in running after this fellow,' said the guide, 'and could not catch him at last. It is strange that, if he came to look for us, he should run away so when he had found us! I do not think he meant us any harm, after all, else he might have done it easily enough in that dark passage; instead whereof he only took to his heels!'

'Silence!' said Schedoni, 'fewer words, friend.'

'Well, Signor, he's peppered now, however; so we need not be afraid; his wings are clipped for one while, so he cannot overtake us. We need not be in such a hurry, Signor, we shall get to the inn in good time yet. It is upon a mountain yonder, whose top you may see upon that red streak in the west. He cannot come after us; I myself saw his arm was wounded.'

'Did you so?' said Schedoni, sharply: 'and pray where was you when you saw so much? It was more than I saw.'

'I was close at your heels, Signor, when you fired the pistol.'

'I do not remember to have heard you there,' observed the Confessor: 'and why did you not come forward, instead of retreating? And where, also, did you hide yourself while I was searching for the fellow, instead of assisting me in the pursuit?'

The guide gave no answer, and Ellena, who had been attentively observing him during the whole of this conversation, perceived that he was now considerably embarrassed; so that her former suspicions as to his integrity began to revive, notwithstanding the several circumstances, which had occurred to render them improbable. There was, however, at present no opportunity for farther observation, Schedoni having, contrary to the advice of the guide, immediately quickened his pace, and the horses continuing on the full gallop, till a steep ascent compelled them to relax their speed.

Contrary to his usual habit, Schedoni now, while they slowly ascended, appeared desirous of conversing with this man, and asked him several questions relative to the villa they had left; and, whether it was that he really felt an interest on the subject, or that he wished to discover if the man had deceived him in the circumstances he had already narrated, from which he might form a judgment as to his general character, he pressed his inquiries with a patient minuteness, that somewhat surprized Ellena. During this conversation, the deep twilight would no longer permit her to notice the countenances of either Schedoni, or the guide, but she gave much attention to the changing tones of their voices, as different circumstances and emotions seemed to affect them. It is to be observed, that during the whole of this discourse, the guide rode at the side of Schedoni.

While the Confessor appeared to be musing upon something, which the peasant had related respecting the Baróne di Cambrusca, Ellena inquired as to the fate of the other inhabitants of the villa.

'The falling of the old tower was enough for them,' replied the guide; 'the crash waked them all directly, and they had time to get out of the new buildings, before the second and third shocks laid them also in ruins. They ran out into the woods for safety, and found it too, for they happened to take a different road from the earthquake. Not a soul suffered, except the Baróne, and he deserved it well enough. O! I could tell such things that I have heard of him!——'

'What became of the rest of the family?' interrupted Schedoni.

'Why, Signor, they were scattered here and there, and every where; and they none of them ever returned to the old spot. No! no! they had suffered enough there already, and might have suffered to this day, if the earthquake had not happened.'

'If it had *not* happened?' repeated Ellena.

'Aye, Signora, for that put an end to the Baróne. If those walls could but speak, they could tell strange things, for they have looked upon sad doings: and that chamber, which I shewed you, Signora, nobody ever went into it but himself, except the servant, to keep it in order, and that he would scarcely suffer, and always staid in the room the while.'

'He had probably treasure secreted there,' said Ellena.

'No, Signora, no treasure! He had always a lamp burning there; and sometimes in the night he has been heard—Once, indeed, his valet happened to—'

'Come on,' said Schedoni, interrupting him; 'keep pace with me. What idle dream are you relating now?'

'It is about the Baróne di Cambrusca, Signor, him that you was asking me so much about just now. I was saying what strange ways he had, and how that, on one stormy night in December, as my cousin Francisco told my father, who told me, and he lived in the family at the time it happened—'

'What happened?' said Schedoni, hastily.

'What I am going to tell, Signor. My cousin lived there at the time; so, however *unbelievable* it may seem, you may depend upon it, it is all true. My father knows I would not believe it myself till—'

'Enough of this,' said Schedoni; 'no more. What family had this Baróne—had he a wife at the time of this destructive shock?'

'Yes, truly, Signor, he had, as I was going to tell, if you would but condescend to have patience.'

'The Baróne had more need of that, friend; I have no wife.'— 'The Baróne's wife had most need of it, Signor, as you shall hear. A good soul, they say, was the Baronessa! but luckily she died many years before. He had a daughter, also, and, young as she was, she had lived too long, but for the earthquake which set her free.'

'How far is it to the inn?' said the Confessor, roughly.

'When we get to the top of this hill, Signor, you will see it on the next, if any light is stirring, for there will only be the hollow between us. But do not be alarmed, Signor, the fellow we left cannot overtake us. Do you know much about him, Signor?'

Schedoni inquired whether the trombone was charged; and, discovering that it was not, ordered the man to load immediately.

'Why, Signor, if you knew as much of him as I do, you could not be more afraid!' said the peasant, while he stopped to obey the order.

'I understood that he was a stranger to you!' observed the Confessor, with surprize.

'Why, Signor, he is, and he is not; I know more about him than he thinks for.'

'You seem to know a vast deal too much of other persons affairs,' said Schedoni, in a tone that was meant to silence him.

'Why, that is just what he would say, Signor; but bad deeds will out, whether people like them to be known or not. This man comes to our town sometimes to market, and nobody knew where he came from for a long while; so they set themselves to work and found it out at last.'

'We shall never reach the summit of this hill,' said Schedoni, testily.

'And they found out, too, a great many strange things about him,' continued the guide.

Ellena, who had attended to this discourse with a degree of curiosity that was painful, now listened impatiently for what might be farther mentioned concerning Spalatro, but without daring to invite, by a single question, any discovery on a subject which appeared to be so intimately connected with Schedoni.

'It was many years ago,' rejoined the guide, 'that this man came to live in that strange house on the sea-shore. It had been shut up ever since—'

'What are you talking of now?' interrupted the Confessor.

'Why, Signor, you never will let me tell you. You always snap me up so short at the beginning, and then ask—what am I talking about! I was going to begin the story, and it is a pretty long one. But first of all, Signor, who do you suppose this man belonged to! And what do you think the people determined to do, when the report was first set a-going? only they could not be sure it was true, and any body would be unwilling enough to believe such a shocking—'

'I have no curiosity on the subject,' replied the Confessor, sternly interrupting him; 'and desire to hear no more concerning it.'

'I meant no harm, Signor,' said the man; 'I did not know it concerned you.'

'And who says that it does concern me!'

'Nobody, Signor, only you seemed to be in a bit of a passion, and so I thought——But I meant no harm, Signor, only as he happened to be your guide part of the way, I guessed you might like to know something of him.'

'All that I desire to know of my guide is, that he does his duty,' replied Schedoni, 'that he conducts me safely, and understands when to be silent.'

To this the man replied nothing, but slackened his pace, and slunk behind his reprover.

The travellers reaching, soon after, the summit of this long hill, looked out for the inn of which they had been told; but darkness now confounded every object, and no domestic light twinkling, however distantly, through the gloom, gave signal of security and comfort. They descended dejectedly into the hollow of the mountains, and found themselves once more immerged in woods. Schedoni again called the peasant to his side, and bade him keep abreast of him, but he did not discourse; and Ellena was too thoughtful to attempt conversation. The hints, which the guide had thrown out respecting Spalatro, had increased her curiosity on that subject; but the conduct of Schedoni, his impatience, his embarrassment, and the decisive manner in which he had put an end to the talk of the guide, excited a degree of surprize, that bordered on astonishment. As she had, however, no clue to lead her conjectures to any point, she was utterly bewildered in surmise, understanding only that Schedoni had been much more deeply connected with Spalatro than she had hitherto believed.

The travellers having descended into the hollow, and commenced the ascent of the opposite height, without discovering any symptom of a neighbouring town, began again to fear that their conductor had deceived them. It was now so dark that the road, though the soil was a limestone, could scarcely be discerned, the woods on either side forming a 'close dungeon of innumerous boughs,' that totally excluded the twilight of the stars.

While the Confessor was questioning the man, with some severity, a faint shouting was heard from a distance, and he stopped the horses to listen from what quarter it came.

'That comes the way we are going, Signor,' said the guide.

'Hark!' exclaimed Schedoni, 'those are strains of revelry!'

A confused sound of voices, laughter, and musical instruments, was heard, and, as the air blew stronger, tamborines and flutes were distinguished.

'Oh! Oh! we are near the end of our journey!' said the peasant; 'all this comes from the town we are going to. But what makes them all so merry, I wonder!'

Ellena, revived by this intelligence, followed with alacrity the sudden speed of the Confessor; and presently reaching a point of the mountain, where the woods opened, a cluster of lights on another summit, a little higher, more certainly announced the town.

They soon after arrived at the ruinous gates, which had formerly led to a place of some strength, and passed at once from darkness and desolated walls, into a market place, blazing with light and resounding with the multitude. Booths, fantastically hung with lamps, and filled with merchandize of every kind, disposed in the gayest order, were spread on all sides, and peasants in their holiday cloaths, and parties of masks crowded every avenue. Here was a band of musicians, and there a group of dancers; on one spot the *outré** humour of a zanni* provoked the never-failing laugh of an Italian rabble, in another the *improvisatore,** by the pathos of his story, and the persuasive sensibility of his strains, was holding the attention of his auditors, as in the bands of magic. Farther on was a stage raised for a display of fireworks, and near this a theatre, where a mimic opera, the 'shadow of a shade,' was exhibiting, whence the roar of laughter, excited by the principal *buffo** within, mingled with the heterogeneous voices of the venders of ice, maccaroni, sherbet, and diavoloni,* without.

The Confessor looked upon this scene with disappointment and ill-humour, and bade the guide go before him, and shew the way to the best inn; an office which the latter undertook with great glee, though he made his way with difficulty. 'To think I should not know it was the time of the fair!' said he, 'though, to say truth, I never was at it but once in my life, so it is not so surprizing, Signor.'

'Make way through the crowd,' said Schedoni.

'After jogging on so long in the dark, Signor, with nothing at all to be seen,' continued the man, without attending to the direction, 'then to come, all of a sudden, to such a place as this, why it is like coming out of purgatory into paradise! Well! Signor, you have forgot all your quandaries now; you think nothing now about that old ruinous place where we had such a race after the man, that would not murder us; but that shot I fired did his business.'

'You fired!' said Schedoni, aroused by the assertion.

'Yes, Signor, as I was looking over your shoulder; I should have thought you must have heard it!'

'I should have thought so, too, friend.'

'Aye, Signor, this fine place has put all that out of your head, I warrant, as well as what I said about that same fellow; but, indeed, Signor, I did not know he was related to you, when I talked so of him. But, perhaps, for all that, you may not know the piece of his story I was going to tell you, when you cut me off so short, though you are better acquainted with one another than I guessed for; so, when I come in from the fair, Signor, if you please,

I will tell it you; and it is a pretty long history, for I happen to know the whole of it; though, where you cut me short, when you was in one of those quandaries, was only just at the beginning, but no matter for that, I can begin it again, for——'

'What is all this!' said Schedoni, again recalled from one of the thoughtful moods in which he had so habitually indulged, that even the bustle around him had failed to interrupt the course of his mind. He now bade the peasant be silent; but the man was too happy to be tractable, and proceeded to express all he felt, as they advanced slowly through the crowd. Every object here was to him new and delightful; and, nothing doubting that it must be equally so to every other person, he was continually pointing out to the proud and gloomy Confessor the trivial subjects of his own admiration. 'See! Signor, there is Punchinello,* see! how he eats the hot maccaroni! And look there, Signor! there is a juggler! O! good Signor, stop one minute, to look at his tricks. See! he has turned a monk into a devil already, in the twinkling of an eye!'

'Silence! and proceed,' said Schedoni.

'That is what I say, Signor:—silence! for the people make such a noise that I cannot hear a word you speak.—Silence, there!'

'Considering that you could not hear, you have answered wonderfully to the purpose,' said Ellena.

'Ah! Signora! is not this better than those dark woods and hills? But what have we here? Look, Signor, here is a fine sight!'

The crowd, which was assembled round a stage on which some persons grotesquely dressed, were performing, now interrupting all farther progress, the travellers were compelled to stop at the foot of the platform. The people above were acting what seemed to have been intended for a tragedy, but what their strange gestures, uncouth recitation, and incongruous countenances, had transformed into a comedy.

Schedoni, thus obliged to pause, withdrew his attention from the scene; Ellena consented to endure it, and the peasant, with gaping mouth and staring eyes, stood like a statue, yet not knowing whether he ought to laugh or cry, till suddenly turning round to the Confessor, whose horse was of necessity close to his, he seized his arm, and pointing to the stage, called out, 'Look! Signor, see! Signor, what a scoundrel! what a villain! See! he has murdered his own daughter!'

At these terrible words, the indignation of Schedoni was done away by other emotions; he turned his eyes upon the stage, and perceived that the actors were performing the story of Virginia.*

It was at the moment when she was dying in the arms of her father, who was holding up the poniard, with which he had stabbed her. The feelings of Schedoni, at this instant, inflicted a punishment almost worthy of the crime he had meditated.

Ellena, struck with the action, and with the contrast which it seemed to offer to what she had believed to have been the late conduct of Schedoni towards herself, looked at him with most expressive tenderness, and as his glance met her's, she perceived, with surprize, the changing emotions of his soul, and the inexplicable character of his countenance. Stung to the heart, the Confessor furiously spurred his horse, that he might escape from the scene, but the poor animal was too spiritless and jaded, to force its way through the crowd; and the peasant, vexed at being hurried from a place where, almost for the first time in his life, he was suffering under the strange delights of artificial grief, and half angry, to observe an animal, of which he had the care, ill treated, loudly remonstrated, and seized the bridle of Schedoni, who, still more incensed, was applying the whip to the shoulders of the guide, when the crowd suddenly fell back and opened a way, through which the travellers passed, and arrived, with little further interruption, at the door of the inn.

Schedoni was not in a humour which rendered him fit to encounter difficulties, and still less the vulgar squabbles of a place already crowded with guests; yet it was not without much opposition that he at length obtained a lodging for the night. The peasant was not less anxious for the accommodation of his horses; and, when Ellena heard him declare, that the animal, which the Confessor had so cruelly spurred, should have a double feed, and a bed of straw as high as his head, if he himself went without one, she gave him, unnoticed by Schedoni, the only ducat she had left.

CHAPTER II

But, if you be afraid to hear the worst,
Then let the worst, unheard, fall on your head.
SHAKESPEARE*

SCHEDONI passed the night without sleep. The incident of the preceding evening had not only renewed the agonies of remorse, but excited those of pride and apprehension. There was something in the conduct of the peasant towards him, which he could not clearly understand, though his suspicions were sufficient to throw his mind into a state of the utmost perturbation. Under an air of extreme simplicity, this man had talked of Spalatro, had discovered that he was acquainted with much of his history, and had hinted that he knew by whom he had been employed; yet at the same time appeared unconscious, that Schedoni's was the master-hand, which had directed the principal actions of the ruffian. At other times, his behaviour had seemed to contradict the supposition of his ignorance on this point; from some circumstances he had mentioned, it appeared impossible but that he must have known who Schedoni really was, and even his own conduct had occasionally seemed to acknowledge this, particularly when, being interrupted in his history of Spalatro, he attempted an apology, by saying, he did not know it concerned Schedoni: nor could the conscious Schedoni believe that the very pointed manner, in which the peasant had addressed him at the representation of Virginia, was merely accidental. He wished to dismiss the man immediately, but it was first necessary to ascertain what he knew concerning him, and then to decide on the measures to be taken. It was, however, a difficult matter to obtain this information, without manifesting an anxiety, which might betray him, if the guide had, at present, only a general suspicion of the truth; and no less difficult to determine how to proceed towards him, if it should be evident that his suspicions rested on Spalatro. To take him forward to Naples, was to bring an informer to his home; to suffer him to return with his discovery, now that he probably knew the place of Schedoni's residence, was little less hazardous. His death only could secure the secret.

After a night passed in the tumult of such considerations, the

Confessor summoned the peasant to his chamber, and, with some short preface, told him he had no further occasion for his services, adding, carelessly, that he advised him to be on his guard as he re-passed the villa, lest Spalatro, who might yet lurk there, should revenge upon him the injury he had received. 'According to your account of him, he is a very dangerous fellow,' said Schedoni; 'but your information is, perhaps, erroneous.'

The guide began, testily, to justify himself for his assertions, and the Confessor then endeavoured to draw from him what he knew on the subject. But, whether the man was piqued by the treatment he had lately received, or had other reasons for reserve, he did not, at first, appear so willing to communicate as formerly.

'What you hinted of this man,' said Schedoni, 'has, in some degree, excited my curiosity: I have now a few moments of leisure, and you may relate, if you will, something of the wonderful history you talked of.'

'It is a long story, Signor, and you would be tired before I got to the end of it,' replied the peasant; 'and, craving your pardon, Signor, I don't much like to be snapped up so!'

'Where did this man live?' said the Confessor. 'You mentioned something of a house at the sea side.'

'Aye, Signor, there is a strange history belonging to that house, too; but this man, as I was saying, came there all of a sudden, nobody knew how! and the place had been shut up ever since the Marchese——'

'The Marchese!' said Schedoni, coldly, 'what Marchese, friend?'
—'Why, I mean the Baróne di Cambrusca, Signor, to be sure, as I was going to have told you, of my own accord, if you would only have let me. Shut up ever since the Baróne——I left off there, I think.'

'I understood that the Baróne was dead!' observed the Confessor.

'Yes, Signor,' replied the peasant, fixing his eyes on Schedoni; 'but what has his death to do with what I was telling? This happened before he died.'

Schedoni, somewhat disconcerted by this unexpected remark, forgot to resent the familiarity of it. 'This man, then, this Spalatro, was connected with the Baróne di Cambrusca?' said he.

'It was pretty well guessed so, Signor.'

'How! no more than guessed?'

'No, Signor, and that was more than enough for the Baróne's liking, I warrant. He took too much care for any thing certain to appear against him, and he was wise so to do, for if it had—it would have been worse for him. But I was going to tell you the story, Signor.'.

'What reasons were there for believing this was an agent of the Baróne di Cambrusca, friend?'

'I thought you wished to hear the story, Signor.'

'In good time; but first what were your reasons?'

'One of them is enough, Signor, and if you would only have let me gone straight on with the story, you would have found it out by this time, Signor.'

Schedoni frowned, but did not otherwise reprove the impertinence of the speech.

'It was reason enough, Signor, to my mind,' continued the peasant, 'that it was such a crime as nobody but the Baróne di Cambrusca could have committed; there was nobody wicked enough, in our parts, to have done it but him. Why is not this *reason* enough, Signor? What makes you look at me so? why the Baróne himself could hardly have looked worse, if I had told him as much!'

'Be less prolix,' said the Confessor, in a restrained voice.

'Well then, Signor, to begin at the beginning. It is a good many years ago that Marco came first to our town. Now the story goes, that one stormy night——'

'You may spare yourself the trouble of relating the story,' said Schedoni, abruptly, 'Did you ever see the Baróne you was speaking of, friend?'

'Why did you bid me tell it, Signor, since you know it already! I have been here all this while, just a-going to begin it, and all for nothing!'

'It is very surprising,' resumed the artful Schedoni, without having noticed what had been said, 'that if this Spalatro was known to be the villain you say he is, not any step should have been taken to bring him to justice! how happened that? But, perhaps, all this story was nothing more than a report.'   •

'Why, Signor, it was every body's business, and nobody's, as one may say; then, besides, nobody could prove what they had heard, and though every body believed the story just the same as if they had seen the whole, yet that, they said, would not do in law, but they should be made to prove it. Now, it is not one time in ten that any thing can be proved, Signor, as you well know, yet we none of us believe it the less for that!'

'So, then, you would have had this man punished for a

murder, which, probably, he never committed!' said the Confessor.

'A murder!' repeated the peasant.

Schedoni was silent, but, in the next instant, said, 'Did you not say it was a murder?'

'I have not told you so, Signor!'

'What was the crime, then?' resumed Schedoni, after another momentary pause, 'you said it was atrocious, and what more so than—murder?' His lip quivered as he pronounced the last word.

The peasant made no reply, but remained with his eyes fixed upon the Confessor, and, at length, repeated, 'Did I say it was murder, Signor?'

'If it was not that, say what it was,' demanded the Confessor, haughtily; 'but let it be in two words.'

'As if a story could be told in two words, Signor!'

'Well, well, be brief.'

'How can I, Signor, when the story is so long!'

'I will waste no more time,' said Schedoni, going.

'Well, Signor, I will do my best to make it short. It was one stormy night in December, that Marco Torma had been out fishing. Marco, Signor, was an old man that lived in our town when I was a boy; I can but just remember him, but my father knew him well, and loved old Marco, and used often to say——'

'To the story!' said Schedoni.

'Why I am telling it, Signor, as fast as I can. This old Marco did not live in our town at the time it happened, but in some place, I have forgot the name of it, near the sea shore. What can the name be! it is something like——'

'Well, what happened to this old dotard?'

'You are out there, Signor, he was no old dotard; but you shall hear. At that time, Signor, Marco lived in this place that I have forgot the name of, and was a fisherman, but better times turned up afterwards, but that is neither here nor there. Old Marco had been out fishing; it was a stormy night, and he was glad enough to get on shore, I warrant. It was quite dark, as dark, Signor, I suppose, as it was last night, and he was making the best of his way, Signor, with some fish along the shore, but it being so dark, he lost it notwithstanding. The rain beat, and the wind blew, and he wandered about a long while, and could see no light, nor hear any thing, but the surge near him, which sometimes seemed as if it was coming to wash him away. He got as far off it as he could, but he knew there were high rocks over the beach, and he was afraid he should run his head against them, if he went too far, I suppose. However, at last, he went up close to them, and as he got a little shelter, he resolved to try no further for the present. I tell it you, Signor, just as my father told it me, and he had it from the old man himself.'

'You need not be so particular,' replied the Confessor; 'speak to the point.'

'Well, Signor, as old Marco lay snug under the rocks, he thought he heard somebody coming, and he lifted up his head, I warrant, poor old soul! as if he could have seen who it was; however, he could hear, though it was so dark, and he heard the steps coming on; but he said nothing yet, meaning to let them come close up to him, before he discovered himself. Presently he sees a little moving light, and it comes nearer and nearer, till it was just opposite to him, and then he saw the shadow of a man on the ground, and then spied the man himself, with a dark lanthorn, passing along the beach.'

'Well, well, to the purpose,' said Schedoni.

'Old Marco, Signor, my father says, was never stout-hearted, and he took it into his head this might be a robber, because he had the lanthorn, though, for that matter, he would have been glad enough of a lanthorn himself, and so he lay quiet. But, presently, he was in a rare fright, for the man stopped to rest the load he had upon his back, on a piece of rock near him, and old Marco saw him throw off a heavy sack, and heard him breathe hard, as if he was hugely tired. I tell it, Signor, just as my father does.'

'What was in the sack?' said Schedoni, coolly.

'All in good time, Signor; perhaps old Marco never found out; but you shall hear. He was afraid, when he saw the sack, to stir a limb, for he thought it held booty. But, presently, the man, without saying a word, heaved it on his shoulders again, and staggered away with it along the beach, and Marco saw no more of him.'

'Well! what has he to do with your story, then?' said the Confessor, 'Was this Spalatro?'

'All in good time, Signor; you put me out. When the storm was down a little, Marco crept out, and, thinking there must be a village, or a hamlet, or a cottage, at no great distance, since this man had passed, he thought he would try a little further. He had better have staid where he was, for he wandered about a long while, and could see nothing, and what was worse, the storm came on louder than before, and he had no rocks to shelter him now. While he was in this quandary, he sees a light at a distance, and it came into his head this might be the lantern again, but he determined to go on notwithstanding, for if it was, he could stop short, and if it was not, he should get shelter, perhaps; so on he went, and I suppose I should have done the same, Signor.'

'Well! this history never will have an end!' said Schedoni.

'Well! Signor, he had not gone far when he found out that it was no lantern, but a light at a window. When he came up to the house he knocked softly at the door, but nobody came.'

'What house?' inquired the Confessor, sharply.

'The rain beat hard, Signor, and I warrant poor old Marco waited a long time before he knocked again, for he was main patient, Signor. O! how I have seen him listen to a story, let it be ever so long!'

'I have need of his patience!' said Schedoni.

'When he knocked again, Signor, the door gave way a little, and he found it was open, and so, as nobody came, he thought fit to walk in of his own accord.'

'The dotard! what business had he to be so curious?' exclaimed Schedoni.

'Curious! Signor, he only sought shelter! He stumbled about in the dark, for a good while, and could find nobody, nor make nobody hear, but, at last, he came to a room where there was some fire not quite out, upon the hearth, and he went up to it, to warm himself, till somebody should come.'

'What! was there nobody in the house?' said the Confessor.

'You shall hear, Signor. He had not been there, he said, no, he was sure, not above two minutes, when he heard a strange sort of a noise in the very room where he was, but the fire gave such a poor light, he could not see whether any body was there.'

'What was the noise?'

'You put me out, Signor. He said he did not much like it, but what could he do! So he stirred up the fire, and tried to make it blaze a little, but it was as dusky as ever; he could see nothing. Presently, however, he heard somebody coming, and saw a light, and then a man coming towards the room where he was, so he went up to him to ask shelter.'

'Who was this man?' said Schedoni.

'Ask shelter. He says the man, when he came to the door of the room, turned as white as a sheet, as well he might, to see a stranger, to find a stranger there, at that time of the night. I suppose I should have done the same myself. The man did not seem very willing to let him stay, but asked what he did there, and such like; but the storm was very loud, and so Marco did not let a little matter daunt him, and, when he shewed the man what fine fish he had in his basket, and said he was welcome to it, he seemed more willing.'

'Incredible!' exclaimed Schedoni, 'the blockhead!'

'He had wit enough for that matter, Signor; Marco says he appeared to be main hungry——'

'Is that any proof of his wit?' said the Confessor, peevishly.

'You never will let me finish, Signor; main hungry; for he put more wood on the fire directly, to dress some of the fish. While he was doing this, Marco says his heart, somehow, misgave him, that this was the man he saw on the beach, and he looked at him pretty hard, till the other asked him, crossly, what he stared at him so for; but Marco took care not to tell. While he was busy making ready the fish, however, Marco had an opportunity of eying him the more, and every time the man looked round the room, which happened to be pretty often, he had a notion it was the same.'

'Well, and if it was the same,' said Schedoni.

'But when Marco happened to spy the sack, lying in a corner, he had no doubt about the matter. He says his heart then misgave him sadly, and he wished himself safe out of the house, and determined, in his own mind, to get away as soon as he could, without letting the man suspect what he thought of him. He now guessed, too, what made the man look round the room so often, and, though Marco thought before it was to find out if he had brought any body with him, he now believed it was to see whether his treasure was safe.'

'Aye, likely enough,' observed Schedoni.

'Well, old Marco sat not much at his ease, while the fish was preparing, and thought it was "out of the fryingpan into the fire"* with him; but what could he do?'

'Why get up and walk away, to be sure,' said the Confessor, 'as I shall do, if your story lasts much longer.'

'You shall hear, Signor; he would have done so, if he had thought this man would have let him, but——'

'Well, this man was Spalatro, I suppose,' said Schedoni, impatiently, 'and this was the house on the shore you formerly mentioned.'

'How well you have guessed it, Signor! though to say truth, I have been expecting you to find it out for this half hour.'

Schedoni did not like the significant look, which the peasant assumed while he said this, but he bade him proceed.

'At first, Signor, Spalatro hardly spoke a word, but he came to by degrees, and by the time the fish was nearly ready, he was talkative enough.'

Here the Confessor rose, with some emotion, and paced the room.

'Poor old Marco, Signor, began to think better of ·him, and when he heard the rain at the casements, he was loath to think of stirring. Presently Spalatro went out of the room for a plate to eat the fish on.——'

'Out of the room?' said Schedoni, and checked his steps.

'Yes, Signor, but he took care to carry the light with him. However, Marco, who had a deal of curiosity to——'

'Yes, he appears to have had a great deal, indeed!' said the Confessor, and turning away, renewed his pace.

'Nay, Signor, I am not come to that yet, he has shewn none yet; —a great deal of curiosity to know what was in the sack, before he consented to let himself stay much longer, thought this a good opportunity for looking, and as the fire was now pretty bright, he determined to see. He went up to the sack, therefore, Signor, and tried to lift it, but it was too heavy for him though it did not seem full.'

Schedoni again checked his steps, and stood fixed before the peasant.

'He raised it, however, a little, Signor, but it fell from his hands, and with such a heavy weight upon the floor, that he was sure it held no common booty. Just then, he says, he thought he heard Spalatro coming, and the sound of the sack was enough to have frightened him, and so Marco quitted it; but he was mistaken, and he went to it again. But you don't seem to hear me, Signor, for you look as you do when you are in those quandaries, so busy a-thinking, and I——'

'Proceed,' said Schedoni, sternly, and renewed his steps, 'I hear you.'

'Went to it again,'—resumed the peasant, cautiously taking up the story at the last words he had dropped. 'He untied the string, Signor, that held the sack, and opened the cloth a little way, but think, Signor, what he must have thought, when he felt—cold flesh! O, Signor! and when he saw by the light of the fire, the face of a corpse within! O, Signor!'—

The peasant, in the eagerness with which he related this circumstance, had followed Schedoni to the other end of the chamber, and he now took hold of his garment, as if to secure his attention to the remainder of the story. The Confessor, however, continued his steps, and the peasant kept pace with him, still loosely holding his garment.

'Marco,' he resumed, 'was so terrified, as my father says, that he hardly knew where he was, and I warrant, if one could have seen him, he looked as white, Signor, as you do now.'

The Confessor abruptly withdrew his garment from the peasant's grasp, and said, in an inward voice, 'If I am shocked at the mere mention of such a spectacle, no wonder he was, who beheld it!' After the pause of a moment, he added,—'But what followed?'

'Marco says he had no power to tie up the cloth again, Signor, and when he came to his thoughts, his only fear was, lest Spalatro should return, though he had hardly been gone a minute, before he could get out of the house, for he cared nothing about the storm now. And sure enough he heard him coming, but he managed to get out of the room, into a passage another way from that Spalatro was in. And luckily, too, it was the same passage he had come in by, and it led him out of the house. He made no more ado, but ran straight off, without stopping to chuse which way, and many perils and dangers he got into among the woods, that night, and——'

'How happened it, that this Spalatro was not taken up, after this discovery?' said Schedoni. 'What was the consequence of it?'

'Why, Signor, old Marco had like to have caught his death that night; what with the wet, and what with the fright, he was laid up with a fever, and was light-headed, and raved of such strange things, that people would not believe any thing he said when he came to his senses.'

'Aye,' said Schedoni, 'the narrative resembles a delirious dream, more than a reality; I perfectly accord with them in their opinion of this feverish old man.'

'But you shall hear, Signor; after a while they began to think better of it, and there was some stir made about it; but what could poor folks do, for nothing could be proved! The house was searched, but the man was gone, and nothing could be found! From that time the place was shut up; till many years after, this Spalatro appeared, and old Marco then said he was pretty sure he was the man, but he could not swear it, and so nothing could be done.'

'Then it appears, after all, that you are not certain that this long history belongs to this Spalatro!' said the Confessor; 'nay, not even that the history itself is any thing more than the vision of a distempered brain!'

'I do not know, Signor, what you may call certain; but I know what we all believe. But the strangest part of the story is to come yet, and that which nobody would believe, hardly, if——'

'I have heard enough,' said Schedoni, 'I will hear no more!'

'Well but, Signor, I have not told you half yet; and I am sure when I heard it myself, it so terrified me.'

'I have listened too long to this idle history,' said the Confessor, 'there seems to be no rational foundation for it. Here is what I owe you; you may depart.'

'Well, Signor, 'tis plain you know the rest already, or you never would go without it. But you don't know, perhaps, Signor, what an unaccountable—I am sure it made my hair stand on end to hear of it, what an unaccountable——'

'I will hear no more of this absurdity,' interrupted Schedoni, with sternness. 'I reproach myself for having listened so long to such a gossip's tale, and have no further curiosity concerning it. You may withdraw; and bid the host attend me.'

'Well, Signor, if you are so easily satisfied,' replied the peasant, with disappointment, 'there is no more to be said, but——'

'You may stay, however, while I caution you,' said Schedoni, 'how you pass the villa, where this Spalatro may yet linger, for, though I can only smile at the story you have related——'

'Related, Signor! why I have not told it half; and if you would only please to be patient——'

'Though I can only smile at that simple narrative,'—repeated Schedoni in a louder tone.

'Nay, Signor, for that matter, you can frown at it too, as I can testify,' muttered the guide.

'Listen to me!' said the Confessor, in a yet more insisting voice. 'I say, that though I give no credit to your curious history, I think this same Spalatro appears to be a desperate fellow, and, therefore, I would have you be on your guard. If you see him, you may depend upon it, that he will attempt your life in revenge of the injury I have done him. I give you, therefore, in addition to your trombone, this stiletto to defend you.'

Schedoni, while he spoke, took an instrument from his bosom, but it was not the one he usually wore, or, at least, that he was seen to wear. He delivered it to the peasant, who received it with a kind of stupid surprise, and then gave him some directions as to the way in which it should be managed.

'Why, Signor,' said the man, who had listened with much attention, 'I am kindly obliged to you for thinking about me, but is there any thing in this stiletto different from others, that it is to be used so?'

Schedoni looked gravely at the peasant for an instant, and then replied, 'Certainly not, friend, I would only instruct you to use it to the best advantage;—farewell!'

'Thank you kindly, Signor, but—but I think I have no need of it, my trombone is enough for me.'

'This will defend you more adroitly,' replied Schedoni, refusing to take back the stiletto, 'and moreover, while you were loading the trombone, your adversary might use his poniard to advantage. Keep it, therefore, friend; it will protect you better than a dozen trombones. Put it up.'

Perhaps it was Schedoni's particular look, more than his argument, that convinced the guide of the value of his gift; he received it submissively, though with a stare of stupid surprise; probably it had been better, if it had been suspicious surprise. He thanked Schedoni again, and was leaving the room, when the Confessor called out, 'Send the landlord to me immediately, I shall set off for Rome without delay!'

'Yes, Signor,' replied the peasant, 'you are at the right place, the road parts here; but I thought you was going for Naples!'

'For Rome,' said Schedoni.

'For Rome, Signor! Well, I hope you will get safe, Signor, with all my heart!' said the guide, and quitted the chamber.

While this dialogue had been passing between Schedoni and the peasant, Ellena, in solitude, was considering on the means of prevailing with the Confessor to allow her to return either to Altieri, or to the neighbouring cloister of 'Our Lady of Pity,' instead of placing her at a distance from Naples, till he should think proper to acknowledge her. The plan, which he had mentioned, seemed to her long-harrassed mind to exile her forever from happiness, and all that was dear to her affections; it appeared like a second banishment to San Stefano, and every abbess, except that of the Santa della Pieta, came to her imagination in the portraiture of an inexorable jailor. While this subject engaged her, she was summoned to attend Schedoni, whom she found impatient to enter the carriage, which at this town they had been able to procure. Ellena, on looking out for the guide, was informed that he had already set off for his home, a circumstance, for the suddenness of which she knew not how to account.

The travellers immediately proceeded on their journey; Schedoni, reflecting on the late conversation, said little, and Ellena read not in his countenance any thing that might encourage her to introduce the subject of her own intended solicitation. Thus separately occupied, they advanced, during some hours, on the

road to Naples, for thither Schedoni had designed to go, notwithstanding his late assertion to the guide, whom it appears, for whatever reason, he was anxious to deceive, as to the place of his actual
residence.

They stopped to dine at a town of some consideration, and,
when Ellena heard the Confessor inquire concerning the numerous
convents it contained, she perceived that it was necessary for her
no longer to defer her petition. She therefore represented immediately what must be the forlornness of her state, and the anxiety of
her mind, if she were placed at a distance from the scenes and the
people, which affection and early habit seemed to have consecrated; especially at this time, when her spirits had scarcely
recovered from the severe pressure of long-suffering, and when to
soothe and renovate them, not only quiet, but the consciousness
of security, were necessary; a consciousness which it was impossible, and especially so after her late experience, that she could
acquire among strangers, till they should cease to be such.

To these pleadings Schedoni thoughtfully attended, but the
darkness of his aspect did not indicate that his compassion was
touched; and Ellena proceeded to represent, secondly, that which,
had she been more artful, or less disdainful of cunning, she would
have urged the first. As it was, she had begun with the mention of
circumstances, which, though the least likely to prevail with
Schedoni, she felt to be most important to herself; and she concluded with representing that, which was most interesting to him.
Ellena suggested, that her residence in the neighbourhood of
Altieri might be so managed, as that his secret would be as effectually preserved, as if she were at an hundred miles from Naples.

It may appear extraordinary, that a man of Schedoni's habitual
coolness, and exact calculation, should have suffered fear, on this
occasion, to obscure his perceptions; and this instance strongly
proved the magnitude of the cause, which could produce so
powerful an effect. While he now listened to Ellena, he began to
perceive circumstances that had eluded his own observation; and
he, at length, acknowledged, that it might be safer to permit her
to return to the Villa Altieri, and that she should from thence go,
as she had formerly intended, to the *Santa della Pieta*, than to
place her in any convent, however remote, where it would be
necessary for himself to introduce her. His only remaining objection to the neighbourhood of Naples, now rested on the chance it
would offer the Marchesa di Vivaldi of discovering Ellena's abode,
before he should judge it convenient to disclose to her his family;

and his knowledge of the Marchesa justified his most horrible suspicion, as to the consequence of such a premature discovery.

Something, however, it appeared, must be risked in any situation he might chuse for Ellena; and her residence at the *Santa della Pieta*, a large convent, well secured, and where, as she had been known to them from her infancy, the abbess and the sisters might be supposed to be not indifferent concerning her welfare, seemed to promise security against any actual violence from the malice of the Marchesa; against her artful duplicity every place would be almost equally insufficient. Here, as Ellena would appear in the character she had always been known in, no curiosity could be excited, or suspicion awakened, as to her family; and here, therefore, Schedoni's secret would more probably be preserved, than elsewhere. As this was, after all, the predominant subject of his anxiety, to which, however unnatural it may seem, even the safety of Ellena was secondary, he finally determined, that she should return to the *Santa della Pieta*; and she thanked him almost with tears, for a consent which she received as a generous indulgence, but which was in reality little more than an effect of selfish apprehension.

The remainder of the journey, which was of some days, passed without any remarkable occurrence: Schedoni, with only short intervals, was still enveloped in gloom and silence; and Ellena, with thoughts engaged by the one subject of her interest, the present situation and circumstances of Vivaldi, willingly submitted to this prolonged stillness.

As, at length, she drew near Naples, her emotions became more various and powerful; and, when she distinguished the top of Vesuvius peering over every intervening summit, she wept as her imagination charactered all the well-known country it overlooked. But when, having reached an eminence, that scenery was exhibited to her senses, when the Bay of Naples, stretching into remotest distance, was spread out before her; when every mountain of that magnificent horizon, which enclosed her native landscape, that country which she believed Vivaldi to inhabit, stood unfolded, how affecting, how overwhelming were her sensations! Every object seemed to speak of her home, of Vivaldi, and of happiness that was passed! and so exquisitely did regret mingle with hope, the tender grief of remembrance with the interest of expectation, that it were difficult to say which prevailed.

Her expressive countenance disclosed to the Confessor the course of her thoughts and of her feelings, feelings which, while he contemned, he believed he perfectly comprehended, but of which, having never in any degree experienced them, he really understood nothing. The callous Schedoni, by a mistake not uncommon, especially to a mind of his character, substituted words for truths; not only confounding the limits of neighbouring qualities, but mistaking their very principles. Incapable of perceiving their nice distinctions, he called the persons who saw them, merely fanciful; thus making his very incapacity an argument for his superior wisdom. And, while he confounded delicacy of feeling with fatuity of mind, taste with caprice, and imagination with error, he yielded, when he most congratulated himself on his sagacity, to illusions not less egregious, because they were less brilliant, than those which are incident to sentiment and feeling.

The better to escape observation, Schedoni had contrived not to reach Naples till the close of evening, and it was entirely dark before the carriage stopped at the gate of the Villa Altieri. Ellena, with a mixture of melancholy and satisfaction, viewed, once more, her long-deserted home, and while she waited till a servant should open the gate, remembered how often she had thus waited when there was a beloved friend within, to welcome her with smiles, which were now gone for ever. Beatrice, the old housekeeper, at length, however, appeared, and received her with an affection as sincere, if not as strong, as that of the relative for whom she mourned.

Here Schedoni alighted, and, having dismissed the carriage, entered the house, for the purpose of relinquishing also his disguise, and resuming his monk's habit. Before he departed, Ellena ventured to mention Vivaldi, and to express her wish to hear of his exact situation; but, though Schedoni was too well enabled to inform her of it, the policy which had hitherto kept him silent on this subject still influenced him; and he replied only, that if he should happen to learn the circumstances of his condition, she should not remain ignorant of them.

This assurance revived Ellena, for two reasons; it afforded her a hope of relief from her present uncertainty, and it also seemed to express an approbation of the object of her affection, such as the Confessor had never yet disclosed. Schedoni added, that he should see her no more, till he thought proper to acknowledge her for his daughter; but that, if circumstances made it necessary, he should, in the mean time, write to her; and he now gave her a direction by which to address him under a fictitious name, and at a place remote from his convent. Ellena, though assured of the necessity for this conduct, could not yield to such disguise, without an aversion that was strongly expressed in her manner, but of which Schedoni took no notice. He bade her, as she valued her existence, watchfully to preserve the secret of her birth; and to waste not a single day at Villa Altieri, but to retire to the *Santa della Pieta*; and these injunctions were delivered in a manner so solemn and energetic, as not only deeply to impress upon her mind the necessity of fulfilling them, but to excite some degree of amazement.

After a short and general direction respecting her further conduct, Schedoni bade her farewell, and, privately quitting the villa, in his ecclesiastical dress, repaired to the Dominican convent, which he entered as a brother returned from a distant pilgrimage. He was received as usual by the society, and found himself, once more, the austere father Schedoni of the Spirito Santo.

The cause of his first anxiety was the necessity for justifying himself to the Marchesa di Vivaldi, for ascertaining how much he might venture to reveal of the truth, and for estimating what would be her decision, were she informed of the whole. His second step would be to obtain the release of Vivaldi; and, as his conduct in this instance would be regulated, in a great degree, by the result of his conference with the Marchesa, it would be only the second. However painful it must be to Schedoni to meet her, now that he had discovered the depth of the guilt, in which she would have involved him, he determined to seek this eventful conference on the following morning: and he passed this night partly in uneasy expectation of the approaching day, but chiefly in inventing circumstances and arranging arguments, that might bear him triumphantly towards the accomplishment of his grand design.

CHAPTER III

Beneath the silent gloom of Solitude
Tho' Peace can sit and smile, tho' meek Content
Can keep the cheerful tenor of her soul,
Ev'n in the loneliest shades, yet let not Wrath
Approach, let black Revenge keep far aloof,
Or soon they flame to madness.

ELFRIDA*

SCHEDONI, on his way to the Vivaldi palace, again reviewed and arranged every argument, or rather specious circumstance, which might induce the Marchesa's consent to the nuptials he so much desired. His family was noble, though no longer wealthy, and he believed that as the seeming want of descent had hitherto been the chief objection to Ellena, the Marchesa might be prevailed with to overlook the wreck of his fortune.

At the palace he was told, that the Marchesa was at one of her villas on the bay; and he was too anxious not to follow her thither immediately. This delightful residence was situated on an airy promontory, that overhung the water, and was nearly embosomed among the woods, that spread far along the heights, and descended, with great pomp of foliage and colouring, to the very margin of the waves. It seemed scarcely possible that misery could inhabit so enchanting an abode; yet the Marchesa was wretched amidst all these luxuries of nature and art, which would have perfected the happiness of an innocent mind. Her heart was possessed by evil passions, and all her perceptions were distorted and dis-coloured by them, which, like a dark magician, had power to change the fairest scenes into those of gloom and desolation.

The servants had orders to admit father Schedoni at all times, and he was shewn into a saloon, in which the Marchesa was alone. Every object in this apartment announced taste, and even magni-ficence. The hangings were of purple and gold; the vaulted ceiling was designed by one of the first painters of the Venetian school; the marble statues that adorned the recesses were not less exquisite, and the whole symmetry and architecture, airy, yet rich; gay, yet chastened; resembled the palace of a fairy, and seemed to possess almost equal fascinations. The lattices were thrown open, to admit the prospect, as well as the air loaded with fragrance from an orangery, that spread before them. Lofty palms and plantains* threw their green and refreshing tint over the windows, and on the lawn that sloped to the edge of the precipice, a shadowy perspective, beyond which appeared the ample waters of the gulf, where the light sails of feluccas,* and the spreading canvas of larger vessels, glided upon the scene and passed away, as in a camera obscura.* Vesuvius and the city of Naples were seen on the coast beyond, with many a bay and lofty cape of that long tract of bold and gaily-coloured scenery, which extends toward Cape Campanella, crowned by fading ranges of mountains, lighted up with all the magic of Italian sunshine. The Marchesa reclined on a sofa before an open lattice; her eyes were fixed upon the prospect without, but her attention was wholly occupied by the visions that evil passions painted to her imagination. On her still beautiful features was the languor of discontent and indisposition; and, though her manners, like her dress, displayed the elegant negligence of the graces, they concealed the movements of a careful, and even a tortured heart. On perceiving Schedoni, a faint smile lightened upon her countenance, and she held forth her hand to him; at the touch of which he shuddered.

'My good father, I rejoice to see you,' said the Marchesa; 'I have felt the want of your conversation much, and at this moment of indisposition especially.'

She waved the attendant to withdraw; while Schedoni, stalking to a window, could with difficulty conceal the perturbation with which he now, for the first time, consciously beheld the willing destroyer of his child. Some farther compliment from the Marchesa recalled him; he soon recovered all his address, and approaching her, said,

'Daughter! you always send me away a worse Dominican than I come; I approach you with humility, but depart elated with pride, and am obliged to suffer much from self-infliction before I can descend to my proper level.'

After some other flatteries had been exchanged, a silence of several moments followed, during which neither of the parties seemed to have sufficient courage to introduce the subjects that engaged their thoughts, subjects upon which their interests were now so directly and unexpectedly opposite. Had Schedoni been less occupied by his own feelings, he might have perceived the extreme agitation of the Marchesa, the tremor of her nerves, the faint flush that crossed her cheek, the wanness that succeeded, the languid movement of her eyes, and the laborious sighs that interrupted her breathing, while she wished, yet dared not ask, whether Ellena was no more, and averted her regards from him, whom she almost believed to be a murderer.

Schedoni, not less affected, though apparently tranquil, as sedulously avoided the face of the Marchesa, whom he considered with a degree of contempt almost equal to his indignation: his feelings had reversed, for the present, all his opinions on the subject of their former arguments, and had taught him, for once, to think justly. Every moment of silence now increased his embarrassment, and his reluctance even to name Ellena. He feared to tell that she lived, yet despised himself for suffering such fear, and shuddered at a recollection of the conduct, which had made any assurance concerning her life necessary. The insinuations, that he had discovered her family to be such as would not degrade that of the Marchesa, he knew not how to introduce with such delicacy of gradation as might win upon the jealousy of her pride, and soothe her disappointment; and he was still meditating how he might lead to this subject, when the Marchesa herself broke the silence.

'Father,' she said, with a sigh, 'I always look to you for consolation, and am seldom disappointed. You are too well acquainted with the anxiety which has long oppressed me; may I understand that the cause of it is removed?' She paused, and then added, 'May I hope that my son will no longer be led from the observance of his duty?'

Schedoni, with his eyes fixed on the ground, remained silent, but, at length, said, 'The chief occasion of your anxiety is certainly removed;'—and he was again silent.

'How!' exclaimed the Marchesa, with the quick-sightedness of suspicion, while all her dissimulation yielded to the urgency of her fear, 'Have you failed? Is she not dead?'

In the earnestness of the question, she fixed her eyes on Schedoni's face, and, perceiving there symptoms of extraordinary emotion, added, 'Relieve me from my apprehensions, good father, I entreat; tell me that you have succeeded, and that she has paid the debt of justice.'

Schedoni raised his eyes to the Marchesa, but instantly averted them; indignation had lifted them, and disgust and stifled horror turned them away. Though very little of these feelings appeared, the Marchesa perceived such expression as she had never been accustomed to observe in his countenance; and, her surprize and impatience increasing, she once more repeated the question, and with a yet more decisive air than before.

'I have not failed in the grand object,' replied Schedoni: 'your son is no longer in danger of forming a disgraceful alliance.'

'In what, then, have you failed?' asked the Marchesa; 'for I perceive that you have not been completely successful.'

'I ought not to say that I have failed in any respect,' replied Schedoni, with emotion, 'since the honour of your house is preserved, and —— a life is spared.'

His voice faultered as he pronounced the last words, and he seemed to experience again the horror of that moment, when, with an uplifted poniard in his grasp, he had discovered Ellena for his daughter.

'Spared!' repeated the Marchesa, doubtingly; 'explain yourself, good father!'

'She lives,' replied Schedoni; 'but you have nothing, therefore, to apprehend.'

The Marchesa, surprized no less by the tone in which he spoke, than shocked at the purport of his words, changed countenance, while she said, impatiently—'You speak in enigmas, father.'

'Lady! I speak plain truth—she lives.'

'I understand that sufficiently,' said the Marchesa; 'but when you tell me, I have nothing to apprehend——'

'I tell you truth, also,' rejoined the Confessor; 'and the benevolence of your nature may be permitted to rejoice, for justice no longer has forbade the exercise of mercy.'

'This is all very well in its place,' said the Marchesa, betrayed by the vexation she suffered; 'such sentiments and such compliments are like gala suits, to be put on in fine weather. My day is cloudy; let me have a little plain strong sense: inform me of the circumstances which have occasioned this change in the course of your observations, and, good father! be brief.'

Schedoni then unfolded, with his usual art, such circumstances relative to the family of Ellena as he hoped would soften the aversion of the Marchesa to the connection, and incline her, in consideration of her son's happiness, finally to approve it; with which disclosure he mingled a plausible relation of the way, in which the discovery had been made.

The Marchesa's patience would scarcely await the conclusion of his narrative, or her disappointment submit to the curb of discretion. When, at length, he had finished his history, 'Is it possible,' said she, with fretful displeasure, 'that you have suffered yourself to be deceived by the plausibility of a girl, who might have been expected to utter any falshood, which should appear likely to protect her! Has a man of your discernment given faith to the idle and improbable tale! Say, rather, father, that your resolution failed in the critical moment, and that you are now anxious to form excuses to yourself for a conduct so pusillanimous.'

'I am not apt to give an easy faith to appearances,' replied Schedoni, gravely, 'and still less, to shrink from the performance of any act, which I judge to be necessary and just. To the last intimation, I make no reply; it does not become my character to vindicate myself from an implication of falshood.'

The Marchesa, perceiving that her passion had betrayed her into imprudence, condescended to apologize for that which she termed an effect of her extreme anxiety, as to what might follow from an act of such indiscreet indulgence; and Schedoni as willingly accepted the apology, each believing the assistance of the other necessary to success.

Schedoni then informed her, that he had better authority for what he had advanced than the assertion of Ellena; and he mentioned some circumstances, which proved him to be more anxious for the reputation than for the truth of his word. Believing that his origin was entirely unknown to the Marchesa, he ventured to disclose some particulars of Ellena's family, without apprehending that it could lead to a suspicion of his own.

The Marchesa, though neither appeased nor convinced, commanded her feelings so far as to appear tranquil, while the Confessor represented, with the most delicate address, the unhappiness of her son, and the satisfaction, which must finally result to herself from an acquiescence with his choice, since the object of it was known to be worthy of his alliance. He added, that, while he had believed the contrary, he had proved himself as strenuous to prevent, as he was now sincere in approving their marriage; and concluded with gently blaming her for suffering prejudice and some remains of resentment to obscure her excellent understanding. 'Trusting to the natural clearness of your perceptions,' he added, 'I doubt not that when you have maturely considered the subject, every objection will yield to a consideration of your son's happiness.'

The earnestness, with which Schedoni pleaded for Vivaldi, excited some surprize; but the Marchesa, without condescending to reply either to his argument or remonstrance, inquired whether Ellena had a suspicion of the design, with which she had been

carried into the forests of the Garganus, or concerning the identity
of her persecutor. Schedoni, immediately perceiving to what these
questions tended, replied, with the facility with which he usually
accommodated his conscience to his interest, that Ellena was
totally ignorant as to who were her immediate persecutors, and
equally unsuspicious of any other evil having been intended her,
than that of a temporary confinement.

The last assertion was admitted by the Marchesa to be probable,
till the boldness of the first made her doubt the truth of each, and
occasioned her new surprize and conjecture as to the motive,
which could induce Schedoni to venture these untruths. She then
inquired where Ellena was now disposed of, but he had too much
prudence to disclose the place of her retreat, however plausible
might be the air with which the inquiry was urged; and he endeavoured to call off her attention to Vivaldi. The Confessor did not,
however, venture, at present, to give a hint as to the pretended
discovery of his situation in the inquisition, but reserved to a more
favourable opportunity such mention, together with the zealous
offer of his services to extricate the prisoner. The Marchesa, believing that her son was still engaged in pursuit of Ellena, made many
inquiries concerning him, but without expressing any solicitude
for his welfare; resentment appearing to be the only emotion she
retained towards him. While Schedoni replied with circumspection
to her questions, he urged inquiries of his own, as to the manner
in which the Marchesa endured the long absence of Vivaldi; thus
endeavouring to ascertain how far he might hereafter venture to
appear in any efforts for liberating him, and how shape his conduct
respecting Ellena. It seemed that the Marchese was not indifferent
as to his son's absence; and, though he had at first believed the
search for Ellena to have occasioned it, other apprehensions
now disturbed him, and taught him the feelings of a father. His
numerous avocations and interests, however, seemed to prevent
such anxiety from preying upon his mind; and, having dismissed
persons in search of Vivaldi, he passed his time in the usual
routine of company and the court. Of the actual situation of his
son it was evident that neither he, nor the Marchesa, had the least
apprehension, and this was a circumstance, which the Confessor
was very careful to ascertain.

Before he took leave, he ventured to renew the mention of
Vivaldi's attachment, and gently to plead for him. The Marchesa,
however, seemed inattentive to what he represented, till, at length,
awaking from her reverie, she said—'Father, you have judged

ill——,' and, before she concluded the sentence, she relapsed again into thoughtful silence. Believing that he anticipated her meaning, Schedoni began to repeat his own justification respecting his conduct towards Ellena.

'You have judged erroneously, father,' resumed the Marchesa, with the same considering air, 'in placing the girl in such a situation; my son cannot fail to discover her there.'

'Or wherever she may be,' replied the Confessor, believing that he understood the Marchesa's aim. 'It may not be possible to conceal her long from his search.'

'The neighbourhood of Naples ought at least to have been avoided,' observed the Marchesa.

Schedoni was silent, and she added, 'So near, also, to his own residence! How far is the *Santa della Piéta* from the Vivaldi palace?'

Though Schedoni had thought that the Marchesa, while displaying a pretended knowledge of Ellena's retreat, was only endeavouring to obtain a real one, this mention of the place of her actual residence shocked him; but he replied almost immediately, 'I am ignorant of the distance, for, till now, I was unacquainted that there is a convent of the name you mention. It appears, however, that this *Santa della Piéta* is the place, of all other, which ought to have been avoided. How could you suspect me, lady, of imprudence thus extravagant!'

While Schedoni spoke, the Marchesa regarded him attentively, and then replied, 'I may be allowed, good father, to suspect your prudence in this instance, since you have just given me so unequivocal a proof of it in another.'

She would then have changed the subject, but Schedoni, believing this inclination to be the consequence of her having assured herself, that she had actually discovered Ellena's asylum, and too reasonably suspecting the dreadful use she designed to make of the discovery, endeavoured to unsettle her opinion, and mislead her as to the place of Ellena's abode. He not only contradicted the fact of her present residence at the *Santa della Piéta*, but, without scruple, made a positive assertion, that she was at a distance from Naples, naming, at the same time, a fictitious place, whose obscurity, he added, would be the best protection from the pursuit of Vivaldi.

'Very true, father,' observed the Marchesa; 'I believe that my son will not readily discover the girl in the place you have named.'

Whether the Marchesa believed Schedoni's assertion or not, she expressed no farther curiosity on the subject, and appeared considerably more tranquil than before. She now chatted with ease on general topics, while the Confessor dared no more to urge the subject of his secret wishes; and, having supported, for some time, a conversation most uncongenial with his temper, he took his leave, and returned to Naples. On the way thither, he reviewed, with exactness, the late behaviour of the Marchesa, and the result of this examination was a resolution—never to renew the subject of their conversation, but to solemnize, without her consent, the nuptials of Vivaldi and Ellena.

The Marchesa, meanwhile, on the departure of Schedoni, remained in the attitude in which he had left her, and absorbed by the interest, which his visit excited. The sudden change in his conduct no less astonished and perplexed, than disappointed her. She could not explain it by the supposition of any principle, or motive. Sometimes it occurred to her, that Vivaldi had bribed him with rich promises, to promote the marriage, which he contributed to thwart; but, when she considered the high expectations she had herself encouraged him to cherish, the improbability of the conjecture was apparent. That Schedoni, from whatever cause, was no longer to be trusted in this business, was sufficiently clear, but she endeavoured to console herself with a hope that a more confidential person might yet be discovered. A part of Schedoni's resolution she also adopted, which was, never again to introduce the subject of their late conversation. But, while she should silently pursue her own plans, she determined to conduct herself towards Schedoni in every other respect, as usual, not suffering him to suspect that she had withdrawn her confidence, but inducing him to believe that she had relinquished all farther design against Ellena.

CHAPTER IV

——————————————————————— We
Would learn the private virtues; how to glide
Through shades and plains, along the smoothest stream
Of rural life; or, snatch'd away by hope,
Through the dim spaces of futurity,
With earnest eye anticipate those scenes
Of happiness and wonder, where the mind,
In endless growth and infinite ascent,
Rises from state to state, and world to world.

THOMSON*

ELLENA, obedient to the command of Schedoni, withdrew from her home on the day that followed her arrival there, to the *Santa della Piéta*. The Superiour, who had known her from her infancy, and, from the acquaintance which such long observation afforded, had both esteemed and loved her, received Ellena with a degree of satisfaction proportionate to the concern she had suffered when informed of her disastrous removal from the Villa Altieri.

Among the quiet groves of this convent, however, Ellena vainly endeavoured to moderate her solicitude respecting the situation of Vivaldi; for, now that she had a respite from immediate calamity, she thought with more intense anxiety as to what might be his sufferings, and her fears and impatience increased, as each day disappointed her expectation of intelligence from Schedoni.

If the soothings of sympathy and the delicate arts of benevolence could have restored the serenity of her mind, Ellena would now have been peaceful; for all these were offered her by the abbess and the sisters of the *Santa della Piéta*. They were not acquainted with the cause of her sorrow, but they perceived that she was unhappy, and wished her to be otherwise. The society of *Our Lady of Pity*, was such as a convent does not often shroud; to the wisdom and virtue of the Superiour, the sisterhood was principally indebted for the harmony and happiness which distinguished them. This lady was a shining example to governesses of religious houses, and a striking instance of the influence, which a virtuous mind may acquire over others, as well as of the extensive good that it may thus diffuse. She was dignified without haughtiness, religious without

bigotry, and mild, though decisive and firm. She possessed penetration to discover what was just, resolution to adhere to it, and
temper to practise it with gentleness and grace; so that even cor-
rection from her, assumed the winning air of courtesy: the person,
whom she admonished, wept in sorrow for the offence, instead of
being secretly irritated by the reproof, and loved her as a mother,
rather than feared her as a judge. Whatever might be her failings,
they were effectually concealed by the general benevolence of her
heart, and the harmony of her mind; a harmony, not the effect of
torpid feelings, but the accomplishment of correct and vigilant
judgment. Her religion was neither gloomy, nor bigotted; it was
the sentiment of a grateful heart offering itself up to a Deity, who
delights in the happiness of his creatures; and she conformed to the
customs of the Roman church, without supposing a faith in all of
them to be necessary to salvation. This opinion, however, she was
obliged to conceal, lest her very virtue should draw upon her the
punishment of a crime, from some fierce ecclesiastics, who contradicted in their practice the very essential principles, which the
christianity they professed would have taught them.

In her lectures to the nuns she seldom touched upon points of
faith, but explained and enforced the moral duties, particularly
such as were most practicable in the society to which she belonged;
such as tended to soften and harmonize the affections, to impart
that repose of mind, which persuades to the practice of sisterly
kindness, universal charity, and the most pure and elevated
devotion. When she spoke of religion, it appeared so interesting,
so beautiful, that her attentive auditors revered and loved it as a
friend, a refiner of the heart, a sublime consoler; and experienced
somewhat of the meek and holy ardour, which may belong to
angelic natures.

The society appeared like a large family, of which the lady
abbess was the mother, rather than an assemblage of strangers;
and particularly when gathered around her, they listened to the
evening sermon, which she delivered with such affectionate
interest, such persuasive eloquence, and sometimes with such
pathetic energy, as few hearts could resist.

She encouraged in her convent every innocent and liberal pursuit, which might sweeten the austerities of confinement, and
which were generally rendered instrumental to charity. The
Daughters of Pity particularly excelled in music; not in those difficulties of the art, which display florid graces, and intricate execution, but in such eloquence of sound as steals upon the heart, and

awakens its sweetest and best affections. It was probably the well-regulated sensibility of their own minds, that enabled these sisters to diffuse through their strains a character of such finely-tempered taste, as drew crowds of visitors, on every festival, to the church of the *Santa della Piéta*.

The local circumstances of this convent were scarcely less agreeable than the harmony of its society was interesting. These extensive domains included olive-grounds, vineyards, and some corn-land; a considerable tract was devoted to the pleasures of the garden, whose groves supplied walnuts, almonds, oranges, and citrons, in abundance, and almost every kind of fruit and flower, which this luxurious climate nurtured. These gardens hung upon the slope of a hill, about a mile within the shore, and afforded extensive views of the country round Naples, and of the gulf. But from the terraces, which extended along a semicircular range of rocks, that rose over the convent, and formed a part of the domain, the prospects were infinitely finer. They extended on the south to the isle of Capræa, where the gulf expands into the sea; in the west, appeared the island of Ischia, distinguished by the white pinnacles of the lofty mountain Epomeo; and near it Prosida, with its many-coloured cliffs, rose out of the waves. Overlooking many points towards Puzzuoli, the eye caught beyond other promontories, and others further still, to the north, a glimpse of the sea, that bathes the now desolate shores of Baia; with Capua, and all the towns and villas, that speckle the garden-plains between Caserta and Naples.

In the nearer scene were the rocky heights of Pausilippo, and Naples itself, with all its crowded suburbs ascending among the hills, and mingling with vineyards and overtopping cypress; the castle of San Elmo, conspicuous on its rock, overhanging the magnificent monastery of the Chartreux; while in the scene below appeared the *Castel Nuovo*, with its clustered towers, the long-extended Corso, the mole, with its tall pharos, and the harbour gay with painted shipping, and full to the brim with the blue waters of the bay. Beyond the hills of Naples, the whole horizon to the north and east was bounded by the mountains of the Appenine, an amphitheatre proportioned to the grandeur of the plain, which the gulf spread out below.

These terraces, shaded with acacias and plane-trees, were the favourite haunt of Ellena. Between the opening branches, she looked down upon Villa Altieri, which brought to her remembrance the affectionate Bianchi, with all the sportive years of her childhood; and where some of her happiest hours had been passed in the society of Vivaldi. Along the windings of the coast, too, she could distinguish many places rendered sacred by affection, to which she had made excursions with her lamented relative, and Vivaldi; and, though sadness mingled with the recollections a view of them restored, they were precious to her heart. Here, alone and unobserved, she frequently yielded to the melancholy which she endeavoured to suppress in society; and at other times tried to deceive, with books and the pencil, the lingering moments of uncertainty concerning the state of Vivaldi; for day after day still elapsed without bringing any intelligence from Schedoni. Whenever the late scenes connected with the discovery of her family recurred to Ellena, she was struck with almost as much amazement as if she was gazing upon a vision, instead of recalling realities. Contrasted with the sober truth of her present life, the past appeared like romance; and there were moments when she shrunk from the relationship of Schedoni with unconquerable affright. The first emotions his appearance had excited were so opposite to those of filial tenderness, that she perceived it was now nearly impossible to love and revere him as her father, and she endeavoured, by dwelling upon all the obligations, which she believed he had lately conferred upon her, to repay him in gratitude, what was withheld in affection.

In such melancholy considerations, she often lingered under the shade of the accacias, till the sun had sunk behind the far distant promontory of Miseno, and the last bell of vespers summoned her to the convent below.

Among the nuns, Ellena had many favourites, but not one that she admired and loved equally with Olivia of San Stefano, the remembrance of whom was always accompanied with a fear lest she should have suffered from her generous compassion, and a wish that she had taken up her abode with the happy society of the *Daughters of Pity*, instead of being subjected to the tyranny of the abbess of San Stefano. To Ellena, the magnificent scenes of the *Santa della Piéta* seemed to open a secure, and, perhaps, a last asylum; for, in her present circumstances, she could not avoid perceiving how menacing and various were the objections to her marriage with Vivaldi, even should Schedoni prove propitious to it. The character of the Marchesa di Vivaldi, such as it stood unfolded by the late occurrences, struck her with dismay, for her designs appeared sufficiently atrocious, whether they had extended to the utmost limit of Ellena's suspicions, or had stopped where the

affected charity of Schedoni had pointed out. In either case, the
pertinacity of her aversion, and the vindictive violence of her
nature, were obvious.

In this view of her character, however, it was not the incon-
venience threatened to those who might become connected with
her, that principally affected Ellena, but the circumstance of such
a woman being the mother of Vivaldi; and, to alleviate so afflicting
a consideration, she endeavoured to believe all the palliating suggestions of Schedoni, respecting the Marchesa's late intentions.
But if Ellena was grieved on discovering crime in the character of
Vivaldi's parent, what would have been her suffering, had she
suspected the nature of Schedoni?—what, if she had been told that
he was the adviser of the Marchesa's plans?—if she had known that
he had been the partner of her intentional guilt? From such suffering she was yet spared, as well as from that, which a knowledge of
Vivaldi's present situation, and of the result of Schedoni's efforts
to procure a release from the perils, among which he had precipitated him, would have inflicted. Had she known this, it is probable that in the first despondency of her mind, she would have
relinquished what is called the world, and sought a lasting asylum
with the society of the holy sisters. Even as it was, she sometimes
endeavoured to look with resignation upon the events which might
render such a step desirable; but it was an effort that seldom
soothed her even with a temporary self-delusion. Should the veil,
however, prove her final refuge, it would be by her own choice;
for the lady abbess of the *Santa della Piéta* employed no art to win
a recluse, nor suffered the nuns to seduce votaries to the order.

CHAPTER V

Sullen and sad to fancy's frighted eye
Did shapes of dun and murky hue advance,
In train tumultuous, all of gesture strange,
And passing horrible.

CARACTACUS*

WHILE the late events had been passing in the Garganus, and at Naples, Vivaldi and his servant Paulo remained imprisoned in distinct chambers of the Inquisition. They were again separately interrogated. From the servant no information could be obtained; he asserted only his master's innocence, without once remembering to mention his own; clamoured, with more justness than prudence, against the persons who had occasioned his arrest; seriously endeavouring to convince the inquisitors, that he himself had *no other motive* in having demanded to be brought to these prisons than that he might comfort his master, he gravely remonstrated on the injustice of separating them, adding, that he was sure when they knew the rights of the matter, they would order him to be carried to the prison of Signor Vivaldi.

'I do assure your *Serenissimo Illustrissimo*,' continued Paulo, addressing the chief inquisitor with profound gravity, 'that this is the last place I should have thought of coming to, on any other account; and if you will only condescend to ask your officials, who took my master up, they will tell you *as good*. They knew well enough all along, what I came here for, and if they had known it would be all in vain, it would have been but civil of them to have told me as much, and not have brought me; for this is the last place in the world I would have come to, otherwise, of my own accord.'

Paulo was permitted to harangue in his own way, because his examiners hoped that his prolixity would be a means of betraying circumstances connected with his master. By this view, however, they were misled, for Paulo, with all his simplicity of heart, was both vigilant and shrewd in Vivaldi's interest. But, when he perceived them really convinced, that his sole motive for visiting the Inquisition was that he might console his master, yet still persisting in the resolution of separately confining him, his indignation knew no bounds. He despised alike their reprehension, their thundering menaces, and their more artful exhibitions; told them of all they had to expect both here and hereafter, for their cruelty to his dear master, and said they might do what they would with him; he defied them to make him more miserable than he was.

It was not without difficulty that he was removed from the chamber; where he left his examiners in a state of astonishment at his rashness, and indignation of his honesty, such as they had, probably, never experienced before.

When Vivaldi was again called up to the table of the Holy Office, he underwent a longer examination than on a former occasion. Several inquisitors attended, and every art was employed to induce him to confess crimes, of which he was suspected, and to draw from him a discovery of others, which might have eluded even suspicion. Still the examiners cautiously avoided informing him of the subject of the accusation on which he had been arrested, and it was, therefore, only on the former assurances of the Benedictine, and the officials in the chapel of San Sebastian, that Vivaldi understood he was accused of having carried off a nun. His answers on the present occasion were concise and firm, and his whole deportment undaunted. He felt less apprehension for himself, than indignation of the general injustice and cruelty, which the tribunal was permitted to exercise upon others; and this virtuous indignation gave a loftiness, a calm heroic grandeur to his mind, which never, for a moment, forsook him, except when he conjectured what might be the sufferings of Ellena. Then, his fortitude and magnanimity failed, and his tortured spirit rose almost to frenzy.

On this, his second examination, he was urged by the same dark questions, and replied to them with the same open sincerity, as during the first. Yet the simplicity and energy of truth failed to impress conviction on minds, which, no longer possessing the virtue themselves, were not competent to understand the symptoms of it in others. Vivaldi was again threatened with the torture, and again dismissed to his prison.

On the way to this dreadful abode, a person passed him in one of the avenues, of whose air and figure he thought he had some recollection; and, as the stranger stalked away, he suddenly knew him to be the prophetic monk, who had haunted him among the ruins of Paluzzi. In the first moment of surprize, Vivaldi lost his presence of mind so far, that he made no attempt to interrupt him. In the next instant, however, he paused and looked back, with an intention of speaking; but this mysterious person was already at the extremity of the avenue. Vivaldi called, and besought him to stop. Without either speaking, or turning his head, however, he immediately disappeared beyond a door that opened at his approach. Vivaldi, on attempting to take the way of the monk, was withheld by his guards, and, when he inquired who was the stranger he had seen, the officials asked, in their turn, what stranger he alluded to.

'He who has just passed us,' replied Vivaldi.

The officials seemed surprized, 'Your spirits are disordered, Signor,' observed one of them, 'I saw no person pass!'

'He passed so closely,' said Vivaldi, 'that it was hardly possible you could avoid seeing him!'

'I did not even hear a footstep!' added the man.

'I do not recollect that I did,' answered Vivaldi, 'but I saw his figure as plainly as I now see your's; his black garments almost touched me! Was he an inquisitor?'

The official appeared astonished; and, whether his surprize was real, or affected for the purpose of concealing his knowledge of the person alluded to, his embarrassment and awe seemed natural. Vivaldi observed, with almost equal curiosity and surprize, the fear which his face expressed; but perceived also, that it would avail nothing to repeat his questions.

As they proceeded along the avenue, a kind of half-stifled groan was sometimes audible from a distance. 'Whence come those sounds?' said Vivaldi, 'they strike to my heart!'

'They should do so,' replied the guard.

'Whence come they?' repeated Vivaldi, more impatiently, and shuddering.

'From the place of torture,' said the official.

'O God! O God!' exclaimed Vivaldi, with a deep groan.

He passed with hasty steps the door of that terrible chamber, and the guard did not attempt to stop him. The officials had brought him, in obedience to the customary orders they had received, within hearing of those doleful sounds, for the purpose of impressing upon his mind the horrors of the punishment, with which he was threatened, and of inducing him to confess without incurring them.

On this same evening, Vivaldi was visited, in his prison, by a man whom he had never consciously seen before. He appeared to be between forty and fifty; was of a grave and observant physiognomy, and of manners, which, though somewhat austere, were not alarming. The account he gave of himself, and of his motive for this visit, was curious. He said that he also was a prisoner in the inquisition, but, as the ground of accusation against him was light, he had been favoured so far as to be allowed some degree of liberty within certain bounds; that, having heard of Vivaldi's situation, he had asked and obtained leave to converse with him, which he had done in compassion, and with a desire of assuaging his sufferings, so far as an expression of sympathy and commiseration might relieve them.

While he spoke, Vivaldi regarded him with deep attention, and the improbability that these pretensions should be true, did not escape him; but the suspicion which they occasioned he prudently concealed. The stranger conversed on various subjects. Vivaldi's answers were cautious and concise; but not even long pauses of silence wearied the compassionate patience of his visitor. Among other topics he, at length, introduced that of religion.

'I have, myself, been accused of heresy,' said he, 'and know how to pity others in the same situation.'

'It is of heresy, then, that I am accused!' interrupted Vivaldi, 'of heresy!'

'It availed me nothing that I asserted my innocence,' continued the stranger, without noticing Vivaldi's exclamation, 'I was condemned to the torture. My sufferings were too terrible to be endured! I confessed my offence——'

'Pardon me,' interrupted Vivaldi, 'but allow me to observe, that since your sufferings were so severe, your's, against whom the ground of accusation was light, what may be the punishment of those, whose offences are more serious?'

The stranger was somewhat embarrassed. 'My offence was slight,' he continued, without giving a full answer.

'Is it possible,' said Vivaldi, again interrupting him, 'that heresy can be considered as a slight offence before the tribunal of the Inquisition?'

'It was only of a slight degree of heresy,' replied the visitor, reddening with displeasure, 'that I was suspected, and ——'

'Does then the Inquisition allow of degrees in heresy?' said Vivaldi.

'I confessed my offence,' added the stranger with a louder emphasis, 'and the consequence of this confession was a remission of punishment. After a trifling penance I shall be dismissed, and probably, in a few days, leave the prison. Before I left it, I was desirous of administering some degree of consolation to a fellow sufferer; if you have any friends whom you wish to inform of your situation, do not fear to confide their names and your message to me.'

The latter part of the speech was delivered in a low voice, as if the stranger feared to be overheard. Vivaldi remained silent, while he examined, with closer attention, the countenance of his visitor. It was of the utmost importance to him, that his family should be made acquainted with his situation; yet he knew not exactly how to interpret, or to confide in this offer. Vivaldi had heard that informers sometimes visited the prisoners, and, under the affectation of kindness and sympathy, drew from them a confession of opinions, which were afterwards urged against them; and obtained discoveries relative to their connections and friends, who were, by these insidious means, frequently involved in their destruction. Vivaldi, conscious of his own innocence, had, on his first examination, acquainted the inquisitor with the names and residence of his family; he had, therefore, nothing new to apprehend from revealing them to this stranger; but he perceived that if it should be known he had attempted to convey a message, however concise and harmless, the discovery would irritate the jealous inquisitors against him, and might be urged as a new presumption of his guilt. These considerations, together with the distrust which the inconsistency of his visitor's assertions, and the occasional embarrassment of his manner, had awakened, determined Vivaldi to resist the temptation now offered to him; and the stranger, having received his thanks, reluctantly withdrew, observing, however, that should any unforeseen circumstance detain him in the Inquisition longer than he had reason to expect, he should beg leave to pay him another visit. In reply to this, Vivaldi only bowed, but he remarked that the stranger's countenance changed, and that some dark brooding appeared to cloud his mind, as he quitted the chamber.

Several days elapsed, during which Vivaldi heard no more of his new acquaintance. He was then summoned to another examination, from which he was dismissed as before; and some weeks of solitude and of heavy uncertainty succeeded, after which he was a fourth time called up to the table of the Holy Office. It was then surrounded by inquisitors, and a more than usual solemnity appeared in the proceedings.

As proofs of Vivaldi's innocence had not been obtained, the suspicions of his examiners, of course, were not removed; and, as he persisted in denying the truth of the charge which he understood would be exhibited against him, and refused to make any confession of crimes, it was ordered that he should, within three hours, be put to the *question*.* Till then, Vivaldi was once more dismissed to his prison chamber. His resolution remained unshaken, but he could not look, unmoved, upon the horrors which might be preparing for him. The interval of expectation between the sentence and the accomplishment of this preliminary punishment, was, indeed, dreadful. The seeming ignominy of his situation, and his ignorance as to the degree of torture to be applied, overcame the calmness he had before exhibited, and as he paced his cell, cold damps, which hung upon his forehead, betrayed the agony of his mind. It was not long, however, that he suffered from a sense of ignominy; his better judgment shewed him, that innocence cannot suffer disgrace from any situation or circumstance, and he once more resumed the courage and the firmness which belong to virtue.

It was about midnight, that Vivaldi heard steps approaching, and a murmur of voices at the door of his cell. He understood these to be the persons come to summon him to the torture. The door was unbarred, and two men, habited in black, appeared at it. Without speaking, they advanced, and throwing over him a singular kind of mantle, led him from the chamber.

Along the galleries, and other avenues through which they passed, not any person was seen, and, by the profound stillness that reigned, it seemed as if death had already anticipated his work in these regions of horror, and had condemned alike the tortured and the torturer.

They descended to the large hall, where Vivaldi had waited on the night of his entrance, and thence through an avenue, and down a long flight of steps, that led to subterranean chambers. His conductors did not utter a syllable during the whole progress; Vivaldi knew too well that questions would only subject him to greater severity, and he asked none.

The doors, through which they passed, regularly opened at the touch of an iron rod, carried by one of the officials, and without the appearance of any person. The other man bore a torch, and the passages were so dimly lighted, that the way could scarcely have been found without one. They crossed what seemed to be a burial vault, but the extent and obscurity of the place did not allow it to be ascertained; and, having reached an iron door, they stopped. One of the officials struck upon it three times with the rod, but it did not open as the others had done. While they waited, Vivaldi thought he heard, from within, low intermitting sounds, as of persons in their last extremity, but, though within, they appeared to come from a distance. His whole heart was chilled, not with fear, for at that moment he did not remember himself, but with horror.

Having waited a considerable time, during which the official did not repeat the signal, the door was partly opened by a person whom Vivaldi could not distinguish in the gloom beyond, and with whom one of his conductors communicated by signs; after which the door was closed.

Several minutes had elapsed, when tones of deep voices aroused the attention of Vivaldi. They were loud and hoarse, and spoke in a language unknown to him. At the sounds, the official immediately extinguished his torch. The voices drew nearer, and, the door again unfolding, two figures stood before Vivaldi, which, shewn by a glimmering light within, struck him with astonishment and dismay. They were cloathed, like his conductors, in black, but in a different fashion, for their habits were made close to the shape. Their faces were entirely concealed beneath a very peculiar kind of cowl, which descended from the head to the feet; and their eyes only were visible through small openings contrived for the sight. It occurred to Vivaldi that these men were torturers; their appearance was worthy of demons. Probably they were thus habited, that the persons whom they afflicted might not know them; or, perhaps, it was only for the purpose of striking terror upon the minds of the accused, and thus compelling them to confess without further difficulty. Whatever motive might have occasioned their horrific appearance, and whatever was their office, Vivaldi was delivered into their hands, and in the same moment heard the iron door shut, which enclosed him with them in a narrow passage, gloomily lighted by a lamp suspended from the arched roof. They walked in silence on each side of their prisoner, and came to a second door, which admitted them instantly into another passage. A third door, at a short distance, admitted them to a third avenue, at the end of which one of his mysterious guides struck upon a gate, and they stopped. The uncertain sounds that Vivaldi had fancied he heard, were now more audible, and he distinguished, with inexpressible horror, that they were uttered by persons suffering.

The gate was, at length, opened by a figure habited like his conductors, and two other doors of iron, placed very near each other, being also unlocked, Vivaldi found himself in a spacious chamber, the walls of which were hung with black, duskily lighted by lamps that gleamed in the lofty vault. Immediately on his entrance, a strange sound ran along the walls, and echoed among other vaults, that appeared, by the progress of the sound, to extend far beyond this.

It was not immediately that Vivaldi could sufficiently recollect himself to observe any object before him; and, even when he did so, the gloom of the place prevented his ascertaining many appearances. Shadowy countenances and uncertain forms seemed to flit through the dusk, and many instruments, the application of which he did not comprehend, struck him with horrible suspicions. Still he heard, at intervals, half-suppressed groans, and was looking round to discover the wretched people from whom they were extorted, when a voice from a remote part of the chamber, called on him to advance.

The distance, and the obscurity of the spot whence the voice issued, had prevented Vivaldi from noticing any person there, and he was now slowly obeying, when, on a second summons, his conductors seized his arms, and hurried him forward.

In a remote part of this extensive chamber, he perceived three persons seated under a black canopy, on chairs raised several steps from the floor, and who appeared to preside there in the office of either judges or examiners, or directors of the punishments. Below, at a table, sat a secretary, over whom was suspended the only lamp that could enable him to commit to paper what should occur during the examination. Vivaldi now understood that the three persons who composed the tribunal were the vicar general, or grand inquisitor, the advocate of the exchequer, and an ordinary inquisitor, who was seated between the other two, and who appeared more eagerly to engage in the duties of his cruel office. A portentous obscurity enveloped alike their persons and their proceedings.

At some distance from the tribunal stood a large iron frame, which Vivaldi conjectured to be the rack, and near it another, resembling, in shape, a coffin, but, happily, he could not distinguish, through the remote obscurity, any person undergoing actual suffering. In the vaults beyond, however, the diabolical decrees of the inquisitors seemed to be fulfilling; for, whenever a distant door opened for a moment, sounds of lamentation issued forth, and men, whom he judged to be familiars, habited like those who stood beside him, were seen passing to and fro within.

Vivaldi almost believed himself in the infernal regions; the dismal aspect of this place, the horrible preparation for punishment, and, above all, the disposition and appearance of the persons that were ready to inflict it, confirmed the resemblance. That any human being should willingly afflict a fellow being who had never injured, or even offended him; that, unswayed by passion, he should deliberately become the means of torturing him, appeared to Vivaldi nearly incredible! But when he looked at the three persons who composed the tribunal, and considered that they had not only voluntarily undertaken the cruel office they fulfilled, but had probably long regarded it as the summit of their ambition, his astonishment and indignation were unbounded.

The grand inquisitor, having again called on Vivaldi by name, admonished him to confess the truth, and avoid the suffering that awaited him.

As Vivaldi had on former examinations spoken the truth, which was not believed, he had no chance of escaping present suffering, but by asserting falshood: in doing so, to avoid such monstrous injustice and cruelty, he might, perhaps, have been justified, had it been certain that such assertion could affect himself alone; but since he knew that the consequence must extend to others, and, above all, believed that Ellena di Rosalba must be involved in it, he did not hesitate for an instant to dare whatever torture his firmness might provoke. But even if morality could have forgiven falshood, in such extraordinary circumstances as these, policy, after all, would have forbidden it, since a discovery of the artifice would probably have led to the final destruction of the accused person.

Of Ellena's situation he would now have asked, however desperate the question; would again have asserted her innocence, and supplicated for compassion, even to inquisitors, had he not perceived that, in doing so, he should only furnish them with a more exquisite means of torturing him than any other they could apply; for if, when all the terrors of his soul concerning her were understood, they should threaten to increase her sufferings, as the punishment of what was termed his obstinacy, they would, indeed, become the masters of his integrity, as well as of his person.

The tribunal again, and repeatedly, urged Vivaldi to confess himself guilty; and the inquisitor, at length, concluded with saying, that the judges were innocent of whatever consequence might ensue from his obstinacy; so that, if he expired beneath his sufferings, himself only, not they, would have occasioned his death.

'I am innocent of the charges which I understand are urged against me,' said Vivaldi, with solemnity; 'I repeat, that I am innocent! If, to escape the horrors of these moments, I could be weak enough to declare myself guilty, not all your racks could alter truth, and make me so, except in that assertion. The consequence of your tortures, therefore, be upon your own heads!'

While Vivaldi spoke, the vicar general listened with attention, and, when he had ceased to speak, appeared to meditate; but the inquisitor was irritated by the boldness of his speech, instead of being convinced by the justness of his representation; and made a signal for the officers to prepare for the *question*. While they were obeying, Vivaldi observed, notwithstanding the agitation he suffered, a person cross the chamber, whom he immediately knew to be the same that had passed him in an avenue of the inquisition on a former night, and whom he had then fancied to be the mysterious stranger of Paluzzi. Vivaldi now fixed his eyes upon him, but his own peculiar situation prevented his feeling the interest he had formerly suffered concerning him.

The figure, air, and stalk, of this person were so striking, and so strongly resembled those of the monk of Paluzzi, that Vivaldi had no longer a doubt as to their identity. He pointed him out to one of the officials, and inquired who he was. While he spoke, the stranger was passing forward, and, before any reply was given, a door leading to the farther vaults shut him from view. Vivaldi, however, repeated the inquiry, which the official appeared unable to answer, and a reproof from the tribunal reminded him that he must not ask questions there. Vivaldi observed that it was the grand inquisitor who spoke, and that the manner of the official immediately changed.

The familiars, who were the same that had conducted Vivaldi into the chamber, having made ready the instrument of torture, approached him, and, after taking off his cloak and vest, bound him with strong cords. They threw over his head the customary black garment, which entirely enveloped his figure, and prevented his observing what was farther preparing. In this state of expectation, he was again interrogated by the inquisitor.

'Was you ever in the church of the Spirito Santo, at Naples?' said he.

'Yes,' replied Vivaldi.

'Did you ever express there a contempt for the Catholic faith?'

'Never,' said Vivaldi.

'Neither by word or action?' continued the inquisitor.

'Never, by either!'

'Recollect yourself,' added the inquisitor. 'Did you never insult there a minister of our most holy church?'

Vivaldi was silent: he began to perceive the real nature of the charge which was to be urged against him, and that it was too plausible to permit his escape from the punishment, which is adjudged for heresy. Questions so direct and minute had never been put to him here on his former examinations; they had been reserved for a moment when it was believed he could not evade them; and the real charge had been concealed from him, that he might not be prepared to elude it.

'Answer!' repeated the inquisitor.—'Did you ever insult a minister of the Catholic faith, in the church of the Spirito Santo, at Naples?'

'Did you not insult him while he was performing an act of holy penance?' said another voice.

Vivaldi started, for he instantly recollected the well-known tones of the monk of Paluzzi. 'Who asks the question?' demanded Vivaldi.

'It is you who are to answer here,' resumed the inquisitor. 'Answer to what I have required.'

'I have offended a minister of the church,' replied Vivaldi, 'but never could intentionally insult our holy religion. You are not acquainted, fathers, with the injuries that provoked——'

'Enough!' interrupted the inquisitor; 'speak to the question. Did you not, by insult and menace, force a pious brother to leave unperformed the act of penance in which he had engaged himself? Did you not compel him to quit the church, and fly for refuge to his convent?'

'No,' replied Vivaldi. ''Tis true, he left the church, and that in consequence of my conduct there; but the consequence was not necessary; if he had only replied to my inquiry, or promised to restore her of whom he had treacherously robbed me, he might have remained quietly in the church till this moment, had that depended upon my forbearance.'

'What!' said the vicar-general, 'would you have compelled him to speak, when he was engaged in silent penance? You confess, that you occasioned him to leave the church. That is enough.'

'Where did you first see Ellena di Rosalba?' said the voice, which had spoken once before.

'I demand again, who gives the question,' answered Vivaldi.

'Recollect yourself,' said the inquisitor, 'a criminal cannot make a demand.'

'I do not perceive the connection between your admonition and your assertion,' observed Vivaldi.

'You appear to be rather too much at your ease,' said the

inquisitor. 'Answer to the question which was last put to you, or the familiars shall do their duty.'

'Let the same person ask it,' replied Vivaldi.

The question was repeated in the former voice.

'In the church of San Lorenzo, at Naples,' said Vivaldi, with a heavy sigh, 'I first beheld Ellena di Rosalba.'

'Was she then professed?' asked the vicar general.

'She never accepted the veil,' replied Vivaldi, 'nor ever intended to do so.'

'Where did she reside at that period?'

'She lived with a relative at Villa Altieri, and would yet reside there, had not the machinations of a monk occasioned her to be torn from her home, and confined in a convent, from which I had just assisted to release her, when she was again seized, and upon a charge most false and cruel.—O reverend fathers! I conjure, I supplicate——' Vivaldi restrained himself, for he was going to have betrayed, to the mercy of inquisitors, all the feelings of his heart.

'The name of the monk?' said the stranger, earnestly.

'If I mistake not,' replied Vivaldi, 'you are already acquainted with it. The monk is called father Schedoni. He is of the Dominican convent of the Spirito Santo, in Naples, and the same who accuses me of having insulted him in the church of that name.'

'How did you know him for your accuser?' asked the same voice.

'Because he is my only enemy,' replied Vivaldi.

'Your enemy!' observed the inquisitor; 'a former deposition says, you were unconscious of having one! You are inconsistent in your replies.'

'You were warned not to visit Villa Altieri,' said the unknown person. 'Why did you not profit by the warning?'

'I was warned by yourself,' answered Vivaldi. 'Now I know you well.'

'By me!' said the stranger, in a solemn tone.

'By you!' repeated Vivaldi: 'you who also foretold the death of Signora Bianchi; and you are that enemy—that father Schedoni, by whom I am accused.'

'Whence come these questions?' demanded the vicar general. 'Who has been authorised thus to interrogate the prisoner?'

No reply was made. A busy hum of voices from the tribunal succeeded the silence. At length, the murmuring subsided, and the monk's voice was heard again.

'I will declare thus much,' it said, addressing Vivaldi; 'I am not father Schedoni.'

The peculiar tone and emphasis, with which this was delivered, more than the assertion itself, persuaded Vivaldi that the stranger spoke truth; and, though he still recognized the voice of the monk of Paluzzi, he did not know it to be that of Schedoni. Vivaldi was astonished! He would have torn the veil from his eyes, and once more viewed this mysterious stranger, had his hands been at liberty. As it was, he could only conjure him to reveal his name, and the motives for his former conduct.

'Who is come amongst us?' said the vicar general, in the voice of a person, who means to inspire in others the awe he himself suffers.

'Who is come amongst us?' he repeated, in a louder tone. Still no answer was returned; but again a confused murmur sounded from the tribunal, and a general consternation seemed to prevail. No person spoke with sufficient pre-eminence to be understood by Vivaldi; something extraordinary appeared to be passing, and he awaited the issue with all the patience he could command. Soon after he heard doors opened, and the noise of persons quitting the chamber. A deep silence followed; but he was certain that the familars were still beside him, waiting to begin their work of torture.

After a considerable time had elapsed, Vivaldi heard footsteps advancing, and a person give orders for his release, that he might be carried back to his cell.

When the veil was removed from his eyes, he perceived that the tribunal was dissolved, and that the stranger was gone. The lamps were dying away, and the chamber appeared more gloomily terrific than before.

The familiars conducted him to the spot at which they had received him; whence the officers who had led him thither, guarded him to his prison. There, stretched upon his bed of straw, in solitude and in darkness, he had leisure enough to reflect upon what had passed, and to recollect with minute exactness every former circumstance connected with the stranger. By comparing those with the present, he endeavoured to draw a more certain conclusion as to the identity of this person, and his motives for the very extraordinary conduct he had pursued. The first appearance of this stranger, among the ruins of Paluzzi, when he had said that Vivaldi's steps were watched, and had cautioned him against returning to Villa Altieri, was recalled to his mind. Vivaldi re-considered, also, his second appearance on the same spot, and his second warning; the circumstances, which had attended his own adventures within the fortress;—the monk's prediction of Bianchi's death, and his evil tidings respecting Ellena, at the very hour when she had been seized and carried from her home. The longer he considered these several instances, as they were now connected in his mind, with the certainty of Schedoni's evil disposition towards him, the more he was inclined to believe, notwithstanding the voice of seeming truth which had just affirmed the contrary, that the unknown person was Schedoni himself, and that he had been employed by the Marchesa, to prevent Vivaldi's visits to Villa Altieri. Being thus an agent in the events of which he had warned Vivaldi, he was too well enabled to predict them. Vivaldi paused upon the remembrance of Signora Bianchi's death; he considered the extraordinary and dubious circumstances that had attended it, and shuddered as a new conjecture crossed his mind.—The thought was too dreadful to be permitted, and he dismissed it instantly.

Of the conversation, however, which he had afterwards held with the Confessor in the Marchesa's cabinet, he recollected many particulars that served to renew his doubts as to the identity of the stranger; the behaviour of Schedoni when he was obliquely challenged for the monk of Paluzzi, still appeared that of a man unconscious of disguise; and above all, Vivaldi was struck with the seeming candour of his having pointed out a circumstance, which removed the probability that the stranger was a brother of the *Santa del Pianto*

Some particulars, also, of the stranger's conduct did not agree with what might have been expected from Schedoni, even though the Confessor had really been Vivaldi's enemy; a circumstance which the latter was no longer permitted to doubt. Nor did those particular circumstances accord, as he was inclined to believe, with the manner of a being of this world; and, when Vivaldi considered the suddenness and mystery, with which the stranger had always appeared and retired, he felt disposed to adopt again one of his earliest conjectures, which undoubtedly the horrors of his present abode disposed his imagination to admit, as those of his former situation in the vaults of Paluzzi, together with a youthful glow of curiosity concerning the marvellous, had before contributed to impress them upon his mind.

He concluded his present reflections as he had begun them—in doubt and perplexity; but at length found a respite from thought and from suffering in sleep.

Midnight had been passed in the vaults of the Inquisition; but it was probably not yet two o'clock, when he was imperfectly awakened by a sound, which he fancied proceeded from within his chamber. He raised himself to discover what had occasioned the noise; it was, however, impossible to discern any object, for all was dark, but he listened for a return of the sound. The wind only, was heard moaning among the inner buildings of the prison, and Vivaldi concluded, that his dream had mocked him with a mimic voice.

Satisfied with this conclusion, he again laid his head on his pillow of straw, and soon sunk into a slumber. The subject of his waking thoughts still haunted his imagination, and the stranger, whose voice he had this night recognized as that of the monk of Paluzzi, appeared before him. Vivaldi, on perceiving the figure of this un-known, felt, perhaps, nearly the same degrees of awe, curiosity, and impatience that he would have suffered, had he beheld the substance of this shadow. The monk, whose face was still shrouded, he thought advanced, till, having come within a few paces of Vivaldi, he paused, and, lifting the awful cowl that had hitherto concealed him, disclosed—not the countenance of Schedoni, but one which Vivaldi did not recollect ever having seen before! It was not less interesting to curiosity, than striking to the feelings. Vivaldi at the first glance shrunk back;—something of that strange and indescribable air, which we attach to the idea of a super-natural being, prevailed over the features; and the intense and fiery eyes resembled those of an evil spirit, rather than of a human character. He drew a poniard from beneath a fold of his garment, and, as he displayed it, pointed with a stern frown to the spots which discoloured the blade; Vivaldi perceived they were of blood! He turned away his eyes in horror, and, when he again looked round in his dream, the figure was gone.

A groan awakened him, but what were his feelings, when, on looking up, he perceived the same figure standing before him! It was not, however, immediately that he could convince himself the appearance was more than the phantom of his dream, strongly impressed upon an alarmed fancy. The voice of the monk, for his face was as usual concealed, recalled Vivaldi from his error; but his emotion cannot easily be conceived, when the stranger, slowly lifting that mysterious cowl, discovered to him the same awful countenance, which had characterized the vision in his slumber.

Unable to inquire the occasion of this appearance, Vivaldi gazed in astonishment and terror, and did not immediately observe, that, instead of a dagger, the monk held a lamp, which gleamed over every deep furrow of his features, yet left their shadowy markings to hint the passions and the history of an extraordinary life.

'You are spared for this night,' said the stranger, 'but for to-morrow'——he paused.

'In the name of all that is most sacred,' said Vivaldi, endeavouring to recollect his thoughts, 'who are you, and what is your errand?'

'Ask no questions,' replied the monk, solemnly;—'but answer *me*.'

Vivaldi was struck by the tone, with which he said this, and dared not to urge the inquiry at the present moment.

'How long have you known father Schedoni?' continued the stranger, 'Where did you first meet?'

'I have known him about a year, as my mother's confessor,' replied Vivaldi. 'I first saw him in a corridor of the Vivaldi palace; it was evening, and he was returning from the Marchesa's closet.'

'Are you certain as to this?' said the monk, with peculiar emphasis. 'It is of consequence that you should be so.'

'I am certain,' repeated Vivaldi.

'It is strange,' observed the monk, after a pause, 'that a circumstance, which must have appeared trivial to you at the moment, should have left so strong a mark on your memory! In two years we have time to forget many things!' He sighed as he spoke.

'I remember the circumstance,' said Vivaldi, 'because I was struck with his appearance; the evening was far advanced—it was dusk, and he came upon me suddenly. His voice startled me; as he passed he said to himself—"It is for vespers." At the same time I heard the bell of the Spirito Santo.'

'Do you know who he is?' said the stranger, solemnly.

'I know only what he appears to be,' replied Vivaldi.

'Did you never hear any report of his past life?'

'Never,' answered Vivaldi.

'Never any thing extraordinary concerning him,' added the monk.

Vivaldi paused a moment; for he now recollected the obscure and imperfect story, which Paulo had related while they were confined in the dungeon of Paluzzi, respecting a confession made in the church of the Black Penitents; but he could not presume to affirm, that it concerned Schedoni. He remembered also the monk's garments, stained with blood, which he had discovered in the vaults of that fort. The conduct of the mysterious being, who now stood before him, with many other particulars of his own adventures there, passed like a vision over his memory. His mind resembled the glass of a magician, on which the apparitions of long-buried events arise, and as they fleet away, point portentously to shapes half-hid in the duskiness of futurity.* An unusual dread seized upon him; and a superstition, such as he had never before admitted in an equal degree, usurped his judgment. He looked up to the shadowy countenance of the stranger; and almost believed he beheld an inhabitant of the world of spirits.

The monk spoke again, repeating in a severer tone, 'Did you never hear any thing extraordinary concerning father Schedoni?'

'Is it reasonable,' said Vivaldi, recollecting his courage, 'that I should answer the questions, the minute questions, of a person who refuses to tell me even his name?'

'My name is passed away—it is no more remembered,' replied the stranger, turning from Vivaldi,—'I leave you to your fate.'

'What fate?' asked Vivaldi, 'and what is the purpose of this visit? I conjure you, in the tremendous name of the Inquisition, to say!'

'You will know full soon; have mercy on yourself!'

'What fate?' repeated Vivaldi.

'Urge me no further,' said the stranger; 'but answer to what I shall demand. Schedoni——'

'I have told all that I certainly know concerning him,' interrupted Vivaldi, 'the rest is only conjecture.'

'What is that conjecture? Does it relate to a confession made in the church of the Black Penitents of the Santa Maria del Pianto?

'It does!' replied Vivaldi with surprise.

'What was that confession?'

'I know not,' answered Vivaldi.

'Declare the truth,' said the stranger, sternly.

'A confession,' replied Vivaldi, 'is sacred, and forever buried in the bosom of the priest to whom it is made. How, then, is it to be supposed, that I can be acquainted with the subject of this?'

'Did you never hear, that father Schedoni had been guilty of some great crimes, which he endeavours to erase from his conscience by the severity of penance?'

'Never!' said Vivaldi.

'Did you never hear that he had a wife—a brother?'

'Never!'

'Nor the means he used—no hint of—murder, of——'

The stranger paused, as if he wished Vivaldi to fill up his meaning, Vivaldi was silent and aghast.

'You know nothing then, of Schedoni,' resumed the monk after a deep pause—'nothing of his past life?'

'Nothing, except what I have mentioned,' replied Vivaldi.

'Then listen to what I shall unfold!' continued the monk, with solemnity. 'To-morrow night you will be again carried to the place of torture; you will be taken to a chamber beyond that in which you were this night. You will there witness many extraordinary things, of which you have not now any suspicion. Be not dismayed; I shall be there, though, perhaps, not visible.'

'Not visible!' exclaimed Vivaldi.

'Interrupt me not, but listen.—When you are asked of father Schedoni, say—that he has lived for fifteen years in the disguise of a monk, a member of the Dominicans of the Spirito Santo, at Naples. When you are asked who he is, reply—Ferando Count di Bruno. You will be asked the motive, for such disguise. In reply to this, refer them to the *Black Penitents* of the Santa Maria del Pianto, near that city; bid the inquisitors summon before their tribunal one father Ansaldo di Rovalli, the grand penitentiary of the society, and command him to divulge the crimes confessed to him in the year 1752, on the evening of the twenty-fourth of April, which was then the vigil of Santo Marco, in a confessional of the Santa del Pianto.'

'It is probable he may have forgotten such confession, at this distance of time,' observed Vivaldi.

'Fear not but he will remember,' replied the stranger.

'But will his conscience suffer him to betray the secrets of a confession?' said Vivaldi.

'The tribunal command, and his conscience is absolved,' answered the monk, 'He may not refuse to obey! You are further to direct your examiners to summon father Schedoni, to answer for the crimes which Ansaldo shall reveal.' The monk paused, and seemed waiting the reply of Vivaldi, who, after a momentary consideration, said,

'How can I do all this, and upon the instigation of a stranger! Neither conscience nor prudence will suffer me to assert what I cannot prove. It is true that I have reason to believe Schedoni is my bitter enemy, but I will not be unjust even to him. I have no proof that he is the Count di Bruno, nor that he is the perpetrator of the crimes you allude to, whatever those may be; and I will not be made an instrument to summon any man before a tribunal, where innocence is no protection from ignominy, and where suspicion alone may inflict death.'

'You doubt, then, the truth of what I assert?' said the monk, in a haughty tone.

'Can I believe that of which I have no proof?' replied Vivaldi.

'Yes, there are cases which do not admit of proof; under your peculiar circumstances, this is one of them; you can act only upon assertion. I attest,' continued the monk, raising his hollow voice to a tone of singular solemnity, 'I attest the powers which are beyond this earth, to witness to the truth of what I have delivered!'

As the stranger uttered this adjuration, Vivaldi observed, with emotion, the extraordinary expression of his eyes; Vivaldi's presence of mind, however, did not forsake him, and, in the next moment, he said, 'But who is he that thus attests? It is upon the assertion of a stranger that I am to rely, in defect of proof! It is a stranger who calls upon me to bring solemn charges against a man, of whose guilt I know nothing!'

'You are not required to bring charges, you are only to summon him who will.'

'I should still assist in bringing forward accusations, which may be founded in error,' replied Vivaldi. 'If you are convinced of their truth, why do not you summon Ansaldo yourself!'

'I shall do more,' said the monk.

'But why not summon also?' urged Vivaldi.

'I shall *appear*,' said the stranger, with emphasis.

Vivaldi, though somewhat awed by the manner, which accompanied these words, still urged his inquiries, 'As a witness?' said he.

'Aye, as a dreadful witness!' replied the monk.

'But may not a witness summon others before the tribunal of the inquisition?' continued Vivaldi, faulteringly.

'He may,' said the stranger.

'Why then,' observed Vivaldi, 'am I, a stranger to you, called upon to do that which you could perform yourself?'

'Ask no further,' said the monk, 'but answer, whether you will deliver the summons?'

'The charges, which must follow,' replied Vivaldi, 'appear to be of a nature too solemn to justify my promoting them. I resign the task to you.'

'When *I* summon,' said the stranger, '*you* shall obey!'

Vivaldi, again awed by his manner, again justified his refusal, and concluded with repeating his surprize, that he should be required to assist in this mysterious affair, 'Since I neither know you, father,' he added, 'nor the Penitentiary Ansaldo, whom you bid me admonish to appear.'

'You shall know me hereafter,' said the stranger, frowningly; and he drew from beneath his garment a dagger!

Vivaldi remembered his dream.

'Mark those spots,' said the monk.

Vivaldi looked, and beheld blood!

'This blood,' added the stranger, pointing to the blade, 'would have saved your's! Here is some print of truth! To-morrow night you will meet me in the chambers of death!'

As he spoke, he turned away; and, before Vivaldi had recovered from his consternation, the light disappeared. Vivaldi knew that the stranger had quitted the prison, only by the silence which prevailed there.

He remained sunk in thought, till, at the dawn of day, the man, on watch, unfastened the door of his cell, and brought, as usual, a jug of water, and some bread. Vivaldi inquired the name of the stranger who had visited him in the night. The centinel looked surprized, and Vivaldi repeated the question before he could obtain an answer.

'I have been on guard since the first hour,' said the man, 'and no person, in that time, has passed through this door!'

Vivaldi regarded the centinel with attention, while he made this assertion, and did not perceive in his manner any consciousness of falshood; yet he knew not how to believe what he had affirmed. 'Did you hear no noise, either?' said Vivaldi. 'Has all been silent during the night?'

'I have heard only the bell of San Dominico strike upon the hour,' replied the man, 'and the watch word of the centinels.'

'This is incomprehensible!' exclaimed Vivaldi, 'What! no footsteps, no voice?'

The man smiled contemptuously. 'None, but of the centinels,' he replied.

'How can you be certain you heard only the centinels, friend?' added Vivaldi.

'They speak only to pass the watch word, and the clash of their arms is heard at the same time.'

'But their footsteps!—how are they distinguished from those of other persons?'

'By the heaviness of their tread; our sandals are braced with iron. But why these questions, Signor?'

'You have kept guard at the door of this chamber?' said Vivaldi.

'Yes, Signor.'

'And you have not once heard, during the whole night, a voice from within it?'

'None, Signor.'

'Fear nothing from discovery, friend; confess that you have slumbered.'

'I had a comrade,' replied the centinel, angrily, 'has he, too, slumbered! and if he had, how could admittance be obtained without our keys?'

'And those might easily have been procured, friend, if you were overcome with sleep. You may rely upon my promise of secrecy.'

'What!' said the man, 'have I kept guard for three years in the Inquisition, to be suspected, by an heretic, of neglecting my duty?'

'If you were suspected by an heretic,' replied Vivaldi, 'you ought to console yourself by recollecting that his opinions are considered to be erroneous.'

'We were watchful every minute of the night,' said the centinel, going.

'This is incomprehensible!' said Vivaldi, 'By what means could the stranger have entered my prison?'

'Signor, you still dream!' replied the centinel, pausing, 'No person has been here.'

'*Still* dream!' repeated Vivaldi, 'how do you know that I have dreamt at all?' His mind deeply affected by the extraordinary circumstances of the dream, and the yet more extraordinary incident that had followed, Vivaldi gave a meaning to the words of the centinel, which did not belong to them.

'When people sleep, they are apt to dream,' replied the man, dryly. 'I supposed *you* had slept, Signor.'

'A person, habited like a monk, came to me in the night,' resumed Vivaldi, and he described the appearance of the stranger. The centinel, while he listened, became grave and thoughtful.

'Do you know any person resembling the one I have mentioned,' said Vivaldi.

'No!' replied the guard.

'Though you have not seen him enter my prison,' continued Vivaldi, 'you may, perhaps, recollect such a person, as an inhabitant of the Inquisition.'

'San Dominico forbid!'

Vivaldi, surprized at this exclamation, inquired the reason for it.

'I know him not,' replied the centinel, changing countenance, and he abruptly left the prison. Whatever consideration might occasion this sudden departure, his assertion that he had been for three years a guard of the Inquisition could scarcely be credited, since he had held so long a dialogue with a prisoner, and was, apparently, insensible of the danger he incurred by so doing.

CHAPTER VI

———— Is it not dead midnight?
Cold fearful drops stand on my trembling flesh,
What do I fear?

SHAKESPEARE *

A T about the same hour, as on the preceding night, Vivaldi heard persons approaching his prison, and, the door unfolding, his former conductors appeared. They threw over him the same mantle as before, and, in addition, a black veil, that completely muffled his eyes; after which, they led him from the chamber. Vivaldi heard the door shut, on his departure, and the centinels followed his steps, as if their duty was finished, and he was to return thither no more. At this moment, he remembered the words of the stranger when he had displayed the poniard, and Vivaldi apprehended the worst, from having thwarted the designs of a person apparently so malignant: but he exulted in the rectitude, which had preserved him from debasement, and, with the magnanimous enthusiasm of virtue, he almost welcomed sufferings, which would prove the firmness of his justice towards an enemy; for he determined to brave every thing, rather than impute to Schedoni circumstances, the truth of which he possessed no means of ascertaining.

While Vivaldi was conducted, as on the preceding night, through many passages, he endeavoured to discover, by their length, and the abruptness of their turnings, whether they were the same he had traversed before. Suddenly, one of his conductors cried 'Steps!' It was the first word Vivaldi had ever heard him utter. He immediately perceived that the ground sunk, and he began to descend; as he did which, he tried to count the number of the steps, that he might form some judgment whether this was the flight he had passed before. When he had reached the bottom, he inclined to believe that it was not so; and the care which had been observed in blinding him, seemed to indicate that he was going to some new place.

He passed through several avenues, and then ascended; soon after which, he again descended a very long stair-case, such as he had not any remembrance of, and they passed over a considerable extent of level ground. By the hollow sounds which his steps returned, he judged that he was walking over vaults. The footsteps of the centinels who had followed from the cell were no longer heard, and he seemed to be left with his conductors only. A second flight appeared to lead him into subterraneous vaults, for he perceived the air change, and felt a damp vapour wrap round him. The menace of the monk, that he should meet him in the chambers of death, frequently occurred to Vivaldi.

His conductors stopped in this vault, and seemed to hold a consultation, but they spoke in such low accents, that their words were not distinguishable, except a few unconnected ones, that hinted of more than Vivaldi could comprehend. He was, at length, again led forward; and soon after, he heard the heavy grating of hinges, and perceived that he was passing through several doors, by the situation of which Vivaldi judged they were the same he had entered the night before, and concluded, that he was going to the hall of the tribunal.

His conductors stopped again, and Vivaldi heard the iron rod strike three times upon a door; immediately a strange voice spoke from within, and the door was unclosed. Vivaldi passed on, and imagined that he was admitted into a spacious vault; for the air was freer, and his steps sounded to a distance.

Presently, a voice, as on the preceding night, summoned him to come forward, and Vivaldi understood that he was again before the tribunal. It was the voice of the inquisitor who had been his chief examiner.

'You, Vincentio di Vivaldi,' it said, 'answer to your name, and to the questions which shall be put to you, without equivocation, on pain of the torture.'

As the monk had predicted, Vivaldi was asked what he knew of father Schedoni, and, when he replied, as he had formerly done to his mysterious visitor, he was told that he knew more than he acknowledged.

'I *know* no more,' replied Vivaldi.

'You equivocate,' said the inquisitor. 'Declare what you have heard, and remember that you formerly took an oath to that purpose.'

Vivaldi was silent, till a tremendous voice from the tribunal commanded him to respect his oath.

'I do respect it,' said Vivaldi; 'and I conjure you to believe that I also respect truth, when I declare, that what I am going to relate, is a report to which I give no confidence, and concerning even the probability of which I cannot produce the smallest proof.'

'Respect truth!' said another voice from the tribunal, and Vivaldi fancied he distinguished the tones of the monk. He paused a moment, and the exhortation was repeated. Vivaldi then related what the stranger had said concerning the family of Schedoni, and the disguise which the father had assumed in the convent of the Spirito Santo; but forbore even to name the penitentiary Ansaldo, and any circumstance connected with the extraordinary confession. Vivaldi concluded, with again declaring, that he had not sufficient authority to justify a belief in those reports.

'On what authority do you repeat them?' said the vicar-general.

Vivaldi was silent.

'On what authority?' inquired the inquisitor, sternly.

Vivaldi, after a momentary hesitation, said, 'What I am about to declare, holy fathers, is so extraordinary——'

'Tremble!' said a voice close to his ear, which he instantly knew to be the monk's, and the suddenness of which electrified him. He was unable to conclude the sentence.

'What is your authority for the reports?' demanded the inquisitor.

'It is unknown, even to myself!' answered Vivaldi.

'Do not equivocate!' said the vicar-general.

'I solemnly protest,' rejoined Vivaldi, 'that I know not either the name or the condition of my informer, and that I never even beheld his face, till the period when he spoke of father Schedoni.'

'Tremble!' repeated the same low, but emphatic voice in his ear. Vivaldi started, and turned involuntarily towards the sound, though his eyes could not assist his curiosity.

'You did well to say, that you had something extraordinary to add,' observed the inquisitor. ' 'Tis evident, also, that you expected something extraordinary from your judges, since you supposed they would credit these assertions.'

Vivaldi was too proud to attempt the justifying himself against so gross an accusation, or to make any reply.

'Why do you not summon father Ansaldo?' said the voice. 'Remember my words!'

Vivaldi, again awed by the voice, hesitated, for an instant, how to act, and in that instant his courage returned.

'My informer stands beside me!' said Vivaldi, boldly; 'I know his voice! Detain him; it is of consequence.'

'Whose voice?' demanded the inquisitor. 'No person spoke but myself!'

'Whose voice?' said the vicar-general.

'The voice was close beside me,' replied Vivaldi. 'It spoke low, but I knew it well.'

'This is either the cunning, or the frenzy of despair!' observed the vicar-general.

'Not any person is now beside you, except the familiars,' said the inquisitor, 'and they wait to do their office, if you shall refuse to answer the questions put to you.'

'I persist in my assertion,' replied Vivaldi; 'and I supplicate that my eyes may be unbound, that I may know my enemy.'

The tribunal, after a long private consultation, granted the request; the veil was withdrawn, and Vivaldi perceived beside him—only the familiars! Their faces, as is usual, were concealed. It appeared that one of these torturers must be the mysterious enemy, who pursued him, if, indeed, that enemy was an inhabitant of the earth! and Vivaldi requested that they might be ordered to uncover their features. He was sternly rebuked for so presumptuous a requisition, and reminded of the inviolable law and faith, which the tribunal had pledged, that persons appointed to their awful office should never be exposed to the revenge of the criminal, whom it might be their duty to punish.

'Their duty!' exclaimed Vivaldi, thrown from his guard by strong indignation. 'And is faith held sacred with demons!'

Without awaiting the order of the tribunal, the familiars immediately covered Vivaldi's face with the veil, and he felt himself in their grasp. He endeavoured, however, to disentangle his hands, and, at length, shook these men from their hold, and again unveiled his eyes; but the familiars were instantly ordered to replace the veil.

The inquisitor bade Vivaldi to recollect in whose presence he then was, and to dread the punishment which his resistance had incurred, and which would be inflicted without delay, unless he could give some instance, that might tend to prove the truth of his late assertions.

'If you expect that I should say more,' replied Vivaldi, 'I claim, at least, protection from the unbidden violence of the men who guard me. If they are suffered, at their pleasure, to sport with the misery of their prisoner, I will be inflexibly silent; and, since I must suffer, it shall be according to the laws of the tribunal.'

The vicar-general, or, as he is called, the grand inquisitor, promised Vivaldi the degree of protection he claimed, and demanded, at the same time, what were the words he had just heard.

Vivaldi considered, that, though justice bade him avoid accusing an enemy of suspicious circumstances, concerning which he had no proof, yet, that neither justice nor common sense required he should make a sacrifice of himself to the dilemma in which he was placed: he, therefore, without further scruple, acknowledged, that the voice had bidden him require of the tribunal to summon one father Ansaldo, the grand penitentiary of the Santa del Pianto, near Naples, and also father Schedoni, who was to answer to extraordinary charges, which would be brought against him by Ansaldo. Vivaldi anxiously and repeatedly declared, that he knew not the nature of the charges, nor that any just grounds for them existed.

These assertions seemed to throw the tribunal into new perplexity. Vivaldi heard their busy voices in low debate, which continued for a considerable time. In this interval, he had leisure to perceive the many improbabilities that either of the familiars should be the stranger who so mysteriously haunted him; and among these was the circumstance of his having resided so long at Naples.

The tribunal, after some time had elapsed in consultation, proceeded on the examination, and Vivaldi was asked what he knew of father Ansaldo. He immediately replied, that Ansaldo was an utter stranger to him, and that he was not even acquainted with a single person residing in the Santa del Pianto or who had any knowledge of the penitentiary.

'How!' said the grand inquisitor. 'You forget that the person, who bade you require of this tribunal to summon Ansaldo, has knowledge of him.'

'Pardon me, I do not forget,' replied Vivaldi; 'and I request it may be remembered that I am not acquainted with that person. If, therefore, he had given me any account of Ansaldo, I could not have relied upon its authenticity.' Vivaldi again required of the tribunal to understand that he did not summon Ansaldo, or any other person, before them, but had merely obeyed their command, to repeat what the stranger had said.

The tribunal acknowledged the justness of this injunction, and exculpated him from any harm that should be the consequence of the summons. But this assurance of safety for himself was not sufficient to appease Vivaldi, who was alarmed lest he should be the means of bringing an innocent person under suspicion. The grand inquisitor again addressed him, after a general silence had been commanded in the court.

'The account you have given of your informer,' said he, 'is so extraordinary, that it would not deserve credit, but that you have discovered the utmost reluctance to reveal the charges he gave you, from which, it appears, that, on your part, at least, the summons is not malicious. But are you certain that you have not deluded yourself, and that the voice beside you was not an imaginary one, conjured up by your agitated spirits?'

'I am certain,' replied Vivaldi, with firmness.

'It is true,' resumed the grand inquisitor, 'that several persons were near you, when you exclaimed, that you heard the voice of your informer; yet no person heard it besides yourself!'

'Where are those persons now?' demanded Vivaldi.

'They are dispersed; alarmed at your accusation.'

'If you will summon them,' said Vivaldi, 'and order that my eyes may be uncovered, I will point out to you, without hesitation, the person of my informer, should he remain among them.'

The tribunal commanded that they should appear, but new difficulties arose. It was not remembered of whom the crowd consisted; a few individuals only were recollected, and these were summoned.

Vivaldi, in solemn expectation, heard steps and the hum of voices gathering round him, and impatiently awaited for the words that would restore him to sight, and, perhaps, release him from uncertainty. In a few moments, he heard the command given; the veil was once more removed from his eyes, and he was ordered to point out the accuser. Vivaldi threw an hasty glance upon the surrounding strangers.

'The lights burn dimly,' said he, 'I cannot distinguish these faces.'

It was ordered that a lamp should be lowered from the roof, and that the strangers should arrange themselves on either side of Vivaldi. When this was done, and he glanced his eyes again upon the crowd, 'He is not here!' said Vivaldi; 'not one of these countenances resembles the monk of Paluzzi. Yet, stay; who is he that stands in the shade behind those persons on the left? Bid him lift his cowl!'

The crowd fell back, and the person, to whom Vivaldi had pointed, was left alone within the circle.

'He is an officer of the Inquisition,' said a man near Vivaldi, 'and he may not be compelled to discover his face, unless by an express command from the tribunal.'

'I call upon the tribunal to command it!' said Vivaldi.

'Who calls!' exclaimed a voice, and Vivaldi recognized the tones of the monk, but he knew not exactly whence they came.

'I, Vincentio di Vivaldi,' replied the prisoner, 'I claim the privilege that has been awarded me, and bid you unveil your countenance.'

There was a pause of silence in the court, except that a dull murmur ran through the tribunal. Meanwhile, the figure within the circle stood motionless, and remained veiled.

'Spare him,' said the man, who had before addressed Vivaldi; 'he has reasons for wishing to remain unknown, which you cannot conjecture. He is an officer of the Inquisition, and not the person you apprehend.'

'Perhaps I *can* conjecture his reasons,' replied Vivaldi, who, raising his voice, added, 'I appeal to this tribunal, and command you, who stand alone within the circle, you in black garments, to unveil your features!'

Immediately a loud voice issued from the tribunal, and said,

'We command you, in the name of the most holy Inquisition, to reveal yourself!'

The stranger trembled, but, without presuming to hesitate, up-lifted his cowl. Vivaldi's eyes were eagerly fixed upon him; but the action disclosed, not the countenance of the monk! but of an official whom he recollected to have seen once before, though exactly on what occasion he did not now remember.

'This is not my informer!' said Vivaldi, turning from him with deep disappointment, while the stranger dropped his cowl, and the crowd closed upon him. At the assertion of Vivaldi, the members of the tribunal looked upon each other doubtingly, and were silent, till the grand inquisitor, waving his hand, as if to command attention, addressed Vivaldi.

'It appears, then, that you *have* formerly seen the face of your informer!'

'I have already declared so,' replied Vivaldi.

The grand inquisitor demanded when, and where, he had seen it.

'Last night, and in my prison,' answered Vivaldi.

'In your prison!' said the ordinary inquisitor, contemptuously, who had before examined him, 'and in your dreams, too, no doubt!'

'In your prison!' exclaimed several members of the lower tribunal.

'He dreams still!' observed an inquisitor. 'Holy fathers! he abuses your patience, and the frenzy of terror has deluded his credulity. We neglect the moments.'

'We must inquire further into this,' said another inquisitor. 'Here is some deception. If you, Vincentio di Vivaldi, have asserted a falshood—tremble!'

Whether Vivaldi's memory still vibrated with the voice of the monk, or that the tone in which this same word was now pronounced did resemble it, he almost started, when the inquisitor had said *tremble!* and he demanded who spoke then.

'It is ourself,' answered the inquisitor.

After a short conversation among the members of the tribunal, the grand inquisitor gave orders that the centinels, who had watched on the preceding night at the prison door of Vivaldi, should be brought into the hall of justice. The persons, who had been lately summoned into the chamber, were now bidden to withdraw, and all further examination was suspended till the arrival of the centinels; Vivaldi heard only the low voices of the inquisitors, as they conversed privately together, and he remained silent, thoughtful, and amazed.

When the centinels appeared, and were asked who had entered the prison of Vivaldi during the last night, they declared, without hesitation, or confusion, that not any person had passed through the door after the hour when the prisoner had returned from examination, till the following morning, when the guard had carried in the usual allowance of bread and water. In this assertion, they persisted, without the least equivocation, notwithstanding which they were ordered into confinement, till the affair should be cleared up.

The doubts, however, which were admitted, as to the integrity of these men, did not contribute to dissipate those, which had prevailed over the opposite side of the question. On the contrary, the suspicions of the tribunal, augmenting with their perplexity, seemed to fluctuate equally over every point of the subject before them, till, instead of throwing any light upon the truth, they only served to involve the whole in deeper obscurity. More doubtful than before of the honesty of Vivaldi's extraordinary assertions, the grand inquisitor informed him, that if, after further inquiry into this affair, it should appear he had been trifling with the credulity of his judges, he would be severely punished for his audacity; but that, on the other hand, should there be reason to believe that the centinels had failed in their duty, and that some person had entered his prison during the night, the tribunal would proceed in a different manner.

Vivaldi, perceiving that, to be believed, it was necessary he should be more circumstantial, described, with exactness, the person and appearance of the monk, without, however, mentioning the poniard which had been exhibited. A profound silence reigned in the chamber, while he spoke; it seemed a silence not merely of attention, but of astonishment. Vivaldi himself was awed, and, when he had concluded, almost expected to hear the voice of the monk uttering defiance, or threatening vengeance; but all remained hushed, till the inquisitor, who had first examined him, said, in a solemn tone,

'We have listened with attention to what you have delivered, and will give the case a full inquiry. Some points, on which you have touched, excite our amazement, and call for particular regard. Retire whence you came—and sleep this night without fear;—*you will soon know more.*'

Vivaldi was immediately led from the chamber, and, still blindfolded, re-conducted to the prison to which he had supposed it was designed he should return no more. When the veil was withdrawn, he perceived that his guard was changed.

Again left to the silence of his cell, he reviewed all that had passed in the chamber of justice; the questions which had been put to him; the different manners of the inquisitors; the occurrence of the monk's voice; and the similarity, which he had fancied he perceived between it and that of an inquisitor, when the latter pronounced the word *tremble*; but the consideration of all these circumstances did not in any degree relieve him from his perplexity. Sometimes he was inclined to think that the monk was an inquisitor, and the voice had more than once appeared to proceed from the tribunal; but he remembered, also, that, more than once, it had spoken close to his ear, and he knew that a member of this tribunal might not leave his station during the examination of a prisoner, and that, even if he had dared to do so, his singular dress would have pointed him out to notice, and consequently to suspicion, at the moment when Vivaldi had exclaimed, that he heard the voice of his informer.

Vivaldi, however, could not avoid meditating, with surprize,

on the last words which the inquisitor, who had been his chief
examiner, had addressed to him, when he was dismissed from
before the tribunal. These were the more surprizing, because they
were the first from him that had in any degree indicated a wish to
console or quiet the alarm of the prisoner; and Vivaldi even fancied
that they betrayed some fore-knowledge that he would not be disturbed this night by the presence of his awful visitor. He would
entirely have ceased to apprehend, though not to expect, had he
been allowed a light, and any weapon of defence, if, in truth, the
stranger was of a nature to fear a weapon; but, to be thus exposed
to the designs of a mysterious and powerful being, whom he was
conscious of having offended, to sustain such a situation, without
suffering anxiety, required somewhat more than courage, or less
than reason.

CHAPTER VII

—It came o'er my soul as doth the thunder,
While distant yet, with an unexpected burst,
It threats the trembling ear. Now to the trial.
                              CARACTACUS *

IN consequence of what had transpired at the last examination of
Vivaldi, the grand penitentiary Ansaldo, together with the father
Schedoni, were cited to appear before the table of the holy office.

Schedoni was arrested on his way to Rome, whither he was
going privately to make further efforts for the liberation of Vivaldi,
whose release he had found it more difficult to effect, than his
imprisonment; the person upon whose assistance the Confessor
relied in the first instance, having boasted of more influence than
he possessed, or perhaps thought it prudent to exert. Schedoni
had been the more anxious to procure an immediate release for
Vivaldi, lest a report of his situation should reach his family, notwithstanding the precautions, which are usually employed to
throw an impenetrable shroud over the prisoners of this dreadful
tribunal, and bury them for ever from the knowledge of their
friends. Such premature discovery of Vivaldi's circumstances,
Schedoni apprehended might include also a discovery of the persecutor, and draw down upon himself the abhorrence and the
vengeance of a family, whom it was now, more than ever, his wish

and his interest to conciliate. It was still his intention, that the nuptials of Vivaldi and Ellena should be privately solemnized immediately on the release of the prisoner, who, even if he had reason to suspect Schedoni for his late persecutor, would then be interested in concealing his suspicions for ever, and from whom therefore, no evil was to be apprehended.

How little did Vivaldi foresee, that in repeating to the tribunal the stranger's summons of father Schedoni, he was deferring, or, perhaps, wholly preventing his own marriage with Ellena di Rosalba! How little, also, did he apprehend what would be the further consequences of a disclosure, which the peculiar circumstances of his situation had hardly permitted him to withhold, though, could he have understood the probable event of it, he would have braved all the terrors of the tribunal, and death itself, rather than incur the remorse of having promoted it.

The motive for his arrestation was concealed from Schedoni, who had not the remotest suspicion of its nature, but attributed the arrest, to a discovery, which the tribunal had made of his being the accuser of Vivaldi. This disclosure he attributed to his own imprudence, in having stated, as an instance of Vivaldi's contempt for the Catholic faith, that he had insulted a priest while doing penance in the church of the Spirito Santo. But by what art the tribunal had discovered that he was the priest alluded to, and the author of the accusation, Schedoni could by no means conjecture. He was willing to believe that this arrest was only for the purpose of obtaining proof of Vivaldi's guilt; and the Confessor knew that he could so conduct himself in evidence, as in all probability to exculpate the prisoner, from whom, when he should explain himself, no resentment on account of his former conduct was to be apprehended. Yet Schedoni was not perfectly at ease; for it was possible that a knowledge of Vivaldi's situation, and of the author of it, had reached his family, and had produced his own arrest. On this head, however, his fears were not powerful; since, the longer he dwelt upon the subject, the more improbable it appeared that such a disclosure, at least so far as it related to himself, could have been affected.

Vivaldi, from the night of his late examination, was not called upon, till Schedoni and father Ansaldo appeared together in the hall of the tribunal. The two latter had already been separately examined, and Ansaldo had privately stated the particulars of the confession he had received on the vigil of the Santo Marco, in the year 1752, for which disclosure he had received formal absolution.

What had passed at that examination does not appear, but on this his second interrogation, he was required to repeat the subject and the circumstances of the confession. This was probably with a view of observing its effect upon Schedoni and on Vivaldi, which would direct the opinion of the tribunal as to the guilt of the Confessor, and the veracity of the young prisoner.

On this night a very exact inquiry was made, concerning every person, who had obtained admission into the hall of justice; such officials as were not immediately necessary to assist in the cere-monies of the tribunal were excluded, together with every other person belonging to the Inquisition not material to the evidence, or to the judges. When this scrutiny was over, the prisoners were brought in, and their conductors ordered to withdraw. A silence of some moments prevailed in the hall; and, however different might be the reflections of the several prisoners, the degree of anxious expectation was in each, probably, nearly the same.

The grand-vicar having spoken a few words in private to a person on his left hand, an inquisitor rose.

'If any person in this court,' said he, 'is known by the name of father Schedoni, belonging to the Dominican society of the Spirito Santo at Naples, let him appear!'

Schedoni answered to the summons. He came forward with a firm step, and, having crossed himself, and bowed to the tribunal, awaited in silence its commands.

The penitentiary Ansaldo was next called upon. Vivaldi observed that he faultered as he advanced; and that his obeisance to the tribunal was more profound than Schedoni's had been. Vivaldi himself was then summoned; his air was calm and digni-fied, and his countenance expressed the solemn energy of his feel-ings, but nothing of dejection.

Schedoni and Ansaldo were now, for the first time, confronted. Whatever might be the feelings of Schedoni on beholding the penitentiary of the *Santa del Pianto*, he effectually concealed them.

The grand-vicar himself opened the examination, 'You, father Schedoni, of the Spirito Santo,' he said, 'answer and say, whether the person who now stands before you, bearing the title of grand penitentiary of the order of the *Black Penitents*, and presiding over the convent of the *Santa Maria del Pianto* at Naples, is known to you.'

To this requisition Schedoni replied with firmness in the negative.

'You have never, to your knowledge, seen him before this hour?'
'Never!' said Schedoni.

'Let the oath be administered,' added the grand-vicar. Schedoni having accepted it, the same questions were put to Ansaldo concerning the Confessor, when, to the astonishment of Vivaldi and of the greater part of the court, the penitentiary denied all knowledge of Schedoni. His negative was given, however, in a less decisive manner than that of the Confessor, and when the usual oath was offered, Ansaldo declined to accept it.

Vivaldi was next called upon to identify Schedoni: he declared, that the person who was then pointed out to him, he had never known by any other denomination than that of father Schedoni; and that he had always understood him to be a monk of the Spirito Santo; but Vivaldi was at the same time careful to repeat, that he knew nothing further relative to his life.

Schedoni was somewhat surprized at this apparent candour of Vivaldi towards himself, but accustomed to impute an evil motive to all conduct, which he could not clearly comprehend, he did not scruple to believe, that some latent mischief was directed against him in this seemingly honest declaration.

After some further preliminary forms had passed, Ansaldo was ordered to relate the particulars of the confession, which had been made to him on the eve of the Santo Marco. It must be remembered, that this was still what is called in the Inquisition, a *private* examination.

After he had taken the customary oaths to relate neither more nor less than the truth of what had passed before him, Ansaldo's depositions were written down nearly in the following words; to which Vivaldi listened with almost trembling attention, for, besides the curiosity which some previous circumstances had excited respecting them, he believed that his own fate in a great measure depended upon a discovery of the fact to which they led. What, if he had surmised how much! and that the person, whom he had been in some degree instrumental in citing before this tremendous tribunal, was the father of his Ellena di Rosalba!

Ansaldo, having again answered to his name and titles, gave his deposition as follows:

'It was on the eve of the twenty-fifth of April, and in the year 1752, that as I sat, according to my custom, in the confessional of San Marco, I was alarmed by deep groans, which came from the box on my left hand.'

Vivaldi observed, that the date now mentioned agreed with that recorded by the stranger, and he was thus prepared to believe what might follow, and to give his confidence to this extraordinary and unseen personage.

Ansaldo continued, 'I was the more alarmed by these sounds, because I had not been prepared for them; I knew not that any person was in the confessional, nor had even observed any one pass along the aisle—but the duskiness of the hour may account for my having failed to do so; it was after sun-set, and the tapers at the shrine of San Antonio as yet burned feebly in the twilight.'

'Be brief, holy father,' said the inquisitor who had formerly been most active in examining Vivaldi; 'speak closely to the point.'

'The groans would sometimes cease,' resumed Ansaldo, 'and long pauses of silence follow; they were those of a soul in agony, struggling with the consciousness of guilt, yet wanting resolution to confess it. I tried to encourage the penitent, and held forth every hope of mercy and forgiveness which my duty would allow, but for a considerable time without effect;—the enormity of the sin seemed too big for utterance, yet the penitent appeared equally unable to endure the concealment of it. His heart was bursting with the secret, and required the comfort of absolution, even at the price of the severest penance.'

'Facts!' said the inquisitor, 'these are are only surmises.'

'Facts will come full soon!' replied Ansaldo, and bowed his head, 'the mention of them will petrify you, holy fathers! as they did me, though not for the same reasons. While I endeavoured to encourage the penitent, and assured him, that absolution should follow the acknowledgment of his crimes, however heinous those crimes might be, if accompanied by sincere repentance, he more than once began his confession, and abruptly dropt it. Once, indeed, he quitted the confessional; his agitated spirit required liberty; and it was then, as he walked with perturbed steps along the aisle, that I first observed his figure. He was in the habit of a white friar, and, as nearly as I can recollect, was about the stature of him, the father Schedoni, who now stands before me.'

As Ansaldo delivered these words, the attention of the whole tribunal was turned upon Schedoni, who stood unmoved, and with his eyes bent towards the ground.

'His face,' continued the penitentiary, 'I did not see; he was, with good reason, careful to conceal it; other resemblance, there-fore, than the stature, I cannot point out between them. The voice, indeed, the voice of the penitent, I think I shall never forget; I should know it again at any distance of time.'

'Has it not struck your ear, since you came within these walls?' said a member of the tribunal.

'Of that hereafter,' observed the inquisitor, 'you wander from the point, father.'

The vicar-general remarked, that the circumstances just related were important, and ought not to be passed over as irrelevant. The inquisitor submitted to this opinion, but objected that they were not pertinent to the moment; and Ansaldo was again bidden to repeat what he had heard at confession.

'When the stranger returned to the steps of the confessional, he had acquired sufficient resolution to go through with the task he had imposed upon himself, and a thrilling voice spoke through the grate the facts I am about to relate.'

Father Ansaldo paused, and was somewhat agitated; he seemed endeavouring to recollect courage to go through with what he had begun. During this pause, the silence of expectation rapt the court, and the eyes of the tribunal were directed alternately to Ansaldo and Schedoni, who certainly required something more than human firmness to support unmoved the severe scrutiny, and the yet severer suspicions, to which he stood exposed. Whether, however, it was the fortitude of conscious innocence, or the hardihood of atrocious vice, that protected the Confessor, he certainly did not betray any emotion. Vivaldi, who had unceasingly observed him from the commencement of the depositions, felt inclined to believe that he was not the penitent described. Ansaldo, having, at length, recollected himself, proceeded as follows:

'"I have been through life," said the penitent, "the slave of my passions, and they have led me into horrible excesses. I had once a brother!"—He stopped, and deep groans again told the agony of his soul; at length, he added—"That brother had a wife!—Now listen, father, and say, whether guilt like mine may hope for absolution! She was beautiful—I loved her; she was virtuous, and I despaired. You, father," he continued in a frightful tone, "never knew the fury of despair! It overcame or communicated its own force to every other passion of my soul, and I sought to release myself from its tortures by any means. My brother died!"—The penitent paused again,' continued Ansaldo, 'I trembled while I listened; my lips were sealed. At length, I bade him proceed, and he spoke as follows.—"My brother died at a distance from home."—Again the penitent paused, and the silence continued so long, that I thought it proper to inquire of what disorder the brother had expired. "Father, I was his murderer!" said the penitent in a voice which I never can forget; it sunk into my heart.'

Ansaldo appeared affected by the remembrance, and was for a moment silent. At the last words Vivaldi had particularly noticed Schedoni, that he might judge by their effect upon him, whether he was guilty; but he remained in his former attitude, and his eyes were still fixed upon the ground.

'Proceed, father!' said the inquisitor, 'what was your reply to this confession?'

'I was silent,' said Ansaldo; 'but at length I bade the penitent go on. "I contrived" said he, "that my brother should die at a distance from home, and I so conducted the affair, that his widow never suspected the cause of his death. It was not till long after the usual time of mourning had expired, that I ventured to solicit her hand: but she had not yet forgotten my brother, and she rejected me. My passion would no longer be trifled with. I caused her to be carried from her house, and she was afterwards willing to retrieve her honour by the marriage vow. I had sacrificed my conscience, without having found happiness;——she did not even condescend to conceal her disdain. Mortified, exasperated by her conduct, I begun to suspect that some other emotion than resentment occasioned this disdain; and last of all jealousy—jealousy came to crown my misery—to light up all my passions into madness!"'

'The penitent,' added Ansaldo, 'appeared by the manner in which he uttered this, to be nearly frantic at the moment, and convulsive sobs soon stifled his words. When he resumed his confession, he said, "I soon found an object for my jealousy. Among the few persons, who visited us in the retirement of our country residence, was a gentleman, who, I fancied, loved my wife; I fancied too, that, whenever he appeared, an air of particular satisfaction was visible on her countenance. She seemed to have pleasure in conversing with, and shewing him distinction. I even sometimes thought, she had pride in displaying to me the preference she entertained for him, and that an air of triumph, and even of scorn, was addressed to me, whenever she mentioned his name. Perhaps, I mistook resentment for love, and she only wished to punish me, by exciting my jealousy. Fatal error! she punished herself also!"'

'Be less circumstantial, father,' said the inquisitor.

Ansaldo bowed his head, and continued. '"One evening," continued the penitent, "that I returned home unexpectedly, I was told that a visitor was with my wife! As I approached the apartment where they sat, I heard the voice of Sacchi; it seemed mournful and supplicating. I stopped to listen, and distinguished enough to fire me with vengeance. I restrained myself, however, so far as to step softly to a lattice that opened from the passage, and overlooked the apartment. The traitor was on his knee before her. Whether she had heard my step, or observed my face, through the high lattice, or that she resented his conduct, I know not, but she rose immediately from her chair. I did not pause to question her motive; but, seizing my stiletto, I rushed into the room, with intent to strike it to the villain's heart. The supposed assassin of my honour escaped into the garden, and was heard of no more."— But your wife? said I. "Her bosom received the poniard!" replied the penitent.'

Ansaldo's voice faultered, as he repeated this part of the confession, and he was utterly unable to proceed. The tribunal, observing his condition, allowed him a chair, and, after a struggle of some moments, he added, 'Think, holy fathers, O think! what must have been my feelings at that instant! I was myself the lover of the woman, whom he confessed himself to have murdered.'

'Was she innocent?' said a voice; and Vivaldi, whose attention had latterly been fixed upon Ansaldo, now, on looking at Schedoni, perceived that it was he who had spoken. At the sound of his voice, the penitentiary turned instantly towards him. There was a pause of general silence, during which Ansaldo's eyes were earnestly fixed upon the accused. At length, he spoke, 'She was innocent!' He replied, with solemn emphasis, 'She was most virtuous!'

Schedoni had shrunk back within himself; he asked no further. A murmur ran through the tribunal, which rose by degrees, till it broke forth into audible conversation; at length, the secretary was directed to note the question of Schedoni.

'Was that the voice of the penitent, which you have just heard?' demanded the inquisitor of Ansaldo. 'Remember, you have said that you should know it again!'

'I think it was,' replied Ansaldo; 'but I cannot swear to that.'

'What infirmity of judgment is this!' said the same inquisitor, who himself was seldom troubled with the modesty of doubt, upon any subject. Ansaldo was bidden to resume the narrative.

'On this discovery of the murderer,' said the penitentiary, 'I quitted the confessional, and my senses forsook me before I could deliver orders for the detection of the assassin. When I recovered, it was too late; he had escaped! From that hour to the present, I have never seen him, nor dare I affirm that the person now before me is he.'

The inquisitor was about to speak, but the grand-vicar waved his hand, as a signal for attention, and, addressing Ansaldo, said, 'Although you may be unacquainted with Schedoni, the monk of the Spirito Santo, reverend father, can you not recollect the person of the Count di Bruno, your former friend?'

Ansaldo again looked at Schedoni, with a scrutinizing eye; he fixed it long; but the countenance of Schedoni suffered no change.

'No!' said the penitentiary, at length, 'I dare not take upon me to assert, that this is the Count di Bruno. If it is he, years have wrought deeply on his features. That the penitent was the Count di Bruno I have proof; he mentioned my name as his visitor, and particular circumstances known only to the Count and myself; but that father Schedoni was the penitent, I repeat it, I dare not affirm.'

'But that dare I!' said another voice; and Vivaldi, turning towards it, beheld the mysterious stranger advancing, his cowl now thrown back, and an air of menace overspreading every terrific feature. Schedoni, in the instant that he perceived him, seemed agitated; his countenance, for the first time, suffered some change.

The tribunal was profoundly silent, but surprize, and a kind of restless expectation, marked every brow. Vivaldi was about to exclaim, 'That is my informer!' when the voice of the stranger checked him.

'Dost thou know me?' said he, sternly, to Schedoni, and his attitude became fixed.

Schedoni gave no reply.

'Dost thou know me?' repeated his accuser, in a steady solemn voice.

'Know thee!' uttered Schedoni, faintly.

'Dost thou know this?' cried the stranger, raising his voice, as he drew from his garment what appeared to be a dagger. 'Dost thou know these indelible stains?' said he, lifting the poniard, and, with an outstretched arm, pointing it towards Schedoni.

The Confessor turned away his face; it seemed as if his heart sickened.

'With this dagger was thy brother slain!' said the terrible stranger. 'Shall I declare myself?'

Schedoni's courage forsook him, and he sunk against a pillar of the hall for support.

The consternation was now general; the extraordinary appearance and conduct of the stranger seemed to strike the greater part of the tribunal, a tribunal of the inquisition itself! with dismay. Several of the members rose from their seats; others called aloud for the officials, who kept guard at the doors of the hall, and inquired who had admitted the stranger, while the vicar-general and a few inquisitors conversed privately together, during which they frequently looked at the stranger and at Schedoni, as if they were the subjects of the discourse. Meanwhile the monk remained with the dagger in his grasp, and his eyes fixed on the Confessor, whose face was still averted, and who yet supported himself against the pillar.

At length, the vicar-general called upon the members who had arisen to return to their seats, and ordered that the officials should withdraw to their posts.

'Holy brethren!' said the vicar, 'we recommend to you, at this important hour, silence and deliberation. Let the examination of the accused proceed; and hereafter let us inquire as to the admittance of the accuser. For the present, suffer him also to have hearing, and the father Schedoni to reply.'

'We suffer him!' answered the tribunal, and bowed their heads.

Vivaldi, who, during the tumult, had ineffectually endeavoured to make himself heard, now profited by the pause which followed the assent of the inquisitors, to claim attention: but the instant he spoke several members impatiently bade that the examination should proceed, and the grand-vicar was again obliged to command silence, before the request of Vivaldi could be understood. Permission to speak being granted him, 'That person,' said he, pointing to the stranger, 'is the same who visited me in my prison; and the dagger the same he now displays! It was he, who commanded me to summon the penitentiary Ansaldo, and the father Schedoni. I have acquitted myself, and have nothing further to do in this struggle.'

The tribunal was again agitated, and the murmurs of private conversation again prevailed. Meanwhile Schedoni appeared to have recovered some degree of self-command; he raised himself, and, bowing to the tribunal, seemed preparing to speak; but waited till the confusion of sound that filled the hall should subside. At length he could be heard, and, addressing the tribunal, he said,

'Holy fathers! the stranger who is now before you is an impostor! I will prove that my accuser was once my friend;—you may perceive how much the discovery of his perfidy affects me. The charge he brings is most false and malicious!'

'*Once* thy friend!' replied the stranger, with peculiar emphasis, 'and what has made me thy enemy! View these spots,' he continued, pointing to the blade of the poniard, 'are they also false and malicious? are they not, on the contrary, reflected on thy conscience?'

'I know them not,' replied Schedoni, 'my conscience is unstained.'

'A brother's blood *has* stained it!' said the stranger, in a hollow voice.

Vivaldi, whose attention was now fixed upon Schedoni, observed a livid hue overspread his complexion, and that his eyes were averted from this extraordinary person with horror: the spectre of his deceased brother could scarcely have called forth a stronger expression. It was not immediately that he could command his voice; when he could, he again appealed to the tribunal.

'Holy fathers!' said he, 'suffer me to defend myself.'

'Holy fathers!' said the accuser, with solemnity, 'hear! hear what I shall unfold!'

Schedoni, who seemed to speak by a strong effort only, again addressed the inquisitors; 'I will prove,' said he, 'that this evidence is not of a nature to be trusted.'

'I will bring *such* proof to the contrary!' said the monk. 'And here,' pointing to Ansaldo, 'is sufficient testimony that the Count di Bruno did confess himself guilty of murder.'

The court commanded silence, and upon the appeal of the stranger to Ansaldo, the penitentiary was asked whether he knew him. He replied, that he did not.

'Recollect yourself,' said the grand inquisitor, 'it is of the utmost consequence that you should be correct on this point.'

The penitentiary observed the stranger with deep attention, and then repeated his assertion.

'Have you never seen him before?' said an inquisitor.

'Never, to my knowledge!' replied Ansaldo.

The inquisitors looked upon each other in silence.

'He speaks the truth,' said the stranger.

This extraordinary fact did not fail to strike the tribunal, and to astonish Vivaldi. Since the accuser confirmed it, Vivaldi was at a loss to understand the means by which he could have become acquainted with the guilt of Schedoni, who, it was not to be supposed, would have acknowledged crimes of such magnitude as those contained in the accusation, to any person, except, indeed, to his confessor, and this confessor, it appeared, was so far from having betrayed his trust to the accuser, that he did not even know him. Vivaldi was no less perplexed as to what would be the nature of the testimony with which the accuser designed to support his charges: but the pause of general amazement, which had permitted Vivaldi these considerations, was now at an end; the tribunal resumed the examination, and the grand inquisitor called aloud,

'You, Vincentio di Vivaldi, answer with exactness to the questions that shall be put to you.'

He was then asked some questions relative to the person, who had visited him in prison. In his answers, Vivaldi was clear and concise, constantly affirming, that the stranger was the same, who now accused Schedoni.

When the accuser was interrogated, he acknowledged, without hesitation, that Vivaldi had spoken the truth. He was then asked his motive for that extraordinary visit.

'It was,' replied the monk, 'that a murderer might be brought to justice.'

'This,' observed the grand inquisitor, 'might have been accomplished by fair and open accusation. If you had known the charge to be just, it is probable that you would have appealed directly to this tribunal, instead of endeavouring insidiously to obtain an influence over the mind of a prisoner, and urging him to become the instrument of bringing the accused to punishment.'

'Yet I have not shrunk from discovery,' observed the stranger, calmly; 'I have voluntarily appeared.'

At these words, Schedoni seemed again much agitated, and even drew his hood over his eyes.

'That is just,' said the grand inquisitor, addressing the stranger: 'but you have neither declared your name, or whence you come!'

To this remark the monk made no reply; but Schedoni, with reviving spirit, urged the circumstance, in evidence of the malignity and falshood of the accuser.

'Wilt thou compel me to reveal my proof?' said the stranger: 'Darest thou to do so?'

'Why should I fear thee?' answered Schedoni.

'Ask thy conscience!' said the stranger, with a terrible frown.

The tribunal again suspended the examination, and consulted in private together.

To the last exhortation of the monk, Schedoni was silent. Vivaldi observed, that during this short dialogue, the Confessor had never once turned his eyes towards the stranger, but apparently avoided him, as an object too affecting to be looked upon. He judged, from this circumstance, and from some other appearances in his conduct, that Schedoni was guilty; yet the consciousness of guilt alone did not perfectly account, he thought, for the strong emotion, with which he avoided the sight of his accuser—unless, indeed, he knew that accuser to have been, not only an accomplice in his crime, but the actual assassin. In this case, it appeared natural even for the stern and subtle Schedoni to betray his horror, on beholding the person of the murderer, with the very instrument of crime in his grasp. On the other hand, Vivaldi could not but perceive it to be highly improbable, that the very man who had really committed the deed should come voluntarily into a court of justice, for the purpose of accusing his employer; that he should dare publicly to accuse him, whose guilt, however enormous, was not more so than his own.

The extraordinary manner, also, in which the accuser had proceeded in the commencement of the affair, engaged Vivaldi's consideration; his apparent reluctance to be seen in this process, and the artful and mysterious plan by which he had caused Schedoni to be summoned before the tribunal, and had endeavoured that he should be there accused by Ansaldo, indicated, at least to Vivaldi's apprehension, the fearfulness of guilt, and, still more, that malice, and a thirst of vengeance, had instigated his conduct in the prosecution. If the stranger had been actuated only by a love of justice, it appeared that he would not have proceeded toward it in a way thus dark and circuitous, but have sought it by the usual process, and have produced the proofs, which he even now asserted he possessed, of Schedoni's crimes. In addition to the circumstances, which seemed to strengthen a supposition of the guiltlessness of Schedoni, was that of the accuser's avoiding to acknowledge who he was, and whence he came. But Vivaldi paused again upon this point; it appeared to be inexplicable, and he could not imagine why the accuser had adopted a style of secrecy, which, if he persisted in it, must probably defeat the very purpose of the accusation; for Vivaldi did not believe that the tribunal would condemn a prisoner upon the testimony of a person who, when called upon, should publicly refuse to reveal himself, even to them. Yet the accuser must certainly have considered this circumstance before he ventured into court; notwithstanding which, he had appeared!

These reflections led Vivaldi to various conjectures relative to the visit he had himself received from the monk, the dream that had preceded it, the extraordinary means by which he had obtained admittance to the prison, the declaration of the centinels, that not any person had passed the door, and many other unaccountable particulars; and, while Vivaldi now looked upon the wild physiognomy of the stranger, he almost fancied, as he had formerly done, that he beheld something not of this earth.

'I have heard of the spirit of the murdered,' said he, to himself—'restless for justice, becoming visible in our world——' But Vivaldi checked the imperfect thought, and, though his imagination inclined him to the marvellous, and to admit ideas which, filling and expanding all the faculties of the soul, produce feelings that partake of the sublime, he now resisted the propensity, and dismissed, as absurd, a supposition, which had begun to thrill his every nerve with horror. He awaited, however, the result of the examination, and what might be the further conduct of the stranger, with intense expectation.

When the tribunal had, at length, finally determined on the method of their proceedings, Schedoni was first called upon, and examined as to his knowledge of the accuser. It was the same inquisitor who had formerly interrogated Vivaldi, that now spoke. 'You, father Schedoni, a monk of the Spirito Santo convent, at Naples, otherwise Ferando Count di Bruno, answer to the questions which shall be put to you. Do you know the name of this man who now appears as your accuser?'

'I answer not to the title of Count di Bruno,' replied the Confessor, 'but I will declare that I know this man. His name is Nicola di Zampari.'

'What is his condition?'

'He is a monk of the Dominican convent of the Spirito Santo,' replied Schedoni. 'Of his family I know little.'

'Where have you seen him?'

'In the city of Naples, where he has resided, during some years, beneath the same roof with me, when I was of the convent of San Angiolo, and since that time, in the Spirito Santo.'

'You have been a resident at the San Angiolo?' said the inquisitor.

'I have,' replied Schedoni; 'and it was there that we first lived together in the confidence of friendship.'

'You now perceive how ill placed was that confidence,' said the inquisitor, 'and repent, no doubt, of your imprudence?'

The wary Schedoni was not entrapped by this observation.

'I must lament a discovery of ingratitude,' he replied, calmly, 'but the subjects of my confidence were too pure to give occasion for repentance.'

'This Nicola di Zampari was ungrateful, then? You had rendered him services?' said the inquisitor.

'The cause of his enmity I can well explain,' observed Schedoni, evading, for the present, the question.

'Explain,' said the stranger, solemnly.

Schedoni hesitated; some sudden consideration seemed to occasion him perplexity.

'I call upon you, in the name of your deceased brother,' said the accuser, 'to reveal the cause of my enmity!'

Vivaldi, struck by the tone in which the stranger spoke this, turned his eyes upon him, but knew not how to interpret the emotion visible on his countenance.

The inquisitor commanded Schedoni to explain himself; the latter could not immediately reply, but, when he recovered a self-command, he added,

'I promised this accuser, this Nicola di Zampari, to assist his preferment with what little interest I possessed; it was but little. Some succeeding circumstances encouraged me to believe that I could more than fulfil my promise. His hopes were elevated, and, in the fulness of expectation—he was disappointed, for I was myself deceived, by the person in whom I had trusted. To the disappointment of a choleric man, I am to attribute this unjust accusation.'

Schedoni paused, and an air of dissatisfaction and anxiety appeared upon his features. His accuser remained silent, but a malicious smile announced his triumph.

'You must declare, also, the services,' said the inquisitor, 'which merited the reward you promised.'

'Those services were inestimable to me,' resumed Schedoni, after a momentary hesitation; 'though they cost di Zampari little: they were the consolations of sympathy, the intelligence of friendship, which he administered, and which gratitude told me never could be repaid.'

'Of sympathy! of friendship!' said the grand-vicar. 'Are we to believe that a man, who brings false accusation of so dreadful a nature as the one now before us, is capable of bestowing the consolations of sympathy, and of friendship? You must either acknowledge, that services of a less disinterested nature won your promises of reward; or we must conclude that your accuser's charge is just. Your assertions are inconsistent, and your explanation too trivial, to deceive for a moment.'

'I have declared the truth,' said Schedoni, haughtily.

'In which instance?' asked the inquisitor; 'for your assertions contradict each other!'

Schedoni was silent. Vivaldi could not judge whether the pride which occasioned his silence was that of innocence, or of remorse.

'It appears, from your own testimony,' said the inquisitor, 'that the ingratitude was your's, not your accuser's, since he consoled you with kindness, which you have never returned him!—Have you any thing further to say?'

Schedoni was still silent.

'This, then, is your only explanation?' added the inquisitor.

Schedoni bowed his head. The inquisitor then, addressing the accuser, demanded what he had to reply.

'I have nothing to reply,' said the stranger, with malicious triumph; 'the accused has replied for me!'

'We are to conclude, then, that he has spoken truth, when he asserted you to be a monk of the Spirito Santo, at Naples?' said the inquisitor.

'You, holy father,' said the stranger, gravely, appealing to the inquisitor, 'can answer for me, whether I am.'

Vivaldi listened with emotion.

The inquisitor rose from his chair, and with solemnity replied, 'I answer, then, that you are not a monk of Naples.'

'By that reply,' said the vicar-general, in a low voice, to the inquisitor, 'I perceive you think father Schedoni is guilty.'

The rejoinder of the inquisitor was delivered in so low a tone, that Vivaldi could not understand it. He was perplexed to interpret the answer given to the appeal of the stranger. He thought that the inquisitor would not have ventured an assertion thus positive, if his opinion had been drawn from inference only; and that he should know the accuser, while he was conducting himself towards him as a stranger, amazed Vivaldi, no less than if he had understood the character of an inquisitor to be as artless as his own. On the other hand, he had so frequently seen the stranger at Paluzzi, and in the habit of a monk, that he could hardly question the assertion of Schedoni, as to his identity.

The inquisitor, addressing Schedoni, said, 'Your evidence we know to be in part erroneous; your accuser is not a monk of Naples, but a servant of the most holy Inquisition. Judging, from this part of your evidence, we must suspect the whole.'

'A servant of the Inquisition!' exclaimed Schedoni, with unaffected surprise. 'Reverend father! your assertion astonishes me! You are deceived, however strange it may appear, trust me, you are deceived! You doubt the credit of my word; I, therefore, will assert no more. But inquire of Signor Vivaldi; ask him, whether he has not often, and lately, seen my accuser at Naples, and in the habit of a monk.'

'I have seen him at the ruins of Paluzzi, near Naples, and in the ecclesiastical dress,' replied Vivaldi, without waiting for the regular question, 'and under circumstances no less extraordinary than those which have attended him here. But, in return for this frank acknowledgment, I require of you, father Schedoni, to answer some questions which I shall venture to suggest to the tribunal—By what means were you informed that I have often seen the stranger at Paluzzi—and was you interested or not in his mysterious conduct towards me there?'

To these questions, though formally delivered from the tribunal, Schedoni did not deign to reply.

'It appears, then,' said the vicar-general, 'that the accuser and the accused were once accomplices.'

The inquisitor objected, that this did not certainly appear; and that, on the contrary, Schedoni seemed to have given his last questions in despair; an observation which Vivaldi thought extra-ordinary from an inquisitor.

'Be it *accomplices*, if it so please you,' said Schedoni, bowing to the grand-vicar, without noticing the inquisitor: 'you may call us accomplices, but I say, that we were *friends*. Since it is necessary to my own peace, that I should more fully explain some circum-stances attending our intimacy, I will own that my accuser was occasionally my agent, and assisted in preserving the dignity of an illustrious family at Naples, the family of the Vivaldi. And there, holy father,' added Schedoni, pointing to Vincentio, 'is the son of that ancient house, for whom I have attempted so much!'

Vivaldi was almost overwhelmed by this confession of Schedoni, though he had already suspected a part of the truth. In the stranger he believed he saw the slanderer of Ellena, the base instrument of the Marchesa's policy, and of Schedoni's ambition; and the whole of his conduct at Paluzzi, at least, seemed now intelligible. In Schedoni he beheld his secret accuser, and the inexorable enemy whom he believed to have occasioned the imprisonment of Ellena. At this latter consideration, all circumspection, all prudence for-sook him: he declared, with energy, that, from what Schedoni had just acknowledged to be his conduct, he knew him for his secret accuser, and the accuser, also, of Ellena di Rosalba; and he called upon the tribunal to examine into the Confessor's motives for the accusation, and afterwards to give hearing to what he would him-self unfold.

To this, the grand-vicar replied, that Vivaldi's appeal would be taken into consideration; and he then ordered that the present business should proceed.

The inquisitor, addressing Schedoni, said, 'The disinterested nature of your friendship is now sufficiently explained, and the degree of credit, which is due to your late assertions understood. Of you we ask no more, but turn to father Nicola di Zampari, and demand what he has to say in support of his accusation. What are your proofs, Nicola di Zampari, that he who calls himself father Schedoni is Ferando Count di Bruno; and that he has been guilty of murder, the murder of his brother, and of his wife? Answer to our charge!'

'To your first question,' said the monk, 'I reply that he has himself acknowledged to me, on an occasion, which it is not necessary to mention, that he was the Count di Bruno; to the last, I produce the poniard which I received, with the dying confession of the assassin whom he employed.'

'Still, these are not proofs, but assertions,' observed the vicar-general, 'and the first forbids our confidence in the second.— If, as you declare, Schedoni himself acknowledged to you that he was Count di Bruno, you must have been to him the intimate friend he has declared you were, or he would not have confided to you a secret so dangerous to himself. And, if you were that friend, what confidence ought we to give to your assertions respecting the dagger? since, whether your accusations be true or false, you prove yourself guilty of treachery in bringing them forward at all.'

Vivaldi was surprized to hear such candour from an inquisitor.

'Here is my proof,' said the stranger, who now produced a paper, containing what he asserted to be the dying confession of the assassin. It was signed by a priest of Rome, as well as by himself, and appeared from the date to have been given only a very few weeks before. The priest, he said, was living, and might be summoned. The tribunal issued an order for the apprehension of this priest, and that he should be brought to give evidence on the following evening; after which, the business of this night proceeded, without further interruption, towards its conclusion.

The vicar-general spoke again, 'Nicola di Zampari, I call upon you to say, why, if your proof of Schedoni's guilt is so clear, as the confession of the assassin himself must make it,—why you thought it necessary to summon father Ansaldo to attest the criminality of the Count di Bruno? The dying confession of the assassin is certainly of more weight than any other evidence.'

'I summoned the father Ansaldo,' replied the stranger, 'as a means of proving that Schedoni is the Count di Bruno. The confession of the assassin sufficiently proves the Count to have been the instigator of the murder, but not that Schedoni is the Count.'

'But that is more than I will engage to prove,' replied Ansaldo, 'I know it was the Count di Bruno who confessed to me, but I do not know that the father Schedoni, who is now before me, was the person who so confessed.'

'Conscientiously observed!' said the vicar-general, interrupting the stranger, who was about to reply, 'but you, Nicola di Zampari, have not on this head been sufficiently explicit.—How do you know that Schedoni is the penitent who confessed to Ansaldo on the vigil of San Marco?'

'Reverend father, that is the point I was about to explain,' replied the monk. 'I myself accompanied Schedoni, on the eve of San Marco, to the church of the *Santa Maria del Pianto*, at the very hour when the confession is said to have been made. Schedoni told me he was going to confession; and, when I observed to him his unusual agitation, his behaviour implied a consciousness of extraordinary guilt; he even betrayed it by some words, which he dropt in the confusion of his mind. I parted with him at the gates of the church. He was then of an order of white friars, and habited as father Ansaldo has described. Within a few weeks after this confession, he left his convent, for what reason I never could learn, though I have often surmised it, and came to reside at the Spirito Santo, whither I also had removed.'

'Here is no proof,' said the vicar-general, 'other friars of that order might confess at the same hour, in the same church.'

'But here is strong presumption for proof,' observed the inquisitor. 'Holy father, we must judge from probabilities, as well as from proof.'

'But probabilities themselves,' replied the vicar-general, 'are strongly against the evidence of a man, who would betray another by means of words dropped in the unguarded moments of powerful emotion.'

'Are these the sentiments of an inquisitor!' said Vivaldi to himself, 'can such glorious candour appear amidst the tribunal of an Inquisition!' Tears fell fast on Vivaldi's cheek while he gazed upon this just judge, whose candour, had it been exerted in his cause, could not have excited more powerful sensations of esteem and admiration. 'An inquisitor!' he repeated to himself, 'an inquisitor!'

The inferior inquisitor, however, was so far from possessing any congeniality of character with his superior, that he was evidently disappointed by the appearance of liberality, which the vicar-general discovered, and immediately said, 'Has the accuser any thing further to urge in evidence, that the father Schedoni is the penitent, who confessed to the penitentiary Ansaldo?'

'I have,' replied the monk, with asperity. 'When I had left Schedoni in the church, I lingered without the walls for his return, according to appointment. But he appeared considerably sooner than I expected, and in a state of disorder, such as I had never witnessed in him before. In an instant he passed me, nor could my voice arrest his progress. Confusion seemed to reign within the church and the convent, and, when I would have entered, for the purpose of inquiring the occasion of it, the gates were suddenly closed, and all entrance forbidden. It has since appeared, that the monks were then searching for the penitent. A rumour afterwards reached me, that a confession had caused this disturbance; that the father-confessor, who happened at that time to be the grand penitentiary Ansaldo, had left the chair in horror of what had been divulged from the grate, and had judged it necessary that a search should be made for the penitent, who was a white friar. This report, reverend fathers, excited general attention; with me it did more—for I thought I knew the penitent. When on the following day, I questioned Schedoni as to his sudden departure from the church of the Black Penitents, his answers were dark, but emphatic, and he extorted from me a promise, thoughtless that I was! never to disclose his visit of the preceding evening to the *Santa del Pianto*. I then certainly discovered who was the penitent.'

'Did he, then, confess to you also?' said the vicar-general.

'No father. I understood him to be the penitent to whom the report alluded, but I had no suspicion of the nature of his crimes, till the assassin began his confession, the conclusion of which clearly explained the subject of Schedoni's; it explained also his motive for endeavouring ever after to attach me to his interest.'

'You have now,' said the vicar-general, 'you have now, confessed yourself a member of the convent of the Spirito Santo at Naples, and an intimate of the father Schedoni; one whom for many years he has endeavoured to attach to him. Not an hour has passed since you denied all this; the negative to the latter circumstance was given, it is true, by implication only; but to the first a direct and absolute denial was pronounced!'

'I denied that I *am* a monk of Naples,' replied the accuser, 'and I appealed to the Inquisitor for the truth of my denial.

He has said, that I am now a servant of the most holy Inquisition.'

The vicar-general, with some surprise, looked at the inquisitor for explanation; other members of the tribunal did the same; the rest appeared to understand more than they had thought it necessary to avow. The inquisitor, who had been called upon, rose, and replied,

'Nicola di Zampari has spoken the truth. It is not many weeks since he entered the holy office. A certificate from his convent at Naples bears testimony to the truth of what I advance, and procured him admittance here.'

'It is extraordinary that you should not have disclosed your knowledge of this person before!' said the vicar-general.

'Holy father, I had reasons,' replied the inquisitor, 'you will recollect that the accused was present, and you will understand them.'

'I comprehend you,' said the vicar-general, 'but I do neither approve of, nor perceive any necessity for your countenancing the subterfuge of this Nicola di Zampari, relative to his identity. But more of this in private.'

'I will explain all there,' answered the inquisitor.

'It appears then,' resumed the vicar-general, speaking aloud, 'that this Nicola di Zampari was formerly the friend and confidant of father Schedoni, whom he now accuses. The accusation is evidently malicious; whether it be also false, remains to be decided. A material question naturally arises out of the subject—Why was not the accusation brought forward before this period?'

The monk's visage brightened with the satisfaction of anticipated triumph, and he immediately replied,

'Most holy father! as soon as I ascertained the crime, I prepared to prosecute the perpetrator of it. A short period only has elapsed since the assassin gave his confession. In this interval I discovered, in these prisons, Signor Vivaldi, and immediately comprehended by whose means he was confined. I knew enough both of the accuser and accused, to understand which of these was innocent, and had then a double motive for causing Schedoni to be summoned;—I wished equally to deliver the innocent and punish the criminal. The question as to the motive for my becoming the enemy of him, who was once my friend, is already answered; —it was a sense of justice, not a suggestion of malice.'

The grand-vicar smiled, but asked no further; and this long examination concluded with committing Schedoni again into close custody, till full evidence should be obtained of his guilt, or his innocence should appear. Respecting the manner of his wife's death, there was yet no other evidence than that which was asserted to be his own confession, which, though perhaps sufficient to condemn a criminal before the tribunal of the Inquisition, was not enough to satisfy the present vicar-general, who gave direction that means might be employed towards obtaining proof of each article of the accusation; in order that, should Schedoni be acquitted of the charge of having murdered his brother, documents might appear for prosecuting him respecting the death of his wife.

Schedoni, when he withdrew from the hall, bowed respectfully to the tribunal, and whether, notwithstanding late appearances, he were innocent, or that subtlety enabled him to reassume his usual address, it is certain his manner no longer betrayed any symptom of conscious guilt. His countenance was firm and even tranquil, and his air dignified. Vivaldi, who, during the greater part of this examination, had been convinced of his criminality, now only doubted his innocence. Vivaldi was himself reconducted to his prison, and the sitting of the tribunal was dissolved.

CHAPTER VIII

The time shall come when Glo'ster's heart shall bleed
In life's last hours with horrors of the deed;
When dreary visions shall at last present
Thy vengeful image. ——

                                          COLLINS*

WHEN the night of Schedoni's trial arrived, Vivaldi was again summoned to the hall of the tribunal. Every circumstance was now arranged according to the full ceremonies of the place; the members of the tribunal were more numerous than formerly at the examinations; the chief inquisitors wore habits of a fashion different from those, which before distinguished them, and their turbans, of a singular form and larger size, seemed to give an air of sterner ferocity to their features. The hall, as usual, was hung with black, and every person who appeared there, whether inquisitor, official, witness or prisoner, was habited in the same dismal hue, which, together with the kind of light diffused through the chamber from lamps hung high in the vaulted roof, and from torches held by parties of officials who kept watch at the several doors, and in different parts of this immense hall, gave a character of gloomy solemnity to the assembly, which was almost horrific.

Vivaldi was situated in a place, whence he beheld the whole of the tribunal, and could distinguish whatever was passing in the hall. The countenance of every member was now fully displayed to him by the torchmen, who, arranged at the steps of the platform on which the three chief inquisitors were elevated, extended in a semicircle on either hand of the place occupied by the inferior members. The red glare, which the torches threw upon the latter, certainly did not soften the expression of faces, for the most part sculptured by passions of dark malignity, or fiercer cruelty; and Vivaldi could not bear even to examine them long.

Before the bar of the tribunal, he distinguished Schedoni, and little did he suspect, that in him, a criminal brought thither to answer for the guilt of murder—the murder of a brother, and of a wife, he beheld the parent of Ellena di Rosalba!

Near Schedoni was seated the penitentiary Ansaldo; the Roman priest, who was to be a principal witness, and father Nicola di Zampari, upon whom Vivaldi could not even now look without experiencing somewhat of the awe, which had prevailed over his mind when he was inclined to consider the stranger, rather as the vision of another world, than as a being of this. The same wild and indescribable character still distinguished his air, his every look and movement, and Vivaldi could not but believe that something in the highest degree extraordinary would yet be discovered concerning him.

The witnesses being called over, Vivaldi understood that he was placed among them, though he had only repeated the words which father Nicola had spoken, and which, since Nicola himself was present as a witness against Schedoni, he did not perceive could be in the least material on the trial.

When Vivaldi had, in his turn, answered to his name, a voice, bursting forth from a distant part of the hall, exclaimed, 'It is my master! my *dear* master!' and on directing his eyes whence it came, he perceived the faithful Paulo struggling with his guard. Vivaldi called to him to be patient, and to forbear resistance, an exhortation, however, which served only to increase the efforts of the servant for liberty, and in the next instant he broke from the grasp of the officials, and, darting towards Vivaldi, fell at his feet, sobbing, and clasping his knees, and exclaiming, 'O my master! my master! have I found you at last?'

Vivaldi, as much affected by this meeting as Paulo, could not immediately speak. He would, however, have raised and embraced his affectionate servant, but Paulo, still clinging to his knees and sobbing, was so much agitated that he scarcely understood any thing said to him, and to the kind assurances and gentle remonstrances of Vivaldi, constantly replied as if to the officers, whom he fancied to be forcing him away.

'Remember your situation, Paulo,' said Vivaldi, 'consider mine also, and be governed by prudence.'

'You shall not force me hence!' cried Paulo, 'you can take my life only once; if I must die, it shall be here.'

'Recollect yourself, Paulo, and be composed. Your life, I trust, is in no danger.'

Paulo looked up, and again bursting into a passion of tears, repeated, 'O! my master! my master! where have you been all this while? are you indeed alive? I thought I never should see you again! I have dreamt an hundred times that you were dead and buried! and I wished to be dead and buried with you. I thought you was gone out of this world into the next. I feared you was gone to heaven, and so believed we should never meet again. But now, I see you once more, and know that you live! O! my master! my master!'

The officers who had followed Paulo, now endeavouring to withdraw him, he became more outrageous.

'Do your worst at once,' said he; 'but you shall find tough work of it, if you try to force me from hence, so you had better be contented with killing me here.'

The incensed officials were laying violent hands upon him, when Vivaldi interposed. 'I entreat, I supplicate you,' said he, 'that you will suffer him to remain near me.'

'It is impossible,' replied an officer, 'we dare not.'

'I will promise that he shall not even speak to me, if you will only allow him to be near,' added Vivaldi.

'Not speak to you, master!' exclaimed Paulo, 'but I will stay by you, and speak to you as long as I like, till my last gasp. Let them do their worst at once; I defy them all, and all the devils of inquisitors at their heels too, to force me away. I can die but once, and they ought to be satisfied with that,—so what is there to be afraid of? Not speak!'

'He knows not what he says,' said Vivaldi to the officials, while he endeavoured to silence Paulo with his hand, 'I am certain that he will submit to whatever I shall require of him, and will be entirely silent; or, if he does speak now and then, it shall be only in a whisper.'

'A whisper!' said an officer sneeringly, 'do you suppose Signor, that any person is suffered to speak in a whisper here?'

'A whisper!' shouted Paulo, 'I scorn to speak in a whisper. I will speak so loud, that every word I say shall ring in the ears of all those old black devils on the benches yonder; aye, and those on that mountebank stage too, that sit there looking so grim and angry as if they longed to tear us in pieces. They'——

'Silence,' said Vivaldi with emphasis, 'Paulo, I command you to be silent.'

'They shall know a bit of my mind,' continued Paulo, without noticing Vivaldi, 'I will tell them what they have to expect for all their cruel usage of my poor master. Where do they expect to go when they die, I wonder? Though for that matter, they cannot go to a worse place than they are in already, and I suppose it is, knowing that, which makes them not afraid of being ever so wicked. They shall hear a little plain truth, for once in their lives, however, they shall hear'——

During the whole of this harangue, Vivaldi, alarmed for the consequence of such imprudent, though honest indignation, had been using all possible effort to silence him, and was the more alarmed, since the officials made no further attempt to interrupt Paulo, a forbearance, which Vivaldi attributed to malignity, and to a wish that Paulo might be entrapped by his own act. At length he made himself heard.

'I *entreat*,' said Vivaldi.

Paulo stopped for a moment.

'Paulo!' rejoined Vivaldi earnestly, 'do you love your master?'

'Love my master!' said Paulo resentfully, without allowing Vivaldi to finish his sentence, 'Have I not gone through fire and water for him? or, what is as good, have I not put myself into the Inquisition, and all on his account? and now to be asked, "Do I love my master!" If you believe, Signor, that any thing else made me come here, into these dismal holes, you are quite entirely out; and when they have made an end of me, as I suppose they will do, before all is over, you will, perhaps, think better of me than to suspect that I came here for my own pleasure.'

'All that may be as you say, Paulo,' replied Vivaldi coldly, while he with difficulty commanded his tears, 'but your immediate submission is the only conduct that can convince me of the sincerity of your professions. I *entreat* you to be silent.'

'*Entreat* me!' said Paulo, 'O my master! what have I done that it should come to this? *Entreat* me!' he repeated, sobbing.

'You will then give me this proof of your attachment?' asked Vivaldi.

'Do not use such a heart-breaking word again, master,' replied Paulo, while he dashed the tears from his cheek, 'such a heart-breaking word, and I will do any thing.'

'You submit to what I require then, Paulo?'

'Aye, Signor, if—if it is even to kneel at the feet of that devil of an inquisitor, yonder.'

'I shall only require you to be silent,' replied Vivaldi, 'and you may then be permitted to remain near me.'

'Well, Signor, well; I will do as you bid me, then, and only just say'——

'Not a syllable! Paulo,' interrupted Vivaldi.

'Only just say, master'——

'Not a word I entreat you!' added Vivaldi, 'or you will be removed immediately.'

'His removal does not depend on that,' said one of the officials, breaking from his watchful silence, 'he must go, and that without more delay.'

'What! after I have promised not to open my lips!' said Paulo, 'do you pretend to break your agreement?'

'There *is* no pretence, and there *was* no agreement,' replied the man sharply, 'so obey directly, or it will be the worse for you.'

The officials were provoked, and Paulo became still more enraged and clamorous, till at length the uproar reached the tribunal at the other end of the hall, and silence having been commanded, an inquiry was made into the cause of the confusion. The consequence of this was, an order that Paulo should withdraw from Vivaldi; but as at this moment he feared no greater evil, he gave his refusal to the tribunal with as little ceremony as he had done before to the officials.

At length, after much difficulty, a sort of compromise was made, and Paulo being soothed by his master into some degree of compliance, was suffered to remain within a short distance of him.

The business of the trial soon after commenced. Ansaldo the penitentiary, and father Nicola, appeared as witnesses, as did, also, the Roman priest, who had assisted in taking the depositions of the dying assassin. He had been privately interrogated, and had given clear and satisfactory evidence as to the truth of the paper produced by Nicola. Other witnesses, also, had been subpœnaed,* whom Schedoni had no expectation of meeting.

The deportment of the Confessor, on first entering the hall, was collected and firm; it remained unchanged when the Roman priest was brought forward; but, on the appearance of another witness, his courage seemed to faulter. Before this evidence was, however, called for, the depositions of the assassin were publicly read. They stated, with the closest conciseness, the chief facts, of which the following is a somewhat more dilated narrative.

It appeared, that about the year 1742, the late Count di Bruno had passed over into Greece, a journey which his brother, the present Confessor, having long expected, had meditated to take advantage of. Though a lawless passion had first suggested to the dark mind of Schedoni the atrocious act, which should destroy a brother, many circumstances and considerations had conspired to urge him towards its accomplishment. Among these was the conduct of the late Count towards himself, which, however reasonable, as it had contradicted his own selfish gratifications, and added strong reproof to opposition, had excited his most inveterate hatred. Schedoni, who, as a younger brother of his family, bore, at that time, the title of Count di Marinella, had dissipated his small patrimony at a very early age; but, though suffering might then have taught him prudence, it had only encouraged him in duplicity, and rendered him more eager to seek a temporary refuge in the same habits of extravagance which had led to it. The Count di Bruno, though his fortune was very limited, had afforded frequent supplies to his brother; till, finding that he was incorrigible, and that the sums which he himself spared with difficulty from his family were lavished, without remorse, by Marinella, instead of being applied, with economy, to his support, he refused further aid than was sufficient for his absolute necessities.

It would be difficult for a candid mind to believe how a conduct so reasonable could possibly excite hatred in any breast, or that the power of selfishness could so far warp any understanding, as to induce Marinella, whom we will, in future, again call Schedoni, to look upon his brother with detestation, because he had refused to ruin himself that his kinsman might revel! Yet it is certain that Schedoni, terming the necessary prudence of di Bruno to be meanness and cold insensibility to the comfort of others, suffered full as much resentment towards him from system, as he did from passion, though the meanness and the insensibility he imagined in his brother's character were not only real traits in his own, but were displaying themselves in the very arguments he urged against them.

The rancour thus excited was cherished by innumerable circumstances, and ripened by envy, that meanest and most malignant of the human passions; by envy of di Bruno's blessings, of an unencumbered estate,* and of a beautiful wife, he was tempted to perpetrate the deed, which might transfer those blessings to himself. Spalatro, whom he employed to this purpose, was well known to him, and he did not fear to confide the conduct of the crime to this man, who was to purchase a little habitation on the remote shore of the Adriatic, and, with a certain stipend, to reside there. The ruinous dwelling, to which Ellena had been carried, as its solitary situation suited Schedoni's views, was taken for him.

Schedoni, who had good intelligence of all di Bruno's movements, acquainted Spalatro, from time to time, with his exact situation; and it was after di Bruno, on his return, had crossed the Adriatic, from Ragusi to Manfredonia, and was entering upon the woods of the Garganus, that Spalatro, with his comrade, overtook him. They fired at the Count and his attendants, who were only a valet, and a guide of the country; and, concealed among the thickets, they securely repeated the attack. The shot did not immediately succeed, and the Count, looking round to discover his enemy, prepared to defend himself, but the firing was so rapidly sustained, that, at length, both di Bruno and his servant fell, covered with wounds. The guide fled.

The unfortunate travellers were buried by their assassins on the spot; but, whether the suspicion which attends upon the consciousness of guilt, prompted Spalatro to guard against every possibility of being betrayed by the accomplice of his crime, or whatever was the motive, he returned to the forest alone; and, shrouded by night, removed the bodies to a pit, which he had prepared under the flooring of the house where he lived; thus displacing all proof, should his accomplice hereafter point out to justice the spot in which he had assisted to deposit the mangled remains of di Bruno.

Schedoni contrived a plausible history of the shipwreck of his brother upon the Adriatic, and of the loss of the whole crew; and, as no persons but the assassins were acquainted with the real cause of his death, the guide, who had fled, and the people at the only town he had passed through, since he landed, being ignorant even of the name of di Bruno, there was not any circumstance to contradict the falshood. It was universally credited, and even the widow of the Count had, perhaps, never doubted its truth; or if, after her compelled marriage with Schedoni, his conduct did awaken a suspicion, it was too vague to produce any serious consequence.

During the reading of Spalatro's confession, and particularly at the conclusion of it, the surprize and dismay of Schedoni were too powerful for concealment; and it was not the least considerable part of his wonder, that Spalatro should have come to Rome for the purpose of making these depositions; but further consideration gave him a conjecture of the truth.

The account, which Spalatro had given of his motive for this journey to the priest, was, that, having lately understood Schedoni to be resident at Rome, he had followed him thither, with an intention of relieving his conscience by an acknowledgment of his own crimes, and a disclosure of Schedoni's. This, however, was not exactly the fact. The design of Spalatro was to extort money from the guilty Confessor; a design, from which the latter believed he had protected himself, as well as from every other evil consequence, when he misled his late accomplice, respecting his place of residence; little foreseeing that the very artifice, which should send this man in search of him to Rome, instead of Naples, would be the means of bringing his crimes before the public.

Spalatro had followed the steps of Schedoni as far as the town at which he slept, on the first night of his journey; and, having there passed him, had reached the villa di Cambrusca, when, perceiving the Confessor approaching, he had taken shelter from observation, within the ruin. The motive, which before made him shrink from notice, had contributed, and still did so, to a suspicion that he aimed at the life of Schedoni, who, in wounding him, believed he had saved himself from an assassin. The wounds, however, of Spalatro did not so much disable him, but that he proceeded towards Rome from the town whence the parting road had conducted his master towards Naples.

The fatigue of a long journey, performed chiefly on foot, in Spalatro's wounded condition, occasioned a fever, that terminated together his journey and his life; and in his last hours he had unburdened his conscience by a full confession of his guilt. The priest, who, on this occasion, had been sent for, alarmed by the importance of the confession, since it implicated a living person, called in a friend as witness to the depositions. This witness was father Nicola, the former intimate of Schedoni, and who was of a character to rejoice in any discovery, which might punish a man from whose repeated promises he had received only severe disappointments.

Schedoni now perceived that all his designs against Spalatro had failed, and he had meditated more than have yet been fully disclosed. It may be remembered, that on parting with the peasant, his conductor, the Confessor, gave him a stiletto to defend him, as he said, from the attack of Spalatro, in case of encountering him on the road. The point of this instrument was tipped with poison; so that a scratch from it was sufficient to inflict death. Schedoni had for many years secretly carried about him such an envenomed instrument, for reasons known only to himself. He had hoped, that, should the peasant meet Spalatro, and be provoked to defend himself, this stiletto would terminate the life of his accomplice, and relieve him from all probability of discovery, since the other assassin, whom he employed, had been dead several years. The expedient failed in every respect; the peasant did not even see Spalatro; and, before he reached his home, he luckily lost the fatal stiletto, which, as he had discovered himself to be acquainted with some circumstances connected with the crimes of Schedoni, the Confessor would have wished him to keep, from the chance, that he might some time injure himself in using it. The poniard, as he had no proper means of fastening it to his dress, had fallen, and was carried away by the torrent he was crossing at that moment.

But, if Schedoni had been shocked by the confession of the assassin, his dismay was considerably greater, when a new witness was brought forward, and he perceived an ancient domestic of his house. This man identified Schedoni for Ferando Count di Bruno, with whom he had lived as a servant after the death of the Count his brother. And not only did he bear testimony to the person of Schedoni, but to the death of the Countess, his wife. Giovanni declared himself to be one of the domestics who had assisted in conveying her to her apartment, after she had been struck by the poniard of Schedoni, and who had afterwards attended her funeral in the church of the Santa del Miracoli, a convent near the late residence of di Bruno. He further affirmed, that the physicians had reported her death to be in consequence of the wound she had received, and he bore witness to the flight of his master, previous to the death of the Countess, and immediately upon the assassination, and that he had never publicly appeared upon his estate since that period.

An inquisitor asked, whether any measures had been taken by the relations of the deceased lady, toward a prosecution of the Count.

The witness replied, that a long search had been made for the

Count, for such a purpose, but that he had wholly eluded discovery, and that, of course, no further step had been taken in the affair. This reply appeared to occasion dissatisfaction; the tribunal was silent, and seemed to hesitate; the vicar-general then addressed the witness.

'How can you be certain that the person now before you, calling himself father Schedoni, is the Count di Bruno, your former master, if you have never seen him during the long interval of years you mention?'

Giovanni, without hesitation, answered, that, though years had worn the features of the Count, he recollected them the moment he beheld him; and not the Count only, but the person of the penitentiary Ansaldo, whom he had seen a frequent visitor at the house of di Bruno, though his appearance, also, was considerably changed by time, and by the ecclesiastical habit which he now wore.

The vicar-general seemed still to doubt the evidence of this man, till Ansaldo himself, on being called upon, remembered him to have been a servant of the Count, though he could not identify the Count himself.

The grand-inquisitor remarked, that it was extraordinary he should recollect the face of the servant, yet forget that of the master, with whom he had lived in habits of intimacy. To this Ansaldo replied, that the stronger passions of Schedoni, together with his particular habits of life, might reasonably be supposed to have wrought a greater change upon the features of the Count than the character and circumstances of Giovanni's could have effected on his.

Schedoni, not without reason, was appalled, on the appearance of this servant, whose further testimony gave such clearness and force to some other parts of the evidence, that the tribunal pronounced sentence upon Schedoni, as the murderer of the Count his brother; and as this, the first charge, was sufficient for his condemnation to death, they did not proceed upon the second, that which related to his wife.

The emotion betrayed by Schedoni, on the appearance of the last witness, and during the delivery of the evidence, disappeared when his fate became certain; and when the dreadful sentence of the law was pronounced, it made no visible impression on his mind. From that moment, his firmness or his hardihood never forsook him.

Vivaldi, who witnessed this condemnation, appeared infinitely more affected by it than himself, and, though in revealing the circumstance of father Nicola's summons, which had eventually led to the discovery of Schedoni's crimes, he had not been left a choice in his conduct, he felt, at this moment, as miserable as if he had actually borne witness against the life of a fellow being: what, then, would have been his feelings, had he been told that this Schedoni, thus condemned, was the father of Ellena di Rosalba! But, whatever these might be, he was soon condemned to experience them. One of the most powerful of Schedoni's passions appeared even in this last scene; and as, in quitting the tribunal, he passed near Vivaldi, he uttered these few words—'In me you have murdered the father of Ellena di Rosalba!'

Not with any hope that the intercession of Vivaldi, himself also a prisoner, could in the least mitigate a sentence pronounced by the Inquisition, did he say this, but for the purpose of revenging himself for the evil, which Vivaldi's evidence had contributed to produce, and inflicting the exquisite misery such information must give. The attempt succeeded too well.

At first, indeed, Vivaldi judged this to be only the desperate assertion of a man, who believed his last chance of escaping the rigour of the law to rest with him; and, at the mention of Ellena, forgetting every precaution, he loudly demanded to know her situation. Schedoni, throwing upon him an horrible smile of triumph and derision, was passing forward without replying, but Vivaldi, unable to support this state of uncertainty, asked permission of the tribunal to converse, for a few moments, with the prisoner; a request which was granted with extreme reluctance, and only on condition that the conversation should be public.

To Vivaldi's questions, as to the situation of Ellena, Schedoni only replied, that she was his daughter, and the solemnity, which accompanied these repeated assertions, though it failed to convince Vivaldi of this truth, occasioned him agonizing doubt and apprehension: but when the Confessor, perceiving the policy of disclosing her place of residence to Vivaldi, softened from his desire of vengeance to secure the interest of his family, and named the *Santa della Piéta* as her present asylum, the joy of such intelligence overcame, for a time, every other consideration.

To this dialogue, however, the officials put a speedy conclusion; Schedoni was led back to his cell, and Vivaldi was soon after ordered to his former close confinement.

But Paulo became again outrageous, when he was about to be separated from his master, till the latter, having petitioned the tribunal, that his servant might accompany him to his prison, and received an absolute refusal, endeavoured to calm the violence of his despair. He fell at his master's feet, and shed tears, but he uttered no further complaints. When he rose, he turned his eyes in silence upon Vivaldi, and they seemed to say, 'Dear master! I shall never see you more!' and with this sad expression, he continued to gaze on him till he had left the hall.

Vivaldi, notwithstanding the various subjects of his distress, could not bear to meet the piteous looks of this poor man, and he withdrew his eyes; yet, at every other step he took, they constantly returned to his faithful servant, till the doors folded him from sight.

When he had quitted the hall, Vivaldi pleaded, however hopelessly, to the officials, in favour of Paulo, entreating that they would speak to the persons, who kept guard over him, and prevail with them to shew him every allowable indulgence.

'No indulgence can be allowed him,' replied one of the men, 'except bread and water, and the liberty of walking in his cell.'

'No *other!*' said Vivaldi.

'None,' repeated the official. 'This prisoner has been near getting one of his guards into a scrape already, for, somehow or other, he so talked him over, and won upon him, (for he is but a young one here) that the man let him have a light, and a pen and ink; but, luckily, it was found out, before any harm was done.'

'And what became of this honest fellow?' inquired Vivaldi.

'Honest! he was none so honest, either, Signor, if he could not mind his duty.'

'Was he punished, then?'

'No, Signor,' replied the man, pausing, and looking back upon the long avenue they were passing, to inquire whether he was observed to hold this conversation with a prisoner: 'no, Signor, he was a younker,* so they let him off for once, and sent him to guard a man, who was not so full of his coaxing ways.'

'Paulo made him merry, perhaps?' asked Vivaldi. 'What were the coaxing ways you spoke of?'

'Merry, Signor! no! he made him cry, and that was as bad.'

'Indeed!' said Vivaldi. 'The man must have been here, then, a very short time.'

'Not more than a month, or so, Signor.'

'But the coaxing ways you talked of,' repeated Vivaldi, 'what were they?—a ducat, or so?'

'A ducat!' exclaimed the man, 'no! not a *paolo!*'*

'Are you *sure* of that?' cried Vivaldi, shrewdly.

'Aye, sure enough, Signor. This fellow is not worth a ducat in the world!'

'But his master is, friend,' observed Vivaldi, in a very low voice, while he put some money into his hand.

The officer made no answer, but concealed the money, and nothing further was said.

Vivaldi had given this as a bribe, to procure some kindness for his servant, not from any consideration of himself, for his own critical situation had ceased at this time to be a subject of anxiety with him. His mind was at present strangely agitated between emotions the most opposite in their nature, the joy which a discovery of Ellena's safety inspired, and the horrible suspicion that Schedoni's assurances of relationship occasioned. That his Ellena was the daughter of a murderer, that the father of Ellena should be brought to ignominious death, and that he himself, however unintentionally, should have assisted to this event, were considerations almost too horrible to be sustained! Vivaldi sought refuge from them in various conjectures as to the motive, which might have induced Schedoni to assert a falshood in this instance; but that of revenge alone appeared plausible; and even this surmise was weakened, when he considered that the Confessor had assured him of Ellena's safety, an assurance which, as Vivaldi did not detect the selfish policy connected with it, he believed Schedoni would not have given, had his general intent towards him been malicious. But it was possible, that this very information, on which all his comfort reposed, might be false, and had been given only for the purpose of inflicting the anguish a discovery of the truth must lead to! With an anxiety so intense, as almost to overcome his faculty of judging, he examined every minute probability relative to this point, and concluded with believing that Schedoni had, in this last instance, at least, spoken honestly.

Whether he had done so in his first assertion was a question, which had raised in Vivaldi's mind a tempest of conjecture and of horror; for, while the subject of it was too astonishing to be fully believed, it was, also, too dreadful, not to be apprehended even as a possibility.

CHAPTER IX

O holy nun! why bend the mournful head?
Why fall those tears from lids uplift in pray'r?
Why o'er thy pale cheek steals the feeble blush,
Then fades, and leaves it wan as the lily
On which a moon-beam falls?

WHILE these events were passing in the prisons of the Inquisition at Rome, Ellena, in the sanctuary of *Our Lady of Pity*, remained ignorant of Schedoni's arrest, and of Vivaldi's situation. She understood that the Confessor was preparing to acknowledge her for his daughter, and believed that she comprehended also the motive for his absence; but, though he had forbidden her to expect a visit from him till his arrangement should be completed, he had promised to write in the mean time, and inform her of all the present circumstances of Vivaldi; his unexpected silence had excited, therefore, apprehensions as various, though not so terrible, as those which Vivaldi had suffered for her; nor did the silence of Vivaldi himself appear less extraordinary.

'His confinement must be severe indeed,' said the afflicted Ellena, 'since he cannot relieve my anxiety by a single line of intelligence. Or, perhaps, harassed by unceasing opposition, he has submitted to the command of his family, and has consented to forget me. Ah! why did I leave the opportunity for that command to his family; why did I not enforce it myself!'

Yet, while she uttered this self-reproach, the tears she shed contradicted the pride which had suggested it; and a conviction lurking in her heart that Vivaldi could not so resign her, soon dissipated those tears. But other conjectures recalled them; it was possible that he was ill—that he was dead!

In such vague and gloomy surmise her days passed away; employment could no longer withdraw her from herself, nor music, even for a moment, charm away the sense of sorrow; yet she regularly partook of the various occupations of the nuns; and was so far from permitting herself to indulge in any useless expression of anxiety, that she had never once disclosed the sacred subject of it; so that, though she could not assume an air of cheerfulness, she never appeared otherwise than tranquil. Her most soothing, yet perhaps most melancholy hour, was when about sun-set she could withdraw unnoticed, to the terrace among the rocks, that overlooked the convent, and formed a part of its domain. There, alone and relieved from all the ceremonial restraints of the society, her very thoughts seemed more at liberty. As, from beneath the light foliage of the accacias, or the more majestic shade of the plane-trees that waved their branches over the many-coloured cliffs of this terrace, Ellena looked down upon the magnificent scenery of the bay, it brought back to memory, in sad yet pleasing detail, the many happy days she had passed on those blue waters, or on the shores, in the society of Vivaldi and her departed relative Bianchi; and every point of the prospect marked by such remembrance, which the veiling distance stole, was rescued by imagination, and pictured by affection in tints more animated than those of brightest nature.

One evening Ellena had lingered on the terrace later than usual. She had watched the rays retiring from the highest points of the horizon, and the fading imagery of the lower scene, till, the sun having sunk into the waves, all colouring was withdrawn, except an empurpling and reposing hue, which overspread the waters and the heavens, and blended in soft confusion every feature of the landscape. The roofs and slender spires of the Santa della Pieta, with a single tower of the church rising loftily over every other part of the buildings that composed the convent, were fading fast from the eye; but the solemn tint that invested them accorded so well with their style, that Ellena was unwilling to relinquish this interesting object. Suddenly she perceived through the dubious light an unusual number of moving figures in the court of the great cloister, and listening, she fancied she could distinguish the murmuring of many voices. The white drapery of the nuns rendered them conspicuous as they moved, but it was impossible to ascertain who were the individuals engaged in this bustle. Presently the assemblage dispersed; and Ellena, curious to understand the occasion of what she had observed, prepared to descend to the convent.

She had left the terrace, and was about to enter a long avenue of chesnuts that extended to a part of the convent, communicating immediately with the great court, when she heard approaching steps, and, on turning into the walk, perceived several persons advancing in the shady distance. Among the voices, as they drew nearer, she distinguished one whose interesting tone engaged all her attention, and began also to awaken memory. She listened, wondered, doubted, hoped, and feared! It spoke again! Ellena thought she could not be deceived in those tender accents, so full of intelligence, so expressive of sensibility and refinement. She proceeded with quicker steps, yet faltered as she drew near the group, and paused to discern whether among them was any figure that might accord with the voice and justify her hopes.

The voice spoke again; it pronounced her name; pronounced it with the tremblings of tenderness and impatience, and Ellena scarcely dared to trust her senses, when she beheld Olivia, the nun of San Stefano, in the cloisters of the Della Pieta!

Ellena could find no words to express her joy and surprise on beholding her preserver in safety, and in these quiet groves; but Olivia repaid all the affectionate caresses of her young friend, and, while she promised to explain the circumstance that had led to her present appearance here, she, in her turn, made numerous inquiries relative to Ellena's adventures after she had quitted San Stefano. They were now, however, surrounded by too many auditors to allow of unreserved conversation; Ellena, therefore, led the nun to her apartment, and Olivia then explained her reasons for having left the convent of San Stefano, which were indeed sufficient to justify, even with the most rigid devotee, her conduct as to the change. This unfortunate recluse, it appeared, persecuted by the suspicions of the abbess, who understood that she had assisted in the liberation of Ellena, had petitioned the bishop of her diocese for leave to remove to the Santa della Pieta. The abbess had not proof to proceed formally against her, as an acomplice in the escape of a novice, for though Jeronimo could have supplied the requisite evidence, he was too deeply implicated in this adventure to do so without betraying his own conduct. From his having withheld such proof, it appears, however, that accident rather than design had occasioned his failure on the evening of Ellena's departure from the monastery. But, though the abbess had not testimony enough for legal punishment, she was acquainted with circumstances sufficient to justify suspicion, and had both the inclination and the power to render Olivia very miserable.

In her choice of the Santa della Pieta, the nun was influenced by many considerations, some of which were the consequence of conversations she had held with Ellena respecting the state of that society. Her design she had been unable to disclose to her friend, lest, by a discovery of such correspondence, the abbess of San Stefano should obtain grounds on which to proceed against her. Even in her appeal to the bishop the utmost caution and secrecy had been necessary, till the order for her removal, procured not without considerable delay and difficulty, arrived, and when it came, the jealous anger of the superior rendered an immediate departure necessary.

Olivia, during many years, had been unhappy in her local circumstances, but it is probable she would have concluded her days within the walls of San Stefano, had not the aggravated oppression of the abbess aroused her courage and activity, and dissipated the despondency, with which severe misfortune had obscured her views.

Ellena was particular in her inquiries whether any person of the monastery had suffered for the assistance they had given her; but learned that not one, except Olivia, had been suspected of befriending her; and then understood, that the venerable friar, who had dared to unfasten the gate which restored her with Vivaldi to liberty, had not been involved by his kindness.

'It is an embarrassing and rather an unusual circumstance,' concluded Olivia, 'to change one's convent; but you perceive the strong reasons which determined me upon a removal. I was, however, perhaps, the more impatient of severe treatment, since you, my sister, had described to me the society of *Our Lady of Pity*, and since I believed it possible that you might form a part of it. When, on my arrival here, I learned that my wishes had not deceived me on this point, I was impatient to see you once more, and as soon as the ceremonies attending an introduction to the superior were over, I requested to be conducted to you, and was in search of you when we met in the avenue. It is unnecessary for me to insist upon the satisfaction, which this meeting gives me; but you may not, perhaps, understand how much the manners of our lady abbess, and of the sisterhood in general, as far as a first interview will allow me to judge of them, have re-animated me. The gloom, which has long hung over my prospects, seems now to open, and a distant gleam promises to light up the evening of my stormy day.'

Olivia paused and appeared to recollect herself; this was the first time she had made so direct a reference to her own misfortunes; and, while Ellena silently remarked it, and observed the dejection, which was already stealing upon the expressive countenance of the nun, she wished, yet feared to lead her back towards the subject of them.

Endeavouring to dismiss some painful remembrance, and assuming a smile of languid gaiety, Olivia said, 'Now that I have related the history of my removal, and sufficiently indulged my egotism, will you let me hear what adventures have befallen you, my young friend, since the melancholy adieu you gave me in the gardens of San Stefano.'

This was a task, to which Ellena's spirits, though revived by the presence of Olivia, were still unequal. Over the scenes of her past distress Time had not yet drawn his shadowing veil; the colours were all too fresh and garish for the meek dejection of her eye, and the subject was too intimately connected with that of her present anxiety, to be reviewed without very painful feelings. She therefore requested Olivia to spare her from a detail of particulars, which she could not recollect but with extreme reluctance; and, scrupulously observing the injunction of Schedoni, she merely mentioned her separation from Vivaldi upon the banks of the Celano, and that a variety of distressing circumstances had intervened before she could regain the sanctuary of the della Pieta.

Olivia understood too well the kind of feelings, from which Ellena was desirous of escaping, willingly to subject her to a renewal of them; and felt too much generous compassion for her sufferings not to endeavour to soothe the sense of them by an exertion of those delicate and nameless arts which, while they mock detection, fascinate the weary spirit as by a charm of magic!

The friends continued in conversation, till a chime from a chapel of the convent summoned them to the last vespers; and, when the service had concluded, they separated for the night.

With the society of the Santa della Pieta, Olivia had thus found an asylum such as till lately she had never dared to hope for; but, though she frequently expressed her sense of this blessing, it was seldom without tears; and Ellena observed, with some surprise and more disappointment, within a very few days after her arrival, a cloud of melancholy spreading again over her mind.

But a nearer interest soon withdrew Ellena's attention from Olivia to fix it upon Vivaldi; and, when she saw her infirm old servant, Beatrice, enter a chamber of the convent, she anticipated that the knowledge of some extraordinary, and probably unhappy, event had brought her. She knew too well the circumspection of Schedoni to believe that Beatrice came commissioned from him; and as the uncertain situation of Vivaldi was so constantly the subject of her anxiety, she immediately concluded that her servant came to announce some evil relative to him.—His indisposition, perhaps his actual confinement in the Inquisition, which lately she had sometimes been inclined to think might not have been a mere menace to Vivaldi, though it had proved to be no more to herself;—or possibly she came to tell of his death—his death in those prisons! This last was a possibility that almost incapacitated her for inquiring what was the errand of Beatrice.

The old servant, trembling and wan, either from the fatigue of her walk, or from a consciousness of disastrous intelligence, seated herself without speaking, and some moments elapsed before she could be prevailed with to answer the repeated inquiries of Ellena.

'O Signora!' said she, at length, 'you do not know what it is to walk up hill such a long way, at my age! Well! heaven protect you, I hope you never will!'

'I perceive you bring ill news,' said Ellena; 'I am prepared for it, and you need not fear to tell me all you know.'

'Holy San Marco!' exclaimed Beatrice, 'if death be ill news, you have guessed right, Signora, for I do bring news of that, it is certain. How came you, Lady, to know my errand? They have been beforehand with me, I see, though I have not walked so fast up hill this many a day, as I have now, to tell you what has happened.'

She stopped on observing the changing countenance of Ellena, who tremulously called upon her to explain what had happened—who was dead; and entreated her to relate the particulars as speedily as possible.

'You said you was prepared, Signora,' said Beatrice, 'but your looks tell another tale.'—

'What is the event you would disclose?' said Ellena, almost breathless. 'When did it happen?—be brief.'

'I cannot tell exactly when it happened, Signora, but it was an own servant of the Marchese's that I had it from.'

'The Marchese's?' interrupted Ellena in a faltering voice.

'Aye, Lady; you will say that is pretty good authority.'

'Death! and in the Marchese's family!' exclaimed Ellena.

'Yes, Signora, I had it from his own servant. He was passing by the garden-gate just as I happened to be speaking to the maccaroni-man.—But you are ill, Lady!'—

'I am very well, if you will but proceed,' replied Ellena, faintly, while her eyes were fixed upon Beatrice, as if they only had power to enforce her meaning.

'"Well, dame," he says to me, "I have not seen you of a long time." "No," says I, "that is a great grievance truly! for old women now-a-days are not much thought of; out of sight out of mind with them, now-a-days!"'—

'I beseech you to the purpose,' interrupted Ellena. 'Whose death did he announce?' She had not courage to pronounce Vivaldi's name.

'You shall hear, Signora. I saw he looked in a sort of a bustle, so I asked him how all did at the Palazzo: so he answers, "Bad enough, Signora Beatrice, have not you heard?" "Heard," says I; "what should I have heard?" "Why," says he, "of what has just happened in our family."'

'O heavens!' exclaimed Ellena, 'he is dead! Vivaldi is dead!'

'You shall hear, Signora,' continued Beatrice.

'Be brief!' said Ellena, 'answer me simply yes or no.'

'I cannot, till I come to the right place, Signora; if you will but have a little patience, you shall hear all. But if you fluster me so, you will put me quite out.'

'Grant me patience!' said Ellena, endeavouring to calm her spirits.

'With that, Signora, I asked him to walk in and rest himself, and tell me all about it. He answered, he was in a great hurry, and could not stay a moment, and a great deal of that sort; but I, knowing that whatever happened in that family, Signora, was something to you, would not let him go off so easily; and so, when I asked him to refresh himself with a glass of lemon-ice, he forgot all his business in a minute, and we had a long chat.'

And Beatrice might now have continued her circumlocution, perhaps as long as she had pleased, for Ellena had lost all power to urge inquiry, and was scarcely sensible of what was said. She neither spoke, nor shed a tear; the one image that possessed her fancy, the image of Vivaldi dead seemed to hold all her faculties, as by a spell.

'So when I asked him,' added Beatrice, 'again what had happened, he was ready enough to tell all about it. "It is near a month ago," said he, "since she was first taken; the Marchesa had been"'——

'The Marchesa!' repeated Ellena, with whom that one word had dissolved the spell of terror—'the Marchesa!'

'Yes Signora, to be sure. Who else did I say it was!'

'Go on, Beatrice; the Marchesa?'—

'What makes you look so glad all of a sudden, Signora? I thought just now you was very sorry about it. What! I warrant you was thinking about my young lord, Vivaldi.'

'Proceed,' said Ellena.

'Well!' added Beatrice, '"It was about a month ago that the Marchesa was first taken," continued the varlet. "She had seemed poorly a long time, but it was from a *conversazione** at the di Voglio palazzo, that she came home so ill. It is supposed she had been long in a bad state of health, but nobody thought her so near her end, till the doctors were called together; and then matters looked very bad indeed. They found out that she had been dying, or as good, for many years, though nobody else had suspected it, and the Marchesa's own physician was blamed for not finding it out before. But he," added the rogue, "had a regard for my lady. He was very obstinate, too, for he kept saying almost to the last, there was no danger, when every body else saw how it was going. The other doctors soon made their words good, and my lady died."'

'And her son'—said Ellena, 'was he with the Marchesa when she expired?'

'What, Signor Vivaldi, lady? No, the Signor was not there.'

'That is very extraordinary!' observed Ellena with emotion. 'Did the servant mention him?'

'Yes, Signora; he said what a sad thing it was that he should be out of the way at that time, and nobody know where!'

'Are his family then ignorant where he is?' asked Ellena, with increased emotion.

'To be sure they are, lady, and have been for these many weeks. They have heard nothing at all of the Signor, or one Paulo Mendrico, his servant, though the Marchesa's people have been riding post after them from one end of the kingdom to the other all the time!'

Shocked with the conviction of a circumstance, which, till lately she scarcely believed was possible, the imprisonment of Vivaldi in the Inquisition, Ellena lost for a while all power of further inquiry; but Beatrice proceeded.

'The Lady Marchesa seemed to lay something much to heart, as the man told me, and often inquired for Signor Vincentio.'

'The Marchesa you are sure then was ignorant where he was?' said Ellena, with new astonishment and perplexity as to the person who, after betraying him into the Inquisition, could yet have suffered her, though arrested at the same time, to escape.

'Yes, Signora, for she wanted sadly to see him. And when she was dying, she sent for her Confessor, one father Schedoni, I think they call him, and'—

'What of him?' said Ellena incautiously.

'Nothing, Signora, for he could not be found.'

'Not be found!' repeated Ellena.

'No, Signora, not just then; he was Confessor, I warrant, to other people beside the Marchesa, and I dare say they had sins enough to confess, so he could not get away in a hurry.'

Ellena recollected herself sufficiently to ask no further of Schedoni; and, when she considered the probable cause of Vivaldi's arrest, she was again consoled by a belief that he had not fallen into the power of real officials, since the comrades of the men who had arrested him, had proved themselves otherwise; and she thought it highly probable, that, while undiscovered by his family, he had been, and was still engaged in searching for the place of her confinement.

'But I was saying,' proceeded Beatrice, 'what a bustle there was when my lady, the Marchesa was dying. As this father Schedoni was not to be found, another Confessor was sent for, and shut up with her for a long while indeed! And then my Lord Marchese was called in, and there seemed to be a deal going forward, for my Lord was heard every now and then by the attendants in the antichamber, talking loud, and sometimes my Lady Marchesa's voice was heard too, though she was so ill! At last all was silent, and after some time my Lord came out of the room, and he seemed very much flustered, they say, that is, very angry and yet very sorrowful. But the Confessor remained with my Lady for a long while after; and, when he departed, my Lady appeared more unhappy than ever. She lived all that night and part of the next day, and something seemed to lie very heavy at her heart, for she sometimes wept, but oftener groaned, and would look so, that it was piteous to see her. She frequently asked for the Marchese, and when he came, the attendants were sent away, and they held long conferences by themselves. The Confessor also was sent for again, just at the last, and they were all shut up together. After this, my Lady appeared more easy in her mind, and not long after she died.'

Ellena, who had attended closely to this little narrative, was prevented for the present from asking the few questions which it had suggested, by the entrance of Olivia, who, on perceiving a stranger, was retiring, but Ellena, not considering these inquiries as important, prevailed with the nun to take a chair at the embroidery frame she had lately quitted.

After conversing for a few moments with Olivia, she returned to a consideration of her own interests. The absence of Schedoni still appeared to her as something more than accidental; and, though she could not urge any inquiry with Beatrice, concerning the monk of the Spirito Santo, she ventured to ask whether she had lately seen the stranger, who had restored her to Altieri, for Beatrice knew him only in the character of Ellena's deliverer.

'No, Signora,' replied Beatrice rather sharply, 'I have never seen his face since he attended you to the villa, though for that matter, I did not see much of it there; and then how he contrived to let himself out of the house that night without my seeing him, I cannot divine, though I have thought of it often enough since. I am sure he need not to have been ashamed to have shewn his face to me, for I should only have blessed him for bringing you safe home again!'

Ellena was somewhat surprised to find that Beatrice had noticed a circumstance apparently so trivial, and replied, that she had herself opened the door for her protector.

While Beatrice spoke, Olivia raising her eyes from the embroidery, had fixed them upon the old servant, who respectfully withdrew her's; but, when the nun was again engaged on her work, she resumed her observation. Ellena fancied she perceived something extraordinary in this mutual examination, although the curiosity of strangers towards each other might have accounted for it.

Beatrice then received directions from Ellena as to some drawings, which she wished to have sent to the convent, and when the servant spoke in reply, Olivia again raised her eyes, and fixed them on her face with intense curiosity.

'I certainly ought to know that voice,' said the nun with great emotion, 'though I dare not judge from your features. Is it,—can it be possible!—is it Beatrice Olca, to whom I speak? So many years have passed'——

Beatrice with equal surprize answered, 'It is, Signora; you are right in my name. But, lady, who are you that know me?'

While she earnestly regarded Olivia, there was an expression of dismay in her look, which increased Ellena's perplexity. The nun's complexion varied every instant, and her words failed when she attempted to speak. Beatrice meanwhile exclaimed, 'My eyes deceive me! yet there is a strange likeness. Santa della Pieta! how it has fluttered me! my heart beats still—you are so like her, lady, yet you are very different too.'

Olivia, whose regards were now entirely fixed upon Ellena, said in a voice that was scarcely articulate, while her whole frame seemed sinking beneath some irresistible feeling, 'Tell me, Beatrice, I conjure you, quickly say, who is this?'—— She pointed to Ellena, and the sentence died on her lips.

Beatrice, wholly occupied by interests of her own, gave no reply, but exclaimed, 'It is in truth the Lady Olivia! It is herself! In the name of all that is sacred, how came you here? O! how glad you must have been to find one another out!' She looked, still gasping with astonishment, at Olivia, while Ellena, unheard, repeatedly inquired the meaning of her words, and in the next moment found herself pressed to the bosom of the nun, who seemed better to have understood them, and who weeping, trembling, and almost fainting, held her there in silence.

Ellena, after some moments had thus passed, requested an explanation of what she witnessed, and Beatrice at the same time demanded the cause of all this emotion. 'For can it be that you did not know one another?' she added.

'What new discovery is this?' said Ellena, fearfully to the nun. 'It is but lately that I have found my father! O tell me by what tender name I am to call you?'

'Your father!' exclaimed Olivia.

'Your father, lady!' echoed Beatrice.

Ellena, betrayed by strong emotion into this premature mention of Schedoni, was embarrassed and remained silent.

'No, my child!' said Olivia, softening from amazement into tones of ineffable sorrow, while she again pressed Ellena to her heart—'No!—thy father is in the grave!'

Ellena no longer returned her caresses; surprize and doubt suspended every tender emotion; she gazed upon Olivia with an intenseness that partook of wildness. At length she said slowly— 'It is my mother, then, whom I see! When will these discoveries end!'

'It is your mother!' replied Olivia solemnly, 'a mother's blessing rests with you!'

The nun endeavoured to soothe the agitated spirits of Ellena, though she was herself nearly overwhelmed by the various and acute feelings this disclosure occasioned. For a considerable time they were unable to speak but in short sentences of affectionate exclamation, but joy was evidently a more predominant feeling with the parent than with the child. When, however, Ellena could weep, she became more tranquil, and by degrees was sensible of a degree of happiness, such as she had perhaps never experienced.

Meanwhile Beatrice seemed lost in amazement mingled with fear. She expressed no pleasure, notwithstanding the joy she witnessed, but was uniformly grave and observant.

Olivia, when she recovered some degree of composure, inquired for her sister Bianchi. The silence and sudden dejection of Ellena indicated the truth. On this mention of her late mistress, Beatrice recovered the use of speech.

'Alas! lady,' said the old servant, 'she is now where I believed you were! and I should as soon have expected to see my dear mistress here as yourself!'

Olivia, though affected by this intelligence, did not feel it with the acuteness she would have done probably at any other moment. After she had indulged her tears, she added, that from the unusual silence of Bianchi, she had suspected the truth, and particularly since not any answer had been returned to the letter she had sent to Altieri upon her arrival at the Santa della Pieta.

'Alas!' said Beatrice, 'I wonder much my lady abbess failed to tell you the sad news, for she knew it too well!—My dear mistress is buried in the church here! as for the letter, I have brought it with me for Signora Ellena to open.'

'The lady abbess is not informed of our relationship,' replied Olivia, 'and I have particular reasons for wishing that at present she should remain ignorant of it. Even you, my Ellena, must appear only as my friend, till some inquiries have been made, which are essential to my peace.'

Olivia required an explanation of Ellena's late extraordinary assertion respecting her father, but this was a request made with emotions very different from those which hope or joy inspire. Ellena, believing that the same circumstances which had deceived herself during so many years, as to his death, had also misled Olivia, was not surprized at the incredulity her mother had shewn, but she was considerably embarrassed how to answer her inquiries. It was now too late to observe the promise of secrecy extorted from her by Schedoni; the first moments of surprize had betrayed her; yet, while she trembled further to transgress his injunction, she perceived that a full explanation was now unavoidable. And, since Ellena considered, that as Schedoni could not have foreseen her present peculiar situation, his command had no reference to her mother, her scruples on this head disappeared. When, therefore, Beatrice had withdrawn, Ellena repeated her assertion, that her father still lived; which, though it increased the amazement of Olivia, did not vanquish her incredulity. Olivia's tears flowed fast, while in contradiction to this assurance, she mentioned the year in which the Count de Bruno died, with some circumstances relative to his death; which, however, as Ellena understood that her mother had not witnessed it, she still believed had not happened. To confirm her late assertion, Ellena then related a few particulars of her second interview with Schedoni, and as some confirmation that he lived, offered to produce the portrait, which he had claimed as his own. Olivia, in great agitation, requested to see the miniature, and Ellena left the apartment in search of it.

Every moment of her absence was to Olivia's expectation lengthened to an hour; she paced the room; listened for a footstep; endeavoured to tranquillize her spirits, and still Ellena did not return. Some strange mystery seemed to lurk in the narrative she had just heard, which she wished, yet dreaded to develope; and when, at length, Ellena appeared with the miniature, she took it in trembling eagerness, and having gazed upon it for an instant, her complexion faded and she fainted.

Ellena had now no doubt respecting the truth of Schedoni's declaration, and blamed herself for not having more gradually prepared her mother for the knowledge of a circumstance, which she believed had overwhelmed her with joy. The usual applications, however, soon restored Olivia, who, when she was again alone with her daughter, desired to behold once more the portrait. Ellena, attributing the strong emotion, with which she still regarded it, to surprize, and fear lest she was admitting a fallacious hope, endeavoured to comfort her by renewed assurances, that not only the Count di Bruno yet existed, but that he lived at this very time in Naples, and further, that he would probably be in her presence within the hour, 'When I quitted the room for the miniature,' added Ellena, 'I dispatched a person with a note, requesting to see my father immediately, being impatient to realize the joy, which such a meeting between my long lost parents must occasion.'

In this instance Ellena had certainly suffered her generous sympathy to overcome her discretion, for, though the contents of the note to Schedoni could not positively have betrayed him, had he even been in Naples at this time, her sending it to the Spirito Santo, instead of the place which he had appointed for his letters, might have led to a premature inquiry respecting herself.

While Ellena had acquainted Olivia that Schedoni would probably be with them soon, she watched eagerly for the joyful surprize she expected would appear on her countenance; how severe then was her disappointment when only terror and dismay were expressed there! and, when, in the next moment, her mother uttered exclamations of distress and even of despair!

'If he sees me,' said Olivia, 'I am irrecoverably lost! O! unhappy Ellena! your precipitancy has destroyed me. The original of this portrait is not the Count di Bruno, *my* dear lord, nor your parent, but his brother, the cruel husband'——

Olivia left the sentence unfinished, as if she was betraying more than was at present discreet; but Ellena, whom astonishment had kept silent, now entreated that she would explain her words, and the cause of her distress.

'I know not,' said Olivia, 'by what means that portrait has been conveyed to you; but it is the resemblance of the Count Ferando di Bruno, the brother of my lord, and my'——second husband she should have said, but her lips refused to honour him with the title.

She paused and was much affected, but presently added—

'I cannot at present explain the subject more fully, for it is to me a very distressing one. Let me rather consider the means of avoiding an interview with di Bruno, and even of concealing, if possible, that I exist.'

Olivia was, however, soothed when she understood that Ellena had not named her in the note, but had merely desired to see the Confessor upon a very particular occasion.

While they were consulting upon the excuse it would be necessary to form for this imprudent summons, the messenger returned with the note unopened, and with information, that father Schedoni was abroad on a pilgrimage, which was the explanation the brothers of the Spirito Santo chose to give of his absence; judging it prudent, for the honour of their convent, to conceal his real situation.

Olivia, thus released from her fears, consented to explain some points of the subject so interesting to Ellena; but it was not till several days after this discovery, that she could sufficiently command her spirits to relate the whole of her narrative. The first part of it agreed perfectly with the account delivered in the confession to the penitentiary Ansaldo; that which follows was known only to herself, her sister Bianchi, a physician, and one faithful servant, who had been considerably entrusted with the conduct of the plan.

It may be recollected that Schedoni left his house immediately after the act, which was designed to be fatal to the Countess his wife, and that she was carried senseless to her chamber. The wound, as appears, was not mortal. But the atrocity of the intent determined her to seize the opportunity thus offered by the absence of Schedoni, and her own peculiar circumstances, to release herself from his tyranny without having recourse to a court of justice, which would have covered with infamy the brother of her first husband. She withdrew, therefore, from his house for ever, and with the assistance of the three persons before mentioned, retired to a remote part of Italy, and sought refuge in the convent of San Stefano, while at home the report of her death was confirmed by a public funeral. Bianchi remained for some time after the departure of Olivia, in her own residence near the Villa di Bruno, having taken under her immediate care the daughter of the Countess and of the first Count di Bruno, as well as an infant daughter of the second.

After some time had elapsed, Bianchi withdrew with her young charge, but not to the neighbourhood of San Stefano. The indulgence of a mother's tenderness was denied to Olivia, for Bianchi could not reside near the convent without subjecting her to the hazard of a discovery, since Schedoni, though he now believed the report of her death, might be led to doubt it, by the conduct of Bianchi, whose steps would probably be observed by him. She chose a residence, therefore, at a distance from Olivia, though not yet at Altieri. At this period, Ellena was not two years old; the daughter of Schedoni was scarcely as many months, and she died before the year concluded. It was this his child, for whom the Confessor, who had too well concealed himself to permit Bianchi to acquaint him with her death, had mistaken Ellena, and to which mistake his own portrait, affirmed by Ellena to be that of her father, had contributed. This miniature she had found in the cabinet of Bianchi after her aunt's decease, and, observing it inscribed with the title of Count di Bruno, she had worn it with a filial fondness ever since that period.

Bianchi, when she had acquainted Ellena with the secret of her birth, was withheld, both by prudence and humanity, from intrusting her with a knowledge that her mother lived; but this, no doubt, was the circumstance she appeared so anxious to disclose on her death-bed, when the suddenness of her disorder had deprived her of the power. The abruptness of that event had thus contributed to keep the mother and daughter unknown to each other, even when they afterwards accidentally met, to which concealment the name of Rosalba, given to Ellena from her infancy by Bianchi, for the purpose of protecting her from discovery by her uncle, had assisted. Beatrice, who was not the domestic intrusted with the escape of Olivia, had believed the report of her death, and thus, though she knew Ellena to be the daughter of the Countess di Bruno, she could never have been a means of discovering them to each other, had it not happened that Olivia recognized this ancient servant of Bianchi, while Ellena was present.

When Bianchi came to reside in the neighbourhood of Naples, she was unsuspicious that Schedoni, who had never been heard of since the night of the assassination, inhabited there; and she so seldom left her house, that it is not surprising she should never happen to meet him, at least consciously; for her veil, and the monk's cowl, might easily have concealed them from each other if they had met.

It appears to have been the intention of Bianchi to disclose to Vivaldi the family of Ellena, before their nuptials were solemnized; since, on the evening of their last conversation, she had declared, when her spirits were exhausted by the exertion she had made, that much remained for her to say, which weakness obliged her to defer till another opportunity. Her unexpected death prevented any future meeting. That she had not sooner intended to make a communication, which might have removed, in a considerable degree, the objection of the Vivaldi to a connection with Ellena, appears extraordinary, till other circumstances of her family, than that of its nobility, are considered. Her present indigence, and yet more, the guilt attached to an individual of the di Bruno, it was reasonable to suppose would operate as a full antidote to the allurement of rank, however jealous of birth the Vivaldi had proved themselves.

Ferando di Bruno had contrived, even in the short interval between the death of his brother and the supposed decease of his wife, again to embarrass his affairs, and soon after his flight, the income arising from what remained of his landed property had been seized upon by his creditors, whether lawfully or not, he was then in a situation which did not permit him to contest, and Ellena was thus left wholly dependent upon her aunt. The small fortune of Bianchi had been diminished by the assistance she afforded Olivia, for whose admittance into the convent of San Stefano it had been necessary to advance a considerable sum; and her original income was afterwards reduced by the purchase of the villa Altieri. This expenditure, however, was not an imprudent one, since she preferred the comforts and independence of a pleasant home, with industry, to the indulgence of an indolence which must have confined her to an inferior residence; and was acquainted with the means of making this industry profitable without being dishonourable. She excelled in many elegant and ingenious arts, and the productions of her pencil and needle were privately disposed of to the nuns of the Santa della Pieta. When Ellena was of an age to assist her, she resigned much of the employment and the profit to her niece, whose genius having unfolded itself, the beauty of her designs and the elegance of her execution, both in drawings and embroidery, were so highly valued by the purchasers at the grate of the convent, that Bianchi committed to Ellena altogether the exercise of her art.

Olivia meanwhile had dedicated her life to devotion in the

monastery of San Stefano, a choice which was willingly made while her mind was yet softened by grief for the death of her first lord, and wearied by the cruelty she had afterwards experienced. The first years of her retirement were passed in tranquillity, except when the remembrance of her child, whom she did not dare to see at the convent, awakened a parental pang. With Bianchi she, however, corresponded as regularly as opportunity would allow, and had at least the consolation of knowing, that the object most dear to her lived, till, within a short period of Ellena's arrival at the very asylum chosen by her mother, her apprehensions were in some degree excited by the unusual silence of Bianchi.

When Olivia had first seen Ellena in the chapel of San Stefano, she was struck with a slight resemblance she bore to the late Count di Bruno, and had frequently afterwards examined her features with a most painful curiosity; but, circumstanced as she was, Olivia could not reasonably suspect the stranger to be her daughter. Once, however, a sense of this possibility so far overcame her judgment, as to prompt an inquiry for the sirname of Ellena; but the mention of Rosalba had checked all further conjecture. What would have been the feelings of the nun, had she been told when her generous compassion was assisting a stranger to escape from oppression that she was preserving her own child! It may be worthy of observation, that the virtues of Olivia, exerted in a general cause, had thus led her unconsciously to the happiness of saving her daughter; while the vices of Schedoni had as unconsciously urged him nearly to destroy his niece, and had always been preventing, by the means they prompted him to employ, the success of his constant aim.

CHAPTER X

Those hours, which lately smil'd, where are they now?
Pallid to thought and ghastly!

YOUNG*

THE Marchesa di Vivaldi, of whose death Beatrice had given an imperfect account, struck with remorse of the crime she had meditated against Ellena, and with terror of the punishment due to it, had sent, when on her death-bed, for a Confessor, to whom she unburthened her conscience, and from whom she hoped to receive, in return, an alleviation of her despair. This Confessor was a man of good sense and humanity; and, when he fully understood the story of Vivaldi and Ellena di Rosalba, he declared, that her only hope of forgiveness, both for the crime she had meditated, and the undeserved sufferings she had occasioned, rested upon her willingness to make those now happy, whom she had formerly rendered miserable. Her conscience had already given her the same lesson; and, now that she was sinking to that grave which levels all distinctions, and had her just fear of retribution no longer opposed by her pride, she became as anxious to promote the marriage of Vivaldi with Ellena as she had ever been to prevent it. She sent, therefore, for the Marchese; and, having made an avowal of the arts she had practised against the peace and reputation of Ellena, without, however, confessing the full extent of her intended crimes, she made it her last request, that he would consent to the happiness of his son.

The Marchese, however, shocked as he was at this discovery of the duplicity and cruelty of his wife, had neither her terror of the future, or remorse for the past, to overcome his objection to the rank of Ellena; and he resisted all her importunity, till the anguish of her last hours overcame every consideration but that of affording her relief; he then gave a solemn promise, in the presence of the Confessor, that he would no longer oppose the marriage of Vivaldi and Ellena, should the former persist in his attachment to her. This promise was sufficient for the Marchesa, and she died with some degree of resignation. It did not, however, appear probable, that the Marchese would soon be called upon to fulfil the engagements, into which he had so unwillingly entered, every inquiry after Vivaldi having been hitherto in-effectual.

During the progress of this fruitless search for his son, and while the Marchese was almost lamenting him as dead, the inhabitants of the Vivaldi palace were, one night, aroused from sleep by a violent knocking at the great gate of the court. The noise was so loud and incessant, that, before the porter could obey the summons, the Marchese, whose apartment looked upon the court, was alarmed, and sent an attendant from his anti-room, to inquire the occasion of it.

Presently a voice was heard from the first anti-chamber, exclaiming, 'I must see my Lord Marchese directly; he will not be angry to be waked, when he knows all about it;' and, before the Marchese could order that no person, on whatever pretence, should be admitted, Paulo, haggard, ragged, and covered with dirt, was in the chamber. His wan and affrighted countenance, his disordered dress, and his very attitude, as on entering he half turned to look back upon the anti-rooms, like one, who, just escaped from bondage, listens to the fancied sounds of pursuit, were altogether so striking and terrific, that the Marchese, anticipating some dreadful news of Vivaldi, had scarcely power to inquire for him. Paulo, however, rendered questions unnecessary; for, without any circumlocution, or preface, he immediately informed the Marchese, that the Signor, his dear master, was in the prisons of the Inquisition, at Rome, if, indeed, they had not put an end to him before that time.

'Yes, my Lord,' said Paulo, 'I am just got out myself, for they would not let me be with the Signor, so it was of no use to stay there any longer. Yet it was a hard matter with me to go away, and leave my dear master within those dismal walls; and nothing should have persuaded me to do so, but that I hoped, when your Lordship knew where the Signor was, you might be able to get him out. But there is not a minute to be lost, my Lord, for when once a gentleman has got within the claws of those inquisitors, there is no knowing how soon they may take it in their heads to tear him in pieces. Shall I order horses for Rome, my Lord? I am ready to set off again directly.'

The suddenness of such intelligence, concerning an only son, might have agitated stronger nerves than those of the Marchese, and so much was he shocked by it, that he could not immediately determine how to proceed, or give any answer to Paulo's repeated questions. When, however, he became sufficiently recollected to make further inquiry into the situation of Vivaldi, he perceived the necessity of an immediate journey; but first it would be prudent to consult with some friends, whose connections at Rome might be a means of greatly facilitating the important purpose, which led him thither, and this could not be done till the following morning. Yet he gave orders, that preparation should be made for his setting out at a moment's notice; and, having listened to as full an account as Paulo could give of the past and present circumstances of Vivaldi, he dismissed him to repose for the remainder of the night.

Paulo, however, though much in want of rest, was in too great an agitation of spirits either to seek or to find it; and the fear he had indicated, on entering the Marchese's apartment, proceeded from the hurry of his mind, rather than from any positive apprehension of new evil. For his liberty he was indebted to the young centinel, who had on a former occasion been removed from the door of his prison, but who, by means of the guard, to whom Vivaldi had given money, as he returned one night from the tribunal, had since been able to communicate with him. This man, of a nature too humane for his situation, was become wretched in it, and he determined to escape from his office before the expiration of the time, for which he had been engaged. He thought that to be a guard over prisoners was nearly as miserable as being a prisoner himself. 'I see no difference between them,' said he, 'except that the prisoner watches on one side of the door, and the centinel on the other.'

With the resolution to release himself, he conferred with Paulo, whose good nature and feeling heart, among so many people of a contrary character, had won his confidence and affection, and he laid his plan of escape so well, that it was on the point of succeeding, when Paulo's obstinacy in attempting an impossibility had nearly counteracted the whole. It went to his heart, he said, to leave his master in prison, while he himself was to march off in safety, and he would run the risk of his neck, rather than have such a deed upon his head. He proposed, therefore, as Vivaldi's guards were of too ferocious a nature to be tampered with, to scale a wall of the court into which a grate of Vivaldi's dungeon looked. But had this lofty wall been practicable, the grate was not; and the attempt had nearly cost Paulo not only his liberty, but his life.

When, at length, he had made his way through the perilous avenues of the prison, and was fairly beyond the walls, he could hardly be prevailed upon by his companion to leave them. For near an hour, he wandered under their shade, weeping and exclaiming, and calling upon his dear master, at the evident hazard of being retaken; and probably would have remained there much longer, had not the dawn of morning rendered his companion desperate. Just, however, as the man was forcing him away, Paulo fancied he distinguished, by the strengthening light, the roof of that particular building, in whose dungeon his master was confined, and the appearance of Vivaldi himself could scarcely have occasioned a more sudden burst of joy; succeeded by one of grief. 'It is the roof, it is the very roof!' exclaimed Paulo, vaulting from the ground, and clapping his hands; 'it is the roof, the roof! O, my master, my master! the roof, the roof!' He continued alternately to exclaim, 'My master! the roof! my master! the roof!' till his companion began to fear he was frantic, while tears streamed down his cheeks, and every look and gesture expressed the most extravagant and whimsical union of joy and sorrow. At length, the absolute terror of discovery compelled his companion to force him from the spot; when, having lost sight of the building which inclosed Vivaldi, he set off for Naples with a speed that defied all interruption, and arrived there in the condition, which has been mentioned, having taken no sleep, and scarcely any sustenance, since he left the Inquisition. Yet though in this exhausted state, the spirit of his affection remained unbroken, and when, on the following morning, the Marchese quitted Naples, neither his weariness, nor the imminent danger, to which this journey must expose him, could prevent his attending him to Rome.

The rank of the Marchese, and the influence he was known to possess at the court of Naples, were circumstances that promised to have weight with the Holy Office, and to procure Vivaldi a speedy release; but yet more than these, were the high connections which the Count di Maro, the friend of the Marchese, had in the church of Rome.

The applications, however, which were made to the inquisitors, were not so soon replied to as the wishes of the Marchese had expected, and he had been above a fortnight in that city, before he was even permitted to visit his son. In this interview, affection predominated on both sides over all remembrance of the past. The condition of Vivaldi, his faded appearance, to which the wounds he had received at Celano, and from which he was scarcely recovered, had contributed; and his situation in a melancholy and terrible prison, were circumstances that awakened all the tenderness of the father; his errors were forgiven, and the Marchese felt disposed to consent to all that might restore him to happiness, could he but be restored to liberty.

Vivaldi, when informed of his mother's death, shed bitter tears of sorrow and remorse, for having occasioned her so much uneasiness. The unreasonableness of her claims was forgotten, and her faults were extenuated; happily, indeed, for his peace, the extent of her criminal designs he had never understood; and when he learned that her dying request had been intended to promote his happiness, the cruel consciousness of having interrupted her's, occasioned him severe anguish, and he was obliged to recollect her former conduct towards Ellena at San Stefano, before he could become reconciled to himself.

CHAPTER XI

Your's in the ranks of death.
SHAKESPEARE*

NEAR three weeks had elapsed since the Marchese's arrival at Rome, and not any decisive answer was returned by the Inquisition to his application, when he and Vivaldi received at the same time a summons to attend father Schedoni in his dungeon. To meet the man who had occasioned so much suffering to his family, was extremely painful to the Marchese, but he was not allowed to refuse the interview; and at the hour appointed he called at the chamber of Vivaldi; and, followed by two officials, they passed on together to that of Schedoni.

While they waited at the door of the prison-room, till the numerous bars and locks were unfastened, the agitation, which Vivaldi had suffered, on receiving the summons, returned with redoubled force, now that he was about to behold, once more, that wretched man, who had announced himself to be the parent of Ellena di Rosalba. The Marchese suffered emotions of a different nature, and with his reluctance to see Schedoni, was mingled a degree of curiosity as to the event, which had occasioned this summons.

The door being thrown open, the officials entered first, and the Marchese and Vivaldi, on following, discovered the Confessor lying on a mattress. He did not rise to receive them, but, as he lifted his head, and bowed it in obeisance, his countenance, upon which the little light admitted through the triple grate of his dungeon gleamed, seemed more than usually ghastly; his eyes were hollow, and his shrunk features appeared as if death had already touched them. Vivaldi, on perceiving him, groaned, and averted his face; but, soon recovering a command of himself, he approached the mattress.

The Marchese, suppressing every expression of resentment towards an enemy, who was reduced to this deplorable condition, inquired what he had to communicate.

'Where is father Nicola?' said Schedoni to an official, without attending to the question: 'I do not see him here. Is he gone so soon, and without having heard the purport of my summons? Let him be called.'

The official spoke to a centinel, who immediately left the chamber.

'Who are these that surround me?' said Schedoni. 'Who is he that stands at the foot of the bed?' While he spoke, he bent his eyes on Vivaldi, who rested in deep dejection there, and was lost in thought, till, aroused by Schedoni's voice, he replied,

'It is I, Vincentio di Vivaldi; I obey your requisition,* and inquire the purpose of it?'

The Marchese repeated the demand. Schedoni appeared to meditate; sometimes he fixed his eyes upon Vivaldi, for an instant, and when he withdrew them, he seemed to sink into deeper thoughtfulness. As he raised them once again, they assumed a singular expression of wildness, and then settling, as if on vacancy, a sudden glare shot from them, while he said—'Who is he, that glides there in the dusk?'

His eyes were directed beyond Vivaldi, who, on turning, perceived the monk, father Nicola, passing behind him.

'I am here,' said Nicola: 'what do you require of me?'

'That you will bear testimony to the truth of what I shall declare,' replied Schedoni.

Nicola, and an inquisitor who had accompanied him, immediately arranged themselves on one side of the bed, while the Marchese stationed himself on the other. Vivaldi remained at its foot.

Schedoni, after a pause, began: 'That which I have to make known relates to the cabal* formerly carried on by him, the father Nicola, and myself, against the peace of an innocent young woman, whom, at my instigation, he has basely traduced.'

At these words, Nicola attempted to interrupt the Confessor, but Vivaldi restrained him.

'Ellena di Rosalba is known to you?' continued Schedoni, addressing the Marchese.

Vivaldi's countenance changed at this abrupt mention of Ellena, but he remained silent.

'I have heard of her,' replied the Marchese, coldly.

'And you have heard falsely of her,' rejoined Schedoni. 'Lift your eyes, my lord Marchese, and say, do you not recollect that face?' pointing to Nicola.

The Marchese regarded the monk attentively, 'It is a face not easily to be forgotten,' he replied; 'I remember to have seen it more than once.'

'Where have you seen him, my Lord?'

'In my own palace, at Naples; and you yourself introduced him to me there.'

'I did,' replied Schedoni.

'Why, then, do you now accuse him of falshood,' observed the Marchese, 'since you acknowledge yourself to have been the instigator of his conduct?'

'O heavens!' said Vivaldi, 'this monk, then, this father Nicola, is, as I suspected, the slanderer of Ellena di Rosalba!'

'Most true,' rejoined Schedoni; 'and it is for the purpose of vindicating——'

'And you acknowledge yourself to be the author of those infamous slanders!' passionately interrupted Vivaldi;—'you, who but lately declared yourself to be her father!'

In the instant, that Vivaldi had uttered this, he became sensible of his indiscretion, for till now he had avoided informing the Marchese, that Ellena had been declared the daughter of Schedoni. This abrupt disclosure, and at such a moment, he immediately perceived might be fatal to his hopes, and that the Marchese would not consider the promise he had given to his dying wife, however solemn, as binding, under circumstances so peculiar and unforeseen as the present. The astonishment of the Marchese, upon this discovery, cannot easily be imagined; he looked at his son for an explanation of what he had heard, and then with increased detestation at the Confessor; but Vivaldi was not in a state of mind to give any explanation at this moment, and he requested his father to suspend even his conjectures till he could converse with him alone.

The Marchese desisted for the present from further inquiry, but it was obvious that his opinion and his resolution, respecting the marriage of Vivaldi, was already formed.

'You, then, are the author of those slanders!' repeated Vivaldi.

'Hear me!' cried Schedoni, in a voice which the strength of his spirit contending with the feebleness of his condition, rendered hollow and terrible—'Hear me!'

He stopped, unable to recover immediately from the effect of the exertion he had made. At length, he resumed,

'I have declared, and I continue to declare, that Ellena di Rosalba, as she has been named for the purpose, I conjecture, of concealing her from an unworthy father, is my daughter!'

Vivaldi groaned in the excess of his despair, but made no further attempt to interrupt Schedoni. The Marchese was not equally passive. 'And was it to listen to a vindication of your daughter,' said he, 'that I have been summoned hither? But let this Signora Rosalba, be who she may, of what importance can it be to me whether she is innocent or otherwise!'

Vivaldi, with the utmost difficulty, forbore to express the feelings, which this sentence excited. It appeared to recall all the spirit of Schedoni. 'She is the daughter of a noble house,' said the Confessor, haughtily, while he half raised himself from his mattress. 'In me you behold the last of the Counts di Bruno.'

The Marchese smiled contemptuously.

Schedoni proceeded. 'I call upon you, Nicola di Zampari, who have declared yourself, on a late occasion, so strenuous for justice, I call upon you now to do justice in this instance, and to acknowledge, before these witnesses, that Ellena Rosalba is innocent of every circumstance of misconduct, which you have formerly related to the Marchese di Vivaldi!'

'Villain! do you hesitate,' said Vivaldi to Nicola, 'to retract the cruel slanders which you have thrown upon her name, and which have been the means of destroying her peace, perhaps for ever? Do you persist——'

The Marchese interrupted his son:—'Let me put an end to the difficulty, by concluding the interview; I perceive that my presence has been required for a purpose that does not concern me.'

Before the Confessor could reply, the Marchese had turned from him to quit the chamber; but the vehemence of Vivaldi's distress prevailed with him to pause, and thus allowed him to understand from Schedoni, that the justification of the innocent Ellena, though it had been mentioned first, as being the object nearest to his heart, was not the only one that had urged him to require this meeting.

'If you consent,' added Schedoni, 'to listen to the vindication of my child, you shall afterwards perceive, Signor, that I, fallen though I am, have still been desirous of counteracting, as far as remains for me, the evil I have occasioned. You shall acknowledge, that what I then make known is of the utmost consequence to the repose of the Marchese di Vivaldi, high in influence, and haughty in prosperity as he now appears.'

The latter part of this assurance threatened to overcome the effect of the first; the pride of the Marchese swelled high; he took some steps towards the door, but then stopped, and, conjecturing that the subject, to which Schedoni alluded, concerned the liberation of his son, he consented to attend to what Nicola should disclose.

This monk, meanwhile, had been balancing the necessity for acknowledging himself a slanderer, against the possibility of avoiding it; and it was the resolute manner of Vivaldi, who appeared to have no doubt as to his guilt in this instance, that made him apprehend the consequence of persisting in falshood, not either remorse of conscience, or the appeal of Schedoni. He acknowledged then, after considerable circumlocution, in which he contrived to defend himself, by throwing all the odium of the original design upon the Confessor, that he had been prevailed upon by his arts to impose on the credulity of the Marchese, respecting the conduct of Ellena di Rosalba. This avowal was made upon oath, and Schedoni, by the questions he put to him, was careful it should be so full and circumstantial that even the most prejudiced hearer must have been convinced of its truth; while the most unfeeling must have yielded for once to indignation against the asperser,* and pity of the aspersed. Its effect upon the present auditors was various. The Marchese had listened to the whole explanation with an unmoved countenance, but with profound attention. Vivaldi had remained in a fixed attitude, with eyes bent on father Nicola, in such eager and stern regard, as seemed to search into his very soul; and, when the monk concluded, a smile of triumphant joy lighted up his features, as he looked upon the Marchese, and claimed an acknowledgment of his conviction, that Ellena had been calumniated. The cold glance, which the Marchese returned, struck the impassioned and generous Vivaldi to the heart, who perceived that he was not only totally indifferent as to the injustice, which an innocent and helpless young woman had suffered, but fancied that he was unwilling to admit the truth, which his judgment would no longer allow him to reject.

Schedoni, meanwhile, appeared almost to writhe under the agony, which his mind inflicted upon him, and it was only by strong effort, that he sustained his spirit so far as to go through with the interrogations he had judged it necessary to put to Nicola. When the subject was finished, he sunk back on his pillow, and, closing his eyes, a hue so pallid, succeeded by one so livid, overspread his features, that Vivaldi for an instant believed he was dying; and in this supposition he was not singular, for even an official was touched with the Confessor's condition, and had advanced to assist him, when he unclosed his eyes, and seemed to revive.

The Marchese, without making any comment upon the avowal of father Nicola, demanded, on its conclusion, the disclosure, which Schedoni had asserted to be intimately connected with his peace; and the latter now inquired of a person near him, whether a secretary of the Inquisition was in the chamber, who he had requested might attend, to take a formal deposition of what he should declare. He was answered, that such an one was already in waiting. He then asked, what other persons were in the room, adding, that he should require inquisitorial witnesses to his deposition; and was answered, that an inquisitor and two officials were present, and that their evidence was more than sufficient for his purpose.

A lamp was then called for by the secretary; but, as that could not immediately be procured, the torch of one of the centinels, who watched in the dark avenue without, was brought in its stead, and this discovered to Schedoni the various figures assembled in his dusky chamber, and to them the emaciated form and ghastly visage of the Confessor. As Vivaldi now beheld him by the stronger light of the torch, he again fancied that death was in his aspect.

Every person was now ready for the declaration of Schedoni; but he himself seemed not fully prepared. He remained for some moments reclining on his pillow in silence, with his eyes shut, while the changes in his features indicated the strong emotion of his mind. Then, as if by a violent effort, he half raised himself, and made an ample confession of the arts he had practised against Vivaldi. He declared himself to be the anonymous accuser, who had caused him to be arrested by the Holy Office, and that the charge of heresy, which he had brought against him, was false and malicious.

At the moment when Vivaldi received this confirmation of his suspicions, as to the identity of his accuser, he discovered more fully that the charge was not what had been stated to him at the chapel of San Sebastian, in which Ellena was implicated; and he demanded an explanation of this circumstance. Schedoni acknowledged, that the persons, who had there arrested him, were not officers of the Inquisition, and that the instrument of arrest, containing the charge of elopement with a nun, was forged by himself, for the purpose of empowering the ruffians to carry off Ellena, without opposition from the inhabitants of the convent, in which she was then lodged.

To Vivaldi's inquiry, why it had been thought necessary to employ stratagem in the removal of Ellena, since, if Schedoni had only claimed her for his daughter, he might have removed her without any, the Confessor replied, that he was then ignorant of the relationship which existed between them. But to the further inquiries, with what design, and whither Ellena had been removed, and the means by which he had discovered her to be his daughter, Schedoni was silent; and he sunk back, overwhelmed by the recollections they awakened.

The depositions of Schedoni having been taken down by the secretary, were formally signed by the inquisitor and the officials present; and Vivaldi thus saw his innocence vindicated by the very man who had thrown him among the perils of the Inquisition. But the near prospect of release now before him failed to affect him with joy, while he understood that Ellena was the daughter of Schedoni, the child of a murderer, whom he himself had been in some degree instrumental in bringing to a dreadful and ignominious death. Still, however, willing to hope, that Schedoni had not spoken the truth concerning his relationship to Ellena, he claimed, in consideration of the affection he had so long cherished for her, a full explanation of the circumstances connected with the discovery of her family.

At this public avowal of his attachment, a haughty impatience appeared on the countenance of the Marchese, who forbade him to make further inquiry on the subject, and was immediately retiring from the chamber.

'My presence is no longer necessary,' he added: 'the prisoner has concluded the only detail which I could be interested to hear from him; and, in consideration of the confession he has made as to the innocence of my son, I pardon him the suffering, which his false charge has occasioned to me and my family. The paper containing his depositions is given to your responsibility, holy father,' addressing the inquisitor; 'and you are required to lay it upon the table of the Holy Office, that the innocence of Vincentio di Vivaldi may appear, and that he may be released from these prisons without further delay. But first, I demand a copy of those declarations, and that the copy also shall be signed by the present witnesses.'

The secretary was now bidden to copy them, and, while the Marchese waited to receive the paper, (for he would not leave the chamber till he had secured it) Vivaldi was urging his claim for an explanation respecting the family of Ellena, with unconquerable perseverance. Schedoni, no longer permitted to evade the inquiry, could not, however, give a circumstantial explanation, without partly disclosing, also, the fatal designs which had been meditated by him and the late Marchesa di Vivaldi, of whose death he was ignorant; he related, therefore, little more respecting Ellena than that a portrait, which she wore as being her father's, had first led to the discovery of her family.

While the Confessor had been giving this brief explanation, Nicola, who was somewhat withdrawn from the circle, stood gazing at him with the malignity of a demon. His glowing eyes just appeared under the edge of his cowl, while, rolled up in his dark drapery, the lower features of his face were muffled; but the inter-mediate part of his countenance, receiving the full glare of the torch, displayed all its speaking and terrific lines. Vivaldi, as his eye glanced upon him, saw again the very monk of Paluzzi, and he thought he beheld also a man capable of the very crimes of which he had accused Schedoni. At this instant, he remembered the dreadful garment that had been discovered in a dungeon of the fortress; and, yet more, he remembered the extraordinary circum-stances attending the death of Bianchi, together with the immediate knowledge which the monk had displayed of that event. Vivaldi's suspicions respecting the cause of her death being thus revived, he determined to obtain, if possible, either a relief from, or a confirmation of them; and he solemnly called upon Schedoni, who, already condemned to die, had no longer any thing to fear from a disclosure of the truth, whatever it might be, to declare all that he knew on the subject. As he did so, he looked at Nicola, to observe the effect of this demand, whose countenance was, however, so much shrouded, that little of its expression could be seen; but Vivaldi remarked, that, while he had spoken, the monk drew his garment closer over the lower part of his face, and that he had immediately turned his eyes from him upon the Confessor.

With most solemn protestations, Schedoni declared himself to be both innocent and ignorant of the cause of Bianchi's death.

Vivaldi then demanded by what means his agent, Nicola, had obtained such immediate information, as the warning he had delivered at Paluzzi proved him to have, of an event, in which it appeared that he could be so little interested; and why that warning had been given.

Nicola did not attempt to anticipate the reply of Schedoni, who, after a momentary silence, said, 'That warning, young man, was given to deter you from visiting Altieri, as was every circumstance of advice or intelligence, which you received beneath the arch of Paluzzi.'

'Father,' replied Vivaldi, 'you have never loved, or you would have spared yourself the practice of artifices so ineffectual to mislead or to conquer a lover. Did you believe that an anonymous adviser could have more influence with me than my affection, or that I could be terrified by such stratagems into a renunciation of its object?'

'I believed,' rejoined the Confessor, 'that the disinterested advice of a stranger might have some weight with you; but I trusted more to the impression of awe, which the conduct and seeming foreknowledge of that stranger were adapted to inspire in a mind like your's; and I thus endeavoured to avail myself of your prevailing weakness.'

'And what do you term my prevailing weakness,' said Vivaldi, blushing.

'A susceptibility which renders you especially liable to superstition,' replied Schedoni.

'What! does a monk call superstition a weakness!' rejoined Vivaldi. 'But grant he does, on what occasion have I betrayed such weakness?'

'Have you forgotten a conversation which I once held with you on invisible spirits?' said Schedoni.

As he asked this, Vivaldi was struck with the tone of his voice; he thought it was different from what he had remembered ever to have heard from him; and he looked at Schedoni more intently, that he might be certain it was he who had spoken. The Confessor's eyes were fixed upon him, and he repeated slowly in the same tone, 'Have you forgotten?'

'I have not forgotten the conversation to which you allude,' replied Vivaldi, 'and I do not recollect that I then disclosed any opinion that may justify your assertion.'

'The opinions you avowed were rational,' said Schedoni, 'but the ardour of your imagination was apparent, and what ardent imagination ever was contented to trust to plain reasoning, or to the evidence of the senses? It may not willingly confine itself to the dull truths of this earth, but, eager to expand its faculties, to fill its capacity, and to experience its own peculiar delights, soars after new wonders into a world of its own!'

Vivaldi blushed at this reproof, now conscious of its justness; and was surprised that Schedoni should so well have understood the nature of his mind, while he himself, with whom conjecture had never assumed the stability of opinion, on the subject to which the Confessor alluded, had been ignorant even of its propensities.

'I acknowledge the truth of your remark,' said Vivaldi, 'as far as it concerns myself. I have, however, inquiries to make on a point less abstracted, and towards explaining which the evidence of my senses themselves have done little. To whom belonged the bloody garments I found in the dungeon of Paluzzi, and what became of the person to whom they had pertained?'

Consternation appeared for an instant on the features of Schedoni. 'What garments?' said he.

'They appeared to be those of a person who had died by violence,' replied Vivaldi, 'and they were discovered in a place frequented by your avowed agent, Nicola, the monk.'

As he concluded the sentence, Vivaldi looked at Nicola, upon whom the attention of every person present was now directed.

'They were my own,' said this monk.

'Your own! and in that condition!' exclaimed Vivaldi. 'They were covered with gore!'

'They were my own,' repeated Nicola. 'For their condition, I have to thank you,—the wound your pistol gave me occasioned it.'

Vivaldi was astonished by this apparent subterfuge. 'I had no pistol,' he rejoined, 'my sword was my only weapon!'

'Pause a moment,' said the monk.

'I repeat that I had no fire-arms,' replied Vivaldi.

'I appeal to father Schedoni,' rejoined Nicola, 'whether I was not wounded by a pistol shot.'

'To me you have no longer any right of appeal,' said Schedoni. 'Why should I save you from suspicions, that may bring you to a state like this, to which you have reduced me!'

'Your crimes have reduced you to it,' replied Nicola, 'I have only done my duty, and that which another person could have effected without my aid—the priest to whom Spalatro made his last confession.'

'It is, however, a duty of such a kind,' observed Vivaldi, 'as I would not willingly have upon my conscience. You have betrayed the life of your former friend, and have compelled me to assist in the destruction of a fellow being.'

'You, like me, have assisted to destroy a destroyer,' replied the monk. 'He has taken life, and deserves, therefore, to lose it. If, however, it will afford you consolation to know that you have not materially assisted in his destruction, I will hereafter give you proof for this assurance. There were other means of shewing that Schedoni was the Count di Bruno, than the testimony of Ansaldo, though I was ignorant of them when I bade you summon the penitentiary.'

'If you had sooner avowed this,' said Vivaldi, 'the assertion would have been more plausible. Now, I can only understand that it is designed to win my silence, and prevent my retorting upon you your own maxim—that he who has taken the life of another, deserves to lose his own.—To whom did those bloody garments belong?'

'To myself, I repeat,' replied Nicola, 'Schedoni can bear testimony that I received at Paluzzi a pistol wound.'

'Impossible,' said Vivaldi, 'I was armed only with my sword!'

'You had a companion,' observed the monk, 'had not he fire-arms?'

Vivaldi, after a momentary consideration, recollected that Paulo had pistols, and that he had fired one beneath the arch of Paluzzi, on the first alarm occasioned by the stranger's voice. He immediately acknowledged the recollection. 'But I heard no groan, no symptom of distress!' he added. 'Besides, the garments were at a considerable distance from the spot where the pistol was fired! How could a person, so severely wounded as those garments indicated, have silently withdrawn to a remote dungeon, or, having done so, is it probable he would have thrown aside his dress!'

'All that is nevertheless true,' replied Nicola. 'My resolution enabled me to stifle the expression of my anguish; I withdrew to the interior of the ruin, to escape from you, but you pursued me even to the dungeon, where I threw off my discoloured vestments, in which I dared not return to my convent, and departed by a way which all your ingenuity failed to discover. The people who were already in the fort, for the purpose of assisting to confine you and your servant during the night on which Signora Rosalba was taken from Altieri, procured me another habit, and relief for my wound. But, though I was unseen by you during the night, I was not entirely unheard, for my groans reached you more than once from an adjoining chamber, and my companions were entertained with the alarm which your servant testified.—Are you now convinced?'

The groans were clearly remembered by Vivaldi, and many other circumstances of Nicola's narration accorded so well with others, which he recollected to have occurred on the night alluded to, that he had no longer a doubt of its veracity. The suddenness of Bianchi's death, however, still occasioned him suspicions as to its cause; yet Schedoni had declared not only that he was innocent, but ignorant of this cause, which it appeared from his unwilling-ness to give testimony in favour of his agent, he would not have affirmed, had he been conscious that the monk was in any degree guilty in this instance. That Nicola could have no inducement for attempting the life of Bianchi other than a reward offered him by Schedoni, was clear; and Vivaldi, after more fully considering these circumstances, became convinced that her death was in consequence of some incident of natural decay.

While this conversation was passing, the Marchese, impatient to put a conclusion to it, and to leave the chamber, repeatedly urged the secretary to dispatch; and, while he now earnestly renewed his request, another voice answered for the secretary, that he had nearly concluded. Vivaldi thought that he had heard the voice on some former occasion, and on turning his eyes upon the person who had spoken, discovered the stranger to be the same who had first visited him in prison. Perceiving by his dress, that he was an officer of the Inquisition, Vivaldi now understood too well the purport of his former visit, and that he had come with a design to betray him by affected sympathy into a confession of some heretical opinions. Similar instances of treachery Vivaldi had heard were frequently practised upon accused persons, but he had never fully believed such cruelty possible till now, that it had been attempted towards himself.*

The visit of this person bringing to his recollection the subse-quent one he had received from Nicola, Vivaldi inquired whether the centinels had really admitted him to his cell, or he had entered it by other means; a question to which the monk was silent, but the smile on his features, if so strange an expression deserved to be called a smile, seemed to reply, 'Do you believe that I, a servant of the Inquisition, will betray its secrets?'

Vivaldi, however, urged the inquiry, for he wished to know whether the guard, who appeared to be faithful to their office, had escaped the punishment that was threatened.

'They were honest,' replied Nicola, 'seek no further.'

'Are the tribunal convinced of their integrity?'

Nicola smiled again in derision, and replied, 'They never doubted it.'

'How!' said Vivaldi. 'Why were these men put under arrest, if their faithfulness was not even suspected?'

'Be satisfied with the knowledge, which experience has given you of the secrets of the Inquisition,' replied Nicola solemnly, 'seek to know no more!'

'It has terrible secrets!' said Schedoni, who had been long silent. 'Know, young man, that almost every cell of every prisoner has a concealed entrance, by which the ministers of death may pass unnoticed to their victims. This Nicola is now one of those dreadful summoners, and is acquainted with all the secret avenues, that lead to murder.'

Vivaldi shrunk from Nicola in horror, and Schedoni paused; but while he had spoken, Vivaldi had again noticed the extraordinary change in his voice, and shuddered at its sound no less than at the information it had given. Nicola was silent; but his terrible eyes were fixed in vengeance on Schedoni.

'His office has been short,' resumed the Confessor, turning his heavy eyes upon Nicola, 'and his task is almost done!' As he pronounced the last words his voice faltered, but they were heard by the monk, who drawing nearer to the bed, demanded an explanation of them. A ghastly smile triumphed in the features of Schedoni; 'Fear not but that an explanation will come full soon,' said he.

Nicola fixed himself before the Confessor, and bent his brows upon him as if he would have searched into his very soul. When Vivaldi again looked at Schedoni, he was shocked on observing the sudden alteration in his countenance, yet still a faint smile of triumph lingered there. But, while Vivaldi gazed, the features suddenly became agitated; in the next instant his whole frame was convulsed, and heavy groans laboured from his breast. Schedoni was now evidently dying.

The horror of Vivaldi, and of the Marchese, who endeavoured to leave the chamber, was equalled only by the general confusion that reigned there; every person present seemed to feel at least a momentary compassion, except Nicola, who stood unmoved beside Schedoni, and looked stedfastly upon his pangs, while a smile of derision marked his countenance. As Vivaldi observed, with detestation, this expression, a slight spasm darted over Nicola's face, and his muscles also seemed to labour with sudden contraction; but the affection was transient, and vanished as abruptly as it had appeared. The monk, however, turned from the miserable spectacle before him, and as he turned he caught involuntarily at the arm of a person near him, and leaned on his shoulder for support. His manner appeared to betray that he had not been permitted to triumph in the sufferings of his enemy, without participating at least in their horror.

Schedoni's struggles now began to abate, and in a short time he lay motionless. When he unclosed his eyes, death was in them. He was yet nearly insensible; but presently a faint gleam of recollection shot from them, and gradually lighting them up, the character of his soul appeared there; the expression was indeed feeble, but it was true. He moved his lips as if he would have spoken, and looked languidly round the chamber, seemingly in search of some person. At length, he uttered a sound, but he had not yet sufficient command of his muscles, to modulate that sound into a word, till by repeated efforts the name of Nicola became intelligible. At the call, the monk raised his head from the shoulder of the person on whom he had reclined, and turning round, Schedoni, as was evident from the sudden change of expression in his countenance, discovered him; his eyes, as they settled on Nicola seemed to recollect all their wonted fire, and the malignant triumph, lately so prevalent in his physiognomy, again appeared as in the next moment, he pointed to him. His glance seemed suddenly impowered with the destructive fascination attributed to that of the basilisk, for while it now met Nicola's, that monk seemed as if transfixed to the spot, and unable to withdraw his eyes from the glare of Schedoni's; in their expression he read the dreadful sentence of his fate, the triumph of revenge and cunning. Struck with this terrible conviction a pallid hue overspread his face; at the same time an involuntary motion convulsed his features, cold trembling seized upon his frame, and, uttering a deep groan, he fell back, and was caught in the arms of the people near him. At the instant of his fall, Schedoni uttered a sound so strange and horrible, so convulsed, yet so loud, so exulting, yet so unlike any human voice, that every person in the chamber, except those who were assisting Nicola, struck with irresistible terror, endeavoured to make their way out of it. This, however, was impracticable, for the door was fastened, until a physician, who had been sent for, should arrive, and some investigation could be made into this mysterious affair. The consternation of the Marchese and of Vivaldi, compelled to witness this scene of horror, cannot easily be imagined.

Schedoni, having uttered that demoniacal sound of exultation, was not permitted to repeat it, for the pangs he had lately suffered returned upon him, and he was again in strong convulsions, when the physician entered the chamber. The moment he beheld

Schedoni, he declared him to be poisoned; and he pronounced a similar opinion on father Nicola; affirming, also, that the drug, as appeared from the violence of the effect, was of too subtle and inveterate a nature to allow of antidote. He was, however, willing to administer the medicine usual in such cases.

While he was giving orders to an attendant, with respect to this, the violence of Schedoni's convulsions once more relaxed; but Nicola appeared in the last extremity. His sufferings were incessant, his senses never for a moment returned, and he expired, before the medicine, which had been sent for, could be brought. When it came, however, it was administered with some success to Schedoni, who recovered not only his recollection, but his voice; and the first word he uttered was, as formerly, the name of Nicola.

'Does he live?' added the Confessor with the utmost difficulty, and after a long pause. The persons around him were silent, but the truth, which this silence indicated, seemed to revive him.

The inquisitor, who had attended, perceiving that Schedoni had recovered the use of his intellects, now judged it prudent to ask some questions relative to his present condition, and to the cause of Nicola's death.

'Poison,' replied Schedoni readily.

'By whom administered?' said the inquisitor, 'consider that, while you answer, you are on your death-bed.'

'I have no wish to conceal the truth,' rejoined Schedoni, 'nor the satisfaction'—he was obliged to pause, but presently added, 'I have destroyed him, who would have destroyed me, and—and I have escaped an ignominious death.'

He paused again; it was with difficulty that he had said thus much, and he was now overcome by the exertion he had made. The secretary, who had not been permitted to leave the chamber, was ordered to note Schedoni's words.

'You avow then,' continued the inquisitor, 'that the poison was administered, both in the case of father Nicola and in your own, by yourself?'

Schedoni could not immediately reply; but when he did, he said, 'I avow it.'

He was asked by what means he had contrived to procure the poison, and was bidden to name his accomplice.

'I had no accomplice,' replied Schedoni.

'How did you procure the poison, then?'

Schedoni, slowly and with difficulty, replied, 'It was concealed in my vest.'

'Consider that you are dying,' said the inquisitor, 'and confess the truth. We cannot believe what you have last asserted. It is improbable that you should have had an opportunity of providing yourself with poison after your arrest, and equally improbable that you should have thought such provision necessary before that period. Confess who is your accomplice.'

This accusation of falshood recalled the spirit of Schedoni, which, contending with, and conquering, for a moment, corporeal suffering, he said in a firmer tone, 'It was the poison, in which I dip my poniard, the better to defend me.'

The inquisitor smiled in contempt of this explanation, and Schedoni, observing him, desired a particular part of his vest might be examined, where would be found some remains of the drug concealed as he had affirmed. He was indulged in his request, and the poison was discovered within a broad hem of his garment.

Still it was inconceivable how he had contrived to administer it to Nicola, who, though he had been for some time alone with him on this day, would scarcely have so far confided in an enemy, as to have accepted any seeming sustenance that might have been offered by him. The inquisitor, still anxious to discover an accomplice, asked Schedoni who had assisted to administer the drug to Nicola, but the Confessor was no longer in a condition to reply. Life was now sinking apace; the gleam of spirit and of character that had returned to his eyes, was departed, and left them haggard and fixed; and presently a livid corse was all that remained of the once terrible Schedoni!

While this awful event had been accomplishing, the Marchese, suffering under the utmost perturbation, had withdrawn to the distant grate of the dungeon, where he conversed with an official as to what might be the probable consequence of his present situation to himself; but Vivaldi, in an agony of horror, had been calling incessantly for the medicine, which might possibly afford some relief to the anguish he witnessed; and when it was brought, he had assisted to support the sufferers.

At length, now that the worst was over, and when the several witnesses had signed to the last avowal of Schedoni, every person in the chamber was suffered to depart; and Vivaldi was re-conducted to his prison, accompanied by the Marchese, where he was to remain till the decision of the holy office respecting his innocence, as asserted by the deposition of Schedoni, should be known. He was too much affected by the late scene to give the Marchese any explanation at present, respecting the family of Ellena di Rosalba, and the Marchese, having remained for some time with his son, withdrew to the residence of his friend.

CHAPTER XII*

Master, go on, and I will follow thee
To the last gasp, with truth and loyalty.
                    SHAKESPEARE*

IN consequence of the dying confession of Schedoni, an order was sent from the holy office for the release of Vivaldi, within a few days after the death of the Confessor; and the Marchese conducted his son from the prisons of the Inquisition to the mansion of his friend the Count di Maro, with whom he had resided since his arrival at Rome.

While they were receiving the ceremonious congratulations of the Count, and of some nobles assembled to welcome the emancipated prisoner, a loud voice was heard from the anti-chamber exclaiming, 'Let me pass! It is my master, let me pass! May all those who attempt to stop me, be sent to the Inquisition themselves!'

In the next instant Paulo burst into the saloon, followed by a group of lacqueys, who, however, paused at the door, fearful of the displeasure of their lord, yet scarcely able to stifle a laugh; while Paulo, springing forward, had nearly overset some of the company, who happened at that moment to be bowing with profound joy to Vivaldi.

'It is my master! it is my dear master!' cried Paulo, and, sending off a nobleman with each elbow, as he made his way between them, he hugged Vivaldi in his arms, repeating, 'O, my master! my master!' till a passion of joy and affection overcame his voice, and he fell at his master's feet and wept.

This was a moment of finer joy to Vivaldi, than he had known since his meeting with his father, and he was too much interested by his faithful servant, to have leisure to apologize to the astonished company for his rudeness. While the lacqueys were repairing the mischief Paulo had occasioned, were picking up the rolling snuff-boxes he had jerked away in his passage, and wiping the snuff from the soiled clothes, Vivaldi was participating in all the delight, and returning all the affection of his servant, and was so wholly occupied by these pleasurable feelings as scarcely to be sensible that any persons besides themselves were in the room. The Marchese, meanwhile was making a thousand apologies for the disasters Paulo had occasioned; was alternately calling upon him to recollect in whose presence he was, and to quit the apartment immediately; explaining to the company that he had not seen Vivaldi since they were together in the Inquisition, and remarking profoundly, that he was much attached to his master. But Paulo, insensible to the repeated commands of the Marchese, and to the endeavours of Vivaldi to raise him, was still pouring forth his whole heart at his master's feet. 'Ah! my Signor,' said he, 'if you could but know how miserable I was when I got out of the Inquisition!'——

'He raves!' observed the Count to the Marchese, 'you perceive that joy has rendered him delirious!'

'How I wandered about the walls half the night, and what it cost me to leave them! But when I lost sight of them, Signor, O! San Dominico! I thought my heart would have broke. I had a great mind to have gone back again and given myself up; and, perhaps, I should too, if it had not been for my friend, the centinel, who escaped with me, and I would not do him an injury, poor fellow! for he meant nothing but kindness when he let me out. And sure enough, as it has proved, it was all for the best, for now I am here, too, Signor, as well as you; and can tell you all I felt when I believed I should never see you again.'

The contrast of his present joy to his remembered grief again brought tears into Paulo's eyes; he smiled and wept, and sobbed and laughed with such rapid transition, that Vivaldi began to be alarmed for him; when, suddenly becoming calm, he looked up in his master's face and said gravely, but with eagerness, 'Pray Signor, was not the roof of your little prison peaked, and was there not a little turret stuck up at one corner of it? and was there not a battlement round the turret? and was there not'——Vivaldi, after regarding him for a moment, replied smilingly. 'Why truly, my good Paulo, my dungeon was so far from the roof, that I never had an opportunity of observing it.'

'That is very true, Signor,' replied Paulo, 'very true indeed; but I did not happen to think of that. I am certain, though, it was as I say, and I was sure of it at the time. O Signor! I thought that roof would have broke my heart, O how I did look at it! and now to think that I am here, with my dear master once again!'

As Paulo concluded, his tears and sobs returned with more violence than before; and Vivaldi, who could not perceive any necessary connection between this mention of the roof of his late prison, and the joy his servant expressed on seeing him again, began to fear that his senses were bewildered, and desired an explanation of his words. Paulo's account, rude and simple as it was, soon discovered to him the relation of these apparently heterogeneous circumstances to each other; when Vivaldi, overcome by this new instance of the power of Paulo's affection, embraced him with his whole heart, and, compelling him to rise, presented him to the assembly as his faithful friend, and chief deliverer.

The Marchese, affected by the scene he had witnessed, and with the truth of Vivaldi's words, condescended to give Paulo a hearty shake by the hand, and to thank him warmly for the bravery and fidelity he had displayed in his master's interest. 'I never can fully reward your attachment,' added the Marchese, 'but what remains for me to do, shall be done. From this moment I make you independent, and promise, in the presence of this noble company, to give you a thousand sequins, as some acknowledgement of your services.'

Paulo did not express all the gratitude for this gift which the Marchese expected. He stammered, and bowed and blushed, and at length burst into tears; and when Vivaldi inquired what distressed him, he replied, 'Why, Signor, of what use are the thousand sequins to me, if I am to be independent! what use if I am not to stay with you?'

Vivaldi cordially assured Paulo, that he should always remain with him, and that he should consider it as his duty to render his future life happy. 'You shall henceforth,' added Vivaldi, 'be placed at the head of my houshold; the management of my servants, and the whole conduct of my domestic concerns shall be committed to you, as a proof of my entire confidence in your integrity and attachment; and because this is a situation which will allow you to be always near me.'

'Thank you, my Signor,' replied Paulo, in a voice rendered almost inarticulate by his gratitude, 'Thank you with my whole heart! if I stay with you, that is enough for me, I ask no more. But I hope my Lord Marchese will not think me ungrateful for refusing to accept of the thousand sequins he was so kind as to offer me, if

I would but be independent, for I thank him as much as if I had received them, and a great deal more too.'

The Marchese, smiling at Paulo's mistake, rejoined, 'As I do not perceive, my good friend, how your remaining with your master can be a circumstance to disqualify you from accepting a thousand sequins, I command you, on pain of my displeasure, to receive them; and whenever you marry, I shall expect that you will shew your obedience to me again, by accepting another thousand from me with your wife, as her dower.'

'This is too much, Signor,' said Paulo sobbing—'too much to be borne!' and ran out of the saloon. But amidst the murmur of applause which his conduct drew from the noble spectators, for Paulo's warm heart had subdued even the coldness of their pride, a convulsive sound from the anti-chamber betrayed the excess of emotion, which he had thus abruptly withdrawn himself to conceal.

In a few hours, the Marchese and Vivaldi took leave of their friends, and set out for Naples, where they arrived, without any interruption, on the fourth day. But it was a melancholy journey to Vivaldi, notwithstanding the joy of his late escape; for the Marchese, having introduced the mention of his attachment to Ellena di Rosalba, informed him, that, under the present unforeseen circumstances, he could not consider his late engagement to the Marchesa on that subject as binding, and that Vivaldi must relinquish Ellena, if it should appear that she really was the daughter of the late Schedoni.

Immediately on his arrival at Naples, however, Vivaldi, with a degree of impatience, to which his utmost speed was inadequate, and with a revived joy so powerful as to overcome every fear, and every melancholy consideration, which the late conversation with his father had occasioned, hastened to the *Santa della Piéta*.

Ellena heard his voice from the grate, inquiring for her of a nun, who was in the parlour, and in the next instant they beheld each other yet once again.

In such a meeting, after the long uncertainty and terror, which each had suffered for the fate of the other, and the dangers and hardships they had really incurred, joy was exalted almost to agony. Ellena wept, and some minutes passed before she could answer to Vivaldi's few words of tender exclamation: it was long ere she was tranquil enough to observe the alteration, which severe confinement had given to his appearance. The animated expression of his countenance was unchanged; yet, when the first glow of joy had faded from it, and Ellena had leisure to observe its wanness, she understood, too certainly, that he had been a prisoner in the Inquisition.

During this interview, he related, at Ellena's request, the particulars of his adventures, since he had been separated from her in the chapel of San Sebastian; but, when he came to that part of the narration where it was necessary to mention Schedoni, he paused in unconquerable embarrassment and a distress not unmingled with horror. Vivaldi could scarcely endure even to hint to Ellena any part of the unjust conduct, which the Confessor had practised towards him, yet it was impossible to conclude his account, without expressing much more than hints; nor could he bear to afflict her with a knowledge of the death of him who he believed to be her parent, however the dreadful circumstances of that event might be concealed. His embarrassment became obvious, and was still increased by Ellena's inquiries.

At length, as an introduction to the information it was necessary to give, and to the fuller explanation he wished to receive upon a subject, which, though it was the one that pressed most anxiously upon his mind, he had not yet dared to mention, Vivaldi ventured to declare his knowledge of her having discovered her parent to be living. The satisfaction immediately apparent upon Ellena's countenance heightened his distress, and his reluctance to proceed; believing, as he did, that the event he had to communicate must change her gladness to grief.

Ellena, however, upon this mention of a topic so interesting to them both, proceeded to express the happiness she had received from the discovery of a parent, whose virtues had even won her affection long before she understood her own interest in them. It was with some difficulty, that Vivaldi could conceal his surprize at such an avowal of prepossession; the manners of Schedoni, of whom he believed her to speak, having certainly never been adapted to inspire tenderness. But his surprize soon changed its object, when Olivia, who had heard that a stranger was at the grate, entered the parlour, and was announced as the mother of Ellena di Rosalba.

Before Vivaldi left the convent, a full explanation, as to family, was given on both sides, when he had the infinite joy of learning, that Ellena was not the daughter of Schedoni; and Olivia had the satisfaction to know that she had no future evil to apprehend from him who had hitherto been her worst enemy. The manner of his death, however, with all the circumstances of his character, as unfolded by his late trial, Vivaldi was careful to conceal.

When Ellena had withdrawn from the room, Vivaldi made a full acknowledgment to Olivia of his long attachment to her daughter, and supplicated for her consent to their marriage. To this application, however, Olivia replied, that, though she had long been no stranger to their mutual affection, or to the several circumstances which had both proved its durability, and tried their fortitude, she never could consent that her daughter should become a member of any family, whose principal was either insensible of her value, or unwilling to acknowledge it; and that in this instance it would be necessary to Vivaldi's success, not only that he, but that his father should be a suitor; on which condition only, she allowed him to hope for her acquiescence.

Such a stipulation scarcely chilled the hopes of Vivaldi, now that Ellena was proved to be the daughter not of the murderer Schedoni, but of a Count di Bruno, who had been no less respectable in character than in rank; and he had little doubt that his father would consent to fulfil the promise he had given to the dying Marchesa.

In this belief he was not mistaken. The Marchese, having attended to Vivaldi's account of Ellena's family, promised, that if it should appear there was no second mistake on the subject, he would not longer oppose the wishes of his son.

The Marchese immediately caused a private inquiry to be made as to the identity of Olivia, the present Countess di Bruno; and, though this was not pursued without difficulty, the physician, who had assisted in the plan of her escape from the cruelty of Ferando di Bruno, and who was living, as well as Beatrice, who clearly remembered the sister of her late mistress, at length rendered Olivia's identity unquestionable. Now, therefore, that the Marchese's every doubt was removed, he paid a visit to the *Santa della Piéta*, and solicited, in due form, Olivia's consent to the nuptials of Vivaldi with Ellena; which she granted him with an entire satisfaction. In this interview, the Marchese was so much fascinated by the manners of the Countess, and pleased with the delicacy and sweetness, which appeared in those of Ellena, that his consent was no longer a constrained one, and he willingly relinquished the views of superior rank and fortune, which he had formerly looked to for his son, for those of virtue and permanent happiness that were now unfolded to him.

On the twentieth of May, the day on which Ellena completed

her eighteenth year, her nuptials with Vivaldi were solemnized in the church of the *Santa Maria della Piéta*, in the presence of the Marchese and of the Countess di Bruno. As Ellena advanced through the church, she recollected, when on a former occasion she had met Vivaldi at the altar, and, the scenes of San Sebastian rising to her memory, the happy character of those, which her present situation opposed to them, drew tears of tender joy and gratitude to her eyes. Then, irresolute, desolate, surrounded by strangers, and ensnared by enemies, she had believed she saw Vivaldi for the last time; now, supported by the presence of a beloved parent, and by the willing approbation of the person, who had hitherto so strenuously opposed her, they were met to part no more; and, as a recollection of the moment when she had been carried from the chapel glanced upon her mind, that moment when she had called upon him for succour, supplicated even to hear his voice once more, and when a blank silence, which, as she believed, was that of death, had succeeded; as the anguish of that moment was now remembered, Ellena became more than ever sensible of the happiness of the present.

Olivia, in thus relinquishing her daughter so soon after she had found her, suffered some pain, but she was consoled by the fair prospect of happiness, that opened to Ellena, and cheered, by considering, that, though she relinquished, she should not lose her, since the vicinity of Vivaldi's residence to *La Piéta*, would permit a frequent intercourse with the convent.

As a testimony of singular esteem, Paulo was permitted to be present at the marriage of his master, when, as perched in a high gallery of the church, he looked down upon the ceremony, and witnessed the delight in Vivaldi's countenance, the satisfaction in that of my 'old Lord Marchese,' the pensive happiness in the Countess di Bruno's, and the tender complacency of Ellena's, which her veil, partly undrawn, allowed him to observe, he could scarcely refrain from expressing the joy he felt, and shouting aloud, '*O! giorno felíce! O! giorno felíce!*'*

* O happy day! O happy day!

CHAPTER XIII

Ah! where shall I so sweet a dwelling find!
For all around, without, and all within,
Nothing save what delightful was and kind,
Of goodness favouring and a tender mind,
E'er rose to view.

THOMSON *

THE fête which, some time after the nuptials, was given by the Marchese, in celebration of them, was held at a delightful villa, belonging to Vivaldi, a few miles distant from Naples, upon the border of the gulf, and on the opposite shore to that which had been the frequent abode of the Marchesa. The beauty of its situation and its interior elegance induced Vivaldi and Ellena to select it as their chief residence. It was, in truth, a scene of fairy-land. The pleasure-grounds extended over a valley, which opened to the bay, and the house stood at the entrance of this valley, upon a gentle slope that margined the water, and commanded the whole extent of its luxuriant shores, from the lofty cape of Miseno to the bold mountains of the south, which, stretching across the distance, appeared to rise out of the sea, and divided the gulf of Naples from that of Salerno.

The marble porticoes and arcades of the villa were shadowed by groves of the beautiful magnolia, flowering ash, cedrati, camellias, and majestic palms; and the cool and airy halls, opening on two opposite sides to a colonade, admitted beyond the rich foliage all the seas and shores of Naples, from the west; and to the east, views of the valley of the domain, withdrawing among winding hills wooded to their summits, except where cliffs of various-coloured granites, yellow, green, and purple, lifted their tall heads, and threw gay gleams of light amidst the umbrageous landscape.

The style of the gardens, where lawns and groves, and woods varied the undulating surface, was that of England,* and of the present day, rather than of Italy; except 'Where a long alley peeping on the main,'* exhibited such gigantic loftiness of shade, and grandeur of perspective, as characterize the Italian taste.

On this jubilee, every avenue and grove, and pavilion was richly illuminated. The villa itself, where each airy hall and arcade was resplendent with lights, and lavishly decorated with flowers and the most beautiful shrubs, whose buds seemed to pour all Arabia's perfumes upon the air, this villa resembled a fabric called up by enchantment, rather than a structure of human art.

The dresses of the higher rank of visitors were as splendid as the scenery, of which Ellena was, in every respect, the queen. But this entertainment was not given to persons of distinction only, for both Vivaldi and Ellena had wished that all the tenants of the domain should partake of it, and share the abundant happiness which themselves possessed; so that the grounds, which were extensive enough to accommodate each rank, were relinquished to a general gaiety. Paulo was, on this occasion, a sort of master of the revels; and, surrounded by a party of his own particular associates, danced once more, as he had so often wished, upon the moon-light shore of Naples.

As Vivaldi and Ellena were passing the spot, which Paulo had chosen for the scene of his festivity, they paused to observe his strange capers and extravagant gesticulation, as he mingled in the dance, while every now-and-then he shouted forth, though half breathless with the heartiness of the exercise, '*O! giorno felice!* * *O! giorno felice!*'

On perceiving Vivaldi, and the smiles with which he and Ellena regarded him, he quitted his sports, and advancing, 'Ah! my dear master,' said he, 'do you remember the night, when we were travelling on the banks of the Celano, before that diabolical accident happened in the chapel of San Sebastian; don't you remember how those people, who were tripping it away so joyously, by moon-light, reminded me of Naples and the many merry dances I had footed on the beach here?'

'I remember it well,' replied Vivaldi.

'Ah! Signor *mio*, you said at the time, that you hoped we should soon be here, and that then I should frisk it away with as glad a heart as the best of them. The first part of your hope, my dear master, you was out in, for, as it happened, we had to go through purgatory before we could reach paradise; but the second part is come at last;—for here I am, sure enough! dancing by moonlight, in my own dear bay of Naples, with my own dear master and mistress, in safety, and as happy *almost* as myself; and with that old mountain yonder, Vesuvius, which I, forsooth! thought I was never to see again, spouting up fire, just as it used to do before we got ourselves put into the Inquisition! O! who could have foreseen all this! *O! giorno felice! O! giorno felice!*'

'I rejoice in your happiness, my good Paulo,' said Vivaldi, 'almost as much as in my own; though I do not entirely agree with you as to the comparative proportion of each.'

'Paulo!' said Ellena, 'I am indebted to you beyond any ability to repay; for to your intrepid affection your master owes his present safety. I will not attempt to thank you for your attachment to him; my care of your welfare shall prove how well I know it; but I wish to give to all your friends this acknowledgment of your worth, and of my sense of it.'

Paulo bowed, and stammered, and writhed and blushed, and was unable to reply; till, at length, giving a sudden and lofty spring from the ground, the emotion which had nearly stifled him burst forth in words, and '*O ! giorno felice! O ! giorno felice!*' flew from his lips with the force of an electric shock. They communicated his enthusiasm to the whole company, the words passed like lightning from one individual to another, till Vivaldi and Ellena withdrew amidst a choral shout, and all the woods and strands of Naples re-echoed with—'*O ! giorno felice! O ! giorno felice!*'

'You see,' said Paulo, when they had departed, and he came to himself again, 'you see how people get through their misfortunes, if they have but a heart to bear up against them, and do nothing that can lie on their conscience afterwards; and how suddenly one comes to be happy, just when one is beginning to think one never is to be happy again! Who would have guessed that my dear master and I, when we were clapped up in that diabolical place, the Inquisition, should ever come out again into this world! Who would have guessed when we were taken before those old devils of Inquisitors, sitting there all of a row in a place under ground, hung with black, and nothing but torches all around, and faces grinning at us, that looked as black as the gentry aforesaid; and when I was not so much as suffered to open my mouth, no! they would not let me open my mouth to my master!—who, I say, would have guessed we should ever be let loose again! who would have thought we should ever know what it is to be happy! Yet here we are all abroad once more! All at liberty! And may run, if we will, straight forward, from one end of the earth to the other, and back again without being stopped! May fly in the sea, or swim in the sky, or tumble over head and heels into the moon! For remember, my good friends, we have no lead in our consciences to keep us down!'

'You mean swim in the sea, and fly in the sky, I suppose,'

observed a grave personage near him, 'but as for tumbling over head and heels into the moon! I don't know what you mean by that!'

'Pshaw!' replied Paulo, 'who can stop, at such a time as this, to think about what he means! I wish that all those, who on this night are not merry enough to speak before they think, may ever after be grave enough to think before they speak! But you, none of you, no! not one of you! I warrant, ever saw the roof of a prison, when your master happened to be below in the dungeon, nor know what it is to be forced to run away, and leave him behind to die by himself. Poor souls! But no matter for that, you can be tolerably happy, perhaps, notwithstanding; but as for guessing how happy I am, or knowing any thing about the matter.——O! it's quite beyond what you can understand. *O! giorno felice! O! giorno felice!*' repeated Paulo, as he bounded forward to mingle in the dance, and '*O! giorno felice!*' was again shouted in chorus by his joyful companions.

THE END

EXPLANATORY NOTES

Title page Unheard, unknown, unsearchable!: source unidentified. Radcliffe generally adds brief attributions to epigraphs taken from other texts. There is no indication of the source in the case of this, and seven other epigraphs in *The Italian*; nor has it been possible to trace any of this group through the Chadwyck-Healey English Poetry Database or other standard reference works. It seems likely that Radcliffe wrote them herself, specifically for the novel.

1 *Santa Maria del Pianto*: translated as 'Our Lady of Tears' on p. 80.

2 *by no means an uncommon one*: see the Introduction, p. xiv.

5 *Mysterious Mother*: epigraph from Horace Walpole, *The Mysterious Mother* (1768), I. iii.

8 *plaintains*: a tall tropical plant with a fruit related to the banana; not native to Europe. Radcliffe's occasional inaccuracies were sometimes noted by contemporary reviewers; nowhere more ferociously than in an unsigned letter to the editor with the title 'Terrorist Novel Writing': 'Besides, the tedious monotony of her descriptions, she affects in the most disgusting manner a knowledge of languages, countries, customs, and objects of art of which she is lamentably ignorant. . . . She covers the kingdom of Naples with India figs because *St Pierre* has introduced these tropical plants in his tales, of which the scene is laid in Italy' (*The Spirit of the Public Journals for 1797*, i (1798), 223–5).

10 *Vesuvius*: a volcano situated close to Naples. It had long been a place of pilgrimage for British tourists, writers and artists. Addison said of it, 'there is nothing about *Naples*, nor indeed in any Part of Italy, which deserves our Admiration so much as this Mountain' (*Remarks on Several Parts of Italy* (London, 1706), 235). From 1766 it began a period of notable activity. An eruption in June 1794 was one of the most violent on record.

23 *Twelfth Night*: epigraph from Shakespeare, *Twelfth Night*, I. v. 271–80.

24 *Herculaneum*: an ancient Roman city destroyed by the eruption of Vesuvius in AD 79. Excavations began at Herculaneum in 1738 and at nearby Pompeii ten years later. The remains discovered there stimulated the fashion for neoclassical art and design.

cabinet: 'a room devoted to the arrangement or display of works of art or objects of vertu', obsolete (*OED*).

26 *Lazaroni*: 'One of the lowest class at Naples, who lounge about the streets, living by odd jobs or by begging' (*OED*). They were a feature of the city frequently noted by travel writers. Samuel Sharp in *Letters from Italy* (1767) describes them as 'such miserable wretches as are not to be seen in any other town in *Europe*' (92). Radcliffe shares the more picturesque view of Hester Thrale Piozzi in *Observations and Reflections* (1789; Ann Arbor, 1967), who notes that they are the favoured subject of the painter Schidone [*sic*]: 'for a *Lazarone* at Naples, like a sailor at Portsmouth, is no mean character, though he is a coarse one' (261); see note to p. 34.

game of maro: probably a reference to the game 'la mor(r)a', similar to the 'stone, scissors, paper' game in England and often a basis for gambling.

33 *closet*: 'a room for privacy or retirement' (*OED*).

34 *Schedoni*: it is likely that the name was borrowed from the Neapolitan painter Bartolomeo Schedoni, discussed by Hester Thrale Piozzi in her *Observations and Reflections Made in the Course of a Journey through France, Italy and Germany* (1789; 1967), 261.

36 *Julius Cæsar*: epigraph from Shakespeare, *Julius Caesar*, IV. iii. 277–80; 'stand' is substituted for 'stare' in line 279.

38 *mole*: a breakwater.

45 *Santa Maria della Pieta*: Our Lady of Pity.

48 *Mysterious Mother*: epigraph from Walpole, *The Mysterious Mother*, I. V.

49 *the fortress of Paluzzi was worthy of being added to her collection*: see Introduction, p. xi.

54 *Shakespeare*: epigraph from Shakespeare, *Romeo and Juliet*, IV. iii. 24–5.

56 *Shakespeare*: epigraph from Shakespeare, *Julius Caesar*, II. i. 276–8.

62 *'unused to pity or be pitied'*: adapted from Shakespeare, *As You Like It*, II. vii. 117.

63 *the objects . . . to the soul*: the idea that a sensitive observer could internalize some of the greatness of sublime objects—such as a mountainous landscape—was an important aspect of eighteenth-century aesthetic theory. Compare Edmund Burke's remarks on the 'swelling' self-love which accompanies ambition in his *Philosophical Enquiry into the Origin of our Ideas of the Sublime and the Beautiful*: 'this swelling is never more perceived, nor operates with more force, than when without danger we are conversant with terrible objects, the mind always claiming to itself some part of the dignity and importance of the things which it contemplates' (Oxford, 1987; 50–1).

Radcliffe's version of the sublime tends towards a more selfless and spiritual exaltation.

65 *grey stuff*: grey was the original colour of the habit of the Franciscan order.

70 *Shakespeare*: epigraph from Shakespeare, *Hamlet*, I. i. 39.

72 *Maestro*: Radcliffe mistakenly uses a title commonly applied to master craftsmen, artists, or musicians.

73 *Lazaro*: a variant of 'lazzarone'; see note to p. 26.

80 *grand penitentiary*: 'The penitentiary is a harbour against the prosecutions of the inquisition. It takes cognisance of all possible crimes, and grants absolution for them' (Pierre Jean Grosley, *New Observation on Italy and its Inhabitants* (2 vols.; London, 1769), ii, 54).

81 *white friar*: member of the order of Carmelites.

86 *Guido*: Guido Reni (1575–1642), Italian painter. He painted in an idealizing, sentimental style especially admired by eighteenth-century connoisseurs.

90 *Tavogliere di Puglia*: 'tableland' or plateau in the region of Puglia (modern form, Apulia).

94 *Guicciardini's history*: Francesco Guicciardini (1482–1540), Italian politician and historian. *Storia d'Italia* (1561–4) is his most celebrated work. It was translated into English in the eighteenth century by Austin Parke Goddard.

Tasso: Torquato Tasso (1544–95), Italian poet. The melancholy cast of his poetry and his unhappy life, which included periods of imprisonment and insanity, made him a celebrated emblem of tormented genius in the eighteenth century.

98 *Mysterious Mother*: epigraph from Walpole, *The Mysterious Mother*, I. i; slightly altered.

109 *Shakespeare*: epigraph from Shakespeare, *The Merchant of Venice*, IV. i. 69.

114 *a party of pilgrims seated on the grass*: J. M. S. Tompkins has suggested that this passage, and the scene of the Carnival at Rome (p. 194), contain echoes of Grosley's *New Observations on Italy and its Inhabitants*, which Radcliffe had certainly used as a source for *The Mysteries of Udolpho* ('Ramond de Carbonnières, Grosley and Mrs. Radcliffe', *Review of English Studies* (July, 1929), 294–301).

scrip: wallet or purse.

Father-director: a priest qualified to give spiritual guidance; more usually associated with the sacrament of confession than with pilgrimage.

115 *partly inhabited by nuns*: the interchangeable use of 'monastery' and 'convent' was not uncommon at the time, but Radcliffe's provision of joint accommodation for monks and nuns was a notorious error she persisted in throughout her novel-writing career.

120 *Abate*: abbot.

123 *waving woods*: John Milton, *Comus* (1634), lines 86–8, adjusted to the past tense.

129 *coup-d'œil*: the impression made by a view.

133 *mattin*: matin; one of the seven canonical hours or divine offices from the Roman Catholic breviary, traditionally sung or recited at a service held between midnight and daybreak. The fact that Radcliffe refers to 'first mattin'—when by definition matin only takes place once per day—is an instance of her well-known vagueness concerning Catholic practices; cf. note to p. 115.

139 *You are not now to learn*: 'As you already know'; an obsolete turn of phrase.

143 *pensile*: overhanging.

149 *Milton*: epigraph from Milton, *Lycidas* (1637), lines 186–7 and 190–1. Lines 188–9 have been omitted, 'unletter'd' substituted for 'uncouth' and 'forth' for 'out'.

150 *Arcadian manners*: Arcadia was a rural paradise of Greek myth, inhabited by shepherds, herdsmen and divinities under the rule of the god Pan. In the genre of pastoral romance, from classical through to modern times, Arcadia is associated with innocent pleasures and romantic love.

153 *Torpedo*: a fish with a numbing sting.

157 *tabor*: 'a small drum beaten with one stick to accompany a pipe' (Johnson).

hautboy: an early form of oboe.

159 *throw out fire!*: the varying responses of Vivaldi, Ellena, and Paolo are apparently designed to illustrate the way gender and class distinctions govern aesthetic appreciation of nature: Vivaldi points out the sublime heights of the landscape; Ellena dwells on the cultivated beauty of the valleys; while Paolo is interested in the scenery only insofar as it reminds him of home. Elsewhere, however, Ellena shows herself to be a fervent enthusiast for the sublime.

'fallen from his high estate': John Dryden, *Alexander's Feast* (1697), line 78.

'no horizontal beam . . . life's dusty day': source unidentified.

160 *worthy of the furies!*: the celebrations were described by Tacitus in *Annals of Imperial Rome*.

165 *Milton*: epigraph from Milton, *Comus* (1634), lines 160–4.

179 *Milton*: epigraph from Milton, 'On the Morning of Christ's Nativity' (1645), lines 181–8; 'thicket' is substituted for 'thickets'.

186 *holy Inquisition!*: an ecclesiastical tribunal, founded by the Papacy in the thirteenth century for the detection and suppression of heresy. It was at various times active in Italy, France, the Netherlands, Spain, Portugal, and the Spanish and Portuguese colonies, reaching a peak of activity in Spain in the sixteenth century. It was abolished in France in 1772 and in Spain in 1834, but survives in Rome to the present day in a modified form.

187 *Holy Office*: established by Pope Paul III in 1542 as the central governing body of the Inquisition. This congregation of Cardinals were invested with powers to act as the 'final court of appeal in trials for heresy' (*Oxford Dictionary of the Christian Church*).

192 *Ode to Fear*: epigraph from William Collins, 'Ode to Fear' (1746), lines 26–9. A key poem for Radcliffe; she quotes from it twice in *The Romance of the Forest* and once in *The Mysteries of Udolpho*.

196 *the Poet*: Thomas Gray, 'Ode on a Distant Prospect of Eton College' (1748), line 69.

201 *The officer, at length, appeared . . . a deep recess*: these two paragraphs, and the description of torturers on p. 310, correspond very closely to passages and an illustration in Phillipus van Limborch's *The History of the Inquisition*, trans. S. Chandler (2 vols.; London, 1731). See John Thomson, 'Ann Radcliffe's Use of Phillipus Van Limborch's *The History of the Inquisition*', *English Language Notes*, 18 (1980), 31–3.

208 *flageolets*: small wind instruments.

215 *Shakespeare*: epigraph from Shakespeare, *Othello*, v. ii. 37–8, 43–6.

219 '*many-sounding waves*': source unidentified.

223 *trepan*: to ensnare.

225 *Shakespeare*: epigraph from Shakespeare, *Macbeth*, I. vii. 80–1.

234 *lawn*: fine linen.

241 *Milton*: epigraph from Milton, *Comus*, lines 36–9.

256 *trombone*: blunderbuss; a gun introduced in the mid-seventeenth century.

261 *palmetos*: 'palmeto', palm grove. Radcliffe has invented a plural form.

268 *pistol*: small hand-gun introduced in the late sixteenth century.

273 *outré*: exaggerated.

    zanni: clown.

    improvisatore: 'One of the greatest curiosities you meet with in Italy is the Improvisatore; such is the name given to certain individuals, who have the suprising talent of reciting verses extempore, on any subject you propose' (Tobias Smollett, *Travels Through Italy and France* (1766; Oxford, 1979), 231). Modern spelling: 'improvvisatore'.

273 *buffo*: comic. Not usually a term for actors, but *opera buffo* was a musical comedy entertainment very popular at the time.

diavoloni: sugar plums.

274 *Punchinello*: 'the principle character in a puppet-show of Italian origin, the prototype of Punch' (*OED*).

the story of Virginia: according to Roman tradition, Virginia was killed by her father Verginius to prevent her being ravished by Appius Claudius. Petrarch, Chaucer, and John Webster are among the authors who retold her story. In the eighteenth century , John Dennis, Samuel Crisp, and Frances Brooke all published dramatic versions.

276 *Shakespeare*: epigraph from Shakespeare, *King John*, IV. ii. 135–7.

282 *'out of the frying pan into the fire'*: a proverb current from the sixteenth century.

291 *Elfrida*: epigraph from William Mason, *Elfrida* (1752), lines 128–9. Mason's dramas *Elfrida* and *Caractacus*, set in Saxon England and modelled on Greek Tragedy, were immensely popular in the period, going through many editions. Radcliffe had previously drawn on them for epigraphs in *The Romance of the Forest* and *The Mysteries of Udolpho*.

292 *plantains*: see note for p. 8.

feluccas: small sailing boats 'used chiefly in the Mediterranean' (*OED*).

camera obscura: 'a darkened chamber or box, into which light is admitted through a double lens, forming an image of external objects on paper, glass, etc., placed at the focus of the lens' (*OED*). This optical device was used by artists and craftsmen of the day for greater accuracy in drawing. Radcliffe perhaps has in mind Canaletto's detailed topographical paintings of Venice.

299 Thomson: epigraph from James Thomson, 'Winter', *The Seasons* (1746), lines 600–8.

304 *Caractacus*: epigraph from William Mason, *Caractacus* (1759), lines 797–800.

309 *the question*: 'the application of torture as part of a judicial examination' (*OED*).

320 *His mind resembled . . . duskiness of futurity*: Shakespeare, *Macbeth*, IV. i. 69–124, is a possible source of the image.

325 *Shakespeare*: epigraph from Shakespeare, *Richard III*, V. iii. 181–3. Line 181 is changed from statement to question.

334 *Caractacus*: epigraph from William Mason, *Caractacus*, lines 927–9.

355 *Collins*: epigraph from William Collins, 'An Epistle: Addressed to Sir Thomas Hanmer, on his Edition of Shakespeare's Works' (1743), lines 87–90.

360 *subpœnaed*: from 'subpoena', a writ summoning a witness to a court of justice, under threat of a penalty for non-appearance.

361 *unencumbered estate*: an estate without debts.

366 *younker*: 'young person: in contempt' (Johnson).

   paolo!: a silver coin, named after Pope Paul.

374 *conversazione*: 'In Italy, an evening assembly for conversation, and recreation', but also current in England in the 1790s for gatherings of an intellectual nature (*OED*).

385 *Young*: epigraph from Edward Young, *Night Thoughts* (1742–5), Night II, lines 368–9.

389 *Shakespeare*: epigraph from Shakespeare, *King Lear*, IV. ii. 25.

390 *requisition*: a formal demand.

   cabal: 'A private intrigue of a sinister character formed by a small body of persons' (*OED*).

393 *asperser*: slanderer.

400 *Similar instances of treachery . . . attempted toward himself*: there are comparable scenes, featuring an *agent provocateur* or '*mosca*' acting to ensnare obdurate prisoners of the Inquisition into confession, in William Godwin, *St Leon* (Oxford, 1994), 327–34; and Charles Maturin, *Melmoth the Wanderer* (Oxford, 1989), 227–39.

405 *Chapter XII*: wrongly numbered 'XI' in the 1797 edition. The numbering of this and the following chapter have been corrected in the present edition.

   Shakespeare: epigraph from Shakespeare, *As You Like It*, II. iii. 69–70.

412 *Thomson*: epigraph from James Thomson, *The Castle of Indolence* (1748), Canto II, lines 2–6.

   style of the gardens . . . was that of England: the relatively informal landscaped gardens popularized by 'Capability' Brown carried potent political and nationalist meanings. They involved a 'liberal' *refinement* of nature, in contrast to the regimented garden design of Continental Europe, connoting autocracy.

   '*Where a long alley peeping on the main*': source unidentified.

413 *giorno felice!*: happy day.

*Veils how
hide from
all seeing
Perception of
society — of
the church*

American Literature

British and Irish Literature

Children's Literature

Classics and Ancient Literature

Colonial Literature

Eastern Literature

European Literature

History

Medieval Literature

Oxford English Drama

Poetry

Philosophy

Politics

Religion

The Oxford Shakespeare

A complete list of Oxford Paperbacks, including Oxford World's Classics, OPUS, Past Masters, Oxford Authors, Oxford Shakespeare, Oxford Drama, and Oxford Paperback Reference, is available in the UK from the Academic Division Publicity Department, Oxford University Press, Great Clarendon Street, Oxford OX2 6DP.

In the USA, complete lists are available from the Paperbacks Marketing Manager, Oxford University Press, 198 Madison Avenue, New York, NY 10016.

Oxford Paperbacks are available from all good bookshops. In case of difficulty, customers in the UK can order direct from Oxford University Press Bookshop, Freepost, 116 High Street, Oxford OX1 4BR, enclosing full payment. Please add 10 per cent of published price for postage and packing.